20 GUINNESS WORLD RECORDS 03

ISBN 085112-1470

MANAGING EDITOR
Claire Folkard

VP CONTENT MANAGEMENT
Chris Sheedy

KEEPER OF THE RECORDS
Stewart Newport

RESEARCH TEAM
Stuart Claxton
Jerramy Fine
David Hawksett
Keely Hopkins
Della Howes
Kim Lacey
Hein Le Roux
Chris Marais
Sue Morrison
Jo Violette

PROOFREADING
Alyse Dar
Sasha Heseltine
Carla Masson

AMERICANIZATION
Mary Sutherland

SENIOR EDITOR
Jackie Freshfield

EDITORS
Rob Dimery
Peter Watts

DESIGN CONCEPT
Office Group NYC

COVER DESIGN
Ron Callow at Design 23

DESIGN
Karen Wilks

DTP
Juliet MacDonald

HEAD OF PICTURE/MEDIA DESK
Betty Halvagi

PHOTO ASSISTANT/DESIGNER
James Thackwell

LIBRARIAN/ARCHIVIST
Roger Wemyss Brooks

PICTURE RESEARCH
Maureen Kane
ilumi

PRODUCTION DIRECTOR
Patricia Langton

PRODUCTION CO-ORDINATOR
David D'Arcy

FULFILMENT CO-ORDINATOR
Katie Stephens

PRINTING AND BINDING
Printer Industria Grafica, SA,
Barcelona, Spain

COLOUR ORIGINATION
Colour Systems,
London, UK

INDEX
Indexing Specialists

ACCREDITATION Guinness World Records Ltd has a very thorough accreditation system for records verification. However, whilst every effort is made to ensure accuracy, Guinness World Records Ltd cannot be held responsible for any errors contained in this work. Feedback from our readers on any point of accuracy is always welcomed.

ABBREVIATIONS AND MEASUREMENTS GUINNESS WORLD RECORDS uses both metric and imperial measurements (US imperial in brackets). The only exception is for some scientific data, where metric measurements only are universally accepted, and for some sports data. All currency values are shown in dollars with the sterling equivalent in brackets except where transactions took place in the United Kingdom, when this is reversed. Where a specific date is given the exchange rate is calculated according to the currency values that were in operation at the time. Where only a year date is given the exchange rate is calculated from December of that year. The billion conversion is one thousand million.'GDR' (the German Democratic Republic) refers to the East German state which unified with West Germany in 1990. The abbreviation is used for sports records broken before 1990. The Union of Soviet Socialist Republics split into a number of parts in 1991, the largest of these being Russia. The Commonwealth of Independent States replaced it and the abbreviation 'CIS' is used mainly for sporting records broken at the 1992 Olympic Games.

GENERAL WARNING Attempting to break records or set new records can be dangerous. Appropriate advice should be taken first and all record attempts are undertaken entirely at the participant's risk. In no ircumstances will Guinness World Records Ltd have any liability for death or injury suffered in any record attempts. Guinness World Records Ltd has complete discretion over whether or not to include any particular records in the book.

GULLANE
ENTERTAINMENT

A Gullane Entertainment company

20

GUINNESS
WORLD
RECORDS™

03

Welcome to Guinness World Records 2003!
With over 1,000 new records and hundreds of exciting new pictures, this year's book is one of the brightest and best yet. We've added new chapters on Modern Society and Buildings and Structures, which offer a fascinating glimpse into our modern world, and the Sport section has been expanded to include a huge range of every activity imaginable, from international soccer to elephant polo!

But the old favourites haven't been forgotten. There are mind-bending records on everything from the wonders of the human body to awe-inspiring facts on the natural world.

So delve into the wonderful world that is Guinness World Records and prepare to be astounded and inspired by the people that have deservedly claimed their place in history!

What could you break...?

Pictures from far left: a delighted Halle Berry with her Oscar at this year's Academy Awards; Rudolph Giuliani as Mayor of New York City; Edward Peter Hannaford with his record-winning French knitting; Olympic skier Janica Kostelic, holder of three gold medals.

FASTEST COMPUTER

The NEC Earth Simulator (below, right) at the Yokohama Institute for Earth Sciences in Japan is capable of carrying out 35.6 trillion calculations per second – around five times the speed of the previous record holder. Built by HNSX Supercomputers, a division of NEC, the computer is designed to simulate Earth's complex climate in order to predict climate change and global warming, both of which have serious implications for Japan. Its 5,104 processors are housed in cabinets that cover an area equivalent to four tennis courts.

FASTEST MEN'S 1,000-M SPEED SKATING

Gerard van Velde (Netherlands, below) skated 1,000 m in 1:07.16 at Salt Lake City, Utah, USA, on 16 February 2002.

LARGEST CURRENCY INTRODUCTION

On 1 January 2002, 15 billion euro banknotes and 50 billion euro coins (with a value of more than €664 billion – £407 billion or $592 billion) were put into circulation in Austria, Belgium, Finland, France, Germany, Greece, Ireland, Italy, Luxembourg, The Netherlands, Portugal and Spain, affecting 290 million people. Put end to end, the new euro banknotes would stretch to the Moon and back two and a half times.

MOST SPACEFLIGHTS BY AN ASTRONAUT

On 8 April 2002, 54-year-old US astronaut Jerry Ross began his seventh space mission. He was flying as a crew member aboard the STS 110 mission of the space shuttle *Atlantis*, on a construction flight to the International Space Station. All of Ross's flights have been on the space shuttle. A retired Air Force Colonel, he was selected as an astronaut in 1980 and his first spaceflight was in 1985.

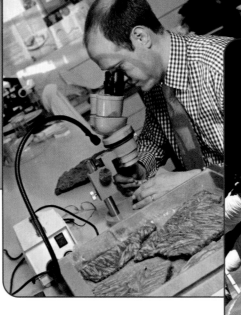

OLDEST VOMIT

On 12 February 2002 a team of palaeontologists led by Prof Peter Doyle (UK) announced the discovery of the fossilized vomit (right) of an ichthyosaur (ancient marine reptile). Found in a quarry in Peterborough, Cambs, UK, the 160-million-year-old vomit may provide an insight into ichthyosaurs' feeding habits.

FASTEST TIME TO COMPLETE A MARATHON FOR WOMEN ONLY

Paula Radcliffe (UK, left) finished the women's race in the London Marathon on 14 April 2002 in London, UK, in 2 hr 18 min 56 sec.

OLDEST PERSON TO CLIMB EVEREST

Tamae Watanabe (Japan, left b. 21 November 1938) reached the summit of Mt Everest aged 63 at 9:55 am on 16 May 2002. Watanabe reached the summit on its busiest day ever, when 54 other climbers reached the top of the 8,848 m (29,028 ft) peak.

OLDEST ROYAL

HM Queen Elizabeth the Queen Mother (UK, 1900–2002, below right) was the oldest member of the British royal family. She married Prince Albert (UK, later George VI) on 26 April 1923 and on his coronation became the first British-born Queen Consort since Tudor times, as well as the Last Empress of India. She died on 30th March 2002 aged 101. Her daughter, Queen Elizabeth II (below, left) celebrated her Golden Jubilee in 2002.

FASTEST $100-MILLION GROSS FOR AN ANIMATED FEATURE FILM

The computer-animated film *Monsters, Inc.* (USA, 2001, above) from Walt Disney Pictures and Pixar Animation Studios reached the $100-million (£68,636,036) mark at the US box office in just nine days after its release on 2 November 2001.

LARGEST SIMULTANEOUS JUMP

To celebrate the launch of UK Science Year on 7 September 2001 at precisely 11:00 am, 559,493 people began jumping up and down in 2,171 schools all over the UK for one minute (right). The total number of participants was 569,069. The extra numbers were made up by disabled pupils who contributed by dropping objects on the ground or hitting the ground with their fists.

BE A RECORD BREAKER

SO YOU WANT TO BE A RECORD BREAKER?
Guinness World Records 2003 is packed with extraordinary people achieving extraordinary feats. If reading this year's book has whetted your appetite to break a record or create a new one, then read on. Applying to become a record breaker has never been so easy. All you need to do is log on to www.guinnessworldrecords.com. But before you do, here are some things you may want to consider:

I COULD BREAK A RECORD – BUT WHICH ONE?
If you think you're made of record-breaking material but don't quite know which record to go for, it's time to get your thinking cap on.

The thousands of unusual records held in our database prove that being a record breaker is not just about being a top athlete or movie star! Maybe you could start a wonderful collection? This doesn't have to be expensive either – current record holders have collected sick bags or chewing gum wrappers! If you are interested in doing a group record, you could organize a huge poetry reading or do something that would help improve the environment, such as picking up litter.

You may even be a record breaker without knowing it. We have records for the most blood donated and the longest legs!

Another option is to create a record that is unique and requires an entirely new category. Our team is constantly on the look out for new categories, particularly those that will be an inspiration to other people. What we look for is a challenge that is interesting, safe and requires skill.

APPLY EARLY
Whatever your record, it is important that you apply to us early and contact us before your attempt. This is to give our researchers time to evaluate your suggestion and, if necessary, draw up new guidelines and consult experts who have specialist knowledge in that field.

You should also check with us shortly before you do your attempt to make sure that the record hasn't recently been set or broken. If you think you may already have set a world record, then contact us so we can decide whether your record is potentially valid before you send in any documentation.

GUIDELINES
For most of our current categories, Guinness World Records has specific guidelines to ensure that all potential record holders make their attempts according to the same conditions that applied to previous challengers.

Your attempt has to be measurable, quantifiable and breakable so that we can make fair comparisons with other record attempts. If the record you are interested in is not a current category and is of interest to us we will draw up specific guidelines to ensure that we can consider it fairly.

DOCUMENTATION

Although some people break their record in front of millions of viewers on the Guinness World Records TV shows, the majority of potential record holders are obliged to follow our rules and regulations, and provide evidence of this with a clearly labelled VHS video tape (with the official timekeeper or continually running clock in view where appropriate). High quality colour photographs or transparencies should also be submitted as documentation. If possible, get a local newspaper or radio station interested in your record so they can cover the event and, preferably, be present during the attempt.

All claims must be well documented. At least two independent witnesses are required, and these should be someone of standing in your local community such as a doctor, lawyer or police officer. Any such witness must not be related to you. Choose someone who is relevant to your record. For example if your record is to do with sport, invite someone from an appropriate sporting body. Witnesses must be able to state they have seen the record take place successfully and that the guidelines have been followed. Guinness World Records cannot supply staff to invigilate all record attempts but reserves the right to do so if it deems it necessary.

TAKING CARE

Safety precautions are another important factor. It is important to note that all record attempts are undertaken at the sole risk of the competitor. Guinness World Records cannot be held responsible for any (potential) liability whatsoever arising out of any such attempt, whether to the claimant or any third party.

CERTIFICATE

Everyone who breaks or sets a record receives a special certificate, acknowledging membership of an exclusive official body – Guinness World Record holders. Details of your record will also be added to our world famous database for potential use in our book, website or related material.

WILL I BE IN THE BOOK?

With tens of thousands of records in existence we are unable to publish all of them. We publish a different selection each year that we believe will be of most interest.

HOW TO APPLY

Our online service is the best way to submit your claim. Visit our website at: http://www.guinnessworldrecords.com. All you need to do is fill in a simple form and follow the instructions to send us your application. You'll get an immediate response from us and when you register your record attempt online, we'll give you a personal ID number so you can track your claim's progress via our website, where the most up to date information is held.

IF YOU DON'T HAVE ONLINE ACCESS

If you do not have access to a computer, you can also contact Guinness World Records in one of the following ways:

Call us: 0870 241 6632 (+44 870 241 6632 if calling from outside the UK). Calls are currently charged at national call rate if dialling from within the UK.

Fax us: 020 7891 4501 (+44 20 7891 4501 from outside the UK)

Or write to us: GUINNESS WORLD RECORDS
338 EUSTON ROAD
LONDON NW1 3BD
UNITED KINGDOM

RECORD-BREAKING TALENT

THE FASTEST PENNY FARTHING IN THE WEST

Colorado's Steve Stevens is a major fan of Victorian penny farthings – he now owns 31 of them – but carried out his first US coast-to-coast ride on a conventional push-bike in 1985. "Afterwards I started reading about Thomas Stevens, who was the first man to ride across America on a penny farthing," says Steve. More than a century later, Steve set out to follow in his hero's penny farthing tracks.

He left San Francisco on 26 May 2000 and arrived in Boston 29 days later, setting the record for the fastest trans-America ride on a penny farthing in the process.

It must have been punishing work to face strong headwinds on a penny farthing, while enduring the 100°F (38°C) heat. But Steve insists that he never even thought about giving up.

For his next ruse Steve is planning to participate in a Victorian Iron Man contest. He intends to sport a woollen Victorian swimsuit and ride a penny farthing in the cycling event!

The penny farthing was named after the smallest and largest UK coins in existence at the time of the bike's invention. Its name reflects the considerable difference in the size of the rear and front wheels.

THE FABULOUS BIKER BOYS

Political turmoil in Colombia and kidnapping threats threw Nick Alcock's and Hugh Sinclair's trans-America record attempt into jeopardy in 2001. The British biker boys had clocked up 6,000 miles in the month following their departure from Alaska on 29 August 2001, but when they arrived in Panama they were warned about

the dangerous situation over the border in Colombia. "The areas we'd planned to pass through are controlled entirely by volatile armed rebel forces," said Nick at the time. The record attempt was in doubt until Guinness World Records approved a third route that omitted Colombia. The boys flew the bikes to Quito, Ecuador, then drove north to the Colombian border and continued south. The trip ended in Ushuaia, Argentina, on 15 October 2001, by which time the pair had covered around 24,000 km (15,000 miles).

FROM STRENGTH TO STRENGTH

English iron man Paddy Doyle began his prolific record-breaking career in 1987, when he completed 4,100 full press-ups with a 22.7-kg (50-lb) weight strapped to his back. He's broken numerous strength and endurance records since.

Paddy powered his way to yet another Guinness World Record this year. The martial arts expert and all-round strongman threw an incredible 4,104 full-contact punches and 1,560 martial arts kicks in just one hour. That works out at over three strikes every two seconds! Each strike was impacted on kick pads worn by one of Paddy's seven assistants – who had to alternate regularly because of the explosive force of the blows!

Paddy's planning to retire from record breaking in November 2002. And as a finale he has a string of speed endurance records planned.

ROLLIN', ROLLIN', ROLLIN'!

When most folks were washing the car, Texans Geoff Ackles and John Landers were pushing their full-weight Chevrolet Sprint around laps of the local neighbourhood, in a bid to smash the record for 24-hour car pushing. In just over 17 hours of nonstop pushing the powerful pair managed to notch up a distance of 54.2 km (33.7 miles) – smashing the previous record held by two Italians, who pushed their car a distance of 52.5 km (32.6 miles) in 24 hours.

"My son was determined that we should break a record – and he suggested car pushing," Geoff says. "At first I thought it would be impossible but then slowly things started coming together. My neighbour, John Landers, agreed to help us and I managed to get hold of a car that was really close to the minimum weight limit of 840.5 kg (1,853 lb) set by Guinness World Records."

Geoff was quietly confident after a test push – "but that was without a driver in as well". Five drivers took turns at front-seat duties during the record attempt. "Towards the end I was pushing with my eyes closed, I was just so tired," recalls the Texan record breaker. "When we crossed the finish line it was just about all I could do to raise my hands in the air."

LAWN MOWER MAN

Gary Hatter (USA) has been interested in lawn mowers since the age of 10. However, it wasn't until a back injury at 24 – which left him unable to continue working as a long-distance truck driver – that the idea of his record-breaking feat occurred to him. Gary needed surgery to prevent paralysis, an operation that would cost $100,000.

Having spent four years planning a trip to raise funds for his treatment, he set off on a $11,500 stock Kubota BX2200-60 mower, with a top speed of 14.5 km/h (9 mph), on 31 May 2000 from Portland, Maine, USA. He drove through 48 continuous states as well as Canada and Mexico and finally, after spending 260 days on the road, arrived at Daytona Beach, Florida on 14 February 2001. Gary covered 23,487.5 km (14,594.5 miles) on his trek, breaking the previous record by more than 17,702.8 km (11,000 miles) and gaining himself a world record. Gary's machine clocked up 22.5 km (14 miles) to the gallon; the trip wore out three sets of rear tyres and four sets of front tyres.

Gary had his mower fitted with new equipment and lights to make it roadworthy. The only thing missing was the cruise-control, a problem he overcame by using a block of wood!

IS THE FORCE WITH YOU?

Jason Joiner, of Ealing, London, UK, a special effects expert who has worked on the recently made Star Wars films, has a collection of more than 20,000 Star Wars toys. And as if that wasn't enough, Jason also has one of the original C-3PO robots, an original R2-D2 and an original Darth Vader costume.

Just before his early teens, Jason developed an interest in the Star Wars movies and everything related to them. Like many of his peers, he began purchasing various types of memorabilia (including action figures, toys, books and cards) with his hard-earned pocket money. But Jason's enthusiasm has not faded with time.

Jason has invested considerable time and money in organizing Star Wars collectors' fairs in England that help to fund his growing collection. He also heads a club of more than 2,000 Star Wars buffs. It just goes to show what a combination of passion, drive and ingenuity can achieve!

THE CHAIN GANG

We've all made paper chains at least once during our lives – but it seems that some people just don't know when to stop! Sixty people made their way into the record books by constructing a paper chain measuring an incredible 83.36 km (51.8 miles) long and comprising 584,000 links – and all in 24 hours.

The feat took place at Alvin Community College, Alvin, Texas, USA, on 23–24 October 1998. It had initially been proposed by ACC Child Laboratory School as part of the college's 50th anniversary celebrations.

The successful attempt beat the proposed target by 2.9 km (1.8 miles) and the previous record by 9.7 km (6 miles)! It also united the campus and the community as senior citizens, families, girl scouts and church youth groups all joined forces to work four- and five-hour shifts apiece. Local businesses donated both the staples that were used to join the strips and food provisions for the participants, and the event was covered by local radio. The sponsorship and T-shirt sales from the event raised more than $5,000 for student scholarships.

RECORD-BREAKING FAITH

Ashrita (formerly Keith) Furman was born on 16 September 1954 in Brooklyn, New York, USA. Ashrita confesses that he was a bit of a wimp as an adolescent and lacked direction until he embraced the teachings of the spiritual leader Sri Chinmoy. In 1974, by now a devout follower, he adopted the name Ashrita, which means 'protected by God' in Sanskrit.

In 1978 Sri Chinmoy suggested that Ashrita attempt a 24-hour cycling marathon. The marathon enabled Ashrita to discover the resources that he could tap into through meditation.

Ashrita set his first world record in 1979 by carrying out 27,000 jumping jacks. Since then he has set around 60 world records, but now holds 14, as many have been broken. Ashrita has broken more world records than any other person. If he suffers extreme pain during a feat, he uses mantras to guide him and help him overcome it. By breaking records Ashrita believes he can free himself from his conscious mind and reach a spiritual plane.

SO WHAT'S NEW?

This year, your favourite records are just a click away. Log on for details of thousands of incredible record attempts, keep up to date with all the latest record-breaking news, and choose from hundreds of amazing video clips.

Plus, if you want to be a record breaker, apply online for all the information and rules you need. You can even track the progress of your record using our new online claim system. Who knows… this time next year you might be a Guinness World Record holder!

FIND A RECORD
Looking for a specific record? Use our keyword search to find one of the thousands of Guinness World Records in the database

BREAK A RECORD
Want to set a new world record? Click here to tell us about your suggestion. If it's approved by our researchers, we'll send you the relevant rules and guidelines

TRACK YOUR RECORD
Once you've applied to break a record, follow the progress of your application using our new tracking system

VIDEO VAULT
Choose from hundreds of exciting video clips and see some of the greatest Guinness World Records come to life

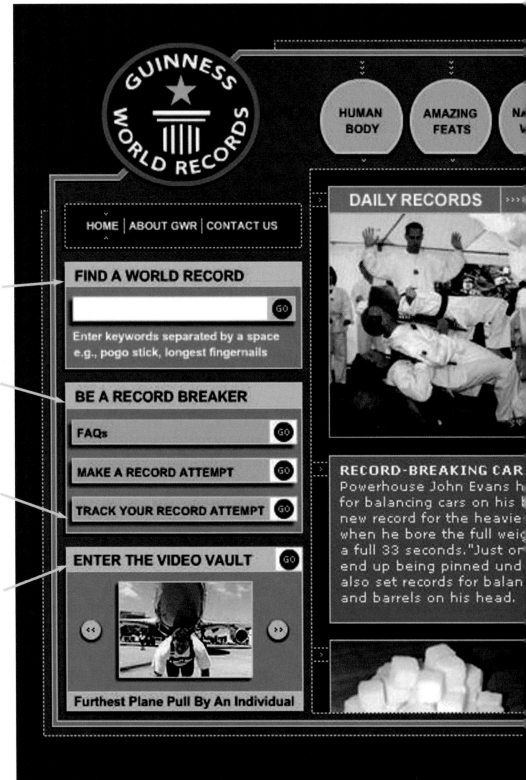

HOME | ABOUT GWR | CONTACT US

HUMAN BODY   AMAZING FEATS

FIND A WORLD RECORD

GO

Enter keywords separated by a space e.g., pogo stick, longest fingernails

BE A RECORD BREAKER

FAQs   GO

MAKE A RECORD ATTEMPT   GO

TRACK YOUR RECORD ATTEMPT   GO

ENTER THE VIDEO VAULT   GO

Furthest Plane Pull By An Individual

DAILY RECORDS

RECORD-BREAKING CAR
Powerhouse John Evans h
for balancing cars on his I
new record for the heavie
when he bore the full weig
a full 33 seconds. "Just on
end up being pinned und
also set records for balan
and barrels on his head.

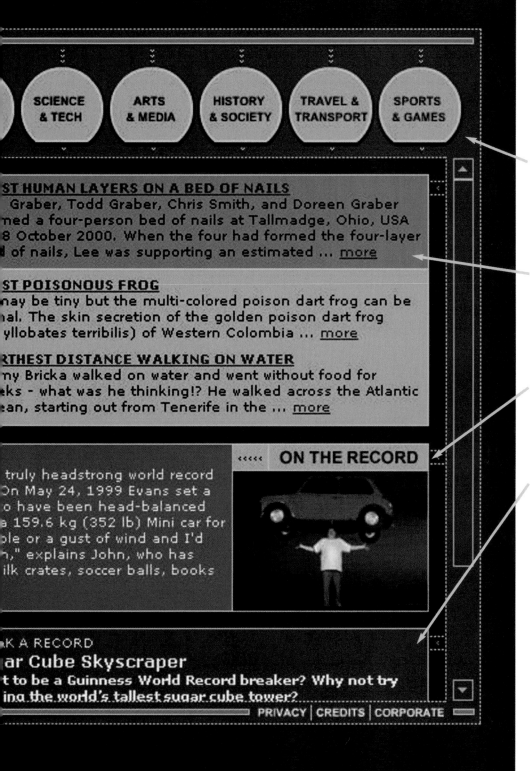

SCIENCE & TECH ARTS & MEDIA HISTORY & SOCIETY TRAVEL & TRANSPORT SPORTS & GAMES

ST HUMAN LAYERS ON A BED OF NAILS
Graber, Todd Graber, Chris Smith, and Doreen Graber
med a four-person bed of nails at Tallmadge, Ohio, USA
8 October 2000. When the four had formed the four-layer
of nails, Lee was supporting an estimated ... more

ST POISONOUS FROG
nay be tiny but the multi-colored poison dart frog can be
al. The skin secretion of the golden poison dart frog
yllobates terribilis) of Western Colombia ... more

RTHEST DISTANCE WALKING ON WATER
ny Bricka walked on water and went without food for
ks - what was he thinking!? He walked across the Atlantic
an, starting out from Tenerife in the ... more

<<<< ON THE RECORD

truly headstrong world record
On May 24, 1999 Evans set a
o have been head-balanced
159.6 kg (352 lb) Mini car for
le or a gust of wind and I'd
," explains John, who has
lk crates, soccer balls, books

K A RECORD
ar Cube Skyscraper
t to be a Guinness World Record breaker? Why not try
ina the world's tallest sugar cube tower?

PRIVACY | CREDITS | CORPORATE

CHOOSE YOUR CATEGORY
Delve into the online archive and browse
through our collection of the world's most
amazing records – just choose the subject
area that interests you most

DAILY RECORDS
Our researchers are always on the hunt for
the most astonishing, incredible, gobsmacking
record attempts. Read our favourite stories
here each day

ON THE RECORD
Dozens of new records are attempted
each week, so check back regularly
for all the latest news and updates

PLUS...
Discover top tips for breaking a record,
read interviews with record holders
and meet the Keeper of the Records

There have been several TV series loosely based on Guinness World Records in the past – most notably, BBC TV's *Record Breakers*, and Sir David Frost's *The Spectacular World of Guinness Records*. However, in 1998 we produced a major new series in the US, *Guinness World Records: Primetime*. Since its launch, the American show has been screened in 28 different countries. It was closely followed by shows in Germany, the UK, Finland, Sweden, Denmark, Norway, France, Spain and Japan. Every show is presided over by an official Guinness World Records judge who ensures that all rules are observed, and attempts are accurately measured and timed. There are no tricks or illusions in the show, just real people achieving incredible things.

1.
Vitaly Schnikers (Latvia) carried out 48 'Thomas Flanks' in one minute. His moment of gymnastic glory took place on the set of *Guinness – Die Show Der Rekorde* in Munich, Germany, on 15 February 2002.

2.
Superbiker Joachim Hindren (Finland) is definitely going up in the world. At the studios of *Guinness World Records*, Helsinki, Finland, on 20 October 2001, Hindren climbed a wall on to a platform 3.01 m (9.87 ft) high astride his trial motorbike.

3.
Tireless footwear tugger Teo, a Border collie, pulled 18 socks off the feet of a selection of people on the set of *Guinness – Die Show Der Rekorde*, on 26 April 2002.

4.
Bundesliga team Energie Cottbus's Under-16 team scored 54 goals in two minutes with a header relay. Each team member headed the ball to the next team-mate, and the last player headed the ball into a goal on the set of *Guinness – Die Show Der Rekorde*, on 26 April 2002.

5.
Peter Wetzelsperger (Germany) smashed his way through a total of 64 coconuts in one minute with his bare hands on the set of *Guinness – Die Show Der Rekorde* on 15 February 2002.

6.
Olympic diver Jan Hempel (Germany) executed a backwards jump reaching a distance of 2.01 m (6 ft 7.1 in) on the set of *Guinness – Die Show Der Rekorde*, on 15 February 2002.

8.
Dean Sheldon (USA) held a total of 21 scorpions in his mouth for a time of 18 seconds on *Guinness Rekord TV*, on 24 November 2001. His fearless feat broke his own record of 20 scorpions in the mouth.

9.
Soap bubble artist Fan Yang (Canada) created a world record 12 soap bubble domes inside one another at the *Guinness World Records* studios, Helsinki, Finland, on 20 October 2001.

7.
Slavisa Pajkic 'Biba' (Yugoslavia) has developed the ability to pass an electric current through himself to power everyday household objects. On 24 November 2001 'Biba' heated up a 15-ml (0.5-fl oz) cup of water from 25ºC to 97ºC (77ºF to 20ºF) in a record-breaking time of 1 min 37 sec on the set of *Guinness Rekord TV*, Stockholm, Sweden.

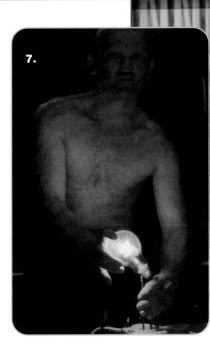

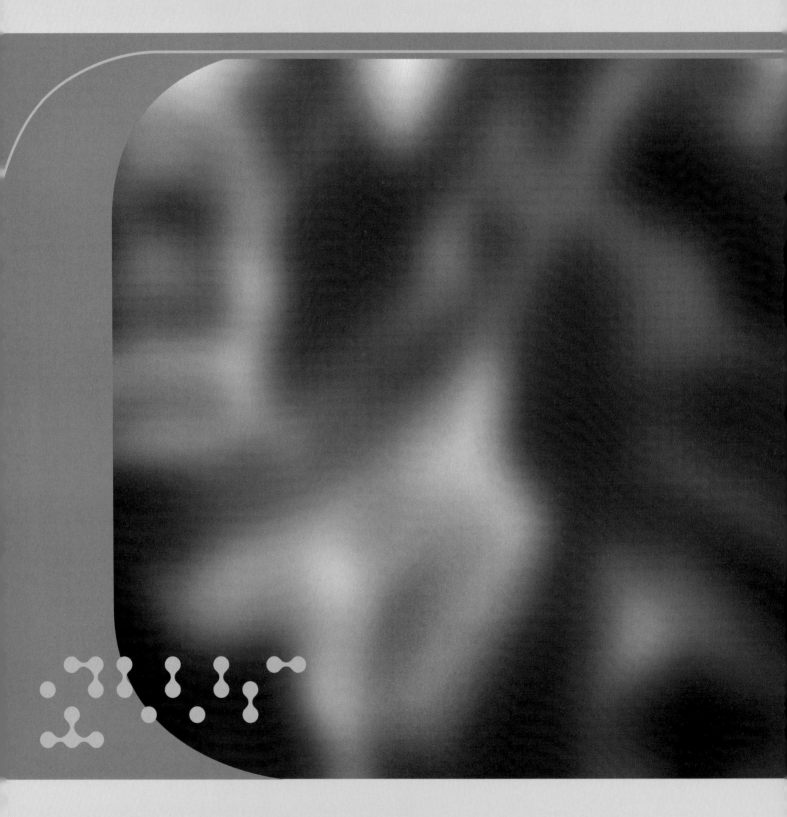

HUMAN ACHIEVEMENT

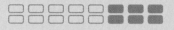

MOST MONEY RAISED FOR CHARITY IN A SPORTING EVENT

The Flora London Marathon (above), run annually since 1981 through the streets of London, UK, raises more money for charity than any other single sporting event in the world. Around £156 million ($224 million) has been raised so far.

YOUNGEST GALLANTRY AWARD

At the age of 4 years 52 days, Ryan Woods (UK) became the youngest person to receive a bravery award when he was awarded The Royal Humane Society's 'Testimonial on Parchment' in recognition of his brave actions during an accident in Portugal in July 1997. Ryan saved his grandmother's life by climbing for help when their car plunged down a steep cliff.

MOST DECORATED WAR HERO

Best known as a film actor, Audie Murphy (USA) was also the most decorated soldier in US history, winning 24 medals including the Congressional Medal of Honor. His exploits were the subject of the film *To Hell and Back* (USA, 1956), in which he starred as himself.

MOST CIVILIAN AWARDS

Reginald H Blanchford (UK) has received the following awards for life-saving on land and at sea: MBE for gallantry in 1950; Queen's Commendation in 1957; Life Saving Medal of The Order of St John in Gold in 1957, with gold bar in 1963; George Medal in 1958; Carnegie Hero Fund's Bronze Medallion in 1959; the OBE in 1961. He was made a Knight of Grace of The Order of St John in 1970 and received the American Biographical Institute's Silver Shield of Valor in 1992.

YOUNGEST RECIPIENT OF THE VICTORIA CROSS

The earliest established age for the winner of a Victoria Cross is 15 years 100 days for hospital apprentice Andrew Fitzgibbon (USA). He was born on 13 May 1845 and received his medal for acts of bravery carried out when he was a member of the Indian Medical Service serving in northern China on 21 August 1860.

YOUNGEST RECIPIENT OF AN OFFICIAL GALLANTRY AWARD

Julius Rosenberg (Canada) was given the Medal of Bravery on 30 March 1994 for foiling a black bear that attacked his three-year-old sister on 20 September 1992. Aged five at the time of the incident, he managed to save his sister by growling at the bear.

YOUNGEST NOBEL PEACE PRIZE WINNER

In 1992, Rigoberta Menchú Tum (Guatemala), an active political worker in labour and human rights groups, was awarded the Nobel Peace Prize, "in recognition of her work for social justice and ethnocultural reconciliation based on respect for the rights of indigenous people". At the age of 33, she was the youngest prize winner ever to receive this honour.

DEEPEST UNDERWATER RESCUE

Roger R Chapman and Roger Mallinson (both UK) were rescued from the submersible *Pisces III* after being trapped for 76 hours when it sank to 480 m (1,575 ft), 241 km (150 miles) off the Irish coast on 29 August 1973. It was hauled up on 1 September by the *John Cabot* after work by *Pisces V*, *Pisces II* and the remote-control recovery vessel *Curv* (Controlled Underwater Recovery Vehicle).

MOST MONEY RAISED BY AN INDIVIDUAL IN A MARATHON

Retired executive John Spurling (UK) raised £1.13 million ($1.87 million) for the Animal Health Trust and Lords Taverners by running the London Marathon on 18 April 1999.

LARGEST VOLUNTEER AMBULANCE ORGANIZATION

Abdul Sattar Edhi (Pakistan) began his ambulance service in 1948. Today, his radio-linked ambulance fleet is 500 vehicles strong and operates all over Pakistan, through $5 million (£3.05 million) funding raised annually.

GREATEST RESCUE WITHOUT LOSS OF LIFE

The greatest rescue without any loss of life was from the American vessel *Susan B Anthony*, which was carrying 2,689 people – all of whom survived – when it was sunk off Normandy, France, on 7 June 1944, while being used as a troop ship.

EARLIEST MID-AIR RESCUE

Dolly Shepherd and Louie May (both UK) were part of a performing troupe who leapt out of balloons wearing parachutes. However, on 9 June 1908, Louie's ripcord jammed following a jump from a hot-air balloon at 3,352 m (11,000 ft) above Longton, Staffs, UK. Dolly saved her by bringing her down on her own single parachute.

LOWEST MID-AIR RESCUE

Eddie Turner saved an unconscious Frank Farnan (both USA), who had been injured in a collision after jumping out of an aircraft at 3,962 m (13,000 ft). Turner pulled Farnan's ripcord at 548 m (1,800 ft), less than 10 seconds from impact with the ground, over Clewiston, Florida, USA, on 16 October 1988.

LARGEST FUNDRAISING CHARITY

For eight consecutive years, the Salvation Army, USA (above), has raised more funds annually than any other charity. For the year ending September 1999, the total was $1,402 million (£855.22 million), the highest amount it has ever raised.

LARGEST SINGLE DONATION TO AIDS RESEARCH

The largest single donation to research into AIDS and HIV of $25 million (£15.08 million) was made by Bill Gates, founder of Microsoft, and his wife Melinda (both USA), in May 1999.

LARGEST MEDICAL CHARITY

The Wellcome Trust, established in 1936 as part of the will of Sir Henry Wellcome (UK), has an asset base of £12 billion ($19.46 billion). This large amount is due to the merger of Wellcome plc with Glaxo in 1995, which left the Wellcome Trust with a 4.7% stake in the new company, Glaxo Wellcome. The Trust has an annual expenditure of £400 million ($648 million).

OLDEST LIFE-SAVING ORGANIZATION

Britain's Royal National Lifeboat Institution (RNLI) was formed by royal edict in March 1824. Its lifeboatmen have to date saved over 135,000 lives.

MOST LIFEBOAT MEDALS

Sir William Hillary (UK), founder of the RNLI in 1824, was awarded a record four RNLI Gold Medals, in 1825, 1828 and twice in 1830.

MOST ARTISTS SAVED

Varian Fry (USA), known as 'The Artists' Schindler', journeyed from the USA to France in 1940 with a list of 200 prominent intellectuals and artists known to be in areas of Nazi-occupied Europe. He subsequently helped to save around 4,000 people from the Gestapo (the Nazi secret police), including some of the 20th century's most famous cultural figures: Marc Chagall, André Breton (both France), Max Ernst and Nobel Prize-winning chemist Otto Meyerhof (both Germany).

OLDEST LIFEGUARD

James Janssen (USA, b. 1921) is the world's oldest lifeguard. A retired priest, James guards The Outing Club pool, Davenport, Iowa, USA, and teaches swimming and water aerobics.

LONGEST CAREER IN FIRE DEPARTMENT

Gustave Ebers (USA) served in the Rhinebeck Fire Department, New York, USA, as a volunteer fireman and treasurer from November 1932 until 1997. He died in 1998.

MOST FIRE PERSONNEL LOST IN ONE INCIDENT

According to the International Association of Fire Fighters, a total of 343 New York City fire personnel (surviving fire officers shown below) lost their lives in the unprecedented tragedy of 11 September 2001, when two hijacked aeroplanes crashed into the twin towers of the World Trade Center in New York City, USA. The fire fighters' gallant rescue efforts saved thousands of lives. This was the largest single-event loss of life sustained by modern-day fire service personnel in war or peace time.

MOST VIEWERS FOR A SIMULTANEOUS CHARITY ROCK CONCERT

Live Aid, the largest simultaneous charity rock concert in terms of viewers, was organized by musician Bob Geldof (Ireland, above). Held in London, UK, and Philadelphia, USA, on 13 July 1985, more than 60 of rock music's biggest acts played for free to approximately 1.5 billion TV viewers watching via satellite. The event was staged to raise money for famine relief in Africa.

OLDEST MALE ASTRONAUT

The oldest man to have travelled into space is John Glenn Jr (USA), who was 77 years 103 days old when he flew with the crew of STS 95 *Discovery* on 29 October 1998. The mission lasted 11 days, returning to Earth on 7 November 1998. In February 1962, Glenn became the first American to orbit Earth, in the spacecraft *Friendship 7*.

OLDEST FEMALE ASTRONAUT

The oldest woman in space to date is Shannon Lucid (USA), who was 53 years old when she took part in the space shuttle mission ST 76 *Atlantis* in March 1996.

She also has the distinction of being the only woman to have taken part in five spaceflights.

FIRST FEMALE PRIME MINISTER

The first woman prime minister was Sirimavo Bandaranaike (Sri Lanka), who became premier of Sri Lanka on 21 July 1960 and also from 1970 to 1977 and from 1994 to 2000. Her daughter Chandrika Bandaranaike Kumaratunga (Sri Lanka) has been Sri Lanka's president since 1994.

OLDEST INTERNATIONAL HUMAN RIGHTS ORGANIZATION

Anti-Slavery International is the world's oldest human rights organization. Its roots stretch back to 1787, when the first abolitionist society was formed. The British and Foreign Anti-Slavery Society (BFASS) was officially created on 17 April 1839 to crusade against slavery and the slave trade throughout the world. To this day, the organization continues the fight against human trafficking, traditional slavery, child prostitution and all forms of forced and bonded labour.

LARGEST ENVIRONMENTAL FUNDRAISING EVENT

The Rainforest Foundation UK, established in 1989 by the musician Sting and his wife Trudie Styler (both UK) , held a celebrity benefit concert in Carnegie Hall, New York City, USA, in April 1998. The concert included performances by Madonna, Elton John and Billy Joel, and the street sign outside Carnegie Hall was renamed 'Rainforest Way' to help promote Rainforest Awareness Week. The concert raised a record $2 million (£1.2 million) gross to provide aid for indigenous people worldwide and contribute towards the preservation of the world's rainforests.

LARGEST SIMULTANEOUS BLOOD DONATION

The American Red Cross/University of Missouri Blood Drive, which was held at the Hernesh Center Field House, Columbia, Missouri, USA, on 7 April 1999, attracted a record 3,539 donors in one day. The drive yielded 3,155 productive units of blood in total.

LARGEST RALLY FOR RACIAL EQUALITY

On 28 August 1963 civil rights leader Martin Luther King, Jr (USA) led more than 250,000 demonstrators down The Mall in Washington DC, USA. Following the march, King delivered his inspirational "I have a dream ..." speech before the Lincoln Memorial. The rally was organized to promote equal civil rights for all Americans, irrespective of their race or colour.

LARGEST LITTER COLLECTION

The greatest number of volunteers to collect litter in one location on one day is 50,405, along the coast of California, USA, on 2 October 1993, in conjunction with the International Coastal Cleanup.

LARGEST AUDIENCE FOR A SPACE EVENT

The broadcast of the first moonwalk by the *Apollo 11* astronauts Neil Armstrong and Edwin 'Buzz' Aldrin (both USA) on 20 July 1969 was watched by an estimated 600 million people worldwide (about one fifth of the world's population at that time).

MOST FAN MAIL

After his solo nonstop transatlantic flight in May 1927, Charles Lindbergh (USA) received 3,500,000 letters. Although fan mail is usually associated with film idols and pop stars, no actor or musician has matched such a figure in his or her career.

BEST-SELLING DIARY

The Diary of Anne Frank has sold more than 25 million copies and has been translated into 55 languages. The diary is an autobiographical account of events that took place while young Anne and her family hid in an attic in Amsterdam, The Netherlands, to escape Nazi persecution during World War II. The book was first published by Anne's father, Otto (Germany), the only survivor of the family.

LONGEST INCARCERATION OF A FUTURE PRESIDENT

Nelson Rolihlahla Mandela (above) spent almost 27 years in prison in South Africa from 1964 until his release on 11 February 1990. On 10 May 1994, he became the first democratically elected president in South Africa's history.

ROYAL PATRON TO THE MOST CHARITIES

As of December 2000, Princess Anne, the Princess Royal (UK), was patron of 233 charity organizations. She is best known for her charity work with Save the Children UK, of which she has been president since 1970, and for her own Princess Royal Trust for Carers, which raises awareness of the UK's estimated 6 million carers.

EARLIEST ROCKET LAUNCH

On 16 March 1926 at Auburn, MA, USA, Dr Robert Hutchings Goddard (USA) launched a liquid-fuelled rocket to an altitude of 12.5 m (41 ft) and over a distance of 56 m (184 ft). This feat effectively marked the first step towards spaceflight, transforming humanity's perception of the universe.

LARGEST RADIO AUDIENCE FOR RELIGIOUS PROGRAMME

Decision Hour, a religious broadcast by the Baptist evangelist Billy Graham (USA), has been broadcast regularly since 1957, attracting an average radio audience of 20 million.

MOST CONDOLENCES POSTED ON THE INTERNET

A total of 580,000 people left messages on the memorial page of the official website of the British monarchy in September 1997, following the death of Diana, Princess of Wales.

MOST CAREER GOALS BY A FOOTBALLER

The most goals scored in a specific period is 1,279 by Edson Arantes do Nascimento (Brazil), known as Pelé, from 7 September 1956 to 1 October 1977 in 1,363 games. His best year was 1959, when he scored 126 times. The Milésimo (1,000th) came from

a penalty for Pelé's club Santos at the Maracanã Stadium, Rio de Janeiro, Brazil, on 19 November 1969, in his 909th first-class match. He added two more goals in special appearances.

Pelé has been actively involved in leprosy elimination campaigns in Brazil and has carried out extensive work for children's causes through the United Nations Children's Fund (UNICEF). Since his retirement in 1977, he has become an international ambassador for sport, working to promote peace and understanding through friendly athletic competition.

LARGEST FOOD DRIVE BY A NON-CHARITABLE ORGANIZATION

The 1,400 students of San Mateo High School, CA, USA, put together the largest food drive by a non-charitable organization between 3–17 December 1999, collecting 97,892.2 kg (214,713 lb) of non-perishable food for the poor and homeless of San Mateo County.

LARGEST DONATION TO A SINGLE UNIVERSITY

The greatest donation to one university is $250 million (£176 million) to the University of Colorado, by the

chairman and co-founder of software manufacturer BEA Systems, Bill Coleman, and his wife Claudia (both USA) in January 2001. The money will be used to set up the Coleman Institute for Cognitive Disabilities.

MOST OSCARS

Walter (Walt) Elias Disney (USA) has won 26 Oscars from 64 nominations. His studio's prolific output, including a host of classic cartoons as well as Oscar-winning documentaries, has had a major and lasting effect on the development of popular culture.

YOUNGEST ELECTED US PRESIDENT

At the age of 43, John F Kennedy (USA) became the youngest man ever to win the American presidency, as Democratic victor in the 1960 US presidential election. Winning by a narrow margin over Richard Nixon in the popular vote, Kennedy had the distinction of becoming the first Roman Catholic president. He was also the youngest president to die in office.

LARGEST DROP IN CRIME

In 1993, Rudolph Giuliani (USA, left) was elected the 107th mayor of New York City, USA. Under his indomitable leadership, New York City experienced an unprecedented reduction in overall crime. According to preliminary crime statistics from the New York City Police Department, between 1993 and 2001 murders in the city decreased by 66.63% and rapes dropped by 49.52%, while robberies fell by 67.56%. This is the largest drop in crime in more than 28 years of available data.

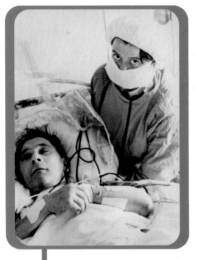

FIRST HEART TRANSPLANT PATIENT

The first heart transplant operation was performed on 55-year-old Louis Washkansky (South Africa, above left) at the Groote Schuur Hospital, Cape Town, South Africa, from 1 am to 6 am on 3 December 1967 by a team of 30 led by Prof Christiaan Barnard (South Africa). Washkansky lived for 18 days.

LONGEST SURVIVAL WITHOUT FOOD AND WATER

Andreas Mihavecz (Austria) survived for 18 days without food and water. Mihavecz had been put into a holding cell on 1 April 1979 in a local government building in Höchst, Austria, but the police subsequently forgot that he was there. On 18 April 1979 he was finally discovered, close to death.

LONGEST ARTIFICIAL HEART TRANSPLANT SURVIVAL

William J Schroeder (USA) is the longest surviving artificial heart transplant patient to date. He survived for 620 days at Louisville, Kentucky, USA, from 25 November 1984 to 7 August 1986.

LONGEST TIME SURVIVED WITHOUT A PULSE

Julie Mills (UK) managed to last three days without a pulse in her vascular system, when she suffered severe heart failure and viral myocarditis on 14 August 1998. Cardiac surgeons at the John Radcliffe Hospital, Oxford, UK, used a non-pulsatile blood pump (AB180) to support her for one week, during which her heart recovered and the pump was removed.

HIGHEST NON-VOLUNTARY G-FORCE ENDURED

Racing driver David Purley (UK) survived a deceleration from 173 km/h (108 mph) to zero in a distance of just 66 cm (26 in) in a crash at Silverstone, Northants, UK, on 13 July 1977. He withstood a force of 179.8 g and suffered 29 fractures, three dislocations, and six heart stoppages.

HIGHEST PARACHUTE ESCAPE

Royal Air Force officers Flt Lt J de Salis and Fg Off P Lowe (both UK) made the highest ever escape in a parachute at 17,100 m (56,102 ft), over Monyash, Derby, UK, on 9 April 1958.

LOWEST PARACHUTE ESCAPE

Sqn Ldr Terence Spencer (UK) made the lowest ever aircraft escape, at a height of 9–12 m (30–40 ft) at Wismar Bay, Germany, on 19 April 1945. Spencer was blown out of his aircraft while attacking enemy planes in the Bay of Wismar. He landed in the sea and managed to swim ashore.

LONGEST FALL SURVIVED BY AN INFANT

In November 1997, 18-month-old baby Alejandro (Spain) survived a 20-m (65-ft 7-in) fall from the seventh-floor kitchen window of a flat in Murcia, Spain. He suffered only bruising, a broken tooth and split lip.

MOST HOSTAGES HELD

The largest group of hostages held by a terrorist organization numbered more than 500 people. They were detained by Tupac Amaru terrorists at the Japanese Embassy in Lima, Peru, on 17 December 1996. Most of the hostages were released over time and the final 72 were rescued when Peruvian commandos stormed the embassy on 22 April 1997 killing all four rebels, including their leader, Nestor Cerpa (Peru).

MOST LIGHTNING STRIKES SURVIVED

A single lightning strike is made up of several 100 million volts (with peak current in the order of 20,000 amps). The only person to be struck seven times by lightning was ex-park ranger Roy C Sullivan (USA), the 'human lightning conductor'. His attraction for lightning began in 1942, when he lost a big toenail as the result of a strike. A second strike in 1969 resulted in the loss of his eyebrows and in July 1970 his left shoulder was seared by a third strike. A fourth strike, on 16 April 1972, set his hair on fire and a fifth, on 7 August 1973, set his new hair on fire and seared his legs. His ankle was injured on 5 June 1976 in strike number six and on 25 June 1977 he suffered chest and stomach burns with the seventh strike. In the USA, the average number of deaths from lightning is just over 100 a year.

LONGEST SOLO SURVIVAL ON A RAFT

Second Steward Poon Lim (Hong Kong) of the British Merchant Navy survived for 133 days after his ship, the *SS Ben Lomond*, was torpedoed in the Atlantic on 23 November 1942. A Brazilian fishing boat rescued him off Salinópolis, Brazil, on 5 April 1943, and he was strong enough to walk ashore.

LONGEST FALL SURVIVED IN A LIFT

Office workers Shameka Peterson and Joe Mascora (both USA) dropped 40 floors (the equivalent of 121 m, or 400 ft) in four seconds down the Empire State Building, New York City, USA, when the cable of the lift they were travelling in failed on 25 January 2000. Stopping just four floors from the ground, both suffered only minor bruising during their ordeal.

HIGHEST FALL SURVIVED WITHOUT A PARACHUTE

Vesna Vulovic (former Yugoslavia, above) survived a fall from 10,160 m (33,333 ft) over Srbsk, Kamenice, Czechoslovakia (now Czech Republic), on 26 January 1972, after the Boeing DC-9 she was working aboard exploded.

MOST LABOUR CAMP ESCAPES

A former Soviet citizen, Tatyana Mikhailovna Russanova, now living in Haifa, Israel, escaped from various Stalinist labour camps in the former Soviet Union on 15 separate occasions between 1943 and 1954, being recaptured and sentenced 14 times.

LONGEST UNDERWATER SURVIVAL

In 1986 two-year-old Michelle Funk (USA) spent 66 minutes underwater, having fallen into a swollen creek. She went on to make a full recovery.

LONGEST MARCH

The longest march in military history was the Long March by the Chinese Communists, which lasted 368 days – of which 268 days were spent on the move – from October 1934 to October 1935. A force of around 100,000 people covered 9,700 km (6,000 miles) from Ruijin, in Jiangxi, to Yan'an, in Shaanxi. They crossed 18 mountain ranges and 24 rivers, reaching Yan'an with approximately 8,000 survivors as a result of continual rearguard actions against nationalist Guomindang (GMD) forces.

OLDEST EX-SERVICEMAN

The longest-lived soldier on record is John B Salling (USA) of the US Confederate Army; he is also the last accepted survivor of the US Civil War (1861–65). Salling died in Kingsport, Tennessee, USA, on 16 March 1959, aged 112 years 305 days.

SURVIVOR OF LONGEST FALL DOWN A LIFT SHAFT

Stuart Jones (New Zealand) fell 23 storeys, a distance of 70 m (229 ft 7 in), down a lift shaft while carrying out structural work on the roof of a temporary lift car at the Midland Park Building, Wellington, New Zealand, in May 1998. Jones survived his dramatic fall, but sustained multiple injuries, including a broken hip, a compound fracture in his left leg, a broken left kneecap and a broken rib.

LONGEST TIME TRAPPED IN A LIFT

On 28 December 1997 Kiveli Papaioannou, who had recently moved from New York City, USA, to Limassol, Cyprus, found herself trapped in her apartment block lift for six days while she was on her way back from a shopping trip. The 76-year-old overcame dehydration and the cold by rationing the fruit, vegetables and bread that she had in her shopping bag.

LONGEST HELD HOSTAGE

Terry Anderson (USA, below with his daughter Sulome) was held hostage in Beirut, Lebanon, for 2,454 days (6 years 264 days) by Hezbollah terrorists, until his release on 4 December 1991.

FIRST WOMAN TO CLIMB MOUNT EVEREST

Junko Tabei (Japan, above) reached the summit of Mount Everest on 16 May 1975. The first woman to climb the 'Seven Summits' (the highest peak on each continent), she has also climbed 70 of the world's major peaks.

LONGEST SCUBA DIVE IN OPEN FRESH WATER

Between 31 August and 3 September 2001 Daniel Misiaszek (USA) spent 60 hr 24 min submerged in Spring Lake, San Marcos, Texas, USA, using air only from underwater breathing tanks. The tanks were replaced throughout the record attempt by a team of 22 divers.

GREATEST DISTANCE WALKED IN 24 HOURS

At Albuquerque, New Mexico, USA, over 24 hours from 18 to 19 September 1976, Jesse Castenda (USA) walked 228.93 km (142.25 miles).

The greatest distance walked over 24 hours by a woman is 211.25 km (131.27 miles) by Annie van der Meer-Timmermann (Netherlands) at Rouen, France, between 10 and 11 May 1986.

LONGEST NON-STOP WALK

Georges Holtyzer (Belgium) walked 673.48 km (418.49 miles) in 6 days 10 hr 58 min, completing 452 laps of a 1.49-km (0.92-mile) circuit at Ninove, Belgium, from 19 to 25 July 1986. He was not permitted any stops for rest and was moving 98.78% of the time.

LONGEST WALK BY A WOMAN

The longest walk by a woman was one of 30,321 km (18,840 miles) by Ffyona Campbell (UK) who walked round the world in five phases, covering four continents and 20 countries. She left John O'Groats, Highland, UK, on 16 August 1983, returning there on 14 October 1994.

FASTEST TRANS-AMERICA WALK

John Lees (UK) walked 4,628 km (2,876 miles) across the USA from City Hall, Los Angeles, California, to City Hall, New York City, in 53 days 12 hr 15 min between 11 April and 3 June 1972. He averaged 86.49 km (53.75 miles) a day.

LONGEST DISTANCE WALKED ON STILTS

The greatest distance ever walked on stilts is 4,841 km (3,008 miles), from Los Angeles, California, USA, to Bowen, Kentucky, USA, by Joe Bowen (USA) from 20 February to 26 July 1980.

GREATEST DISTANCE COVERED IN 24 HOURS IN A WHEELCHAIR

Iran-born Nik Nikzaban (Canada) wheeled himself over 124.86 km (77.58 miles) in 24 hours from 6 to 7 April 2000. The endurance event took place on Handsworth Secondary School track, in North Vancouver, Canada. The track lane that Nik used was 415.4 m (1,362 ft 10.2 in) in length and he completed 301 laps of the track.

FURTHEST ROUND-THE-WORLD WALK

The greatest distance claimed for a round-the-world walker is 55,524 km (34,501 miles) by Arthur Blessitt (USA), in more than 33 years since 25 December 1969. He has been to all seven continents, including Antarctica, carrying a 3.66-m (12-ft) cross and preaching throughout his walk.

LONGEST TIGHTROPE WALK

The longest walk by any funambulist (tightrope walker) was by Henri Rochetain (France), on a wire 3,465 m (11,368 ft) long, across a gorge at Clermont Ferrand, France, on 13 July 1969. The crossing took 3 hr 20 min.

FIRST PEOPLE TO REACH THE NORTH POLE

Arctic explorer Robert Peary (USA) is widely regarded as being the first person to reach the North Pole. Peary set off on his expedition from Cape Columbia, Ellesmere Island, Canada, on 1 March 1909 with his associate Matt Henson (USA). On 6 April Peary made observations indicating that he had reached his destination. Although Frederick Cook (also USA) challenged his claim, asserting that he had reached the pole earlier that month, the US Congress acknowledged Peary's achievement in 1911.

FIRST SOLO EXPEDITION TO THE NORTH POLE

Japanese explorer and mountaineer Naomi Uemura became the first person to reach the North Pole in a solo trek across the Arctic sea-ice at 4:45 am GMT on 1 May 1978. He travelled 725 km (450 miles), setting out on 7 March from Cape Edward, Ellesmere Island in northern Canada. In February 1984, Uemura died attempting to become the first person to climb Mt McKinley, Alaska, USA, alone in winter.

FASTEST ASCENT OF MOUNT EVEREST

On 21 May 2000 Babu Chhiri Sherpa (Nepal) made the fastest ascent of Mount Everest from base camp to its 8,848-m (29,028-ft) summit, via the south side of the mountain, in 16 hr 56 min.

During the same ascent, he also completed the longest ever stay (21 hours) at Everest's peak without the use of bottled oxygen.

MOST SOUTHERLY DIVE

On 17 February 2000 nine members of *HMS Endurance* ship's company (above) undertook a dive at 77.11ºS, 32.59ºW in the Weddell Sea, Antarctica. The 10-m dive (32-ft 9.6-in) was in a water temperature of -1.5ºC (29.3ºF).

FASTEST SOLO CIRCUMNAVIGATION BY A YACHTSWOMAN

Ellen MacArthur (UK) circumnavigated the globe in 94 days 4 hr 25 min 40 sec during the 2000 Vendée Globe yacht race, starting and finishing at Les Sables d'Olonne, France. She covered 38,600 km (24,000 miles) in her yacht *Kingfisher* from 5 November 2000 to 11 February 2001.

FASTEST SEVEN-SUMMIT ASCENT

Andrew Salter (UK) climbed the highest peak on each continent in 290 days. Between 16 May 2000, when he reached the top of Mt Everest, Nepal, and 28 February 2001, when he ascended Aconcagua, Argentina, he climbed Mt McKinley, Alaska, USA, on 21 June 2000; Kilimanjaro, Tanzania, on 12 July 2000; Elbrus, Russia, on 1 September 2000; Puncak Jaya, Indonesia, on 24 October 2000 and Vinson Massif, Antarctica, in November 2000.

MOST SOUTHERLY MARATHON

The Antarctica Marathon and Half-Marathon is the only sporting event held on the most southerly continent. Operating since 1995, it takes place on King George Island, just off the Antarctic peninsula. Because the race only takes place in perfect weather, runners can use ordinary running shoes in the snowy conditions.

DEEPEST NO LIMITS FREE DIVE BY A WOMAN

The record depth for the dangerous sport of no limits free-diving by a woman is 125 m (411 ft) – deeper than Japanese submarines reached during World War II – by Audrey Mestre Ferrera (France) at La Palma, Canary Islands, Spain, on 13 May 2000. Taking just a single breath she was underwater for 2 min 3 sec.

DEEPEST SEAWATER SCUBA DIVE

The deepest ever scuba dive was 307.8 m (1,010 ft) by John Bennett (UK) on 6 November 2001. The dive took place off Escarcia Point, Puerto Galera, Philippines. The descent on a weighted sled took just over 12 minutes but the ascent took 9 hr 36 min.

FASTEST SOLO ROW ACROSS THE ATLANTIC FROM EAST TO WEST

From December 1969 to July 1970 Sidney Genders (UK) rowed from Las Palmas, Canary Islands, Spain, to Antigua, West Indies – a distance of 6,115 km (3,800 miles) – in 73 days 8 hours.

EARLIEST MANNED SPACEFLIGHT

The earliest manned spaceflight – ratified by the world governing body, the Fédération Aeronautique Internationale (FAI) – was by Cosmonaut Flight Major Yuri Alekseyevich Gagarin (USSR) in *Vostok 1* on 12 April 1961. The take-off was from the Baikonur Cosmodrome, Kazakhstan, at 6:07 am GMT and the landing occurred near Smelovka, near Engels, in the Saratov region of Russia, some 115 minutes later. Gagarin landed by parachute separately from his spacecraft 118 minutes after the launch, having ejected 108 minutes into the flight as planned.

MOST CONQUESTS OF MOUNT EVEREST

Apa Sherpa (Nepal) has successfully reached the summit of Mount Everest 12 times between 1990 and 2002.

YOUNGEST PERSON TO VISIT BOTH POLES

The youngest person to have visited both geographical poles is Jonathan Silverman (USA, b. 13 June 1990, above), who reached the North Pole on 25 July 1999 and the South Pole on 10 January 2002, aged 11 years 211 days. He travelled to the North Pole via a Russian ice-breaker and landed at the South Pole by aircraft from Chile.

FASTEST MICROLIGHT CIRCUMNAVIGATION

Colin Bodill (UK, above right) flew around the world in a Mainair Blade 912 Flexwing microlight in 99 days from 31 May to 6 September 2000. Bodill was accompanying Jennifer Murray (UK, above centre) as she set the record for the fastest solo helicopter circumnavigation by a female. Along with co-pilot Quentin Smith (UK, above left), Murray had previously become the first female to pilot a helicopter around the globe – their 97-day journey lasted from 10 May 1997 to 15 August 1997.

LONGEST UNAIDED CROSSING OF ANTARCTICA

Alain Hubert and Dixie Dansercoer (Belgium) are the only people to have crossed Antarctica – from the now defunct Belgian King Baudouin Base to the US McMurdo Base on the Ross Sea – with only a pair of skis and a parafoil. The 3,900-km (2,423-mile) journey began on 4 November 1997 and ended on 9 February 1998 after 99 days of struggling against ice storms and temperatures of below -10°C (14°F).

FASTEST CIRCUMNAVIGATION OF THE WORLD IN A HELICOPTER

John Williams and Ron Bower (both USA) flew round the world in a Bell 430 helicopter in a record time of 17 days 6 hr 14 min 25 sec, at an average speed of 91.76 km/h (57.02 mph). They left Fair Oaks, London, UK, on 17 August 1996 and flew west, against prevailing winds, finally arriving back at Fair Oaks on 3 September 1996.

FIRST POLE-TO-POLE CIRCUMNAVIGATION OF THE WORLD

Ranulph Fiennes and Charles Burton (both UK) of the British Trans-Globe Expedition were the first people to achieve a pole-to-pole surface circumnavigation of the world. Fiennes and Burton set out from Greenwich, London, UK, on 2 September 1979, crossing the South Pole on 15 December 1980 and the North Pole on 10 April 1982. They returned to Greenwich on 29 August 1982, having completed a 56,000-km (35,000-mile) trek.

GREATEST MANNED DISTANCE IN A BALLOON

The official Fédération Aéronautique Internationale (FAI) record for the furthest balloon journey is 40,814 km (25,361 miles) set by Bertrand Piccard (Switzerland) and Brian Jones (UK). The two piloted the *Breitling Orbiter 3* from 1–21 March 1999.

When *Breitling Orbiter 3* crossed the 'finishing line' of 9.27°W over Mauritania, north-west Africa, after a journey of 15 days 10 hr 24 min, it also became the first balloon to circle the world nonstop. As the first people to accomplish this feat, Jones and Piccard are also the holders of the record for the fastest circumnavigation of the globe in a balloon.

LONGEST LIFEBOAT JOURNEY

After his ship the *Endurance* became trapped by sea ice in Antarctica, Ernest Shackleton (UK) decided to abandon it, taking with him his 28-man crew. Their three lifeboats headed for Elephant Island, 161 km (100 miles) north. Once there, and knowing that a rescue expedition was unlikely, Shackleton chose five of his best men to sail the largest lifeboat, the 6.85-m-long (22.5-ft) *James Caird*, to a whaling station in South Georgia, 1,287 km (800 miles) away. They reached the island after 17 days, on 19 May 1916.

GREATEST DISTANCE FLOWN BY A SOLO BALLOONIST

Steve Fossett (USA) flew 22,909 km (14,235 miles), launching in Mendoza, Argentina, and crash-landing in the Pacific Ocean, 800 km (500 miles) off the coast of Australia. The flight lasted from 7–16 August 1998.

FASTEST ROUND-THE-WORLD JOURNEY BY CAR

Driving a Metrocab taxi, Jeremy Levine, James Burke and Mark Aylett (all UK) circumnavigated the world in 19 days 10 hr 10 min. The trio started at Buckingham Palace, London, UK, on 16 June 2000 and arrived back on 11 October 2000 after a journey of 29,159 km (18,119 miles). This total excludes time spent aboard ships between countries and continents.

The record for the first and fastest circumnavigation of the world by car, under the rules applicable in 1989 and 1991, embracing more than an equator's length of driving (40,074 km, or 24,901 road miles), is held by Mohammed Salahuddin Choudhury and his wife Neena (both India). The journey took 69 days 19 hr 5 min from 9 September to 17 November 1989. The couple drove a 1989 Hindustan 'Contessa Classic', starting and finishing in Delhi, India.

LONGEST SOLO CYCLE JOURNEY

The greatest mileage amassed in a cycle tour was in excess of 646,960 km (402,000 miles) and was achieved by itinerant lecturer Walter Stolle (Czech Republic) from 24 January 1959 to 12 December 1976. He visited 159 countries, starting from Romford, Essex, UK.

LONGEST WIND-POWERED LAND JOURNEY

Robert Torline (USA, above) travelled from Brownsville, Texas, USA (on the Mexican border), to Maida, North Dakota, USA (on the Canadian border), covering 3,410 km (2,119 miles) on his wind-powered Streetsailor from 29 April to 16 June 2001.

LONGEST JOURNEY BY WHEELCHAIR

Rick Hansen (Canada), who was paralysed from the waist down in 1973 after a motor accident, wheeled his wheelchair for 40,075.16 km (24,901.55 miles) through four continents and 34 countries during his 'Man in Motion World Tour'. The journey started in Vancouver, British Columbia, Canada, on 21 March 1985 and finished at the same location on 22 May 1987. Hansen undertook his demanding feat in an effort to promote a greater awareness of the potential of disabled people and succeeded in raising $24 million (£14.7 million) for spinal cord injury research.

GREATEST DISTANCE COVERED ON IN-LINE SKATES

Jari Koistinen and V-P Poikonen (both Finland) travelled 2,815 km (1,749 miles) on in-line skates between 29 May and 22 June 2000. The pair travelled from Helsinki to Utsjoki, Finland, and back, using in-line skates and ski poles, a technique commonly known as 'Nordic blading'.

FASTEST CROSSING OF THE BERING STRAIT ON SKIS AND BY FOOT

The first and fastest crossing of the Bering Strait by skis and on foot was completed by Dmitry Shparo and his son Matvey (both Russia), when they reached Chariot, Alaska, USA, on 20 March 1998. They had begun their journey from Mys Dezhneva (East Cape), Russia, on 1 March that year and travelled a total distance of approximately 290 km (180 miles).

FASTEST CAPE TOWN TO CAIRO RUN

Nicholas Bourne (UK) completed the first and fastest run from Cape Town, South Africa, to Cairo, Egypt. Leaving Cape Town on 21 January 1998, Bourne covered more than 12,069 km (7,500 miles), passing through South Africa, Botswana, Zambia, Tanzania, Kenya, Ethiopia, Sudan and Egypt, arriving at the Great Pyramids, Giza, Cairo, on 5 December 1998.

FIRST ANTARCTIC CROSSING

The first ever surface crossing of Antarctica ended at 1:47 pm on 2 March 1958, after a 3,473-km (2,158-mile) trek. The journey, from Shackleton Base to Scott Base via the South Pole, lasted 99 days, and began on 24 November 1957. The party consisted of 12 people and was led by Vivian Ernest Fuchs (UK).

FASTEST CROSSING OF THE AMERICAS BY MOTORCYCLE

Nick Alcock and Hugh Sinclair (both UK, below) rode a pair of Honda Africa Twin 742-cc motorcycles from Prudhoe Bay, Alaska, USA, to Ushuaia, Argentina, in 47 days 12 hr from 29 August to 15 October 2001, a distance of around 24,000 km (15,000 miles). Alcock and Sinclair embarked on the challenge to raise funds for Action Aid.

AMAZING FEATS

LONGEST RIDE WEARING A SUIT OF ARMOUR IN MODERN TIMES

Dick Brown (UK, above) rode a total of 334.7 km (208 miles) in a full suit of steel armour from Edinburgh Castle, Lothian, UK, to Dumfries, UK, from 10–14 June 1989. The suit weighed 30.84 kg (68 lb).

LONGEST MAGGOT BATH

Christine Martin (UK) immersed herself in a bath of maggots for a period of 1 hour 30 min in April 2002 to raise cash for a trek to Nepal organized by medical charity Action Research. Ten gallons of maggots were poured over Martin as she sat in the tub wearing only a swimsuit. The maggots used in the record attempt were sponsored by The National Bait Company.

LONGEST SIDE-WHEEL CAR DRIVE

Bengt Norberg (Sweden) drove a Mitsubishi Colt GTi-16V on two side wheels nonstop for a distance of 310.391 km (192.873 miles) in a time of 7 hr 15 min 50 sec. Norberg also achieved a distance of 44.808 km (27.842 miles) in one hour on two side wheels at Rattvik Horse Track, Sweden, on 24 May 1989.

FASTEST EGG-AND-SPOON MARATHON

Dale Lyons (UK) ran the London Marathon, London, UK, (a distance of 42.195 km, or 26 miles 385 yd) while carrying a dessertspoon with a fresh egg on it. He completed the marathon in 3 hr 47 min on 23 April 1990.

GREATEST DISTANCE COVERED WALKING BACKWARDS IN 24 HOURS

The longest distance covered walking backwards for a period of 24 hours is 153.52 km (95.40 miles) by Anthony Thornton (USA) in Minneapolis, Minnesota, USA, from 31 December 1988 to 1 January 1989. His average speed was 6.4 km/h (3.9 mph).

FASTEST MARATHON RUNNING BACKWARDS

Timothy Bud Badyna (USA) completed a marathon (26 miles 385 yd, or 42.195 km) running backwards in 3 hr 53 min 17 sec in Toledo, Ohio, USA, on 24 April 1994.

FASTEST STAIR CLIMB

The record for climbing the 1,336 stairs (73 floors) of the world's tallest hotel, the Westin Stamford Hotel, Singapore, is 6 min 55 sec by Balvinder Singh (Singapore). The feat was attained during the hotel's 3rd Annual Vertical Marathon on 4 June 1989.

LONGEST NONSTOP CONCERT BY A CHOIR

The longest continuous concert by a choral group lasted 20 hr 23 sec and was performed by the 120 members of the Turtle Creek Chorale (USA), directed by Dr Timothy Seelig (USA). The performance took place at the Lakewood Theater in Dallas, Texas, USA, from 14–15 August 1999. The choir was split into four groups. Each group sang for 30 minutes per hour and they overlapped each other in 15-minute segments.

LONGEST BACKWARDS WALK

Plennie L Wingo (USA) is the greatest exponent of reverse pedestrianism. He completed his 12,875-km (8,000-mile) trans-continental walk from Santa Monica, California, USA, to Istanbul, Turkey, from 15 April 1931 to 24 October 1932.

LONGEST HANDBELL RINGING SESSION

The longest nonstop handbell ringing by a group of nine players lasted 12 hr 1 min 7 sec and was carried out by the St Columba Harmony Handbell Ensemble of Durango, Colorado, USA, on 18 June 1999 in Durango.

LONGEST MOVIE-WATCHING MARATHON

An audience of 14 people consisting of Chinnawatra Boonrasri, Sirirat Kampongsa, Nuntiya Thammajinda, Nitipol Charoenkool, Pongsakorn Kerdpan, Pongsak Jamonchote, Suwat Kamvisuth, Yuthana Eakpornwut, Wuttichai Leelasvattanakul, Chalee Yongsamith, Sumalee Suwannapatch, Kodchapong Sarobon, Sonravit Eonvonsakun and Apiradee Phantong (all Thailand) watched 25 films, lasting 50 hr 55 min, at The Grand EGV Cinemas, Bangkok, Thailand, from 18–20 February 2000. The audience was allowed to move to a designated room for five minutes between films, and to have a 15-minute eating break after every three movies. The marathon began with 369 film fans, but all except the final 14 subsequently dropped out.

LONGEST VIDEO-WATCHING MARATHON

At an event organized by Court TV, Kevin Keaveny (USA) watched 51 episodes of *NYPD Blue* over 46 hr 30 min 50.91 sec between 31 August and 2 September 2001 in New York City, USA.

LONGEST INDIVIDUAL KEYBOARD-PLAYING MARATHON

From 30 March to 1 April 2001, Ginés Borges Belza (Spain) played a Yamaha MC-600 electric organ for 49 hr 15 min (including six breaks of 15 minutes) at the Royal Nautical Club of Santa Cruz de Tenerife, Canary Islands, Spain. Belza played a total of 800 individual arrangements, each lasting around three minutes.

LONGEST KISS

Rich Langley and Louisa Almedovar (both USA, above centre and right) hold the record for the world's longest kiss, which lasted for 30 hr 59 min 27 sec on 5 December 2001 at the TV studios of *Ricki Lake*, New York City, USA.

LONGEST IRONING SESSION

Eufemia Stadler (Switzerland) ironed 228 shirts in one 40-hour session while standing at an ironing board from 16–18 September 1999. Stadler was only allowed breaks of 15 minutes every eight hours.

LONGEST TIME SPENT JUGGLING THREE OBJECTS

Terry Cole (UK) juggled three objects, without dropping any of them, for 11 hr 4 min 22 sec in 1995.

LONGEST CARD GAME

Rolando Fasani, Ivano Pancera, Claudio Zanelli, Andrea Zanelli, Mauro Rossi, Armando von Bürer, Eros Zanelli, and Daniele Fiore (all Italy) played the card game 'Jass' for 28 hours continuously at the Bellavista Restaurant, Sant'Abbondio, Switzerland, from 17–18 March 2001.

LONGEST TIME SPENT ON A BED OF NAILS

The duration record for nonstop lying on a bed of nails (15.2 cm, or 6 in, in length and 5 cm, or 2 in, apart) is 274 hr 2 min by Inge Wilda Svingen (Norway) on 3 November 1984.

The same duration record for a female is 30 hours, set by Geraldine Williams (UK) on 18–19 May 1977.

LONGEST TREE SITTING

The official duration record for staying in a tree is 21 years, by Bungkas (Indonesia), who first climbed up into a 17-m-high (55-ft-9.24-in) palm tree in the Indonesian village of Bengkes, in the district of Pakong, in 1970, remaining there until 1991.

LONGEST TIME POLE-SITTING IN A BARREL

Vernon Kruger (South Africa) stayed in a barrel (maximum capacity 682 litres, or 150 gal) at the top of a pole at Dullstroom, Mpumalanga, South Africa, for 67 days 14 minutes from 17 March to 23 May 1997. Kruger's pole was situated in the middle of the town square and tourists often stopped off to see him on their way to the Kruger National Wildlife Park.

LONGEST DURATION SITTING IN A SHACK ON A POLE

Mellissa Sanders (USA) lived in a shack measuring 1.8 m x 2.1 m (5 ft 10.8 in x 6 ft 9.6 in) on top of a pole in Indianapolis, Indiana, USA, from 26 October 1986 to 24 March 1988, a total of 516 days.

LONGEST WING-WALKING MARATHON

Roy Castle (UK) flew on the wing of a Boeing Stearman biplane for 3 hr 23 min on 2 August 1990, taking off from Gatwick, W Sussex, UK, and landing at Le Bourget, near Paris, France. At the time Castle was host of the UK's *Record Breakers* television programme.

GREATEST DISTANCE SAILED IN A BATH TUB OVER 24 HOURS

The greatest distance covered by paddling a hand-propelled bath tub on still water in 24 hours is 145.6 km (90.5 miles), by 13 members of Aldington Prison Officers Social Club (UK) on 28–29 May 1983.

GREATEST DISTANCE TO DRIBBLE A BASKETBALL

The greatest distance covered in 24 hours while simultaneously dribbling a basketball is 156.71 km (97.37 miles). The feat was carried out by Suresh Joachim (Australia) at Vulkanhallen, Oslo, Norway, from 30–31 March 2001.

LONGEST TENNIS BALL-HEADING

Luis Silva (Portugal, below) headed a tennis ball continuously for 59 min 53 sec in Folgosa do Douro, Portugal, on 10 June 2001. Silva began training for the record attempt when he was 15 years old, around four years before he successfully achieved his goal.

HIGHEST EIGHT-PERSON TIGHTROPE PYRAMID
Circus troupe The Flying Wallendas (USA, above) performed an eight-person pyramid suspended at a height of 7.62 m (25 ft) at Sarasota, Florida, USA, on 20 February 2001.

LONGEST DRUMMING MARATHON
Paskaran Sreekaram (Singapore), Selvapandian Shunmuga Sundaram (Singapore) and Mirajkar Nawaz Mohammad (India) banged a set of drums continuously for 27 hr 45 min at Kolam Ayer Community Club, Singapore, from 2–3 February 2001.

FASTEST BED-MAKING
The fastest time for making a bed with one blanket, two sheets, an undersheet, an uncased pillow, one pillowcase, one counterpane and hospital corners is 14 seconds by Sister Sharon Stringer and Nurse Michelle Benkel (both UK) of the Royal Masonic Hospital, London, UK, at Canary Wharf, London, UK, on 26 November 1993.

MOST POTATOES PEELED
The greatest quantity of potatoes peeled by five people to a recognized cookery standard and using kitchen knives is 482.8 kg (1,064 lb 6 oz) in 45 minutes by Marj Killian, Terry Anderson, Barbara Pearson, Marilyn Small and Janene Utkin (all USA) at the 64th Annual Idaho Spud Day celebration. The event took place at Shelley, Idaho, USA, on 19 September 1992.

FASTEST CROSSING OF FLORIDA STRAITS BY PADDLEBOARD
The fastest crossing of the 180-km (110-mile) Florida Straits between Havana, Cuba, and Key West, Florida, on a paddleboard, is 19 hr 19 min 52 sec by Michael Lee, Jeff Horn, Derek Levy and Michael O'Shaughnessey (all USA), paddling in relay, on 23 June 2000.

MOST BEER CRATES STACKED IN PYRAMID
On 21–22 June 1997 a team of 86 people from Villeroy & Boch Nederland, Anklaarsewg, The Netherlands, stacked 53,955 beer crates to form a pyramid in 15 hr 57 min. The record was achieved in Loo, The Netherlands.

GREATEST DISTANCE TO PUSH A PRAM IN 24 HOURS
A 10-man team from the Royal Marines School of Music, Deal, Kent, UK, pushed a pram containing an adult dressed as a baby a distance of 437.3 km (271.7 miles) in 24 hours from 22–23 November 1990.

HEAVIEST WEIGHT PULLED BY A DOG-SLED TEAM
On 22 October 2000 in Whitehorse, Yukon, Canada, 210 dogs pulled a sled attached to both a Kenworth tractor and a seven-axle rail trailer combination, the latter with a track mounted drill – adding up to a total weight of 65,910 kg (145,302 lb). The vehicle reached 15 km/h (9 mph) and travelled a distance of six blocks.

FURTHEST DISTANCE TO PUSH A LAWN MOWER IN 24 HOURS
From 13–14 September 1997, four members of the Stowmarket and District Round Table, Suffolk, UK, pushed a standard lawn mower 162.936 km (101 miles 429 yd) around a course at Chilton Fields, Suffolk, UK.

GREATEST DISTANCE TO PULL A BOEING 747
A team of 60 British policemen pulled a Boeing 747-400 aeroplane weighing 205 tonnes (451,947 lb) a distance of 100 m (328 ft) in just 53.33 sec at London Heathrow Airport, London, UK, on 27 September 2000.

FURTHEST DISTANCE TO ROLL A BARREL IN 24 HOURS
A team of 10 from Groningen, The Netherlands, rolled a 63.5-kg (140-lb) barrel 263.9 km (163 miles) in 24 hours on 28–29 November 1998 at Stadspark, Rotterdam, The Netherlands.

MOST TRAMPOLINE SOMERSAULTS IN ONE HOUR
The most complete somersaults performed in one hour by a team is 7,043 by 10 members of the Kirklees Rebound Trampoline Club, using two trampolines at Huddersfield Sports Centre, Huddersfield, West Yorkshire, UK, on 24 July 1999.

HAND-WALKING RELAY
A four-man relay team walking on their hands covered 1.6 km (1 mile) in 24 min 48 sec on 15 March 1987 at Knoxville, Tennessee, USA.

FASTEST OPENING OF 300 BEER BOTTLES
The fastest time to open 300 bottles of beer by a team of three is 1 min 47 sec. The leader of the team was Alois Unertl (Germany) of the German Unertl Brewery in Munich, Germany, on 2 April 1999.

MOST CANS STACKED IN A PYRAMID IN 30 MINUTES
A team of Malaysian students constructed a pyramid from 9,455 aluminium cans in 24 minutes on 23 September 2000 at Midvalley Mega Mall, Kuala Lumpur, Malaysia. The pyramid had a square base of 30 x 30 cans, measuring 1.98 x 1.98 m (6.5 x 6.5 ft), and reached a height of 3.36 m (11.02 ft).

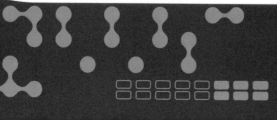

LONGEST GAME OF HUMAN TABLE FOOTBALL
On 5 August 2001 in Ilhavo, Portugal, 360 people took part in a game of human table football (above) that lasted 12 hours. Human table football is played with people tied to huge rotatable poles on a giant football pitch.

FASTEST THREE-LEGGED MARATHON

Identical twins Nick and Alastair Benbow (UK) set a three-legged running record in the London Marathon, London, UK, with a time of 3 hr 40 min 16 sec on 26 April 1998. They were tied together at the wrist and shared a three-legged pair of trousers for the duration of their run.

MOST REVOLUTIONS ON A THRILL SWING

Paavo Lahtinen and Martti Pohjosaho (Finland) completed 212 continuous 360-degree revolutions on a thrill-swing fairground ride measuring 3.8 m (12.46 ft) tall and 2.85 m (9.35 ft) wide on 7 July 2000 at Karstula, Finland.

MOST CARS DRIVEN ON TWO WHEELS SIMULTANEOUSLY

A team from Renault drove a continuous line of 16 cars on two wheels simultaneously at a military base at Evreux, France, on 26 November 2000. The stunt was filmed for the TV show *L'Émission des Records* that was screened on 23 December 2000.

FURTHEST DISTANCE PUSHING A BATH TUB IN 24 HOURS

The greatest distance covered in 24 hours pushing a wheeled bath tub containing one passenger is 513.32 km (318.96 miles), by a team of 25 from Tea Tree Gully Baptist Church, Westfield, WA, Australia, on 11–12 March 1995.

MOST SHOES SHINED IN EIGHT HOURS

Four teenagers polished off eight hours shining 14,975 shoes at the London Church of Christ at Leicester Square, London, UK, on 15 June 1996.

MOST PEOPLE ON A SINGLE PAIR OF SKIS

The greatest number of people to travel on one pair of skis is 64, at the Norwegian Giant Ski Event in Ottawa, Ontario, Canada, on 4 February 2001 (below). The participants covered 120 m (400 ft) on the skis, which, at 64 m (210 ft), are the longest pair ever made.

MOST PEOPLE FLOSSING SIMULTANEOUSLY ON THE SAME LENGTH OF FLOSS
On 31 July 2001, 297 people flossed for 45 seconds with a 457.2-m-long (1,500-ft) piece of dental floss to the tune 'Eye of the Tiger' at Lake Geneva Youth Camp, Illinois, USA (above). There was a minimum of 60 cm (2 ft) of floss between each person. Dental personnel were on hand to ensure the attempt was executed safely and correctly.

MOST PEOPLE BRUSHING TEETH SIMULTANEOUSLY
On 9 September 2001 in 'The Great American Brush Off' at Coors Baseball Field in Denver, Colorado, USA, 1,586 baseball fans broke the world record for most people simultaneously brushing their teeth using innovative 'eBrushes' supplied by Waterpik Technologies, Inc (USA). The fans were supplied with an eBrush, a tube of toothpaste, a bottle of water and a spitting receptacle, and each participant brushed for a full minute.

LARGEST MOBILE PHONE RING
The world's largest mobile phone ring took place in Leicester Square, London, UK, on 5 September 2001, when the mobile phones of 260 people played the same ring tone (cinema advertiser Pearl and Dean's theme tune) simultaneously.

LARGEST WALK
The New Paper Big Walk 2000 had 77,500 participants and started from the National Stadium, Singapore, on 21 May 2000. It was organized by The Singapore Press Holdings, The Singapore Amateur Athletic Association and The Singapore Sports Council. The purpose of the walk was to promote healthy living in Singapore.

LARGEST SIMULTANEOUS JUMP
The largest simultaneous jump occurred on 7 September 2001 to celebrate the launch of Science Year in the UK. At precisely 11:00 am, 559,493 people began jumping up and down in 2,171 schools all over the UK for one minute. The total number of participants was 569,069. The extra numbers were made up by disabled pupils who contributed to the seismic activity by dropping objects on the ground or hitting the ground with their fists.

LARGEST TWIST
A total of 1,055 people danced the Twist for five minutes at Coquina Beach, Bradenton, Florida, USA, on 31 December 1999. The event was organized by the *Manatee Herald Tribune* for the Millennium festivities.

LARGEST GAME OF MUSICAL CHAIRS
On 5 August 1989 the largest game of musical chairs began with 8,238 participants at the Anglo-Chinese School in Singapore. Three-and-a-half hours later, the game ended with the lucky 15-year-old winner Xu Chong Wei (Singapore) on the last chair. He won the first prize of a trip for two to Bali.

LARGEST HUG
On 16 October 2001 staff and students from the Rocori Area Schools, Minnesota, USA, broke the world record for the largest hug, with 2,903 participants. The circle was continuous and the participants held the hug for 15 seconds.

LARGEST GAME OF CHINESE WHISPERS
The largest ever game of Chinese Whispers (aka 'Telephone') took place at Wembley Conference Centre, London, UK, on 22 May 2002. The group of record-breaking whisperers was made up of 296 employees of Procter & Gamble UK and Ireland MDO.

LARGEST IRISH DANCE
A total of 6,971 people danced for five minutes at the Dublin Irish Festival, Dublin, Ohio, USA, on 1 August 1998. Professional ceilidh dance callers presided at the event and Irish bands played traditional jig music.

LARGEST TEA PARTY
The world's largest tea party took place on 19 August 2001 at the Fort Canning Park, Singapore. It was organized by Care Community Services and Dairy Farm Singapore and was attended by 7,121 people. Altogether, 20,700 cups of hot and cold Lipton tea were served on the day, along with 6,500 goodie bags, 20,000 pieces of cake and 19,500 pieces of fruit. A total of SG$145,000 (£57,535 or $78,985) was raised for charity through ticket sales and individual donations.

LARGEST GATHERING OF CLOWNS
In 1991 at Bognor Regis, Dorset, UK, 850 clowns, including 430 from North America, assembled for their annual convention, which was arranged by Clowns International, the largest and oldest clown organization. The first clown convention was held in 1946.

MOST PEOPLE WEARING GROUCHO MARX GLASSES AT ONE TIME
The largest recorded number of people simultaneously wearing Groucho Marx-style glasses, nose and moustache at one location is 522 on an enclosed tennis court in Pittsfield, New Hampshire, USA, on 14 July 2001.

MOST PEOPLE SKIPPING SIMULTANEOUSLY
On 24 September 2000, 1,060 students (above) skipped rope for three minutes at the Tamar Site, Hong Kong, for World Heart Day. The event was organized by The Hong Kong College of Cardiology and the Tung Wah Group of Hospitals.

MOST PEOPLE BLOWING BUBBLES AT ONE TIME

On 16 May 1999, 23,680 people blew glycerine bubbles into the air for one full minute prior to West Ham's home Premier League fixture against Middlesbrough FC at the Boleyn Ground, Upton Park, London, UK. West Ham United FC's anthem is 'I'm Forever Blowing Bubbles'. The song was inspired by William Murray, who played for West Ham in the 1920s and resembled a child in a Pears' soap advertisement who was pictured blowing bubbles!

LARGEST EASTER EGG HUNT

On 14 April 2001 Hershey Canada and Canadian Niagara Hotels, Inc organized the world's largest Easter egg hunt. The event featured 8,200 children aged between six and 12, who hunted for 254,000 eggs in Queen Victoria Park, Niagara Falls, Ontario, Canada. The eggs were made from 11,340 kg (25,000 lb) of chocolate. Laid end to end, they would be two-and-a-half times higher than Mount Everest.

LARGEST MASS BUNGEE JUMP

On 6 September 1998, 25 people bungee-jumped simultaneously from a platform suspended 52 m (170 ft) above the ground, in front of the headquarters of Deutsche Bank, Frankfurt, Germany. The event, which was organized by Sanver Bungee on behalf of Frankfurt City Council, was part of a 'skyscraper festival' to draw public attention to the city's modern architecture and burgeoning business district.

LARGEST HUMAN LOGO

On 24 July 1999 a total of 34,309 people gathered at the National Stadium of Jamor, Lisbon, Portugal, to create the Portuguese logo for Euro 2004, as part of Portugal's successful bid to hold the UEFA football championships in 2004. The event was organized by Realizar Eventos Especiais (Portugal).

MOST COUPLES KISSING SIMULTANEOUSLY

On 11 February 2000, 1,588 couples kissed simultaneously for 10 seconds as part of 'The Big Kiss' sponsored by Radio Sarnia Lambton, Ontario, Canada.

GREATEST SIMULTANEOUS LEAPFROG

On 22 May 2002 at the Wembley Conference Centre, London, UK, 415 employees from Procter & Gamble UK and Ireland MDO broke the world record for most people leapfrogging at one time in one location.

LONGEST DISTANCE LEAP-FROGGED

A team of 14 students from Stanford University, Stanford, California, USA, covered 1,603.2 km (996.2 miles) leapfrogging for 244 hr 43 min in May 1991.

LOUDEST CROWD SCREAM

On 5 July 1998 at The Party in the Park, Hyde Park, London, UK, Trevor Lewis (UK) of CEL Instruments Ltd (UK) measured a scream by the crowd at a volume of 126.3 dBA.

MOST NATIONALITIES IN A SAUNA

On 8 March 2002 in Halmstad, Sweden, 29 male participants from 29 different countries crammed into the same sauna and shut the door for 10 minutes – setting the record for most nationalities simultaneously in a sauna.

FASTEST ONE-MILE BARREL ROLL
The record for rolling a full 163.6-litre (36-gal) metal beer barrel over a mile is 8 min 7.2 sec, by Phillip Randle, Steve Hewitt, John Round, Trevor Bradley, Colin Barnes and Ray Glover (all UK) of Haunchwood Collieries Institute and Social Club, Nuneaton, Warwks, UK, on 15 August 1982.

MOST BEER KEGS LIFTED IN SIX HOURS
Tom Gaskin (Ireland) raised a keg of beer weighing 62.5 kg (137 lb 8 oz) above his head 902 times in six hours at Liska House, Newry, Co Down, UK, on 26 October 1996.

HIGHEST BEER KEG TOSS
Juha Rasanen (Finland) threw a 12.3-kg (27-lb 1.6-oz) beer keg over a bar that was set at a height of 6.93 m (22 ft 8.76 in) on the set of *El Show de los Récords*, Madrid, Spain, on 21 September 2001.

LONGEST WASHING MACHINE THROW
Miguel Ballesteros and José Francisco Dopcio de Pablo (both Spain) managed to throw a washing machine weighing 47 kg (103 lb 9.8 oz) a distance of 6.37 m (20 ft 10.68 in) at the studios of *El Show de los Récords*, Madrid, Spain, on 23 October 2001.

HEAVIEST DEADLIFT WITH LITTLE FINGER
The heaviest deadlift with the little finger is 89.6 kg (197 lb 8.54 oz) by Barry Anderson (UK) on 14 October 2000 at the Bass Museum, Burton-upon-Trent, Staffs, UK.

HEAVIEST BOAT PULLED
David Huxley (Australia) pulled the 1,006-tonne (221,785-lb) *Delphin*, with a cargo of passengers and 175 cars over 7 m (23 ft) on 19 November 1998 in Rostock, Germany.

HEAVIEST CAR BALANCED ON THE HEAD
On 24 May 1999 former hod-carrier John Evans (UK, above) balanced a gutted Mini car, weighing a total of 159.6 kg (352 lb), on his head for 33 seconds at the London Studios, London, UK.

MOST WATERMELONS CRUSHED
Leonardo D'Andrea (Italy) crushed 16 watermelons with his head in one minute in Madrid, Spain, on 18 October 2001. For each melon to count toward the record, it had to be broken into two pieces.

HEAVIEST TRAIN PULLED
Juraj Barbaric (Slovakia) single-handedly pulled a 20 freight-car train weighing 1,000 tonnes (2.2 million lb) a distance of 4.5 m (14 ft 9 in) along a railway track at Kosice, Slovakia, on 1 June 1999.

HEAVIEST WEIGHT LIFTED WITH TEETH
Walter Arfeuille (Belgium) lifted weights totalling 281.5 kg (620 lb 10 oz) a distance of 17 cm (6.75 in) off the ground with his teeth in Paris, France, on 31 March 1990.

LONGEST AEROPLANE RESTRAINT
Using ropes looped around his arms, Ilkka Nummisto (Finland) prevented the take-off of two Cessna planes pulling in opposite directions for 54 seconds at Räyskälä Airport, Finland, on 1 August 2001.

FASTEST TYRE-FLIPPING OVER 20 METRES
Flipping a Michelin Radial Steel Cord X26.5R25 (XHA) tyre weighing 420 kg (925 lb 14.4 oz), Israel Garrido Sanguinetti (Spain), completed a 20-m (65-ft 7.3-in) course (10 m or 32 ft 9.6 in each way) in 56.3 seconds on *El Show de los Récords*, Madrid, Spain, on 11 December 2001.

GREATEST WEIGHT BROKEN ON CHEST WHILE LYING ON BED OF NAILS
On 23 June 2001, while lying on a bed of nails, Lee Graber (USA) had concrete blocks weighing a total of 222.07 kg (489 lb 9.76 oz) placed on his chest and then broken with a 6.35-kg (14-lb) sledgehammer. The event took place at Ontario Place, Toronto, Ontario, Canada.

MOST CONCRETE BLOCKS BROKEN USING HAN MOO DO TECHNIQUE
Jani Käkelä (Finland) broke 11 stacked concrete blocks with one blow, using the Han Moo Do technique, in Helsinki, Finland, on 11 October 2000. Each block had a minimum density of 650 kg/m^3 (40 lb/ft^3).

MOST BASEBALL BATS BROKEN IN ONE MINUTE
On 31 March 2001 in Munich, Germany, Markus Böck (Germany) broke 23 baseball bats with his shin in a minute.

MOST WEIGHT LIFTED WITH EARS, NIPPLES AND TONGUE
The most weight lifted using ears, tongue and nipples simultaneously is 13.19 kg (29 lb 1.6 oz) by Joe Hermann (USA), a member of the Jim Rose Circus. He lifted two standard 1.04-kg (2-lb 4.8-oz) steam irons with his earlobes, picked up a 2.26-kg (5-lb) car battery with his tongue and supported the weight of a 7.12-kg (15-lb 11.2-oz) cinder block from his nipples to earn the record in Los Angeles, California, USA, on 25 September 1998.

FASTEST WORLD WIFE-CARRYING CHAMPIONSHIP RUN
The fastest time to complete the annual 235-m (771-ft) obstacle course of the World Wife-Carrying Championships, held in Sonkajärvi, Finland, is 55.5 seconds by Margo Uusorg and Birgit Ulricht (both Estonia, above) on 1 July 2000.

FASTEST TIME TO BEND AN IRON BAR AND FIT IT INTO A SUITCASE

The fastest time to bend a 6-m-long (19-ft 7.2-in) iron bar which has a diameter of 12 mm (0.47 in) and fit it into a Samsonite suitcase measuring 50 x 70 x 20 cm (19.6 x 27.5 x 7.87 in) is 44 seconds, by Thomas Bleiker (Switzerland) in Munich, Germany, on 20 January 2000. He bent the bar a total of 23 times.

HEAVIEST WEIGHT LIFTED BY A HUMAN BEARD

The heaviest weight lifted by a human beard is 61.3 kg (135 lb) when Antanas Kontrimas lifted Ruta Cekyte (both Lithuania) off the ground for 15 seconds on 18 August 2001 at the VIII International Country Festival 2001, Visaginas, Lithuania.

MOST BRICKS LIFTED

Russell Bradley (UK) lifted 31 bricks – laid side-by-side – off a table, raising them to chest height and holding them for two seconds on 14 June 1992.

GREATEST WEIGHT OF BRICKS LIFTED

Fred Burton (UK) lifted the greatest weight of bricks ever, when he held 20 bricks, weighing 102.73 kg (226 lb 7 oz) for two seconds on 5 June 1998.

HEAVIEST BRICKS BALANCED ON HEAD

John Evans (UK) balanced 101 bricks, weighing a total of 188.7 kg (416 lb), on his head for 10 seconds at the BBC Television Centre, London, UK, on 24 December 1997.

MOST WEIGHT ON BODY

The most weight sustained on the body is 1,381.19 kg (3,045 lb) by Master Kahled Dahdouh (USA) on 13 August 1999. The weight was made up of cinder blocks measuring 40.6 x 20.3 x 20.3 cm (16 x 8 x 8 in) and three bodybuilders, placed on his chest for five seconds.

MOST CONSECUTIVE ONE-ARM CHIN-UPS

Robert Chisholm (Canada) completed 22 consecutive one-arm chin-ups at Queen's University, Kingston, Ontario, Canada, on 3 December 1982.

HEAVIEST TRUCK PULL

The heaviest truck pulled over 30.48 m (100 ft) weighed 24,640 kg (54,321 lb) and was pulled by Kevin Fast (Canada, below) at Cobourg, Ontario, Canada, on 30 June 2001.

FASTEST TOMATO KETCHUP DRINKER
Dustin Phillips (USA, above) drank a standard 400-g (14-oz) bottle of Heinz tomato ketchup through a 0.64-cm-diameter (0.25-in) drinking straw in 33 seconds on the set of *Guinness World Records: Primetime* in Los Angeles, California, USA, on 23 September 1999. He consumed around 91% of the bottle's contents.

FASTEST BACKWARDS RUN FROM LOS ANGELES TO NEW YORK
Between 18 August and 3 December 1984 Arvind Pandya (India) ran backwards across America from Los Angeles to New York City. His 107-day journey covered around 2,400 km (1,500 miles) at an average of 22.5 km (14 miles) per day.

FASTEST REVERSE DRIVING
Darren Manning (UK) attained a speed of 165.08 km/h (102.58 mph) driving backwards in a Caterham 7 Fireblade, at Kemble Airfield, Gloucester, UK, on 22 October 2001.

FASTEST BED PUSH
The fastest time for the annual 3.27-km (2.04-mile) Knaresborough Bed Race (established 1966) in North Yorks, UK, is 12 min 9 sec. The record feat was achieved by the Vibroplant team on 9 June 1990.

FASTEST WHEELBARROW RACE
The fastest time attained in a 1.609-km (1-mile) wheelbarrow race is 4 min 48.51 sec, by Piet Pitzer and Jaco Erasmus (both South Africa) at Transvalia High School, Vanderbijlpark, South Africa, on 3 October 1987. One was running, pushing the barrow, while the other remained seated in the barrow.

FASTEST 50-M 31-LEGGED RACE
Students from the Ogori-minami school in Yamaguchi, Japan, ran a 31-legged race over a total of 50 m (160.04 ft) in 9.12 seconds on 5 December 1999.

FASTEST HUMAN CALCULATOR
Scott Flansburg (USA) correctly added a randomly selected two-digit number (38) to itself 36 times in 15 seconds without the use of a calculator on 27 April 2000.

MOST RICE GRAINS EATEN IN 3 MINUTES
Tae Wah Gooding (South Korea) ate 64 grains of rice, one by one, using chopsticks, in 3 minutes at Peterborough Regional College, Peterborough, Cambs, UK, on 7 November 2000.

MOST GRAPES EATEN IN 3 MINUTES
The record for the largest amount of grapes eaten in 3 minutes is held by Mat Hand (UK), who consumed a total of 133 grapes in this time on 8 November 2001.

FASTEST RUN UP THE EMPIRE STATE BUILDING
Paul Crake (Australia) ascended the 1,576 steps of the Empire State Building in 9 min 53 sec at the 23rd Annual Empire State Building Run-Up, New York City, USA, on 23 February 2000.

Belinda Soszyn (Australia) is the fastest woman to achieve the same feat. In 1996 she completed a run-up in 12 min 19 sec.

MOST SALMONS FILLETED IN 10 MINUTES
Per-Arne Korshag (Sweden) filleted 228.3 kg (503.31 lb) of salmon in 10 minutes on 13 December 1998.

MOST OYSTERS OPENED IN ONE MINUTE
Marcel Lesoille (France) opened 29 oysters in one minute on the set of *El Show de los Récords*, Madrid, Spain, on 15 November 2001.

FASTEST TIME TO SOLVE A RUBIK CUBE
Vietnamese refugee Minh Thai won the World Rubik Cube Championship in Budapest, Hungary, on 5 June 1982.

His winning time was 22.95 seconds. Ernö Rubik's (Hungary) cube, which has 43,252,003,274,489,856,856,000 combinations, was patented in 1977.

FASTEST WINE BOTTLE OPENER
Alain Dorotte (France) opened 13 wine bottles with a 'T-handled' corkscrew (non-leverage) in one minute on 18 April 2001.

MOST SURGICAL GLOVES INFLATED IN 2 MINUTES
Susanne 'Tussen' Formgren (Sweden) inflated three pre-powdered procedure surgical gloves until they burst, in a time of 2 minutes, at the studios of *Guinness Rekord TV*, Stockholm, Sweden, on 1 February 2001.

FASTEST PANTOMIME HORSE
On 3 August 1999 at St Andrews School, Cobham, Surrey, UK, Geoff Seale and Stuart Coleman (both UK) won the pantomime horse race, which was run over a distance of 100 m (328.08 ft) in a time of 16.7 seconds. Seven other 'horses' competed. The race marked the pair's debut as a pantomime horse.

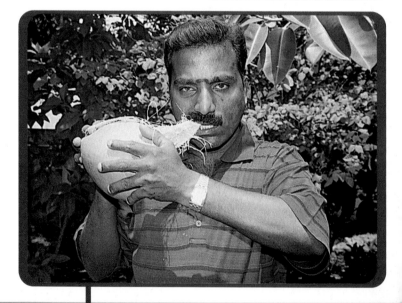

FASTEST COCONUT HUSKER
Using his teeth, Raman Andiappan (India, above) husked a coconut with a 46-cm (18.125-in) circumference and weighing 4.64 kg (10 lb 3.66 oz) in 37.67 seconds on *Guinness World Records: Primetime*, Los Angeles, USA, on 11 March 2001.

MOST SAUSAGES EATEN IN ONE MINUTE

The record for the most sausages eaten in one minute is held by Stefan Paladin (New Zealand), who ate eight whole sausages at the Ericsson Stadium, Auckland, New Zealand, on 22 July 2001. The sausages were 10 cm (3.94 in) long and 2 cm (0.79 in) wide.

FASTEST TALKER

Steve Woodmore (UK) spoke a total of 595 words in 56.01 seconds – a rate of 637.4 words per minute – on the UK's ITV programme *Motor Mouth* on 22 September 1990. Most people speak at a rate of about 60 words per minute – around a word a second. In an excited state, a person may reach 120 to 150 words per minute.

FASTEST RAP ARTIST

Rebel X.D. (USA, real name Seandale Price) beat his own record by rapping 683 syllables in 54.501 seconds on the set of *Guinness World Records: Primetime* in Los Angeles, California, USA, on 24 June 1998.

MOST WORDS SPOKEN BACKWARDS IN A MINUTE

Sara Jokinen (Finland) spoke 47 words backwards in one minute in Helsinki, Finland, on 19 October 2001.

FASTEST HAIRCUT

Trevor Mitchell (UK) cut a full head of hair in 1 min 13 sec on 26 November 1999 at the Southampton City Guildhall, Hants, UK, as part of BBC TV's *Children in Need* event.

FASTEST TIME TO MAKE 1 LITRE OF ICE CREAM

On 20 March 2002 Peter Barnham (UK) broke his previous record by making the fastest litre of ice cream in 20.91 seconds. The successful record attempt was carried out on location for the Discovery Channel's *Kitchen Chemistry*, in Maidenhead, Berks, UK.

FASTEST CONSTRUCTION OF A 30-LEVEL JENGA TOWER

The fastest time to build a stable Jenga tower 30 levels high within the rules of the game is 12 min 27 sec by Simon Spalding and Ali Malik (both UK) at Highclere Castle, Hampshire, UK, on 17 August 1997.

FASTEST MUSIC VIDEO (FILM TO BROADCAST)

The fastest time in which a music video has been filmed and then broadcast is 3 hr 46 min 19 sec. The video, which featured the band Electric Soft Parade (UK), was made using Microsoft Windows XP at HMV, London, UK, on 25 October 2001.

FASTEST FURNITURE

'The Casual Lofa', a motorized sofa built by Edd China (UK, below) and David Davenport (UK), has a top speed of 140 km/h (87 mph). Powered by a Mini 1300-cc engine, it is licensed for use on UK roads and is steered by means of turning a medium-sized pizza pan. It has a seating capacity for one driver with two passengers sitting alongside. The car has covered 10,008.5 km (6,219 miles) since it was built.

YOUNGEST PUBLISHED COOK

Justin Miller (USA, above, b. 1990) became famous for his cooking prowess at the age of five after appearing on the *David Letterman Show*. Two years later he published his cookbook, *Cooking with Justin: Recipes for Kids (and Parents)*. He now advises the Marriott hotel chain on its children's menus.

YOUNGEST CONSULTANT

On 15 April 2000 supermarket chain Tesco announced that it had procured the services of seven-year-old Laurie Sleator (UK), to advise senior executives on the *Pokemon* cartoon craze then sweeping the globe.

YOUNGEST PERSON TO HAVE RESEARCH PUBLISHED

Emily Rosa (USA) became the youngest person to have serious research published in a scientific or medical journal when an article she co-authored at the age of 11 appeared in the *Journal of the American Medical Association* on 1 April 1998. The article reported an experiment on Touch Therapy conceived by Emily when she was only eight years old.

The fourth-grader's project created an uproar at the time as the therapy she was questioning was being used in over 80 hospitals throughout the USA.

OLDEST FILM DIRECTOR

George Cukor (USA, 1899–1983) made his 50th and final film, *Rich and Famous* (USA,1981) at the age of 81.

YOUNGEST AUTHOR

The youngest commercially published author on record is Dorothy Straight (USA) who wrote *How the World Began* in 1962 at the age of four. It was published in August 1964 by Pantheon Books.

OLDEST MOTORCYCLIST

On 2 May 2000 Len Vale Onslow (UK) rode his motorcycle 194.9 km (121 miles) to the gates of Buckingham Palace, London, UK, to receive his congratulatory telegram from HM The Queen on the occasion of his 100th birthday. Len has been riding motorcycles since he was seven years old and still rides regularly.

OLDEST CHORUS LINE MEMBER

The oldest 'showgirl' still regularly performing in a chorus line is Beverly Allen (USA, b. 4 November 1917). A member of The Fabulous Palm Springs Follies, her jitterbug routine – in which her partner lifts her over his head – is a favourite with audiences.

OLDEST PERSON TO ABSEIL DOWN A BUILDING

On 25 November 2000 Dorothy Williams (UK, b. 26 January 1916), successfully abseiled down a 30.48-m (100-ft) building in Flintshire, Wales, UK. The event was sponsored by the North East Wales Search and Rescue Team and raised £2,071 ($3,000) for cancer research. Dorothy plans to become the world's oldest free-fall parachute jumper.

OLDEST COMPETITIVE BALLROOM DANCER

The oldest competitive ballroom dancer was Albert J Sylvester (UK, 1889–1989) who retired at the age of 94. In addition to being a record-breaking ballroom dancer, Sylvester was the personal secretary to UK prime minister David Lloyd-George.

OLDEST OPERA SINGER

The Ukrainian bass Mark Reizen (1895–1992) sang the role of Prince Gremin in Tchaikovsky's *Eugene Onegin* at the Moscow's Bolshoi Theatre on his 90th birthday in 1985, highlighting his 70-year opera career.

OLDEST PRACTISING BARBER

Born in 1910, Leamon Ward (USA) has been cutting hair professionally since July 1927, when he was 17 – that's over 70 years of continuous barbering. In many cases he has cut the hair of several generations of families.

OLDEST ADOPTION

Paula Louise Daly Winter Dolan (USA, b. 1940) became the oldest person to be adopted on 5 November 1998 when, aged 58 years, 5 months and 17 days, she was adopted by her aunt and uncle, John A Winter and Elizabeth R Winter (both USA).

OLDEST MALE PARACHUTIST

Norwegian Bjarne Mæland (b. 1899) made his first tandem parachute jump (in which two parachutists jump at the same time) at the age of 100 years 21 days. He jumped from a height of 3,200 m (10,499 ft) above Stavanger Airport, Sola, Norway, on 8 September 1999.

OLDEST WING WALKER

On 23 December 1999, 87-year-old Martha Ritchie (South Africa, b. 5 April 1912), performed an eight-minute wing walk on a 1942 Boeing Stearman over Port Elizabeth Airport, South Africa.

OLDEST BEST MAN

On 14 August 1999, Philip Hicks (UK, b. 26 March 1906) served as best man at his daughter's wedding at the age of 93. At the civil ceremony in St Michel de Vax, France, Phillip proudly gave his daughter away before promptly moving to the right to become the best man of his future son-in-law.

YOUNGEST BILLIONAIRE

Taiwan-born Jerry Yang (USA, above), co-founder of internet search engine Yahoo! Inc, became a billionaire in 1997 when aged 29. According to *Forbes* magazine, in 2002 Yang's net worth dropped to an estimated $730 million (£520 million).

OLDEST BAREFOOT WATER-SKIER

On 10 February 2002, George Blair, (USA, below), successfully water-skied barefoot on Lake Florence, Winter Haven, Florida, USA, aged 87 years 18 days. George had already set the record for the oldest snowboarder on 22 January 2001 when he hit the snowy slopes of Steamboat Springs, Colorado, USA, with his snowboard.

OLDEST PERSON TO FLY IN A HOT-AIR BALLOON

Florence Laine (UK, 1894–1999) flew in a hot-air balloon aged 102 years 92 days. The balloon travelled 3 km (1.86 miles) over Cust, New Zealand, on 26 September 1996.

OLDEST PILOT

Col Clarence Cornish (USA, 1898–1995) was flying aircraft at the age of 97, the last occasion being when he flew a Cessna 172 on 4 December 1995. His first flight had been on 6 May 1918, and he made his first solo flight 21 days later. Col Cornish died 18 days after his last flight.

YOUNGEST DJ

Llewellyn Owen (UK, b. 21 February 1992), aka 'DJ Welly', headlined at London's Warp Club on 1 May 2000 when aged 8 years 70 days. A native Londoner, DJ Welly is paid the same as popular DJs five times his age – approximately £125 ($190) per hour. Since his professional debut, he has headlined at famous clubs such as London's Ministry of Sound and played at the Glastonbury Music Festival.

OLDEST BRIDESMAID

Flossie Bennett (UK, b. 9 August 1902) was matron of honour when aged 97 years 6 months at the wedding of her close friends Leonard and Edna Petchey on 6 February 1999 at St Peter's Church, Holton, Suffolk, UK. Len's 12-year-old granddaughter was the other bridesmaid at the service, creating an 85-year age gap between Edna's two bridesmaids.

MOST CHAINSAW JUGGLING ROTATIONS
The greatest number of rotations of three juggled chainsaws is 12 (36 throws) by Karoly Donnert (Hungary, above) on the set of *Guinness Rekord TV*, Stockholm, Sweden on 30 January 2001.

FASTEST TIME TO BOIL WATER THROUGH BODY
With electricity passing through his body, Slavisa Pajkic 'Biba' (Yugoslavia) was able to heat a 15-ml (0.5-fl-oz) cup of water from 25°C to 97°C (77°F to 206°F) in a time of 1 min 37 sec on 24 November 2001.

FURTHEST SPAGHETTI NASAL EJECTION
Kevin Cole (USA) holds the record for the longest spaghetti strand blown out of a nostril in a single blow. On 16 December 1998 Cole successfully achieved a record distance of 19 cm (7.5 in) in Los Angeles, California, USA.

LONGEST GRAPE BLOWING
Marianne Gille (Sweden) kept a grape suspended in the air above her mouth for 4.81 seconds in Stockholm, Sweden, on 29 November 2001.

LONGEST FRYING PAN SPIN ON FINGER
Anders Björklund (Sweden) was able to spin a frying pan on his finger for 14 minutes on 29 November 2001.

HEAVIEST EAR WEIGHTLIFT
The heaviest weight lifted using only the ear is 50 kg (110 lb 1.6 oz) by Li Jian Hua (China) who lifted a column of bricks hanging from a clamp attached to his ear and held the weight for 9.3 seconds on 17 December 1998.

MOST TENNIS BALLS HELD IN THE HAND
Roberto Barra-Chicote (Spain) was able to place 16 tennis balls in his hand and hold them for five seconds at the studios of *L'Émission des Records* on 30 November 2001.

HIGHEST GOLF BALL STACK
Don Athey (USA) stacked nine golf balls vertically without the use of adhesives on 4 October 1998.

MOST FACES SHAVED BY A SAFETY RAZOR
Denny Rowe (UK) shaved 1,994 men in 60 minutes with a safety razor at Herne Bay, Kent, UK, on 19 June 1988, taking on average 1.8 second per man and drawing blood four times.

FASTEST UNDERPANT JUMPER
Matthieu Bommier (France) jumped into and out of a pair of underpants a total of 27 times in a minute on the set of *L'Émission des Records*, Paris, France, on 18 April 2001.

MOST BEER BOTTLE CAPS REMOVED WITH TEETH IN ONE MINUTE
José Ivan Hernandez (USA) removed 56 beer bottle caps with his teeth in one minute in the TV studios of *Ricki Lake*, New York City, USA, on 5 December 2001.

MOST STOREYS IN A HOUSE OF CARDS
On 6 November 1999 architecture graduate Bryan Berg (USA) built a free-standing house of standard playing cards that had 131 storeys. The house was built to a height of 7.71 m (25 ft 3.48 in) using 91,800 cards in the casino at Potsdammer Platz, Berlin, Germany. The total weight of the 1,765 packs of cards used was 110 kg (242 lb 8 oz). No adhesives of any kind are used on the playing cards when constructing these creations.

MOST BEER MATS FLIPPED
Dean Gould (UK) flipped a pile of 111 beer mats each 1.2 mm (0.05 in) thick through 180º and caught them at Edinburgh, Lothian, UK, on 13 January 1993.

MOST BARRELS JUMPED
The men's record for barrel jumping (circling an ice rink to gain speed, before jumping a row of barrels laid down side by side) is 18 barrels, by Yvon Jolin Junior (Canada) – the first Triple Crown Barrel Jumping Champion in the history of barrel jumping – at Terrebonne, Quebec, Canada on 12 April 1980. The distance jumped was 8.43 m (27 ft 8 in). The women's record is 6.84 m (22 ft 5 in) over 13 barrels, by Marie-Jose Houle (Canadian) at Lasalle, Quebec, Canada, on 1 March 1987.

FURTHEST FIRE BREATHING DISTANCE
Reg Morris (UK) blew a flame from his mouth to a distance of 9.4 m (31 ft) at The Miner's Rest, Chasetown, Staffs, UK, on 29 October 1986.

HIGHEST FIRE BREATHING FLAME
Henrik Segelstrom (Sweden) blew a flame to a height of 3 m (9 ft 9.6 in) on the set of *Guinness Rekord TV*, Stockholm, Sweden, on 28 November 2001.

MOST HULA HOOPING HOOPS
The record for 'hula hooping' the most hoops simultaneously is 83, held by Cia Grangér (Finland) in Helsinki, Finland, on 25 October 1999. She sustained three full revolutions of the standard size and weight hula hoops between her shoulders and her hips.

BOWLING BALL STACKING
Dave Kremer (USA, above) stacked 10 bowling balls vertically without the use of adhesives on the set of *Guinness World Records: Primetime*, Los Angeles, California, USA, on 19 November 1998.

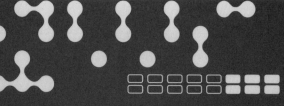

LEAPFROG OVER THE MOST STANDING PEOPLE

In September 2000 Andy Wiltz (USA) leapfrogged over 10 standing people during a local variety show at Seaman High School, Topeka, Kansas, USA. All ten people were over age 16 and over 1.53 m (5 ft) tall. Wiltz did not have a trampoline or any other assistance, but he had a running start before he pushed off the shoulders of the first person in line and flew through the air over all ten of their heads.

MOST CLOTHES PEGS CLIPPED ON A FACE

Pub landlord Garry Turner (UK, left) clipped 133 ordinary wooden clothes pegs on his face at the offices of *Guinness World Records*, London, UK, on 3 August 2001.

LONGEST DURATION SITTING IN A GLASS CAGE OF SCORPIONS

Nor Malena Hassan (Malaysia), 'Scorpion Queen', sat in a glass cage measuring 12 m^2 (130 ft^2) which contained 2,000 scorpions for 30 days from 1 July to 30 July 2001 in the Kelantan State Museum, Kota Baru, Malaysia. After 19 days she asked for 700 more scorpions to be added to the 2,000. During the attempt she was stung seven times, but only twice seriously.

WEIRD TALENTS
AMAZING FEATS

MOST LIVE RATTLESNAKES HELD IN THE MOUTH
On 19 May 2001 Jackie Bibby (USA, above) held eight live rattlesnakes in his mouth by their tails for 12.5 seconds without assistance at the Guinness World Records Experience, Orlando, Florida, USA. Each rattlesnake measured 74 cm (29 in) long.

LONGEST CONTINUOUS SKID ON A BICYCLE
On 17 April 2001 James David (USA) performed a continuous 130-m (425-ft 3-in) skid on his bicycle on a flat surface at the Spokane Raceway Park, Washington, USA.

MOST HAIR-CUTTING SCISSORS IN ONE HAND
On 12 January 1998 Danny Bar-Gil (Israel), professionally known as Danny Figaro, successfully styled hair using seven pairs of scissors in one hand, controlling each pair independently.

MOST HANDCUFFED MAN
Since 1954 escapologist Nick Janson (UK) has escaped from 1,680 pairs of handcuffs securely locked on his wrists by police officers.

MOST SWORDS SWALLOWED AND TWISTED
Brad Byers (USA), swallowed 10 swords each 68.5-cm (27-in) long and rotated them 180° in his oesophagus on 13 August 1999 on the set of *Guinness World Records: Primetime* in Los Angeles, California, USA.

MOST SWORDS SWALLOWED BY A WOMAN
The most 35.5–53-cm (14–21-in) swords swallowed by a female is six, by Amy Saunders (UK) on the set of *El Show de los Récords*, Madrid, Spain, on 27 November 2001.

LONGEST DURATION FOR A SWORD-TO-SWORD BALANCE
Ali Bandbaz balanced his brother Massoud (both Iran) above his head on the blade tips of two 36.5-cm (14.5-in) steel swords, holding the position for 30 seconds at the studios of *L'Émission des Records*, Paris, France, on 26 October 2000.

MOST CARDS HELD IN A FAN
Ralf Laue (Germany) held 326 standard playing cards in a fan in one hand, so that the value and colour of each one was visible, at Leipzig, Germany, on 18 March 1994.

FASTEST HUMAN CRAB
In the 'bridge', or crab position, Agnès Brun (France) covered 20 m (65 ft) in 33.3 seconds. The record was set on *L'Émission des Records*, Paris, France, on 30 November 2001.

FURTHEST DISTANCE AN ARROW HAS BEEN SHOT USING THE FEET
The furthest distance an arrow has been shot into a target using feet to control the bow is 5.5 m (18 ft 4.8 in), by Claudia Gomez (Argentina) on the set of *El Show de los Récords*, Madrid, Spain, on 15 November 2001.

MOST WATCHES EATEN
On 18 December 1998 on the set of *Guinness World Records: Primetime* in Los Angeles, California, USA, Kim Seung Do (South Korea) ate five watches (the entire watch with the exception of the wristband) in a time of 1 hr 34 min 7 sec.

MOST ARROWS CAUGHT BY HAND
Anthony Kelly (Australia) caught 10 arrows in two minutes standing at a distance of 13 m (42 ft) from the archer at the studios of *El Show de los Récords*, Madrid, Spain, on 5 December 2001.

MOST CIGAR BOXES BALANCED ON THE CHIN
Terry Cole (UK) balanced 220 unmodified cigar boxes on his chin for nine seconds on 24 April 1992.

FURTHEST DISTANCE CARRYING BEER STEINS
On 10 July 1992, in a contest at Cadillac, Michigan, USA, Duane Osborn (USA) covered a distance of 15 m (50 ft) in 3.65 seconds with five full steins of beer in each hand.

MOST CHERRY STEMS KNOTTED IN THREE MINUTES
Al Gliniecki (USA) tied 39 cherry stems into knots in three minutes, using his tongue at the Guinness World Records Experience, Orlando, Florida, on 26 January 1999.

MOST DOMINOES TOPPLED SINGLE-HANDEDLY
The greatest number of dominoes set up single-handedly and toppled is 281,581 out of 320,236, by Klaus Friedrich (Germany) at Fürth, Germany, on 27 January 1984. The dominoes fell in 12 min 57.3 sec, having taken 10 hours a day, for a period of 31 days, to set up.

MOST COINS REGURGITATED ON REQUEST
Stevie Starr (UK) swallowed 11 Spanish 100-peseta pieces, each with a different year of minting, and regurgitated them at will, one by one, on request from 11 different members of the studio audience at *El Show de los Récords*, Madrid, Spain, on 5 December 2001.

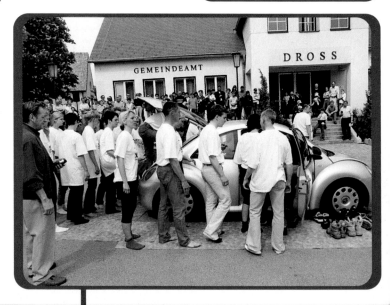

CAR CRAMMING A VOLKSWAGEN BEETLE
On 29 April 2000, 25 people crammed themselves into a standard VW Beetle car (above) in Kremser, Austria. To break this record, all the car windows and doors must be closed and no body parts can protrude from the car.

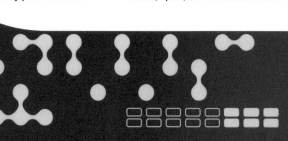

LONGEST DURATION SPINNING A FOOTBALL ON THE FOREHEAD

On 25 November 2001 Tommy Baker (UK) spun a Nike FIFA-approved football on his forehead for 11.9 seconds after transferring it from his finger on the set of *Guinness Rekord TV*, Stockholm, Sweden.

FULL-BODY ICE CONTACT ENDURANCE

Wearing only swimming trunks, Wim Hof (Netherlands) endured standing in a tube filled with ice cubes for 1 hr 6 min 4 sec on the set of *Tomorrow's World*, at BBC TV Centre, London, UK, on 13 March 2002.

HAMBURGER STUFFING

The record for stuffing the most regulation size hamburgers (including buns) in the mouth at one time is three. Johnny Reitz (USA) performed the feat on the set of *Guinness World Records: Primetime* on 17 June 1998. The rules require the participant not to swallow any of the hamburger.

MOST FISH CAUGHT WITH ONE HAND IN 30 SECONDS

On 11 March 2001 Justin Hall (USA) caught 16 salmon weighing between 1.81 and 2.72 kg (4 and 6 lb) with one hand, which were thrown by Jaison Scott (USA) from a distance of 5.48 m (18 ft).

MOST CANS SCOOPED WHEN SIDE-DRIVING

Sven-Erik Söderman (Sweden) picked up 15 full food cans whilst driving his car on two wheels, at Mora Siljan Flygplats, Mora, Sweden, on 12 September 2001. The rules state that the cans must be set out on opposite sides of a 3-m-wide (10-ft) track, forcing the driver to zig-zag on two wheels.

MOST STRAWS IN THE MOUTH

Marco Hort (Switzerland, below) stuffed 210 drinking straws, each with a diameter of 6.4 mm (0.25 in), into his mouth and held them there for the required 10 seconds on 21 February 2002 on the set of *Guinness – Die Show der Rekorde* in Munich, Germany.

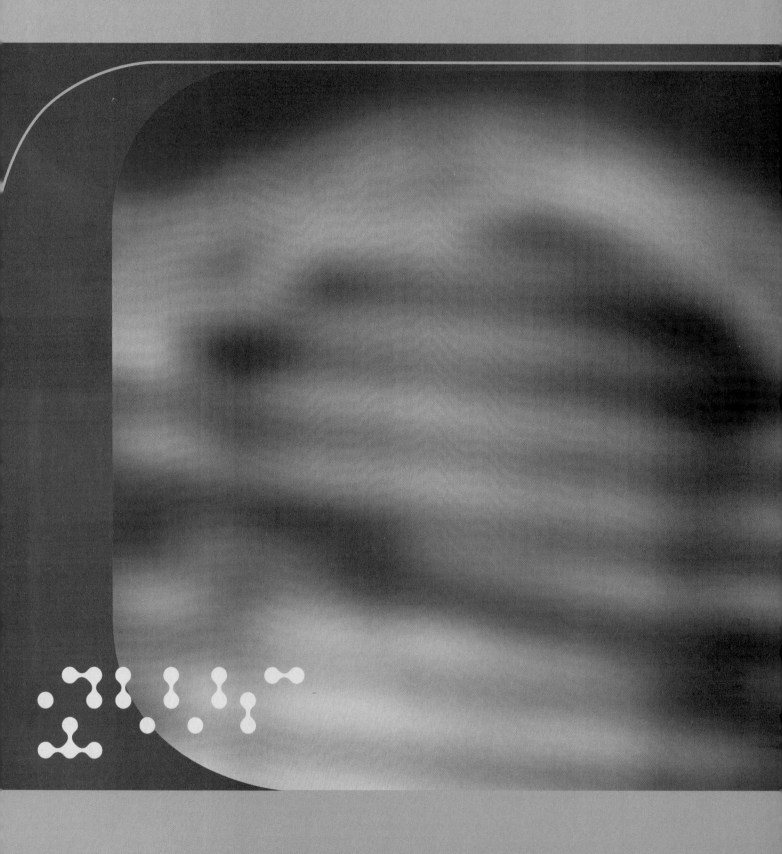

THE HUMAN BODY

LARGEST HANDS

Somalian-born Hussain Bisad (above), who lives in the UK, has the largest hands of any living person. His hands measure 26.9 cm (10.59 in) from the wrist to the tip of his middle finger. Robert Wadlow (USA), who died in 1940, had the largest hands ever. His hands measured 32.3 cm (12.75 in) from the wrist to the tip of his middle finger. He wore a size 25 ring.

LARGEST NATURAL BREASTS

Annie Hawkins-Turner (USA) has an under-breast measurement of 1.09 m (43 in) and an around-chest-over-nipple measurement of 1.79 m (70 in). She currently wears a US size 52-I bra, the largest made. These measurements would put her in a 48-V bra, which is not manufactured. She currently lives and works in Washington DC, USA.

MOST VARIABLE STATURE

At the age of 21 in 1920, Adam Rainer (Austria) measured 1.18 m (3 ft 10.5 in). He then had a rapid growth spurt and by 1931 he had reached 2.18 m (7 ft 1.75 in). As a result of this, he became so weak that he was bedridden for the rest of his life. When he died in 1950, he measured 2.34 m (7 ft 8 in) and remains the only person to have been both a dwarf and a giant.

GREATEST WEIGHT GAIN

The greatest weight gain by a woman was achieved by Doris James (USA) who is alleged to have gained 147 kg (23 st 3 lb) in the 12 months before her death at the age of 38 in August 1965. At her death she weighed 306 kg (48 st 3 lb). She was only 1.57 m (5 ft 2 in) tall.

The equivalent weight-gain record for a male is held by Arthur Knorr (USA), who gained 133 kg (21 st) in 1960 over the last six months of his life.

GREATEST WEIGHT LOSS

The record for weight loss for men is held by Jon Brower Minnoch (USA) with a weight of 635 kg (100 st) – the highest weight ever recorded for a man. He had reduced to 216 kg (34 st) by July 1979: a weight loss of at least 419 kg (66 st) over a 16-month period.

Rosalie Bradford (USA) went from a weight of 544 kg (85 st) in January 1987 (the highest weight ever recorded for a woman) to 128 kg (20 st 3 lb) in February 1994, a record weight loss of 416 kg (64 st 11 lb).

TALLEST WOMAN

When Zeng Jinlian (China) died on 13 February 1982, she measured 2.48 m (8 ft 1.75 in). This figure represented her height with assumed normal spinal curvature, as she had severe scoliosis (curvature of the spine) and could not stand up straight. She began to grow abnormally from the age of four months and stood 1.56 m (5 ft 1.5 in) before her fourth birthday and 2.17 m (7 ft 1.5 in) at 13.

Standing 2.32 m (7 ft 7.25 in), Sandy Allen (USA) is currently the tallest living woman. Her abnormal growth began soon after birth and by the age of 10 she stood an amazing 1.91 m (6 ft 3 in) tall.

LONGEST NOSE

There are accounts that Thomas Wedders (UK) who lived during the 1770s and was a member of a travelling freak circus, had a nose measuring 19 cm (7.5 in) long. The record for the longest nose on a living person belongs to Mehmet Ozyurek (Turkey). His nose was 8.8 cm (3.46 in) long from the bridge to the tip when measured on 31 January 2001.

TALLEST TWINS

Non-identical twins Michael and James Lanier (USA) both stand 2.23 m (7 ft 3 in) tall and hold the record for the world's tallest living twins. The tallest identical male twins ever recorded were the Knipe brothers (UK) who both measured 2.18 m (7 ft 2 in). The world's tallest living female twins (who are also identical) are Heather and Heidi Burge (USA) who are both 1.95 m (6 ft 4.75 in) tall.

LONGEST TONGUE

Umar Alvi (UK) has a tongue (when stuck out) measuring 5.65 cm (2.22 in) from the tip to the centre of his closed top lip. The measurement was taken on 15 November 2001.

TALLEST MAN

The world's tallest-ever man, Robert Wadlow (USA), stood an amazing 2.72 m (8 ft 11.1 in) when measured before his death aged 22 in June 1940.

The tallest living man is Radhouane Charbib (Tunisia) who measured 2 m 35.9 cm (7 ft 8.9 in) as a result of seven measurements taken between 22–23 April 1999 in Tunis.

OLDEST MAN EVER

Shigechiyo Izumi (Japan) lived to 120 years 237 days. Born on 29 June 1865, he is recorded as a six-year-old in Japan's first census in 1871. He died from pneumonia on 21 February 1986.

STRONGEST HUMAN BITE

In August 1986 Richard Hofmann (USA) achieved a bite strength of 442 kg (975 lb) for around two seconds in a research test using a gnathodynamometer at the College of Dentistry, University of Florida, Florida, USA. This is more than six times the normal human biting strength and is due to his unusually powerful masseter muscles.

OLDEST MAN LIVING

Yukichi Chuganji (b. 23 March 1889, above) of Ogori, Fukuoka Prefecture, Japan, became the oldest man in Japan on 18 January 2000 and took the world-record title on 4 January 2002 at the age of 112 years 288 days.

OLDEST WOMAN

The greatest fully authenticated age to which any human has ever lived is 122 years 164 days. This was achieved by Jeanne Louise Calment (France). She was born on 21 February 1875 and died on 4 August 1997.

The oldest living woman in the world whose date of birth can be fully authenticated is Kamato Hongo (Japan), born 16 September 1887. She took the title aged 114 years 183 days on the death of Maude Farris-Luse (USA) who died on 18 March 2002.

OLDEST DWARF

Hungarian-born dwarf Susanna Bokonyi (USA) died at the age of 105 on 24 August 1984. She was only 1.015 m (3 ft 4 in) tall.

SHORTEST WOMAN

The shortest-ever female was Pauline Musters (Netherlands) who measured 30 cm (1 ft) at her birth in 1876. When she died on 1 March 1895, a post-mortem examination showed her to be 61 cm (2 ft) tall (although there was some elongation of her body after death).

LIGHTEST BRAIN

The lightest 'normal' or non-atrophied brain on record weighed just 680 g (1 lb 8 oz). It belonged to Daniel Lyon (Ireland), who died in New York, USA, in 1907 aged 46. He was just over 1.5 m (5 ft) tall and weighed 66 kg (10 st 4.9 lb).

HEAVIEST BRAIN

The heaviest brain ever recorded weighed 2.3 kg (5 lb 1.1 oz) and had belonged to a 30-year-old male. The record was reported by the Dept of Pathology and Laboratory Medicine at the University of Cincinnati, Ohio, USA, in December 1992.

SHORTEST MAN

The shortest living man is Younis Edwan (Jordan, below) who is believed to be 65 cm (2 ft 1.5 in) tall. The shortest mature man of whom there is independent evidence was Gul Mohammed (India), who measured 57 cm (1 ft 10.5 in) tall. He died in 1997 aged 39.

FURTHEST EYEBALL POPPER
Kim Goodman (USA, above) can pop out her eyeballs to a protrusion of 11 mm (0.43 in) beyond her eye sockets. Her startling record was set on 13 June 1998.

STRETCHIEST SKIN
Public house landlord Garry Turner (UK) stretched the skin of his stomach a measured length of 15.8 cm (6.25 in) in Los Angeles, California, USA, on 29 October 1999. Another bizarre but favourite trick of his is to stretch his neck skin over his mouth to create a 'human turtleneck'.

OLDEST UNDISCOVERED TWIN
In July 1997, a foetus was discovered in the abdomen of 16-year-old Hisham Ragab (Egypt), who had been complaining of stomach pains. A swollen sac found pressing against his kidneys turned out to be Hisham's identical twin. The foetus, 18 cm (7 in) in length and weighing 2 kg (4 lb 6 oz), had been growing inside Hisham and had lived to the age of 32 or 33 weeks.

LOUDEST SNORING
Kåre Walkert (Sweden) who has the breathing disorder apnea, recorded snoring sound-levels of 93 dBA (about the same noise level as a busy street) on 24 May 1993.

MOST FINGERS AND TOES
At an inquest held in London, UK, on 16 September 1921, it was reported that a baby boy had 14 fingers and 15 toes. Polydactylism is quite common, with as many as two in 1,000 births affected. Extra digits are usually fleshy bumps without any bones, but can be complete fingers or toes.

With 10 fingers and two thumbs, Godfrey Hill (UK) has the most fingers on a living person. Godfrey found his hands an advantage at school, topping the class at adding up in the days when 12 pennies made a shilling.

LARGEST BRAIN TUMOUR
Dr Deepak S Kulkarni (India) removed a primary fibrosarcoma tumour weighing 570 g (20.1 oz) from the brain of four-year-old Kaushal Choudhary (India) at Curewell Hospital, Indore, India, on 25 May 2000.

LARGEST TUMOUR AT BIRTH
The largest tumour at birth weighed 0.311 kg (11 oz) and was pressing against the windpipe of Ryan James Shannon (USA). He was born on 2 January 1996 weighing 2.77 kg (6 lb 2 oz), with the tumour weighing 10% of his bodyweight. Nine days after birth, he underwent a four-hour operation to remove the tumour.

LARGEST TUMOUR REMOVED INTACT
The largest-ever tumour removed intact was a multicystic mass of the right ovary that had a diameter of 1 m (3 ft) and weighed 137.6 kg (21st 8.9 lb). The massive growth was removed in its entirety from the abdomen of an unnamed 34-year-old woman in a six-hour operation performed by Prof Katherine O'Hanlan (USA) in October 1991. The patient left the operating theatre on one stretcher and the cyst on another.

LONGEST LIFE WITH A BULLET IN THE HEAD
Satoru Fushiki (Japan) was accidentally hit in his left eye by an air-gun pellet on 23 January 1943 near his home in Kasuga Jinya. He was hospitalized for a month, but the bullet was not removed and he remains blind in that eye as of 25 September 2001.

LARGEST TUMOUR EVER OPERATED ON
In 1905 Dr Arthur Spohn (USA) had a patient with an ovarian cyst, estimated to weigh a staggering 148.7 kg (23 st 6 lb). It was drained during the week prior to the surgical removal of the cyst shell and after the operation the patient made a full recovery.

LONGEST ATTACK OF HICCUPS
Charles Osborne (USA) started hiccupping in 1922 while trying to weigh a hog before slaughtering it. He was unable to find a cure, but led a normal life, had two wives and fathered eight children. His hiccups continued until they stopped naturally one morning in February 1990.

HAIRIEST FAMILY
Victor 'Larry' and Gabriel 'Danny' Ramos Gomez (Mexico) are 98% covered with a thick coat of hair. They are two of a family of 19 that spans five generations who all have hypertrichosis or 'werewolf syndrome'. The women are covered with a light-to-medium coat of hair while the men have thick hair on every inch of their body (apart from the palms of their hands and soles of their feet).

MOST KIDNEY STONES PRODUCED
Don Winfield (Canada) produced and passed 3,711 kidney stones between 20 February 1986 and 30 June 2001.

LONGEST SURVIVAL WITH AN EXPOSED HEART
Christopher Wall (USA), born on 19 August 1975, is the longest-known survivor of the condition *ectopia cordis*, where the heart lies outside the body. Most patients die within 48 hours. *Ectopia* occurs in between 5.5 and 7.9 for every one million live births, according to the American Heart Association. He still lives with the condition.

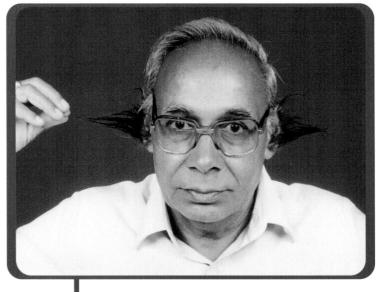

LONGEST EAR HAIR
B D Tyagi (India, above) has hair sprouting from the centre of his pinna (outer ear) that measures 10.2 cm (4 in) at its longest point.

LONGEST BEARD ON A FEMALE

American 'Bearded Lady' Janice Deveree had a beard that measured 36 cm (14 in) in 1884.

In 1990, Vivian Wheeler (USA) stopped trimming back her unusual facial growth to let her beard grow. She is the current record-holder for the longest beard on a living female, with the longest hair from follicle to tip measuring 27.9 cm (11 in) in 2000.

FEWEST TOES

Some of the Wadomo tribe of the Zambezi Valley, Zimbabwe, and the Kalanga tribe of the eastern Kalahari Desert, Botswana, have only got two toes. This syndrome is inherited via a single mutated gene.

MOST ALBINO SIBLINGS

The most albino children in one family is three – Ayonote, Osimo and Atinuk (UK, below), born to Cynthia and Dixkson Unoarumhi. All have the rare genetic condition, albinism. Both parents, who are black, carry the faulty gene, giving a one-in-four chance that their children would be born with reduced or non-existent pigmentation. All three children have translucent skin, light hazel-green eyes and pale golden hair.

MOST CAESAREAN SECTIONS

Kristina House (USA, above centre) gave birth to 11 children by Caesarean section – in which the child is delivered via an incision in the mother's abdomen – between 15 May 1979 and 20 November 1998. A woman's body takes over a year to recover from a Caesarean and it is recommended to have no more than three during a lifetime.

LONGEST SURVIVING KIDNEY TRANSPLANT

Johanna Leanora Rempel (Canada) was given a kidney from her identical twin sister Lana Blatz on 28 December 1960. The transplant operation was performed at the Peter Bent Brigham Hospital, Boston, Massachusetts, USA. Both Johanna and her sister have enjoyed excellent health and both have had healthy children.

RECIPIENT OF MOST BLOOD

When undergoing open-heart surgery at the Michael Reese Hospital, Chicago, Illinois, USA, in December 1970, 50-year-old haemophiliac Warren C Jyrich (USA) required a staggering 2,400 donor units of blood. This is equivalent to 1,080 litres (1,900 pints). On average, every human body contains around 5 litres (8.8 pints) of blood.

LOWEST BODY TEMPERATURE

The lowest authenticated body temperature is 14.2°C (57.5°F), the rectal temperature for two-year-old Karlee Kosolofski (Canada) taken on 23 February 1994. Karlee had accidentally been locked out of her home for six hours in a temperature of -22°C (-8°F). The normal human temperature is around 37°C (98.6°F) and mild hypothermia sets in under 35°C (95°F). Despite frostbite leading to the amputation of her left leg she made a full recovery.

HIGHEST BODY TEMPERATURE

Body temperatures above 42.7°C (109°F) can prove fatal, but when 52-year-old Willie Jones (USA) was admitted to Grady Memorial Hospital, Atlanta, Georgia, USA, on 10 July 1980 with heatstroke, his temperature reached 46.5°C (115.7°F). He was discharged after 24 days.

MOST ARTIFICIAL JOINTS

By the age of 47 Anne Davison (UK) had 12 major joints (elbows, wrists, both shoulders, hips, knees and ankles) and three knuckles replaced.

Charles Wedde (USA), who has rheumatoid arthritis, also had 12 major joints replaced between 1979 and 1995.

YOUNGEST HEART SURGERY PATIENT

Pioneering surgery to correct a defective heart valve was performed on a foetus aged only 23 weeks by team of 10 doctors at the Children's Hospital, Boston, Mass, USA. The baby (named Jack) was born six weeks early in November 2001 at Brigham and Women's Hospital, Boston, Mass, USA, with a healthy heart and weighing 2.49 kg (5 lb 8 oz).

YOUNGEST TRANSPLANT PATIENT

On 8 November 1996 one-hour-old Cheyenne Pyle (USA) became the youngest-ever transplant patient when she received a donor heart at Jackson Children's Hospital, Miami, Florida, USA. The six-hour operation involved draining Cheyenne's blood and cooling her body to 17°C (62.6°F), the temperature at which organs cease to function. The transplant had to be completed within an hour to prevent damage to her other organs.

LONGEST SURVIVOR OF A PORCINE AORTIC VALVE REPLACEMENT

Harry Driver (UK) received a porcine (pig's) aortic valve replacement on 12 April 1978 under surgeon Mr John Keats. It is still in full working order. He is also the oldest living recipient.

HEAVIEST SINGLE BIRTH

Anna Bates (Canada) who stood 2.27 m (7 ft 5.5 in) tall, gave birth to a boy weighing a massive 10.8 kg (23 lb 12 oz) at her home in Seville, Ohio, USA, on 19 January 1879. The baby died 11 hours later.

LIGHTEST SINGLE BIRTH

The lowest birthweight recorded for a surviving infant is 283 g (10 oz) for Marian Taggart (UK) in 1938. She was born six weeks prematurely and was fed hourly for the first 30 hours via a fountain pen filled with brandy, glucose and water. At three weeks she weighed 821 g (1 lb 13 oz) and by her first birthday she was 6.3 kg (13 lb 14 oz).

MOST PREMATURE BABY

James Elgin Gill (Canada) was born 128 days prematurely on 20 May 1987, weighing 624 g (1 lb 6 oz); the normal human gestation period is 280 days. James's parents were told that he had no chance of survival. Much of his body was still developing; including his skin, hands and feet, while his eyes were still fused shut. James is now a healthy 15-year-old.

HIGHEST BLOOD SUGAR LEVEL

On 21 November 1995, 12-year-old Michael Dougherty (USA) had a blood-sugar level of 2,350 while still conscious. The normal blood sugar range is between 80–120 so this is 19 times above average.

LONGEST DISTANCE BETWEEN PATIENT AND SURGEON

On 7 September 2001, a robot removed Madeleine Schaal's (France) gall bladder in Strasbourg, France, while her surgeons (above) operated the robot remotely from New York, USA, a total distance of 6,222 km (3,866 miles) away.

MOST SURVIVING CHILDREN DELIVERED AT A SINGLE BIRTH

A set of septuplets – four boys and three girls – were born to Bobbie McCaughey (USA) on 19 November 1997 at University Hospital, Iowa, USA. The babies were conceived by IVF and delivered by Caesarean section at 31 weeks in the space of 16 minutes. They weighed between 1.048 kg and 1.474 kg (2 lb 5 oz and 3 lb 4 oz).

Another set of surviving septuplets (four boys and three girls) were born eight weeks premature on 14 January 1998 to 40-year-old Hasna Mohammed Humair (Saudi Arabia). The smallest weighed just under 907 g (2 lb).

LONGEST FOETAL SURVIVAL OUTSIDE THE WOMB

Triplet Ronan Ingram (UK) survived outside his mother's womb for an amazing 29 weeks. Six weeks after conception, his mother's fallopian tube ruptured and the rogue fertilized egg attached itself to the exterior wall of her uterus, developing its own placenta while his two sisters developed normally in the womb. The three babies were delivered at 29 weeks by a Caesarean section. Doctors cut 1.09-kg (2-lb 4-oz) baby Ronan free after his two sisters were born. The chances of having two babies in the uterus and another outside are about one in 60–100 million.

EARLIEST BRAIN-CELL TRANSPLANT

The first brain-cell transplant was performed at the University of Pittsburgh Medical Center, Penn, USA, on 23 June 1998. The operation aimed to reverse the stroke damage suffered by 62-year-old Alma Cerasini (USA), who had suffered some speech loss and paralysis.

EARLIEST DOUBLE ARM TRANSPLANT

In January 2000, Professor Jean-Michel Dubernard (France) headed an international team of 18 surgeons and 32 staff who successfully transplanted two arms just below the elbow on to a 33-year-old French explosives worker who had lost his arms in a rocket accident four years previously.

GREATEST PERCENTAGE OF BURNS TO BODY SURVIVED

David Chapman (UK) survived 90% burns to his body following an accident on 2 July 1996. A petrol canister he was holding exploded and turned him into a human fireball. Surgeons at St Andrew's Hospital, Billericay, Essex, UK, spent 36 hours removing his dead skin and he spent seven hours in the operating theatre every two days for three weeks. After nine months in a UK hospital undergoing skin grafts donated by members of his family, the 16-year-old flew with his parents to Houston, Texas, USA, on 14 April 1997 to obtain specialist treatment.

EARLIEST SUCCESSFUL KIDNEY TRANSPLANT

RH Lawler (USA) performed the groundbreaking surgery at Little Company of Mary Hospital, Chicago, Illinois, USA, on 17 June 1950.

YOUNGEST PERSON TO HAVE A PAIR OF BIONIC ARMS FITTED
Kyle Barton (UK, below) was eight years old when he was fitted with his second bionic arm at the Northern General Hospital, Sheffield, UK, in February 2002. Kyle had to have both his arms and legs amputated after he contracted meningitis in 1998.

LARGEST LIP PLATE
The women of the Surma (above) and Mursi tribes of Ethiopia make lip plates from clay, colour them with ochre and charcoal and fire-bake them. The process of inserting the plates starts about a year before marriage. The final size indicates the number of cattle required from her future husband in return for her hand. The plates can reach up to 15 cm (6 in) in diameter.

MOST PIERCED WOMAN
As of 9 August 2001, Scottish-born Elaine Davidson (UK) has had her body adorned with a total of 720 piercings. Her record amount of body decoration includes 192 piercings on her ears, forehead, eyebrows, chin, nose and tongue and 56 piercings on her stomach, breasts and hands. Elaine had her first piercing in January 1997.

MOST PIERCED MAN
Antonio Agüero (Cuba) has 230 piercings on his body and head. His face alone holds over 175 rings. It has taken Antonio since 1990 to pierce his ears, cheeks, lips, chin, nostrils and forehead with the rings, plus the two rods that slide through the bridge of his nose. Agüero charges a nominal fee for photographs of himself in order to help with the upkeep of his large family.

MOST BODY PIERCINGS IN ONE SESSION
On 22 September 2001, American Greg Thompson received a total of 227 new piercings to his body without an anaesthetic. All piercings were executed by Beaker Trigg (USA) in one continuous six-hour session at Area 51 Tattoo and Body Piercing, Colorado Springs, Colorado, USA.

MOST BODY PIERCINGS USING SURGICAL NEEDLES
Jerome Abramovitch (Canada) holds the record for most body piercings using surgical needles. On a TV show recorded on 31 October 1999, he inserted 200 3.81-cm-long (1.5-in) surgical needles (all 22 gauge) into his chest, neck and arms.

MOST TATTOOED WOMAN
The world's most tattooed woman is strip artiste Krystyne Kolorful (Canada) who has tattoos decorating 95% of her body. They cost approximately CAN$15,000 (£6,667 or $9,486), took 10 years to complete and are the work of 13 different artists. The largest design on Krystyne's body is a dragon that wraps around her chest and back. The dragon alone took 40 hours to do.

LONGEST TATTOO SESSION
Kevin Gill (UK) tattooed Dave Sheldrick (UK) for a continuous 27 hr 12 min at Kev's Tattoo Parlour, Welling, Kent, UK, between 15 and 17 March 2001.

LONGEST BEARD
Norwegian Hans N Langseth's beard measured an impressive 5.33 m (17 ft 6 in) – the longest ever recorded – at the time of his burial at Kensett, Iowa, USA, in 1927.

The record for the longest beard on a living male is held by Shamsher Singh (India). By 18 August 1997 his beard measured 1.83 m (6 ft) from the end of his chin to its tip.

LONGEST MOUSTACHE
The record holder for the world's longest moustache is Kalyan Ramji Sain (India), who has been growing his impressive moustache since 1976. By July 1993 it spanned 3.39 m (11 ft 1 in); the right side is 1.72 m (5 ft 7 in) long and the left side is 1.67 m (5 ft 5 in) long. Dedicated moustache-growers use mustard, oil, butter and cream to keep their 'taches in top condition.

MOST RHINESTONES TO ADORN A BODY
The record for the most rhinestones to adorn a body was set by Maria Rosa Pons Abad (Spain), who attached 30,361 rhinestones to the body of a model on 22 November 2001.

LONGEST TOENAILS
In 1991 the combined length of Louise Hollis's (USA) 10 toenails was 221 cm (7 ft 3 in). Louise was inspired to grow her toenails in 1982 after seeing a TV programme featuring the longest fingernails. The mother of 12 rarely wears shoes and keeps all of her broken toenails. Currently, each of her toenails are approximately 15.24 cm (6 in) long.

LONGEST FINGERNAILS
On 8 July 1998 the total length of the five nails on the left hand of Shridhar Chillal (India) was a record-breaking 6.15 m (20 ft 2.25 in). He last cut his fingernails in 1952.

The longest fingernails on a female belong to Lee Redmond (USA), who has been growing them for 19 years. Their total length is 6.62 m (21 ft 9 in). The longest nail (on her left thumb) measures 68.58 cm (2 ft 3 in).

LARGEST BICEP
Denis Sester's (USA) right bicep is 77.8 cm (30 in) when cold. He built up his huge muscles by doing arm curls with a 68-kg (150-lb) sand bucket.

MOST BREAST ENLARGEMENTS
The late Lolo Ferrari, aka Eve Valois (France), had a bust measuring 1.80 m (71 in) and a 54-G bra size – the result of 22 enlargements. Her breasts were first increased to 1.17 m (46 in), but she later found an aeronautical engineer who designed 1.3-m (51-inch) moulds for her. Lolo's breasts eventually weighed more than 11.7 kg (26 lb).

MOST TATTOOED MAN
Around 99.9% of Tom Leppard's (UK, above) body is tattooed. Tom's tattoo portrays a leopard-skin design – dark spots on a yellow background. He estimates that he has spent over £5,000 ($7,000) on his stunning bodywork.

LONGEST HAIR

The world's longest recorded hair belongs to Hoo Sateow (Thailand) who has not had a haircut in over 70 years as he believes his hair holds the key to his healing powers. On 21 November 1997 it was unravelled and officially measured at 5.15 m (16 ft 11 in).

MOST PLASTIC SURGERY

Since 1979, Cindy Jackson (USA) has spent $99,600 (£69,104) on 28 cosmetic operations. Jackson has had three full facelifts, two nose operations, knee, waist, abdomen and jawline surgery, thigh liposuction, breast reduction and augmentation, and semi-permanent make-up.

MOST WOMEN WITH BOUND FEET

Foot-binding, which began in 10th-century China and was banned in 1911, prevented women's feet from growing over 10 cm (3.9 in). The feet were bound with cloth strips, so their shape would resemble lotus flowers. A study in 1997 of 193 women (93 over 80 years old and 100 aged 70–79) in Beijing, China, by the University of California, San Francisco, USA, found that 38% in the over-80 group and 18% of those in the 70–79 group had their feet deformed by the process.

SMALLEST WAIST

The smallest waist recorded on a person of normal stature was 33 cm (13 in), on Ethel Granger (UK), who went from a waist of 56 cm (22 in) to a tiny 33 cm (13 in) between 1929 and 1939. The same size was claimed for French actress Emile Marie Bouchand.

The smallest waist on a living person belongs to Cathie Jung (USA), whose waist measures 38.1 cm (15 in).

The women wore corsets to achieve their records.

LONGEST NECK

The maximum known extension of a human neck is 40 cm (15.75 in), created by the fitting of copper coils, as practised by women of the Padaung, or Kareni, tribe of Myanmar (Burma, below) as a sign of beauty. Subsequent removal of the coils can prove fatal.

MOST BLOODTHIRSTY PARASITE

The eggs of the *Ancylostoma duodenale* and *Necator americanus* hookworms (above) are found in the faeces of 1.3 billion people worldwide. In bad infestations, the gut lining is so thickly covered that it looks like carpet pile. Bleeding caused by the worms' feeding adds up to 10 million litres (2.6 million gal) of blood worldwide every day.

MOST PREVALENT ALLERGIC DISEASE

Bronchial asthma affects up to 150 million people around the world (roughly the population of Russia) with deaths from the condition reaching a tragic 180,000 each year. Worldwide it is estimated that the economic costs associated with treating the sufferers of this disease exceed those of tuberculosis and HIV/AIDS combined.

MOST RESURGENT DISEASE

The resurgence of diphtheria has been caused mainly by the deterioration in health services and medical supplies following the 1991 collapse of the Soviet Union. There were 2,000 cases of diphtheria in the Soviet Union in 1991 but by 1997 there were between 150,000 and 200,000 cases in the countries of the former USSR, according to Red Cross estimates.

DEADLIEST DISEASE

AIDS (Acquired Immune Deficiency Syndrome) and rabies encephalitis, a virus infection of the central nervous system, are generally considered to be universally fatal. In 2001 there was a total of three million deaths from AIDS – 580,000 of which were children under the age of 15. The annual number of deaths worldwide caused by rabies is estimated to be between 40,000 and 70,000 – with 10 million people receiving treatment after being exposed to suspect animals.

MOST COMMON INFECTIOUS DISEASE

The cold is the most common infectious disease. This condition is almost universal, afflicting everyone but those living in isolated communities or in Antarctica (no virus will survive the extreme cold). There are at least 40 cold viruses that are airborne or transmitted by direct contact.

LEADING CAUSE OF DEATH

In industrialized countries the most common cause of death is cardiovascular disease, which causes fatal strokes and heart attacks in over 50% of all deaths. The main factors which put an individual at risk from coronary disease are cigarette smoking, high blood pressure and high levels of cholesterol in food.

FASTEST GROWING DISEASE

In 2001 there were around 14,000 new HIV infections a day, the majority of which occurred among young people aged 15 to 24. By the beginning of 2002, an estimated 40 million people were living with HIV.

EARLIEST AIDS CASE WITH AN HIV DIAGNOSIS

The earliest AIDS case for which an HIV diagnosis has been confirmed was that of a US youth who died in 1969.

WIDEST E. COLI OUTBREAK

More than 9,500 cases of *E. coli* (*Escherichia coli*) food poisoning were reported in Japan in 1996, and 11 people died. The infection is not always fatal but can lead to kidney failure. The worst case was in 1996 when 21 people died and 500 became ill after eating meat infected with *E. coli* from a butcher's shop in Wishaw, Lanarkshire, UK.

WORST PANDEMIC

The 'Black Death', the pneumonic form of the plague, killed around a third of the population of Europe and some 75 million people worldwide in 1347–51.

MOST VIRULENT VIRAL DISEASE

Ebola haemorrhagic fever (EHF), is said to kill 90% of those who contract it. It causes massive internal bleeding that 'melts' internal organs and there is no cure. It was first identified in Zaire (now Democratic Republic of Congo) in 1976 and is named after the river where the outbreak occurred. There have been around 1,500 reported cases and over 1,000 deaths.

HIGHEST PREVALENCE OF LEPROSY

The WHO (World Health Organization) listed India as having 577,200 registered leprosy sufferers at the start of 1999. By July 1999, that figure had increased by a further 634,901. Leprosy mainly affects the skin, the peripheral nerves and eyes. It causes mutilation of the body with victims suffering exclusion from society.

MOST DEADLY BUG

The bacterium *Yersinia pestis* caused the death of 25 million people in 14th-century Europe. Identified in 1894, it causes bubonic plague – the killer disease transmitted by fleas and rats.

MOST DANGEROUS PARASITE

According to 1998 WHO estimates, malaria causes over one million deaths a year and is a public-health problem in 90 countries. The malarial parasites of the genus *Plasmodium* carried by mosquitoes of the genus *Anopheles*, have, excluding wars and accidents, probably been responsible for half of all human deaths since the Stone Age.

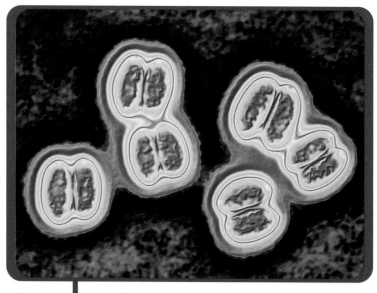

LARGEST MENINGITIS OUTBREAK

In Africa in 1996, an incredible 187,000 cases of meningitis (cells of which are shown above) were reported. The largest outbreak occurred in São Paulo, Brazil, in 1974, where there were 30,000 cases.

MOST SURVIVABLE CANCER

Non-melanoma skin cancer has a 97% survival rate for both male and female patients.

OLDEST DISEASE

Cases of leprosy were described in ancient Egypt as early as 1350 BC. Egyptian mummies from the twentieth dynasty (1250–1000 BC) have exhibited traces of *Tuberculosis schistosomiasi*, an infectious disease of the lungs. Other ancient diseases include plague and cholera, which are both referred to in the Old Testament of the Bible.

MOST NOTORIOUS TYPHOID CARRIER

Swiss-born Mary Mallon, known as 'Typhoid Mary', emigrated to the USA in 1868. In her job as a cook, she was the source of 53 typhoid outbreaks, including the 1903 epidemic of 1,400 cases and three deaths in Ithaca, New York. She was detained at Riverside Hospital, New York, from 1915 until her death on 11 November 1938.

WORST INFLUENZA EPIDEMIC

Between 1918 and 1919, 21,640,000 people died worldwide of influenza. The infection is viral and is commonly spread by coughing and sneezing.

MOST DANGEROUS MALARIAL INFECTION

Plasmodium falciparum causes malignant tertian malaria, which affects the brain, causing fits, coma or even sudden death.

MOST MALARIA EPIDEMICS IN A YEAR

According to the WHO, 1991 saw 144 epidemics of malaria worldwide. Recently, the malaria virus has adapted to antimalarial treatments.

LONGEST QUARANTINED ISLAND

In 1942, Gruinard Island, Scotland, UK, was quarantined after a test release of anthrax (*Bacillus anthracis*) that killed a flock of sheep. The test was carried out to gather chemical warfare data. The quarantine was lifted 48 years later, on 24 April 1990. Worldwide, 2,000 cases of human infection from anthrax are reported annually.

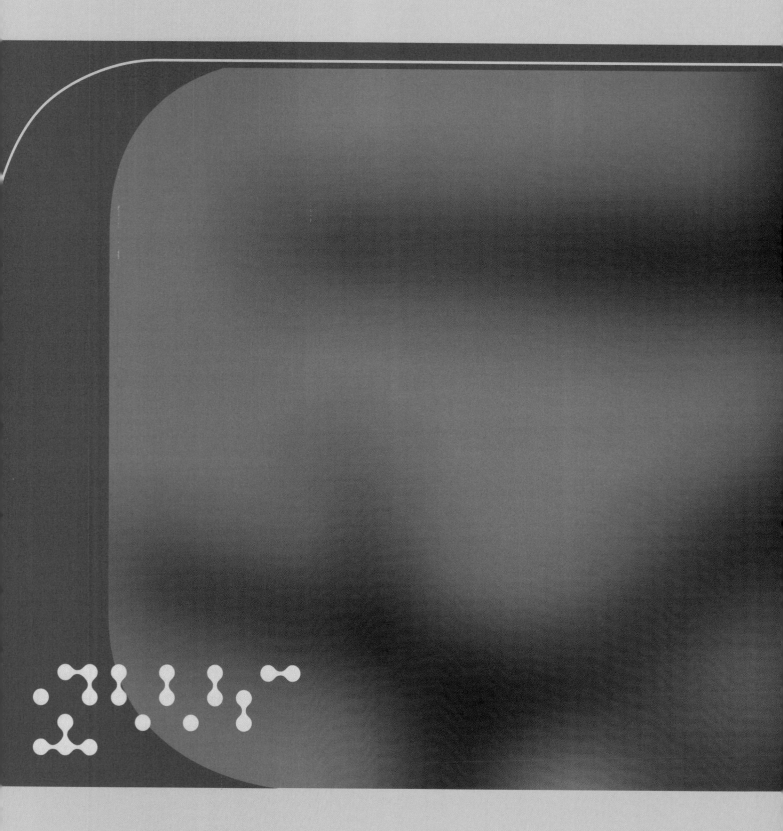

POWERFUL WORLD

LARGEST CARVED SAPPHIRE

The 'Millennium Sapphire' (above), which weighs 61,500 carats, was carved by designer Alessio Boschi (Italy) with images that celebrate milestones in human achievement. It is currently on display at the Dallas Fort Worth Metroplex, Texas, USA.

LARGEST DIAMOND

On 26 January 1905, the 'Cullinan', a 3,106-carat diamond, was found at the Premier Diamond Mine, near Pretoria, South Africa. It was given to the reigning British monarch, Edward VII and, cut into 106 polished diamonds, produced the largest cut fine quality diamond, the 'Star of Africa', which weighs 530.2 carats and tops the Royal Sceptre, part of the British Crown Jewels.

LARGEST GOLD NUGGET

The Holtermann Nugget weighed 235.14 kg (7,560 troy oz). It was discovered on 19 October 1872 in the Beyers & Holtermann Star of Hope Mine, Hill End, NSW, Australia. The nugget was crushed soon after its discovery and 82.11 kg (2,640 troy oz) of gold was extracted from it.

LARGEST SINGLE EMERALD CRYSTAL

The largest known single emerald crystal of gem quality in the world weighs 7,025 carats. It was discovered in Colombia in 1969 at the Cruces Mine, near Gachala, and is currently owned by a private mining concern.

LARGEST GOLD BAR

The world's largest manufactured pure gold bar weighs 200 kg (441 lb) and was made in Japan by the Mitsubishi Materials Corporation at the Naoshima Refinery, Kagawa, Japan, on 15 December 1999. The gold is certified 99.99% pure, while the bar itself measures 19.5 cm (7.7 in) wide and 40.5 cm (15.9 in) long at its base. It was purchased by Toi Marine Kanko Corporation (Japan) on 20 December 1999 and is currently on display at the Toi Gold Mine, Shizuoka, Japan. It has an estimated value of ¥20 million (£140,000 or $200,000).

DEEPEST ICE DRILLING

In July 1993, the deepest-ever ice borehole was reported to have reached the bottom of the Greenland ice sheet, a depth of 3,053.51 m (10,018 ft). This milestone was achieved after five years' drilling by US researchers.

DEEPEST OCEAN DRILLING

In 1993, the Ocean Drilling Program's vessel *JOIDES Resolution* carried out the deepest recorded drilling below the sea bed, descending to 2,111 m (6,926 ft in the eastern equatorial Pacific). The greatest amount of core recovered during a single leg of the Ocean Drilling Program's work was 6,731 m (22,083 ft) in 1995.

OLDEST MINE

The world's oldest mine is the chert (silica) mine in at Nazlet Sabaha, Garb, Egypt. Mining first took place there around 100,000 years ago.

DEEPEST PENETRATION INTO THE EARTH'S CRUST

The deepest penetration into the Earth's crust is an exploratory geological borehole near Zapolyarny on the Kola peninsula of Arctic Russia. Work began on 24 May 1970, and the hole had reached a depth of 12,261 m (40,236 ft) by 1983, when work stopped due to lack of funds. The temperature of the rocks at the bottom of the hole is about 210°C (410°F).

DEEPEST WATER BORE

The Stensvad Water Well 11-W1, is a record-breaking 2,231 m (7,320 ft) deep. It was drilled by the Great Northern Drilling Co Inc (USA) in Rosebud County, Montana, USA, between October and November 1961.

Begun in 1955, the Thermal Power Co geothermal steam well in Sonoma County, California, USA, has reached a depth of 2,752 m (9,029 ft).

DEEPEST UNDERGROUND NUCLEAR EXPLOSION

On 18 June 1985, a 2.5-kiloton nuclear device was detonated at the bottom of a shaft 2,850 m (9,350 ft) deep at a site 60 km (37 miles) south of Nefte-yugamsk, Siberia, in the former USSR. The detonation was an attempt to stimulate oil production.

DEEPEST MINE

On 12 July 1977, miners reached a depth of 3,581 m (11,749 ft) at the Western Deep Levels Gold Mine in Carletonville, Transvaal, South Africa. The mine is unpleasantly warm at its lowest levels because of geothermal heating and miners are kept cool with water hoses. The mine has a hoisting shaft 2,072 m (6,800 ft) deep with a lift that winds at an ear-popping maximum speed of 1,095 m (3,595 ft) per minute.

LARGEST PLATINUM NUGGET

The largest existing platinum nugget weighs 7,860.5 g (252.7 troy oz) and is known as the 'Ural Giant'. It is presently in the care of the Diamond Foundation in the Kremlin, Moscow, Russia.

The largest-ever platinum nugget was found in 1843, in Russia's Ural Mountains. It weighed 9,635 g (309.7 troy oz) and was melted down shortly after its discovery.

LARGEST ENERGY CONSUMPTION

The USA is the largest consumer of fossil fuels and commercial energy (fossil fuels plus hydro and nuclear power). In 1998 it consumed 1,937 million tonnes of oil equivalent (Mtoe) of fossil fuels and 2,147 Mtoe of commercial energy.

LARGEST GOLD PRODUCER

AngloGold Ltd of Johannesburg, South Africa, is the world's largest gold producer. It has 24 operations worldwide and in 2000 produced 217.7 million g (7 million troy oz) of gold, almost twice the output of its nearest rival. The company holds 2.73 million kg (88 million troy oz) of gold in reserves and also has 12.37 million kg (398 million troy oz) of gold in resources.

LARGEST OIL GUSHER

The largest known 'wildcat' oil gusher blew near Qum, Iran, on 26 August 1956. The uncontrolled oil gushed to a height of 52 m (170 ft), at a rate of 120,000 barrels per day. The gusher was closed after 90 days' work by B Mostofi and Myron Kinley (USA).

WORST RESERVOIR-INDUCED LANDSLIDE

Up to 2,500 people were killed on 9 October 1963 when 240 million m³ (8,475 million ft³) of rock slipped from the side of Mount Toc in the Italian Alps and tumbled into a reservoir behind the Vaiont Dam. The 266.7-m-high (875-ft) dam held firm, but a wave of water around 100 m (330 ft) high flowed over the top, wiping out the nearby community of Longarone. Construction work on the dam had severely affected the levels of the local water table and this factor was later regarded as the primary cause of the disaster.

LARGEST MARBLE PRODUCER

The world's largest marble mining company (based on weight extracted) is R K Marbles Ltd of Rajasthan, India. In 2000 it produced 890,603.33 tonnes (1,963,441,913 lb) of marble blocks.

LARGEST OIL FIELD

The Ghawar field in Saudi Arabia, which was developed by Aramco (Saudi Arabia), is 240 km (150 miles) long and 35 km (22 miles) wide. As of May 2000, the oil field was estimated to contain between 70–85 billion barrels of proven reserves.

MOST ACCURATE 3-D MAP OF EARTH

A 3-D map of Earth, covering 80% of the world's land masses, has been compiled by NASA using data collected during the 11-day STS-99 mission of the space shuttle *Endeavour*. Using two large radar antennae, one in the cargo bay and another on a 60-m (197-ft) mast, the shuttle crew collected eight terabytes (roughly equivalent to 160 million pages of text) of precise topographical data on Earth's physical geography, with a horizontal resolution of 10 m (33 ft) and a vertical resolution of 10 m. NASA began releasing the map in August 2001.

EARLIEST GEOLOGICAL MAP

The first geological map was drawn up by William Smith (UK) and was compiled in 1799. Smith's map covered the area surrounding the city of Bath, Avon, UK, and today it is stored in the archives of the Department of Earth Sciences, University of Oxford, Oxford, UK. In 1801, Smith also drew up the oldest geological map of England and Wales.

LARGEST MAN-MADE EXCAVATION

The Bingham Canyon Copper Mine near Salt Lake City, Utah, USA, (below) measures 4 km (2.5 miles) across, 0.8 km (0.5 mile) deep and is visible from space. Since 1906, when work began in the mine, more than 5.4 billion tonnes of rock have been excavated and it has produced over 14.5 million tonnes of copper, 630,000 kg (1.6 million troy lb) of gold and 5.9 million kg (15.8 million troy lb) of silver.

MOST DEVASTATING AIR POLLUTION

On 3 December 1984, a poisonous cloud of methyl isocyanate escaped from the Union Carbide pesticide plant (above) near Bhopal, capital of Madhya Pradesh, India. More than 6,300 people died and thousands of the survivors have since suffered from long-term damage to their brain, lungs, liver and kidneys, as well as being blinded.

WORST MARINE POLLUTION

A fertilizer factory on Minamata Bay, Kyushu, Japan, continually deposited mercury waste into the sea between 1953 and 1967. Up to 20,000 people were affected by 'Minamata disease', 4,500 seriously, and 43 people died. A further 800 deaths were attributed to mercury poisoning from related sources, while 111 others suffered permanent damage.

MOST POLLUTED CITY

Mexico City, Mexico, exceeds the World Health Organization (WHO) guidelines in sulphur dioxide, ozone, suspended particulate matter and carbon monoxide. It also has moderate-to-heavy lead and nitrogen dioxide pollution. The mountains surrounding the city trap the pollution, building it up to extremely toxic levels.

HIGHEST CARBON DIOXIDE EMISSIONS

The USA has the highest emissions of CO_2, one of the key gases responsible for the 'greenhouse effect'. In 2000, the USA emitted 5,800 million tonnes (11,600 billion lb) of CO_2, a 3.1% increase on the previous year.

LOWEST CARBON DIOXIDE EMISSIONS

Of the major industrialized nations in the western hemisphere, France has the lowest emissions of CO_2. In 1999, France emitted 400 million tonnes (800 billion lb) of CO_2. France's commitment to nuclear power helps cut fossil fuel-related CO_2 emissions.

WORST OIL TANKER SPILL

The collision of the *Atlantic Empress* with the *Aegean Captain* off Tobago in the Caribbean Sea on 19 July 1979, resulted in the loss of 161.6 million litres (35.5 million gal) of oil.

WORST MARINE OIL POLLUTION

When Saddam Hussein (Iraq) retreated from Kuwait in the 1991 Gulf War, he ordered a Kuwaiti refinery to release 908 million litres (200 million gal) of oil into the Gulf: 25 times more than in the *Exxon Valdez* disaster in 1989.

LARGEST DEFORESTATION

Between 1990 and 2000, Brazil cleared an average of 22,264 km² (8,596 miles²) of forests every year – an area approximately the size of El Salvador – to meet demands for land and timber. Between 1994 and 1995, deforestation rates in Brazil nearly doubled to about 29,000 km² (11,197 miles²) annually, representing the greatest increase in the rate of deforestation ever recorded. Since then, deforestation rates have gone back to the levels of the late 1980s and early 1990s – about 13,000 km² (5,000 miles²) per year.

LARGEST ENVIRONMENTAL PETITION

In 1995, the international and independent environmental organization Greenpeace (founded in 1971) collected a record-breaking 8.5 million signatures worldwide to call upon the then President Chirac to end French nuclear testing in Mururoa in the South Pacific. Despite the petition, six nuclear tests went ahead as planned, but as France had initially intended to perform eight tests, Greenpeace declared the protest a success.

FASTEST FOREST DEPLETION

In Burundi, central Africa, forested areas were depleted at an average rate of 9% every year between 1990 and 2000. If this rate is sustained, Burundi's forests will have completely disappeared in just over 11 years.

LARGEST HOLE IN THE OZONE LAYER

The ozone layer is found in the stratosphere (about 12–45 km or 7–28 miles above the ground) and it shields the Earth's surface from the Sun's damaging ultraviolet (UV-B) rays.

In September 2000, NASA scientists detected the largest hole so far seen in the ozone layer – around 28.3 million km² (11 million miles²). This hole above Antarctica is roughly three times the area of the USA.

HIGHEST GLASS RECYCLING RATE

Switzerland leads the world in recycling glass, with an estimated 91% of the glass products sold being recycled. Switzerland's tradition of recycling and its network of free collection points account for the high percentage. Also, collection for non-recyclable material carries a charge.

LOWEST EMISSION-PRODUCING NATURAL GAS-FUELLED CAR

Introduced in 1998, the Honda Civic GX is the world's most eco-friendly natural gas vehicle. Emissions of CO, HC and NOx from the car have been reduced to almost zero, while CO_2 emissions have been reduced by about 20%. The Civic GX has 98% fewer emissions overall compared to a standard low-emission vehicle.

LARGEST REFORESTATION

Between 1990 and 2000, China (above) replanted enough trees to cover an average area of 18,063 km² (6,974 miles²) every year (equivalent to the size of Kuwait). Loans from the World Bank support China's reforestation programmes.

MOST ACIDIC ACID RAIN

With pH 7 being a neutral reading (the lower the number, the higher the acid level), the lowest pH level ever recorded for acid precipitation is a reading of 1.87 at Inverpolly Forest, Scotland, UK, in 1983. This area receives the most acidic acid rain.

WORST ACID RAIN ENVIRONMENTAL DAMAGE

Atmospheric fallout from industrial pollution causes acid rain. The Czech Republic has the greatest forest damage due to acid rain with 71% of its forests affected. The problem is particularly acute in northern Bohemia, where the pollution is caused by the large amounts of fossil fuels burned by Polish and east German industries.

WORST NUCLEAR REACTOR DISASTER

A nuclear reactor disaster at Chernobyl No 4 in the former USSR (now the Ukraine) on 26 April 1986, resulted in an official Soviet death toll of 31 people. No systematic records were kept of subsequent deaths, but over 1.7 million people were exposed to radiation. Up to 135,000 people were evacuated but another 850,000 are still living in the affected areas. Contamination was experienced over 28,200 km^2 (10,900 miles^2). No records were kept of how many of the 200,000 people involved in the clean-up operation died in the five-year period following the disaster.

WORST NUCLEAR WASTE ACCIDENT

In December 1957, a nuclear waste container overheated at a complex at Kyshtym, Russia, causing an explosion. Radioactive compounds were dispersed over 23,000 km^2 (8,900 miles^2). More than 30 small communities within a 1,200-km^2 (460-mile^2) radius were eliminated from maps of the USSR in the three years following the accident, and about 17,000 people were evacuated. A 1992 report indicated that 8,015 people died over a 32-year observation period as a result of the discharges.

LARGEST SOLAR ENERGY ROOF

The world's largest photovoltaic solar energy roof measures 10,000 m^2 (108,000 ft^2). It belongs to the Nordrhine-Westfalen Mont-Cenis Academy in Herne, Germany. The one-megawatt roof has 3,185 solar cells, connected by 55 km (34 miles) of cabling, and yields over twice the annual power consumption of the building. The electricity is fed to the public grid, while the heat is used in the nearby houses and hospital.

MOST ENVIRONMENTALLY FRIENDLY COUNTRY

Finland heads the Environmental Sustainability Index (ESI) compiled in 2001 by the World Economic Forum. It is based on 22 core indicators covering five areas, including environmental systems (eg air and water quality) and reducing human vulnerability to environmental degradation. Finland scored 80.5 out of 100. The lowest, Kyrgyzstan, scored 39.6.

LARGEST WIND FARM

The Pacific Gas and Electric Company's wind farm at Altamont Pass, California, USA (below), covers 140 km^2 (54 miles^2). Since 1981, its 7,300 turbines have produced over 6 billion kilowatt-hours of electricity – enough to power 800,000 homes for one year.

WARMEST YEAR ON RECORD
The warmest year since records began (in around 1880) was 1998, when it was 0.57ºC (1.03ºF) warmer than the average global temperature (measured between 1961 and 1990). The 1990s was in fact the warmest decade on record: the six warmest years ever were all in the 1990s.

HOTTEST PLACE ON EARTH
The hottest place on Earth is the air around a lightning strike. For a fraction of a second, the air is heated to an incredible 30,000ºC (54,000ºF). This is roughly equivalent to five times hotter than the visible surface of the Sun.

HIGHEST BAROMETRIC PRESSURE
Barometric pressure is the physical pressure exerted by all the air above us, with pressure decreasing as you gain altitude. It is measured in millibars or inches of mercury. The highest ever recorded was 1,083.8 mb (32 in) at Agata, Siberia, Russia, on 31 December 1968. This pressure corresponds to being at nearly 600 m (2,000 ft) below sea level, even though Agata is 262 m (826 ft) above sea level.

The lowest barometric pressure was 870 mb (25.69 in) recorded 483 km (300 miles) west of Guam in the Pacific Ocean on 12 October 1979.

DRIEST PLACE ON EARTH
Between 1964 and 2001 the average annual rainfall for the meteorological station in Quillagua (above, situated at lat 21° 38'S, long 69° 33'W), in the Atacama Desert, Chile, was just 0.5 mm (0.02 in). This discovery was made during the making of the documentary series *Going to Extremes*, by Keo Films in 2001.

LEAST SUNSHINE
At the South Pole there is no sunshine for 182 days every year and at the North Pole the same applies for 176 days per year. This is due to their geographical locations, which means that for half of the year the Sun never rises above the horizon.

EARLIEST IMAGE OF A SPRITE
Sprites are atmospheric electrical phenomena associated with lightning. These unusual flashes shoot upwards from the tops of thunderstorms to altitudes of around 100 km (60 miles) above the Earth's surface. Historical reports of these phenomena were not taken seriously until the first image was captured – accidentally – in 1989, when a low-level-light TV camera was pointed above a thunderstorm. Video footage of sprites has been taken from the space shuttle.

HEAVIEST HAILSTONES
The heaviest hailstones ever recorded weighed up to 1 kg (2 lb 2.4 oz) each. They are reported to have killed 92 people when they fell in the Gopalganj district of Bangladesh on 14 April 1986.

MOST POWERFUL NATURAL CLIMATE CHANGE
The El-Niño Southern Oscillation occurs due to cyclic warming of the eastern and central Pacific Ocean. Apart from natural seasonal changes, it is the Earth's most powerful short-term natural climate change. The entire cycle of El Niño and La Niña (its cooler opposite) lasts between three and seven years, causing unusual weather conditions worldwide; notable were the 1982/83 and 1997/98 events.

LONGEST SEA-LEVEL FOGS
Fogs with visibility under around 900 m (3,000 ft) persist for weeks on the Grand Banks, Newfoundland, Canada, with their average durations being more than 120 days per year.

MOST ROCKETS LAUNCHED BY LIGHTNING
In June 1987, a lightning strike at NASA's launch facility at Wallops Island, Virginia, USA, inadvertently triggered the launch of three unmanned rockets. Two of them began to follow their planned trajectories while the third rocket splashed into the ocean around 90 m (300 ft) from the launch pad. Ironically, the third rocket was designed to study thunderstorms.

LARGEST SNOWFLAKE
It is reported that on 28 January 1887 at Fort Keogh, Montana, USA, ranch owner Matt Coleman (USA) measured a snowflake that was 38 cm (15 in) wide and 20 cm (8 in) thick, which he later described as being 'larger than milk pans'.

MOST FREAKISH TEMPERATURE RISE
The freakiest temperature rise was 27ºC (49ºF) in two minutes, recorded at Spearfish, South Dakota, USA, from -20ºC (-4ºF) at 7:30 am to 7ºC (45ºF) at 7:32 am on 22 January 1943.

LONGEST-LASTING RAINBOW
A rainbow over Wetherby, Yorkshire, UK, on 14 March 1994 was visible for six hours continuously from 9:00 am to 3:00 pm. Most rainbows last much less than one hour.

OLDEST FOSSILIZED RAINDROPS
On 15 December 2001 Chirananda De (India) announced his discovery of the fossilized imprints of raindrops in ancient rocks in the Vindhyan range, Madhya Pradesh, India. These rocks prove that rain fell on Earth at least 1.6 billion years ago.

HIGHEST ATMOSPHERIC PHENOMENA
The very highest visible phenomena are the beautiful shimmering lights of the aurorae (above), the lowest of which occur at altitudes of around 100 km (60 miles), while the highest extend up to around 400 km (250 miles).

HIGHEST CLOUDS

The highest clouds in the atmosphere are noctilucent clouds. Best seen in the lower and higher latitudes, these beautiful, tenuous phenomena form above 99.9% of the atmosphere at altitudes of around 80 km (50 miles). They can be seen after sunset, when, due to their high altitude, they are still illuminated by the Sun's rays. They are believed to form from a mixture of ice crystals and dust from meteors.

STRONGEST JETSTREAM

Jetstreams are narrow, fast-flowing currents of air that exist in the upper atmosphere. The fastest-ever jetstream wind speeds – up to an incredible 500 km/h (310 mph) – have been recorded over Japan during the winter season, when tropical air from northern India flows north-eastwards over the islands.

HIGHEST WATERSPOUT

Waterspouts are essentially tornadoes over water. The highest waterspout of which there is a reliable record was one observed on 16 May 1898 off Eden, NSW, Australia. A surveyor's reading from the shore gave its height as 1,528 m (5,014 ft) and it was about 3 m (10 ft) in diameter. Waterspouts have been known to suck up fish from the sea and rain them back down on nearby towns.

LONGEST LIGHTNING FLASH

At any one time, around 100 lightning bolts per second hit the Earth. Typically, the actual length of these bolts can be around 9 km (5.5 miles). However, in 1956 meteorologist Myron Ligda (USA) used radar to record a lightning flash that covered a horizontal distance of 150 km (93 miles) inside clouds.

GREATEST DISPLAY OF SOLAR HALOS

On 11 January 1999, at least 24 types of solar halo were witnessed by scientists at the geographic South Pole. Solar halos are formed when sunlight is reflected and refracted by ice crystals in the atmosphere, causing rings around the Sun and brightly coloured patches in the sky. Atmospheric conditions at the pole are conducive to this type of phenomenon.

LARGEST PIECE OF FALLEN ICE

On 13 August 1849 a piece of ice 6 m (20 ft) long was reported to have fallen from the sky in Scotland, UK. The ice was clear but looked as though it was composed of smaller pieces, possibly hailstones (left). An explanation is that the hailstones were fused together by a bolt of lightning. The mass of ice reportedly fell after a crash of thunder.

WORST LIGHTNING STRIKE DEATH TOLL
A total of 81 people aboard a Boeing 707 jet airliner died when their plane was struck by lightning when flying near Elkton, Maryland, USA, on 8 December 1963.

WORST HOMELESS TOLL FOR A CYCLONE DISASTER
Hurricane Mitch, which struck Central America (Honduras and Nicaragua) between 26 October and 4 November 1998, left around 2.5 million people dependent on international aid efforts when it destroyed 93,690 homes.

HIGHEST FLOOD DEATH TOLL
When the Huang He (Yellow River), Huayan Kou, China, flooded in October 1887, it is estimated that 900,000 people were killed.

WORST TORNADO DEATH TOLL
On 26 April 1989 the town of Shaturia in Bangladesh was wiped out by a huge tornado. About 1,300 people died and as many as 50,000 people were made homeless.

HIGHEST TSUNAMI DEATH TOLL
Up to 27,000 people drowned when a giant tsunami (seismically-induced wave) inundated the Japanese coastline on the Sea of Japan in 1896.

The most deadly tsunami of modern times occurred in the Moro Gulf region of the Philippines on 17 August 1976. Caused by an earthquake, this massive wave was responsible for an estimated death toll of 8,000.

COSTLIEST YEAR FOR NATURAL DISASTERS
The year ending 31 December 1995 was the costliest ever in terms of natural disasters, with a bill amounting to $180 billion (then £114.05 billion). Much of this was accounted for by the earthquake in Kobe, Japan, which occurred in January of that year.

WORST DEVASTATION DUE TO AN EARTHQUAKE
After an earthquake with a magnitude of 8.19 on the Kanto plain, Japan, on 1 September 1923, 575,000 homes were destroyed in Tokyo and Yokohama and 142,807 people were listed as killed or missing. The entire city of Yokohama was wrecked and fires broke out in both cities, adding to the devastation. At Misaki, south of Yokohama, the ground rose up by up to 7.3 m (24 ft), changing the shape of the coastline. After 72 hours the ground began to sink to its former position. In addition to the terrible loss of life, the damage toll was estimated to be $1 billion (then £210 million).

HIGHEST EARTHQUAKE DEATH TOLL
The highest death toll in modern times was in the Tangshan earthquake (magnitude 7.9) in China on 28 July 1976. It is estimated that at least 255,000 people were killed.

MOST DESTRUCTIVE GEOMAGNETIC STORM
The 'Great Geomagnetic Storm' of 13 March 1989 was classified G5 (the most severe rating) on the space weather scale. It caused large-scale disruption to the power grid in North America, changed the orbit of a satellite and caused dazzling auroral displays. These 'storms' occur when the Earth's magnetic field is buffeted by vast quantities of particles released after a Solar eruption.

WORST FLOOD DAMAGE
According to official figures, flooding from the Hwai and Yangtze rivers in China in August 1950 destroyed 890,000 homes and left 490 people dead and 10 million homeless. A total of 2 million ha (5 million acres) of land was left under water, rendering 1.4 million ha (3.5 million acres) unworkable for the planting season.

HIGHEST CYCLONE DEATH TOLL
A tropical cyclone that hit the Ganges Delta Islands, Bangladesh, between 12 and 13 November 1970, is thought to have killed one million people. Less than half the population survived.

WORST LANDSLIDE DEATH TOLL
On 31 May 1970, a landslide of rock debris from Mt Huascarán, Peru, killed over 18,000 people in the town of Yungay. It began with a sliding mass of rock and glacial ice around 900 m (3,000 ft) wide and 1.6 km (1 mile) long and travelled at an average speed of around 160 km/h (100 mph) before hitting the town of Yungay, 14.4 km (9 miles) down-slope.

WORST HAILSTORM DISASTER
A total of 246 people were killed during a hailstorm at Moradabad, Uttar Pradesh, India, on 20 April 1888.

LONGEST POST-EARTHQUAKE SURVIVAL BY A CAT
In December 1999, 80 days after the earthquake that struck Taiwan on 21 September, killing an estimated 2,400 people, a cat was discovered alive but trapped in the rubble of a building in Taichung, Taiwan. The cat, dehydrated and barely breathing, weighed less than half the weight of a healthy cat. It was rushed to a veterinary hospital where it made a full recovery.

WORST CYCLONE DISASTER DAMAGE
Hurricane Andrew (the results of which are shown above), which hit Homestead, Florida, USA, between 23 and 26 August 1992, was estimated to have caused $15.5 billion (£7.8 billion) worth of damage in terms of insured losses.

WORST DAMAGE BY AN ICE STORM

The most damaging ice storm on record was one experienced in the first week of January 1998 in eastern Canada and adjoining parts of the USA. The storm, which began on 6 January, shut down airports and trains, blocked highways and cut off power to three million people – almost 40% of the population of Québec. Over five days, freezing rain coated power lines with 10 cm (4 in) of ice, more weight than they could carry. Tens of thousands of poles were toppled. The bill was estimated at a massive CAN$1 billion ($650 million or £406 million).

HIGHEST DEATH TOLL FROM A VOLCANIC ERUPTION

Around 92,000 people were killed when the Tambora volcano in Sumbawa, Indonesia (then Dutch East Indies) erupted in 1815.

LARGEST GEYSER DEATH TOLL

Four people were killed in New Zealand in August 1903 during one of the geyser Waimangu's violent eruptions. The hydrothermal system that powers this activity was formed in 1886 when the nearby volcano Tarawera erupted. The victims were standing 27 m (90 ft) from the geyser, but their bodies were found up to 800 m (0.5 mile) away. One was jammed between two rocks, one in a hole in the ground, one suspended in a tree and the fourth was found on flat ground.

WORST DAMAGE BY A HAILSTORM

A massive hailstorm in Munich, Germany, in July 1984, wreaked damage on trees, buildings and vehicles, leading to insurance losses of $500 million (£378 million). The final bill, including losses to the economy caused by damage to uninsured buildings, was estimated at $1 billion (£756 million).

WORST HOMELESS TOLL FROM A FLOOD DISASTER

In September 1978, monsoon rains in the Indian state of Bengal caused such extensive river-flooding that around 15 million people out of a total population of 44 million were made homeless. This is equal to almost twice the population of London. In addition, 1,300 people and 26,687 cattle drowned and economic losses were put at $11.3 million (£5.7 million).

BIGGEST LAVA FLOW DIVERTED

In 1973 the Eldfell volcano on the Icelandic island of Heimaey erupted, causing lava to flow towards the town of Vestmannaeyjar. A third of the town was destroyed, but the inhabitants defended the rest of the town, using fire hoses and water pumps to cool and solidify the lava and form a natural dam. This barrier successfully diverted the flow away from the village into the sea.

SMOOTHEST SURFACE IN THE SOLAR SYSTEM

Jupiter's icy moon, Europa, orbits 670,900 km (416,900 miles) above the planet. Its surface (above) is smoother than any solid body in our Solar System. Ridges up to 800 m (2,600 ft) in height form the only relief on the moon's surface.

BRIGHTEST STAR CLUSTER

The Pleiades (M45), or Seven Sisters, contains around 500 individual stars in a region of space around 20 light years across and at an average distance from Earth of approximately 380 light years. The brightest star in the Pleiades is Alcyone, with an apparent magnitude (brightness as seen from Earth) of 2.87; the Sun's apparent magnitude is -26.5.

HIGHEST VOLCANIC ERUPTION

On 6 August 2001 NASA's *Galileo* spacecraft performed a close flyby of Jupiter's volcanically active moon, Io. Over the next few months, as the data was transmitted back to Earth, scientists realized that the spacecraft had passed through the top of a 500-km-high (310-mile) volcanic plume – the highest ever seen in the Solar System.

PLANET WITH THE LONGEST DAY

While the Earth takes 23 hr 56 min 4 sec to complete one rotation on its axis, Venus takes a very slow 243.16 'Earth days' to spin once through 360 degrees. Venus is closer to the Sun than the Earth is, meaning that a year on the planet is shorter than an Earth year, lasting 224.7 days. Therefore a Venus 'day' is actually longer than a Venus 'year'.

CLOSEST MOON TO A PLANET

Of all the moons in the Solar System, the one that orbits closest to its planet is the Martian satellite Phobos. This tiny moon lies 9,378 km (5,827 miles) from the centre of Mars, which corresponds to 5,981 km (3,716 miles) above the Martian surface. In comparison, the Moon is 384,400 km (238,855 miles) from the Earth, which corresponds to 376,284 km (233,812 miles) surface to surface.

LARGEST FLOOD CHANNEL IN THE SOLAR SYSTEM

The enormous north-western slope valleys on Mars have a width of around 200 km (120 miles) and were probably formed by catastrophic floods of water bursting through the surface around 3.5 billion years ago. The valleys were discovered by James Dohm (USA, University of Arizona) and colleagues in 2001, using data collected from NASA's *Mars Global Surveyor* spacecraft.

DENSEST PLANET

Earth is the densest planet in the Solar System, with an average density of 5.517 times that of water. Formed approximately 4.6 billion years ago, the planet is composed of a core of iron and nickel, an outer core of liquid iron and nickel, a rocky mantle and a thin, rocky crust.

MOST DISTANT OBSERVED SUPERNOVA

In April 2001, astronomers using data from the orbiting Hubble Space Telescope announced that they had discovered the most distant observed supernova. The light from this exploding star originates from a distance of 10 billion light years from Earth. One light year is the distance light travels in a year, about 9.5 trillion km (6 trillion miles).

HOTTEST PLACE IN THE SOLAR SYSTEM

The very centre of the Sun is the hottest place in the Solar System. Latest estimates put the temperature there at 15,600,000°C. The immense pressure in the core is around 250 billion times the pressure at sea level on Earth. It is here that around 600 million tonnes of hydrogen are fused into helium every second. This ongoing nuclear reaction is what makes the Sun shine.

NEAREST NEUTRON STAR

Observations of the star RX J185635-3754 by the Hubble Space Telescope have revealed it to be the closest neutron star (a star, composed only of neutrons, that has collapsed under its own gravity) to the Solar System. A remnant of a supernova around one million years ago, this star is only 200 light years away.

MOST DISTANT PLANET WITH AN ATMOSPHERE

On 27 November 2001, astronomers using the Hubble Space Telescope announced the discovery of an atmosphere on a planet orbiting another star. This as-yet-unnamed planet orbits the star HD 209458, 150 light years away from Earth. Astronomers were first alerted to the planet's presence in 1999, by the slight wobble its gravity inflicts upon HD 209458, as it orbits the star.

LARGEST STRUCTURE IN THE UNIVERSE

The largest structure discovered to date in the universe is the Great Wall. This giant sheet, or filament, of galaxies was found in 1989 by Margaret Geller and John Huchra (both USA). The Great Wall has been estimated at approximately 270 x 700 million light years in extent, and is thought to be around 15 million light years thick.

HEAVIEST BLACK HOLE

On 28 November 2001, a black hole (above) with a mass 14 times that of the Sun was discovered by a team at the European Southern Observatory's Paranal Observatory. It is approximately 40,000 light years from Earth.

BRIGHTEST SUPERNOVA

The supernova SN 1006, noted in April 1006 near the star Beta Lupi, flared for two years and reached a magnitude of -9.5. This titanic cosmic explosion was bright enough to be seen with the naked eye for 24 months and, at its brightest, was 1,500 times brighter than Sirius, the brightest star in the night sky. The supernova was around 3,260 light years away, or about 137,000,000,000,000,000 km (85,000,000,000,000,000 miles).

BRIGHTEST NEBULA

The Orion Nebula is the brightest nebula (a hazy cloud of particles and gases) in the sky. Located in the 'sword' of the constellation of Orion, the nebula is easily visible to the naked eye.

MOST LUMINOUS OBJECT

Quasar (short for 'quasi-stellar object') APM08279+5255 was discovered in March 1998 by a team of astronomers at La Palma in the Canary Islands, Spain, using the 2.5-m Isaac Newton Telescope. This quasar is 4–5 million billion times brighter than the Sun and is estimated to be more than 10 times brighter than any known quasar. The light we see from the quasar left it around 11 billion years ago.

DARKEST OBJECT IN THE SOLAR SYSTEM

The darkest body so far discovered in the Solar System is Comet Borrelly. This 8-km-long (5-mile) comet nucleus was imaged by the *Deep Space 1* unmanned spacecraft on 22 September 2001. The surface of Borrelly reflects less than 3% of the sunlight it receives. (Earth reflects around 30% of the sunlight that it receives.) The comet's darkness is due to dark dust that coats its surface.

LARGEST RECORDED SOLAR FLARE

On 2 April 2001 at 9:51 pm GMT, the largest solar flare ever recorded erupted from the Sun's surface, emitting billions of tonnes of electrified gas and radiation. Some of this matter hit Earth's atmosphere, creating an aurora (shifting pattern of light) in the sky.

MOST WIDELY INVESTIGATED PLANET

There have been 28 missions to Venus (above) and 26 missions to Mars. The most recent spacecraft to visit Venus was *Cassini-Huygens*, which flew by in 1998 and 1999 to pick up speed from the planet's orbit around the Sun. The craft is now en route to Saturn and will arrive in July 2004.

OLDEST OPERATING INTERPLANETARY SPACECRAFT

The unmanned space probe *Pioneer 6* was launched on 16 December 1965. After achieving solar orbit between Earth and Venus, it determined the structure and flow of the solar wind, the million-mile-an-hour stream of charged particles from the Sun. It is still in operation 35 years later, but is no longer collecting data.

LONGEST SPACEWALK

American astronauts Jim Voss and Susan Helms spent 8 hr 56 min in space on 11 March 2001. Their job was to make sufficient room on the International Space Station for the Italian cargo module *Leonardo*, which was carried into space by the space shuttle *Discovery*. *Leonardo*'s payload included around 5 tonnes (11,000 lb) of supplies and equipment for the space station.

MOST PEOPLE IN SPACE AT ONCE

On 14 March 1995, a record 13 people were in space at the same time: seven Americans aboard the space shuttle *Endeavour*, three Russian cosmonauts aboard the *Mir* space station and two Commonwealth of Independent States (CIS) cosmonauts and a US astronaut aboard the CIS *Soyuz* TM21.

BOUNCIEST LANDING ON A PLANET'S SURFACE

Upon its arrival at Mars on 4 July 1997, the *Mars Pathfinder* space probe (USA) used a combination of a parachute and retro rockets to slow down after entering the atmosphere. The lander then cut away from the parachute and fell to the surface of Mars, wrapped in inflatable airbags. Upon impact at 4:57 pm (UT) it rebounded to a height of around 15 m (50 ft), then bounced 15 times before coming to rest on the Martian surface.

MOST DISTANT SOLAR-POWERED SPACECRAFT

In April 2002, NASA's solar-powered *Stardust* spacecraft, en route to sample comet Wild 2 in January 2004, was 407 million km (253 million miles) from the Sun. Solar-powered spacecraft usually only explore the inner Solar System, as more distant planets do not receive enough sunlight to power the craft.

MOST DISTANT IMAGE OF EARTH

On 4 February 1990, after 12.5 years in space, the camera on NASA's *Voyager 1* spacecraft turned back towards the Sun and its planets and took a picture of Earth from a distance of almost 6.5 billion km (4 billion miles). The images were transmitted back to NASA and showed the Sun as a bright star and the Earth as a pale blue dot.

MOST REMOTE GOLF SHOT

In February 1971, at the end of the *Apollo 14* mission, astronaut Alan Shepard (USA) struck two golf balls in the Fra Mauro region on the Moon. He used a club that was made from a tool used to sample lunar material, with a six-iron attached to it. One of the golf balls travelled for a distance of around 15 m (50 ft).

OLDEST OPERATING MANNED SPACECRAFT

Columbia, the earliest of NASA's fleet of four operating space shuttles, was first launched into space on 12 April 1981. Its maiden flight proved the viability of the concept of a reusable, winged spaceplane. The commander for *Columbia*'s first mission was John Young (USA), who was already a veteran of four previous spaceflights, including two Apollo missions to the Moon.

MOST SPACEFLIGHTS BY AN ASTRONAUT

On 8 April 2002, 54-year-old US astronaut Jerry Ross began his seventh space mission. He was flying as a crew member aboard the STS 110 mission of the space shuttle *Atlantis*, on a construction flight to the International Space Station. All of Ross's flights have been on the space shuttle. He was selected as an astronaut in 1980 and his first spaceflight was in 1985.

MOST ACCURATE STAR MAP

The European Space Agency's (ESA) *Hipparcos* satellite plotted the relative positions of more than 100,000 stars with an accuracy 200 times greater than that of any previous measurements. The results, published by ESA in 1997, filled 16 bound volumes, along with a three-volume millennium star atlas. The mission was in operation from 1989 to 1993.

LONGEST SPACEFLIGHT BY A WOMAN

The longest spaceflight achieved by a woman lasted 188 days 4 hr 14 sec. Shannon Lucid (USA) was launched to the *Mir* space station aboard the US space shuttle *Atlantis* on 22 March 1996. She returned to Earth aboard *Atlantis* on 26 September the same year. Her stay in space is also the longest by any US astronaut.

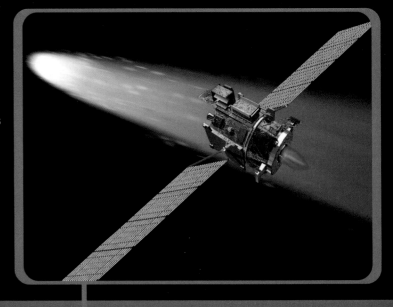

CLEAREST IMAGE OF A COMET

On 22 September 2001, NASA's probe *Deep Space 1* (above) passed within 2,000 km (1,243 miles) of Comet Borrelly. Its camera photographed the comet's rock-and-ice nucleus, revealing some details only 45 m (150 ft) across.

FASTEST ATMOSPHERIC ENTRY

On 7 December 1995, a small probe from the *Galileo* spacecraft began a fiery descent into Jupiter's atmosphere. The 339-kg (747-lb) mini-spacecraft was equipped with a heat shield to allow it to enter the atmosphere without burning up in the 15,500°C (28,000°F) heat caused by the friction of its entry. Due to Jupiter's intense gravity, the probe was accelerated to enormous speeds before entering the planet's atmosphere. During this – the most difficult atmospheric entry ever – the *Galileo* probe reached the astonishing speed of 170,000 km/h (106,000 mph).

MOST POWERFUL TELESCOPES

The Chandra X-Ray Telescope, which was launched in July 1999, has a resolving power equivalent to the ability to read a stop sign at a distance of 19.3 km (12 miles). Its sensitivity is due to the size and smoothness of its mirrors. Chandra orbits the Earth at a distance 200 times higher than that of NASA's Hubble telescope – more than a third of the way to the Moon.

Launched in 1991, the Compton Gamma Ray Observatory is the most powerful gamma-ray telescope invented. Following nine years of observations it re-entered the Earth's atmosphere and burned up on 4 June 2000.

The largest infrared telescope dedicated solely to infrared astronomy is the UKIRT (United Kingdom Infrared Telescope) on Mauna Kea, Hawaii, USA. The telescope features a 3.74-m (147-in) mirror, and is so powerful that it can be used for visual work as well as for infrared investigations.

MOST MISSIONS BY A SINGLE SPACECRAFT

The space shuttle *Discovery* (right) was launched on 10 August 2001 at 4:10 pm (CDT) on a mission to deliver the *Leonardo* cargo module and a new crew to the International Space Station. This was the 30th mission for *Discovery*, which has been in operation since 1984.

MOST COMPREHENSIVE GALACTIC SURVEY

The 2dF (two-degree field) survey of more than 100,000 galaxies is the largest and most detailed galactic study that has been carried out to date. Using one of the most complex astronomical instruments in the world, the Anglo-Australian Telescope (NSW, Australia), the survey enabled the international team of astronomers to construct a 3-D 'map' that revealed the large-scale structure of the universe in unprecedented detail.

MOST PLANETS VISITED BY A SPACECRAFT

NASA's *Voyager 2* spacecraft, which was launched in 1977, visited all four of the Solar System's outer gas giants – Jupiter, Saturn, Uranus and Neptune – between the years 1979 and 1989.

LONGEST STAY ON A CELESTIAL BODY

During the course of *Apollo 17*'s mission, astronauts Eugene A Cernan and Harrison H Schmitt (both USA) spent a total of 74 hr 59 min 40 sec on the surface of the Moon. *Apollo 17* was the last of the USA's manned missions to the Moon. The duration of the mission, from its launch on 7 December 1972 to the splashdown on 19 December 1972, was 12 days 13 hr 52 min.

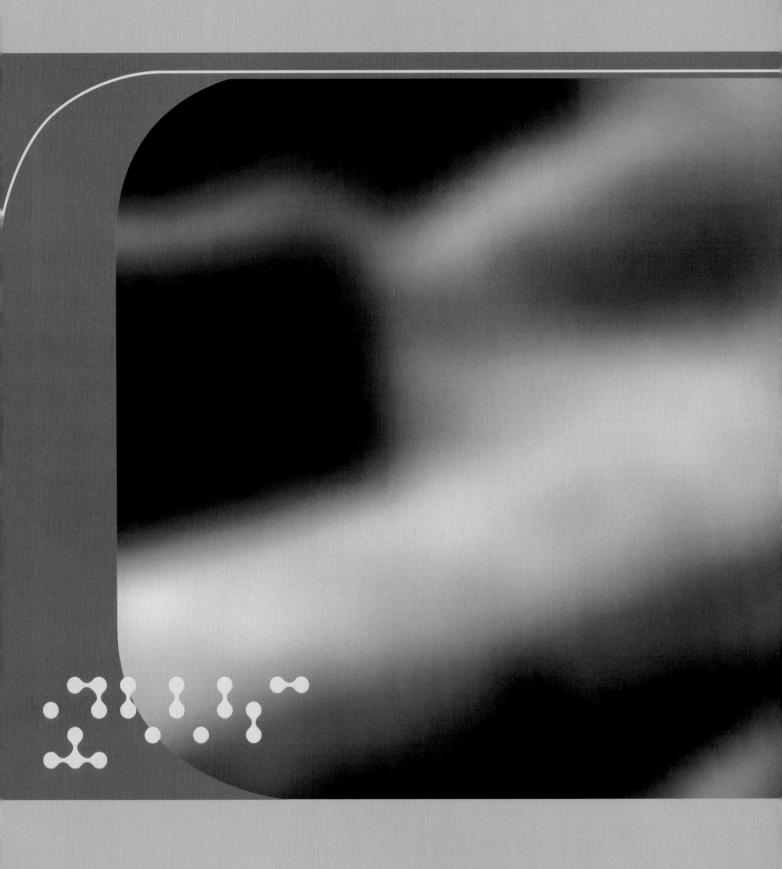

AMAZING NATURE

GREATEST PLATEAU
The world's most extensive plateau is the Tibetan Plateau in Central Asia (above). Its average altitude is 4,900 m (16,000 ft) and its area is 1,850,000 km^2 (715,000 miles^2).

LONGEST-BURNING FIRE
The world's longest-burning fire is a burning coal seam beneath Mt Wingen, NSW, Australia. It is believed to have started around 5,000 years ago when lightning struck the coal seam at the Earth's surface. Today, the fire is now burning around 30 m (100 ft) underground as it has slowly eaten its way back down the seam.

LARGEST IMPACT CRATER
Approximately 150 impact craters have been identified so far on Earth. The largest is the Vredefort Crater, near Johannesburg, South Africa, with an estimated diameter of around 300 km (186 miles). This huge eroded structure was formed around two billion years ago, when either an asteroid or comet collided with the Earth.

LARGEST ACTIVE VOLCANO
Mauna Loa, Hawaii, USA, which last erupted in 1984, rises 4,170 m (13,680 ft) above sea level, has the shape of a broad gentle dome and is 120 km (75 miles) long and 50 km (31 miles) wide. It has a total volume of 42,500 km^3 (10,200 miles^3) of which 84.2% is below sea level. Its caldera (volcano crater), Mokuaweoweo, measures 10.5 km^2 (4 miles^2) and is 150–180 m (500–600 ft) deep.

LARGEST VOLCANO CRATER
The Toba caldera in Sumatra, Indonesia, covers 1,775 km^2 (685 miles^2). It last erupted around 75,000 years ago.

LOUDEST NOISE
The loudest noise ever recorded was the eruption of the island-volcano Krakatoa in the Sunda Strait between Sumatra and Java, Indonesia, on 27 August 1883. The sound was heard 5,000 km (3,100 miles) away. With 26 times the power of the largest H-bomb test, it is estimated that the noise was heard over 8% of the Earth.

GREATEST MASS EXTINCTION
A mass extinction 248 million years ago wiped out around 90% of all marine species and 70% of all land animals. Possible causes include asteroid or comet impact, global climate change, or changes in ocean composition. This period was the end of the line for many species, but for fish and the dinosaur's ancestors, it was a pivotal moment in evolution.

HIGHEST MOUNTAIN
Mount Everest, on the Tibet–Nepal border in the Himalayas, has a height of 8,848 m (29,028.8 ft). Officially recognized as the world's highest mountain in 1856, the mountain was named after Colonel Sir George Everest, Surveyor-General of India from 1830 to 1843.

LARGEST STEAM RINGS
Europe's tallest and most active volcano – Mount Etna on the island of Sicily, Italy – emits steam rings of around 200 m (650 ft) across that can last up to around 10 minutes as they slowly drift up to 1,000 m (3,300 ft) above the volcanic vent. It is essentially the same process as a smoker blowing smoke rings, and is thought to be due to the unusual shape of the volcanic vent as it expels hot gases.

LONGEST FULGURITE
In 1996, a huge fulgurite (a tube of glassy mineral matter formed in rocks or sand by lightning) was excavated in Florida, USA. Two branches extended down from the strike point, one 5.2 m (17 ft) and the other 4.9 m (16 ft) long.

LARGEST SANDSTONE MONOLITH
The largest exposed sandstone monolith in the world is Uluru, also known as Ayers Rock, which rises 348 m (1,143 ft) above the desert plain in Northern Territory, Australia. It is 2.5 km (1.5 miles) long and 1.6 km (1 mile) wide.

OLDEST EARTH FRAGMENTS
A tiny zircon crystal discovered in Australia is the oldest fragment of Earth discovered so far. Between 4.3 and 4.4 billion years old, this sample is 100 million years older than any previous discovery, and challenges the theory that the Earth's surface was at that time an ocean of molten magma.

LARGEST CONTINENT EVER
About 250 million years ago, all the continents were joined together as one 'supercontinent' called Pangea (Greek for 'all lands'). Pangea began to break apart due to plate tectonics 180 million years ago, resulting in today's land masses. Evidence can be seen in the matching coastlines of Africa and South America.

FASTEST LAND MASS
Due to convection currents in the Earth's mantle, all the continental plates slowly move either towards or away from each other. The greatest movement occurs at the Tonga microplate, near Samoa, which is moving steadily into the Pacific Ocean at an amazing rate of 24 cm (9.4 in) per year.

HIGHEST CLIFFS
The massive cliffs on the north-east coast of Molokai, Hawaii, USA (above), descend 1,010 m (3,300 ft) to the sea. This equates to just under twice the height of the world's tallest building – the CN Tower in Toronto, Ontario, Canada.

LARGEST DESERT

Nearly an eighth of the world's land surface is arid, with a rainfall of less than 25 cm (10 in) per year. The Sahara in north Africa (below) is the world's largest hot desert. It is 5,150 km (3,200 miles) at its widedst point and between 1,280 and 2,250 km (800 and 1,400 miles) from north to south. With an area of about 9,269,000 km^2 (3,579,000 miles^2), the Sahara is roughly the same size as the USA.

MOST REMOTE ISLAND

The very remote Bouvet Island in the South Atlantic, discovered by JBC Bouvet de Lozier (France) on 1 January 1739, can be found at lat 54°26'S, long 3°24'E. This uninhabited Norwegian dependency is about 1,700 km (1,050 miles) from the nearest land, Queen Maud Land in East Antarctica, which is also uninhabited.

LARGEST PINGO

Pingoes are isolated conical mounds which have a core of ice. They form when lakes in permafrost regions drain. As the residual water in the ground under the lake freezes, it expands, pushing up a mound of land. Ibyuk Pingo, in the Tuktoyaktuk Peninsula on the western Arctic coast of Canada, is the world's largest. It measures around 50 m (160 ft) high and 300 m (990 ft) around its base.

LARGEST UNINHABITED ISLAND

Devon Island, Canada, in the Arctic Circle north of Baffin Island, has an approximate area of 66,800 km^2 (25,800 miles^2). A third of the island is covered with ice and the rest is barren. Its most distinctive feature is the Haughton Crater – a 20-km-wide (12-mile) impact crater formed 23 million years ago. It is home to the Haughton-Mars Project: scientists are using the desolate environment to learn about surviving on Mars.

GREATEST RECORDED IMPACT ON EARTH

On 30 June 1908 an explosion occurred over the basin of the Podkamennaya Tunguska River, Russia. The probable cause was energy released following the disintegration of a common-type stony meteoroid 30 m (98 ft) in diameter, at an altitude of 10 km (6 miles) and travelling at hypersonic velocity at an incoming angle of 45°. Equivalent to 10–15 megatons of high-explosives, it resulted in the devastation of an area of 3,900 km^2 (1,500 miles^2). The shock wave was felt up to 1,000 km (620 miles) away.

LARGEST CAVE

The world's largest cave chamber is the Sarawak Chamber, Lubang Nasib Bagus, in the Gunung Mulu National Park, Sarawak, Malaysia. It was discovered and surveyed by the 1980 British-Malaysian Mulu Expedition. It is 700 m (2,300 ft) long, its average width is 300 m (980 ft) and it is at least 70 m (230 ft) high. This massive underground chamber is large enough to contain St Paul's Cathedral in London.

DEEPEST LAKE

Lake Baikal (above), in the southern part of eastern Siberia, Russia, is the world's deepest lake. In 1974 the depth of the lake's Olkhon Crevice was measured at 1,637 m (5,371 ft), of which 1,181 m (3,875 ft) is below sea level. Lake Baikal is also Earth's oldest freshwater lake, having formed 20–25 million years ago, and contains one fifth of the world's fresh surface water.

SALTIEST LAKE

Don Juan Pond in Wright Valley, Antarctica, has such a high salt content that it remains a liquid even at temperatures as low as -53°C (-63.4°F). At its saltiest, the lake's percentage of salt by weight is 40.2%, compared to 23.1% in the Dead Sea and a 3.38% average in the world's oceans as a whole.

LARGEST OCEAN

Excluding adjacent seas, the Pacific Ocean represents 45.9% of the world's ocean surface. It has a total area of 166,241,700 km² (64,186,000 miles²) and an average depth of 3,940 m (12,925 ft). The Pacific covers over one third of the Earth.

TALLEST HYDROTHERMAL VENTS

A hydrothermal vent (a type of underwater hot spring) produces a column of super-heated water that gushes from the seabed due to volcanic activity. The tallest hydrothermal vent found on the ocean floor measures approximately 55 m (180 ft) in height. It was found by the US research vessel *Atlantis* and its sensing system, *Argo*, in December 2000. The vent was one of a group, dubbed 'The Lost City', which is part of a newly discovered system of vents on the mid-Atlantic Ridge – itself the largest system of these vents discovered so far.

HIGHEST OCEAN TEMPERATURE

The highest temperature recorded in the ocean is 404°C (759°F) for a hydrothermal vent measured by a US research submarine approximately 480 km (300 miles) off the west coast of the USA in 1985.

DEEPEST POINT IN THE OCEAN

The deepest part of the ocean was first pinpointed in 1951 by HM Survey Ship *Challenger* in the Marianas Trench of the Pacific Ocean. The manned US Navy bathyscaphe *Trieste* reached the bottom of the trench on 23 January 1960. The unmanned Japanese probe *Kaiko* reached the trench bottom on 24 March 1995 and recorded a depth of 10,911 m (35,797 ft), the most accurate measurement of this point that has ever been made.

LARGEST ICEBERG

The largest known iceberg was a tabular iceberg measuring over 31,000 km² (12,000 miles²). Tabular icebergs are sections of continental ice sheet that extend far over the sea before breaking off, and are typical of Antarctica. They have flat tops and a

HIGHEST WAVES

The highest recorded sea wave (one dependent on weather or climate) was put at 34 m (112 ft) from trough to crest. It was measured on the night of 6–7 February 1933 by Lt Frederic Margraff (USA) from the *USS Ramapo* while sailing from Manila, Philippines, to San Diego, California, USA, during a hurricane that reached speeds of up to 68 knots (126 km/h or 78.3 mph).

level height. The record-breaking iceberg was 335 km (208 miles) long and 97 km (60 miles) wide (larger than Belgium) and was sighted 240 km (150 miles) west of Scott Island, in the South Pacific Ocean, Antarctica, by the *USS Glacier* on 12 November 1956.

LARGEST LAKE

The world's largest inland sea or lake is the Caspian Sea in Russia, Iran, Turkmenistan, Azerbaijan and Kazakhstan. It is 1,225 km (760 miles) long and has an area of 371,800 km² (143,550 miles²). Around 143,200 km² (55,280 miles²) – or 38.5% of the total area – is in Iran. Its maximum depth is 1,025 m (3,360 ft) and the surface is 28.5 m (93 ft) below sea level.

The total volume of saline water in the lake has been estimated at 89,600 km³ (21,500 miles³).

GREATEST WATERFALL ANNUAL FLOW

The greatest waterfall flow in the world is the Boyoma Falls in Zaïre (now Democratic Republic of Congo). The water at the falls flows at a rate of 17,000 m³/sec (600,000 ft³/sec).

LARGEST HOT SPRING

The largest boiling river issues from hot alkaline springs located at Deildartunguhver, north of Reykjavik, Iceland, at a rate of 245 litres (65 gal) of boiling water per second, heated by volcanic activity underground.

HIGHEST TSUNAMI

The highest tsunami (giant wave) was 524 m (1,719 ft) high and occurred along the fjord-like Lituya Bay, Alaska, USA, on 9 July 1958. It was caused by a giant landslip and moved at 160 km/h (100 mph). The wave was so high it would easily have swamped the Petronas Towers in Kuala Lumpur, Malaysia, which, at around 452 m (1,483 ft), are the world's tallest office buildings.

DEADLIEST LAKE

One night in August 1986, over 1,600 people and many animals died when large quantities of carbon dioxide gas were released from Lake Nyos (above) in Cameroon, west Africa. The source of its mysterious deadly gases is unknown.

HIGHEST WATERFALL

The Salto Angel in Venezuela, on the river Churun – a tributary of the Caroni River – is the world's highest waterfall. It has a total drop of 979 m (3,212 ft) – the longest single drop being one of 807 m (2,648 ft). It is also known as the 'Angel Falls', after US pilot Jimmie Angel, who recorded the waterfall in his log book on 16 November 1933. The falls had originally been reported by Venezuelan explorer Ernesto Sanchez la Cruz in 1910.

LARGEST LAGOON

The Lagoa dos Patos lagoon, located near the seashore in Rio Grande do Sul in southernmost Brazil, is 280 km (174 miles) long, 70 km (44 miles) at its widest point and extends over an area of 9,850 km^2 (3,803 miles^2). The lagoon is separated from the Atlantic Ocean by long sand strips.

LARGEST UNDERGROUND LAKE

The largest known underground lake is in the Drachenhauchloch (Dragon's Breath) cave near Grootfontein, Namibia, Africa, and was discovered in 1986. When it was surveyed in April 1991, the lake's total area was found to be 2.61 ha (6.45 acres). The surface of the lake is around 66 m (217 ft) underground and it is 84 m (276 ft) deep.

LARGEST TIDAL BORE

A tidal bore – a solitary wave that travels with great speed up a narrow river, forcing the flow upstream – is caused when the Sun, Moon and Earth align to form dramatic tidal conditions. Such waves can have devastating effects. The largest tidal bore ever recorded occurred on 18 August 1993 in Hangzhou Bay, China. It reached a height of 9 m (30 ft) and a length of 320 km (200 miles) and forced 9 million litres (2 million gal) of water per second towards the shore, killing around 100 people.

LONGEST RIVER

The Nile and the Amazon both have a claim to the title of the world's longest river. The Nile is officially 6,695 km (4,160 miles) long, but lost a few miles after the formation of Lake Nasser behind the Aswan Dam, Egypt. The end point of the Amazon remains uncertain. Including its furthest mouth – the Para estuary – the river is approximately 6,750 km (4,195 miles) in length.

FASTEST-MELTING GLACIER

A volcanic eruption under Europe's largest glacier, the Vatnajokul glacier (above) in Iceland, during October 1996, topped Lake Grimsvotn with meltwater. The meltwater flowed from the lake at an estimated 45,000 m^3/sec (1.6 million ft^3/sec), making it the fastest melting of a glacier in recorded history.

HIGHEST PLANT

The greatest certain altitude at which any flowering plants have been found is 6,400 m (21,000 ft) on Mt Kamet in the Himalayas. They were *Ermania himalayensis* and *Ranunculus lobatus*, found by ND Jayal (India) in 1955.

GREATEST ROOT DEPTH

The greatest reported depth to which roots have penetrated is calculated to be 120 m (400 ft) for a wild fig tree at Echo Caves, near Ohrigstad, Transvaal, South Africa.

SLOWEST FLOWERING PLANT

The panicle (flower) of the herb *Puya raimondii* (above) only emerges after about 80–150 years. A specimen seen in Bolivia in 1870 was 3,960 m (13,000 ft) above sea level. One planted at sea level in California, USA, in 1958 grew to 7.6 m (25 ft) and bloomed after 28 years in 1986.

OLDEST TREE SPECIES

The earliest surviving species of tree is the maidenhair (*Gingko biloba*) of Zhejiang, China, which first appeared about 160 million years ago during the Jurassic era. Leaf imprints of ancient species of Gingko trees have been found in sedimentary rocks of the Jurassic and Triassic periods – between 135–210 million years ago. Gingko can be used to treat a variety of ailments, including senility.

MOST LETHAL STINGING PLANT

New Zealand's feared tree nettle (*Urtica ferox*) can grow up to 3 m (9.8 ft) in height and has been known to kill dogs and horses. The fine white stinging hairs that line its leaves contain many toxins, including: histamine, 5-hydroxytryptamine, acetylcholine, formic acid and tryffidin. The tree nettle is known to have killed at least one man. This happened in 1961, and the man died just five hours after his skin had been in contact with the plant.

LARGEST TREE EVER

The world's all-time most massive tree was Lindsey Creek Tree, a coast redwood (*Sequoia sempervirens*) in California, USA. It had a minimum trunk volume of 2,549 m³ (90,000 ft³) and a minimum total mass of 3,630 tonnes (8,002,770 lb) including its foliage, branches and roots – roughly the same weight as 890 elephants. The tree blew over in a storm in 1905.

OLDEST PLANT

'King's Holly' (*Lomatia tasmanica*), found in Tasmania's south-western wilderness, is believed to be 43,000 years old. The shrub was carbon dated using a fossil of an identical specimen found nearby. This plant is on the endangered list as it only naturally occurs in this area.

TALLEST LIVING TREE

Currently, the tallest tree standing is the Mendocino Tree, a coast redwood (*Sequoia sempervirens*) at Montgomery State Reserve, Ukiah, California, USA. In September 1998, its height was 112.014 m (368.5 ft) – the same as the length of an average soccer field. This tree is still growing and is estimated to be about 1,000 years old.

SMELLIEST FLOWER

Known as 'the corpse flower', the *Amorphophallus titanum* is the world's smelliest flower. When it blooms (which is rare), it releases an extremely foul odour comparable to rotten flesh which can be smelled half a mile away. A native of the Sumatran rainforests, very few have ever flowered in Europe or the USA since first being discovered in 1878.

TALLEST TREE EVER

An Australian eucalyptus (*Eucalyptus regnans* – usual height 50 m or 164 ft) at Watts River, Vic, Australia, reported in 1872, was 132.6 m tall (435 ft) and may have originally been over 150 m (500 ft).

LARGEST LIVING TREE

'General Sherman', a giant sequoia (*Sequoiadendron giganteum)* in the Sequoia National Park, California, USA, stands 83.82 m (274.9 ft) tall, has a diameter of 11.1 m (36 ft 5 in) and a 31.3-m (102-ft 0.5-in) girth. The trunk volume is 1,487 m³ (52,508 ft³) – the same as 606,100 board-feet of timber, or enough for five billion matches.

LIVING TREE WITH GREATEST GIRTH

'El Arbol del Tule' in Oaxaca state, Mexico is a Montezuma cypress (*Taxodium mucronatum*, 42-m high (137-ft), with a diameter of 14.05 m (46 ft 0.9 in) and a girth (in 1998) of 58 m (190 ft). Roughly 19 cars placed end-to-end in a circle would match this girth. African baobab trees (*Adansonia digitata*) generally have the largest girths – up to 43 m (141 ft).

MOST REMOTE TREE

There is a solitary Norwegian spruce (*Picea abies*) on Campbell Island, Antarctica. Its nearest companions are trees over 222 km (120 nautical miles) away on the Auckland Islands.

LARGEST LEAF

The largest leaves of any plant are those of the raffia palm (*Raffia farinifera*) of the Mascarene Islands in the Indian Ocean, and the Amazonian bamboo palm (*Raffia taedigera*) of South America and Africa. Their leaf blades can be up to 20 m (65 ft 6 in) long, with petioles (the stalk by which a leaf is attached to a plant) measuring 4 m (13 ft).

OLDEST FLOWERING PLANT

A 142-million-year-old flower fossil, dubbed *Archaefructus liaoningensis* was found in north-east China in 1996. The plant was unearthed by Ge Sun (China), from the Institute of Geology and Paleontology in Nanjing, China.

MOST POISONOUS COMMON PLANT

The castor bean (*Ricinus communis*) holds the plant-poison record. A dose of 70 micrograms (2 millionths of an ounce) is enough to kill a 72-kg (11-st 4-lb) human. The poison, ricin, is a protein found in the castor bean's seeds and is approximately 6,000 times more poisonous than cyanide and 12,000 times more poisonous than rattlesnake venom.

OLDEST LIVING TREE

The oldest tree alive is the ancient Bristlecone pine 'Methuselah' (*Pinus longaeva*, above) which is a magnificent 4,767 years old. It was found by Dr Edmund Schulman (USA) in the White Mountains, California, USA, and dated in 1957.

HOTTEST SPICE

The hottest of all spices is believed to be Red Savina Habanero, belonging to the genus *Capsicum*, developed by GNS Spices of Walnut, California, USA. A single dried gram (0.04 oz) will produce detectable heat in 577 kg (1,272 lb) of bland sauce.

MOST MASSIVE PLANT

The most massive organism, as reported in December 1992, is a network of quaking aspen trees (*Populus tremuloides*) in the Wasatch Mountains, Utah, USA. They grow from a single root system covering 43 ha (106 acres) and weigh an estimated 6,000 tonnes (13.2 million lb). The clonal system is genetically uniform and acts as a single organism, with all the component trees changing colour or shedding leaves in unison.

SOUTHERNMOST PLANT

Lichens resembling *Rhinodina frigida* were found in Moraine Canyon near Mount Heekin, Antarctica, at lat 86°09'S, long 157°30'W in 1971 and in the Horlick Mountain area of Antarctica at lat 86°09'S, long 131°14'W in 1965. Lichens continue to grow despite droughts and extreme cold.

NORTHERNMOST PLANT

The yellow poppy (*Papaver radicatum*) and the Arctic willow (*Salix arctica*) survive at lat 83ºN, although the latter exists there in an extremely stunted form.

LARGEST CARNIVOROUS PLANT PREY

The Nepenthaceae family (genus *Nepenthes*, below) digest the largest prey in 'pitchers' up to 30 cm (11.81 in) long. Both *N. rajah* and *N. rafflesiana* have been known to eat frogs, birds and even rats. They are found in the rainforests of Asia, particularly in Indonesia.

LONGEST BILL

Bills on Australian pelicans (above, *Pelicanus conspicillatus*) can be up to 47 cm (18.5 in) long. The longest bill, relative to body length, belongs to the sword-billed hummingbird (*Ensifera ensifera*), which has a 10.2-cm (4-in) beak – longer than its body.

MOST FEARLESS MAMMAL

The ratel or honey badger (*Mellivora capensis*) will defend itself against any animal, especially if they disturb its breeding burrow. Its tough skin is impervious to attacks by bees, porcupines and most snakes and its skin is so loose that if it is held by the scruff of the neck – for example by a leopard – it can turn inside its skin and bite its attacker until released.

HIGHEST G-FORCE

Experiments have shown that the beak of the red-headed woodpecker (*Melanerpes erythrocephalus*) hits the bark of a tree with an impact velocity of 20.9 km/h (13 mph). This motion subjects the brain to a deceleration of about 10 G when the head snaps back.

FASTEST BIRD IN LEVEL FLIGHT

The fastest fliers in level flight are found among ducks and geese (Anatidae). Some powerful species such as the red-breasted merganser (*Mergus serrator*), the eider (*Somateria mollissima*), the canvasback (*Aythya valisineria*) and the spur-winged goose (*Plectropterus gambensis*) can, on rare occasions, reach 90–100 km/h (56–62 mph).

BEST ANIMAL REGENERATION

Sponges (Porifera) have the most remarkable powers of regeneration of any animal. If they lose a segment of their body, it grows right back. If a sponge is forced through a fine-meshed silk gauze, the separate fragments can re-form into a full-size sponge.

FASTEST CREATURES ON LAND

When measured over a short distance, the cheetah (*Acinonyx jubatus*) can maintain a record-breaking steady maximum speed of around 100 km/h (62 mph) on level ground. That's nearly the American highway speed limit!

The American antelope (*Antilocapra americana),* found in parts of the western United States, south-western Canada and parts of northern Mexico, is the fastest land animal when measured steadily over a long distance. The antelope has been witnessed travelling continuously at 56 km/h (35 mph) for as far as 6 km (4 miles).

The fastest bird on land is the ostrich, which, although it cannot fly, can run at a speed of up to 72 km/h (45 mph) when necessary. The ostrich also holds the record for the longest stride, which may exceed 7 m (23 ft) in length when sprinting.

OLDEST ELEPHANT

Lakshmikutty (1913–1997), a female elephant donated to the Guruvayur Sri Krishna temple, Mathrubhami, India, on 17 November 1923, lived to be 84 years old. Standing at 2.76 m (9 ft) tall, she was crowned 'Elephant Queen' in 1983.

HIGHEST FREQUENCY HEARING

Due to their ultrasonic echolocation (sensory perception by which they orientate themselves), bats have the most acute hearing of any terrestrial animal. Most species use frequencies in the 20–80 kHz range, although some can hear frequencies as high as 120–250 kHz, compared with a limit of 20 kHz for humans.

GREATEST DISTANCE FLOWN BY A BIRD

A common tern (*Sterna hirundo*), banded as a juvenile on 30 June 1996 in central Finland, flew a record 26,000 km (16,250 miles) before being recaptured alive at Rotamah Island, Vic, Australia, in January 1997. To have reached there, the bird must have flown an exhausting 200 km (124 miles) per day.

LARGEST LAND MAMMAL

The male African bush elephant (*Loxodonta africana*) has an average shoulder-height of 3–3.7 m (9 ft 10 in –12 ft 2 in) and an average weight of 4–7 tonnes (8,800–15,400 lb). The heaviest recorded specimen was shot in Angola, Africa, on 7 November 1974. It had a projected standing height of 3.96 m (13 ft) and weighed a massive 12.24 tonnes (26,984 lb).

FASTEST WING BEAT

The horned sungem (*Heliactin cornuta*), a hummingbird from tropical South America, has the fastest wing beat at 90 beats/sec. The wings move so fast that you can barely see them.

GREATEST TREE-CLIMBING FISH

The climbing perch (*Anabas testudineus*) from south Asia is remarkable for its ability to walk on land and climb palm trees. It will even walk to search for better habitat. The species has special gills that allow it to absorb atmospheric oxygen. Mudskippers (Perciformes) can also live out of water for short periods and climb trees using their pectoral fins.

NOISIEST LAND MAMMAL

Male howler monkeys (*Alouatta*, above) of Central and South America have an enlarged bony structure at the top of their windpipe that amplifies their shouts. Their noisy calls can be heard over distances of up to 4.8 km (3 miles) away.

SMALLEST OWL
The elf owl (*Micrathene whitneyi*) from south-west USA and Mexico is usually quoted as the smallest owl, averaging a tiny 12–14 cm (4.75–5.5 in) in length and weighing less than 50 g (1.75 oz).

HIGHEST-FLYING BIRDS
The highest altitude recorded for a bird is 11,300 m (37,000 ft) for a Ruppell's vulture (*Gyps rueppellii*), which collided with a commercial aircraft over Abidjan, Ivory Coast, on 29 November 1973. The impact shut down one of the aircraft's engines, but it landed safely. Enough feathers were recovered to make a positive identification of this high-flier, which is rarely seen above 6,000 m (20,000 ft).

LARGEST ANTLERS
The record antler spread, or 'rack', of any living species is 1.99 m (6 ft 6.5 in) on a moose (*Alces alces*) killed near the Stewart River, Yukon, Canada, in October 1897. The rack is on display in Chicago's Field Museum, Illinois, USA.

LARGEST MAMMAL EYES
The Pygmy tarsier (*Tarsius pumilus*) from south-east Asia, which has a head and body length of 8.5–16 cm (3.3– 6.3 in) has huge forward-pointing eyes with a diameter of 1.6 cm (0.6 in). This eye-size is equivalent to humans having eyes the size of grapefruits. Tarsiers are the only primates that can move their heads 180 degrees to the left and right.

LARGEST WINGSPAN
The largest wingspan of any living species of bird was that of a male wandering albatross (*Diomedea exulans*) of the southern oceans, with a wingspan of 3.63 m (11 ft 11 in). It was caught by crew of the Antarctic research ship *USNS Eltanin* in the Tasman Sea on 18 September 1965.

KEENEST VISION
It has been calculated that large birds of prey have the keenest vision. They can detect a target object at a distance three or more times further than that achieved by humans. Under ideal conditions a peregrine falcon (*Falco peregrinus*) can spot a pigeon at a range of over 8 km (5 miles).

LARGEST BIRD EGG
The largest egg on record was an ostrich egg weighing 2.35 kg (5 lb 2 oz), laid in June 1997 at Datong Xinda ostrich farm, Shanxi, China. An ostrich egg normally weighs 1.0–1.78 kg (2.2–3.9 lb) equal to 24 hen's eggs in volume. Although only 1.5 mm (0.06 in) thick, the shell can support the weight of an adult human.

SMALLEST MAMMAL
The world's smallest mammal is the bumblebee bat or Kitti's hog-nosed bat (*Craseonycteris thonglongyai*), which has a body no bigger than a large bumblebee. It has a head-body length of only 29–33 mm (1.14–1.30 in), and a wingspan of approximately 130–145 mm (5.1–5.7 in). It can only be found in the limestone caves on the Kwae Noi River, Thailand.

LARGEST BIRD'S NEST
A nest built by a pair of bald eagles (*Haliaeetus leucocephalus*), near St Petersburg, Florida, USA, measured 2.9 m (9 ft 6 in) wide and 6 m (20 ft) deep. Examined in 1963, it was estimated to weigh more than 2 tonnes (4,400 lb).

GREEDIEST ANIMAL
The larva of the polyphemus moth (*Antheraea polyphemus*, above) of North America eats an amount equal to 86,000 times its own birthweight in its first 56 days. In human terms, this would be the same as a 3.17-kg (7-lb) baby taking on a staggering 273 tonnes (602,000 lb) of nourishment.

MOST INTELLIGENT PARROT

The world's most intelligent parrot, an African grey (*Psittacus erithacus*) called Alex (above), knows the words for more than 35 objects and seven colours. He also has a functional use of phrases and can distinguish between shapes with three, four, five or six sides.

Another contender is a parrot called Smudge, owned by Mark Steiger (Switzerland), who managed to remove 10 keys from an 'S'-shaped keyring on 30 November 2001.

BIRD WITH THE LARGEST VOCABULARY

The bird with the most extensive vocabulary was a budgerigar called Puck, owned by Camille Jordan (USA). Puck knew an estimated 1,728 words by the time of its death in 1994.

LONGEST DOG SWIM

On 2 September 1995, two black Labradors named Kai and Gypsy swam the 'Maui Channel Swim' from Lanai to Maui Island in Hawaii, USA – a distance of 15.2 km (9.5 miles) – in 6 hr 3 min 42 sec. The dogs' owner, Steve Fisher (USA), swam along with them the entire time. Kai and Gypsy are also talented windsurfers and often accompany Steve on his large, modified surfboard.

DOG WITH THE LARGEST REPERTOIRE OF TRICKS

Toy poodle Chanda-Leah, owned and trained by Sharon Robinson (Canada), can perform a repertoire of 469 tricks including playing the piano, knowing her three, four and five times table and riding a skateboard.

HIGHEST JUMP BY A DOG

On 27 September 1993 an 18-month-old lurcher dog named Stag broke the canine high-jump record for a leap-and-scramble over a smooth wooden wall without any climbing aids. The dog, which is owned by Mr and Mrs PR Matthews of Redruth, Cornwall, UK, cleared 3.72 m (12 ft 2.5 in), at the annual Cotswold Country Fair in Cirencester, Glos, UK.

FURTHEST CANINE TREK

In 1979, Jimpa, a Labrador/boxer cross, turned up at his home in Pimpinio, Vic, Australia, after walking 3,220 km (2,000 miles) across the continent. Jimpa's owner, Warren Dumesney (Australia), had taken the dog with him 14 months earlier when he went to work on a farm at Nyabing, WA, Australia. During his extraordinary trek, the dog negotiated the almost waterless Nullarbor Plain, South Australia.

MOST CELEBRATED CANINE RESCUER

The most famous canine rescuer of all time is a St Bernard dog called Barry, who rescued more than 40 people during a 12-year career on the Swiss Alps. His numerous successful rescues included that of a boy who was lying half-frozen under an avalanche in which his mother had perished. Barry spread himself across the boy's body to warm him and licked his face until he succeeded in waking him up. He then carried the youngster back to the nearest dwelling.

MOST NUMERATE CHIMPANZEE

Ai is the first chimpanzee to be able to count from one to nine. She is also able to remember five of these numbers chosen at random and can put them into ascending order in a fraction of a second. Ai was born in west Africa in 1976 and was brought to the Primate Research Institute, Kyoto University, Japan, in December 1977. There, she was nurtured by Prof Tetsuro Matsuzawa (Japan) and her numeracy skills blossomed.

LONGEST SCENT-TRACKING

In 1925 a Doberman pinscher called Sauer, who was trained by Det Sgt Herbert Kruger (South Africa), tracked a stock thief for 160 km (100 miles) over the arid Great Karroo plateau, South Africa, by scent alone.

HIGHEST-ALTITUDE SKYDIVE BY A DOG

On 20 May 1997, Brutus the 'Skydiving Dog' jumped from a large twin-engine plane at 4,572 m (15,000 ft) above sea level, flying high above the town of Lake Elsinore, California, USA, and set a new world record. His owner, Ron Sirull (USA), first began to take Brutus along on his skydives to prevent the dog from chasing his plane down the runway. Brutus, a miniature dachshund, currently boasts 71 separate skydives in his career and has his own custom-made goggles.

ONLY CANONIZED DOG

Guinefort, a French greyhound who was killed while saving a child from a snake, was later made a saint for his brave act. Healing miracles were performed on sickly children at his tomb in the 13th century until Dominican monks quashed the cult.

MOST PROFICIENT SIGNING GORILLA

In 1972, Koko – a gorilla born at San Francisco Zoo – was taught Ameslan (American Sign Language for the Deaf) by Dr Francine Patterson (USA). By 2000 Koko had a working vocabulary of over 1,000 signs and understood around 2,000 words of spoken English. She can refer to the past and future, argue, joke and lie. When Koko was asked by Dr Patterson whether she was an animal or a person, she replied, "Fine animal gorilla".

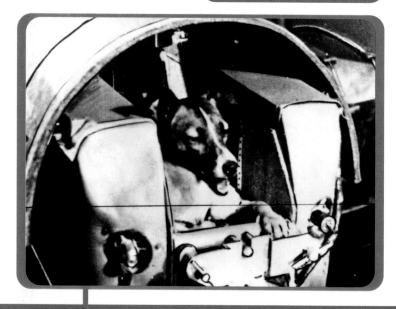

FIRST DOG IN SPACE

A dog called Laika (above) became the first animal in space in November 1957 when she went into orbit on *Sputnik 2*. Sadly, her vehicle was not designed to return to Earth and Laika (meaning 'barker' in Russian) died after a few days.

MOST SUCCESSFUL SNIFFER DOG

Snag, a US customs Labrador retriever trained and partnered by Jeff Weitzmann (USA), has made 118 drug seizures, worth a canine record $810 million (£580 million).

LONGEST SURVIVING HEADLESS CHICKEN

On 10 September 1945 a Wyandotte chicken called Mike was decapitated, but went on to survive for 18 months. The cut had missed the jugular vein and much of the brain stem had been left intact. His owner, Lloyd Olsen (USA), fed and watered the headless chicken directly into his gullet with the aid of an eyedropper. Mike eventually choked to death in an Arizona motel.

FIRST CHIMPANZEE TO OPERATE A COMPUTER

In 1972, Lana the chimpanzee was trained to read and write Yerkish, a language of words represented by abstract symbols on a computer keyboard, at the Yerkes Primate Research Center in Atlanta, Georgia, USA. After three years she had acquired a vocabulary of 120 words and could ask for a cup of coffee in 23 different ways.

LONGEST-SERVING MILITARY MULE

The unit mascot for the 853 AT Coy ASC (MA Mules) was a Spanish mule called Pedongi, who was on active service with the Indian Army from 4 May 1965 until her death at the age of 37 on 5 March 1998. Her name was derived from the first battle area she was sent to, at Pedong in north-east India.

BRAVEST DONKEY

On 19 May 1997, an Australian Army donkey called Murphy, was posthumously awarded the RSPCA Australia Purple Cross on behalf of all the donkeys that had served in the 1915–16 Gallipoli campaign during World War I. Murphy carried thousands of wounded soldiers to field hospitals.

OLDEST PRIMATE

Cheeta the chimpanzee, who appeared in the Tarzan films of the 1930s and 1940s starring Johnny Weissmuller and Maureen O'Sullivan, is the world's oldest living primate. He had reached the age of 69 years and one month by April 2001. Cheeta has been enshrined in the Palm Springs Walk of Stars in Palm Springs, California, USA, and is involved in the promotion of the chimp foundation CHEETA (the Committee to Help Enhance the Environment of Threatened Apes).

LONGEST SURVIVAL BY A SHEEP

On 24 March 1978, Alex Maclennan (UK) found one ewe still alive after he had dug 16 dead sheep out of a snowdrift. The flock was buried for 50 days in Sutherland, Highland, UK, following the great blizzard in January 1978. The sheep's hot breath created air holes in the snow, and the animal had gnawed its own wool for protein.

FASTEST SNAIL

The World Snail Racing Championships have been held outside St Andrew's church in Congham, Norfolk, UK, every July since 1970. Around 150 participants enter each year, racing against each other from the centre of a 33-cm (13-in) circular course to its perimeter. The all-time record holder is Archie, a young snail trained by Carl Bramham (UK), whose record-breaking sprint to the winning post in 1995 took 2 min 20 sec.

MOST SUCCESSFUL POLICE DOG

Police dogs (above) are a vital aid to law enforcement. Although many canine breeds are used in this line of work, the world's top police dog is a golden retriever – Trepp – who is credited with more than 100 arrests up to 1979 and the recovery of over $63 million (£28.6 million) worth of narcotics.

LARGEST SCORPION

The largest scorpion ever seen was one of the *Heterometrus swannerdami* species (above). It was found during World War II and measured a massive 29.2 cm (11.4 in) in overall length from the tips of the pedipalps (pincers) to the end of the sting. This particular species is from southern India. Males frequently attain a length of more than 18 cm (7 in).

MOST VENOMOUS SPIDER

The world's most venomous spiders are the Brazilian wandering spiders of the genus Phoneutria, particularly the Brazilian huntsman (*Phoneutria fera*), which has the most active neurotoxic venom of any living spider. Its venom is so potent that only 0.006 mg (0.00000021 oz) is sufficient to kill a mouse. Fortunately an anti-venom is available.

HEAVIEST SPIDER

Female bird-eating spiders (family Theraphosidae) are more heavily built than males and in February 1985 Charles J Seiderman (USA) captured a female example near Paramaribo, Surinam, which weighed a record 122.2 g (4.3 oz) before it died in January 1986. It had a leg-span of 26.7 cm (10.5 in), a body length of 10.2 cm (4 in) and fangs measuring 2.5 cm (1 in).

MOST VENOMOUS LAND SNAKE

The taipan (*Oxyuranus microlepidotus*), which measures 1.7 m (5 ft 7 in) and is found in Queensland, Australia, can inject 60 mg (0.021 oz) of venom in a single strike – enough to wipe out several human adults. The average venom yield after milking is 44 mg (0.00155 oz) but one male specimen yielded 110 mg (0.00385 oz), enough to kill 250,000 mice or 15 humans.

FASTEST LAND SNAKE

The land-speed record for snakes is held by the aggressive black mamba (*Dendroaspis polylepis*) found in south-eastern tropical Africa. In short bursts over level ground it can reach speeds of 16–19 km/h (10–12 mph).

HEAVIEST SNAKE

The world's heaviest snake is the anaconda (*Eunectes murinus*) found in South America and Trinidad. A female of this species shot in Brazil in 1960 measured an incredible 8.45 m (27 ft 9 in) long with an astounding girth of 1.11 m (44 in). It was estimated to weigh 227 kg (500 lb).

LONGEST SNAKE

The reticulated python (*Python reticulatus*) of Indonesia, south-east Asia, and the Philippines, regularly exceeds 6.25 m (20 ft 6 in), and the record length is 10 m (32 ft 9.5 in) for a specimen shot in Indonesia in 1912.

HEAVIEST INSECT

The world's heaviest insects are the Goliath beetles (family Scarabaeidae) of equatorial Africa. The largest are *Goliathus regius*, *G. meleagris*, *G. goliathus* (=*G. giganteus*) and *G. druryi*. In measurements of one series of males, the lengths from the tips of the frontal horns to the end of the abdomen were 11 cm (4.33 in), with weights of 70–100 g (2.5–3.5 oz).

HEAVIEST LIVING SNAKE

A Burmese python (*Python molurus bivittatus*) that weighed an incredible 182.76 kg (403 lb) on 20 November 1998 is the heaviest living snake. 'Baby' is 21 years old, 8.22 m (27 ft) long with a girth of 71.12 cm (28 in). She lives at the Serpent Safari Park in Gurnee, Illinois, USA, and is owned by Lou Daddano (USA). She eats four to five chickens every two weeks, swallowing them whole.

SMALLEST INSECT

The smallest recorded insects are the 'feather-winged' beetles of the family Ptiliidae (or Trichopterygidae), which measure a tiny 0.25 mm (0.01 in).

MOST HEAT-TOLERANT LAND CREATURE

The *Cataglyphis bicolor*, a scavenger ant from the Sahara desert, Africa, lives in temperatures of over 55ºC (131ºF).

BIGGEST INSECT SWARM

A huge swarm of Rocky Mountain locusts (*Melanoplus spretus*) that occurred in Nebraska, USA, between 20 and 30 July 1874 covered an estimated area of 514,374 km² (198,600 miles²). This swarm of locusts contained a staggering 12.5 trillion insects, weighing 25 million tonnes (50 billion lb).

FASTEST-MOVING INSECT

The fastest land insects are large tropical cockroaches of the family Dictyoptera. The record is a speedy 5.4 km/h (3.36 mph), or 50 body lengths per second, recorded by an American cockroach (*Periplaneta americana*) in 1991 at the University of California at Berkeley, California, USA.

FASTEST LIZARD

The fastest reptile land-speed record is 34.9 km/h (21.7 mph), achieved by *Ctenosaura*, a spiny-tailed iguana from Central America.

MOST DANGEROUS ANT

The world's most dangerous ant is the ferocious bulldog ant (*Myrmecia pyriformis*) found in coastal regions in Australia. When in attack mode it uses its sting and jaws simultaneously. It is extremely aggressive, stinging many times in quick succession, and shows little fear of humans. There have been at least three human fatalities since 1936, the latest a farmer in 1988.

MOST BIOLUMINESCENT INSECT

Fireflies (*Pyrophorus noctilucus,* above) emit the most light naturally. They are unique as almost 100% of their energy is given off as light. In a lightbulb only 10% of the energy is light, with the other 90% given off as heat.

LARGEST CROCODILIAN

The largest reptile in the world is the estuarine or saltwater crocodile (*Crocodylus porosus*), which ranges throughout the tropical regions of Asia and the Pacific. The Bhitarkanika Wildlife Sanctuary in Orissa State, India, houses four protected estuarine crocodiles, each measuring more than 6 m (19 ft 8 in) in length, the largest being over 7 m (23 ft) long. There are several reports of specimens up to 10 m (33 ft) long.

LARGEST LIZARD

The Komodo dragon (*Varanus komodoensis*) is found on the Indonesian islands of Komodo, Rintja, Padar and Flores. Males average a huge 2.25 m (7 ft 5 in) in length and weigh about 59 kg (130 lb). The largest accurately measured specimen was displayed in St Louis Zoological Gardens, Missouri, USA, in 1937. It was 3.1 m (10 ft 2 in) long and weighed 166 kg (365 lb).

MOST DANGEROUS LIZARD

The Gila monster (*Heloderma suspectum*), a large, brightly coloured lizard, measures up to 60 cm (24 in) long, and lives in arid parts of Mexico and the south-western USA. Although relatively harmless, it has eight venom glands in its lower jaws and carries enough venom to kill two adult humans. The venom is not injected but seeps into the wound when the Gila monster bites and chews its victim with its sharp but fragile teeth.

LONGEST LIZARD

The Salvadori or Papuan monitor (*Varanus salvadorii*) of Papua New Guinea can grow to 4.75 m (15 ft 7 in) in length, although 70% of this is the tail.

SMALLEST LIZARD

The title of world's smallest lizard is held by the *Sphaerodactylus parthenopion* and *S. ariasiae* (below), which have both been recorded as having an average snout-to-vent length (ie not including the tail) of a miniscule 1.6 cm (0.6 in).

HEAVIEST BONY FISH

The sunfish (*Mola mola*, above) has a record-breaking average weight of 2 tonnes (4,409 lb) and measures 3 m (11 ft) from fin tip to fin tip (top to bottom). *Mola mola* actually comes from the Latin meaning millstone. These huge fish have an unusual disc-shaped body with tall dorsal and anal fins. Sunfish are found in temperate and tropical regions and feed on plankton and algae.

LONGEST ANIMAL

The jellyfish (siphonophore) *Praya dubia* is considered to be the longest organism as it measures between 30–50 m (100–160 ft) in length. It has large paired transparent swimming bells at the head and long tentacles trailing behind. These are pulled through the water and can deliver a powerful sting. In comparison, a blue whale measures 25 to 27 m (82 to 88 ft) long.

SLOWEST FISH

The 30 species of seahorses (family Syngnathidas) are the slowest underwater creatures. Their swimming ability is limited by their rigid body structure and only the small pectoral and dorsal fins can move rapidly. They are incapable of swimming against the current and hang on to coral and marine plants with their prehensile tails to avoid being swept away.

LARGEST STARFISH

Out of the 1,600 known species, the largest starfish is the very fragile *Midgardia xandaros*. In 1968 one measuring an astonishing 1.38 m (4 ft 6 in) from tip to tip was collected in the Gulf of Mexico by the Texas University vessel *The Alaminos*.

MOST FEROCIOUS FRESHWATER FISH

The South American piranha (family Serrasalmus) with its sharp teeth, is the world's most ferocious freshwater fish. Attracted to blood and frantic splashing, piranhas can strip an animal as large as a horse of its flesh within minutes, leaving only a skeleton. Attacks are swift and comprehensive as they start eating their victims alive. On 19 September 1981 more than 300 people were reportedly killed and eaten by piranha when an overloaded boat capsized as it was docking at the port of Obidos, Brazil.

SMALLEST STARFISH

An asterinid sea star (*Patiriella parvivipara*), found in South Australia in 1975, has a tiny maximum radius of 4.7 mm (0.18 in).

LARGEST RAY

The Atlantic manta ray (*Manta birostris*), has an average wingspan of 5.2–6.8 m (17–22 ft). The largest recorded manta ray wingspan is 9.1 m (30 ft).

LARGEST SQUID

A giant squid (*Architeuthis kirkii*) washed ashore at Wingan Inlet, Vic, Australia, in 1948, was estimated to be 8.53 m (28 ft) long: the tentacles and arms had been torn off at 1.22 m (4 ft).

MOST ABUNDANT FISH

The most abundant fish species is probably the deep-sea bristlemouth (*Cyclothone microdon*), distributed almost worldwide. It would take about 900 of them to weigh 0.45 kg (1 lb).

MOST LIGHT-SENSITIVE EYES

The eyes with the highest light-collecting ability belong to the ostracod *Gigantocypris*. Its eyes have an f-number (indicating the amount of light that can be taken in) of 0.25, whereas human eyes have an f-number of approximately 2.55, and a camera lens an f-number of 1.8. *Gigantocypris* has a diameter of only around 1.5 cm (0.7 in).

LONGEST FIN

All three species of thresher shark (family Alopiidae) have a huge, scythe-shaped caudal fin (tail fin), which is almost as long as the body itself. The largest and most common species, *Alopias vulpinus*, found world-wide in temperate and tropical seas, may grow to a length of 6 m (19 ft 8 in), of which almost 3 m (9 ft 10 in) consists of this greatly elongated upper tail fin; the body itself is small and sleek.

LARGEST PREDATORY FISH

The record-breaking underwater predator is the rare great white shark (*Carcharodon carcharias*). Adult specimens average 4.3–4.6 m (14–15 ft) in length, and weigh 520–770 kg (1,150–1,700 lb). There are claims of huge specimens of up to 10 m (33 ft) in length. Although few have been authenticated, there is evidence to suggest that some great whites grow to more than 6 m (20 ft).

MOST ELECTRIC FISH

The electric eel or paroque (*Electrophorus electricus*), found in rivers in Brazil and the Guianas, is not an eel but a relative of the piranha. Up to 1.8 m (6 ft) in length, the fish is live from head to tail. The shock, which can measure up to 650 volts, is used to immobilize prey and is strong enough to stun an adult human or light an electric bulb.

LARGEST TEETH

Relative to its head size, the fish with the largest teeth is the 28-cm-long (11-in) viperfish (*Chauliodus sloani*) which has teeth half the size of its head. They are so large the fish must open its mouth to make its jaws vertical before it can swallow prey. It eats large prey by lowering the internal skeleton of its gills, allowing the prey to pass into its throat without interference.

MOST VENOMOUS FISH

The stonefish (Synanceidae, above) of the waters of the Indo-Pacific, particularly the *Synanceia horrida*, have the largest venom glands of any fish. Direct contact with its fin spines – which contain a neurotoxic poison – can prove fatal.

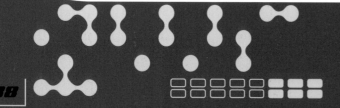

MOST VENOMOUS MARINE SNAKE

The sea snake species *Hydrophis belcheri*, found around Ashmore Reef in the Timor Sea off Australia, has a myotoxic venom many times more toxic than the venom of any land snake. The common beaked sea snake (*Enhydrina schistosa*) is almost as venomous but more dangerous as it is more common and more aggressive.

DEEPEST LIVING FISH

A cuskeel (*Abyssobrotula galatheae*) measuring 20 cm (8 in) has been found living in the Puerto Rico Trench at a depth of 8,370 m (27,455 ft).

LARGEST MOUTH

The largest mouth in the world belongs to the bowhead whale (*Balaena mysticetus*) and can measure 5 m (16 ft) long, 4 m (12 ft) high and 2.5 m (8 ft) wide. Its tongue weighs around 900 kg (2,000 lb).

LARGEST MAMMAL

The world's largest mammal is the blue whale (*Balaenoptera musculus*). Their average length is a massive 35 m (115 ft) and they can weigh up to 130 tonnes (287,000 lb). A huge specimen caught in the Southern Ocean, Antarctica, on 20 March 1947 weighed 190 tonnes (420,000 lb) and measured 27.6 m (90 ft 6 in). The blue whale also has the largest offspring; a newborn calf measures between 6 and 8 m (20 and 26 ft) long and weighs between 2 and 3 tonnes (4,400 and 6,600 lb).

LARGEST SPONGE

Found in seas off the West Indies and Florida, the barrel-shaped loggerhead sponge (*Spheciospongia vesparium*), measures up to 105 cm (3 ft 6 in) in height and 91 cm (3 ft) in diameter.

MOST VENOMOUS JELLYFISH

The deadly Australian sea wasp or box jellyfish (*Chironex fleckeri,* below) has up to 60 tentacles, each one containing millions of poisonous nematocysts (small external cells). It has enough poison to kill 60 humans and is responsible for at least one death a year.

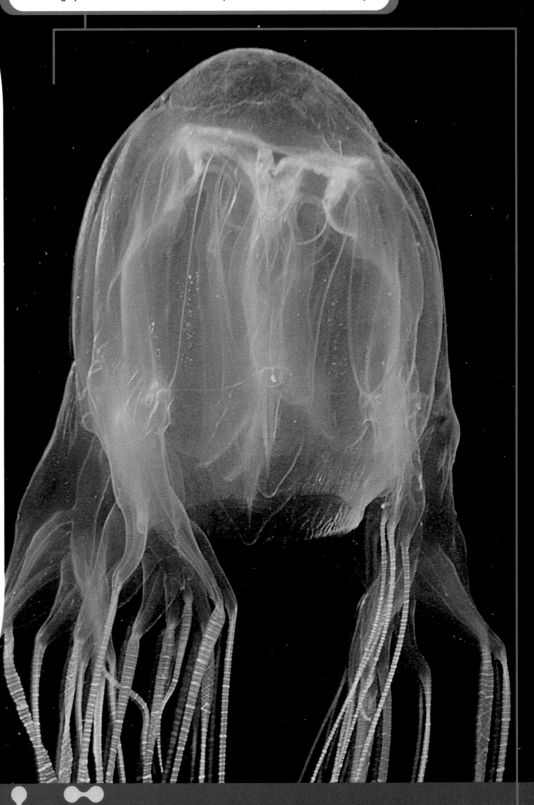

OLDEST VOMIT

On 12 February 2002, a team of palaeontologists led by Prof Peter Doyle (UK) announced the discovery of the fossilized vomit (above) of an ichthyosaur (ancient marine reptile). Found in a quarry in Peterborough, Cambs, UK, the 160-million-year-old vomit may provide an insight into ichthyosaurs' feeding habits.

FASTEST DINOSAUR

In 1981, trackways discovered in the fossil-rich Morrison formation (an area of 2.5 million km^2, or 1 million miles^2, in the western USA), indicated that one carnivorous dinosaur had been capable of speeds of up to 40 km/h (25 mph). The tracks were found in Texas and dated from the Late Jurassic period, 155–145 million years ago.

LARGEST DINOSAUR FOOTPRINT

In 1932, the gigantic footprints of a large bipedal hadrosaurid ('duckbill') measuring 1.36 m (53.5 in) in length and 81 cm (32 in) wide were found in Salt Lake City, Utah, USA.

LONGEST DINOSAUR

The longest vertebrate on record, *Seismosaurus halli*, was a diplodocid (herbivorous long-necked dinosaur) which was excavated from a site in New Mexico, USA, in 1980. Its overall length was estimated at 39–52 m (128–170 ft). The bones were reconstructed in 1999 at the Wyoming Dinosaur Center, and measured 41 m (134.5 ft) long.

LARGEST PREHISTORIC INSECT

The dragonfly *Meganeura monyi* lived about 280 million years ago. Fossil remains discovered at Commentry, France, indicate a wing expanse of up to 70 cm (27.5 in). This compares to the largest dragonfly living today (*Megaloprepus caeruleata*) from Central and South America, which has been measured at up to 12 cm (4.72 in) long, with a wingspan of up to 19.1 cm (7.52 in).

LARGEST PREHISTORIC LAND MAMMAL

Indricotherium (also known as *Baluchitherium* or *Paraceratherium*), a long-necked, hornless member of the family Rhinocerotidae that lived in western Asia and Europe about 35 million years ago, is regarded as the largest prehistoric land mammal. It is known from bones discovered in the Bugti Hills of Baluchistan, Pakistan, in 1907–08. A restoration of the dinosaur in the American Museum of Natural History, New York City, USA, measured 5.41 m (17 ft 9 in) to the top of the shoulder hump and 11.27 m (37 ft) in total.

TALLEST DINOSAUR

Dinosaur remains found in 1994 in Oklahoma, USA, belong to what is believed to be the largest creature ever to have walked the Earth. *Sauroposeidon* ('lizard earthquake god'), was giraffe-like in shape though it was 30 times larger than the largest giraffe. It stood a staggering 18 m (60 ft) tall (the size of a six-storey building) and weighed 60 tonnes (132,300 lb). This lofty dinosaur lived about 110 million years ago, in the Mid-Cretaceous period.

LARGEST CROCODILE

At 225 million years old, the crocodile family is one of the oldest of all animal groups. *Sarchosuchus imperator* was a prehistoric species of crocodile that lived approximately 110 million years ago. Fossilized remains found recently in the Sahara Desert, Africa, suggest that this creature took 50 to 60 years to grow to its full length of around 11–12 m (37–40 ft). It reached a maximum weight of approximately 8 tonnes (17,600 lb).

HEAVIEST DINOSAUR

The heaviest ever land animals were sauropod dinosaurs, a group of long-necked, long-tailed, four-legged herbivores that lived during the Jurassic and Cretaceous periods, approximately 208–65 million years ago. The heaviest of all sauropods was probably *Argentinosaurus* ('Argentina lizard') a dinosaur that in 1994 was estimated to have weighed up to 100 tonnes (220,000 lb) and to have been around 40–42 m (130–140 ft) long. These figures are based on the size of its vast vertebrae, which were 1.5 m (5 ft) high and 1.5 m (5 ft) wide.

LONGEST TAIL

The diplodocid *Diplodocus* ('double beamed', a reference to a special feature of the creature's backbone) was a long-necked sauropod dinosaur that lived during the Late Jurassic period, approximately 155–145 million years ago. *Diplodocus* was 27 m (90 ft) long in total, with much of its size being accounted for by its long neck and lengthy, whip-like tail, which grew up to 13–14 m (43–45 ft) in length. Scientists have estimated that the average weight of *Diplodocus* was 12 tonnes (26,500 lb), but it is possible that it grew to a weight of 18 tonnes (39,700 lb).

LARGEST DINOSAUR EGG

Eggs of the *Hypselosaurus priscus* ('high ridge lizard'), a 12-m-long (40-ft) dinosaur that lived about 80 million years ago, were more than twice the size of the average ostrich egg. Samples found near Aix-en-Provence, France, in October 1961, were 30 cm (12 in, about the height of this page) long, had a diameter of 25.5 cm (10 in) and a capacity of 3.3 litres (5.8 pints).

MOST COMPLETE TYRANNOSAURUS REX SKELETON

The largest, most complete *Tyrannosaurus rex* skeleton (above) found to date is 'Sue', measuring 4 m (13 ft) tall and 12.5 m (41 ft) long. Found in South Dakota, USA, on 12 August 1990 by explorer Sue Hendrickson (USA), 'Sue' is 90% intact.

LARGEST EVER CARNIVORE

A skeleton of the largest predatory dinosaur was discovered in Neuquen, Patagonia, Argentina, in 1995. *Giganotosaurus carolinii* was 12.5 m (40 ft) long, and weighed 8 tonnes (17,600 lb). Its bones suggest that *G. carolinii* was both taller and more heavily built than *Tyrannosaurus rex.*

LARGEST DINOSAUR BRAIN

Troodontids (formerly known as saurornithoidids) had the largest brain-to-body size ratio of all non-avian (bird-like) dinosaurs, possibly making them the most intelligent dinosaurs. They were about 5 ft (1.52 m) long – the size of a small adult human – and are thought to have been fast carnivorous hunters.

LARGEST PREHISTORIC FISH

Scientists believe that the largest fish in prehistoric times was the great shark *Carcharodon megalodon*, which lived 50–4.5 million years ago. Recent studies suggest that it grew to a length of 13.7 m (45 ft).

LARGEST PREHISTORIC BIRD

The flightless *Dromornis stirtoni*, a huge emu-like creature, lived in central Australia between 15 million and 25,000 years ago. Fossil leg bones found near Alice Springs, NT, Australia, in 1974 indicate that the bird stood around 3 m (10 ft) tall and weighed around 500 kg (1,100 lb).

DINOSAUR WITH THE LONGEST NAME

Micropachycephalosaurus is the longest generic name for a dinosaur. Despite its lengthy title, it was quite a small dinosaur; the name means 'small, thick-headed lizard'.

EARLIEST FLYING BIRD

Skeletons of a bird similar in size to a crow, and known as *Archaeopteryx lithographica*, were found in Jurassic sediments in Germany in 1861. They are 153 million years old.

DINOSAUR WITH THE MOST TEETH

The duck-billed hadrosaurs ('bulky lizards') had more teeth than any other dinosaur. Hadrosaurs were herbivores with toothless beaks, but had up to 960 self-sharpening teeth in the side of their strong jaws that enabled them to chew tough plants. They ranged in length from 3 to 12 m (10 to 40 ft).

SMALLEST DINOSAUR

The chicken-sized *Compsognathus* ('pretty jaw') of southern Germany and south-east France measured 60 cm (23 in) from the snout to the tip of the tail and weighed about 3 kg (6 lb 8 oz). *Compsognathus* lived in the Late Jurassic period and ate small animals such as lizards and insects. To date, only two sets of *Compsognathus* fossils have been found.

LARGEST ARMOURED DINOSAUR

The largest armoured dinosaur was *Ankylosaurus* (below), a herbivore that had thick plates covering its skin. It also had a double row of spikes running from the back of its head to its club tail. *Ankylosaurus* was 7.5–10.7 m (24.6–35.1 ft) long, 1.2 m (4 ft) tall and lived in the Late Cretaceous period, 70–65 million years ago. With a width of up to 2.5 m (8 ft), it also holds the record for being the widest dinosaur.

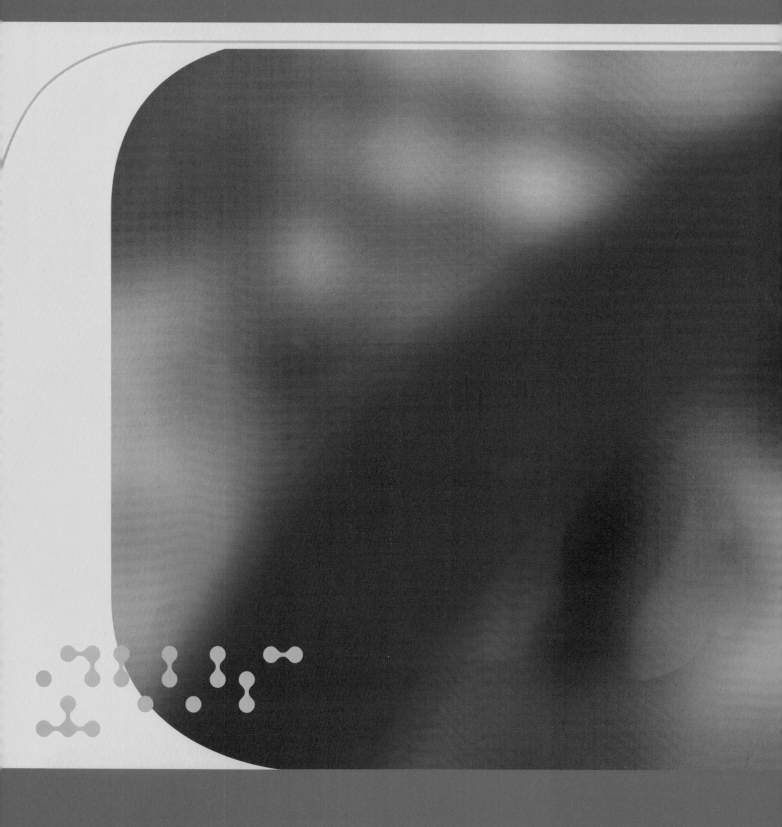

SOCIETY AND POLITICS

MOST OFFICIAL LANGUAGES

The Republic of South Africa (the RSA flag flies above) has 11 official languages. These are: Afrikaans, English, Ndebele, North Sotho, South Sotho, Swazi, Tsonga, Tswana, Venda, Xhosa and Zulu. South Africa has a population of 43,840,000.

MOST LAND BOUNDARIES

China and Russia share the land boundary record, both having 14. China's are: Afghanistan, Bhutan, India, Kazakhstan, Kyrgyzstan, Laos, Mongolia, Myanmar (Burma), Nepal, North Korea, Pakistan, Russia, Tajikistan and Vietnam. Russia's boundaries are with: Azerbaijan, Belarus, China, Estonia, Finland, Georgia, Kazakhstan, Latvia Lithuania, Mongolia, North Korea, Norway, Poland and Ukraine.

OLDEST CAPITAL CITY

The oldest capital city in the world is Damascus (also know as Dimishq), Syria. It has been continuously inhabited since around 2500 BC. In 1998 it had an estimated population of 1,431,821.

NORTHERNMOST CAPITAL CITY

The world's northernmost city, (and also the northernmost national capital), is Reykjavik, Iceland (64°08'N). The most northerly capital of a dependency is Nuuk (formerly Godthåb), Greenland (64°15'N).

SOUTHERNMOST CAPITAL CITY

Wellington, New Zealand, is the southernmost capital city of an independent country (41°17'S). The world's southernmost capital of a dependent territory is Port Stanley, Falkland Islands (51°43'S), with a population of 1,600 (excluding service personnel) in 1999.

LARGEST COUNTRY

Russia takes up 11.5% of the world's surface, with a total area of 17,075,400 km^2 (6,592,848 miles^2). This vast country is 70 times as large as the UK, but with a population of 147,231,000 in 1997, it is only 2.5 times as populated.

MOST DENSELY & SPARSELY POPULATED COUNTRIES

Of those countries with an area over 2,500 km^2 (965 miles^2), the most densely populated is Bangladesh. In 2000, it had a population of 129,194,000 living in 147,570 km^2 (56,977 miles^2) at a density of roughly 875 people per km^2 (2,267 per mile^2).

The most sparsely populated sovereign country is Mongolia, with a population of 2,440,000 (in 1999) in an area of 1,564,116 km^2 (603,908 miles^2). This equates to a density of roughly 1.6 people per km^2 (four per mile^2).

MOST POPULOUS ISLAND

Java, Indonesia, has a population (in 1997) of 118,700,000 living in an area of 132,186 km^2 (51,037 miles^2), or 897 people per km^2 (2,325 per mile^2).

OLDEST AND YOUNGEST POPULATIONS

In the Marshall Islands in the Pacific Ocean, 49.29% of the population is under the age of 15. In July 2001, out of a total population of 70,822, about 34,909 were aged between 0–14 years. In the Gaza Strip (under Palestinian authority), 48.89% of the population is aged under 15. By contrast, in Monaco, 10.8% of the population was aged 75 and over in 1995.

MOST SPARSELY POPULATED CONTINENT

Although there are no native people here, Antarctica has been permanently occupied by relays of scientists since 1943. The seasonal population varies and can reach 4,000. Antarctica is also the coldest, highest, windiest and most remote continent.

MOST DENSELY POPULATED ISLAND

Ap Lei Chau, off the south-west side of Hong Kong, China, has a population of 80,000 living in an area measuring a tiny 1.3 km^2 (0.5 mile^2). The actual population density is a very cramped 60,000 per km^2 (160,000 per mile^2).

MOST IMMIGRANTS

The country that regularly receives the most legal immigrants is the USA. Records show that between 1820 and 1996 the USA received 63,140,227 official immigrants. In 1996, the illegal alien population was 5 million of which 2.7 million were Mexican.

OLDEST TOWN

The town of Dolní Vêstonice in the Czech Republic has been dated to the prehistoric Gravettian culture of 27,000 BC – during the upper Paleolithic age.

LONGEST MARITIME BOUNDARY

The longest maritime boundary is that between the Danish dependent territory of Greenland and Canada at 2,697 km (1,676 miles).

HIGHEST PRISON POPULATION

According to Amnesty International, the prison population in the USA had topped 2 million prisoners by February 2000. This accounts for 25% of the world's prison population, yet the USA accounts for only 5% of the world's population.

LEAST POPULOUS COUNTRY

The Vatican City (above), the world's smallest country, is also the least populous, with just 890 inhabitants in 2001. Situated in Rome, the Vatican City comprises St Peter's Church, St Peter's Square, the Vatican and the Vatican Gardens.

HIGHEST & LOWEST LIFE EXPECTANCY

Japan is the country with the highest life expectancy at birth. The average for the total population is 80.5 years. For males, the life expectancy stands at 77.3 years and for females 83.9 years.

Sierra Leone has the world's lowest life expectancy at birth. The average for the total population is 37.3 years. For males, the life expectancy stands at 35.9 years, and for females 39.8 years.

MOST PLASTIC SURGEONS

The country with the most plastic surgeons in the world is the USA with an approximate total of 5,965 according to The International Confederation for Plastic, Reconstructive and Aesthetic Surgery.

LARGEST SHORTAGE OF WOMEN

With a male population of 66%, men most outnumber women in Qatar.

LARGEST SHORTAGE OF MEN

In Ukraine, 53.7% of the population is female. Worldwide, it is estimated that there are currently 1,015 males for every 1,000 females.

HIGHEST & LOWEST GNI

According to World Bank 2000 figures (using data from 206 countries), the country with the highest GNI (Gross National Income, formerly GNP or Gross National Product) per capita was Luxembourg, with a GNI of $44,340 (£29,302). For the same period, the UK's GNI was $24,500 (£16,191) and the USA's $34,260 (£22,641). GNI is the total value of goods and services produced by a country in one year divided by its population. These figures indicate the proportion of GNI each person would receive if it were divided equally. Second is Liechtenstein, then Switzerland. For 2000, Ethiopia had the world's lowest GNI per capita of $100 (£66).

LOWEST LITERACY RATE

In Niger, only 15% of the total adult population (aged over 15) is literate, and only 6.6% of the adult female population is literate. The literacy rate for females in Afghanistan was 15% in 1999, but the country is now thought to have a similar rate to Niger. The rate of adult female literacy in Afghanistan was set to fall as the fundamentalist Taliban regime banned the education of females. The Taliban fell in 2001, but it is not known how this will affect the literacy rate.

MOST POPULOUS COUNTRY

China is the world's most populated country, with an estimated 1,265,207,000 people in 2000 (Chinese children shown below). The annual rate of increase was 1.3%, or over 16 million people, between 1997 and 1998. Its population is more than that of the whole world 150 years ago. By 2025 it is estimated that China's population will exceed 1.48 billion.

MOST POPULAR POLITICAL CAT

Socks (above), a stray cat rescued by a neighbour of Bill and Hillary Clinton (both USA) when they lived in Little Rock, Arkansas, USA, was adopted by the future First Family in 1991. During his eight-year stint in the White House, Socks was said to receive 75,000 letters and parcels a week. The popular kitty answered his fan mail with help from his personal correspondence staff.

OLDEST ROYAL

HM Queen Elizabeth the Queen Mother (UK, 1900-2002) was the oldest member of the British royal family. She married Prince Albert (UK, later George VI) on 26 April 1923, and on his coronation became the first British-born Queen Consort since Tudor times, as well as the Last Empress of India. She died on 30th March 2002, aged 101.

MOST PRESIDENTIAL PALACES

Saddam Hussein, President of Iraq since 1979, has eight principal palaces, plus other minor residences throughout Iraq. In Babylon, Saddam has a palace that was built alongside the remains of the palace of Nebuchadnezzar II (620–562 BC). Every brick is stamped with the legend 'The Leader, Saddam Hussein, Victor of Allah'.

MOST STATE ROLES HELD BY A MODERN ROYAL

Cambodia's King Norodom Sihanouk was king fom 1941 to 1955, prime minister from 1955 to 1966, head of state from 1960 to 1970, head of the government-in-exile in 1970, president in 1976, president-in-exile from 1982 to 1988, head of the government-in-exile from 1989 to 1991, president of the National Council in 1991 and head of state from 1991 to 1993. In 1993 he was restored as king.

LARGEST POLITICAL PARTY MEMBERSHIP

The Chinese Communist Party, formed in 1920, had a membership of around 59 million in April 2000.

LARGEST PRESIDENTIAL ENTOURAGE

US President Bill Clinton's official visit to China in June 1998 involved an entourage of 1,200 people. They included 200 secret service agents, 150 military personnel, 30 senior delegates, 375 reporters, four TV crews, 150 support staff and 70 senior advisers. Four passenger planes, including Air Force One, were used, and military transport planes flew in 10 armoured limousines, two communication vans, a mobile hospital and a bullet-proof lectern. In comparison, when US President Richard Nixon visited China in 1972, he was accompanied by just 300 people.

LARGEST THEFT FROM A GOVERNMENT

On 23 April 1986 the Philippine government announced that it had finally identified the $860.8 million (£569.5 million) salted away by the former President Ferdinand Marcos and his wife Imelda. The total national loss from November 1965 onwards was thought to be a staggering $5–$10 billion (£3.4–£6.8 billion).

LARGEST GATHERING OF WORLD LEADERS

The 55th session of the United Nations' General Assembly brought together 144 kings, heads of states, prime ministers and presidents for the Millennium Summit held in New York City, USA, from 6 to 8 September 2000. There were over 1,300 official cars at the event, thousands of secret service agents, up to 6,000 police officers and more than 2,500 members of the international media.

HEAVIEST MONARCH

The world's heaviest monarch was the 1.90-m-tall (6-ft 3-in) King Taufa'ahau Tupou IV of Tonga, who in September 1976 recorded a weight of 209.5 kg (33 st or 462 lb). By 1993 he was reported to have slimmed down to 127 kg (20 st or 280 lb), and by 1998 had lost more weight as a result of a fitness programme.

OLDEST TREATY

The oldest treaty still in force is the Anglo-Portuguese Treaty, which was signed in London over 625 years ago on 16 June 1373, making Portugal the UK's oldest ally.

MOST HANDSHAKES BY A NATIONAL POLITICAL FIGURE

On 22 August 1998, US House Speaker Newt Gingrich (USA) shook hands with 3,609 people at the King County Republican Picnic on Vashon Island, Washington, USA. Speaker Gingrich began shaking hands during a photo opportunity at 10:30 am and finished at 3:30 pm.

HIGHEST-PAID PRIME MINISTER

The former Prime Minister of Japan, Yoshiro Mori, who served from 5 April 2000 to 26 April 2001, had an annual salary of ¥69,290,000 ($676,000 or £470,700), including monthly allowances and bonuses.

MONARCH APPEARING ON MOST COINAGE

The image of Her Majesty Queen Elizabeth II (UK) appears on the coinage of at least 35 different countries – more countries than any other living monarch. Elizabeth II has been Queen of the UK and head of the Commonwealth since the death of her father, George VI, in 1952. She celebrated her Golden Jubilee in 2002.

MOST MONEY SPENT PER VOTE IN AN ELECTION

Michael R Bloomberg (USA, above), the Republican candidate in the 2001 mayoral election in New York City, USA, spent $68,968,185 (£49,962,464) on his successful campaign. This equates to $92.60 (£63.65) for each of the 744,757 votes he won.

LONGEST REIGN IN EUROPE

The longest-reigning European monarch was Afonso I Henrique of Portugal, who ascended the throne on 30 April 1112 and died on 6 December 1185 after reigning for 73 years 220 days, first as count and then (after 25 July 1139) as king.

MOST VOTES FOR A CHIMPANZEE

In the 1988 mayoral election campaign in Rio de Janeiro, Brazil, the anti-establishment Brazilian Banana Party presented a chimp called Tião as their candidate. The chimp came third out of twelve candidates, receiving over 400,000 votes. The campaign slogan was 'Vote monkey – get monkey'.

LONGEST-SERVING FEMALE PRIME MINISTER

Sirimavo Bandaranaike (Sri Lanka) was prime minister of Sri Lanka for a total of 17 years 208 days: 21 July 1960 to 25 March 1965; 29 May 1970 to 22 July 1977 and 12 November 1994 to 10 August 2000.

LARGEST ROYAL FAMILY

There are more than 4,200 royal princes and more than 40,000 other relatives in the Saudi royal family.

RICHEST MONARCH

In April 2002, it was estimated that the personal wealth of Prince Alwaleed Bin Talal Alsaud of Saudi Arabia stood at $20 billion (£13.9 billion). King Fahd remains the technical ruler of Saudi Arabia, but the stroke he suffered in 1995 means his half-brother Prince Abdullah rules de facto.

Queen Beatrix of The Netherlands, who ascended the throne in 1980, has an estimated net worth of around £2.43 billion ($3.46 billion), making her the world's wealthiest modern queen. In comparison, Queen Elizabeth II (UK) is worth only £230 million ($330 million).

MOST ACCESSIBLE PRIME MINISTER

With the exception of the leaders of some of the world's micro-states, the most accessible premier was the Danish Prime Minister Poul Nyrup Rasmussen (who served from 1993 to 2001), whose home telephone number was in the public domain. Rasmussen was known to answer telephone queries from Danish citizens personally.

LONGEST-SERVING PRESIDENT TODAY

Omar Bongo has been president of the oil-rich central west African republic of Gabon since 2 December 1967. He was re-elected unopposed at presidential elections every seven years under a single-party system until 1993, when he was returned with a narrow majority following the restoration of a multi-party system.

MOST HIT RECORDS BY A ROYAL

Princess Stephanie of Monaco, the younger daughter of Prince Rainier III and Princess Grace, is the only royal to have had pop music hits in Europe. Her album *Rendez-Vous,* recorded with the record label Success, made it into the German Top 10 and Dutch Top 40, as well as the Italian and French charts.

YOUNGEST LEADER OF THE LABOUR PARTY

In 1994, at the age of 41, Tony Blair (UK, below) became the youngest-ever leader of the British Labour Party. After the UK's 1997 general election, 44-year-old Mr Blair became the youngest British prime minister of the 20th century.

MODERN SOCIETY

LARGEST GAY AND LESBIAN RIGHTS MARCH

On 25 April 1993, 300,000 people gathered in support of the 'March on Washington for Gay, Lesbian and Bi-equal Rights' (above). The event, near the Washington Memorial in Washington DC, USA, was to support legislation granting equal rights for homosexuals in America, including anti-discrimination regulations based on sexual orientation and an end to the ban on homosexuals in the military.

HIGHEST TAXES

In Denmark the highest rate of personal income tax is 63%, with the basic rate starting at 44%. In return for these high taxes, the Danes receive a wide range of governmental benefits, including free health assistance, free higher education and an extensive system of similar social services.

MOST EXPENSIVE MATCHMAKER

Orly the Matchmaker of Beverly Hills, California, USA, has been running an upscale international introductions company for the last 25 years – the most expensive service of its kind in the world. Run by a former model, Orly's world-renowned, old-fashioned matchmaking skills are available for a membership fee that can cost up to $100,000 (£70,000).

MOST BEER CONSUMED

The Czech Republic is the world's leading beer consumer per capita, with each person drinking an average of 160 litres (42.7 gal) in 1998. The population as a whole consumed 1,653 million litres (436.68 million gal) during 1998. The USA consumed the greatest volume of beer in the world in the same year, disposing of some 24,376 million litres (6.439 million gal) – which works out at an average of 89 litres (23.5 gal) per person.

MOST COFFEE CONSUMED

The country that consumes the most coffee per capita is Finland where 11.3 kg (24.91 lb) of coffee per person was consumed in 1998. The total amount of coffee consumed in the country in 1998 was 58,000 tonnes (127.8 million lb). In the same year, the USA consumed the greatest amount of coffee in the world with a total of 1.148 million tonnes (2.5 billion lb) – 4.2 kg per capita (around 646 cups per person).

GREATEST ELECTRICITY CONSUMPTION

The USA used 3,235.9 billion kW per hour in 1999 – which is almost a quarter of the total net electricity consumption used by the entire world (12,832.7 billion kW per hour). The greatest consumers of electricity per capita are the Norwegians, who used 26,956 kW per hour per person in 1995 compared to 12,663 kW per hour per capita in the USA.

HEAVIEST SMOKERS

South Korea has the highest per capita consumption of cigarettes in the world, at 4,153 cigarettes per capita per annum. Japan is second with 2,739 and Hungary third with 2,689. An estimated 4.6 trillion cigarettes were smoked in 1999. If you laid them end to end, they would reach to the Sun and back.

HIGHEST COST OF LIVING

According to *The Economist* Intelligence Unit's bi-annual survey, Tokyo and Osaka/Kobe (both Japan) are the most expensive cities to live in the world, jointly holding the top spot for the first time in nine years (previously Tokyo has held the title alone). After them, the list reads: Hong Kong, Libreville (in Gabon), Oslo, London, New York City and Zurich (jointly), Singapore, Taipei and Tel Aviv (jointly).

HIGHEST BIRTH RATE

In 1998, the highest estimated birth rate for the central African country of Niger was 52 births per 1,000 people. This compares to the United Kingdom, which had 13 births per 1,000 people in 1980 and 12 births per 1,000 people in 1998.

HIGHEST DEATH RATE

The current highest estimated death rate is 25 per 1,000 people for Sierra Leone, a former French colony in western Africa, in 1998. This compares to the UK's rate of 12 deaths per 1,000 people in 1980 and 11 deaths per 1,000 in 1998.

LARGEST HUMAN-RIGHTS ORGANIZATION

Amnesty International, which was first launched in the UK in 1961, now has in excess of 1.2 million members and subscribers in more than 100 countries, national offices in more than 50 countries and more than 4,200 local groups situated on every continent. The human rights organization operates independently of any government, political ideology, economic interest or religion. It believes in releasing prisoners of conscience regardless of their origin, providing fair trials for all political prisoners, abolishing the death penalty, torture and other cruel treatment of prisoners as well as eliminating all types of politically motivated killings and 'disappearances'.

LARGEST EMPLOYER

The world's largest commercial or utility employer is Indian Railways, which had an amazing 1,583,614 regular employees when it was last measured in March 1997. The Indian Railways' wage bill for the period 1996-97 worked out as a massive 105,145,000,000 rupees ($2.1 billion or £1.5 billion).

HIGHEST ANNUAL RACING CLUB BETTING TURNOVER

The total betting turnover of the Hong Kong Jockey Club (stadium, above) for the 1997/98 season was $12.1 billion (£7.3 billion). Approximately one third of Hong Kong's adult population is reported to regularly bet on horse racing.

HIGHEST AND LOWEST UNEMPLOYMENT

In 1996, Bosnia-Herzegovina had the highest rate of unemployment, with 75% of the labour force not in paid employment.

Liechtenstein had the lowest recorded unemployment of any world state in 1997, with 97.3% of its labour force in work.

MOST VALUABLE FOOTBALL CLUB

Manchester United Football Club, who play in the English Premiership, had a market capitalization of more than £1 billion ($1.59 billion) on 8 March 2000, becoming the first football club ever to reach that milestone.

MOST PUBS VISITED

Bruce Masters (UK) has visited 31,751 pubs and a further 1,974 other drinking establishments since 1960, sampling the local brew in each case where available, making a total of 33,725 bar visits by the end of 2000. His busiest year was 1974, when he frequented 3,016 pubs. From his own statistics, the most popular name for a pub is the Red Lion, of which he has visited 480.

LARGEST LOTTERY WINS

The Big Game Lottery, which is composed of seven different US states (Georgia, Illinois, Maryland, Massachusetts, Michigan, New Jersey and Virginia) reached a sky-high jackpot of $350 million (£220 million) on the day it was due to be drawn, 9 May 2000. The winnings were split between two ticket holders.

The largest individual lottery win is $197 million (£122 million) by Maria Grasso (USA) for the Big Game Lottery draw on 13 April 1999.

MOST EXPENSIVE OFFICE LOCATION

As of March 2002, London, UK (below), is the world's most expensive location for office space. Cost per square metre, including rent, taxes and service charges, is £1,074 ($1,525). Tokyo, Japan, is second with £754 ($1,070) per square metre.

LARGEST SPACE FUNERAL

The ashes of 24 space pioneers and enthusiasts, including *Star Trek* creator Gene Roddenberry (USA) and former Nazi rocket scientist Krafft Ehricke (Germany), were sent into orbit on 21 April 1997, on board Spain's *Pegasus* rocket, at a cost of £3,000 each. Held in lipstick-sized capsules (above) inscribed with a name and a personal message, the ashes will orbit for between 18 months and 10 years.

LARGEST MASS CREMATION

In December 1997, at a temple in Smut Scom province, Thailand, 21,347 skulls and thousands of tonnes of bones were cremated to mark the end of urban burials in the overcrowded Thai capital, Bangkok. The bones and skulls represented remains that had been left unclaimed from a former Chinese cemetery in Bangkok.

LONGEST MARRIAGE

China-born William Wen Lung Hsieh (b.1899) and his wife Woo Fung Siu (b.1900, both USA) married on 17 March 1917 and their marriage lasted 84 years 6 months 15 days until William's death on 1 October 2001.

MOST CHILDREN WITH THE SAME BIRTH DATE

The only verified record of a family producing five single children with the same date of birth is that of Catherine (1952), Carol (1953), Charles (1956), Claudia (1961) and Cecilia (1966), born to Carolyn and Ralph Cummins (both USA), all on 20 February.

The three children of the Henriksen family (Norway) – Heidi (1960), Olav (1964) and Lief-Martin (1968) – all celebrate infrequent birthdays: they fall on Leap Year Day – 29 February.

OLDEST BRIDE

The oldest recorded bride is Minnie Munro (Australia), aged 102, who married Dudley Reid (Australia), at the advanced age of 83, at Point Clare, NSW, Australia, on 31 May 1991.

GREATEST HEIGHT DIFFERENTIAL BETWEEN HUSBAND AND WIFE

Fabien Pretou (France), who stands 1.885 m (6 ft 2 in) tall, married Natalie Lucius (France) who was 94 cm (3 ft 1 in) tall, at Seyssinet-Pariset, France, on 14 April 1990 – a height difference of 94.5 cm (37 in). Fabien has to take things easy around the home as it's all adapted for Natalie's size. If he wants to cook her dinner, he has to sit down to be at the right height for the hob.

MOST PROLIFIC MOTHER

The greatest officially recorded number of children born to one mother is an incredible 69, born to the wife of Feodor Vassilyev, an 18th-century Russian peasant. In 27 confinements she gave birth to 16 pairs of twins, seven sets of triplets and four sets of quadruplets. Her husband had 18 more children with a second wife.

LARGEST SINGLE TOMB

The Mount Li tomb, the burial place of China's first emperor, Qin Shi Huangdi, is situated 40 km (25 miles) east of Xian, China. The two walls surrounding the grave measure 2,173 x 974 m (7,129 x 3,195 ft) and 685 x 578 m (2,247 x 1,896 ft). The site has become world-famous for its army of terracotta soldiers, which were arranged in formation in four pits around the emperor's tomb.

LARGEST TV AUDIENCE FOR A LIVE BROADCAST

The worldwide TV audience for the funeral of Diana, Princess of Wales (UK), at Westminster Abbey, London, UK, on 6 September 1997, was estimated at 2.5 billion. An estimated 750 million had watched her wedding to HRH Prince Charles on TV in 1981.

EARLIEST SIAMESE TWINS

Conjoined twins derive the name 'Siamese' from Chang and Eng Bunker (their names mean left and right in Thai) born on 11 May 1811 to Chinese parents. The boys were joined by a cartilaginous band at the chest. In April 1843 they married Sarah and Adelaide Yates (both USA), and fathered 10 and 12 children respectively. The twins died within three hours of each other on 17 January 1874, aged 62.

MOST MARRIAGES

The most monogamous marriages undertaken by one person is 28, by former Baptist minister Glynn 'Scotty' Wolfe (USA), who first married in 1927. He believed he had a total of 41 children.

The most monogamous marriages by a woman is 22, by Linda Essex (USA), who has had 15 different husbands since 1957. Her most recent marriage, in October 1991, also ended in divorce.

MOST VALUABLE PIECE OF WEDDING CAKE

A box containing a piece of the Duke and Duchess of Windsor's (UK) wedding cake from June 1937 sold at Sotheby's, New York City, USA, on 27 February 1998 for a massive $29,900 (then £18,040). It was bought by Benjamin and Amanda Yin (both USA). The lot was originally estimated at $500–$1,000 (£300–£600). Proceeds from the sale were donated to charity.

CITY WITH THE MOST WEDDINGS

Regarded as the world's 'wedding capital', Las Vegas, Nevada, USA (above), has over 100 chapels performing about 8,400 marriages a month – 280 daily or one wedding every 5 min 17 sec. Foreign couples make up 12% of this total.

MOST TIMES MARRIED

Lauren Lubeck Blair and David E Hough Blair (both USA), married each other for the 61st time on 19 April, 2001 at London's Hard Rock Cafe, UK. The Blairs have married each other a total of 59 times since they first got hitched in 1984; all the wedding ceremonies have been in separate locations. In 2000, the Blairs got married 21 times. Their favourite wedding was in Gretna Green, Scotland, UK.

LARGEST CEMETERY

The 400-ha (990-acre) Ohlsdorf Cemetery, Hamburg, Germany, has handled 982,117 burials and 413,589 cremations as at 31 December 1996. It has been in continuous use since 1877.

LARGEST MASS SUICIDE

As reported by 1st-century historian Flavius Josephus (Israel), 960 Jewish zealots committed suicide by cutting each others' throats at Masada, Israel, in 73 AD, as the fortress was being besieged by Romans.

The greatest mass suicide of modern times occurred on 18 November 1978, when 913 members of the People's Temple cult died of cyanide poisoning at Jonestown, Guyana.

TALLEST CEMETERY

The permanently illuminated Memorial Necrópole Ecumônica, in Santos, near Saõ Paulo, Brazil, is 10 storeys high and occupies an area of 1.8 ha (4.4 acres). Begun in March 1983, the first burial was held there on 28 July 1984.

OLDEST COUPLE TO MARRY

On 1 February 2002, French couple Francois Frenandez (b.17 April 1906) and Madeleine Francineau (b.15 July 1907) married at their rest home in Clapiers, France, at the ages of 95 and 94 respectively.

MOST EXPENSIVE WEDDING

The wedding of Mohammed, son of Sheik Rashid Bin Saeed Al Maktoum, to Princess Salama (both UEA) in Dubai in May 1981 lasted seven days and cost around £22 million ($44.5 million). It was held in a purpose-built stadium for 20,000 people.

MOST COUPLES MARRIED SIMULTANEOUSLY

On 25 August 1995, some 35,000 couples were married (right) in the Olympic Stadium in Seoul, South Korea, in a ceremony officiated over by Sun Myung Moon of the Holy Spirit Association for the Unification of World Christianity. In addition, a further 325,000 couples around the world took part in the ceremony through a satellite link.

LARGEST PAPAL CROWD

On 15 January 1995, during his visit to the Philippines, Pope John Paul II (above, centre right) offered Mass to a crowd estimated at between 4 and 5 million people. The Mass took place at Luneta Park, Manila.

LONGEST-SERVING ALTAR BOY

Tommy Kinsella (Ireland) began to serve at Mass in the Church of the Holy Redeemer, Bray, Co Wicklow, Ireland, in April 1917, at the age of 11. He continued working for the same church for 81 years until his death on April 1 1999.

LARGEST RELIGION

Christianity is the world's predominant religion. In 2000 it had approximately 2 billion followers, or one third of the world's entire population.

FASTEST-GROWING RELIGION

Islam is the world's fastest-growing religion. In 1990, 935 million people were Muslims and this figure had escalated to around 1.2 billion by 2000, meaning that around one in five people follow Islam. Although the religion began in Arabia, by 2002 80% of all believers in Islam lived outside the Arab world. In the period 1990–2000, approximately 12.5 million more people converted to Islam than to Christianity.

LARGEST RELIGIOUS BUILDINGS

The largest religious structure is Angkor Wat (City Temple), enclosing 1,626,000 m² (17,502,118.3 ft²) in Cambodia (formerly Kampuchea), built during the period 1113–50. Its external wall measures 1,280 m (4,200 ft), and its population – before it was abandoned in 1432 – stood at 80,000. The whole complex of 72 major monuments extends over 24.8 km (15.4 miles).

The largest synagogue in the world is Temple Emanu-El on Fifth Avenue at 65th Street, New York City, USA, which has an area of 3,523 m² (37,922 ft²). The main sanctuary can accommodate 2,500 people, and the adjoining Beth-El Chapel seats 350. When these and the temple's other three sanctuaries are in use, 5,500 people can fit inside the synagogue.

Srirangam Temple, at Tiruchirappalli, Tamil Nadu, India, is the world's largest Hindu temple. Dedicated to the Hindu god Vishnu, it covers an area of 631,000 m² (6,792,027 ft²) and has a 1.116-km (0.683-mile) perimeter. The temple comprises seven concentric enclosures around the inner sanctum, the highest of which rises to 70.1 m (230 ft).

The world's largest Buddhist temple is Borobudur, Central Java, Indonesia, which was built between 750 and 842AD. The 60,000-m³ (2,118,880-ft³) stone structure is 34.5 m (113 ft) in height and its base measures 123 x 123 m (403 x 403 ft).

The largest mosque complex in the world is Shah Faisal Mosque, near Islamabad, Pakistan. The total area of the complex is 189,700 m² (2,041,913 ft²), with the covered area of the prayer hall measuring 4,800 m² (51,666 ft²). The complex

LARGEST DONATION OF HAIR

Every pilgrim to the Tirupati temple in Andhra Pradesh, India, donates a tonsure of their hair. An estimated 6.5 million people make such donations and over $2.2 million (£1.4 million) is raised in funds through the annual auction of hair. The temple attracts an average of 30,000 visitors per day and 600 barbers are employed to shave the pilgrims' hair 24 hours a day.

can accommodate 100,000 worshippers in the prayer hall and courtyard and a further 200,000 people in the adjacent grounds.

The cathedral church of St John the Divine, New York City, USA, is the largest Anglican cathedral. The Gothic Revival building has a floor area of 11,240 m² (120,986 ft²) and a volume of 476,350 m³ (16,822,141 ft³). At 183.2 m (601 ft), the nave is also longer than that of any other church.

The world's largest church is the Basilica of Our Lady of Peace (Notre Dame de la Paix) at Yamoussoukro, the Ivory Coast's administrative and

legal capital. Completed in 1989 at a cost of $164 million (£93,511,233), it has a total area of 30,000 m² (322,917 ft²), with seating for 7,000 people. Including its gold cross, the church is 158 m (518 ft) high.

SMALLEST CHURCH

The world's smallest church is that of Santa Isabel de Hungría in Colomares Castle, Benalmádena, Spain. The church was consecrated on 7 April 1990 and stands as a monument to the Italian explorer Christopher Columbus. Mass is only held there on special occasions, and, with a total floor area of 1.96 m² (21.09 ft²), only one person can fit in to pray at a time.

MOST PROLIFIC CRYING STATUE

On 14 days between 2 February and 17 March 1995, a 40-cm (15.75-in) plaster statue of the Virgin Mary, standing at the Marian shrine at Medjugorje, Bosnia-Herzegovina, apparently wept tears of blood. One such manifestation was witnessed by the diocesan bishop. Most reports of weeping statues do not receive any form of recognition from the Roman Catholic Church.

LARGEST MONKEY BUFFET

The Kala Temple in Lopburi province, north of Bangkok, Thailand, provides an annual spread of tropical fruit and vegetables weighing 3,000 kg (6,613.86 lb) for around 2,000 local monkeys (above). The buffet is now a major tourist attraction.

LARGEST ROSARY

In January 2001, teachers and students at St Joseph School in Cairo, Illinois, USA, made the world's largest rosary. It measured 52.9 m (173 ft 9 in).

LARGEST UNDERGROUND TEMPLE

The world's largest underground temple has been excavated over a period of 16 years by members of the 800-strong Damanhur religious community living in Baldissero, near Turin, Italy. The temple was excavated from the side of a hill and takes up a total volume of 6,000 m³ (211,888 ft³). The community has carved out its temple – the 'Temple of Humankind' – using only pick-axes and buckets.

LARGEST PILGRIMAGE CENTRES

The House of the Virgin Mary at Loretto, Italy, receives 3.5 million pilgrims (as opposed to tourists) a year, more than three times the number that visit Lourdes, France. Traditionally the Holy House of Loretto was said to have been transported by angels from Palestine to Italy.

The annual pilgrimage (or *hajj*) to Mecca, Saudi Arabia, attracts an average attendance of 2 million people, more than that to any other Islamic holy place.

MOST RECENTLY FOUND BUDDHIST RELIC

The Buddha's ashes were divided into eight lots and sent for safe-keeping to various parts of Asia. In 1981, one of the eight boxes was found at Yunju 75 km (46 miles) from Beijing, China.

OLDEST COMPLETE STAINED GLASS

The oldest intact stained glass in the world depicts the prophets and can be found in a window of the Cathedral of Augsburg, in Germany. It dates from the second half of the 11th century.

OLDEST BIBLE PUBLISHER

The oldest publisher of bibles is Cambridge University Press. Its first bible was the Geneva version of 1591.

MOST EXPENSIVE SACRED OBJECT

The 15th-century gold Buddha in Wat Trimitr Temple, Bangkok, Thailand, has a higher intrinsic value than any other sacred object. It is 3 m (10 ft) tall and weighs around 58 tonnes (127,867 lb). At £260 ($370) per fine ounce (April 1996 prices), the Buddha was valued at £32.7 million ($46 million), or £37.1 million ($53.7 million) in 2001. The gold under the statue's plaster exterior was only found in 1954.

LARGEST RELIGIOUS CROWD

Around 20 million people gathered for the Hindu festival of Ardh Kumbha Mela (below) at Allahabad (Prayag), Uttar Pradesh, India. on 30 January 1995. The site of the gathering was the confluence of the rivers Yamuna, Ganges and the subterranean river Saraswati. Allahabad is one of four different sites between which the festival is rotated every three years.

MOST VISITED TOURIST REGION

According to the World Tourism Organization (WTO), Europe (London shown above) received the most tourists in 2000, with 403,303,000 arrivals. This represents a 57.7% share of the world tourist market. For the same year, the Americas commanded 18.5% of the market.

BUSIEST AIRPORT (INTERNATIONAL PASSENGERS)

In terms of the number of international passengers, the world's busiest airport is London Heathrow (UK). In 2001 it handled 64 million passengers, of which around 56 million arrived from, or departed to, countries other than the UK. Despite being the record holder for international passengers, it is only the fourth busiest airport in the world overall.

LOWEST RATE OF CAR OWNERSHIP

Somalia and Tajikistan jointly have the world's lowest rate of car ownership, with 0.1 cars per 1,000 people, or one car per 10,000 people. By contrast, the European state of Luxembourg has 576 cars per 1,000, or one for every 1.7 people.

LONGEST DRIVEABLE ROAD

The Pan-American Highway, which runs from Fairbanks, Alaska, USA, to Santiago, Chile, then eastward to Brasilia, Brazil, via Buenos Aires, Argentina, is over 24,140 km (15,000 miles) long. However, there is a small section in Panama and Colombia called the Darién Gap, which is incomplete due to political and financial reasons.

HIGHEST ROAD FATALITY RATE

India's roads are rated as the world's most dangerous. Although the country contains only 1% of the world's road vehicles, it accounts for 6% of its road accidents. Of the 9.34 million deaths in India in 1998, 217,000, or 1 in 43, were due to road traffic accidents.

WORLD'S STEEPEST STREET

Baldwin Street in Dunedin, New Zealand, has a maximum gradient of 1:1.266 (38° or 42.2%).

LARGEST AIRPORT

The £2.1-billion ($3.17-billion) King Khalid International Airport outside Riyadh, Saudi Arabia, covers an area of 225 km² (55,040 acres).

HIGHEST TRAFFIC DENSITY

Monaco has the highest number of vehicles in relation to its road network. In 1996, (most recent figures) it had 480 vehicles for each kilometre of road. If they were required to park behind one another on the streets, nearly half would have nowhere to park!

BUSIEST INTERNATIONAL AIR ROUTE

The air route between Hong Kong, China, and Taipei, Taiwan, is the world's busiest. In 1999, 3.96 million passengers flew between the two cities. London, UK, to Dublin, Ireland, was second, with 3.85 million.

FASTEST-GROWING TOURIST REGION

According to the WTO, the region showing the greatest annual growth in the number of tourists in 2000 was east Asia and the Pacific. The area, which includes popular tourist destinations such as Australia, Cambodia, China, Indonesia, Malaysia, Thailand and Vietnam, hosted 111.9 million tourists in 2000, a massive 14.7% increase over the previous year.

BUSIEST INTERCONTINENTAL AIR ROUTE

The busiest intercontinental air route is between London (UK) and New York (USA). In 1999, 3.82 million passengers flew the 5,539 km (3,442 miles) between the two cities, an average of 10,645 air passengers per day, or 26 full Boeing 747s.

BUSIEST AIRPORT (AIRCRAFT AND PASSENGERS)

Hartsfield International Airport, Atlanta, Georgia, USA, is the world's busiest airport when considering passenger numbers, with 80,162,407 people passing through in 2000. This was a 2.7% increase over 1999. It is also the world's busiest airport in terms of the number of aircraft taking off and landing. In 2000, there were 915,454 aircraft landings and departures.

OLDEST CONTINUOUSLY OPERATING AIRPORT

The College Park Airport in Washington DC, USA, is the oldest continuously operating airport in the world. It dates back to 1909.

COUNTRY WITH THE MOST AIRPORTS

The USA has a record-breaking 14,459 airports. Brazil comes a distant second with 3,291.

BIGGEST TOURIST SPENDERS

Americans are the biggest overseas tourism spenders. In 2000, they spent an estimated wallet-emptying $65 billion (£43.5 billion) while on holiday in foreign countries (not including air fares). Germany and the UK come second and third in the spending stakes respectively, with $47.6 billion (£31.5 billion) and $36.6 billion (£24 billion).

LARGEST AIRPORT TERMINAL

The Hong Kong International Airport passenger terminal building (above) is 1.3 km (0.8 mile) long and covers 550,000 m² (136 acres). The baggage hall alone is as big as New York's Yankee Stadium.

LARGEST EXPORT INDUSTRY

Tourism is widely regarded as the world's largest export industry, with $555 billion (£343 billion) flowing into countries through the selling of services to visiting foreign tourists in 1999.

MOST FREQUENT FLIERS

In 2000, Americans clocked up around 1,110.8 billion passenger kilometres (690.2 billion miles) – the sum of the total distance flown by every passenger.

DENSEST ROAD NETWORK

The Mediterranean island republic of Malta is the country with the densest road network (in relation to its size). It has 15.2 km (9.4 miles) of roads per square kilometre (0.38 square mile). As a comparison, the USA, which has the world's largest road network, has a density of only 0.69 km (0.43 mile) of roads per square kilometre because of its immense size.

HIGHEST EARNINGS FROM TOURISM

The undisputed world leader – in terms of earnings from international tourism – is the USA. In the year 2000, the USA earned $85.2 billion (£57 billion) from this lucrative source of revenue – nearly three times as much as its nearest rivals, Spain ($31 billion or £20.5 billion) and France ($29.9 billion or £20 billion). The US tourism total accounted for 17.9% of the entire world earnings, which stand at $476 billion (£318 billion).

HIGHEST AIRPORT

Bangda Airport in eastern Tibet lies 4,739 m (15,548 ft) above sea level, making it the world's highest airport.

LOWEST INTERNATIONAL AIRPORT

Schiphol Airport outside Amsterdam, The Netherlands, lies at 4.5 m (15 ft) below sea level.

LARGEST HELIPORT

The world's largest-ever heliport was located at An Khe, South Vietnam, during the Vietnam War. With an area measuring 6 km^2 (2.32 miles^2), it could take up to 434 helicopters.

MOST POPULAR TOURIST DESTINATION

In 2000, France singlehandedly accounted for 10.8% of all international tourists, with 75.5 million arrivals. This is substantially more than its own population of around 60 million. By comparison, the second most visited country, the USA, has a population of nearly 300 million, but had 50.9 million international tourists, accounting for 7.3% of the total world market.

GREATEST TRAIN ROBBERY

Between 3:03 am and 3:27 am on 8 August 1963, a General Post Office mail train was ambushed at Sears Crossing, Bucks, UK, and robbed at nearby Bridego Bridge. The gang, which included Ronnie Biggs (UK, above), escaped with around 120 mailbags, containing £2,631,784 (then $7,369,784) in banknotes heading for London to be destroyed. Only £343,448 (then $961,757) was ever recovered.

MOST PROLIFIC CANNIBAL

During the 19th century, Ratu Udre Udre, a cannibalistic Fijian chief, reportedly ate between 872 and 999 people. The chief had kept a stone to record each body that he had consumed, and these were placed along his tomb in Rakiraki, northern Viti Levu, Fiji.

COUNTRY WITH THE FEWEST PRISONERS

According to the International Centre for Prison Studies, as of 2001 the country with the fewest prisoners is Indonesia, which has approximately 162,886 prison inmates out of an estimated national population of 214.8 million. Indonesian prisoners represent only 29 out of every 100,000 of the country's population.

COUNTRY WITH THE MOST MURDERS

In 1997, the USA had an estimated 25,000 cases of homicide. The offence rate for homicide was 8.2 per 100,000 of the population.

GREATEST ART ROBBERY

On 14 April 1991, 20 paintings, estimated to be worth $500 million (then £280 million), were stolen from the Van Gogh Museum in Amsterdam, The Netherlands. Only 35 minutes later, they were found in an abandoned car near the museum.

MOST VALUABLE OBJECT EVER STOLEN

Though its price has not been officially calculated, the Mona Lisa is arguably the most valuable object ever stolen. The painting vanished from the Louvre, Paris, France, on 21 August 1911 and was discovered in Florence, Italy, in 1913. Vincenzo Perugia (Italy), a former Louvre employee, was later charged with the theft of the famous art work.

LARGEST JEWEL ROBBERY

On 11 August 1994 at the Carlton Hotel, Cannes, France, a three-man gang carrying machine guns made off with FF250 million ($45 million or £29.1 million) worth of gems from the hotel's jewellery shop.

GREATEST MODERN KIDNAP RANSOM

Two Hong Kong businessmen, Walter Kwok and Victor Li, paid off gangster Cheung Tze-keung, (aka 'Big Spender'), a record total ransom of $206 million (£144 million) in exchange for their freedom after they were kidnapped in 1996 and 1997, respectively.

SURVIVOR OF MOST HANGING ATTEMPTS

The survivor of the greatest number of legal hanging attempts is Joseph Samuel (Australia), a 22-year-old who was sentenced to death for murder in Sydney, NSW, Australia. On 26 September 1803, the first attempt at execution failed when the hangman's rope broke. Another attempt was made, but this was also abandoned, after the rope stretched so much that Samuel's feet touched the ground. At the third attempt, the rope broke again. Samuel was then reprieved.

LARGEST SPEEDING FINE

Anssi Vanjoki (Finland) was fined €116,000 ($104,000 or £71,600) for driving his Harley Davidson motorcycle at 75 km/h (46.6 mph) in a 50 km/h (31 mph) zone in Helsinki, Finland, on October 2001. In keeping with Finnish law, by which speeding offenders are fined according to their annual incomes, Vanjoki, a director of telecommunications company Nokia, was ordered to pay the equivalent of 14 days of his 1999 income of approximately €14 million ($12.5 million or £8.6 million).

LARGEST JAIL BREAK

On 11 February 1979, an Iranian employee of the Electronic Data Systems Corporation (EDS) led a mob into Gasr prison, Tehran, Iran, in an attempt to rescue two American colleagues. The mastermind of the plan was EDS owner and future presidential candidate H Ross Perot. Around 11,000 other prisoners took advantage of the confusion to stage history's largest jail break.

MOST ARRESTED PERSON

By 1998, Tommy Johns (Australia), had been arrested nearly 3,000 times for being drunk and disorderly in a public place.

MOST PEOPLE KILLED IN A TERRORIST ACT

The greatest number of individuals killed in a terrorist act is 2,800 (624 positively identified bodies), in the attack on the World Trade Centre, New York City, USA, on 11 September 2001. The figure includes those killed in the Centre's two towers, 157 aboard the two Boeing 767s that struck them and 479 staff from emergency services. The final toll may never accurately be known.

LARGEST PRISON SYSTEM

The US state of California has the biggest prison system in the industrialized world. The state holds more inmates in its jails and prisons than France, Great Britain, Germany, Japan, Singapore and The Netherlands combined.

MOST PROLIFIC MURDER PARTNERSHIP

The sisters Delfina and María de Jesús Gonzáles (Mexico), who abducted girls to work in their brothel, are known to have murdered at least 90 prostitutes, as well as some of the girls' clients. The two women were sentenced to 40 years' imprisonment in 1964.

LARGEST DAMAGES FOR SEXUAL HARASSMENT

The record individual award in a sexual harassment case was $50 million (£32 million), made to Peggy Kimzey (USA), a former employee of Wal-Mart, the largest retail chain in the United States, on 28 June 1995.

LONGEST-SERVING POLITICAL PRISONER

Kim Sung-myun (South Korea) was imprisoned for 43 years 10 months in Seoul, South Korea, for supporting Communist North Korea. He was freed in August 1995 at the age of 70.

COUNTRY WITH THE MOST EXECUTIONS

According to figures released by Amnesty International in March 2001, China executes more people than the rest of the world combined. During 1999 China executed 1,077 people, while the figure for the rest of the world totalled 736. In 2000, the limited records available to Amnesty International revealed that at least 1,511 death sentences had been passed in China and at least 1,000 executions had been carried out. These are believed to be only a fraction of the true figures.

US STATE WITH THE MOST EXECUTIONS

As of April 2001, Texas had carried out more executions than any other US state. Since 1974, Texas has executed 244 convicted criminals, followed by Virginia, with 82, and Florida, with 51.

MOST PROLIFIC MURDERER

It emerged at his trial that Behram, aka the 'Indian Thug', strangled at least 931 victims with his yellow-and-white cloth strip, or *ruhmal*, in Oudh (now in Uttar Pradesh, India) from 1790–1840.

LONGEST PRISON SENTENCE FOR MURDER

Andrew Aston (UK), who clubbed two senior citizens to death during a series of robberies, was given 26 life sentences on 20 February 2002, during his trial at Birmingham Crown Court, West Midlands, UK. Aston battered 24 other elderly victims in their homes over three months in 2001, posing as a policeman to gain entry and then attacking them for money to feed his cocaine habit.

LARGEST DRUG SEIZURES BY WEIGHT

On 29 September 1989 in Sylmar, California, USA, officers from the Drug Enforcement Administration (DEA) in Alexandria, Virginia, seized 21,570 kg (47,554 lb) of cocaine.

According to the DEA based in Alexandria, Virginia, USA, the largest ever heroin seizure took place in Bangkok, Thailand, on 11 February 1988, when officers impounded 1,277 kg (2,816 lb) of the drug.

LARGEST MINT

The US Treasury, constructed in 1965–69 in Philadelphia, Penn, USA, covers 4.7 ha (11.5 acres). In 2001 it produced 9.5 billion coins – nearly 38 million daily. The Graebner Press, a high-speed stamping machine, can produce coins at a rate of 42,000 per hour, with a record production of 12,647,096,000 coins in 2000. A mint in Denver, Colorado, USA, set a new record for coin-production by a single facility in 2000, producing over 15.4 billion coins.

GREATEST BANKNOTE FORGERY

The German Third Reich's 'Operation Bernhard' during World War II aimed to ruin the British economy with a flood of fake notes. Over nine million counterfeit British notes valued at £130 million ($520 million) were forged by 140 Jewish prisoners at Sachsenhausen concentration camp, Germany. The notes were sent to Nazi-occupied or neutral countries to pay agents or to be exchanged for other currencies.

EARLIEST PAPER MONEY

The earliest recorded use of paper currency can be traced back to the Song dynasty (960–1279) in China. It was utilized by a group of wealthy merchants and businessmen in Szechuan, where the art of printing also originated.

SMALLEST PAPER MONEY BY SIZE

The smallest national note ever issued, in terms of physical size, was the 10-bani note of the Ministry of Finance of Romania in 1917. Its printed area measured 27.5 x 38 mm (1.08 x 1.49 in). This is roughly a tenth the size of a $1 banknote.

OLDEST COIN

The earliest coins recorded are not stamped with a date, but were made during the reign of King Gyges of Lydia, Turkey, around 630 BC. They were composed of electrum, a naturally occurring amalgam of gold and silver.

EARLIEST DATED COINS

A Samian silver tetradrachm struck in Zankle (now Messina), Sicily, Italy, is dated year 1 (494 BC). The date is indicated by the letter 'A' on one side of the coin. The earliest-known dated coins from the Christian era are the Danish 'Bishop of Roskilde' coins, of which six are known. The coins bear the inscription MCCXXXIIII, standing for the year 1234.

LARGEST CHEQUE BY VALUE

The greatest amount paid by a single cheque in the history of banking was £2,474,655,000 ($3,971,821,324). It was issued on 30 March 1995 and signed by Nicholas Morris, Company Secretary of Glaxo plc, UK. The cheque represented a payment by Glaxo plc to Wellcome Trust Nominees Limited in respect of the Trust's share in Wellcome plc. The Lloyds Bank Registrars' computer system could not generate a cheque this large, so it was completed by a Lloyds employee using a typewriter. The typist was so overawed by the responsibility of the task that it took her three attempts to type out the cheque for this massive amount.

LARGEST RETURN OF CASH

In May 1994, Howard Jenkins (USA), a 31-year-old roofing engineer, discovered that a mystery $88 million (£62 million) had been transferred mistakenly into his bank account. Although he initially withdrew $4 million (£2.8 million), his conscience got the better of him shortly afterwards and he returned the $88 million in full.

MOST EXPENSIVE GOLD BAR

The largest known transaction for a single numismatic item took place on 7 November 2001, when an 80-lb (30-kg) pioneer gold assay bar (dubbed the 'Eureka'), retrieved from the 1857 shipwreck *SS Central America*, was bought for $8 million (£5.5 million) by an anonymous buyer.

LONGEST CONTINUOUS ISSUER OF BANKNOTES

The longest continuous issuer of banknotes in the world is the Bank of England, UK. It has been issuing banknotes without interruption since 1694, when it was first established to raise money for King William III's war against the French.

HIGHEST-VALUE BANKNOTES

The highest-value banknote ever issued by the US Federal Reserve System is a $100,000 note, bearing the head of US president Woodrow Wilson, which is used only for transactions between the Federal Reserve and the Treasury Department.

The highest-value notes in circulation were printed when the US Federal Reserve released $10,000 banknotes bearing the head of 19th-century US Supreme Court Chief Justice Salmon P Chase. It was announced in 1969 that no further notes higher than $100 would be issued. Only 200 $10,000 bills remain in circulation or 'unretired'.

TALLEST COIN COLUMN

The tallest single column of coins ever stacked on the edge of a coin was built by Dipak Syal (India) on 3 May 1991 and made up of 253 Indian one-rupee pieces on top of a vertical five-rupee coin. He also balanced 10 one-rupee coins and 10 10-paise coins alternately horizontally and vertically in a single column on 1 May 1991.

LARGEST CORPORATE BANKRUPTCY

In terms of assets, the largest corporate bankruptcy amounted to $63.3 billion (£44.4 billion) filed by US energy-trading company Enron (above) on 2 December 2001. Until this date, Enron had been America's seventh-largest company.

HEAVIEST HOARD OF COINS

The largest-ever hoard of coins in terms of weight was a 43-tonne (96,320-lb) haul of gold (worth £5 million or $23.8 million). It was recovered from the White Star Liner *HMS Laurentic*, which sank after it struck a mine in waters 40 m (132 ft) deep off Malin Head, Donegal, Ireland, on 25 January 1917.

SMALLEST MINT

The single-press mint of the Sovereign Military Order of Malta, in Rome, Italy, is housed in one room and has issued proof coins since 1961.

LARGEST GOLD RESERVES

The US Treasury held approximately 262 million fine ounces of gold during 1996, equivalent to $100 billion (£65 billion) at the June 1996 price of $382 (£249) per fine ounce.

HIGHEST-DENOMINATION BANKNOTE

The Hungarian 100 million B-pengo (100,000,000,000,000,000,000 pengo), issued in 1946, is the highest denomination banknote, though the figure was not printed on it. It was worth around $0.20 (£0.05) at the time.

BANKNOTE WITH THE MOST ZEROS

The Yugoslavian 500-billion dinar note (equivalent to £0.70 or $1), issued in 1993, had 11 zeros printed on it.

MOST CORPORATE DEBT FAILURES

A record 211 companies defaulted on $115.4 billion (£79.5 billion) of debt in 2001 – a record in both number of defaults and total amount. This is an increase of more than 120% from 2000, when 132 companies defaulted on $42.3 billion (£39.1 billion) of debt.

LARGEST CURRENCY INTRODUCTION

On 1 January 2002, 15 billion euro banknotes and 50 billion euro coins (with a value of over €664 billion – £407 billion or $592 billion) were put into circulation in Austria, Belgium, Finland, France, Germany, Greece, Ireland, Italy, Luxembourg, The Netherlands, Portugal and Spain, affecting 290 million people. Put end to end, the new euro banknotes would stretch to the Moon and back two and a half times.

AMAZING OBJECTS

SMALLEST HAND-MADE TEDDY BEAR

Utaho Imaoka (Japan) has created the world's smallest hand-made teddy bear (above), which measures a minuscule 9 mm (0.35 in) long. The bear consists of six main parts: head, body and four limbs, each of which is filled with polyester-cotton. The arms, legs and head are all moveable and the exterior is made of ultra-suede.

SMALLEST COMMERCIALLY AVAILABLE WINE BOTTLE

Steve Klein (USA) of Klein's Designs, California, USA, makes hand-blown miniature wine bottles that stand 3.4 cm (1.37 in) tall. Each bottle is corked, sealed and labelled to show that it contains 0.75 ml (0.026 fl oz) of fine wine.

SMALLEST COMMERCIALLY AVAILABLE STITCHED TEDDY BEAR

The smallest teddy bear available to buy is named 'Titch', and is hand-made from pipe cleaners by Sue Wilkes (UK). The tiny bear is only 1.58 cm (0.62 in) tall and retails at £5.99 ($8.38).

SMALLEST PAIR OF SCISSORS

In 1998 Ramesh Chand Dhiman (India) hand-made a pair of working scissors measuring 3.12 mm (0.12 in) long and 2.17 mm (0.08 in) wide.

SMALLEST BICYCLES

The world's smallest rideable bicycle has a front wheel with an 11-mm (0.43-in) diameter and a rear wheel with a 13-mm (0.51-in) diameter. On 11 August 1999 it was ridden by its constructor, Zbigniew Rózanekit (Poland), for a distance of 5 m (16 ft).

Jacques Puyoou (France) has built a tandem 36 cm (14 in) long, which has been ridden by himself and Madame Puyoou (France).

SMALLEST COCKTAIL AND COCKTAIL SHAKER

On 22 March 2001 José Luis Iriarte Iñigo (Spain) prepared a 7-ml (0.2-fl oz) cocktail called 'Puntito' (Little Point), using eight-year-old rum, strawberry liqueur, pineapple juice, peach juice and ice at the 'Y Punto' bar in Tudela, Navarra, Spain.

A cocktail shaker custom-made for Paul Bordonaba Areizaga (Spain) of the Whisky Museum pub, San Sebastián, Spain, measures just 5 cm (1.9 in) tall with a capacity of 6 cm³ (0.36 in³). The first cocktail mixed in it consisted of a 30-year-old whisky with six small caviar balls (Triple seco) and saffron. It cost a hefty 150,000 pesetas (£552.03 or $787.13).

SMALLEST DOG EVER

The smallest dog on record is a fist-sized dwarf Yorkshire terrier owned by Arthur Marples (UK). Fully grown, this tiny dog stood 6.3 cm (2.8 in) at the shoulder and measured 9.5 cm (3.75 in) from the tip of its nose to the tip of its tail. It died in 1945, just before its second birthday.

SMALLEST NIGHTCLUB

The world's smallest nightclub is The Miniscule of Sound, London, UK, which is a box only 2.4 m (8 ft) long, 1.2 m (4 ft) wide and 2.4 m (8 ft) high. Constructed in August 1998 out of hardboard walls and Dexion shelving, the club contains a full DJ and sound system and a dance floor that is only 2 m² (21.5 ft²). The nightclub's maximum capacity is 14 people, including the DJ.

SMALLEST CAT EVER

The smallest cat on record is a male blue point Himalayan-Persian named Tinker Toy. Fully grown, it is only 7 cm (2.75 in) tall and 19 cm (7.5 in) long. The diminutive feline is owned by Katrina and Scott Forbes (both USA).

SMALLEST COMMERCIAL JIGSAW PUZZLE

The smallest commercially available jigsaw puzzle with a minimum of 1,000 pieces is made by Educa Sallent (Spain) and measures 46 x 30 cm (18 x 11 in). The miniature puzzles are all made from recycled materials and depict a variety of designs, ranging from European landmarks to Walt Disney cartoons and characters from *Sesame Street*. The small puzzles retail for 1,035 pesetas (£3.84 or $5.44). A glow-in-the-dark neon version of the jigsaw puzzle is also available.

SMALLEST SUBMARINE

In 1991 William G Smith (UK) constructed a fully functional submarine that was only 2.95 m (9 ft 8 in) long, 1.15 m (3 ft 9 in) wide and 1.42 m (4 ft 8 in) high. Named *The Water Beatle*, it can reach depths of around 30.4 m (100 ft) and can remain underwater for at least four hours using 2.23-kW (3-hp) air cylinders (or more with the use of two additional external cylinders). The submarine is now being used to locate aircraft wreckage off the Sussex coast of south-eastern England.

SMALLEST FUNCTIONAL VINYL RECORDS

Six records with a 33.3-mm (1.3-in) diameter were recorded by HMV's studio at Hayes, Middlesex, UK, on 26 January 1923, for Queen Mary's dolls' house. Approximately 92,000 copies of these miniature records were pressed, including 35,000 discs of 'God Save The King'.

SMALLEST PUB

The ground floor of The Nutshell (above) in Bury St Edmunds, Suffolk, UK, is 4.82 x 2.28 m (15 ft 10 in x 7 ft 6 in). The pub was reputedly granted a licence personally by a thirsty King Charles II when he was passing by one day.

SMALLEST UNICYCLE

The smallest rideable unicycle measures 30 cm (11.81 in) high with a wheel diameter of 16.5 mm (0.64 in) and has no attachments or extensions. It has been ridden publicly on a number of occasions by Peter Rosendahl (Sweden), the furthest distance covered so far being 11.61 m (38 ft 1.1 in) at the studios of *El Show de los Récords*, Madrid, Spain, on 11 October 2001.

SMALLEST BOOKS

The smallest book ever printed measures 0.95 x 0.95 mm (0.0374 x 0.0374 in). Entitled *The Twelve Horary Signs – Chinese Zodiac*, 100 copies were printed in October 2000 by Toppan Printing Co Ltd under the direction of the Printing Museum, Tokyo, Japan. The 16-page book contains pictograms representing the 12 animals of the Chinese zodiac, and their names in both English and hiragana, the Japanese symbol writing system.

The smallest Qur'an is owned by Neera and Narendra Bhatia (both India) and measures 2 x 1.5 x 1 cm (0.8 x 0.6 x 0.4 in). It is published in an unabridged, bound version, in fine print Arabic, and is 572 pages long.

SMALLEST NEWSPAPER

The monthly journal *Vossa Senhoria*, published by Dolores Nunes Schwindt (Brazil), measures a minute 3.5 x 2.5 cm (1.37 x 0.9 in).

SMALLEST TV SETS

The Seiko TV-Wrist Watch, launched on 23 December 1982 in Japan, has a black-and-white screen measuring 30.5 mm (1.25 in) wide. Together with the receiver unit and headphones, the entire black-and-white system, which costs ¥108,000 (£564.65 or $807.53), weighs only 320 g (11.3 oz).

The smallest single-piece TV set is the Casio-Keisanki TV-10, weighing 338 g (11.9 oz) with a screen 6.85 cm (2.69 in) wide. The tiny television was launched in Tokyo, Japan in July 1983.

The smallest and lightest colour TV set is the Casio CV-1, launched in July 1992 by the Casio Computer Co Ltd (Japan). It measures 60 x 24 x 91 mm (2.4 x 0.9 x 3.6 in) and weighs 168.5 g (6 oz), with its battery. It has a screen size of 35 mm (1.38 in) and sells for ¥40,000 (around £200 or $300).

SMALLEST STEAM ENGINE

The smallest working stationary steam engine, made by Iqbal Ahmed (India), has a flywheel with a diameter of just 6.8 mm (0.27 in). The machine is fed steam from a separate boiler unit via a copper pipe. It stands just 6.8 mm (0.27 in) high, is 16.24 mm (0.64 in) long and weighs 1.72 g (0.06 oz).

SMALLEST CRYSTAL BOWL

A crystal bowl made by Jim Irish (Ireland), a former master cutter at Waterford Crystal, measured 8.55 mm (0.33 in) wide, 4.6 mm (0.18 in) tall and 2.1 mm (0.08 in) thick.

SMALLEST MAP

In 1992 Dr Jonathon Mamin (Switzerland) of IBM's Zürich laboratory used sudden electrical pulses to create a map of the western hemisphere out of atoms. The map has a scale of one trillion to one, and a diameter of approximately one micron (one millionth of a metre), around one hundredth of the diameter of a human hair.

SMALLEST WINE GLASS

On 7 December 2000 the world's smallest wine glass was unveiled. Created by NEC, Prof Shinji Matsui's (Japan) research group at the Himeji Institute of Technology, Himeji, Hyogo, Japan, and Seiko Instruments, this tiny vessel measures just 2,750 nanometres across. This is around 20,000 times smaller than a conventional wine glass.

SMALLEST MOTORIZED CAR

Nippondenso of Kariya, Japan, have made a motorized model of Toyota's first passenger car, the 1936 AA sedan (left), which has a length of only 4.785 mm (0.188 in), a width of 1.730 mm (0.0681 in) and a height of 1.736 mm (0.0683 in). The bumper is 50 microns thick (by way of comparison, a human hair is 100 microns in diameter). The motor (the coil of which is 1 mm, or 0.039 in, in diameter) can power the miniature car to a top speed of 0.018 km/h (0.011 mph).

HIGHEST-HEELED SHOES
The highest-heeled shoes that are commercially available (above) boast 27.9-cm (11-in) platforms and 40.6-cm (16-in) heels. Available in red or black leather, these Vertigo shoes sell for £725 ($1,092). The company that manufactures the shoes, LadyBWear (UK), warns that it is not responsible for anyone who falls while they are wearing the staggering heels.

LARGEST BRA
In September 1990, the company Triumph International Japan Ltd produced a brassiere with an underbust measurement of 24 m (78 ft 8 in) and a bust measurement of 28 m (91 ft 10 in).

LARGEST CHRISTMAS TREE MADE FROM LIGHTS
A Christmas tree made entirely from lights was assembled in the garden of Pietro Cucchi (Italy) in Milan, Italy, on 23 November 1998. The tree measured 51 m (167 ft 3.8 in) tall and 21 m (68 ft 10.8 in) at its widest point; it consisted of 77,300 bulbs. The tree remained illuminated until it was dismantled on 18 January 1999.

LARGEST CHANDELIER
The world's largest set of chandeliers was created by the Kookje Lighting Co Ltd of Seoul, South Korea. It is 12 m (39 ft) high, weighs 10.67 tonnes (23,523 lb) and features 700 bulbs. The colossal chandelier was completed in November 1988 and occupies three floors of the Lotte Chamshil department store in Seoul.

LARGEST ADVENT CALENDAR
The Coca-Cola BlowUP Media advent calendar was 54 m (177 ft 1.9 in) long and 17.3 m (56 ft 9 in) high. It was unveiled by schoolchildren outside Birmingham Town Hall, Birmingham, UK, on 30 November 2001.

LARGEST BOUQUETS
The world's largest bouquet measured 23.4 m (77 ft) in length. Completed on 26 August 2001 by a team led by Ashrita Furman (USA), it was shown in the town of Jamaica, New York, USA.

The largest bouquet sold by a florist (in one order) featured 518 stems, had a diameter of 1.2 m (3 ft 9 in) and weighed 28.49 kg (62 lb 11.3 oz). The record-breaking bouquet was ordered from Flores do Liz, Leiria, Portugal, and delivered on 29 July 2001.

LARGEST BUCKET OF MAPLE SYRUP
Rapid Duct Supply (Canada) made the world's largest maple syrup bucket, measuring 0.91 m (3 ft) in height and 0.96 m (3 ft 2 in) in diameter, with a capacity of 605 litres (133 gal) for the annual Elmira Maple Syrup Festival, Ontario, Canada, held on 1 April 2000.

HEAVIEST CARROT
British-born John Evans grew a carrot that weighed an astonishing 8.61 kg (18 lb 13 oz) when measured at the 1998 Alaska State Fair.

LARGEST GLASS SCULPTURE
The Bellagio in Las Vegas, USA, is the most expensive hotel ever built and can also boast the largest glass sculpture ever created. The floral-design chandelier stretches above the hotel's foyer and measures 9 x 20 m (29 ft 6 in x 65 ft 7 in). It was produced by glass artist Dale Chihuly (USA). Entitled Fiori di Como, the work comprises 4,535 kg (10,000 lb) of steel and 18,143 kg (40,000 lb) of hand-blown glass.

LARGEST BANANA BUNCH
Kabana SA and Tecorone SL (Spain) grew a gigantic bunch of bananas that contained 473 individual fruits on the island of El Hierro, Canary Islands, Spain. When the bunch was measured on 11 July 2001 it weighed in at an impressive 130 kg (287 lb).

LARGEST PUMPKIN
Gerry Checkon (USA) grew a pumpkin that measured 513 kg (1,131 lb) when weighed at the Pennsylvania Pumpkin Bowl, Altoona, Penn, USA, on 2 October 1999. Altoona's Pumpkin Bowl is the official Great Pumpkin Commonwealth weigh-off site.

LARGEST SHIRT
The world's largest shirt, the Tide Shirt, was 45.4 m (148 ft 11.4 in) long, with a chest of 49.6 m (162 ft 8.7 in) and sleeves of 9 x 15 m (29 ft 6.3 in x 49 ft 2.5 in). It was made for Procter & Gamble Romania, makers of Tide detergent, and measured in Bucharest, Romania, on 27 September 2001.

LARGEST FOOTBALL SHIRT
The world's largest ever football shirt measured 35.9 x 34.4 m (118 x 113 ft). It bore the national colours of Trinidad and Tobago and was shown around the two islands in July 2001 as part of the run-up to the FIFA Under-17 World Championships.

LARGEST LEATHER BOOT
Hand-made by Pasquale Tramonta (Italy), the world's largest leather boot measures 4.16 m (13 ft 7.7 in) high, 2.7 m (8 ft 10.2 in) long and 80 cm (31 in) wide. Five years of work went into making it, at a cost of 25 million lire (£7,896 or $11,416). The boot, which weighs 280 kg (617 lb) and was made from 40 leather hides, can accommodate at least three people.

LONGEST GARLIC STRING
The world's longest string of garlic bulbs (above) measured an incredible 110.99 m (364 ft 1.6 in) and was made by Somerfield Stores Ltd (UK). It was displayed at Greenwich Park, London, UK, in November 2001.

LARGEST CONTAINER OF BODY CREAM

The largest body cream container was 2 m (6 ft 6.7 in) in diameter, 53 cm (1 ft 8.8 in) high and held 1,124,490 ml (247.4 gal) of NIVEA Creme. Made by Beiersdorf Hellas, it was unveiled in Athens, Greece, on 15 December 2001. The giant cosmetic was created for NIVEA'S 90th anniversary and was 16,327 times larger than the original.

LARGEST CHRISTMAS CRACKER

The largest functional Christmas cracker ever constructed was 55.45 m (181 ft 11 in) long and 3.6 m (11 ft 9 in) in diameter. It was built by ex-international rugby league footballer Ray Price (Australia), for Australian company Markson Sparks! and pulled in the car park at Westfield Shopping Town, Chatswood, Sydney, NSW, Australia, on 16 December 1998.

LARGEST SWIMMING POOL

The world's largest swimming pool is the seawater Orthlieb Pool, Casablanca, Morocco. It is 480 m (1,574 ft) long, 75 m (246 ft) wide, and has an area of 3.6 ha (8.9 acres).

The largest land-locked pool currently in use is Willow Lake at Warren, Ohio, USA, which is 183 x 46 m (600 x 150 ft) in size.

LARGEST ACOUSTIC GUITAR

The largest playable acoustic guitar in the world measures 16.75 m (59 ft 11 in) long, 7.57 m (24 ft 10 in) wide and 2.67 m (8 ft 9 in) deep. Built in Realizarevents, Porto, Portugal, by a

team that comprised more than 50 people, it weighs 4.064 tonnes (28,818 lb).

LARGEST ELECTRIC GUITAR

The largest playable electric guitar in the world is 13.29 m (43 ft 7.5 in) tall, 5.01 m (16 ft 5.5 in) wide and weighs 907 kg (2,000 lb). Modelled on a 1967 Gibson Flying V and built to a scale of 1:12, it was made by students from Conroe Independent School District Academy of Science and Technology, Conroe, Texas, USA, at a cost of $3,000 (£1,975). Construction of the guitar began in October 1999 and the instrument was played for the first time at the Cynthia Woods Mitchell Pavilion on 6 June 2000, when the opening chord of The Beatles' song 'A Hard Day's Night' was strummed.

LARGEST GRILLED SANDWICH

Cabot Creamery of Vermont, USA, created the world's largest grilled cheese sandwich on 4 November 2000 at the 2nd Annual Everglades Cheese & (Florida) Cracker Festival, Everglades City, Florida, USA. After it had been cooked, the sandwich measured 1.52 m x 3.05 m x 6.35 cm (5 ft x 10 ft 0.5 in x 2.5 in) and 3.42 m (11 ft 2.75 in) across the diagonal.

TALLEST SAND SCULPTURE

On 12 July 2001, the Holland Sand Sculpture company (Netherlands) created a sand sculpture of a fairy castle (left) measuring 20.91 m (68 ft 7.2 in) in height.

LARGEST ICE CREAM SCOOP PYRAMID
Executives, franchisees and flavour experts from ice cream company Baskin-Robbins International (USA) constructed the world's largest ice cream scoop pyramid (above), using 3,100 scoops of ice cream, in Maui, Hawaii, USA, on 18 May 2000. The 21-layer pyramid weighed a massive 362.87 kg (800 lb) and stood about 1.21 m (4 ft) high for approximately 45 minutes.

LARGEST BAG OF CHIPS
On 20 January 2001, Dirk Haverals (Belgium) and a team of 15 people prepared the world's largest bag of chips at Opwijk Heivelds Sportscentre, Belgium. The full bag measured 2.62 m (8 ft 7 in) in height and contained 180.212 kg (397.29 lb) of chips.

LONGEST STRAND OF PASTA
Michael Sorge (USA) cooked a strand of fettuccine pasta measuring 127.4 m (418 ft) long at Sorge's Restaurant, New York City, USA, on 2 June 2001.

LARGEST WATERING CAN
A giant galvanised-steel watering can was delivered to Utica Zoo, Utica, New York, USA, on 5 December 2000. It weighs 900 kg (2,000 lb) and measures 4.7 m (15.5 ft) high, with a diameter of 3.65 m (12 ft).

HEAVIEST CHOCOLATE MODEL
A 4.2 x 4.2 x 2 m (13 x 13 x 6 ft) model of a house made out of chocolate that weighed 5.08 tonnes (11,200 lb), was created by José Rafael Palermo (Argentina) in Córdoba, Argentina, between 8 and 23 March 1997.

LARGEST INDIVIDUAL FIREWORK
The 'Super Crown' firework is 0.6 m (2 ft) tall, has a 41 cm (16 in) shell and is packed with 34 kg (75 lb) of gunpowder and explosives. A hole 2 m (6 ft) deep must be dug to house the mortar. These monsters take about eight seconds to reach 488 m (1,600 ft), before a second charge at the shell's core scatters golden stars across 0.5 km (0.25 mile), each one burning for a further nine seconds.

LONGEST CHOCOLATE SALAMI
The world's longest chocolate salami, measuring 75 m (246 ft), was made at the Torre de Belém, Lisbon, Portugal, on 1 June 2001. Chocolate salami is a popular and easy-to-make local delicacy. The record-breaking salami weighed about 500 kg (1,100 lb) and ingredients included 200 kg (440 lb) biscuits, 50 kg (110 lb) chocolate powder and 2,000 eggs.

LARGEST NUDE PHOTO SHOOT
On 7 October 2001, in Melbourne, Vic, Australia, 4,000 volunteers stripped naked in the morning air for a mass nude photo shoot organised by artist Spencer Tunick (USA).

LARGEST PRETZEL
The world's largest hand-rolled soft pretzel was baked in conjunction with the Children's Miracle Network at a fundraiser in Lake Charles, Louisiana, USA, on 3 June 2000. The pretzel weighed 195 kg (431 lb).

LARGEST STITCHED TEDDY BEAR
The largest stitched teddy bear measured 11.79 m (38 ft 8.5 in) in length on 21 January 2001 and was constructed by Dana Warren (USA) of Edmond, Oklahoma, USA.

LARGEST MURAL
The Pueblo Levee Project in Pueblo, Colorado, USA, has produced the world's largest mural, covering an area 16,554.8 m² (178,200 ft²). Begun in the 1970s, the mural has contributions from thousands of artists aged from five to 65. It costs nothing to add your own art to the mural using recycled paint. The connected murals are almost 3.21 km (2 miles) long and 17.67 m (58 ft) tall.

LARGEST SERVING OF FISH AND CHIPS
James Broughall and Peter Stead (both UK), prepared the world's largest serving of fish and chips on 2 May 2001, from the premises of Fish'n'Chick'n at the Thorley Centre, Bishops Stortford, Herts, UK. The fish, when battered and fried, weighed 5.33 kg (11.75 lb), and the chips weighed 6.35 kg (13.9 lb).

LONGEST SOFA
In September 2001, Industrie Natuzzi SPA (Italy) created the world's longest sofa (which was crescent-shaped). It measured 35.11 m (115 ft 2 in) along the outside edge and 24.86 m (81 ft 6 in) along the inside edge. A total of 250 m² (2,690 ft²) of red leather was used in its construction.

LARGEST DISCO BALL
A disco ball measuring 2.41 m (7 ft 11.25 in) in diameter and weighing 137.89 kg (304 lb), was installed at the Mayan Club, Los Angeles, California, USA. Made by Big Millennium Balls (USA), it consists of 6,900 mirror squares, each measuring 5 x 5 cm (2 x 2 in).

LARGEST WEDDING CAKE
Serendipity 3 Restaurant and World of Chantilly (both USA) created the world's largest wedding cake weighing 693.99 kg (1,530 lb) and measuring 2.74 m (9 ft) tall. It was displayed at Serendipity Restaurant, New York City, USA, on 14 February 2001. Ingredients included 104.3 kg (230 lb) of flour and 181.4 kg (400 lb) of marzipan and icing.

LARGEST COCKTAIL
A margarita (above) measuring 26,645 litres (5,861 gal) was made on 17 May 2001 by staff at Jimmy Buffet's Margaritaville and Mott's Inc, Universal City Walk, Orlando, Florida, USA. It was sold to raise money for local charities.

LARGEST TRUFFLE

A white truffle (*Eutuberaceae tuber*) weighing 1.31 kg (2 lb 8 oz) was found by Giancarlo Zigante (Croatia) on 2 November 1999 near Buje, Croatia. Measuring 19.5 cm (7.67 in) long, 12.4 cm (4.8 in) wide and 13.5 cm (5.3 in) high, it was estimated to be worth £3,175 (then $5,080).

LARGEST TOOTHPICK SCULPTURE

In 2000, the William Adams Middle School Art Club, Alice, Texas, USA, used over one million toothpicks to create a sculpture 0.76 m (2 ft 6 in) wide, 5.18 m (17 ft) long, and 2.28 m (7 ft 6 in) high.

LARGEST ICE CREAM SUNDAE

An ice cream sundae weighing 24.91 tonnes (54,914 lb 13 oz) was made by Palm Dairies Ltd, supervised by Mike Rogiani (Canada), in Edmonton, Alberta, Canada, on 24 July 1988. The ingredients were 20.27 tonnes (44,689 lb 8 oz) of ice cream, 4.39 tonnes (9,688 lb 2 oz) of syrup and 243.7 kg (537 lb 3 oz) of topping.

LARGEST RAVIOLI MEAL

The world's largest ravioli meal consisted of 224,040 Tesco Italiano Fresh Pasta individual raviolis made by Geest Plc (UK), which was served at the pre-race Pasta Party for the Bupa Great North Run, South Shields, Tyne & Wear, UK, on 15 September 2001. A total of 11,202 bowls were served: that's 1.6 tonnes (3,527 lb) of pasta.

LARGEST RANGOLI PATTERN

Rangoli is a form of traditional Indian doorstep art made with rice powder. On 8 July 2000 at Belgrave Mela, Leicester, UK, Pravin Mistry and Sangita Patel (both UK) organized the world's largest Rangoli pattern. It measured 9.16 x 9.16 m (30 ft 1 in x 30 ft 1 in).

LARGEST CHALK PAVEMENT ART

On 23 June 2001 in Canton, Michigan, USA, the Boys and Girls Club of Detroit (USA) teamed up with Boomerang Cartoon Network and Direct TV (both USA) to create the world's largest chalk pavement art, which measured 2,684.89 m^2 (28,900 ft^2). The drawing used 14,000 pieces of coloured chalk and featured cartoon characters 'Huckleberry Hound' and 'Top Cat'.

LARGEST HANDWOVEN CARPET

Forty weavers from the Bakharden Art Carpet-Making Enterprise of Turkmenhaly State Join-Stock Corporation, near Ashgabat, Turkmenistan, created a carpet 14 m (45.9 ft) long and 21.5 m (70.5 ft) wide between 9 February and 10 October 2001. The 301 m^2 (3,240 ft^2) pure wool carpet had 304,000 knots per m^2 (10 ft^2).

LARGEST PAINTING BY ONE ARTIST

Eric Waugh (Canada) unveiled his 3,846.18-m^2 (41,400-ft^2) painting, entitled *Hero*, at the North Carolina Museum of Art, Raleigh, North Carolina, USA, on World AIDS Day, 1 December 2001. *Hero* is twice the height of the Statue of Liberty.

LONGEST SAUSAGE

An incredible 59.14-km (36.75-mile) sausage was made by JJ Tranfield on behalf of Asda Stores Plc (UK), at Sheffield, Yorkshire, UK, between 27 and 29 October 2000.

LARGEST SECURITY LOCK

Sheikh Zafar Iqbal (Pakistan, below) has created the world's largest working lock and key. Made of steel, the security lock measures 67.3 x 39.6 x 12.4 cm (26.5 x 15.6 x 4.9 in) and weighs 96.3 kg (212.3 lb).

LARGEST COLLECTION OF BEATLES MEMORABILIA

By 9 August 2001, Rodolfo Renato Vazquez (Argentina) had amassed 5,612 individual items of Beatle-related memorabilia. Books, posters, stage passes and even life-size figures of the 'Fab Four' are now housed in the attic of his house in Buenos Aires, Argentina. His collection has toured the country and was visited in 1997 by original Beatles drummer Pete Best (UK).

LARGEST COLLECTION OF CELEBRITY HAIR

John Reznikoff (USA) has accumulated a collection of hair from 115 different historical celebrities. This assortment of famous locks is insured for $1 million (£700,000) and includes genuine tresses from the heads of Abraham Lincoln, John F Kennedy, Marilyn Monroe, Albert Einstein, Napoleon, Elvis Presley, King Charles I and Charles Dickens.

LARGEST MODEL CAR COLLECTION

Since 1990, Suhail Mohammed Al Zarooni (UAE) has collected a fleet of more than 1,500 individual miniature model cars.

LARGEST COLLECTION OF ROYAL MEMORABILIA

Anita Atkinson (UK) has accumulated a total number of 1,781 different items of royal memorabilia of the British monarchy, including dishes, commemorative books and magazines.

LARGEST COLLECTION OF GNOMES AND PIXIES

Since 1978, Ann Atkin (UK) has collected a total of 2,010 gnomes and pixies, all of whom live in a 1.61-ha (4-acre) woodland gnome reserve. The reserve enjoys an average of 25,000 visitors per year, who are all encouraged to don hats and temporarily become gnomes for their magical journey through the woodland.

LARGEST KEYRING COLLECTION

Over 20 years, Kurt Meadows (USA) had amassed a total of 24,810 unduplicated keyrings by April 2001.

LARGEST HANDCUFF COLLECTION

Locksmith Chris Gower (UK) has 530 pairs of antique and modern handcuffs, which he has been collecting since 1968. His favourite item in the collection is a famous pair of Plug Lock Figure '8' leg-irons that legendary escapologist Harry Houdini (USA) failed to escape from in 1903.

LARGEST COLLECTION OF COLOURED VINYL RECORDS

Alessandro Benedetti (Italy) has 934 music records made of coloured vinyl. His collection is made up of 647 LPs (601 coloured, 46 with pictures) and 287 singles (255 coloured, 13 with pictures and 19 in unusual shapes).

LARGEST BANDAID COLLECTION

Brian Viner (UK) has 3,750 different types of unused bandaids, varying in colour, style, shape and size.

LARGEST CHAMBER POT COLLECTION

Manfred Klauda (Germany) has amassed a collection of 9,400 chamber pots, the earliest dating from the 16th century. His collection can be seen at the Zentrum für, Aubergewöhnliche Museen, Munich, Germany.

LARGEST CONDOM COLLECTION

Amatore Bolzoni (Italy) has 1,947 condoms, collected since the 1980s. The oldest dates from the 19th-century and is made from a sheep's bowel

LARGEST TIE PIN COLLECTION

Murray Steinberg (USA) has collected 678 tie pins since his bar mitzvah in February 1937, when he was given a pin by his brother.

LARGEST LIPSTICK PRINT COLLECTION

Breakthrough Breast Cancer and Avon Cosmetics accumulated 3,201 lipstick prints as part of their 'Kiss Goodbye to Breast Cancer' campaign. The kisses were collected on a mechandise flyer with a tear slip sent out to Avon customers or on a postcard distributed through retailers. Once imprinted with a lipstick kiss and sent back, the lip prints were presented to 10 Downing Street on 25 October 1999.

LARGEST COLLECTION OF INSTRUMENTS MADE FROM WOODEN MATCHSTICKS

Tony Hall (UK) owns 10 playable musical instruments made entirely from matchsticks. Constructed from used wooden matches by Tony's deceased father Jack, the collection comprises: violin, chin-rest and bow; Neopolitan mandolin; acoustic guitar; flat-back mandolin; tenor banjo; bones (percussion); castanets; descant recorder; drumsticks and ukulele. The first instrument was finished in 1936, and a total of 106,000 matches have been used to construct the collection.

LARGEST COLLECTION OF 'DO NOT DISTURB' SIGNS

Since 1985, Jean Francois Vernetti (Switzerland) has collected 1,750 'Do Not Disturb' signs from hotels in 100 countries across the world. He is aiming to cover all 191 countries.

LARGEST BARBIE DOLL COLLECTION

Tony Mattia (UK, above), has collected 1,125 Barbie dolls – about one half of all the Barbie models produced since 1959, including many versions of Barbie's boyfriend Ken. Tony changes the costume of every doll once a month.

LARGEST COLLECTION OF ROAD CONES

David Morgan (UK) has put together a collection of 137 traffic cones – each of them different. He owns a cone from about two-thirds of all cone types ever made.

LARGEST COLLECTION OF STAR WARS MEMORABILIA

Jason Joiner (UK), a special effects expert who worked on the most recent *Star Wars* films, has a collection of more than 20,000 *Star Wars* items, including toys, cards and books. In addition to this collection, Joiner has one of the original C-3PO robots, an original R2-D2 and an original Darth Vader costume.

LARGEST CLOTHING LABEL COLLECTION

The world's largest collection of clothing labels is owned by Leonie Robroek (Netherlands), who has been collecting them since 1992 and has amassed 1,729 different types.

LARGEST COLLECTION OF NAIL CLIPPERS

André Ludwick (South Africa) has collected 505 pairs of nail clippers since 1971. He began collecting them on a visit to Israel, where he bought some clippers as souvenirs, and now his collection is housed in a huge display cabinet. His favourite pair was hand-made by a blacksmith in 1935 and is one of the oldest in his collection.

LARGEST AEROPLANE SICK-BAG COLLECTION

Niek Vermeulen (Netherlands) has 3,139 airline sickness bags from 470 different airlines, topping a list of over 50 serious airsickness bag collectors. His favourite is a bag from a NASA space shuttle.

LARGEST FRIDGE MAGNET COLLECTION

Louise J Greenfarb (USA) has collected over 29,000 refrigerator magnets in the past 30 years.

LARGEST PIGGY BANK COLLECTION

Since 1957, Ove Nordström (Sweden), has collected 5,111 different piggy banks from 40 different countries.

LARGEST COLLECTION OF CONAN THE BARBARIAN MEMORABILIA

Over a span of 30 years, Robert and Patricia Leffler (both USA, below centre), have amassed a collection of 2,418 items of memorabilia relating to Robert E Howard's (USA) fantasy character Conan the Barbarian. Their collection includes comic books, movie posters, statues and shields.

PENKNIFE WITH THE MOST BLADES

The Year Knife (above), which was originally made in 1822 by cutlers Joseph Rodgers & Sons (UK), initially had 1,822 blades. A blade was then added every year, with occasional gaps. The penknife was acquired by Britain's largest hand-tool manufacturers, Stanley Works Ltd, in 1969. In 1999 the penknife was restored and a final silver blade was added to mark the coming of the year 2000.

PEN WITH THE MOST TOOLS

The PenTool is a pen that features 12 interchangeable attachments. They are: hole punch, short cutting blade, long cutting blade, wire stripper/small nail or staple remover, Phillips-head screwdriver, miniature saw, stainless-steel file, flat-head screwdriver, scraper, tweezers, stainless-steel fork and, of course, a writing pen.

EARLIEST HOVERCRAFT PATENT

The earliest patent relating to air-cushioned craft was applied for in 1877 by Sir John I Thornycroft (UK). The idea was developed by Toivo Kaario (Finland) in 1935.

EARLIEST RADIO PATENT

The first patent for a communication system by means of electro-magnetic waves was granted to the Italian-Irish Marchese Guglielmo Marconi on 2 June 1896.

LARGEST PATENT CASE AWARD

Litton Industries Inc (USA) was awarded $1.2 billion (£799 million) in damages from Honeywell Inc (USA) in Los Angeles, California, USA, on 31 August 1993. The award was made after a jury decided that Honeywell had violated a Litton patent covering airline navigation systems. Litton filed a lawsuit in March 1990 and this was followed by a counterclaim from Honeywell nine months later.

MOST WIDESPREAD FASTENING DEVICE

In 1893 Whitcomb Judson (USA) patented a Clasp Locker, the precursor of the modern zip fastener. Gideon Sundback (Sweden) rose to the position of head designer at Judson's company and after years of refinement he came up with the zip we know today in December 1913, registering a patent in 1917.

FIRST PRODUCTION HELICOPTER

Igor Sikorsky, originally from Ukraine, designed the world's first successful multi-motor aeroplane and the world's first genuine production helicopter. Sikorsky's US patent No 1,994,488, filed on 27 June 1931, marked the crucial breakthrough in helicopter technology.

MOST DIRECTIONAL SOUND SYSTEM

The Audio Spotlight transmits ultrasonic sound waves in a narrow beam of sound. These sound waves then become audible as they travel through the air, and the result is a system that can project sound over 100 m (328 ft), in a beam between two and five degrees wide. Possible uses include art galleries, where an observer in front of a painting could hear a commentary that is totally inaudible to anybody who is around 30 cm (1 ft) to one side.

MOST VERSATILE PEN

The Space Pen range made by Fisher Space Pen Company (USA) use special nitrogen-pressurized cartridges to dispense visco-elastic ink. This allows the pens to work perfectly upside down and under a range of severe environmental conditions, including extreme hot and cold, underwater, and even in the zero gravity of space. The pens were first used in space on the Apollo 7 mission in 1968 and have become the standard pen for astronauts, including those currently on board the International Space Station.

MOST ENERGY-EFFICIENT SHOE

The Electric Shoe Company was founded in March 2000 by British inventor Trevor Baylis and shoemakers Texon International, who are based in Leicester, UK. The company's aim is to develop a shoe that generates electricity through the act of walking. Prototypes were tested in August 2000 by Baylis and Texon's John Grantham (UK) during a 120-km (75-mile) trek into the Namibian desert. At the end of the walk, Baylis was able to make a successful phone call to Richard Branson, the British entrepreneur, using a mobile phone that had been charged by the shoes.

EARLIEST BALLPOINT PEN

The Hungarian journalist László Biro created the first ballpoint pen in 1938, in collaboration with his brother Georg. One of the first organizations to exploit Biro's idea was the British Royal Air Force, whose pilots needed a pen that would not leak at high altitudes. The biro's success with the RAF earned it widespread popularity.

FIRST POWER-DRIVEN FLIGHT

The first controlled and sustained power-driven flight was at Kitty Hawk, North Carolina, USA, at 10:35 am on 17 December 1903, when Orville Wright (USA) flew the Flyer I (above) for 36.5 m (120 ft) for a period of 12 seconds.

EARLIEST RADIO TRANSMISSION

The earliest description of a radio transmission system was written by American Dr Mahlon Laomis on 21 July 1864. It was demonstrated between two kites more than 22 km (14 miles) apart at Bear's Den, Loudoun County, Virginia, USA, in October 1866. He received US patent No 129,971, entitled Improvement in Telegraphing, on 20 July 1872.

EARLIEST TAPE RECORDING

Magnetic recording was invented in 1898 by Valdemar Poulsen (Denmark) with his steel-wire Telegraphone (US patent No 661,619). Inventor Fritz Pfleumer (Germany) introduced tape in 1928 (German patent No 500,900). Tapes were first used at the Blattner Studios (UK) in 1929. Plastic tapes were devised by BASF (Germany) between 1932 and 1935, but were not marketed until 1950 by Recording Associates (USA).

MOST SUCCESSFUL CLOCKWORK RADIO

In 1993 Trevor Baylis (UK) created a radio driven by a spring system that, when wound for several seconds, gave a few minutes of uninterrputed airplay. Freeplay Energy (UK) refined his idea and have now produced more than 2.5 million units of these self-sufficient wind-up radios.

OLDEST EXPLOSIVE

As early as the 13th century AD, 'black powder' was in use in Europe. This mixture of charcoal, potassium nitrate and sulphur is the oldest explosive in the world and was not superseded until 1866, when Alfred Nobel (Sweden), who gave his name to the Nobel prize, found a way to control nitroglycerine.

PUBLICATION WITH THE MOST USELESS INVENTIONS

Chindogu, Japanese for 'weird tool', has been popularized by Kenji Kawakami (Japan). It is the art of creating inventions that appear to be useful at first glance but upon closer inspection reveal their utter uselessness. Kawakami has published two books of *chindogu* inventions. Examples include the camera hat (below), which allows the wearer to take a 360° picture of their immediate surroundings.

MOST EXPENSIVE INSECT

A giant 80-mm (3-in) stag beetle (*Dorcus hopei*) is reported to have been sold for ¥10,035,000 (£57,000 or $90,000) in Tokyo on 19 August 1999. A 36-year-old company president bought it for his collection, but he remains unidentified for fear of being targeted by thieves.

MOST VALUABLE POP MEMORABILIA

John Lennon's (UK) 1965 Phantom V Rolls Royce was bought for $2,229,000 (£1,768,000) at Sotheby's, New York City, USA, on 29 June 1985 by Jim Pattison (Canada), Chairman of the Expo 86 World Fair in Vancouver, BC, Canada.

MOST VALUABLE HOT CROSS BUN

A hot cross bun baked in 1829 in Stepney, London, UK, was bought by Bill Foster (UK) for £155 ($218) at the Antiques for Everyone show at the NEC in Birmingham, West Midlands, UK, on 27 April 2000. It was originally made to hang in the kitchen to ward off evil spirits.

MOST VALUABLE 20TH-CENTURY TEAPOT

A black teapot made by Dame Lucie Rie (UK) in 1938 was sold at Phillips, London, UK, for £11,270 ($18,522) in 1999. This was a record for any 20th-century teapot and also for any piece from Rie's Vienna period.

MOST EXPENSIVE SPORTS SHOES

The most expensive sports shoes ever marketed were mink-lined golf shoes with 18-carat gold embellishments and ruby-tipped spikes. They were made by Stylo Matchmakers International (UK) and cost £13,600 ($20,400) per pair.

MOST VALUABLE BASEBALL ITEMS

The baseball glove used by New York Yankee Lou Gehrig (USA) for his final game on 30 April 1939, was sold for $389,500 (£236,778) at Sotheby's, New York, USA, on 29 September 1999.

On 12 January 1999, a baseball was sold at Guernsey's auction house, New York City, USA, for $3,054,000 (£1,848,780). This famous baseball was the one hit by Mark McGwire (USA) of the St Louis Cardinals for his 70th and final home run in his record-setting 1998 season.

MOST EXPENSIVE BRA

The 'Red Hot Fantasy' bra, created by Victoria's Secret (USA) is priced at $15 million (£10 million). The fiery-red bra contains over 1,300 precious stones, including 300 carats of Thai rubies set among dazzling diamonds.

MOST VALUABLE BISCUIT

At an auction at Christie's, London, UK, on 18 April 2000, art dealer Johnny Van Haeften (UK) bought a biscuit from Sir Ernest Shackleton's (UK) failed 1907–09 expedition to the South Pole. He paid £4,935 ($7,798).

MOST VALUABLE DENIM JACKET

A sleeveless Lee denim jacket owned and worn by Madonna (USA) for a photo shoot by Marcus Leatherdale (Canada) in 1985, was bought for $22,000 (£15,473) on 30 May 2001 at a Sotheby's online auction. Well worn in, the back of the jacket is covered in graffiti. It was auctioned along with a photo of the star wearing it.

MOST VALUABLE CHRISTMAS CARD

The world's most valuable Christmas card was sold at auction in Devizes, Wiltshire, UK, on 24 November 2001, for £20,000 ($28,000). It was bought by an anonymous bidder. Considered to be the world's first Christmas card, it measures 13 x 8 cm (5 x 3 in) and was hand-coloured by the London illustrator John Calcott Horsley. It was sent by Sir Henry Cole (UK) to his grandmother in 1843. Only 1,000 were lithographed and sold at one shilling each. Of the originals, only 12 still exist.

MOST VALUABLE LYRICS

In February 1998 the autographed lyrics to 'Candle In The Wind 1997' sold for $442,500 (£240,963) in Los Angeles, California, USA. The lyrics were rewritten by Bernie Taupin (UK) and the song was performed by Elton John (UK) at the funeral of Diana, Princess of Wales, in September 1997. The three-page signed manuscript, was bought by the Lund Foundation For Children, which funds programmes for disadvantaged children.

MOST VALUABLE FILM SCRIPT

Clark Gable's (USA) personal film script from *Gone With the Wind* (USA, 1939) sold for $244,500 (£152,852) to Steven Spielberg (USA) at Christie's, Los Angeles, California, USA, on 15 December 1996.

MOST VALUABLE FILM POSTER

A one-sheet poster for the Universal film *The Mummy* (USA, 1932) sold for $453,500 (£282,431) at Sotheby's, New York City, USA, on 7 March 1997.

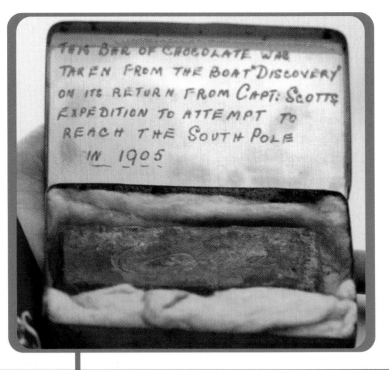

MOST VALUABLE CHOCOLATE BAR

A 100-year-old, 10-cm-long (4-in) Cadbury's chocolate bar (above), which went on Captain Robert Scott's (UK) 1901–04 Antarctic expedition, was bought for £470 ($694) by an anonymous buyer at Christie's, London, UK, on 25 September 2001.

MOST VALUABLE PAIR OF JEANS

A pair of jeans – the oldest known pair – reported to have been sold 120 years ago to a worker for $1, were sold for $46,532 (£33,039) through an internet auction on eBay on 25 May 2001. Bought by jeans maker Levi Strauss, they were discovered buried in the mud of a mining town in Nevada and were probably manufactured in Manchester, New Hampshire, USA, sometime between 1880 and 1885.

MOST VALUABLE DIARY

The journal kept by Dr Alexander Macklin (UK), a surgeon on Sir Ernest Shackleton's (UK) epic *Endurance* expedition of 1914–17, was sold at Christie's, London, UK, on 25 September 2001, for £104,950 ($153,573).

MOST VALUABLE TEDDY BEAR

A 1904 Steiff bear named Teddy Girl sold for £110,000 ($170,830) – more than 18 times the estimate – at Christie's, London, UK, on 5 December 1994.

MOST EXPENSIVE UMBRELLA

Hung Hee Ho (Hong Kong) made six umbrellas from buffalo skin for a US customer in May 1994, at a cost of HKD$2,000 (£167 or $250) each.

MOST EXPENSIVE POST-IT® NOTE

Sold for £640 ($925), the most expensive Post-it® Note features a pastel and charcoal work called *After Rembrandt* by artist RB Kitaj (USA). To celebrate the 20th anniversary of the Post-it® Note, artists were asked to create works of art on Post-it® Notes that were then auctioned online between 13 and 20 December 2000, raising over £5,000 ($7,300) for charity.

MOST VALUABLE TOY SOLDIER

A 1963 prototype GI Joe (right), was purchased by Matt Babek (USA) for $14,000 (£8,747) on 3 December 1999, at an eBay online auction. The original 12-inch GI Joe toys with 21 movable parts were sold between 1964–78 and then cost $4 (£2.50) each. Matt now keeps the figure in a bank vault.

MOST VALUABLE FOOTBALL PROGRAMME

A programme for the FA Charity Shield replay between Manchester United and Queens Park Rangers, played at Stamford Bridge, London, UK, on 29 April 1908, was sold by Phillips at Old Trafford, Manchester, UK, for £8,050 ($12,759) on 10 April 2000. The programme originally cost one penny.

MOST VALUABLE FOOTBALL SHIRT

The No 10 shirt worn by Pelé (Brazil) in the 1970 World Cup final was sold at Christie's, London, UK, on 27 March 2002 for £157,750 ($220,850), over three times the expected price. It was sold by Italian international Roberto Rosato who exchanged shirts with Pelé after Brazil's 4-1 victory.

MOST VALUABLE SCULPTURE BY A LIVING ARTIST

On 15 May 2001 *Michael Jackson and Bubbles* (above), a porcelain sculpture created in 1988 by Jeff Koons (USA), sold for $5,616,750 (£3,945,344) at Sotheby's, New York City, USA. It measures 106.7 x 179.1 x 82.6 cm (42 x 70.5 x 32.5 in).

MOST EXPENSIVE MAGAZINE

Visionaire magazine, created by Stephan Gan (USA), is sold at a starting price of $175 (£120) per issue. However, collectors are said to pay up to $5,000 (£3,500) for hard-to-find issues such as No. 18, which came in its own Louis Vuitton portfolio case.

MOST VALUABLE CIGARS

On 16 November 1997 at Christie's, London, UK, an Asian buyer paid a record £9,980 ($16,349) for 25 Trinidad cigars made by the Cuban National Factory.

MOST VALUABLE COMIC

A first edition copy of *Action Comics*, from June 1938, sold for $100,000 (£68,771) in 1997. Featuring the first appearance of 'Superman', it is now thought to be worth an astonishing $185,000 (£115,625).

MOST VALUABLE DIAMOND, PER CARAT

The highest price paid for a diamond, per carat, is $926,315.79 (£555,678), for a 0.95-carat fancy purple-red stone sold at Christie's, New York City, USA, on 28 April 1987.

MOST VALUABLE JEWELLERY BOX

A Cartier jewelled vanity case, set with a fragment of ancient Egyptian steel, was sold at Christie's, New York City, USA, for $189,000 (£127,651) on 17 November 1993.

MOST EXPENSIVE WALLET

A platinum-cornered, diamond-studded crocodile creation made by Louis Quatorze of Paris and Mikimoto of Tokyo, sold in September 1984 for £56,000 ($74,816).

MOST EXPENSIVE COMMERCIALLY AVAILABLE WRISTWATCH

In 1999 Gianni Vivé Sulman of London, UK (once makers of the world's most expensive perfume), produced a watch costing more than $520,000 (£325,000) plus taxes. Only five are to be made every year.

MOST VALUABLE PEN

A Japanese collector paid a record price of FF1.3 million (£122,677 or $218,007) in February 1988 for the 'Anémone' fountain pen made by Réden, France. It was encrusted with 600 different precious stones, including emeralds, amethysts, rubies, sapphires and onyx, and took craftsmen more than a year to make.

MOST EXPENSIVE PEN

The world's most expensive pen is 'La Modernista Diamonds' made by Caran d'Ache, Geneva, Switzerland, which was on sale in Harrods, London, UK, for £169,000 ($265,000) from September to December 1999.

MOST EXPENSIVE CREDIT CARD

The American Express Centurion credit card, also known as the 'Black Card', has an annual fee of $1,000 (£700) and is only open to those with a minimum income of $215,000 (£150,000) per annum. The Black Card has no spending limits and is offered by invitation only to selected individuals who travel frequently, entertain a great deal, and expect exceptional service.

MOST EXPENSIVE MOBILE PHONE

A mobile phone designed by David Morris International of London, UK, was sold for £66,629 ($104,050) in 1996. Made entirely from 18-carat gold, the one-off mobile had a keypad encrusted with pink and white diamonds.

MOST EXPENSIVE PAIR OF JEANS

Gucci 'genius jeans' – complete with African beading, tribal feathers and strategically placed rips and silver buttons and rivets – were sold in Gucci stores for £1,840 ($3,134) after their launch in Milan, Italy, in October 1998.

MOST EXPENSIVE SINGLE PURCHASE OF WHISKY

On 16 November 2000 Turkey-based businessman Norman Shelley (UK), purchased a collection of 76 bottles of Macallan malt whisky at the current value of £231,417.90 ($341,154). The oldest bottle dated from 1856.

MOST EXPENSIVE SPIRIT

A bottle of 60-year-old Macallan malt whisky sold for £11,000 ($15,663) at Fortnum & Mason, London, UK, in February 2000.

MOST VALUABLE WINE BOTTLE

A record £105,000 ($151,840) was paid for a bottle of 1787 Château Lafite claret, sold to Christopher Forbes (USA) at Christie's, London, UK, on 5 December 1985.

MOST VALUABLE FURNITURE

The highest price paid for a single piece of furniture is £8.58 million ($15.1 million) at Christie's, London, UK, on 5 July 1990. This was the auction price for the 18th-century Italian Badminton cabinet owned by the Duke of Beaufort (UK).

MOST VALUABLE WORK BY SHAKESPEARE

One of only five copies of William Shakespeare's (UK) First Folio, dated 1623, was sold at Christie's, New York City, USA, on 8 October 2001 for $6,166,000 (£4,156,947). This is the highest price ever paid for a 17th-century book.

MOST EXPENSIVE GLASS OF WINE

A somewhat sobering FF8,600 (£982 or $1,382.80) was paid for the first glass of 1993 Beaujolais Nouveau released in Beaune (from Maison Jaffelin), in the wine region of Burgundy, France. It was bought by Robert Denby (UK) at Pickwick's, a British-themed pub in Beaune, on 18 November 1993.

MOST VALUABLE FISH

The high cost of the eggs from the Russian sturgeon (*Huso huso*) make it the world's most expensive fish. One 1,227-kg (2,706-lb) female caught in the Tikhaya Sosna River, Russia, in 1924, yielded 245 kg (540 lb) of best quality caviar, worth nearly $289,000 (£203,000) in today's market.

MOST VALUABLE ILLUSTRATED MANUSCRIPT

Leonardo da Vinci's (Italy) illustrated manuscript known as the *Codex Hammer*, in which he predicted the invention of the submarine and the steam engine, sold for a record $30.8 million (£19,388,141) at Christie's, New York City, USA, on 11 November 1994. The only Leonardo manuscript now in private hands, it was bought by Microsoft boss Bill Gates (USA).

GEMSTONE MOST IN DEMAND

Global sales from the world's largest diamond trading centre in Antwerp, Belgium, totalled £17.2 billion ($25.8 billion) in 2000, a record since trading began in the 15th century. A recent diamond record-breaker was the most valuable piece of jewellery made for a film, a necklace (right) – with 1,308 diamonds – worn by Nicole Kidman (Australia) in the film *Moulin Rouge* (AUS/USA, 2001), valued at $1 million (£660,000).

MOST VALUABLE SCULPTURE SOLD AT AUCTION

The most valuable sculpture sold at auction is Alberto Giacometti's (Italy) *Grande femme debout I*, conceived in 1960 and cast in 1962, which was sold at Christie's, New York City, USA, on 8 November 2000 for $14,306,000 (£10,004,196).

MOST VALUABLE CELLO

The highest ever auction price for a cello is £682,000 ($1,213,278) paid at Sotheby's, London, on 22 June 1988 for a Stradivarius known as the 'Cholmondeley'. The instrument was made in Cremona, Italy, c. 1698.

MOST VALUABLE JAZZ INSTRUMENT

A saxophone once owned by Charlie Parker (USA) sold for £93,500 ($144,500) at Christie's London, UK, on 7 September 1994.

MOST VALUABLE VIOLIN

A violin made by Guarneri del Gesu (Italy) in 1742 and owned by the late Yehudi Menuhin (USA), was sold for an undisclosed amount to an anonymous collector in Zurich, Switzerland, on 29 October 1999. Swiss dealer Musik Hug would not disclose the price but said it was "approximately $1.25 million (£781,250) above what had ever been paid for a violin" – which was £947,500 ($1,360,927) in 1998.

MOST EXPENSIVE PERFUME

'Parfum VI' designed by perfumer Arthur Burnham (UK), which comes in a 10-cm (4-in) bottle (made with platinum, 24-carat gold, rubies and diamonds), was launched in June 2000 at a cost of £47,500 ($71,380). Inspired by the Phantom VI Rolls-Royce, only 173 were made.

TALLEST RESIDENTIAL BUILDING

The Trump World Tower (above) in New York City, USA, is the world's tallest purely residential building, standing 262.5 m (861 ft) high. The tower has 72 storeys, although the luxuriously lofty ceilings make it taller than most other buildings with a similar number of floors.

TALLEST OBSERVATION WHEEL

The 'British Airways London Eye', designed by architects David Marks and Julia Barfield (both UK), has a diameter and height of 135 m (443 ft) and made its first 'flight' on 1 February 2000. It is the fourth-tallest structure in London, UK, and can carry up to 800 passengers.

TALLEST CINEMA

The world's tallest cinema complex is the UGC Cinema, Glasgow, Strathclyde, UK, with an overall height of 62 m (203 ft 4.9 in). It holds 18 screens, has a seating capacity of 4,277 and is 12 storeys high. The cinema opened on 21 September 2001.

TALLEST OPERA HOUSE

The Civic Opera House at 20 North Wacker Drive in Chicago, Illinois, USA, is an imposing 45-storey skyscraper made from limestone and is able to accommodate 3,563 people. The building opened in 1929.

TALLEST OFFICE BUILDING

In March 1996, the Petronas Towers in Kuala Lumpur, Malaysia, overtook the Sears Tower's record as the world's tallest office building. Stainless-steel pinnacles 73.5 m (241 ft) long placed on top of the 88-storey towers brought their height to 451.9 m (1,482 ft 8 in). The Sears Tower has 110 storeys and is 443 m (1,453 ft 6 in) tall.

TALLEST TOTEM POLE

A totem pole 54.94 m (180 ft 3 in) tall, called 'Spirit of Lekwammen' ('land of the winds'), was raised on 4 August 1994 at Victoria, British Columbia, Canada, prior to the Commonwealth Games held there that year.

TALLEST CATHEDRAL SPIRE

The world's tallest cathedral spire is that of the Protestant cathedral of Ulm in Germany. Work on the building began in 1377, but the tower in the centre of the west façade, which is 160.9 m (528 ft) high, was not completed until 1890.

TALLEST MINARET

The tallest minaret in the world is that of the Great Hassan II Mosque, Casablanca, Morocco, which is 200 m (656 ft) high. The cost of the mosque's construction was 5 billion dirhams (£360 million or $513.5 million). Among minarets of earlier centuries the tallest is the Qutb Minar, south of New Delhi, India, built in 1194 to a height of 72.54 m (238 ft).

TALLEST CHIMNEY

The coal power-plant No 2 stack at Ekibastuz, Kazakhstan, completed in 1987, is 420 m (1,378 ft) tall. Its diameter tapers from 44 m (144 ft) at the base to 14.2 m (46 ft 7 in) at the top, and it weighs 60,000 tonnes (132,277,200 lb). The stack is on a par with the world's fourth-tallest office building, Shanghai's Jin Mao Tower, which is 421 m (1,381 ft) tall.

TALLEST BUILDING

The tallest free-standing tower in the world is the $63-million (£28-million) CN Tower in Toronto, Canada, which rises to 553.34 m (1,815 ft 5 in). Excavation for the erection of the 130,000-tonne (286,600,600-lb) reinforced, post-tensioned concrete tower began on 12 February 1973, and the structure was 'topped out' on 2 April 1975. A 416-seat restaurant revolves in the tower's Sky Pod at a height of 351 m (1,150 ft), and visibility can extend to hills 120 km (75 miles) away.

TALLEST MONUMENT

The world's tallest monument is the stainless-steel Gateway to the West arch in St Louis, Missouri, USA, which was completed on 28 October 1965. The monument was erected to mark the westward expansion in the USA following the Louisiana Purchase of 1803, in which the United States bought the state of Louisiana from France. The Gateway is a sweeping arch spanning 192 m (630 ft) and rising to the same height. Designed in 1947 by the Finnish-American architect Eero Saarinen, it cost $29 million (£7 million) at the time.

TALLEST FLAGPOLE

The tallest flagpole in the world is at Panmunjon, North Korea, near the border with South Korea. It is 160 m (525 ft) high and flies a flag 30 m (98.5 ft) long. The flagpole is the result of a propaganda war between the two countries, and was reportedly built in response to a tall flagpole erected in a nearby South Korean village.

TALLEST STATUE

A bronze statue of Buddha measuring 120 m (394 ft) high, was completed in Tokyo, Japan, in January 1993. A joint Japanese-Taiwanese project, which took seven years to complete, it is 35 m (115 ft) wide and weighs 1,000 tonnes (22,204,600 lb).

TALLEST LIGHTHOUSE

The steel 'Marine Tower' lighthouse at Yamashita Park in Yokohama, Japan, stands 106 m (348 ft) high. It has a power of 600,000 candelas (a candela is a basic unit of luminous intensity), a visibility range of 32 km (20 miles) and an observatory 100 m (328 ft) above the ground. It was built to mark the 100th anniversary of the first recorded trade between Yokohama and the West, in 1854.

TALLEST FULLY ROTATING TOWER

The Glasgow Tower (above) at the Glasgow Science Centre, Glasgow, Strathclyde, UK, is 127 m (416 ft) tall and is the tallest tower in the world capable of fully rotating through 360 degrees from base to top. It opened in spring 2001.

TALLEST FOUNTAIN

At its full pressure of 26.3 kg/cm² (375 lb/in²) and a rate of 26,500 litres/min (5,850 gal/min), the fountain at Fountain Hills, Arizona, USA, produces a column of water that reaches a height of 171.2 m (562 ft).

TALLEST FREE-STANDING STRUCTURE

The tallest free-standing structure on Earth is the Petronius oil and gas drilling platform, which stands 570 m (1,870 ft) above the ocean floor in the Gulf of Mexico. Operated by Texaco, it began production on 21 July 2000. The highest point on the platform, the vent boom, is over 610 m (2,000 ft) above the ocean floor, making it more than 50 m (165 ft) taller than Toronto's CN Tower.

TALLEST STRUCTURE EVER

The all-time height record for any structure is the guyed Warszawa Radio mast at Konstantynow, 96 km (60 miles) north-west of the capital of Poland. The mast was designed by Jan Polak and, prior to its fall during renovation work on 10 August 1991, it stood 646.38 m (2,120 ft 8 in) tall and weighed 550 tonnes (1,212,500 lb). It was completed on 18 July 1974 and put into operation on 22 July 1974.

The tallest structure in the world today is a stayed television transmitting tower 629 m (2,063 ft) tall, between Fargo and Blanchard, North Dakota, USA. It was built for Channel 11 of KTHI-TV in 30 days (2 October to 1 November 1963) by 11 men from Hamilton Erection, Inc (USA). From that time until the completion of the Warszawa Radio mast, the tower was the tallest structure in the world, a title that it regained following the collapse of the Warszawa mast.

HIGHEST HABITABLE FLOOR IN A SKYSCRAPER

Chicago's Sears Tower (below) has the highest habitable floor of any skyscraper. Its 110 storeys rise to 443 m (1,454 ft). Although the Petronas Towers in Kuala Lumpur is the world's tallest office building, its top floor (the 88th) is around 60 m (200 ft) lower.

LARGEST MUD BUILDING

The Grand Mosque in Djenne, Mali (above), measuring 100 m (328 ft) long and 40 m (131 ft) wide, is the largest mud building in the world. The present structure was built in 1905 and is based on the design of an 11th-century mosque. Rendered annually, it is surmounted by two massive towers and inside there is a forest of vast columns that take up almost half the floor space.

LARGEST FILM STAGE

The world's largest film stage is the '007' stage at Pinewood Studios, Bucks, UK, which measures 102 x 42 x 12 m (336 x 139 x 41 ft). Designed by Michael Brown (UK), it was built in 1976 for the James Bond film *The Spy Who Loved Me* (UK, 1977), when it accommodated 4.54 million litres (1.2 million gal) of water, a full-scale section of a 544,311-tonne (1.2 million-lb) supertanker and three scaled-down models of nuclear submarines.

LARGEST FREE-STANDING ADVERT

The two faces of an advertising sign at the Hilton Hotel and Casino in Las Vegas, Nevada, USA, have a total area of 6,512.3 m² (70,100 ft²). The sign is 85.03 m (279 ft) high and features more than 9.65 km (6 miles) of neon and fluorescent lights.

LARGEST PLANETARIUM

The planetarium at the Ehime Prefectural Science Museum, in Niihama City, Japan, has a massive dome with a diameter of 30 m (98 ft 5 in). It displays up to 25,000 stars and viewers can also observe space as seen from other planets.

LARGEST AIRPORT ROOF

The Hajj Terminal at the £2.8-billion ($5.6-billion) King Abdul-Aziz airport near Jeddah, Saudi Arabia, designed to cater for the annual influx of pilgrims, is the world's largest roofed structure, covering 1.5 km² (0.6 miles²).

LARGEST STADIA

Strahov Stadium in Prague, Czech Republic, completed in 1934, is the world's largest stadium. It has a seating capacity of 240,000 people.

Opened in 1968, the largest covered stadium is the Aztec Stadium in Mexico City, Mexico. It can accommodate 107,000 football spectators, with nearly all seats under cover.

With a maximum seating capacity of 97,365 for conventions and 76,791 for American football, the Superdome in New Orleans, Louisiana, USA, holds the indoor stadium record. It is 83.2 m (273 ft) tall, covers 5.26 ha (13 acres), and cost $173 million (£78 million). It was completed in May 1975.

LARGEST RETRACTABLE ROOF

The world's largest retractable roof covers the SkyDome in Toronto, Ontario, Canada. Completed in June 1989, the roof covers 3.2 ha (8 acres), spans 209 m (674 ft) at its widest point and rises to 86 m (282 ft). It weighs a massive 11,000 tonnes (24.6 million lb) – the same as 6,000 cars – and takes 20 minutes to open fully. When retracted, the entire field and 91% of the seats are uncovered.

LARGEST NIGHTCLUB

Privilege nightclub in Ibiza, Spain, can hold 10,000 clubbers on its 6,500 m² (69,968 ft²) of dance space, spread over three floors. This is larger than an American football field, which covers 5,500 m² (59,202 ft²). One end of the venue is sheet glass to allow the morning sun to shine through. A swimming pool, fountains and gardens add to the ambience. The club is the venue for the legendary Monday Manumission all-nighters.

LARGEST ART GALLERY

You have to walk an amazing 24 km (15 miles) to visit each of the 322 galleries of the Winter Palace within the State Hermitage Museum in St Petersburg, Russia. The galleries house nearly three million works of art.

LARGEST LIBRARY

Founded in 1800, the US Library of Congress in Washington DC, USA, contains more than 125,198,175 items. The collection includes over 18 million books, 2.5 million recordings, 12 million photographs, 4.5 million maps and 54 million manuscripts on its 856 km (532 miles) of shelving. The library takes up 265,000 m² (2.85 million ft²) of the Capitol Hill buildings, with additional offices world-wide.

LARGEST MUSEUMS

The American Museum of Natural History in New York City, USA, founded in 1869, comprises a total of 23 interconnected buildings. The buildings of the museum and the planetarium contain 111,000 m² (1.2 million ft²) of floor space, accommodating more than 30 million artifacts and specimens, and the museum attracts approximately three million visitors each year.

Comprising 16 museums and the National Zoological Park in Washington DC, USA, the Smithsonian Institution contains over 140 million items and has over 6,000 employees.

LARGEST CINEMA COMPLEX

Kinepolis Madrid, which opened in Madrid, Spain, on 17 September 1998, is the world's largest cinema complex. It has a total seating capacity of 9,200 for its 25 screens, which, individually, can seat between 211 and 996 people.

LARGEST SOCCER STADIUM

The Maracanã Municipal Stadium (above) in Rio de Janeiro, Brazil, has a capacity of 205,000, of whom 155,000 can be seated. Built for the 1950 World Cup, a crowd of 199,854 was accommodated for the Brazil v. Uruguay final.

LARGEST PYRAMID

The largest pyramid, and the largest monument ever constructed, is the Quetzalcóatl Pyramid at Cholula de Rivadavia, 101 km (63 miles) south-east of Mexico City, Mexico. It is 54 m (177 ft) tall, and its base covers an area of nearly 18.2 ha (45 acres). Its total volume has been estimated at 3.3 million m³ (116.5 million ft³), compared with the volume of 2.4 million m³ (84.8 million ft³) for the Pyramid of Khufu (or Cheops), the largest pyramid in Giza, Egypt.

LARGEST WIND GENERATOR

The Mod-5B generator in Oahu, Hawaii, USA, has two giant blades measuring 97.5 m (320 ft) from tip to tip, the same as the height of a 25-storey building. The turbine produces 3,200 kW (4,290 hp) when the wind reaches 51 km/h (32 mph).

LARGEST WIND TUNNEL

The largest test section at the NASA Ames Research Center in Mountain View, Palo Alto, California, USA, measures 36 x 24 m (118 x 79 ft). It is powered by six giant 17,000-kW (22,500-hp) fans with blades measuring 12 m (40 ft) from tip to tip.

MOST CAPACIOUS BUILDING

Boeing's (USA) assembly plant at Everett, Washington, USA, has an indoor floor area of 39.8 ha (98.3 acres) and a total volume of 13.4 million m³ (472 million ft³). Completed in 1968, the building has to be big, because Boeing's 747, 767 and 777 aircraft – among the world's largest – are assembled there.

LARGEST SHOPPING CENTRE

West Edmonton Mall in Edmonton, Alberta, Canada, covers an area of 492,000 m² (5.3 million ft²). It cost CAN$1.2 billion ($789 million or £700 million) and features more than 800 stores and services. Over 20,000 vehicles can park in the world's largest car park. The mall also houses the world's largest indoor amusement park, indoor waterpark and man-made lake.

LARGEST FILM STUDIO

Universal City, Los Angeles, California, USA, is home to the largest film studio complex in the world. The site, called the Back Lot, measures 170 ha (420 acres), and comprises 561 buildings and 34 sound stages. It was built on the site of a chicken ranch in 1915 and the first visitors were able to buy eggs on their way out.

LARGEST AMPHITHEATRE

The Flavian amphitheatre or Colosseum of Rome, Italy (below), completed in 80 AD, covers 2 ha (5 acres) and has a capacity of 87,000. It had a maximum length of 187 m (612 ft) and a maximum width of 175 m (515 ft). At the height of Rome's power, the Colosseum was the venue for battles between gladiators, slaves and wild beasts, and the arena was occasionally flooded to recreate naval battles.

FEATS OF ENGINEERING

BUILDINGS AND STRUCTURES

More than 280,000 vehicles pass along the tunnel's two decks each day. It carries five lanes of traffic on each of its two decks and is so large that a four-storey house could be pulled through it.

LONGEST ROAD TUNNEL
The tunnel on the main road between Bergen and Oslo, Norway, which cuts through the high range of mountains dividing west and east Norway, is 24.5 km (15.2 miles) long. The two-lane Lærdal Tunnel opened in 2001 and reportedly cost $113.1 million (£80.7 million) to construct.

LONGEST BRIDGE-TUNNEL
The Chesapeake Bay bridge-tunnel, which opened to traffic on 15 April 1964, extends 28.4 km (17.65 miles) from the Eastern Shore region of the Virginia Peninsula to Virginia Beach, Virginia, USA. The longest bridged section is Trestle C, at 7.34 km (4.56 miles), while the longest tunnel section is the Thimble Shoal Channel Tunnel, at 1.75 km (1.09 miles).

LARGEST RESERVOIR
The most voluminous man-made reservoir is the Bratskoye Reservoir on the river Angara in Russia. It has a volume of 169.3 km^3 (40.6 miles^3) and an area of 5,470 km^2 (2,112 miles^2), which means that the largest of the Egyptian pyramids at Giza would fit into it nearly 70,000 times. Built between 1961 and 1967, the reservoir is the power source for a sizeable hydroelectric power plant.

HIGHEST CAUSEWAY
In the mid-1990s, a causeway (raised road) was built to replace Bailey Bridge, which spanned Khardungla Pass, Ladakh, India. The bridge had been built in August 1982 and at one time stood at a higher altitude (5,602 m or 18,380 ft) than any other road bridge in the world.

FURTHEST DISTANCE TO MOVE A LIGHTHOUSE
To save the Cape Hatteras Lighthouse (above) in North Carolina, USA, from a receding shoreline, the National Park Service (NPS) decided to move it around 0.8 km (0.5 mile) further inland. After replacing its granite base with steel supports and hydraulic jacks on rollers, engineers began moving the 63-m-high (208-ft) lighthouse along a specially designed track on 17 June 1999. It reached its destination, around 883 m (2,900 ft) from its original location, on 9 July 1999.

DEEPEST ROAD TUNNEL
The Hitra Tunnel in Norway, linking the mainland to the island of Hitra, reaches a depth of 264 m (866 ft) below sea level. The tunnel is 5.6 km (3.8 miles) long, with three lanes, and was opened in December 1994. It is so deep that if you were to use its floor as the foundation for a building, you would need to build a 66-storey tower before reaching the surface of the sea above.

LARGEST ROAD TUNNEL
The road tunnel with the largest diameter in the world is the one that runs through Yerba Buena Island, San Francisco, California, USA. It is 24 m (79 ft) wide, 17 m (56 ft) high and 165 m (541 ft) long.

HIGHEST BRIDGE
The world's highest bridge is suspended 321 m (1,053 ft) above the Royal Gorge of the Arkansas River in Colorado, USA. A suspension bridge with a main span of 268 m (880 ft), the structure took six months to build and opened to the public on 6 December 1929.

HEAVIEST BUILDING RELOCATION
The Cudecom Building, an eight-storey apartment block in Bogotá, Colombia, weighing 7,700 tonnes (16.9 million lb) was moved intact 28.95 m (95 ft) by the company Antonio Paez-Restrepo Cia, Sociedad en Comandita, on 6 October 1974, in order to make way for a road.

OLDEST BRIDGE
The oldest datable bridge still in use today is the slab-stone single-arch bridge over the river Meles in Izmir (formerly Smyrna), Turkey. The bridge is thought to have been constructed in around 850 BC.

Remnants of Mycenaean bridges over the river Havos, dating back to around 1600 BC, exist in Mycenae, Greece.

LONGEST STEEL-ARCH BRIDGE
The New River Gorge Bridge, near Fayetteville, West Virginia, USA, which was completed in 1977, has a record span of 518 m (1,700 ft).

GREATEST DISTANCE A BRIDGE HAS BEEN MOVED
Unable to handle increasing volumes of traffic, London Bridge was auctioned in 1962 and bought for $2,460,000 (then £876,068) by Robert McCulloch (USA). The bridge was dismantled and moved brick-by-brick to Lake Havasu City, Arizona, USA – a total distance of 8,530 km (5,300 miles) – where it was reassembled and opened in 1971. It later transpired that McCulloch bought the wrong bridge – he had presumed that he was buying Tower Bridge.

LIGHTS WITH THE GREATEST RANGE
The lights 332 m (1,089 ft) above the ground on the Empire State Building, New York City, USA, have the greatest range of any lights. Each of the four-arc mercury bulbs is visible 130 km (80 miles) away on the ground and 490 km (300 miles) away in an aircraft.

LARGEST MAN-MADE FLOATING ISLAND
On 10 August 1999, the Mega-Float island (above) opened in Tokyo's Yokosuka Port, Japan. It is 1,000 m (3,280 ft 10 in) long, 121 m (396 ft 11.7 in) wide and 3 m (9 ft 10 in) deep, and is used to simulate disasters and test new aircraft.

LONGEST CABLE-SUSPENSION BRIDGE

The main span of the Akashi-Kaikyo road bridge – which links the Japanese islands of Honshu and Shikoku – is 1,990.8 m (1.23 miles) long. The bridge's overall suspended length, including side spans, totals 3,911.1 m (2.43 miles). Its two towers rise 297 m (974 ft 5 in) above water level and the two main supporting cables are 1.12 m (44 in) in diameter, making both the tower height and the cable diameter world records. Work on the bridge began in 1988 and it opened to traffic on 5 April 1998.

LONGEST WALL

The Great Wall of China is the longest wall in the world. It was first built to repel marauding tribes of Mongol raiders from the north. The main part of the wall is 3,460 km (2,150 miles) long, nearly three times the length of Great Britain, and the structure also features 3,530 km (2,195 miles) of branches and spurs. Construction of the wall began in the reign of Qin Shi Huangdi (221–210 BC), although it did not take on its present-day form until the Ming dynasty (1368–1644). The height of the wall varies from 4.5 m to 12 m (15 ft to 39 ft) and it is up to 9.8 m (32 ft) thick. It runs from Shanhaiguan, on the Gulf of Bohai, west to Yumenguan and Yangguan and was was kept in repair up until the 16th century. Around 51.5 km (32 miles) of the wall have been destroyed since 1966.

WIDEST ROAD

The toll plaza for the San Francisco-Oakland Bay Bridge (below) features 23 traffic lanes – 17 of which are westbound – which serve the bridge in Oakland, California, USA.

LARGEST INHABITED CASTLE
The royal residence at Windsor Castle (above) at Windsor, Berks, UK, is built in the form of a parallelogram measuring 576 x 164 m (1,890 x 540 ft). It was constructed mainly in the 12th century under Henry II.

HIGHEST RESIDENTIAL APARTMENTS
The John Hancock Center in Chicago, Illinois, USA, contains the highest residential apartments in the world. It stands 343.5 m (1,127 ft) high and comprises 100 storeys. Although the building is mixed-use, floors 44 to 92 are residential. The building was completed in 1970 and remodelled in 1995.

LARGEST NON-PALATIAL RESIDENCE
St Emmeram Castle in Regensburg, Germany, has 517 rooms and a floor area of 21,460 m² (231,000 ft²). It belonged to the late Prince Johannes von Thurn und Taxis, whose family use only 95 of the rooms. The castle is valued at over DM 336 million (£122 million or $178 million).

OLDEST HOTEL
The Hoshi Ryokan in the village of Awazu, Japan, is reputedly the oldest hotel in the world. It dates back to 717 AD, when Taicho Daishi built an inn near a hot-water spring that was reputed to have miraculous healing powers. The waters are still celebrated to this day for their recuperative effects. The Ryokan currently has 100 bedrooms.

TALLEST HOTEL
The all-suite Burj Al Arab – The Arabian Tower – located 15 km (9 miles) south of Dubai, United Arab Emirates, is the world's tallest hotel. Measured on 26 October 1999, it stood 320.94 m (1,052 ft) high from ground level to the top of its mast. The hotel, which is built on a man-made island and is shaped like a sail, has 202 suites, 28 'double-height' storeys and has a floor area of 111,480 m² (1.2million ft²).

MOST EXPENSIVE HOTEL APARTMENT
The 10-room Bridge Suite at the Royal Towers of Atlantis in the Bahamas can be rented for $25,000 (£15,084) per night. This price includes a bar lounge, two entertainment centres, a baby grand piano and a dining room with a 22-carat gold chandelier.

HIGHEST DENSITY OF HOTEL ROOMS
Las Vegas, Nevada, USA, boasts an incredible 120,000 hotel and motel rooms, nearly one for every four of its 456,000 inhabitants. The city single-handedly accounts for around 3.33% of all hotel rooms in the USA.

HIGHEST CONCENTRATION OF THEME HOTELS
There are more than 16 theme hotels on the Strip in Las Vegas, Nevada, USA. *The Luxor* has a sphinx, a black pyramid, and an obelisk; *New York New York* features a one-third-scale New York skyline; and *Paris* has a half-scale Eiffel Tower. Other themes include Treasure Island and Venice.

LARGEST HOTEL
The MGM Grand Hotel/Casino in Las Vegas, Nevada, USA, consists of four 30-storey towers on a site covering 45.3 ha (112 acres). The hotel has 5,005 rooms, with suites of up to 560 m² (6,000 ft²) in area, a 15,200-seat arena, and a 13.3-ha (33-acre) theme park.

HIGHEST-ALTITUDE HOTEL
The Hotel Everest View above Namche, Nepal – the village closest to Everest base camp – stands at a record height of 3,962 m (13,000 ft).

LARGEST ICE HOTEL
Sweden's Ice Hotel in Jukkasjärvi, has a total floor area of 4,000 m² (13,124 ft²), comprising 15 suites and 32 bedrooms. Lying 200 km (120 miles) north of the Arctic Circle, the hotel has been rebuilt and expanded every December since 1990. It features ice sculptures, a cinema, saunas, colonnaded halls, a bar made out of ice and an ice chapel. The hotel currently has 120 ice beds, which are covered with thick reindeer pelts. The inside temperature hovers around the -6°C (20°F) mark.

LARGEST WOODEN BUILDING
Built in 1912, Woolloomooloo Bay Wharf, Sydney, NSW, Australia is 400 m (1,312 ft) long and 63 m (206 ft) wide; it stands on 3,600 piles. The building on the wharf is five storeys high, 350.5 m (1,150 ft) long and 43 m (141 ft) wide, with a total floor area of 64,000 m² (688,890 ft²). It has been converted into a hotel, apartments and a marina complex.

LARGEST FORT
Fort George near Ardersier, Highland, UK, is 640 m (2,100 ft) long and has an average width of 189 m (620 ft) on a site 17.2 ha (42 acres) in area. It was built from 1748 to 1769.

LARGEST PALACE
Situated in the centre of Beijing, China, the Imperial Palace covers a rectangular area measuring 960 x 750 m (3,150 x 2,460 ft) over an area of 72 ha (178 acres). Its outline survives from an original construction dating back to the rule of Yongle, the third Ming emperor, in the 15th century. Due to reconstruction work, however, most of the palatial buildings (five halls and 17 palaces) date back only to the 18th century.

LARGEST GARDEN
In the late 17th century, Andre le Notre (France) created a magnificent garden (above) for Louis XIV at Versailles, France. The gardens and parkland take up over 6,070 ha (15,000 acres), of which the formal garden covers 100 ha (247 acres).

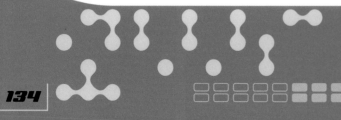

GUINNESS WORLD RECORDS

HIGHEST HOTEL

China's Grand Hyatt Shanghai in Pudong is the highest hotel in the world. It occupies floors 53 to 87 of the 88-storey Jin Mao Tower, China's tallest building, and – at 420 m (1377.9 ft) – one of the world's tallest buildings. The hotel opened for business on 18 March 1999, and offers spectacular views over the Bund financial centre and the adjacent Huang Pu River.

LARGEST TEPEE

Dr Michael Doss (USA) of the Crow Indian Reservation, Montana, USA, is the creator of the world's largest tepee. It stands 12.8 m (42 ft) high, has a 76.8-m (252-ft) circumference and a 15.2-m (50-ft) diameter.

MOST DURABLE RESIDENT

Virginia Hopkins Phillips of Onancock, Virginia, USA, lived in the same house from the time of her birth in 1891 until just after her 102nd birthday in 1993.

MOST EXPENSIVE HOUSE SALE

Businessman Eric Hotung's house at 6–10 Black's Link, Hong Kong, sold for HK$778.88 million (£62,767,500 or $101,909,312) on 12 May 1997.

LARGEST RESIDENTIAL PALACE

The Istana Nurul Iman, the palace of HM the Sultan of Brunei in the capital Bandar Seri Begawan, was completed in January 1984 at a reported cost of £300 million ($422 million).

The palace is the largest residence in the world, with a total floor space of 200,000 m² (2,152,780 ft²), 1,788 rooms and 257 lavatories. The underground garage houses the Sultan's 153 cars.

LARGEST HOLLYWOOD HOME

Hollywood's largest home is the house at 594 Mapleton Drive, Hollywood, California, USA. It occupies 5,253 m² (56,550 ft²) and was extended to 123 rooms by its owner, TV producer Aaron Spelling (USA). The house is valued at $37 million (£26.4 million) and includes a gym, bowling alley, swimming pool and skating rink.

MOST EXPENSIVE ISLAND SOLD

The most expensive island ever sold was Palmyra Island (USA), 1,545 km (960 miles) south-west of Honolulu. In 2000 the island was bought by The Nature Conservancy for $30 million (£21 million) from the Fullard-Leos family. Palmyra is unique in that no settlers have ever colonized it.

MOST EXPENSIVE NON-PALATIAL HOUSE BUILT

Hearst Castle (below), at San Simeon, California, USA, was built between the years 1922 and 1939 for the newspaper tycoon William Randolph Hearst (USA), at a cost of more than $30 million (£6.5 million), the equivalent of over $350 million (£250 million) today. The house has more than 100 rooms, a 32-m-long (104-ft) heated swimming pool, a 25-m-long (83-ft) assembly hall and a garage that can accommodate 25 limousines. The house required 60 servants to maintain it. Today, guided tours of Hearst Castle take place throughout the year.

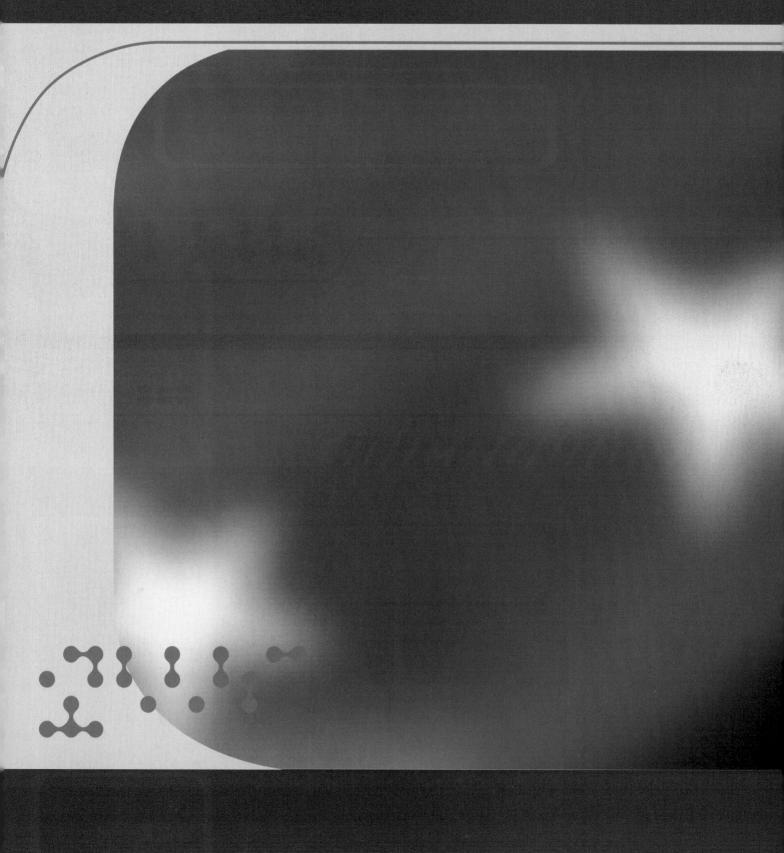

PLANES, TRAINS AND AUTOS

HIGHEST CAPACITY AIRLINER

The jet airliner with the highest capacity is a custom-built Boeing 747-400 (above), which entered service with Northwest Airlines (USA) in January 1989. The plane has a wingspan of 64.9 m (213 ft), a range of 13,340 km (8,290 miles) and can carry 566 passengers.

LONGEST-DURATION FLIGHT BY A MODEL AIRCRAFT

The longest-duration flight by a powered model aircraft is 33 hr 39 min 15 sec by Maynard Hill (USA), on 1 and 2 October 1992.

MOST EXPENSIVE PRIVATE JET

At an amazing price of $45 million (£31 million), the Gulfstream V-SP is the most expensive private jet ever made. It has a range of 12,500 km (7,800 miles) at long-range cruise speeds, and is capable of flying 9,260 km (5,750 miles) at Mach 0.87. It has Rolls-Royce BR-710 engines and airframe drag reduction.

FASTEST PASSENGER AIRLINER

Russia's Tupolev Tu-144, first flown on 31 December 1968, is reported to have reached Mach 2.4 (2,587 km/h or 1,600 mph), although its normal cruising speed was Mach 2.2.

MOST POWERFUL JET ENGINE

A prototype General Electric GE90-115B turbofan engine achieved steady-state thrust of 55,800 kg (123,000 lb) during flight tests in December 2001 – almost twice as much as each of the four engines used by the Boeing 747-400. The engine will eventually be put to use on Boeing 777s, due to enter service in 2003, and will be certified at 52,160 kg (115,000 lb).

SMALLEST JET AIRCRAFT

The smallest jet is *Silver Bullet*, which was built by Bob and Mary Ellen Bishop (USA) in 1976. It is 3.7 m (12 ft) long, has a 5.2-m (17-ft) wingspan, weighs 198 kg (437 lb) and can fly at 483 km/h (300 mph).

SMALLEST MONOPLANE AIRCRAFT

The smallest monoplane is the *Baby Bird*, designed and built by Donald R Stits (USA). It is 3.35 m (11 ft) long, with a wingspan of 1.91 m (6.25 ft) and weighs 114.3 kg (252 lb) when empty. It is powered by a 41.25-kW (55-hp) two-cylinder Hirth engine, giving a top speed of 177 km/h (110 mph). It was first flown by Harold Nemer (USA) on 4 August 1984, at Camarillo, California, USA.

HIGHEST ALTITUDE IN AN AUTOGYRO

On 20 July 1982, over Boscombe Down, Wilts, UK, Wing Commander Kenneth H Wallis (UK) reached an altitude of 5,643.7 m (18,516 ft) in a WA-121/Mc gyrocopter.

AIR-SPEED RECORD

The highest officially recorded air speed is 3,529.56 km/h (2,193.17 mph), by Capt Eldon W Joersz and Maj George T Morgan Jr (both USA), achieved in a Lockheed SR-71A Blackbird near Beale Air Force Base, California, USA, over a 250-km (158-mile) course on 28 July 1976.

LONGEST JOURNEY BY POWERED PARAGLIDER

Bob Holloway (USA) flew his powered paraglider a distance of 2,400 km (1,500 miles), from close to the Canadian border in Washington, USA, to the Mexican border in Arizona, USA, between 15 and 26 June 2001.

FASTEST SPEED IN A HELICOPTER

Under Fédération Aéronautique Internationale (FAI) regulations, the world speed record for helicopters was set by John Eggington and his co-pilot Derek J Clews (both UK), who averaged a remarkable 400.87 km/h (249.09 mph) when in flight over Glastonbury, Somerset, UK, in a Westland Lynx demonstrator helicopter on 11 August 1986.

WORST SINGLE-AIRCRAFT INCIDENT

The worst single-aircraft accident occured on 12 August 1985, when JAL Boeing 747 Flight 123 crashed into Mount Osutaka near Tokyo, Japan, killing 520 of the 524 passengers and crew on board.

HIGHEST-FLYING PROPELLER-DRIVEN AIRCRAFT

The highest altitude reached by a propeller-driven aircraft is 29,413 m (96,500 ft), when the unmanned solar-powered *Helios* prototype flew over the Hawaiian island of Kauai on 13 August 2001. *Helios* is one of a new breed of high-altitude aircraft that could provide an alternative to communications satellites.

MOST WIDELY USED AIRLINER

Launched in 1965, the Boeing 737 has become the world's most widely used airliner. Over 2,800 units are in use worldwide, and in January 2000 it became the first airliner to clock up more than 100 million flight hours.

FASTEST SPEED IN AN AUTOGYRO

Wing Commander Kenneth H Wallis (UK, above) flew a WA-116/F/S gyrocopter with unpowered rotors, to a speed of 193.6 km/h (120.3 mph) over a 3-km (1.86-mile) course in Norfolk, UK, on 18 September 1986.

LONGEST PERIOD SPENT AIRBORNE

Robert Timm and John Cooke (both USA) kept their Cessna 172 Hacienda aloft for 64 days 22 hr 19 min 5 sec from 4 December 1958 to 7 February 1959. They took off at McCarran Airfield, Las Vegas, Nevada, USA, and landed at the same place after covering a distance equivalent to six times round the world, with refuelling taking place in the air.

LONGEST FLIGHT BY POWERED PARACHUTE

The official FAI record for the longest distance flown in a single hop by a powered parachute is 644 km (400 miles), by Juan Ramon Morillas Salmeron (Spain), from Almonte, Huelva, Spain, to Minuesa, Teruel, Spain, on 21 June 1998.

LONGEST DISTANCE FLOWN BY A PAPER AIRCRAFT

The greatest distance flown by a paper aircraft is 58.82 m (193 ft), by Tony Felch (USA), set indoors at La Crosse, Wisconsin, USA, on 21 May 1985.

LONGEST FLIGHT BY AN UNMANNED AIRCRAFT

The longest flight by a full-scale unmanned conventional aircraft is 13,840 km (8,600 miles) by a USAF Northrop Grumman Global Hawk *Southern Cross II* (above) on 22 April 2001. The journey from Edwards Air Force Base, California, USA, to RAAF Base Edinburgh, SA, Australia, took 23 hr 23 min.

LARGEST PASSENGER AIRCRAFT (STILL IN DEVELOPMENT)

The Airbus A380, which was launched in December 2000 and is expected to enter service by 2007, will have a wingspan of 79.8 m (261 ft 10 in) and a length of 73 m (239 ft 6 in). It will be able to carry 555 passengers in considerable comfort and will have a maximum take-off weight of 560 tonnes (1,234,587 lb).

FASTEST RADIO-CONTROLLED MODEL AIRCRAFT

Leonid Lipinski (USSR) flew a model aircraft at 395.64 km/h (245.94 mph) on 6 December 1971.

LARGEST AIRLINE AIRCRAFT FLEET

The airline with the most aircraft is American Airlines (USA), which, in September 2001, operated a fleet of nearly 700 planes. Its nearest two rivals were United and Delta (both USA), with close to 600 planes. The largest non-US airline was British Airways (UK), with 357 aircraft.

LARGEST AIRSHIP

The world's largest airships were the 213.9-tonne (471,568-lb) *Hindenburg* (LZ 129) and the *Graf Zeppelin II* (LZ 130), each of which had a length of 245 m (803 ft 10 in) and had a hydrogen gas capacity of 200,000 m³ (7,062,100 ft³). The *Hindenburg* was launched in 1936, while the *Graf Zeppelin II* made its first flight in the following year. Both airships were built in Germany.

LARGEST AEROSPACE COMPANY

In 2000 Boeing, who are based in Seattle, Washington, USA, made $51.321 billion (£34.381 billion), earning profits of $2.128 billion (£1.425 billion). Boeing's workforce at the time totalled 198,100.

EARLIEST HELICOPTER FLIGHT

In 1935 the Breguet-Dorand Laboratory Gyroplane (France) became the first helicopter to be fully controllable and fly successfully.

LONGEST DURATION FLIGHT IN HUMAN-POWERED VEHICLE

Kanellos Kanellopoulos (Greece) kept his Daedalus 88 aircraft aloft for 3 hr 54 min 59 sec when pedalling the 114.11 km (71.93 miles) between two Greek islands on 23 April 1988.

SMALLEST CARS

The Smart car (above), made by Germany's Daimler-Benz, is the smallest four-wheeled car currently in production. It is slightly less than 2.5 m (8 ft 4 in) long. The smallest road-legal car ever was the Peel P50. It was 134 cm (53 in) long, 99 cm (39 in) wide and 134 cm (53 in) high – smaller than a fairground 'dodgem' car. It was built by Britain's Peel Engineering Co between 1962 and 1965.

GREATEST DISTANCE DRIVEN IN ONE HOUR

Helmut Henzler (Germany) and Keke Rosberg (Finland) hold the record for the greatest distance driven in one hour by a car with an internal combustion engine. They drove a prototype diesel-powered Volkswagen car 353.409 km (219.598 miles) at the Nardo Circuit, Italy, on 18 October 1980.

MOST POWERFUL PRODUCTION CAR

In 1992, McLaren (UK) launched the F1, which can produce a world record power output of 467 kW (627 bhp).

BEST-SELLING TWO-SEATER SPORTS CAR

Mazda (Japan) has produced more than 600,000 MX-5 Miata sports models (as of 19 April 2001) since launch in April 1989.

FASTEST CARS

The highest speed ever recorded by a rocket car is 1,016.086 km/h (631.367 mph) over a measured kilometre by *The Blue Flame*, a rocket-powered four-wheeled car driven by Gary Gabelich (USA) on the Bonneville Salt Flats, Utah, USA, on 23 October 1970. At one point Gabelich's unique vehicle exceeded 1,046 km/h (650 mph). The car was powered by a liquid natural gas/hydrogen peroxide rocket engine that could develop thrust of up to 10,000 kg (22,000 lb).

The fastest a wheel-driven car has ever been driven is 659.808 km/h (409.986 mph) – taken as the average over two runs – with a peak of 696.331 km/h (432.692 mph), by Al Teague (USA) in *Spirit of '76* at Bonneville Salt Flats, Utah, USA, on 21 August 1991. 'Wheel-driven' refers to the power of the engine being transferred through the wheels into forward motion, in contrast to jet- or rocket-powered vehicles.

On 22 October 1999 at Bonneville Salt Flats, Utah, USA, Dempsey's World Record Associates *White Lightning Electric Streamliner*, driven by Patrick Rummerfield (USA), reached a speed of 395.821 km/h (245.523 mph), the fastest ever achieved by an electric car.

A McLaren F1 driven by Andy Wallace (UK) at the Volkswagen Proving Ground, Wolfsburg, Germany, on 31 March 1998, reached 386.7 km/h (2401.1 mph), a world record for a standard production car.

The streamliner *Thermo King-Wynns*, driven by Virgil Snyder (USA) at Bonneville Salt Flats, Utah, USA, on 25 August 1973, attained a speed of 379.413 km/h (235.756 mph), a record for a diesel-engine car.

MOST EXPENSIVE PRODUCTION CAR

The most expensive production car in the world is the German built Mercedes-Benz CLK/LM, valued at $1,547,620 (£957,093.33). The car has a top speed of 320 km/h (200 mph) and does 0–100 km/h (62 mph) in just 3.8 seconds.

LONGEST CAR

Jay Ohrberg (USA) designed a 30.5-m-long (100-ft) 26-wheeled limousine, which came complete with a swimming pool, diving board and a king-sized water bed. The car can be driven as a rigid vehicle but its design also allows it to bend in the middle to help negotiate difficult corners. Its main purpose is for use in films and exhibitions.

FASTEST ACCELERATION BY A PRODUCTION CAR

The highest road-tested acceleration ever reported by a production car is 0–96 km/h (0–60 mph) in just 3.07 seconds by a Ford RS200 Evolution. The British-built car was driven by Graham Hathaway (UK) in tests at the Millbrook Proving Ground in Bedfordshire, UK, on 25 May 1994.

MOST VALUABLE CAR

The greatest confirmed price paid for a car is $15 million (£8.45 million) for the 1931 Bugatti Type 41 Royale Sports Coupé, by Kellner, sold by Nicholas Harley to the Meitec Corporation of Japan in April 1990.

OFFICIAL LAND-SPEED RECORD FOR A CAR

Andy Green (UK) set the one-mile land-speed record when he reached 1,227.985 km/h (763.035 mph) on 15 October 1997 in the Black Rock Desert, Nevada, USA, in *Thrust SSC*. The car has two Rolls-Royce Spey 202 jet engines, which generate 22,680 kg (50,000 lb) of thrust.

LARGEST VEHICLE PRODUCER

General Motors Corporation of Detroit, Michigan, USA, is the world's largest producer of motor vehicles. In 2000, the company sold 8.746 million vehicles, earned $184.632 billion (£122.02 billion) and made a profit of $4.452 billion (£2.94 billion). GM's 17 brands include many well-known names such as Buick, Cadillac, Chevrolet, Isuzu, Vauxhall and Saab.

MOST FUEL-EFFICIENT CAR

The Microjoule team of Lycée La Joliverie (above) of St Sebastien/Loire, France, recorded fuel consumption of 0.02762 litres per 100 km (10,227 mpg) in a Shell Eco Marathon event on 23 June 2001 at Rockingham Motor Speedway, Northants, UK.

MOST WIDESPREAD CAR IN PRODUCTION

Toyota Corolla (Japan) has appeared on more cars than any other name, with 24,986,607 vehicles produced by December 2000. However, the vehicle has been redesigned a number of times since its 1966 launch and cannot be said to be the same car.

More than 21 million 'old-style' VW Beetles (Germany) have been produced since the 1940s. Although the car was given a new look in the 1990s, the 'old-style' Beetle is still being made and sold in Brazil.

MOST CARS WRECKED

Dick Shepherd (UK) wrecked 2,003 cars over 40 years until his eventual retirement in 1993 – not because he was a bad driver, but in his role as a professional stuntman.

LONGEST HORIZONTAL POWER SLIDE

Simon de Banke (UK) performed a horizontal power slide – a controlled skid – for 2 hr 11 min 18 sec on 29 July 2001 at the MIRA Proving Ground, Nuneaton, Warwickshire, UK.

HIGHEST SPEED ON A PUBLIC HIGHWAY

The highest speed reached on a public highway is 334.3896 km/h (207.7801 mph), by Charles 'Chuck' Shafer and Gary Bockman (both USA), on a 145-km (90-mile) stretch of Nevada's Route 318 during the May 2000 Silver State Classic Challenge. This was Shafer's average speed – at times his Chrysler LeBaron-bodied former NASCAR (National Association for Stock Car Auto Racing) Busch series car went at speeds in excess of 355 km/h (220 mph).

LARGEST CAR ENGINE

Three production cars have been developed with engines that measured a huge 13.5 litres – the US Pierce-Arrow 6-66 Raceabout of 1912 to 1918, the US Peerless 6-60 of 1912 to 1914 and the Fageol of 1918.

GREATEST DISTANCE DRIVEN IN ONE HOUR BY AN ELECTRIC VEHICLE

The record distance that an electric car has covered in one hour is 199.881 km (124.2 miles) by Oscar De Vita (Italy) driving a Bertone ZER (Zero Emission Record) prototype at the Nardo Circuit, Italy, on 2 October 1994. The streamlined car, designed and built in Italy, was also the first electric vehicle that was able to break the 300-km/h (186-mph) barrier.

FASTEST RADIO-CONTROLLED MODEL CAR

The top speed ever achieved by a radio-controlled model car is 178.63 km/h (111 mph), set by the 1:10 scale Team Associated RC10L3 Oval Racer car at the Irwindale Speedway, California, USA, on 13 January 2001. The heavily modified stock model was built and driven by Cliff Lett (USA) of Associated Electronics.

LARGEST MOTOR SHOW

Frankfurt, Germany, hosts the biennial International Motor Show for Passenger Cars (IAA), the largest such event in the world. The show in September 2001 drew more than 1,000 exhibitors from 39 countries to a display area of 235,000 m² (2.5 million ft²), where latest models such as the Bugatti Veyron 16/4 (Italy, below) could be seen.

FASTEST ROAD RACE

In the Silver State Classic Challenge on Route 318 in Nevada, USA, competing drivers frequently maintain average speeds that are in excess of 305 km/h (190 mph) over the 145-km (90-mile) course. Held twice a year, it is the world's fastest race on a public highway.

FASTEST PRODUCTION MOTORCYCLE
The Suzuki GSX1300R Hayabusa (above), powered by a 1,298-cc DOHX engine, can reach speeds of 312 km/h (194 mph), making it the fastest bike in the world.

UNSIGHTED MOTORCYCLE SPEED RECORD
Blind motorcyclist Gordon Wilson (UK) reached a record speed of 126.17 km/h (78.4 mph) on an unmodified Triumph Daytona at Elvington airforce base in Yorkshire, UK, on 1 July 2000. He was guided via radio. The record is open to anybody who is riding unsighted, be they blind or blindfolded.

LONGEST TRIKE
The longest trike or three-wheeled motorcycle in the world is *Greenfly*, a 5.48-m-long (18-ft) five-seater vehicle built by Dan Quinlan (UK). The trike, which weighs 1,220 kg (2,690 lb), consists of the rear end of a Rover supported by a custom-built front wheel assembly. It is powered by the car's original 3.5-litre engine.

FASTEST SPEED WHILE SWAPPING PLACES ON A MOTORCYCLE
Riding a Honda CBR600 F2, Lantinen Jouni and Pitkänen Matti (both Finland) swapped places in a time of 4.18 seconds while

travelling at an average of 140 km/h (86.99 mph) from the time they began and ended the manoeuvre on the Paimio to Muuria highway, Finland, on 3 July 2001.

MOST MOTORCYCLISTS IN GLOBE OF DEATH
The most motorcyclists to ride inside a 4.33-m-diameter (14.2-ft) steel sphere is five. All five rode around a central person at the Versailles Theater, Riviera Hotel, Las Vegas, Nevada, USA, on 2 November 1999. The team comprised Gary Lurent, Humberto Fonseca Pinto, Kurtis Kunz and Humberto H Fonseca Pinto Jr and were led by Bela Tabak (all USA).

HIGHEST WALL CLIMB ON A TRIALS MOTORCYCLE
David Cobos (Spain) climbed a vertical wall onto a platform 3.2 m (10.5 ft) high on his trials motorcycle in Madrid, Spain, on 11 October 2001. According to the regulations established for this event, claimants are allowed the aid of a ramp with a maximum height of 50 cm (19.6 in) to give them a boost at the start.

LONGEST NON STOP HANDS-FREE MOTORCYCLE RIDE
On 25 February 2001, Manrique Saenz Cruz (Colombia) rode a Honda 125 XL bike for 213 km (132 miles) non stop without ever touching the handlebars in Girardot, Colombia. Manrique went round the 6.46-km (4-mile) circuit 33 times in a time of 3 hr 28 min 7 sec.

HIGHEST BICYCLE BUNNY HOP
Daniel Comas Riera (Spain) cleared a horizontal bar 116 cm (45.5 in) high without using a ramp at the studio of *El Show de los Récords*, in Madrid, Spain on 15 November 2001 in a bicycle without any suspension.

LONGEST MOTORCYCLE WHEELIE
Japan-born motorcyclist Yasuyuki Kudo covered a distance of 331 km (205.7 miles) while riding only on the rear wheel of his Honda TLM220R bike. This exhibition of precision riding took place at the Japan Automobile Research Institute proving ground, which is based in Tsukuba, Tsuchiura, Japan, on 5 May 1991.

FASTEST MOTORCYCLE SPEED
Dave Campos (USA), on a 7-m-long (23-ft) streamliner *Easyrider*, which was powered by twin 1,500-cc Ruxton Harley-Davidson engines, set American Motorcyclist Association (AMA) and Fédération Internationale de Motorcyclisme (FIM) records with a two-run average of 518.450 km/h (322.150 mph) at Bonneville Salt Flats, Utah, USA, on 14 July 1990. He completed the faster of the runs at 519.609 km/h (322.870 mph).

EARLIEST BICYCLE
The earliest machine propelled by cranks and pedals with connecting rods was built from 1839 to 1840 by

Kirkpatrick Macmillan (UK). A copy of the machine is now at the Science Museum, Kensington, London, UK.

Italian artist Leonardo da Vinci drew a picture of a machine propelled with cranks and pedals in the 1490s.

HIGHEST VERTICAL DROP ON A BICYCLE
Walter Belli (Italy) and David Cachón Labrador (Spain) rode their BMX bicycles off a platform 4 m (13.12 ft) high and continued to cycle upon landing without their feet touching the ground in Madrid, Spain, on 5 December 2001. In accordance with the rules of the event, they were not allowed a run-up before they dropped off the platform into thin air.

MOST 360-DEGREE SPINS ON FRONT WHEEL OF A BMX BIKE
Martti Kuoppa (Finland) completed 95 continuous rotations of his 50.8-cm (20-in) freestyle BMX bike while balancing on the front wheel. The display took place on the set of *Guinness Rekord TV*, filmed in Liljeholmshallen, Stockholm, Sweden, on 6 October 2001.

LARGEST MOTORCYCLE PYRAMID
The Dare Devils Team of the Indian Army Signal Corps built a motorcycle pyramid consisting of 210 men balanced on 10 motorcycles (above) on 5 July 2001 in Jabalpur, India. The pyramid travelled a distance of 129 m (424 ft).

FASTEST BICYCLE SPEED

The highest speed ever achieved on a bicycle is 268.831 km/h (166.944 mph) by Fred Rompelberg (Netherlands) behind a windshield at Bonneville Salt Flats, Utah, USA, on 3 October 1995. Considerable help was provided by the slipstreaming effect of the lead vehicle.

FASTEST BICYCLE WHEELIE — FRONT WHEEL

Bobby Root (USA) reached a top speed of 94.62 km/h (58.8 mph) riding on the front wheel of his bike at Palmdale, California, USA, on 31 January 2001.

LIGHTEST FULL-SIZE RACING BICYCLE

A full-sized racing bicycle weighing 5.45 kg (12 lb 1 oz) was built by Dionisio Coronado (Spain) in San Sebastián, Spain, in 1999. The bicycle's high-tech frame is mostly constructed from military-grade titanium and carbon fibre and is so light it can be lifted by one finger.

GREATEST DISTANCE COVERED BY PENNY-FARTHING IN 24 HOURS

The furthest a penny-farthing has been ridden in 24 hours is 522.504 km (324.668 miles) by Josef Zimovc (Czech Republic) at Brno, Czech Republic, on 20 and 21 June 1996.

LONGEST BICYCLE

The longest true bicycle (one that has only two wheels) ever built is a staggering 25.88 m (84 ft 11 in) long — larger than two standard coaches — and was built by the Super Tandem Club Ceparana (Italy). Forty club members cycled the vehicle 112.2 m (368 ft) at Ceparana, Italy, in September 1998. Cornering continues to be a problem.

GREATEST DISTANCE JUMPED ON A QUAD BIKE

The longest jump on a quad bike (a four-wheeled motorcycle or ATV) is 40.9 m (134 ft) over 14 Honda CRV vehicles by Matt 'Kangaroo Kid' Coulter (Australia, left) at RAF Bentwaters in Suffolk, UK, on 17 April 2000. Quad bikes are more dangerous than normal bikes because they are twice as heavy and therefore harder to control.

HIGHEST SPEED ON A QUAD BIKE

Graham Hicks (UK) reached a top speed of 159.74 km/h (99.26 mph) on a customized 500-cc quad bike at Bruntingthorpe Proving Ground, Leicester, UK, on 21 May 2001. Hicks, who is deaf and blind, drove the vehicle over a quarter-of-a-mile course while Matt Coulter (Australia) rode pillion behind him, prompting him by means of touch.

LARGEST CONTAINER SHIP

The *Hamburg Express* (above), used by Germany's Hapag-Lloyd Container Line, carries the most standard containers – 7,500. The largest ships by size, however, are Maersk Sealand's 'S-Types', at 347 m (1,138.5 ft) long.

LARGEST CAR FERRY

The largest 'roll-on roll-off' passenger ferry is *MV Pride of Rotterdam*, which has a maximum cargo-carrying capacity of 59,925 gross registered tons (grt) and entered service for P&O North Sea Ferries in April 2001. Built in Italy by the Fincantieri company, the ship is 203.88 m (668.89 ft) long and 31.5 m (103.34 ft) wide. It can carry 250 cars and 1,360 passengers in cruise ship luxury.

BUSIEST SHIPPING LANE

Between 500 and 600 ships a day pass through the Dover Strait between the UK and France, making it the world's busiest shipping lane. In 1999, an estimated 1.4 billion tonnes (2,645 billion lb) gross, carried by 62,500 vessels, crossed this part of the English Channel.

FASTEST ATLANTIC CROSSING

The fastest crossing of the Atlantic is 2 days 10 hr 34 min 47 sec by the 68-m (222-ft) luxury yacht *Destriero*, from 6 to 9 August 1992. Despite weighing in the region of 400 tonnes (882,000 lb), the gas turbine-propelled vessel maintained an average speed of 45.7 knots (84.6 km/h or 52.6 mph).

FASTEST SAILING VESSEL

On 26 October 1993 the trifoiler (a catamaran with three short planing hulls) *Yellow Pages Endeavour* reached 46.52 knots (86.21 km/h or 53.57 mph) while on a timed run of 500 m (547 yd) at Sandy Point near Melbourne, Victoria, Australia. This is the highest speed ever attained by any craft under sail on water.

LARGEST VESSEL

The world's largest ship of any kind is the oil tanker *Jahre Viking* (formerly *Happy Giant* and *Seawise Giant*), at 564,763 tonnes (1,245 billion lb) deadweight and 260,815 grt. The tanker is 458.45 m (1,504 ft) long overall, has a beam of 68.8 m (226 ft) and a draught of 24.61 m (80 ft 9 in). Declared irreparable after being disabled by severe bombardment in 1987–88 during the Iran-Iraq War, the tanker underwent extensive renovation in Singapore and the United Arab Emirates, costing some $60 million (£34 million), and was relaunched in November 1991.

FURTHEST DISTANCE TRAVELLED IN 24 HOURS BY A RADIO-CONTROLLED MODEL BOAT

On 17 and 18 August 1991 at Dome Leisure Park, Doncaster, Yorks, UK, members of the Lowestoft Model Boat Club crewed a radio-controlled boat to a 24-hour furthest distance record of 178.93 km (111 miles).

FASTEST HOVERCRAFT

The greatest recorded speed by a hovercraft is 137.4 km/h (85.38 mph) by Bob Windt (USA) at the 1995 World Hovercraft Championships on the Rio Douro river, Peso de Regua, Portugal. Windt was piloting *Jenny II*, a streamlined 5.8-m (19-ft) Universal UH19P hovercraft with an 82-kW (110-hp) V6 car engine driving two fans, one at the rear for propulsion and one underneath for lift.

OLDEST IRON STEAMSHIP

The *SS Great Britain*, launched in Bristol, UK, in 1843, was the first propeller-driven iron vessel to cross the Atlantic Ocean. After being used as a storage vessel in the Falkland Islands, the ship was brought back to Bristol for renovation in the 1970s.

LARGEST FLOATING WOODEN STRUCTURE

Eureka is the last of the traditional wooden side-paddle ferries that served as inland passenger vessels, transporting travellers to connect with the railroad in San Francisco, California, USA. It is 69.19 m (227 ft) long and 13.01 m (42.7 ft) wide.

OLDEST SHIPS FOUND IN THE SEA

Two Phoenician vessels, built around 2,700 years ago, were found off the coast of Israel in June 1998. They were discovered by Dr Robert Ballard (US), who also found the *Titanic* and the *Bismarck* in the 1980s.

FIRST ATLANTIC CROSSING BY A POWER VESSEL

The first Atlantic crossing by a power vessel, as opposed to an auxiliary-engined sailing ship, was by the *Curaçao*, a 38.7-m (127-ft) wooden paddle boat. The 22-day voyage between The Netherlands and the West Indies took place in April 1827.

HIGHEST SPEED ON WATER

The highest speed reached on water is 275.8 knots (511.11 km/h or 317.58 mph) by Ken Warby (Australia) on Blowering Dam Lake, NSW, Australia, on 20 November 1977 in his unlimited hydroplane, *Spirit of Australia*. Warby also reached an estimated but unofficial speed of 300 knots (555 km/h or 344.86 mph) in the same craft on the same lake on 8 October 1978.

FASTEST PROPELLER-DRIVEN BOAT

Russ Wicks (USA) reached 178.61 knots (330.79 km/h or 205.494 mph) in his hydroplane *Miss Freei* (above) on 15 June 2000 at Lake Washington, Seattle, Washington, USA, the highest speed ever attained in a propeller-driven boat.

LARGEST CRUISE SHIP

The 42,000-grt liner *Voyager of the Seas*, owned by Royal Caribbean and launched on 7 November 1999, measures 310 m (1,020 ft) long and 48 m (157.5 ft) wide. The ship has an international crew of 1,181 and can carry a total capacity of 3,114 passengers.

LARGEST CANOE CREW

The 41.1-m-long (135-ft) 'Snake Boat' *Nadubhagóm* from Kerala, southern India, has a crew of 109 rowers and nine 'encouragers'.

EARLIEST FLIGHT BY A HOVERCRAFT

The first flight by a hovercraft was by a 4-tonne (8,800-lb) Saunders-Roe SRN1 at Cowes, Isle of Wight, UK, on 30 May 1959. With a 680-kg (1,500-lb) thrust Viper turbojet engine, the craft reached 68 knots (126 km/h or 78 mph) in June 1961.

LONGEST SOLO NON-STOP YACHTING RACE

The world's longest non-stop solo sailing race is the Vendée Globe Challenge, first held in November 1989, which starts and finishes at Les Sables d'Olonne, France, and claims to be the longest and most difficult competitive yachting event ever devised. The race covers approximately 22,500 nautical miles (41,652 km or 25,881 miles) and is limited to boats between 50-60 ft (15-18 m), sailed single-handed.

LARGEST CIVILIAN HOVERCRAFT

The SRN4 Mk III, a British-built civil hovercraft, weighs 310 tonnes (683,400 lb) and can accommodate 418 passengers and 60 cars. It is 56.38 m (185 ft) in length, and is powered by four Bristol Siddeley Marine Proteus engines, giving a maximum speed that is in excess of the scheduled permitted English Channel operating speed of 65 knots (120 km/h or 75 mph). Cross-channel services ceased in December 2000 when the hovercraft were replaced by the slower but more economical Seacat catamarans.

FASTEST CAR FERRY

Designed in Australia by Advanced Multi-Hull Designs PTY Ltd, the *Luciano Federico L*, operated by Buquebus of Buenos Aires, Argentina, is powered by two 16-mW (21,500-hp) gas turbines and has a loaded speed of 57 knots (105.5 km/h or 65.5 mph), with a top speed of 60 knots (111 km/h or 69 mph).

OLDEST INTERNATIONAL YACHT RACE

In 1848 Queen Victoria (UK) authorized the creation of the 100 Guinea Cup for a yacht race "open to all nations". This was the forerunner of the Americas Cup, the world's oldest international yacht race. It was first won in 1851 by the New York Yacht Club in Cowes on the Isle Of Wight, UK.

FASTEST ATLANTIC CROSSING BY A SAILING VESSEL

The record for the fastest transatlantic sailing, between Ambrose Light Tower, New York, USA, and Lizard Point, Cornwall, UK, is 4 days 17 hr 28 min 6 sec, by the catamaran *Playstation* (left), captained by Steve Fossett (USA) in October 2001. The average speed for the journey was 25.78 knots (47.74 km/h or 29.66 mph).

GREATEST DISTANCE SAILED IN 24 HOURS

The 38.1-m (125-ft) catamaran *Playstation* (left), captained by Steve Fossett (USA), covered a record 687.17 nautical miles (1,272.67 km or 790.8 miles) in 24 hours on 7 October 2001, at an average speed of 28.63 knots (53.02 km/h or 32.94 mph). The record was set on a successful attempt to break the west-to-east transatlantic sailing record.

FASTEST SPEED ON A RAILWAY SYSTEM

The highest speed recorded on any national rail system is 515.3 km/h (320.2 mph) by the French SNCF high-speed train TGV (*Train à Grande Vitesse*) *Atlantique,* between Courtalain and Tours, France, on 18 May 1990.

LONGEST MONORAIL

The Osaka Monorail in Osaka, Japan, has an operational length of 22.2 km (13.8 miles). Fully operational since August 1997, it runs between Osaka International Airport and Hankyu Railway Minami Ibaraki Station, with the second stage running between Hankyu and Keihan Railway Kadomashi Station.

HIGHEST RAILWAY LINE

The world's highest railway line is the standard gauge (1,435-mm or 56.5-in) track on the main line between Lima and La Oroya on the Peruvian State Railway, which reaches 4,818 m (15,806 ft) above sea level at La Cima.

HIGHEST RAILWAY STATION

Opened in 1908, Cóndor station on the metre-gauge (39.37-in) Río Mulatos-Potosí line in Bolivia lies at an altitude of 4,786 m (15,705 ft).

NARROWEST GAUGE RAILWAY

The narrowest gauge on which public rail services are operated is 260 mm (10.25 in). This gauge is used on the Wells Harbour Railway, which runs for 1.12 km (0.7 mile), and the Wells Walsingham Light Railway, which runs for 6.5 km (4 miles) in Norfolk, UK.

SMALLEST RAILWAY SYSTEM

The country with the shortest length of railway track is the Vatican City, which has an 862-m (2,828-ft) spur entering the Holy See from Italy. It is used only for goods and supplies.

BUSIEST UNDERGROUND RAILWAY

At its peak, the beautifully decorated Greater Moscow Metro (above), in Moscow, Russia, saw 3.3 billion passenger journeys in a year, although by 1998 the figure had declined to 2.55 billion. The system, which has been serving the Russian capital since 1935, has 3,135 railcars covering 159 stations and 212 km (132 miles) of track.

LONGEST RAIL TUNNEL

The Seikan rail tunnel is 53.85 km (33.46 miles) long and links Tappi Saki on the main Japanese island of Honshu with Fukushima, on the northern island of Hokkaido, Japan. The first test run through the tunnel took place on 13 March 1988.

LEAST EXTENSIVE UNDERGROUND SYSTEM

The shortest underground system in the world is the Carmelit in Haifa, Israel. Opened in 1959, the Carmelit is just 1,800 m (1.12 miles) long. The only subway in Israel, the Carmelit is a funicular running at a gradient of 12 degrees. Starting at Paris Square, and finishing at Carmel Central, it has just six stations.

LONGEST SUSPENDED MONORAIL SYSTEM

Monorail trains either straddle their rail or are suspended from it, and in most cases they are powered by electricity. The Chiba Urban Monorail near Tokyo, Japan, is the longest suspended monorail train system in the world, at 15.2 km (9.45 miles) long. The first 3.2-km (1.99-mile) stretch opened on 20 March 1979, and the line has been expanded three times since.

LARGEST RAILWAY SYSTEM

The largest railway network is found in the USA, where there are around 225,000 km (140,000 miles) of railway lines. The USA's nearest competitor is Russia, with 149,000 km (92,500 miles) of rails.

LONGEST PASSENGER TRAIN

A passenger train created by the National Belgian Railway Company (NMBS) measured 1,732.9 m (5,685.3 ft) and consisted of 70 coaches pulled by one electric locomotive. On 27 April 1991, it travelled 62.5 km (38.9 miles) from Ghent to Ostend, Belgium.

LARGEST TRAIN STATION BUILDING

The JR Central Towers in Nagoya, Japan, has 410,000 m^2 (4,413,000 ft^2) of floor space. The complex was built by the Central Japan Railway Company to replace the existing Nagoya Station and was completed on 20 December 1999.

OLDEST TRAMS IN REVENUE SERVICE

The oldest trams still in service are cars 1 and 2 of the Manx Electric Railway, which date from 1893. They regularly run on the 28.5-km (17.75-mile) railway between Douglas and Ramsey on the Isle of Man, UK.

LONGEST AND HEAVIEST TRAIN

The longest-ever train was 7.353 km (4.568 miles) long, and consisted of 682 ore-cars pushed by eight powerful diesel-electric locomotives. At 99,732.1 tonnes (220 million lb), it was also the heaviest-ever train. Assembled by BHP Iron Ore, the train travelled 275 km (171 miles) from the company's Newman and Yandi mines to Port Hedland, WA, Australia, on 21 June 2001.

LARGEST RAILWAY STATION BY NUMBER OF PLATFORMS

The world's largest station in terms of platforms is Grand Central Terminal (above), New York City, USA, built between 1903–13, which has 44 platforms. Situated on two levels, there are 41 tracks on the upper level and 26 on the lower.

LONGEST RAIIL JOURNEY WITHOUT CHANGING TRAINS

It is possible to travel an incredible 10,214 km (6,346 miles) from Moscow, Russia, to Pyongyang, North Korea, without changing trains. One train per week makes this long journey, which includes sections of the famous Trans-Siberian line. It is scheduled to take 7 days 20 hr 25 min.

MOST EXTENSIVE UNDERGROUND RAIL SYSTEM

The New York City subway, USA, has a total track mileage of 1,355 km (842 miles), including 299 km (186 miles) of track in yards, shops and storage. With 468 stations (277 of which are underground), it also holds the record for the most underground railway stations. It serves an estimated 4.3 million passengers per day, or 1.3 billion a year.

LONGEST UNDERGROUND PLATFORM

The State Street Center subway platform on 'The Loop' in Chicago, Illinois, USA, measures 1,066 m (3,500 ft) in length.

STEEPEST RAILWAY GRADIENT

The Katoomba Scenic Railway in the Blue Mountains, NSW, Australia, is 311 m (1,020 ft) long, with a gradient of 1:0.82. A 15-kW (20-hp) electric winch takes 1 min 40 sec to haul the car up by steel cables with a 2.2-cm (0.86-in) diameter.

MOST EXTENSIVE TRAM SYSTEM

The city of St Petersburg, Russia, has the most extensive tramway system, with 2,402 cars on 64 routes, covering 690.6 km (429.1 miles) of track.

LONGEST RAILROAD STRAIGHT

The Australian National Railways Trans-Australian line over the Nullarbor Plain, is 478 km (297 miles) dead straight, although not level, from Mile 496 between Nurina and Loongana, Western Australia, to Mile 793 between Ooldea and Watson, South Australia.

LONGEST METRO ESCALATOR

One escalator on the St Petersburg Metro, Russia, has a vertical rise of 50.5 m (195 ft).

LONGEST AND HIGHEST CABLE CAR

The Teleférico Mérida in Venezuela runs from Mérida City at 1,639.5 m (5,379 ft) to the summit of Pico Espejo at 4,763.7 m (15,629 ft), a rise of 3,124 m (10,250 ft). The 12.5-km (7.8-mile) journey takes one hour.

OLDEST STEAM ENGINE IN USE

The steam engine *The Fairy Queen* was built in 1855 by Kitson Thompson Hewitson (UK). Between October 1997 and February 1998, this grand old engine was put into service hauling a twin-coach train between Delhi Cantonment, Delhi, India and Alwar, Rajasthan, India, a journey of 143 km (89 miles).

FASTEST STEAM LOCOMOTIVE

The highest speed ever ratified for a steam locomotive is 201 km/h (125 mph) over 402 m (1,319 ft) by the London North Eastern Railway 'Class A4' (4–6–2) No 4468 *Mallard* (below, later numbered 60022). Seven coaches weighing 243 tonnes (535,723 lb) were hauled down Stoke Bank, near Essendine, between Grantham, Lincolnshire, and Peterborough, Cambridgeshire, UK, on 3 July 1938.

LARGEST BULLDOZER
The massive Komatsu D575A 'Super Dozer' (USA, above) weighs in at a staggering 152.6 tonnes (336,000 lb) – approximately the weight of 120 saloon cars. Its 7.4 x 3.25-m (24.27 x 10.66-ft) blade has a capacity of 69 m³ (2,437 ft³). The 11.72-m-long (38.45-ft) pusher moves on tank-style tracks and is powered by an 858-kW (1,150-hp) turbo-charged diesel engine.

LARGEST FRONT-END LOADER
The largest wheel-driven earthmover is the L-1800, developed by LeTourneau Inc (USA). It is 17.83 m (58 ft 6 in) long, weighs 217.5 tonnes (480,000 lb), has a payload (cargo) capacity of 45.36 tonnes (100,000 lb), and a bucket capacity of 25.2 m³ (889.9 ft³).

TALLEST MOBILE CRANE
The Demag CC 12600 made by Mannesmann Dematic (Germany), is 198 m (649.6 ft) high in its tallest configuration, which consists of a 120-m (393.7-ft) 'fixed jib' attached to a 114-m (374-ft) near-vertical boom. It has a maximum lifting capacity of 1,600 tonnes (3,527,392 lb) at a 22-m (72-ft) radius (ie the distance from the central supporting column) and is so large that it requires 100 trucks to transport all its parts to a site.

LARGEST LAND VEHICLE
The largest land vehicle is the 14,196-tonne (31.3 million-lb) RB293 bucket-wheel excavator, an earth-moving machine manufactured by MAN TAKRAF (Germany). Used at an open-cast coal mine in North Rhine Westphalia, Germany, it is 220 m (722 ft) long, 94.5 m (310 ft) tall, and is capable of shifting 240,000 m³ (8.475 million ft³) of earth per day.

LARGEST FORK-LIFT TRUCK
In 1991, Kalmar LMV (Sweden) manufactured three counterbalanced fork-lift trucks capable of lifting loads of up to 90 tonnes (198,415.8 lb). These monsters weigh in at 116.5 tonnes (256,838 lb) and are 16.6 m (54.1 ft) in length (including forks).

LARGEST HYDRAULIC SHOVEL EXCAVATOR
The RH 400-2000 hydraulic shovel excavator, manufactured by O&K Mining (Germany), is capable of filling the world's largest dumper truck in just six passes. Weighing around 900 tonnes (1,984,158 lb) it has a shovel capacity of 51.7 m³ (1,825.7 ft³). The top of the driver's cab is 10.2 m (33.46 ft) high, the equivalent of three storeys above the ground.

FASTEST TRUCK WHEELIE
Patrick Bourny (France) performed a wheelie in his modified truck cab at a speed of 90 km/h (55.92 mph) in Lure, France, on 21 October 2000.

LARGEST TWO-AXLE DUMPER TRUCK
The T-282, manufactured by the Liebherr Mining Equipment Co (USA), is the world's largest two-axle dumper truck, with a payload capacity of 327 tonnes (720,900 lb). The diesel-electric powered vehicle is 14.4 m (47 ft 6 in) long, 8.7 m (28 ft 7 in) wide, 7.3 m (24 ft) high and weighs 201 tonnes (443,100 lb).

LARGEST HAULAGE COMPANY FAN CLUB
The Eddie Stobart Ltd (UK) haulage company has a fan club with over 25,000 members, including some in Australia and the USA. Founded in 1970, the green, red and gold trucks (each named after a woman) driven by polite, tie-wearing, uniformed drivers, soon attracted the attention of other road users. Club members, or 'Eddie Spotters', as they are known, receive a 'fleet manual' detailing the name, number and type of all 800 trucks.

MOST DEFENSIVE FEATURES ON A PICK-UP TRUCK
The US Army's SmarTruck concept vehicle, based around a standard Ford F-350 truck, has more than 10 'James Bond'-style features to protect its occupants. These include electrified door handles, super-bright lights to blind night-time pursuers, oil slicks and tyre-puncturing tacks which can be dropped, and a retractable laser cannon on the roof to clear any minefields ahead. All its functions are controlled by touch-screen computers that only react to authorized fingerprints.

FASTEST ROCKET-POWERED FIRE TRUCK
The world's fastest fire truck is the jet-powered 'Hawaiian Eagle', owned by Shannen Seydel (USA), which attained a speed of 655 km/h (407 mph) in Ontario, Canada, on 11 July 1998. The truck is a red 1940 Ford, powered by two Rolls-Royce Bristol Viper engines boasting 4,470 kW (6,000 hp) per engine and generating 5,443 kg (12,000 lb) of thrust.

LARGEST TYRE
At 4 m (13 ft 1 in) tall and weighing over 4 tonnes (8,818 lb), the world's largest tyres are manufactured by Michelin (France), to fit on to monster dumper trucks such as Caterpillar's largest model, the 797.

FURTHEST SIDE-WHEEL TRUCK-DRIVING DISTANCE
Sven-Erik Söderman (Sweden) drove a Daf 2800 7.5-tonne (16,536-lb) truck on two wheels and tilted at an angle, for a record-breaking distance of 10.83 km (6.72 miles) at Mora Siljan airport, Mora, Sweden, on 19 May 1991.

LONGEST ROAD TRAIN
On 19 October 2000, a 1,018.2-m-long (3,340-ft) road train (above), made of 79 trailers, was pulled over 8 km (4.9 miles) by a Kenworth C501T truck, driven by Steven Matthews (Australia), near Kalgoorlie, WA, Australia.

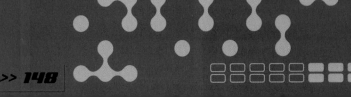

LARGEST DRAGLINE EXCAVATOR

'Big Muskie', a walking earth-moving machine weighing around 13,200 tonnes (29.1 million lb) was the largest-ever dragline excavator and one of the largest mobile machines ever made, weighing as much as nearly 10,000 saloon cars. It stood at Central Ohio Coal Co's open-cast coal mine in Ohio, USA, but was dismantled in 1999. Big Muskie was 46 m (151 ft) wide (the same as an eight-lane highway) and capable of moving 17,500 tonnes (38,580,850 lb) of earth an hour.

LARGEST TOWER CRANE

A typical tower crane stands 80 m (262 ft) tall and can lift around 3.5 tonnes (7,716 lb) at an 82-m (269 ft) radius. The Danish-made Kroll K-10000 is capable of lifting 120 tonnes (264,554 lb) at an 82-m (269 ft) radius. It stands 120 m (393 ft) high on a rotating cylinder just 12 m (39.3 ft) in diameter. It has no support wires, but 223 tonnes (491,630 lb) of counterweights balance out its 84-m-long (275-ft) load-carrying boom.

MOST PRODUCED FOUR-WHEELED VEHICLE

The Ford F-series nameplate has appeared on more vehicles than any other. By January 2002, an estimated 27,257,475 F-series pick-up trucks had been produced. The first in the series, the F-1, was produced in 1948 and an F-150 truck later provided the bodywork for the original 'Bigfoot' monster truck. Between 800,000 and 900,000 F-series trucks are sold annually, largely in North America, accounting for roughly one eighth of Ford's global sales.

LONGEST MONSTER TRUCK RAMP JUMP

'Bigfoot 14', driven by Dan Runte (USA), jumped a record 61.57 m (202 ft)

over a Boeing 727 passenger jet on 11 September 1999, at Smyrna Airport, Tennessee, USA. He set the monster truck speed record of 111.5 km/h (69.3 mph) during the run-up. The Bigfoot monster truck suffered a bent and broken frame, two bent wheels, a bent tie rod and some body damage and Runte walked away with a sore back.

LARGEST MONSTER TRUCK

'Bigfoot 5' is 4.7 m (15 ft 6 in) tall, with 3-m-high (10-ft) Firestone Tundra tyres, and weighs 17.236 tonnes (38,000 lb).

HIGHEST MONSTER RAMP JUMP

Dan Runte (USA) made a record monster ramp jump of 7.3 m (24 ft) in Bigfoot 14 (below), on 14 December 1999. The force of landing snapped one of the truck's front wheels off its axle and bent the other under the truck. Behind the wheels of various Bigfoots, Runte has won three monster truck racing series world championships and set four world jump records.

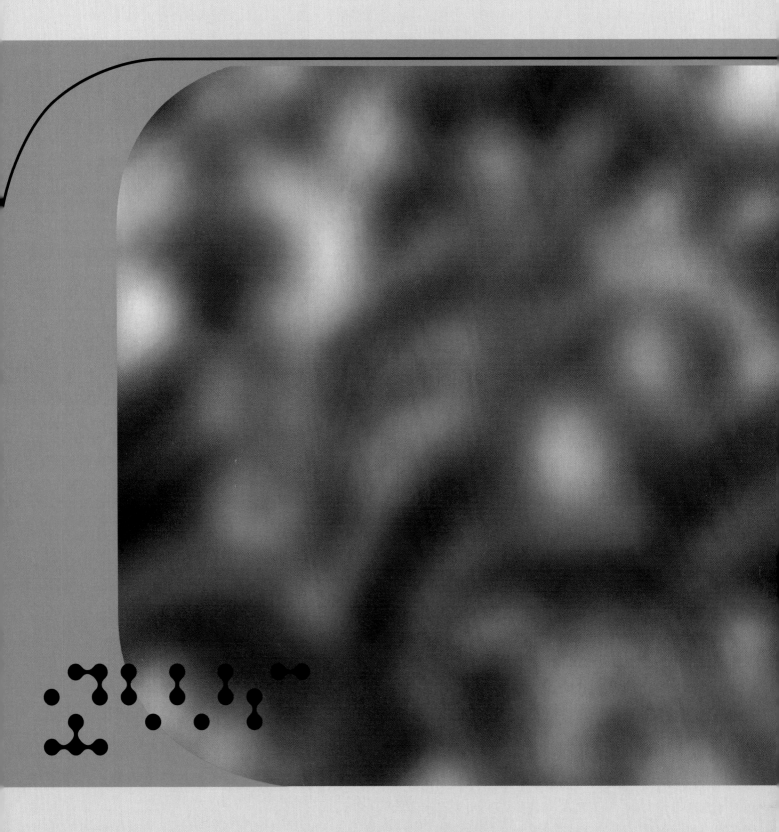

MILITARY SERVICE

OLDEST ARMY

The oldest established military force in the world is the Vatican City's 80–90-strong Pontifical Swiss Guard (above), whose formation can be dated back to 21 January 1506. Its origins, however, predate 1400. The Guard's colourful tunics are said to have been designed by the Italian artist Michelangelo.

LARGEST EVER AIR FORCE

The United States Army Air Corps (now the US Air Force) operated 79,908 aircraft in July 1944 and 2,411,294 personnel in March 1944. By mid-1995, the US Air Force, including strategic missile forces, had 408,700 personnel and 5,900 aircraft in operational duty.

LARGEST NAVY

The United States Navy has a manpower of 570,400, including Marines, as of January 2000.

SHORTEST WAR

The shortest war on record was that between the UK and Zanzibar (now part of Tanzania), which finished at 9:45 am on 27 August 1896, after a battle that lasted just 45 minutes.

LONGEST SIEGE

The siege of Azotus (now Ashdod), Israel, is the longest on reliable record. The Greek historian Herodotus wrote that the city was besieged by Egyptian forces led by Psamtik I for 29 years in the period 664–610 BC.

BLOODIEST WAR

By far the most costly war in terms of human life was World War II (1939 to 1945), in which the total number of military and civilian fatalities of all countries is estimated to have been 56.4 million – in comparison, the UK's population today is 59.5 million. The country that suffered the most in proportion to its population was Poland, with 6 million killed, or 17.2% of its population of 35.1 million.

LARGEST COMMUNAL TOMB

A communal tomb housing 180,000 World War II dead in Okinawa, Japan, was enlarged in 1985 so that it could accommodate another 9,000 bodies thought to be buried on the island.

OLDEST AIR FORCE

The origins of the British Royal Air Force (RAF) can be traced back as far as 1878, when the War Office first commissioned the building of a military balloon. The RAF itself came into existence on 1 April 1918. Balloons had been used for military observation as far back as 1794 by the French at the Battle of Fleurus, during the French Revolutionary Wars.

MOST COSTLY WAR

The material cost of World War II far transcended that of the rest of history's wars put together and has been estimated at the equivalent of £1.04 trillion ($1.5 trillion) today. The cost for the UK is put at £34.42 billion ($49.43 billion), while the USA is estimated to have spent $530 billion (£369 billion) on the war.

MOST FATALITIES IN A CROCODILE ATTACK

On 19 February 1945 an Imperial Japanese Army unit based on the Burmese island of Ramree was outflanked by a British naval force and forced to trek across 16 km (10 miles) of mangrove swamps. The swamps housed thousands of 4.57-m-long (15-ft) saltwater crocodiles (*Crocodylus porosus*). By the morning of 20 February, only 20 of the 1,000 soldiers that entered the swamp had survived.

LONGEST CONTINUOUS WAR

The longest continuous war was the Thirty Years War, a conflict that was fought between various European countries from 1618 to 1648.

LARGEST PEACEKEEPING DEPLOYMENT

The largest peacekeeping mission was UNPROFOR (United Nations Protection Force), which took place in former Yugoslavia from February 1992 to March 1995. The mission reached a full strength of 39,922 personnel in September 1994, including a 'Rapid Reaction Force'.

BLOODIEST SIEGE

The worst siege in history was World War II's 880-day siege of Leningrad, USSR (now St Petersburg, Russia), which was maintained by the German Army from 30 August 1941 until 27 January 1944. The most realistic estimate puts the Russian dead at between 1.3 million and 1.5 million. This includes 641,000 people who died of starvation and 17,000 civilians killed by shelling. More than 150,000 shells and 100,000 bombs were dropped on the city.

MOST AIR FORCE PERSONNEL

China's air force consisted of 470,000 service personnel when counted in January 2000. In comparison, the US Air Force total was 370,022 in 1998.

LARGEST MILITARY EVACUATION

The greatest evacuation in military history was that carried out by 1,200 Allied naval and civil craft from the beachhead at Dunkerque (Dunkirk), France, between 26 May and 4 June 1940. In total, 338,226 men from the British and French armies escaped to safety.

LARGEST ARMY

According to *Jane's World Armies*, China's People's Liberation Army (above) had 2.2 million service personnel as of May 2000. China is downscaling its army, but can still call on a reserve-militia force and an armed police force.

LARGEST CIVILIAN AID CONVOY

From 1 to 4 December 1992 a convoy of 105 privately owned vehicles travelled in the Convoy of Hope from Dover, Kent, UK, to Zagreb, Croatia, carrying food and aid donated to refugees of the war in Bosnia. This was a round trip of about 3,200 km (1,988 miles).

LONGEST SERVING BARRACKS

The longest serving barracks is believed to be the Collins Barracks, formerly the Royal Barracks, in Dublin, Ireland. Completed in 1704, it housed a military presence for 290 years before it became the National Museum of Ireland in 1994.

BLOODIEST MODERN BATTLE

The greatest death toll in a battle in the modern day has been estimated at 1,109,000 in World War II's Battle of Stalingrad, USSR (now Volgograd, Russia), which started in the summer of 1942 and ended with the German surrender on 31 January 1943. In addition to the dead, approximately 650,800 Soviet troops were wounded but survived. World War I's torrid 142-day Battle of the Somme, France (from 1 July to 19 November 1916), produced more than 1.22 million casualties (dead and wounded combined), of which 398,671 were British (57,470 on the first day alone), more than 600,000 were German, and the rest were French.

MOST NATIONALITIES IN A MILITARY FORCE

As of March 2000, the French Foreign Legion numbered some 8,200 soldiers from 120 different countries. Non-French recruits receive a French passport after five years of service with the Legion.

MOST TANKS

The army with the most available tanks, according to figures released in 1997, was the People's Liberation Army of China, with 8,500.

BLOODIEST ANCIENT BATTLE

Roman losses at the Battle of Cannae in 216 BC have been estimated at 48,000–50,000 dead out of a force of about 80,000 men. Hannibal's opposing forces lost just 5,700. Cannae is thus considered to be the bloodiest example of annihilation in ancient warfare. In 479 BC, 250,000 men were reputedly killed at Plataea (Greeks against Persians), but historians consider the source for this and some other ancient battles to be unreliable.

GREATEST AIR AND SEA BATTLE

The Battle of Leyte Gulf, which took place in the Philippines during World War II, involved 218 Allied warships and 64 of their Japanese counterparts over five days in October 1944. In the skies above, 1,280 American and 716 Japanese aircraft engaged in combat. By the end of the fierce battle, 26 Japanese vessels and six US vessels had been sunk.

LONGEST RUNNING PEACEKEEPING MISSION

The longest running United Nations peacekeeping mission is UNTSO (United Nations Truce Supervision Organization, below), which has been in existence since June 1948. UNTSO's main headquarters are in Jerusalem, Israel, but it maintains various military observation posts throughout the Middle East. UNTSO was originally formed to oversee the 1948 truce in Palestine.

MOST EXPENSIVE FIGHTER AIRCRAFT

The US F-22 Raptor (above) was developed by Lockheed Martin Aeronautical Systems and Lockheed Martin Fort Worth (both USA) in the late 1990s. A total of $22.7 billion (£14 billion) was spent on the F-22's development – twice the sum spent on its European counterpart, the Eurofighter. The US Joint Strike Fighter, now in development, will exceed the F-22 in terms of cost.

MOST WIDELY DEPLOYED UNMANNED MILITARY AIRCRAFT

By March 2002, the RQ-1 Predator unmanned aerial vehicle (UAV) had logged over 35,000 hours of flying time, of which more than 8,200 had been in combat situations. It was used by the US military in Kosovo in 1999 and has seen extensive action in Afghanistan. Its advanced on-board cameras and sensors make it a valuable military asset in surveillance, reconnaissance and target-acquisition operations.

FASTEST PROPELLER FIGHTER OF WWII

The German Dornier DO-335 was unique in that it was driven by two motors, one right at the front of the aircraft and the other behind the cockpit. The aircraft could reach a sustained speed of 665 km/h (413 mph) and 765 km/h (477 mph) with emergency boost. Two models of the Dornier existed – the A-1 and the A-6; only 28 were completed before the end of World War II.

FASTEST OPERATIONAL BOMBERS

The US variable-geometry or 'swing-wing' General Dynamics FB-111A has a maximum speed of Mach 2.5 (around 2,655 km/h or 1,650 mph). The Russian swing-wing Tupolev Tu-22M, which is known to NATO as 'Backfire', has an estimated over-target speed of Mach 2 (2,124 km/h or 1,320 mph), but may also be capable of reaching Mach 2.5.

BOMBER WITH THE GREATEST WINGSPAN

The 10-engined Convair B-36J 'Peacemaker' had a total wingspan of 70.1 m (230 ft), the largest ever for a bomber, and a maximum take-off weight of 185 tonnes (407,854.7 lb). Its maiden flight took place in 1946, but the B-36J has been out of service since the late 1950s, when it was replaced by the Boeing B-52. Its top speed was 700 km/h (435 mph).

HEAVIEST BOMBER IN SERVICE

The Russian four-jet Tupolev Tu-160 'Blackjack' bomber, first produced in the Soviet era, has a maximum take-off weight of 275 tonnes (606,270 lb). The bomber's empty weight is 110 tonnes (242,500 lb).

FASTEST COMBAT JET

The fastest combat jet is the Russian Mikoyan MiG-25 fighter (NATO code name 'Foxbat'). The reconnaissance Foxbat-B has been tracked by radar at about Mach 3.2 (3,395 km/h or 2,110 mph). It was designed as a high-altitude interceptor.

SMALLEST SPY PLANE

The palm-sized Black Widow was developed by Aerovironment of Monrovia, California, USA, for possible reconnaissance use by ground-combat troops. It has a wingspan of 15.24 cm (6 in), weighs just 80 g (2.8 oz) and carries a tiny colour video camera weighing 2 g (0.07 oz). The plane is propelled by a battery-powered electric motor.

FIRST JET-ENGINED FLIGHT

The Heinkel He 178 was the first plane to be powered by a turbojet engine. The Heinkel's maiden flight was on 27 August 1939, when its pilot was Flugkapitän Erich Warsitz (Germany), at Marienehe, Germany. Its engine – a Heinkel He S3b – weighed 378 kg (834 lb) and was designed by Dr Hans Pabst von Ohain (Germany).

LONGEST-RANGE AIR ATTACKS

The longest-range attacks by air were undertaken by seven B-52G bombers that took off from Barksdale Air Force Base, Louisiana, USA, on 16 January 1991. The bombers were on their way to deliver air-launched cruise missiles against targets in Iraq shortly after the start of the Gulf War. Each flew 22,500 km (14,000 miles), refuelling four times in flight. The round trip mission lasted around 35 hours.

MOST EXPENSIVE MILITARY AIRCRAFT

The world's most expensive military aircraft is the US-made B-2 Spirit, a stealth bomber, which costs in excess of $1.3 billion (£780 million) per unit.

TOP-SCORING WWII FLYING ACE

The highest officially attributed figure for aircraft shot down by any airman was 352 by Major Erich Hartmann (Germany) during World War II.

LARGEST HELICOPTER IN PRODUCTION

The largest helicopter currently being produced is the Russian Mil Mi-26, which has a maximum take-off weight of 56 tonnes (123,460 lb). Unladen, it weighs 28.2 tonnes (62,170 lb) and its total length is 40.025 m (131 ft). The eight-bladed main rotor has a diameter of 32 m (105 ft) and is powered by two 8,500-kW (11,240-hp) turbo shaft engines.

MOST COMPLEX AIRCRAFT WEAPONS SYSTEM

The US AC-130U gunship (above) has TV, radar and infrared sensors, a 105-mm tank-sized cannon, a 40-mm cannon, a 25-mm Gatling gun, mission computer software with 609,000 lines of code and nine attack countermeasures systems.

LONGEST MILITARY RUNWAY

The longest military runway is at Edwards Air Force Base on the west side of Rogers dry lakebed at Muroc, California, USA, and is 11.92 km (7.41 miles) in length. The *Voyager* aircraft, taking off for its round-the-world unrefuelled flight, used 4.3 km (14,200 ft) of the 4.6-km-long (15,000-ft) main base concrete runway.

TOP SCORING WWI FLYING ACE

The highest figures officially attributed to any air ace in World War I was 80 aircraft shot down by Rittmeister Manfred Freiherr (Baron) von Richthofen (Germany), who was perhaps better known by his nickname 'The Red Baron'.

TOP-SCORING FEMALE AIR ACE

The record number of aircraft shot down by a female fighter pilot is 12 by Jnr Lydia Litvak (USSR) on the Eastern Front, from 1941. She was killed in action on 1 August 1943.

MOST PLANES DOWNED BY ONE PERSON IN A SORTIE

The highest official figure for aircraft shot down by one airman in a single sortie is 13 in 17 minutes by Major Erich Rudorffer (Germany) on the Russian front on 6 November 1943.

MOST SUCCESSFUL AIR ACE AGAINST FLYING BOMBS

The greatest number of successes against flying bombs (also known as V1s) was by Sqn Ldr Joseph Berry DFC (UK), who brought down 60 during the V1 campaign between 13 June and 1 September 1944, 57 of them at night. Sqn Ldr Berry was killed in action on 2 October 1944.

GREATEST NUMBER OF JETS SHOT DOWN

The greatest number of kills claimed in jet-to-jet battles is 21, achieved by Capt Nikolai Vasilevich Sutyagin of the former USSR during the Korean War.

MOST FLYING HOURS BY A MEMBER OF THE MILITARY

Sqn Ldr Bob Henderson logged a total of 18,188.5 hours, flying first with the Royal Canadian Air Force and then the Royal Air Force, between March 1955 and December 1994.

WORST HELICOPTER DISASTER

The worst ever helicopter disaster occurred on 4 February 1997, when two Israeli Sikorsky CH-53 helicopters collided in mid-air near the settlement of Shaar Yishuv in the north of Israel, killing 73 soldiers.

LARGEST AIR FORCE BY NUMBER OF AIRCRAFT

The world's largest air force in terms of aircraft is that of the USA, which had 4,413 combat aircraft as of September 1999. This includes 179 bombers, 1,666 fighter and attack aircraft and 1,279 trainer aircraft.

FASTEST PROPELLER-DRIVEN AIRCRAFT

The Russian Tu-95/142 (NATO code name 'Bear'), originally produced in the Soviet era, has a maximum level speed of Mach 0.82 (925 km/h or 575 mph). The aircraft first flew in 1954 and there are still many Bears in operation.

MOST NUMEROUS WWII FIGHTER PLANE

More than 36,000 Ilyushin Il-2 Sturmovik ground-attack aircraft are said to have been produced in the former Soviet Union before, during and immediately after World War II. This means that the fighter was produced in greater numbers than any other aircraft used during the war and also makes it one of the most numerous combat aircraft of all time.

MOST PRODUCED TILT ROTOR AIRCRAFT

The Boeing/Bell V-22 Osprey tilt rotor aircraft (below) is the first such machine to enter production. The US military had employed 12 Ospreys as test and training aircraft early in 2002, by which time 20 more had been ordered.

NAVY WITH THE MOST AIRCRAFT

The US Navy had more than 4,000 aircraft (EA-6B Prowler, above) in service at the start of 2002. It can boast around 20 different models of fixed-wing aircraft, including carrier-based F-14 Tomcat and F/A-18 Hornet fighters and various models of reconnaissance, transport, anti-submarine and airborne command post aircraft. It also operates six different helicopters and the unique new V-22 Osprey tilt rotor aircraft.

GREATEST MODERN NAVAL BATTLE

The greatest purely naval battle of modern times was the World War I Battle of Jutland on 31 May 1916, in which 151 British Royal Navy warships battled with 101 German warships. The Royal Navy lost 14 ships and 6,097 men, while the German fleet lost 11 ships and 2,545 men.

FASTEST SUBMARINE

The Russian Alpha class nuclear-powered submarines had a reported maximum speed of more than 40 knots (74 km/h or 46 mph), and were thought to be capable of diving to depths of 760 m (2,500 ft). It is believed that only one now remains in service, as a trials boat.

NAVY WITH THE MOST SUBMARINES

The United States Navy has 74 armed submarines, more than any other country. The entire submarine fleet is nuclear powered, and includes more than 50 Seawolf and Los Angeles class attack ships, as well as 18 Ohio class ballistic missile carriers.

WORST SUBMARINE DISASTER

The 2,926-tonne (6,450,718-lb) French submarine *Surcouf* sank with 159 crewmen on board after it had been rammed by US merchantman *Thompson Lykes* in the Caribbean on 18 February 1942.

MOST SUBMARINES SUNK BY ONE SHIP

The highest number of U-boat kills attributed to one ship in World War II was 15, achieved by *HMS Starling* under the command of Capt Frederic John Walker DSO***, RN, CB. Ships under Captain Walker's command sank a total of 20 U-boats between 1941 and his death on 9 July 1944.

HIGHEST DEATH TOLL ON A SINGLE SHIP IN WARTIME

When the liner *Wilhelm Gustloff* (Germany) was torpedoed off Danzig (now known as Gdansk), Poland, by a Soviet S-13 submarine on 30 January 1945, a total of 7,700 people died. There were only 903 survivors.

GREATEST ANCIENT NAVAL BATTLE

The greatest of all ancient naval battles was the Battle of Salamis, Greece, which took place in autumn 480 BC. There were approximately 800 vessels in the defeated Persian fleet and 380 in the victorious fleet of the Athenians and their allies. It is estimated that up to 200,000 men may have been involved in the conflict.

FASTEST DESTROYER

The highest speed ever attained by a destroyer was 45.25 knots (83.42 km/h or 52 mph) by the 2,900-tonne (6.4 million-lb) French ship *Le Terrible* in 1935. Built in Blainville, France, and powered by four Yarrow small tube boilers and two Rateau geared turbines, giving 74,570 kW (100,000 hp), the ship was decommissioned at the end of 1957.

LARGEST TORPEDO

The Russian Type 65 torpedo, which has a 65-cm (25.5-in) diameter, carries either a warhead of nearly one tonne (2,204 lb) of conventional explosive, or a 15-kiloton nuclear warhead. This gives it slightly less explosive power than the atomic bombs that destroyed Hiroshima and Nagasaki in 1945.

FASTEST WARSHIP

The world's fastest-ever warship was the 23.7-m-long (78-ft) 100-tonne (220,000-lb) US Navy test surface-effect ship SES-100B. It attained a world record 91.9 knots (170 km/h or 105 mph) on 25 January 1980 the Chesapeake Bay Test Range, Maryland, USA. Like hovercraft, surface-effect ships travel on a cushion of air, but also have two sharp, rigid hulls that remain in the water. Large fans under the ship create air pressure that is trapped between the hulls and raises the ship, reducing the hull area that is actually submerged and thereby permitting higher speeds and efficiency.

NAVY WITH MOST WARSHIPS

The navy with the largest number of warships is the United States Navy, which in early 2002 had 318 principal vessels, including submarines. These vessels are supported by 380,000 Navy personnel and 183,000 civilians.

LARGEST UNMANNED SUBMARINE

The US Navy LSV-2 *Cutthroat* is the largest unmanned submarine in existence. It is 33.83 m (111 ft) long, 3.05 m (10 ft) wide, and weighs 205 tonnes (451,950 lb). An unarmed experimental craft, the *Cutthroat* is a 1:4 (25%) scale model of the US Navy's Virginia class submarine, which is presently being developed. The *Cutthroat* acts as a platform to test stealth technologies designed for the Virginia class ships.

GREATEST SEABORNE INVASION

In the first three days of the Allied land, air and sea operation (above) on D-day, 6 June 1944, 745 ships, 347 minesweepers and 4,066 landing craft carrying 185,000 men and 20,000 vehicles landed on the French Normandy coast.

LARGEST NAVAL HOVERCRAFT

The Russian Zubr (NATO code name 'Pomornik') is the largest naval hovercraft, and the largest operational hovercraft in the world at present. It is 57 m (187 ft) long, 22.3 m (73 ft 1.2 in) wide and has a full load displacement of 535 tonnes (1.17 million lb). The Zubr is an amphibious landing craft able to deliver 360 troops or three battle tanks onto beaches at speeds of up to 60 knots (111 km/h or 69 mph).

LARGEST AIRCRAFT CARRIER

The warships with the largest full load displacement in the world are the Nimitz class US Navy aircraft carriers USS Nimitz, USS Carl Vinson, USS Dwight D Eisenhower, USS Theodore Roosevelt, USS Abraham Lincoln, USS John C Stennis, USS George Washington, USS Harry S Truman and USS Ronald Reagan, the last five of which displace around 98,550 tonnes (217.2 million lb). The ships are 332.9 m (1,092 ft) long, have 1.82 ha (4.49 acres) of flight deck and, driven by four nuclear-powered 194,000-kW (260,000-hp) geared steam turbines, can reach speeds of over 30 knots (56 km/h or 34.5 mph).

LARGEST BATTLESHIP EVER

The Japanese vessels Yamato and Musashi were the largest battleships ever to be commissioned. Yamato was completed on 16 December 1941 and sunk by 11 torpedoes and seven bombs south-west of Kyushu, Japan, by US planes on 7 April 1945. Musashi was sunk in the Philippine Sea by 20 torpedoes and 17 bombs on 24 October 1944. Both ships had a full load displacement of 71,111 tonnes (156.7 million lb), an overall length of 263 m (863 ft), a beam of 38.7 m (127 ft) and a full load draught of 10.8 m (35 ft 5 in).

LARGEST SURFACE-EFFECT SHIP

The largest surface-effect ships in service today are two Russian Bora class guided missile corvettes, which have a displacement of approximately 1,050 tonnes (2.31 million lb) and a claimed cruising speed of 54 knots (100 km/h or 62 mph). The Bora are 65.6 m (215 ft) long, 18 m (59 ft) wide, and have a full crew complement of 68.

EARLIEST STEALTH SHIP

The earliest known ship to feature stealth technology is the US Navy Sea Shadow, which was completed in the mid-1980s but only revealed to the public in 1993. (Stealth technology is designed to reduce the thermal, radar and acoustic recognizability of military craft or weapons.) The bizarre-looking twin-hulled ship is 49.98 m (164 ft) long, 20.72 m (68 ft) across and has a full load displacement of 569 tonnes (1.25 million lb). The Sea Shadow was built by Lockheed Martin (USA), has a crew of 10 and a top speed of 18.52 km/h (11.5 mph).

LARGEST STEALTH SHIP

The largest ship to incorporate stealth technology is the Swedish Visby class corvette (right), which is around 72 m (236 ft) long and has a displacement of 600 tonnes (1.32 million lb). Developed by the Kockums shipyard, the carbon fibre vessel is considerably lighter than a conventional ship of its size, and has the large flat surfaces used in aircraft to provide low radar visibility. The Visby prototype made her maiden voyage in December 2001.

HIGHEST RATE OF FIRE FOR A MACHINE GUN IN SERVICE
Designed for use in helicopters and armoured vehicles in the late 1960s, the 7.62-mm calibre M134 Minigun (above) is based on the multiple-barrelled Gatling gun. Its six barrels are revolved by an electric motor and fed by a 4,000-round link belt. This permits a firing rate of 6,000 rounds per minute, or 100 rounds per second, about 10 times faster than a standard machine gun.

LARGEST GATHERING OF FORD GPA AMPHIBIANS
Sixteen Ford GPA amphibious vehicles assembled at the 20th National GPA Swim at Corowa, NSW, Australia, on 13 March 1999, the largest gathering of this type of craft since World War II.

EARLIEST USE OF ROCKETS
Propelled by gunpowder, 'flying fireworks' (composed of a charcoal-saltpetre-sulphur mixture) were first described by Zeng Gongliang (China) in 1042. War rockets originated in 1245 near Hangzhou, China. Hangzhou was the Chinese capital between 1127 and 1278.

GREATEST GUN RANGE
The Paris-Geschetz 'Paris Gun' was a famous long-range gun that shelled Paris during World War I. It had a calibre of 21 cm, a designed range of 127.9 km (79.5 miles) and an achieved range of 122 km (76 miles) from the woods at Crepy, France, in March 1918.

During World War II, Germany's little-known V3 static underground firing tubes were built into 50 shafts near Mimoyecques, not far from Calais, France. They were originally designed to bombard London, although they were never operative, and would have fired projectiles a distance of approximately 150 km (95 miles).

LARGEST GUN
In the siege of Sevastopol, USSR (now Ukraine), in July 1942, the German army used an 80-cm-calibre gun with a barrel 28.87 m (94 ft 8 in) long. Named *Schwerer Gustav*, it was one of three guns that were given the general name of 'Dora', although the other two were not finished and so were not used in action. The gun was built by Krupp, and its remains were discovered near Metzenhof, Bavaria, in August 1945. The whole assembly of the gun was 42.9 m (141 ft) in length and weighed 1,344 tonnes (2,963,009 lb); it was manned by a crew of 1,500. The *Schwerer Gustav* was capable of firing an 8.1-tonne (17,857.4-lb) projectile 20.9 km (13 miles), while for a 4.8-tonne (10,582-lb) projectile the range was 46.7 km (29 miles).

LARGEST MORTAR
The two largest mortars ever constructed were 'Mallet's Mortar', which was constructed in the Woolwich Arsenal, London, UK, in 1857, and the 'Little David' of World War II, which was made in the USA. Each had a calibre of 91.4 cm, but neither was ever used in action.

SMALLEST RADAR SYSTEM
American electronics engineer Tom McEwan invented a radar device on a 2-cm^2 (0.79-in^2) silicon chip, with a key component that costs less than $15 (£8.40) to manufacture. It can detect moving objects up to 50 m (164 ft) away and is being used as a virtual dipstick in industrial liquid tanks and as an electronic stethoscope.

MOST ACCURATE PORTABLE ANTI-AIRCRAFT MISSILE
The US-made Stinger missile, introduced in the early 1980s, is 1.5 m (5 ft) long and weighs 9.9 kg (22 lb). It has a range of approximately 4.8 km (3 miles) and a speed of around 2,000 km/h (1,300 mph). Based on figures obtained during the conflict in Afghanistan during the 1980s, it is said to have a 79% success rate.

LARGEST CONVENTIONAL EXPLOSION
The largest single conventional explosive detonation was for the demolition of the German fortifications at Helgoland, Germany, on 18 April 1947. A charge of 4,061 tonnes

(8,952,961 lb) was detonated by Commissioned Gunner EC Jellis (UK) of the Royal Navy demolition team headed by Lt FT Woosnam (UK) aboard *HMS Lasso*, lying 14.5 km (9 miles) out to sea.

EARLIEST TANK
The first tank was produced by William Foster & Co Ltd of Lincoln, Lincs, UK, and was known as 'No. 1 Lincoln' – subsequently modified and renamed 'Little Willie'. It first ran on 6 September 1915. Tanks first saw action with the Heavy Section, Machine Gun Corps, later the Tank Corps, at the Battle of Flers-Courcelette, France, on 15 September 1916.

FASTEST TANK
On 26 March 2002 a standard S 2000 Scorpion Peacekeeper tank achieved a speed of 82.23 km/h (51.1 mph) at the QinetiQ vehicle test track, Chertsey, Surrey, UK. The tank's features include appliqué hull armour, ballistic skirts and a K10000 replaceable rubber pad track, and it is powered by an RS 2133 high-speed diesel engine. It was developed by the UK company Repaircraft plc.

LIGHTEST TANK
The hull of the Advanced Composite Armoured Vehicle Platform (ACAVP) tank (above) is built from E-glass epoxy, a plastic-and-fibreglass composite material. It is 10% lighter than an equivalent in-service metallic-hulled tank.

HEAVIEST TANK

The heaviest tank ever built was the German Panzer Kampfwagen Maus II, which, at 192 tonnes (423,287 lb), weighed as much as 130 modern saloon cars. By 1945 it was still at an experimental stage and was abandoned. The heaviest operational tank used by any army was the 75.2-tonne (165,787.4-lb) 13-man French Char de Rupture 2C bis of 1922. It carried a 15.5-cm (6.1-in) howitzer and was powered by two 186-kW (250-hp) engines.

HEAVIEST CONVENTIONAL BOMB

The heaviest conventional bomb used operationally was the UK Royal Air Force's Grand Slam. The bomb, which weighed 9,980 kg (22,000 lb) and was 7.74 m (25 ft 5 in) long, was first dropped on Bielefeld railway viaduct, Germany, on 14 March 1945. In all, 41 Grand Slam bombs were dropped by 617 Sqn RAF in 1945. In 1949 the US Air Force tested a bomb weighing 19,050 kg (42,000 lb) at Muroc Dry Lake, California, USA.

MOST ACCURATE BOMB

The US-built Joint Direct Attack Munition (JDAM) is the world's most accurate air drop munition (the word 'Joint' refers to the co-funding of the project by the US Air Force and the US Navy). After its release, the JDAM's location is monitored by fixes from satellites. Upon impact, the JDAM is accurate to plus or minus 2 m (6 ft 7 in).

MOST HEAVILY ARMED TANK

The most heavily armed tanks in recent times have been the Russian T-64, T-72, T-80 and T-90, all of which have a 12.5-cm gun-missile system. The American Sheridan light tank mounts a 15.2-cm weapon, which is both a gun and a missile launcher combined, but this is not a long-barrelled, high-velocity gun of the conventional type. The British AVRE Centurion had a 16.5-cm low-velocity demolition gun.

MOST TANKS PRODUCED

The most widespread production of any model of tank was that of the Soviet T-54/55 series. More than 50,000 T-54/55s were constructed during the period 1954–1980 in the former USSR alone. There was further production of the tank in the countries of the one-time Warsaw Pact in central and eastern Europe as well as in China.

EARLIEST WARTIME USE OF A BOUNCING BOMB

The bouncing bomb, designed by Barnes Wallis (UK), was first used in wartime on 16 May 1943, when Guy Gibson of the UK's 617 Sqn RAF released the cylindrical bombs in the Ruhr Valley, Germany, during an attack on the Möhne and Eder dams. Dropped from a height of 18 m (60 ft), at a speed of 386 km/h (240 mph) and spinning at a rate of 500 rpm, the bombs bounced over the water, sank in front of the dam wall and exploded underwater.

MOST WIDELY USED FIREARM IN WARFARE

The Kalashnikov AK-47 (below), and its variants, has been used in over 75 wars – more than any other weapon. Over 100 million units of the AK-47 have been assembled in over 25 countries, some illegally.

MOST RECENT USE OF NERVE GAS WITH MALICE

On 20 March 1995 in Tokyo, Japan, members of the Aum Shinrikyo sect, a Buddhist splinter group, released sarin, a lethal nerve gas, into the subway system (above), killing 11 and injuring more than 5,500. A pin-prick of sarin is enough to kill a human.

LARGEST STOCKPILE OF CHEMICAL WEAPONS

According to the International Institute of Strategic Studies, Russia has the largest stockpile of lethal and non-lethal chemical weapons. The total amount is said to weigh around 40,000 tonnes (88,184,000 lb). The USA, with an estimated total of 25,000 tonnes (55,115,500 lb), has the second largest stockpile in the world.

LARGEST CRATER CAUSED BY A NUCLEAR EXPLOSION

A 104-kiloton nuclear device was detonated at the Semipalatinsk Test Site, Kazakhstan, 178 m (583 ft) beneath the dry bed of the Chagan river on 15 January 1965. The crater caused by the resulting explosion is 408 m (1,338 ft) wide, with a depth of 100 m (328 ft). It is known locally as Lake Chagan.

HIGHEST-ALTITUDE NUCLEAR EXPLOSION

A 1.7-kiloton nuclear weapon was detonated 749 km (466 miles) above the Earth's surface on 6 September 1958, as part of the United States' secret Operation Argus test series. The 98.9-kg (218-lb) W-25 warhead was launched by a three-stage Lockheed X-17A missile fired by the warship USS Norton Sound, which was located in the South Atlantic, 1,770 km (1,100 miles) south-west of Cape Town, South Africa.

MOST POWERFUL NERVE GAS

The nerve gas VX – or, to give its true name, Ethyl S-2-diisopropylamino ethylmethyl-phosphonothiolate – was developed at the Chemical Defence Experimental Establishment, Porton Down, Wilts, UK, in 1952. It is about 300 times more powerful than the phosgene ($COCl_2$) that was used in World War I, and a drop an eighth the size of a raindrop is enough to kill a human. In the 1950s the USA were so keen to get hold of this gas they traded thermonucleur weapons technology with the British.

HIGHEST NUMBER OF NUCLEAR WEAPONS DETONATED AT ONE TIME

A minimum of eight (possibly nine) nuclear weapons were detonated simultaneously in an underground tunnel at the former USSR test site at Novaya Zemyla, deep in the Russian Arctic, on 24 October 1990.

SMALLEST NUCLEAR WEAPON

The W54 fission bomb, deployed by the USA in Europe between 1961 and 1971, is the smallest confirmed nuclear weapon ever made. The bomb had a range of 4 km (2.49 miles) and weighed 34.47 kg (76 lb). Its widest diameter was just 27 cm (11 in).

LONGEST-RUNNING ENVIRONMENTAL CAMPAIGN

Greenpeace has been campaigning against nuclear testing since the group was founded in 1971. The first campaign was directed against nuclear testing off the coast of Alaska, USA. The organization is still campaigning all around the world against nuclear weapons.

FIRST USE OF ATOMIC BOMB

The first atom bomb dropped was on Hiroshima, Japan, by the USA at 8:16 am on 6 August 1945. It had an explosive power equivalent to that of 15 kilotons of trinitrotoluene ($C_7H_5N_3O_6$), or TNT. The first atom bomb test, in New Mexico, USA, was carried out three weeks before this device was deployed. Code-named 'Little Boy', it had a length of 3 m (10 ft) and weighed 4,082 kg (9,000 lb).

HIGHEST DEATH TOLL FROM AN ATOMIC BOMB RAID

On 6 August 1945, 155,200 people were killed when an atomic bomb was dropped on Hiroshima, Japan.

This figure includes radiation deaths within a year. The device exploded 509 m (1,670 ft) above the city and completely devastated at least 10 km² (4 miles²) of Hiroshima as soon as it exploded, damaging 65% of all the city's structures.

MOST DEADLY ANTHRAX EPIDEMIC

The most deadly anthrax epidemic occured in Sverdlovsk, USSR (now Ekaterinberg, Russia), in April 1979. At least 68 people died from inhaling spores spread on the wind. The cause of the epidemic has never been verified.

HIGHEST DEATH TOLL FROM A CHEMICAL WARFARE ATTACK

The greatest number of people killed in a single chemical weapons attack is estimated at around 4,000, although the exact figure may never be known. The victims died when President Saddam Hussein of Iraq attacked members of his country's Kurdish minority at Halabja, Iraq, in March 1988. The attack was ostensibly punishment for the support the Kurds had given to Iran during the Iran–Iraq War.

LARGEST CONVENTIONAL BOMB IN EXISTENCE

The BLU-82B/C-130 weapon system (above), nicknamed 'Daisy Cutter', contains a warhead with 5,715 kg (12,600 lb) of explosives. The bomb has an impact area of 91–274 m (300–900 ft) and was used in Afghanistan in 2001.

EARLIEST USE OF SMALLPOX AS A BIOLOGICAL WEAPON

The earliest documented use of the smallpox virus as a biological weapon occurred during the French And Indian Wars 1754–1763, fought in North America. British soldiers, fighting both French colonists and native Americans, gave blankets that had been contaminated with smallpox to native Americans. In the virus epidemics that followed, more than 50% of the affected tribes were wiped out.

MOST DESTRUCTIVE NUCLEAR ICBM

The most powerful ICBM (intercontinental ballistic missile) is the former Soviet Union's SS-18 Model 5, officially called the RS-20, armed with 10 MIRVs (multiple independently targetable re-entry vehicles), each of 750 kilotons. Another model is rumoured to have had a single 20-megaton warhead. During the Cold War, the RS-20 was the most feared weapon in the Warsaw Pact arsenal, because of its high yield. Each of the 10 MIRVs had an accuracy of 250 m (820 ft).

HEAVIEST NUCLEAR BOMB

The heaviest known nuclear bomb in operational service was the MK 17, which was carried by US B-36 Peacemaker long-range bombers during the mid-1950s. This mammoth device weighed 19,050 kg (42,000 lb) and measured 7.49 m (24 ft 6 in) long. It had a maximum yield of 20 megatons, the equivalent to a 1,000 times the strength of the bomb that the USA dropped on Hiroshima, Japan, during World War II.

MOST POWERFUL NUCLEAR EXPLOSION

The most powerful thermonuclear device so far tested is one dubbed 'Tsar Bomba', which had a power equivalent to that of approximately 57 megatons of TNT. It was detonated by the former Soviet Union in the Novaya Zemlya area at 8:33 am on 30 October 1961. The shockwave circled the world three times, taking 36 hr 27 min for the first circuit.

MOST POWERFUL NUCLEAR EXPLOSION IN SPACE

A 1.45-megaton nuclear explosion took place 399 km (248 miles) above Johnston Island in the Pacific Ocean on 9 July 1962. The 755-kg (1,665-lb) warhead was launched by the US Air Force using a Thor missile. Code-named 'Starfish Prime', the height of the detonation was equivalent to the orbital altitude of the present-day space shuttle and was 100 times more powerful than the blast that hit Hiroshima.

FIRST DOCUMENTED BIOLOGICAL ATTACK

In the 6th century BC, Assyrians, who lived in present-day Iraq, used rye ergot to poison enemy wells. This gave rise to paranoid behaviour among their victims, some who died as a result.

LARGEST STOCKPILE OF THE SMALLPOX VACCINE

The USA has the world's largest stockpile of vaccines to treat the deadly smallpox virus. There are currently 15.4 million doses in storage, but by the end of 2002 the USA will have 286 million doses – enough for each American citizen. This is for protection against possible future acts of bioterrorism.

WORST NUCLEAR SUBMARINE ACCIDENT

The worst nuclear submarine accident in terms of weapons lost occured on 6 October 1986 when the Russian submarine K-219 (Project 667-A Yankee Class) sank in the Atlantic 965 km (599 miles) north of Bermuda. The submarine is now sitting 5,800 m (19,028 ft) beneath the surface of the ocean, with two nuclear reactors and 16 nuclear missiles still on board.

MOST DESTRUCTIVE NON-LETHAL WEAPON

The BLU-114/B 'graphite bomb' (left), used by NATO in Operation Allied Force against Serbia in May 1999, disabled 70% of the country's power grid with minimal 'direct' casualties. A similar device was used to knock out 85% of Iraq's electrical capacity during the Gulf War. The bombs explode ultra-fine short-circuiting carbon-fibre wires over electrical installations.

TECHNOLOGY AND SCIENCE

MOST COMPREHENSIVE CYBERSPACE MAP
Working from the Bell Laboratories, New Jersey, USA, researchers Bill Cheswick and Hal Burch (both USA) created a map of cyberspace (above) featuring 88,000 endpoints. The pair used colours to represent different Internet Service Providers (ISPs). To create the map, Cheswick sent out electronic tracers from his New Jersey-based computer, which 'died' on reaching a terminal destination. At their point of expiry, the messages sent back a 'death notice', which enabled Burch's program to create the map.

FASTEST AROUND-THE-WORLD TEXT MESSAGE
On 20 February 2002 at the 3GSM World Congress in Cannes, France, Logica sent a text message around the world by forwarding it to mobile phones in six countries in six continents, and finally back to the original phone in Cannes. The message was received back in France only 3 min 17.53 sec after the original sender began typing in the message.

EARLIEST E-MAIL
In 1971, the first-ever e-mail was sent by Ray Tomlinson (USA), an engineer working at the computer company Bolt, Beranek & Newman in Cambridge, Massachusetts, USA. The e-mail was initially designed as an experiment by Ray to see if he was able to get two computers to exchange a message. He was also responsible for choosing to use the @ symbol to separate the recipient's name from their location. The first e-mail message was 'QWERTYUIOP'.

HIGHEST NUMBER OF TELEPHONES PER CAPITA
The principality of Monaco holds the record for the most telephones per head of population, with 1,994 for every 1,000 people.

COSTLIEST E-MAIL
In 1997, a subsidiary of US-based petroleum company Chevron Corp paid $2.2 million (£1.3 million) to settle a sexual harassment lawsuit filed against it by four female employees. Evidence presented by the women's lawyers included e-mail records listing 25 reasons why beer is supposedly better than women. In settling, Chevron denied the women's allegations.

OLDEST COMPUTER
The first fully automated, software-driven computer was designed and run by Tom Kilburn and Freddie Williams (both UK) on 21 June 1948. The pair used a 17-instruction program on a machine called 'Baby', which calculated the highest factor of 2 to the power of 18.

COUNTRY WITH THE MOST MOBILE PHONES
The country with the greatest number of cellular telephone users is the USA, with a grand total of 69.209 million subscribers in 1998.

FIRST POLE-TO-POLE TELEPHONE CALL
On April 28 1999, at 10:30 am (GMT), the first phone call between people at the North and the South poles took place, lasting 45 minutes. Taking part were: George Morrow, Tom Carlson, Joel Michalski, Vince Hurley, Mike Comberiate, Ron Ruhlman and Claire Parkinson (all USA). The day before, the same team had carried out the first internet link and webcast from the North Pole.

BUSIEST INTERNATIONAL TELEPHONE ROUTE
The busiest international telephone route is between the USA and Canada. In 2001 there were approximately 10.4 billion minutes of two-way traffic between the two countries.

LARGEST SWITCHBOARD
The world's biggest switchboard is the one in the Pentagon, Arlington, Virginia, USA, which has 34,500 lines that handle nearly one million calls per day through about 160,934 km (100,000 miles) of telephone cable. Its busiest day was 6 June 1994 – the 50th anniversary of D-day – when it took 1,502,415 calls.

LARGEST TELECOMMUNICATIONS COMPANY
The Nippon Telegraph and Telephone Corporation (NTT), Tokyo, Japan, is the world's largest telecommunications company. In 2001, NTT had revenues of $97,956 million (£69,163 million) and profits totalling $2,821 million (£1,991 million). The company had a workforce of 224,000 employees.

LARGEST HOLDER OF DOMAIN NAMES
The US company Namezero holds 1,307,300 domain names, more than any other company in the world.

LARGEST DIGITAL SATELLITE RADIO BROADCASTER
From its two geosynchronous satellites (which orbit the Earth while staying above a fixed point on its surface), WorldSpace broadcasts digital radio channels to Africa, Asia and Europe with a total surface area (or 'footprint') of 80 million km^2 (30.8 million miles^2). Its first satellite, Afristar, began broadcasting in October 1999 and Asiastar began after its launch in March 2000.

LARGEST HOST OF INTERNATIONAL TELEPHONE CALLS
In 2000, US company WorldCom (CEO and president Bernard J Ebbers, above right) was recognized as the world's largest carrier of international telephone calls, in terms of outgoing traffic, with 12.4 billion minutes of communications.

MOST NEW COMPUTER VIRUSES IN A MONTH

The greatest number of new computer viruses to appear in any one month was approximately 16,000, in January 1999. The same year also saw the highest ever number of new computer viruses, with 26,193 entering 'the wild'. The majority of these new viruses were a direct consequence of the circulation on the internet of a new construction kit for viruses.

LONGEST TELEPHONE CABLE

The world's longest submarine telephone cable is FLAG (Fibre-optic Link Around the Globe), which runs for 27,000 km (16,800 miles) from Japan to the United Kingdom. It links three continents (Europe, Africa and Asia) and 11 countries, and is capable of supporting 600,000 simultaneous telephone calls.

SMALLEST COMPUTER VIRUS

The smallest computer virus to date is the TrivialOW.13 virus. With a size of just 13 bytes, this DOS-based virus overwrites data in the files it infects. It was first detected in January 1998 and is no longer active.

MOST POPULAR COUNTRY LEVEL DOMAIN

According to NetNames Ltd, as of March 2001, the most popular country level domain is '.uk' (Britain), with over 2 million domain registrations. Britain is closely followed by Germany. The USA has the most internet sites, but few of them use '.us' in their URL.

MOST POPULAR TOP-LEVEL DOMAIN NAME (TLD)

Of the 35.3 million domain names in existence worldwide (as of April 2001), the most popular is '.com', which is used by 22.3 million hosts.

LARGEST INTERNET SEARCH ENGINE

Google, with around 2.215 billion pages, has the largest continually refreshed webpage index of any search engine in the world. Founded by Larry Page (below left) and Sergey Brin (below right, both USA), Google's first office was a garage in Menlo Park, California, USA, which opened in September 1998 with a staff of four people.

FASTEST COMPUTER

The NEC Earth Simulator at the Yokohama Institute for Earth Sciences in Japan is capable of carrying out 35.6 trillion calculations per second – approximately five times the speed of the previous record holder. Built by HNSX Supercomputers, a division of NEC, the computer is designed to simulate Earth's complex climate in order to predict climate change and global warming, both of which have serious implications for Japan. Its 5,104 processors are housed in cabinets that cover an area equivalent to four tennis courts.

MOST HUMAN-LIKE COMPUTER PROGRAM

A computer program called ALICE, created by Richard Wallace (USA), is the most human-like computer program and won the annual 2001 Loebner Prize. A bronze medal is awarded each year to the program that wins the highest score from a panel of expert judges, who attempt to converse with the competing programs via a keyboard. The silver medal will be awarded to the program that convinces half the judges that it is a human, and a gold medal will be awarded once half the judges are convinced by a program conversing with speech rather than text. Neither the silver nor the gold medal have yet been awarded.

SHORTEST INSTRUCTION MANUAL FOR A COMPUTER

The Apple iMac personal computer comes with an instruction manual that consists of just six pictures and 36 words. The computer therefore certainly lives up to its sales pitch, which states that a user can simply take it out of the box and plug it in.

MOST WIDELY USED INDUSTRIAL ROBOT

Puma (Programmable Universal Machine for Assembly), designed by Vic Schienman in the 1970s and made by Swiss company Staubli Unimation, is the most commonly used robot in university laboratories and automated assembly lines.

FASTEST-SELLING ENTERTAINMENT ROBOT

Sony Corporation's AIBO Entertainment Robot ERS-110, a robotic pet puppy, retailed for $2,066 (£1,289) when it first went on sale on 31 May 1999, and 3,000 were sold within 20 minutes. AIBO is 27.9 cm (11 in) tall and can recognize its surroundings using a built-in sensor. (The word 'Aibo' means 'pal' or 'partner' in Japanese.) It can be programmed to perform tricks or to 'play' on its own. On 1 June 1999, 2,000 AIBOs became available over the internet in America and the initial rush to buy the robot caused web servers to crash. The latest model, the ERS-220, features enhanced touch sensors and word recognition, as well as a motion sensor surveillance mode.

SMALLEST CASSETTE

The NT digital cassette made by the Sony Corporation of Japan for use in dictating machines measures just 30 x 21 x 5 mm (1.18 x 0.82 x 0.19 in).

LARGEST PLASMA SCREEN

Plasma technology is the latest revolution in high-quality computer screens. It features charged gas between two layers of glass, which operate under the same principles as fluorescent lights and neon tubes. The result is a perfectly flat and uniformly focused high-quality image on a slim screen. The largest plasma screen produced to date measures 160 cm (63 in) diagonally and is manufactured by Samsung.

SMALLEST GPS WATCH

The Casio PAT2GP-1V watch measures 58.5 x 51.5 x 21.0 mm (2.3 x 2.0 x 0.8 in). It receives data from the fleet of Global Positioning System (GPS) satellites in order to pinpoint the location of the wearer to within 10 m (33 ft), anywhere on Earth. It can be connected to a home computer to plan map routes, which can be stored in the watch itself.

HIGHEST-JUMPING ROBOT

Sandia National Laboratories, USA, have developed experimental 'hopper' robots that use combustion-driven pistons to jump to heights of 9 m (30 ft). The diminutive robots have potential applications in planetary exploration, where several hoppers could be released by a lander to survey the surrounding landscape.

HIGHEST RESOLUTION MONITOR

The T220, made by IBM, has a higher resolution than any other monitor in the world. With a liquid crystal display (LCD) screen size of 55.5 cm (22.2 in) and a resolution of 3,840 x 2,800 pixels, the T220 has a total of 9.4 million pixels. Its technological superiority enables it to provide around 12 times higher detail than most conventional monitors.

SMALLEST BLACK BOX RECORDER

The smallest 'black box' recorder is the Accu-counter, a device fitted to firearms that records the number and exact time of each shot fired from that weapon. It is typically 2.5 cm (1 in) long, 1.3 cm (0.5 in) wide and 0.6 cm (0.25 in) thick. Made by Accu-counter, Inc (USA), it is expected to be adopted by law enforcement agencies and the military to monitor firearm use.

FASTEST-GROWING ENTERTAINMENT PRODUCT

Since the DVD player launched in 1997 over 627 million DVDs have been sold, according to research and consultancy company Understanding & Solutions. After the launch of CD players in 1983, 256 million CDs sold over the same period.

MOST THERAPEUTIC ROBOT

PARO, a robotic seal designed by Takanori Shibata of the Intelligent Systems Institute (Japan) as a therapeutic robot, can respond to human touch and sound. During a six-week trial, from May to July 2001 in a day care centre for the elderly, tests demonstrated a marked improvement in the levels of stress among patients after interaction with the robot.

images of the Earth's surface at a resolution of 61 cm (24 in) per pixel. QuickBird can also take multispectral images at 2.44 m (8 ft) per pixel. (Multispectral images use different parts of the spectrum, as opposed to monochrome images.)

MOST INTELLIGENT PEN AND PAPER

The Swedish company Anoto has created a digital pen that allows the user to digitally store up to 50 fully written pages in its memory. This information can then be transferred directly to a nearby computer or – via Bluetooth technology – straight to any

computer in the world over the internet. (Bluetooth technology uses short-range radio as a replacement for physical wires, enabling wire-free communications between items such as computers, mobile phones, PDAs and the internet.) The pen writes on special digital paper that enables the pen to know exactly where on the paper it is. The paper is divided into a grid with squares 2 x 2 mm (0.08 x 0.08 in). Inside each square is a pattern of dots that varies according to which area of the paper the user is looking at.

MOST EMOTIONALLY RESPONSIVE ROBOT

Kismet (below), created by Cynthia Breazeal (USA) at Massachusetts Institute of Technology (MIT), is a robotic head powered by 21 motors and 15 networked computers. It is designed to recognize different emotions while interacting with humans, and to respond to them. Nine of the computers are used to control Kismet's vision alone.

LARGEST ROBOT DOG

The Roboscience (UK) RS-01 Robodog, measures 82 x 67 x 37 cm (32 x 26 x 14 in). Strong enough to lift a five-year-old child, the RS-01 is far larger and more powerful than its nearest rivals.

HIGHEST-RESOLUTION COMMERCIALLY AVAILABLE SATELLITE IMAGES

DigitalGlobe's QuickBird Satellite is capable of taking images with a higher resolution than that of any other commercially available satellite images. Launched on 18 October 2001 on a Boeing Delta 2 rocket, QuickBird can take black-and-white

MOST ADVANCED CYBERNETIC LIMB IMPLANT

Prof Kevin Warwick (UK) had a second silicon chip implanted into his arm on 14 March 2002. Linked directly to nerve fibres in his wrist, this tiny device enables him to interact with some objects without touching them. The chip measures his nerve impulses, then transmits them to a computer, which in turn translates them into commands.

LARGEST MOLECULE IN THE CELL
DNA, the double helix-shaped molecule discovered in 1953 by James Watson (UK) and Francis Crick (USA), contains all the genetic code needed to build an individual. Each of the ten trillion cells in the human body contains this code. If a DNA molecule was unwound and stretched out, it would be around 2 m (6 ft) long. If all the DNA in the human body could be stretched out end-to-end, it would reach to the Sun and back more than 600 times.

FURTHEST TRACED DESCENDANT BY DNA
History teacher Adrian Targett (UK) can genetically trace his family back further than any other person. He is a direct descendant, on his mother's side, of 'Cheddar Man', a 9,000-year-old skeleton found in a cave in Cheddar Gorge, Somerset, UK. Scientists took a DNA sample from one of Cheddar Man's molars and found a near perfect match in Targett, who lives less than half a mile away.

OLDEST EXTRACTED HUMAN DNA
In January 2000, it was announced that scientists had extracted DNA from a bone belonging to a 60,000-year-old ancestor of modern humans. The skeleton, nicknamed 'Mungo Man', was unearthed at Lake Mungo, NSW, Australia, in 1974 and was dated (between 56,000 and 68,000 years old) in 1999. Mungo Man's DNA challenges the 'Out of Africa' theory of evolution, which holds that we are all descended from a common ancestor (*Homo erectus*) in Africa. Mungo Man has a skeleton which is anatomically the same as ours, but its DNA appears to have no links with *Homo erectus*.

SPECIES WITH THE MOST CHROMOSOMES
The plant species with the most chromosomes per cell discovered to date is adder's tongue fern (*Ophioglossum reticulatum*, above) which has 630 pairs of chromosomes per cell.

EARLIEST CLONED KIDNEYS
In January 2001, scientists from Advanced Cell Technologies, Mass, USA, revealed that they had successfully grown kidneys using cloning technology for the first time. The technique took a DNA-containing nucleus from a single cow skin cell and fused it with a host egg. The egg multiplied into an embryo rich in stem cells. These cells were then chemically manipulated to grow into kidney cells, using an artifical kidney-shaped scaffold. Several of these miniature kidneys were grown in this way and transplanted back into the cow, where they began to produce urine. Each of the kidneys was several centimetres (a couple of inches) long.

MOST COMPATIBLE ANIMALS FOR ORGAN TRANSPLANTATION INTO HUMANS
Although they share around 95% of their DNA with us, compared to 98.9% for the pygmy chimp, pigs are considered to be the most compatible animals for potential organ transplants into humans. This is because pig organs are more similar in size to human organs and there is also a risk of contracting AIDS from primate organs. There are also ethical problems with the use of primates compared to pigs – in the west, for example, we rear pigs to kill and eat, but not monkeys.

ANIMALS MOST GENETICALLY SIMILAR TO HUMANS
Bonobos (primates similar to chimpanzees), which live only in the rainforests of central Democratic Republic of Congo, share 98.9% of their DNA with humans. This species, often called the 'pygmy chimpanzee', numbers no more than a few tens of thousands of individuals. Chimps share around 98.5% of DNA with humans.

LARGEST CLONED ANIMAL
On 6 January 2000, Xiangzhong Yang (China), from the University of Connecticut, USA, and scientists from the Kagoshima Prefectural Cattle Breeding Development Institute, Japan, announced that they had successfully cloned six calves from skin cells taken from a bull's ear. Some of the calves have now reached adulthood.

OLDEST NATURAL CLONES
Darwinulidae, a family of ostracod (crustaceans around 1 mm or 0.04 in long) reproduce asexually. Fossil records show that this has been happening for at least 100 million years. So every individual alive today is an almost exact clone of an individual from the Cretaceous Period. The only genetic differences are due to genetic mutations in the intervening period and, therefore, their evolution has been extremely slow.

EARLIEST CLONED PRIMATE
Two monkeys were cloned in August 1996 at the Primate Research Center, Beaverton, Oregon, USA. The pair were created from embryos rather than from an adult animal, which means that the monkeys are not genetically identical to any existing animal. The embryos were implanted into the wombs of host mothers using IVF.

MOST GENETICALLY DIVERSE PEOPLE ON EARTH
For some genetic traits, Pygmies and African bushmen (above) have up to 17 genetic variations, whereas most people on Earth have two or three. They may represent the survivors of the original human population.

MOST ADVANCED CLONED HUMAN EMBRYO

In October 2001, a team of scientists at Advanced Cell Technologies, Mass, USA, led by Dr Jose Cibelli (USA), created the first cloned human embryos, using a cumulus cell from a mature human egg. One of these embryos managed to divide into six cells before growth ceased after around five days. The research aims to eventually produce cloned stem cells for use in curing disease.

MOST SUCCESSFUL PLANT-TO-ANIMAL GENE TRANSFER

In January 2002, scientists led by Akira Iritani (Japan) announced that they had successfully implanted genetic vegetable material into an animal. The genetically modified pigs contain a spinach gene that will reportedly make pork meat less fatty and thus more healthy to eat. The pigs were born in mid-1998 and no health problems have been reported.

LONGEST-LIVED HUMAN CELLS

Cells from Henrietta Lacks (USA) are still alive and being grown worldwide in laboratories decades after her death in 1951. Cells from her cervical cancer were removed and subsequently found to lack chromosome 11 – now known as the 'tumour suppressor'. As a result of this error, these cells can divide indefinitely and are essential tools in biomedical research.

LARGEST HUMAN CHROMOSOME SEQUENCED

On 20 December 2001, scientists at the Sanger Centre (UK) announced their completion of the sequence of chromosome 20. This chromosome has nearly 60 million DNA letters and more than 720 genes (about 2% of the three billion letters that make up the human genetic code). Thirty two of the genes are linked to genetic disorders and disorders of the immune system. The smallest human chromosome sequenced is chromosome 21, also mapped at the Sanger Centre (UK) in 1999.

RAREST ANIMAL TO BE SUCCESSFULLY CLONED

On 1 October 2001, scientists announced that a European Mouflon lamb had been cloned and had survived. This rare breed of sheep, found on Cyprus, Sardinia and Corsica, represents the first-ever successful cloning of an endangered species. A European team led by the University of Teramo, Abruzzo, Italy, created the clone. There are fewer than 1,000 Mouflon sheep surviving in the wild.

OLDEST CLONED ANIMAL

Dolly (left), a Finn Dorset sheep cloned from the breast cell of an adult ewe, was born at Edinburgh's Roslin Institute, Midlothian, UK, in July 1996. Her arrival prompted a debate on the ethics of cloning. Named after the US country singer Dolly Parton, she was mated naturally with a Welsh mountain ram in 1997 and gave birth to a healthy lamb called Bonnie on 13 April 1998.

MOST COMMON ELEMENT

Hydrogen is the most common element in both the universe (in which it represents over 90% of all elements) and the Solar System (in which it makes up 70.68% of all elements). Iron is the most common element on Earth, making up 36% of its mass, and molecular nitrogen (N_2) is the most common element in the atmosphere at 75.52% by mass or 78.08% by volume. The picture above, taken by the Hubble space telescope, shows large formations of interstellar dust and molecular hydrogen in the Eagle Nebula.

OLDEST NUCLEAR CHAIN REACTION

On 2 June 1972 French scientists analysing uranium ore in Gabon, west Africa, found tiny anomalies in the ratio of isotopes in the samples. This led to the discovery of the Oklo natural fossil reactors. Around 2 billion years ago, these were active underground nuclear fission reactors, powered by uranium ore that had been concentrated by geological processes, and cooled by ground water. Seventeen such sites have been discovered in Gabon.

HARDEST ELEMENT

The diamond allotrope of carbon (C) has value of 10 on Moh's scale of hardness. Diamonds have historically been mined principally in India, Brazil, South Africa and Russia.

RAREST ELEMENT ON EARTH

The element astatine is the rarest element found in the Earth's crust, with around 25 g (0.9 oz) of the element occurring naturally.

FASTEST SPEED POSSIBLE

The fastest speed possible in the universe is the speed of light. This is achieved only by light and other forms of electromagnetic radiation, such as radio waves, X-rays and infrared radiation. The speed of light varies according to what the light is travelling through. Light moves most rapidly in a vacuum. In such conditions it achieves a velocity of 299,792,458 m/sec (983,571,056.4 ft/sec). As a result, the light we see from the Sun left it around 8.3 minutes beforehand and the light from the Moon takes around 1.3 seconds to reach Earth.

LARGEST MICROBE

The largest known protozoans (forms of minute invertebrates) in terms of volume are the extinct calcareous Foraminifera (Foraminiferida) of the genus *Nummulites*. Individuals up to 150 mm (6 in) wide were found in rocks in Turkey that dated back to the Middle Eocene geological period. (The Eocene era lasted from around 55–38 million years ago.)

LARGEST KNOWN PROTEIN

The largest known single-chain protein is found in muscle cells and is referred to by two different names: titin and connectin. A molecule of titin can reach a length of one micron (0.000001 m or 0.00004 in) and may be larger than some cells.

STRONGEST FORCE IN THE UNIVERSE

There are four fundamental forces in the universe that account for all interactions between matter and energy. They are known as the strong nuclear, weak nuclear, electromagnetic, and gravitational forces. The most powerful of these four is the strong nuclear force, which is 100 times stronger than the next strongest – electromagnetic force. The strong nuclear force operates exclusively within the nucleus of an atom.

WEAKEST FORCE IN THE UNIVERSE

The four fundamental forces in the universe are given relative strength values, with electromagnetic force given the value of 1. Gravitational force, the weakest of the four, has a strength of 10^{-40}, relative to electromagnetism. An illustration of how much weaker gravity is when compared to electromagnetism, for instance, is demonstrated by the fact that it is easy for a toy magnet to pick up a nail, despite the fact that the whole of Earth's gravity is working to pull it back down.

SMALLEST UNIT OF LENGTH

The smallest possible size for anything in the universe is the Planck length. At 1.6×10^{-35} m, it is equivalent to around one millionth of a billionth of a billionth of a billionth of a centimetre across (a decimal point followed by thirty-four zeroes and a one), this is the scale at which quantum foam is believed to exist. (The laws of quantum physics cause minute wormholes to open and close constantly, giving space a rapidly changing, foam-like structure.) Quantum foam is potentially a tremendous source of energy: the power in one cubic centimetre of empty space would be enough to boil all the Earth's oceans.

OLDEST HOMINID FOOTPRINTS

The oldest known human-like footprints were discovered in Laetoli, northern Tanzania, in 1978. They belong to two or three hominids who walked upright on the ashy plains of the area approximately 3.6 million years ago. The trackway consists of approximately 70 footprints in two parallel trails of around 30 m (100 ft) in length.

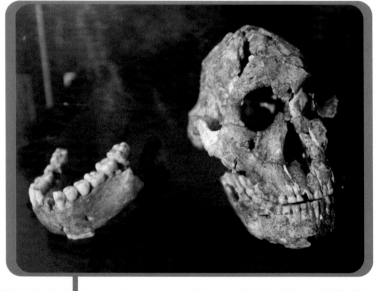

EARLIEST KNOWN HUMAN ANCESTOR

In December 2000 scientists on the Kenya Palaeontology Expedition announced the discovery of 6-million-year-old fossilized hominid remains. *Orrorin tugenensis* (above) walked on two legs and was similar in size to an adult female chimp.

LARGEST KNOWN PRIME NUMBER

Michael Cameron (Canada), a participant in the Great Internet Mersenne Prime Search (GIMPS) announced the discovery of the largest known prime number on 5 December 2001. It is $2^{13,466,917}-1$. Written out in full, the number would have 4,053,946 digits. A reward of $100,000 (£68,568) is on offer to the person who discovers the first 10-million-digit prime number.

LOWEST POSSIBLE TEMPERATURE

The temperature of a substance is determined by the speed at which the atoms or molecules that make up that substance vibrate. Theoretically, the coldest that any substance can be is when there is no such vibration at all, resulting in absolute zero – 0K (zero kelvin) or -273.15°C. This has never been achieved in a laboratory on Earth, and even in the coldest parts of deep space, the temperature is slightly above absolute zero.

FASTEST MICROBE

By means of a polar flagellum (a whip-like outgrowth) rotating 100 times per second, the rod-shaped bacillus *Bdellovibrio bacteriovorus* can travel 50 times its own length of 0.2 micrometres per second. This would be the equivalent of a human sprinter reaching 320 km/h (200 mph), or a swimmer covering 20 miles (32 km) in six minutes.

MOST POWERFUL REACTION

When matter reacts with antimatter, both are annihilated and all of the mass converts to energy. Less than 100 g (3.5 oz) of antimatter would produce energies similar to the power of a hydrogen bomb (below), if annihilated with matter.

MOST PROLIFIC ANTIMATTER PRODUCER

The laboratory Fermilab, in Batavia, Illinois, USA, produces around 100 billion protons of antimatter every hour. This amounts to around one billionth of a gram each year. Antimatter is similar to normal matter, but the charges on the subatomic particles are reversed. For example, an anti-electron, also known as a positron, is the same as an electron but with a positive rather than a negative charge.

FASTEST ATOMIC CLOCK
A team of physicists at the National Institute of Standards and Technology in Boulder, Colorado, USA, have developed an atomic clock (above), which ticks around a quadrillion (million billion) times per second. It is hoped that this clock will eventually be accurate to one second in 100 million years.

LOWEST MAN-MADE TEMPERATURE
In 1995 a team of scientists led by Eric Cornell and Carl Wieman (both USA) cooled atoms of rubidium to a record low temperature of less than 170 billionths of a degree above absolute zero – the coldest temperature possible.

HIGHEST MAN-MADE TEMPERATURE
The highest temperature ever created by man is 5.2×10^8 Kelvin, which works out as almost 30 times the temperature you will find at the centre of the Sun. It was achieved on 19 July 1996 by scientists who were working at the Naka Fusion Research Establishment in Nakamachi, Ibaraki, Japan.

SMALLEST LASER SCULPTURE
In August 2001 researchers at Osaka University, Osaka, Japan, used lasers to create a 3D model of a bull that measured seven thousandths of a millimetre high and ten thousandths of a millimetre long (0.00027 x 0.00039 in) – the same size as a single red blood cell. It is so small that 30 could fit inside the full stop at the end of this sentence.

SLOWEST LIGHT
In January 2001 scientists in Cambridge, Massachusetts, USA, were able to slow down light itself to a complete halt. Light usually travels at the speed of 300,000 km/s (186,000 miles/sec), but naturally slows when it passes through a denser medium such as water or glass.

MOST DENSE MATTER
Scientists at the Brookhaven National Laboratory, Long Island, New York, USA, have created matter 20 times more dense than the nucleus of an atom. By smashing the nucleii of gold atoms together at close to the speed of light, they created subatomic particles that existed for a fraction of a second. Matter this dense may not have existed in the universe since its creation in the 'Big Bang', which physicists believe occurred between 12 and 15 billion years ago.

DEEPEST OPERATING NEUTRINO OBSERVATORY
The Sudbury Neutrino Observatory is located 2,072 m (6,800 ft) below ground in the INCO Creighton Mine, Ontario, Canada. The observatory consists of a 12-m (39-ft) diameter vessel containing around 900 tonnes of heavy water. It is designed to detect neutrinos – neutral elementary particles produced by nuclear fusion in the Sun – and its depth allows it to detect only these particles.

LONGEST RUNNING LAB EXPERIMENT
Since 1930 the University of Queensland, Brisbane, Australia, has been conducting an experiment into the viscosity of black pitch. The pitch was placed in a funnel, out of which it slowly drips. In late 2000 the eighth drop fell, demonstrating that pitch is about 100 billion times more viscous than water. The experiment is expected to continue for at least another 100 years.

LARGEST VAN DE GRAAFF GENERATOR
The largest Van de Graaff generator was built in 1931 by scientists at Cambridge's Massachusetts Institute of Technology, USA. It consists of two columns, each with a 4.57-m (15-ft) hollow aluminium sphere at the top. The two spheres are oppositely charged, causing discharges of 5 million volts. The machine was originally used to smash atoms and research high-energy X-rays. It is currently grounded and on permanent display at the Thomson Theater of Electricity at the Boston Museum of Science, Boston, Massachusetts, USA.

HIGHEST ARCHAEOLOGICAL SITE
Dr Johan Reinhard (USA) and a team sponsored by the National Geographic Society discovered three Inca mummies while exploring the Andes mountain range at Salta, Argentina. The mummies, the frozen remains of children sacrificed an estimated 500 years ago, were found at the peak of the Llullaillaco mountain, at an altitude of 6,706 m (22,000 ft).

MOST NOBEL PRIZES FOR CHEMISTRY AND PHYSICS
American scientists have a total of 51 outright or shared winners of the Nobel prize for chemistry and an additional 52 prizes for physics.

LONGEST RECORDED DREAM
Dream sleep is characterized by rapid eye movements known as REM. The longest recorded period of REM is one of 3 hr 8 min registered by volunteer David Powell (USA) in an experiment at the Puget Sound Sleep Disorder Center, Seattle, Washington, USA, on 29 April 1994. Dream sleep usually lasts around 20 minutes.

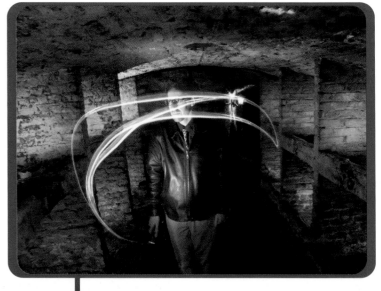

MOST SYSTEMATIC STUDY INTO 'HAUNTED' LOCATIONS
In 2001 Dr Richard Wiseman (UK, above) measured the reactions of 250 people to 'haunted' locations. The data should provide insights into the effects of factors such as magnetic fields, light levels, temperature and low-frequency sound on the mind.

MOST LEAD TURNED TO GOLD

In 1980 Glenn Seaborg (USA) used nuclear physics to turn several thousand atoms of lead into gold at the Lawrence Berkeley Laboratory, Berkeley, California, USA. However, the experimental technique is far too expensive to enable the routine manufacturing of gold from lead.

MOST DETAILED HUMAN DISSECTION

The world's most detailed dissection, the 'Visible Human Project', took place at the University of Colorado, Boulder, USA, from November 1994 to November 1995. A male cadaver was divided into 1,878 slices, 1 mm (0.03 in) thick, and a female cadaver was cut into 5,189 slices, 0.33 mm (0.01 in) thick. Every slice was then photographed by a digital camera to create a virtual anatomy 'text book' for students to experiment upon.

MOST NOBEL PRIZE WINNERS FROM A SINGLE LABORATORY

Eleven researchers have received Nobel prizes for work done while they were based at Bell Laboratories, New Jersey, USA. The first was in 1927 and the most recent came in 1998.

LEAST DENSE SOLID

The solid substance with the lowest density is aerogel – tiny spheres of bonded silicon and oxygen atoms joined into long strands separated by pockets of air. The latest versions of this substance weigh just 3 mg/cm^3, and are produced by the Jet Propulsion Laboratory in Pasadena, California, USA.

SMELLIEST SUBSTANCES

The smelliest substances on Earth are 'US Government Standard Bathroom Malodor', and 'Who-Me', two man-made chemicals which have five and eight chemical ingredients respectively. 'Bathroom Malodor' smells primarily of human faeces and becomes incredibly repellant to people at just two parts per million. The smelliest molecules are ethyl mercaptan and butyl seleno-mercaptan, which smell of a combination of rotting cabbage, garlic, onions, burnt toast and sewers.

SHORTEST FLASH OF LIGHT

The shortest flash of light was a burst recorded at 650 billion-billionths of a second (0.00000000000000065 sec) in 2001 by scientists led by Ferenc Krausz (Austria) based at the Vienna Institute of Technology, Vienna, Austria. The technique will be used to study the behaviour of electrons.

MOST ELEMENTS DISCOVERED

Since Albert Ghiorso (USA) began his scientific career in 1942, he has discovered or co-discovered a record 12 different chemical elements.

STRONGEST MAGNETIC FIELD

In June 2000 the Hybrid Magnet at the National High Magnetic Field Laboratory, Tallahassee, Florida, USA, achieved a DC magnetic field strength of 45T – about 1.5 million times stronger than that of the Earth's magnetic field. The amount of electricity needed to run the magnet at its full field, 27 mW, could supply 1,500 houses.

STRONGEST ACID

Normal solutions of strong acids and alkalis tend towards pH values of 0 and 14 respectively, but this scale is inadequate for superacids, the strongest of which is an 80% solution of antimony pentafluoride in hydrofluoric acid (fluoro-antimonic acid). The acidity function of this solution has not been measured, but even a weaker 50% solution is 1,018 times more powerful than concentrated sulphuric acid.

BEST-SELLING DRIVING SIMULATION GAME

Gran Turismo Real Driving Simulator (above) sold 7 million units worldwide for the Sony PlayStation as of February 2000. *Gran Turismo* was developed by Polyphony Digital, a US-based subsidiary of Sony Computer Entertainment Inc (Japan).

FASTEST-SELLING PC GAME

The role-playing PC game *Diablo II* by Blizzard Entertainment (USA), sold more than one million copies within the first two weeks of being shipped in June 2000. By January 2001, it had sold 2.75 million copies worldwide, making it the fastest-selling PC game.

BEST-SELLING SOCCER GAME

The FIFA series, developed by EA Sports (USA) and launched for the PC on 27 November 1998, has sold more than 16 million units across different platforms. The most recent version, *FIFA 2002*, has commentary provided by UK veteran John Motson and music by DJs based at the Ministry of Sound club.

BEST-SELLING GAMES CONSOLE

The Sony PlayStation console had sold approximately 79.61 million units worldwide by January 2001, making it the best-selling computer games console in the world. The PSone, a revamped model of the original PlayStation, accounts for 5.27 million of these figures. The PSone is smaller than the original, but works with regular PlayStation games and accessories. Sony Computer Entertainment Inc (Japan) has spent more than $300 million (£181 million) developing the PlayStation, which boasts well-known games such as *Tomb Raider* and *Final Fantasy VII*. About 430 million units of PlayStation software have so far been produced.

FASTEST-SELLING VIDEO GAME

The Nintendo Game Boy (Japan) games cartridge *Pokemon Yellow*, based on the popular Japanese children's cartoon, was released in the USA on 18 October 1999 and sold about one million copies in the first ten days it was available.

LONGEST-RUNNING COMPUTER GAME CHARACTER

Nintendo's famous character 'Mario', a plumber by trade, first appeared in the amusement arcade version of *Donkey Kong* in 1981. Since then, Mario has made an appearance in more than 70 different games. In the original, Mario was a carpenter called 'Jumpman', but he was renamed when Nintendo's president in America noticed that the character resembled his landlord, Mario. His distinctive look owes a lot to the limitations of early computer technology. On the low-resolution hardware of the early 1980s, it was easier to animate a moustache than a mouth, and a cap was easier to draw than hair.

BEST-SELLING VIDEO GAMES

More than 40% of American households own a Nintendo game system and the Nintendo game *Super Mario Brothers* has sold 40.23 million copies worldwide. The 26 games featuring Mario in a leading role have sold more than 152 million copies since 1983. It would take 190 years to play all of the 100 million Game Boys in the world for 60 seconds.

EARLIEST COMPUTER GAME

Spacewar was designed and created between 1961 and 1962 by students who worked at the Massachusetts Institute of Technology, Cambridge, Mass, USA, on a PDP-1 computer. It was a space combat game in which two ships, revolving around a central star, had to shoot each other down. Written for fun, this basic game was an important precursor to all modern computer games. The PDP-1 machine first became available in 1960 for $120,000 (£42,735) and 50 units were sold in total. It had a memory of 4K and operators used a keyboard and paper tape to input data.

MOST EXPENSIVE COMPUTER GAME DEVELOPMENT

The Sega Dreamcast computer game *Shenmue* cost more than $20 million (£12.39 million) to develop. The seven-year project was the brainchild of Yu Suzuki (Japan), the head of Japanese company Sega's game-development AM2 division, and was launched in December 1999.

MOST POPULAR HAND-HELD VIDEOGAME SYSTEM

The Nintendo Game Boy sold more than 100 million units in the 11 years between 1989 and 2000. Since its launch, the Game Boy has sold continuously throughout the world at an average rate of more than 1,000 systems every single hour.

MOST ADVANCED ORDERS FOR A VIDEO GAME

More than 325,000 US consumers put down deposits for copies of the Nintendo 64 game *The Legend of Zelda: Ocarina of Time*, to ensure that they received their copy as soon as it arrived in the stores on 23 November 1998.

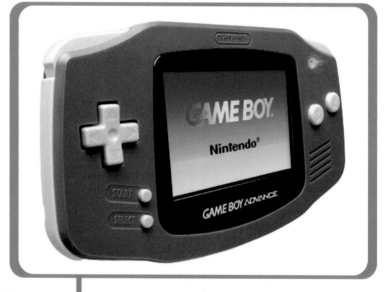

MOST POWERFUL HANDHELD GAMES CONSOLE

Nintendo's Game Boy Advance (above) is powered by a 32-bit ARM chip. It can be linked with three other Game Boy Advances or the Nintendo Game Cube and was launched in Japan on 21 March 2001 and in the USA on 11 June 2001.

MOST COMPLEX CHARACTER IN A COMPUTER GAME

In the PC game *Black and White*, by Lionhead Studios (UK), the player controls a god-like character that in turn trains an artificially intelligent giant creature. During the game, the creature learns from the player and starts to develop its own distinct personality. The size of the creature's mind increases from around 6–7K up to a maximum of 500K. This is the first time that a computer-game character has been programmed with such empathic learning capabilities.

MOST SUCCESSFUL COIN-OPERATED ARCADE GAME

From its launch in 1981 until 1987 a total of 295,992 *Pacman* arcade machines were built and installed in arcade venues around the world. Designed by Tohru Iwatani (Japan) of Namco, the original game took eight people 15 months to complete. Japanese company Namco estimate that *Pacman* has been played more than 10 billion times in its history.

MOST COMPUTER SALES

Unlike modern PCs, which receive regular upgrades to improve their performance, the Commodore 64 desktop computer barely changed between its release date in 1982 and its commerical decline in 1993. In that period it managed to sell more than 30 million units.

GREATEST MARKET SHARE IN GLOBAL GAMING

In March 2000 Sony Computer Entertainment Inc's games consoles – the PlayStation, PSone and the most recent release, the PlayStation 2 – held a 70% share of the world's game console market.

FASTEST-SELLING GAMES CONSOLE

Sales of the Sony PlayStation 2, which originally cost ¥39,800 (£233.50 or $369.62) on release, had reached 980,000 within 48 hours of its launch on 4 March 2000. That is more than 10 times the sales achieved by the original PlayStation console in the same period when it was launched four years previously.

EARLIEST VIDEO ARCADE GAME

Computer Space, a simple space simulation, was designed in 1971 by Nolan Bushnell (USA) of Nutting Associates. Although it sold poorly, Bushnell went on to found Atari and produced the first commerically successful video game, *Pong*.

MOST SUCCESSFUL GAMES PUBLISHER

In 1999 US company Electronic Arts (EA) had sales of $1.2 billion (£750 million) and profits of $73 million (£45 million), making the company the most successful makers of computer games in the world. Their games cover a wide range of genres and are available for many different platforms, including the Sony PlayStation, the Nintendo 64 and for regular PCs.

MOST POWERFUL GAMES CONSOLE

Microsoft's Xbox, which was launched in the USA in November 2001 and the UK in March 2002, is powered by a 733 MHz Intel CPU, the fastest of any current games console. Its graphics processor, a custom-designed chip which runs at 250 MHz, is also the field leader. This is the first time that the US company founded by Bill Gates (USA) has developed a console.

FASTEST FULL-CIRCUIT ROLLER COASTER

The fastest full-circuit roller coaster in the world is the 171.98-km/h (106.86-mph) 'Dodonpa' (above) at Fujikyu Highland Park, Fuji-Yoshida, Japan. The ride is 1,189 m (3,900 ft) long, and at its apex it is 52 m (170 ft 7.2 in) above the ground. Although the ride time is around one minute, the coaster reaches its maximum speed less than two seconds after being launched by high-speed pressurized air.

COUNTRY WITH MOST ROLLER COASTERS

The USA boasts more roller coasters than any other country in the world, with 427. Next comes the UK with 114 and Japan is third, with 66. The first American roller coaster reportedly dates back as far as 1870, when an abandoned mine train in Pennsylvania, USA, was converted to use for entertainment.

OLDEST ROLLER COASTER PASSENGERS

The highest average age of a group of roller-coaster passengers is 69.5, set by 30 riders on the 'Hurricane' coaster, in Dania Beach, Florida, USA, on 25 July 2001. The oldest rider was 84 and the aggregate age of the group was 2,085 years.

MOST ROLLER COASTERS RIDDEN IN 24 HOURS

The greatest number of different roller coasters ridden in a 24-hour period is 74, set by Philip A Guarno, Adam Spivak, John R Kirkwood and Aaron Monroe Rye (all USA) on 9 August 2001. The four rode coasters in 10 parks in four US states, using helicopters to travel between them.

TALLEST ROLLER COASTER

'Superman The Escape', at Six Flags Magic Mountain, Valencia, California, USA, is a dual-track freefall roller coaster, designed by Swiss firm Intamin AG. The ride features 15-seater gondolas that, when launched along the tracks via a Linear Induction Motor (LIM), give riders the experience of 6.5 seconds of 'airtime', or zero-G. The gondolas rise from the horizontal to the vertical plane soon after launch, reaching a height of 126 m (415 ft) before falling vertically back along the same tracks at a design speed of 160 km/h (100 mph).

FASTEST WOODEN ROLLER COASTER

The fastest wooden roller coaster in the world is 'Son of Beast' at Paramount's Kings Island in Kings Mills, Ohio, USA, which reaches a speed of 126 km/h (78.3 mph) and takes three minutes to complete. The first hill rises to 66.4 m (218 ft), making 'Son of Beast' the world's tallest wooden roller coaster.

'The Beast', the forerunner of this ride at the same amusement park, was built in 1979 and is the world's longest traditional wooden roller coaster at 2,256 m (7,400 ft).

AMUSEMENT PARK WITH THE MOST RIDES

Six Flags Great Adventure in Jackson, New Jersey, USA, has a total of 71 different mechanical rides, more than any other theme park in the world. The park, which now boasts 12 roller coasters, opened its doors on 4 July 1974 and covers a total area of 56.6 ha (140 acres).

STEEPEST WOODEN ROLLER COASTER

'Colossos' at Heide-Park near Soltau, Germany, has the steepest drop of any wooden roller coaster, at 61°. The 1,500-m (4,921-ft) ride lasts 2 min 25 sec, during which it can reach speeds of up to 120 km/h (74.6 mph).

TALLEST FULL-CIRCUIT ROLLER COASTER

'Steel Dragon', which opened on 1 August 2000 at Nagashima Spaland, Mie, Japan, is a full-circuit roller coaster that rises to 95 m (311 ft 8 in) above the ground. 'Steel Dragon' is also the world's longest full-circuit roller coaster at 2,479 m (8,133 ft) and the full-circuit roller coaster with the longest drop – 93.5 m (306 ft 9 in).

TALLEST FREE-FALL DROP RIDE

The 'Drop Zone', at Paramount's Kings Island, Ohio, USA, drops riders a record 80 m (262 ft 6 in) from the 96-m (315-ft) vertical lift-tower. The height of the free-fall drop is 43 m (141 ft 2 in) at zero-G, when the ride can reach a top speed of 105 km/h (65 mph). The remaining drop of 37 m (121 ft 4 in) is then completed at an increasingly reduced speed while the brakes are applied.

OLDEST OPERATING CAROUSEL

The 'Vermolen Boden-Karussell' at Efteling Theme Park in Kaatsheuvel, The Netherlands, was built in 1865. It was originally pulled by horses, but is now electrically driven.

TALLEST SPEED WATER SLIDE

The tallest water slide in the world is 'Insane' at Beach Park, Fortaleza, Brazil, which is 41 m (135 ft) high – as tall as an 11-storey building. In only four seconds, the riders – who wear nothing more than bathing suits – reach speeds of up to 104 km/h (64.6 mph).

ROLLER COASTER WITH THE MOST INVERSIONS

'Colossus' (above) at Thorpe Park, Surrey, UK, turns riders upside down 10 times during each 850-m (2,789-ft) run. Launched in March 2002, it has a maximum height of 30 m (98 ft) and a top speed of 65 km/h (40 mph).

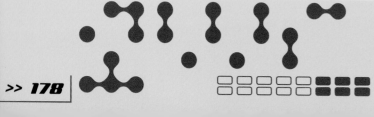

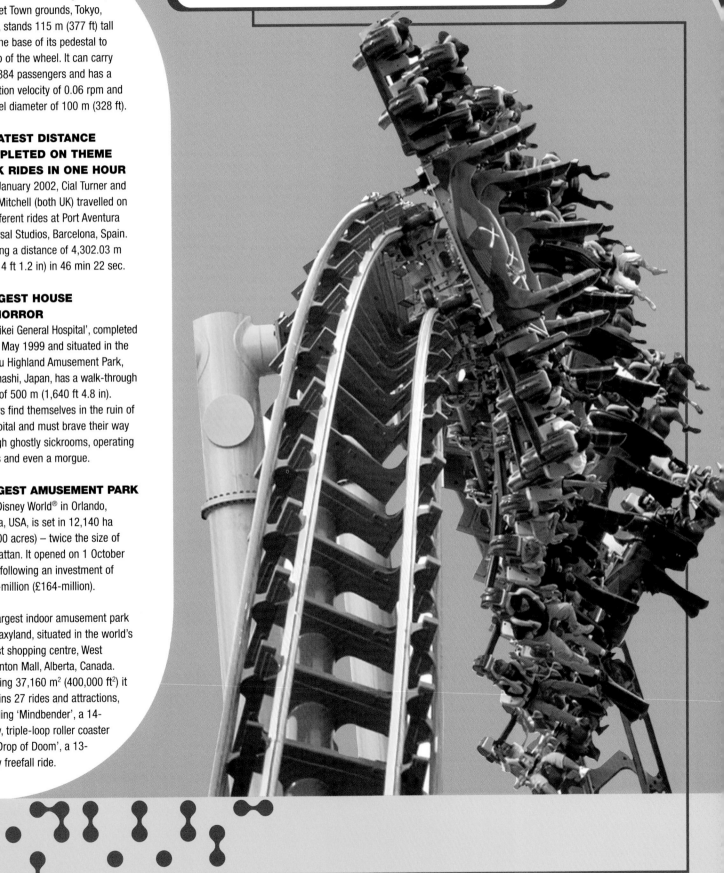

TALLEST FERRIS WHEEL

The 'Dai-Kanransha' big wheel, at Pallet Town grounds, Tokyo, Japan, stands 115 m (377 ft) tall from the base of its pedestal to the top of the wheel. It can carry up to 384 passengers and has a revolution velocity of 0.06 rpm and a wheel diameter of 100 m (328 ft).

GREATEST DISTANCE COMPLETED ON THEME PARK RIDES IN ONE HOUR

On 4 January 2002, Cial Turner and Nigel Mitchell (both UK) travelled on six different rides at Port Aventura Universal Studios, Barcelona, Spain, covering a distance of 4,302.03 m (14,114 ft 1.2 in) in 46 min 22 sec.

LONGEST HOUSE OF HORROR

The 'Jikei General Hospital', completed on 25 May 1999 and situated in the Fujikyu Highland Amusement Park, Yamanashi, Japan, has a walk-through route of 500 m (1,640 ft 4.8 in). Visitors find themselves in the ruin of a hospital and must brave their way through ghostly sickrooms, operating rooms and even a morgue.

LARGEST AMUSEMENT PARK

Walt Disney World® in Orlando, Florida, USA, is set in 12,140 ha (30,000 acres) – twice the size of Manhattan. It opened on 1 October 1971 following an investment of $400-million (£164-million).

The largest indoor amusement park is Galaxyland, situated in the world's largest shopping centre, West Edmonton Mall, Alberta, Canada. Covering 37,160 m² (400,000 ft²) it contains 27 rides and attractions, including 'Mindbender', a 14-storey, triple-loop roller coaster and 'Drop of Doom', a 13-storey freefall ride.

THEME PARK WITH GREATEST NUMBER OF ROLLER COASTERS
Six Flags Magic Mountain, Valencia, California, USA, and Cedar Point in Sandunsky, Ohio, USA, both have 15 roller coasters each ('X', at Valencia, below). Cedar Point is the second oldest amusement park in America and installed its first roller coaster in 1892.

GREATEST AGE SPAN PORTRAYED BY AN ACTOR IN A FILM

In *Little Big Man* (USA, 1970), Dustin Hoffman (USA, above) then aged 33, played 'Jack Crabb' who ages 104 years, from 17 to 121. To achieve the sound of a 120-year-old man, Hoffman is said to have screamed at the top of his voice for an hour before going on set.

LONGEST HOLLYWOOD MARRIAGE

British-born star Bob Hope married Dolores Reade (both USA) in 1934 and the pair are still going strong, 68 years later. They met in 1933, when actor and comedian Hope heard Dolores singing 'Did You Ever See A Dream Walking' in a club in New York City, USA.

MOST OSCAR WINS

Katharine Hepburn (USA) has been nominated for and won more Oscars than any other actor. Nominated 12 times, she won the Best Actress Oscar on four occasions between 1934 and 1982, most recently for *On Golden Pond* (USA, 1981).

OLDEST ACTRESS

Jeanne Louise Calment (France), the oldest woman ever, was 114 when she played herself in *Vincent And Me* (Canada, 1990). The film was about a girl who went back in time to meet the 19th-century Dutch artist Vincent Van Gogh. Ironically, Calment, who was born in 1875, was one of the last people to have met Van Gogh in real life.

OLDEST FILM CAREER EMBARKMENT

Character actress Lydia Yeamans Titus (USA) was 84 when she appeared in her first film, *In The Grasp Of The Law* (USA, 1915). She featured in more than 50 films before her death in 1929.

HIGHEST ANNUAL EARNINGS BY A FILM ACTRESS

Julia Roberts (USA) earned $18.9 million (£13.3 million) in 2000, according to the 2001 *Forbes* Celebrity top 100 List. Roberts also holds the record for the most any actress has ever received for a film, earning $20 million (£12.5 million) for her roles in both *Erin Brockovich* (USA, 2000) and *The Mexican* (USA, 2001).

HIGHEST ANNUAL EARNINGS BY A FILM ACTOR

According to the 2001 *Forbes* Celebrity top 100 List, Bruce Willis (USA) earned $70 million (£46.8 million) in 2000. In 1999, Willis received £100 million (then £61.83 million) for his part in the film *The Sixth Sense* (USA, 1999), the most any actor has been paid for one performance.

MOST LEADING ROLES

Western star John Wayne (USA) starred in 153 movies from *The Drop Kick* (USA, 1927) to *The Shootist* (USA, 1976). In all but 11 of these films he played the lead. He won a Best Actor Oscar for his role in *True Grit* (USA, 1969).

MOST ROLES PLAYED BY AN ACTOR IN ONE FILM

A number of actors have famously taken more than one role in a movie. The two actors topping this long list are Rolf Leslie (UK), who played an astonishing 27 different parts in *Sixty Years A Queen* (UK, 1913), the life story of Queen Victoria, and Lupino Lane (UK), who played all 24 parts in *Only Me* (USA, 1929).

MOST GENERATIONS OF FILM ACTORS IN A FAMILY

Roy Redgrave (UK) was the first of four generations of the Redgrave family to appear on screen. He made his debut in 1911 and was followed by his son, Sir Michael Redgrave, who appeared in many films and who also fathered a further three stars, Vanessa, Lynn and Corin. Vanessa's two daughters, Joely and Natasha, are successful actresses, as is Corin's daughter, Jemma (all UK).

HIGHEST SALARY FOR A DEBUT LEAD ROLE

Billed as Dwayne Johnson, WWF star 'The Rock' (USA) was paid $5.5 million (£3.7 million) for playing the title role in *The Scorpion King* (USA, 2002). He had previously taken fifth billing in *The Mummy Returns* (USA, 2001), playing the same character.

MOST BEST ACTRESS FILMFARE AWARDS

Nutan (India) was named Filmfare Best Actress on five occasions during her 47-year career.

MOST CÉSAR AWARDS WON BY A FILM ACTRESS

Isabelle Adjani (France) won the first of four César Best Actress awards between 1982 and 1995 for *Possession* (France/Germany/Italy, 1981).

LONGEST FILM SERIES WITH THE SAME STAR

All 48 *Tora-jiro Kuruma* (more familiarly known as *Tora-san*) comedy films made by Shochiku Studios, Japan, between August 1969 and December 1995, starred Kiyoshi Atsumi (Japan) in the role of master spy 'Torajiro Kuruma'. At the height of Atsumi's popularity, one film critic claimed that his face was better known than that of the Japanese emperor.

MOST OSCARS FOR PORTRAYAL OF THE SAME CHARACTER

Both Marlon Brando (above) and Robert De Niro (both USA) won Oscars for playing Mafia boss Vito Corleone. Brando was named Best Actor in *The Godfather* (USA, 1972) and De Niro won Best Supporting Actor in *The Godfather Part II* (USA, 1974).

MOST COSTUME CHANGES IN A FILM FOR A CHARACTER

While playing the lead role in *Evita* (USA, 1996), actress and pop star Madonna (USA) changed her costume 85 times, wearing 39 different hats and 45 pairs of shoes. All the outfits were designed by Penny Rose (UK) and were based on originals owned by Eva Peron, the former wife of the Argentine leader Juan Peron.

LONGEST CAREER BY A FILM ACTRESS

Maxine Elliott Hicks (USA) had a film career spanning 78 years. She made her debut in *The Borrowed Finery* (USA, 1914) and her final movie role was in *Beethoven* (USA, 1992).

Lillian Gish (USA) had the longest career as a leading film actress. She made her screen debut in *An Unseen Enemy* (USA, 1912) and played leading roles for another 75 years, until her final film, *The Whales Of August* (USA, 1987).

The longest career as a 'Bollywood' actress belongs to Lalita Pawar (India). She was 12 when she made her acting debut in 1930 and went on to appear in more than 700 films over 70 years.

MOST BEST ACTOR FILMFARE AWARDS

Dilip Kumar (Pakistan) has won eight Filmfare awards for Best Actor and one Lifetime Achievement award in his 50-year career. He received his first award in 1953 and his most recent in 1982.

MOST OSCAR NOMINATIONS BEFORE WINNING

Randy Newman (USA) won the Oscar for Best Music (song) at the 74th Academy Awards held on 24 March 2002 with 'If I Didn't Have You' from the film *Monsters, Inc.* (USA, 2001) – his first win from 16 nominations. He received his first nominations in 1982 for *Ragtime* (USA, 1981) for both Best Song and Best Original Score.

ONLY POSTHUMOUS BEST ACTOR OSCAR

Peter Finch (UK) is the only actor to have won the Best Actor Oscar after his death. Finch, who won for his part in *Network* (USA, 1976), suffered a heart attack two months before the 1977 awards ceremony.

HIGHEST BOX OFFICE GROSS FOR AN ACTRESS

Julia Roberts's (USA) 28 films since 1987 have a total box-office gross of $2,236 million (£1,557 million). Ten of these films have taken over $100 million, the highest-grossing being *Ocean's Eleven* (USA, 2001) with $429,425,628 (£299,042,916).

HIGHEST BOX OFFICE GROSS FOR AN ACTOR

Harrison Ford (USA) has starred in 25 films with a total box office gross of $3,285,111,472 (£2,315,741,909), 10 of which took over $200 million. His highest-grossing film so far is *Star Wars* (USA, 1977), which took $798 million (£555 million).

LOWEST PAID CONTRACT ACTOR IN HOLLYWOOD

Robert Taylor (USA) signed with Hollywood studio MGM for $35 (£7) a week in 1934. He stayed with them for 25 years.

LONGEST OSCAR SPEECH

Greer Garson (UK) made a record 5-min 30-sec speech when she picked up the Best Actress Oscar for *Mrs. Miniver* (USA, 1942). From 1990, speeches were limited to only 45 seconds. The longest speech in recent years was more than four minutes by Halle Berry (USA, left), when she won the Best Actress Oscar (the first black actress to do so) for her role in *Monster's Ball* (USA, 2001) on 24 March 2002.

HIGHEST BOX-OFFICE GROSS FOR FRENCH FILM

Directed by Jean-Pierre Jeunet and starring Audrey Tautou (both France) *Le Fabuleux destin d'Amélie Poulain* (France, 2001, above), (UK title: *Amélie*), which was first released in France on 25 April 2001, went on to take the foreign box office by storm. As of April 2002, the film had amassed $144,488,955 (£101,005,911).

MOST EXPENSIVE REEL OF FILM

A 26-second reel of 8-mm cine film that captured the assassination of President John F Kennedy (USA) in Dallas, Texas, USA, on 22 November 1963, was valued at $16 million (£10 million) by an arbitration panel. The US Government was ordered to pay the amount, the equivalent of $615,384 (£384,615) per second, to the heirs of Abraham Zapruder (USA), for taking his footage into the National Archives.

FASTEST $100-MILLION GROSS AT BOX OFFICE

Two films have taken $100 million at the box office in just five days. *Star Wars: Episode 1 – The Phantom Menace* (USA, 1999), which opened in 2,970 cinemas from 23–28 May 1999, took $100 million (£60.33 million at the time). This broke the previous record held by *Jurassic Park:*

The Lost World (USA, 1997), which passed the $100-million mark in 58 days in July 1997. *Harry Potter and the Philosopher's Stone* (UK, 2001 – released in the USA as *Harry Potter and the Sorcerer's Stone*) opened in 3,672 cinemas across North America and passed through the $100-million (£70,457,268 at the time) mark from 17–21 November 2001.

HIGHEST NON-USA INTERNATIONAL BOX-OFFICE GROSS

Bean – The Ultimate Disaster Movie (UK, 1997) took more than $100 million (£62.5 million) at the international box office – the first time that a film has broken through the official blockbuster threshold without a single cinema ticket being sold in North America.

WIDEST FILM RELEASE

Heyday Films and Warner Brothers' *Harry Potter and the Philosopher's Stone* (UK, 2001) was given the widest film release of any movie in history when it opened on 16 November 2001 in the USA on 8,200 screens (3,672 cinemas). The same release date was also given for the UK, Canada, Malta and Taiwan.

LARGEST FILM BUDGET

The largest production budget ever set aside for any movie before filming started is $145 million (£93 million) for the World War II epic *Pearl Harbor* (USA, 2001).

LARGEST FILM BUDGET TO BOX OFFICE RATIO

The $22,000 (£13,750) Haxan Entertainment production *The Blair Witch Project* (USA, 1999), directed by Daniel Myrick and Eduardo Sánchez (both USA), grossed $240.5 million (then approximately £150 million) worldwide, resulting in a record budget to box office ratio of 1:10,931.

LONGEST CONSTANT FILM SHOOT

Stanley Kubrick's (USA) film *Eyes Wide Shut* (USA/UK, 1999), starring Tom Cruise (USA) and Nicole Kidman (Australia), was in production for more than 15 months, including an unbroken 46-week shoot. Kubrick, who died before the film's release, also holds the record for the most retakes for a dialogue scene, with 127 in *The Shining* (USA, 1980).

LARGEST FILM SET

The largest ever film set, measuring 400 x 230 m (1,312 ft 4 in x 754 ft 7.2 in), was of the Roman Forum. Designed by Veniero Colasanti (Italy) and John Moore (USA) for *The Fall of the Roman Empire* (USA, 1964), it took 1,100 workmen seven months to lay its surface with 170,000 cement blocks. They also erected 601 columns, 350 statues and 27 full-size buildings.

MOST EXPENSIVE FILM

In terms of real costs adjusted for inflation, the most expensive film ever made was *Cleopatra* (USA, 1963). Its $44-million budget (£15,712,602 at the time) would be the equivalent of $306,867,120 (£175,352,640) today.

HIGHEST-INSURED FILM MAKER

Film director, producer and screenwriter Steven Spielberg (USA) was reportedly insured for $1.2 billion (£852.8 million) in July 2001 by DreamWorks, the company he founded with David Geffen and Jeffrey Katzenberg (both USA). The amount is believed to reflect the cost of lost revenue for the company in the event of his death.

LONGEST CAREER FOR A FILM DIRECTOR

King Vidor's (USA) directorial career lasted for 67 years, beginning with *Hurricane in Galveston* (USA, 1913) and culminating in *The Metaphor* (USA, 1980), a documentary.

HIGHEST GROSSING FOREIGN LANGUAGE FILM

First released on 30 June 2000, the martial arts film *Wo Hu Zang Long* (*Crouching Tiger, Hidden Dragon*, TPE, 2000), directed by Ang Lee (Taiwan) and starring Yun-Fat Chow (Hong Kong) and Michelle Yeoh (Malaysia), is the highest grossing foreign language film. As of April 2002 it had taken $209,126,710 (£144,501,285) worldwide.

HIGHEST BOX-OFFICE GROSS ON AN OPENING DAY

Harry Potter and the Philosopher's Stone (UK, 2001, above) took $31.6 million (£22.141 million) on its opening day in the USA, 16 November 2001. By mid-April 2002, it had grossed £317,093,502 (£219,381,142) at the US box office.

EARLIEST FEATURE FILM

The Story of the Kelly Gang was made in Melbourne, Vic, Australia, in 1906. Produced on a budget of £450 (then $2,185.65), this biopic of the armoured bushranger Ned Kelly ran for 60–70 minutes and opened at the Melbourne Town Hall, Australia, on 26 December 1906.

EARLIEST SURVIVING FILM

The earliest surviving piece of film was taken in early October 1888 and is from the camera of Louis Aime Augustin Le Prince (France). It depicts the garden of his father-in-law Joseph Whitley in Roundhay, Leeds, West Yorkshire, UK. The film, a sensitized 53.9-mm-wide (2.1-in) paper roll, runs at 10–12 frames per second.

FIRST USE OF TECHNICOLOR

Rouben Mamoulian's (Russia) film *Becky Sharp* (USA, 1935), based on the classic novel *Vanity Fair*, starring Cedric Hardwicke (UK) and Miriam Hopkins (USA), was the first feature film to use Technicolor.

SHORTEST CLASSIFIED FEATURE FILM

The 8-second advertisement *It's a MINI Adventure*, directed by Chris Palmer (UK), was submitted by its writers, WCRS Ltd, to the British Board of Film Classification as a short feature film and classified as such on 13 June 2001. It aired at UK cinemas from 6 July 2001.

MOST PORTRAYED MOVIE CHARACTER

The most frequently portrayed character on the silver screen is Sherlock Holmes, created by Sir Arthur Conan Doyle (UK). The Baker Street sleuth has been portrayed by around 75 actors in more than 211 films since 1900.

FASTEST $100-MILLION GROSS FOR AN ANIMATED FEATURE FILM

The computer-animated film *Monsters, Inc.* (USA, 2001, below) from Walt Disney Pictures and Pixar Animation Studios reached the $100-million (£68,636,036 at the time) mark at the US box office in nine days from its release on 2 November 2001.

LARGEST MAKE-UP BUDGET

A total of $1 million (then £345,542) was budgeted for the 78 make-up artists working on *Planet of the Apes* (USA, 1968, above). This represents nearly 17% of the total production cost of $5.8 million (£2 million).

LARGEST SPECIAL EFFECTS BUDGET

A total of $6.5 million (£2.2 million) was budgeted for *2001: A Space Odyssey* (USA, 1968) – more than 60% of the total production cost of $10.5 million (£3.6 million). If you compared this to *Star Wars: Episode 1 The Phantom Menace* (USA, 1999) it would be the same as spending $69 million (£48 million) of its $115-million (£81-million) budget just on special effects.

MOST PROLIFIC BOLLYWOOD STUNTWOMAN

In a career spanning 27 years, Mary Evans (Australia), also known as 'Fearless Nadia', acted as a stuntwoman in more than 55 films. Born in 1909 to an English father and Greek mother, she got her first break in Indian films in 1934 in *Desh Deepak* and *Noor-e-Yaman*. Her stunts included jumping from a moving train onto a horse and swinging from chandeliers.

MOST STUNTS BY A LIVING ACTOR

Jackie Chan, the Hong Kong actor, director, producer, stunt co-ordinator and writer, has appeared in more than 90 films, including *The Big Brawl* (USA, 1980) and *Highbinders* (HK/USA, 2002). No insurance company will underwrite Chan's productions as he usually performs all his own stunts.

LONGEST FILM STUNT LEAP IN A CAR

The longest leap in a car propelled by its own engine was performed by stunt driver Gary Davis (USA) in *Smokey and the Bandit II* (USA, 1981). Davis raced a Plymouth up a ramp at 128 km/h (80 mph) and leapt 49.6 m (163 ft) before landing safely.

LONGEST TAKE IN A COMMERCIALLY MADE FILM

In *A Free Soul* (USA, 1931), there is a 14-minute uninterrupted monologue by Lionel Barrymore (USA). Since a reel of camera film only lasted 10 minutes, the take was achieved by using more than one camera.

LARGEST FILM STUNT BUDGET

More than $3 million (then £1.87 million) of the $200-million (£125-million) budget for *Titanic* (USA, 1997) went on stunts. In the most complex scene, 100 stuntpeople leapt, fell and slid 21 m (70 ft) as the sinking ship broke in two and rose out of the sea to a 90° angle.

LARGEST STUNTMAN-TO-ACTOR RATIO IN A FILM

US actor and director Clint Eastwood's *The Rookie* (USA, 1990) featured more than twice as many stuntmen as actors – 87 to 37.

LONGEST MAKE-UP JOB

Rod Steiger (USA) endured 20 hours of make-up each day for his role in *The Illustrated Man* (USA, 1968).

MOST PROLIFIC DUBBING ARTIST

Jun Huzisaki (Japan) has dubbed for 47 actors or animated characters in 54 movies. His career has been extremely varied, ranging from dubbing the voices of US film star Al Pacino to Donald Duck.

MOST PROLIFIC STUNTMAN

Vic Armstrong's (UK) career spans four decades. He has performed stunts in over 200 films and has doubled for every actor portraying James Bond.

LONGEST FULL-LENGTH FILM MADE WITHOUT A CAMERA

José Antonio Sistiaga (Spain) spent 17 months on a 75-minute animated production *Scope, Color, Muda* (Spain, 1970), which he painted frame by frame directly onto film stock.

MOST COMPUTER-GENERATED EFFECTS IN A MOVIE

The film *Pleasantville* (USA, 1998), which incorporates black and white and colour characters in the same scenes, had 1,700 digital visual effect shots, compared to 50 for the average Hollywood film.

FIRST FEATURE-LENGTH CARTOON

The Argentine movie *El Apóstol,* made by Federico Valle (Argentina) in 1917, has long been recognized as the first feature-length cartoon. A political satire about the then president of Argentina, Hipólito Yrigoyen, it was drawn by Quirino Cristiani and Diógenes Taborda (both Argentina). Cristiani was also responsible for the first feature colour cartoon, *Peludópolis,* (Argentina,1931). It was also a satire of President Yrigoyen, who was nicknamed 'El Peludo' ('the hairy one').

LONGEST STOP-MOTION FEATURE FILM

Chicken Run (UK, 2000) runs for 82 minutes and has 118,080 shots – a live-action feature normally has between 500 and 1000 shots. Each Plasticine character on the miniature film set had to be adjusted 24 times for every second of film. As a result, it took an average of two days to shoot four seconds of film and 18 months to complete the whole film. Animators used a record 2,380 kg (5,247 lb) of Plasticine.

MOST EXPENSIVE EXPLOSION SEQUENCE IN A MOVIE

An explosion sequence at the end of *Pearl Harbor* (USA, 2001) involved the destruction of six ships each measuring 120-185 m (400-600 ft). The entire sequence cost $5.5 million (£3,850,000) and was filmed by 12 camera teams.

LONGEST 'TALKIE' CARTOON SERIES

Max Fleisher's (USA) *Popeye The Sailor Man* had 233 one-reelers and a single two-reeler between 1933 and 1957. There were a further 220 *Popeye* cartoons for television between 1960 and 1962, followed by 192 *All New Popeye* cartoons from 1978 to 1983. The series was first aired on TV in September 1956, making it the longest running syndicated cartoon series.

MOST EXPENSIVE CARTOON

DreamWork's *Prince of Egypt* (USA, 1998) took four years to make and cost $60 million (£37.5 million). The 90-minute film has 1,192 special effects.

LONGEST CAREER AS A CARTOON VOICE

Jack Mercer (USA) provided the voice for 294 *Popeye* cartoons over 45 years from 1934.

EARLIEST BLACK AND WHITE FEATURE FILM TO BE CONVERTED TO FULL COLOUR

Special prints of the Oscar-winning biopic of songwriter George M Cohan, *Yankee Doodle Dandy* (USA, 1942), starring James Cagney (USA), was released by MGM on 4 July 1985 with computer-applied colour.

MOST EXPENSIVE AERIAL STUNT

Simon Crane (UK) performed one of the most dangerous aerial stunts ever when he moved between two jet planes at an altitude of 4,572 m (15,000 ft) for the film *Cliffhanger* (USA, 1993). The stunt, performed only once because it was so risky, cost a record $1 million (then £568,000).

MOST LATEX FEET MADE FOR A SINGLE FILM

More than 1,600 pairs of latex feet were used during the shooting of the film *The Lord of the Rings: The Fellowship of the Ring* (NZ/USA, 2001, left). Each foot had to be glued on and then ripped off at the end of the day's filming, so they could only be used once.

BIGGEST RECORD DEAL

In April 2001 Virgin/EMI paid the singer Mariah Carey (USA, above) a 'signing-on bonus' of $21 million (£14.73 million) when she agreed to a four-album deal reported to be worth between $80–$100 million (£56–£70 million). At the time, Virgin/EMI claimed that she was 'the biggest-selling female artist of all time' with worldwide sales of more than 150 million and 15 US No.1 singles. Carey had also spent longer in the US No.1 spot (61 weeks) than any other female. In January 2002 after releasing one album, *Glitter*, Virgin/EMI paid her $29 million (£20.34 million) to end the deal.

BEST-SELLING HIP-HOP ALBUM IN THE USA

The best-selling rap/R&B album ever released in the USA is *CrazySexyCool* by TLC (USA), which has reached sales of 11 million, surpassing MC Hammer's (USA) 10 million-selling *Please Hammer, Don't Hurt 'Em*. One member of the all-female TLC, Lisa 'Left Eye' Lopes was tragically killed in a car accident in April 2002.

BEST-SELLING REGGAE ALBUM

Legend by Bob Marley (Jamaica), released posthumously after Marley died in 1981, is reggae's best-selling album of all time. In the UK, where it topped the charts in 1984, *Legend* has had certified sales of 1.8 million, and although it did not hit the Top 40 in the USA, it has still sold more than 10 million copies Stateside.

BEST-SELLING ALBUM

The best-selling album of all time is *Thriller* by Michael Jackson (USA), with global sales since its release in 1982 of more than 47 million copies.

EARLIEST GOLD DISC MUSIC AWARD

The first actual gold disc was sprayed by RCA Victor for presentation to the US trombonist and band-leader Alton 'Glenn' Miller for his 'Chattanooga Choo Choo' on 10 February 1942.

MOST CHARTED ARTIST ON UK SINGLES CHART

Elvis Presley's (USA) releases spent a cumulative total of 1,173 weeks on the UK singles chart since 'Heartbreak Hotel' debuted on 11 May 1956. Presley's last UK No.1 was 'Way Down' in 1977, the year he died.

MOST CONCERTS PERFORMED IN 12 HOURS

The Bus Station Loonies (UK) played 25 gigs in 12 hours at venues in and around Plymouth, Devon, UK, on 29 September 2001. The four-piece band played 15-minute sets at each venue, were supported by two road crews and raised £1,200 for charity.

MOST CONSECUTIVE NO.1 SINGLES

The KinKi Kids (Japan) have had 13 consecutive singles debut at No.1 on the Japanese charts between 28 July 1997 and 20 November 2001.

MOST EXPENSIVE MUSIC VIDEO

The promotional video for 'Scream', the hit single by siblings Michael and Janet Jackson (both USA), cost about $7 million (£4.4 million) to make in 1995. Directed by Mark Romanek (USA), 'Scream' won the MTV Music Video Award for Dance in 1995 and the Grammy for Music Video Short Form in 1996 and was shot on seven different sound stages. In 1995 'Scream' became the first single to enter the US chart inside the top five.

MOST CONSECUTIVE WEEKS AT NO.1 ON US SINGLES CHART

'One Sweet Day' by Mariah Carey and Boyz II Men (USA), topped the US chart for 16 weeks in 1995 and 1996.

MOST GRAMMY AWARDS WON BY A FEMALE ARTIST

Aretha Franklin (USA) has won 15 Grammys since she received her first award in 1967 for Best R&B Vocal Performance with 'Respect'. She has also won the most Grammys for R&B Female Vocal Performances, claiming 11 awards between 1967 and 1987.

MOST SUCCESSFUL MALE COUNTRY ARTIST

Garth Brooks (USA) is the most successful country music recording artist of all time. Since his debut in 1989, Brooks has registered album sales of more than 100 million.

YOUNGEST SOLO ARTIST AT NO.1 ON US ALBUM CHART

Stevie Wonder (USA) was aged just 13 years 3 months when *Little Stevie Wonder – The Twelve Year Old Genius*, released in 1963, topped the US charts. In 1976 Wonder, who has been blind since just after his birth, signed a contract with the world famous Motown record label worth $13 million (£7.3 million), which at the time was the largest ever deal made in music industry history.

LONGEST STAY ON A US SINGLES CHART

'How Do I Live' by country singer LeAnn Rimes (USA) entered the Top 25 US Country Singles Sales Chart on 21 June 1997 and was still there a massive 250 weeks later in April 2002, having sold more than 3 million copies – a record for a country single.

OLDEST ARTIST TO SELL A MILLION ALBUMS

Compay Segundo (Cuba, above) has sold more than one million albums worldwide since he turned 88 in 1995. Segundo first recorded in the 1930s and found fame with the late-1990s Latin superband Buena Vista Social Club.

LARGEST RAP GROUP
Hip-hop outfit Minority Militia (USA) is the world's largest rap group, with a remarkable 124 members. Each member of the crew plays a full and active part in their recordings, either rapping, singing, playing an instrument or producing on their 2001 album *The People's Army*, released on Lowtown records.

OLDEST RECORDS
The BBC record library contains more than one million records. The oldest records in the library are white wax cylinders dating from 1888. The earliest commercial disc recording was manufactured in 1895.

EARLIEST MILLION-SELLING CD
The first CD to sell one million copies worldwide was UK band Dire Straits' 1986 album *Brother in Arms*, which topped the charts in 22 countries.

MOST MULTI-PLATINUM RIAA CERTIFICATES
Elvis Presley (USA) has 35 multi-platinum Recording Industry Association of America (RIAA) certificates, for singles and albums with more than 2 million sales.

MOST NO.1 SINGLES ON UK CHART
The Beatles (UK) and Elvis Presley (USA) both hold the record for the most No.1 singles on the UK charts, with 17 each. The Beatles (right, clockwise from far left – George Harrison, John Lennon, Ringo Starr and Paul McCartney), scored their successes in the period between 1963 and 1969, while Presley's were spread over 20 years from 1957 to 1977.

BEST-SELLING DVD SINGLE
Madonna's (USA) 'What It Feels Like For A Girl' sold 6,200 copies in its first week of release in May 2001 – the greatest ever registered week's sale for any single released on the DVD format. The previous record was also held by Madonna – full name Madonna Ciccone – with 4,200 sales for 'Music', which was set when it was released in September 2000.

MOST BRIT AWARDS
British band Blur hold the record for winning the most BRIT (British Record Industry Trust) Awards in a year, with four presented to them in 1995.

HIGHEST ANNUAL EARNINGS BY A RAP ARTIST

Rap mogul Dr Dre (USA, above) earned $31.5 million (£21.1 million) in 2000, according to the *Forbes* Celebrity 100 List of 2001. Dre has sold millions of copies of his solo material as well as producing Snoop Dogg and Eminem (both USA).

MOST PERFORMERS ON ONE SINGLE

The greatest number of people to sing on one hit single is 275,000 on British band S Club 7's 'Have You Ever'. The single was released on 19 November 2001 as part of the BBC's Children in Need appeal and features contributions from children at 3,616 UK schools.

FASTEST-SELLING ALBUM

The Beatles' *1*, a compilation of all the British band's No.1 singles in the USA and UK, sold 3.6 million on its first day, 13 November 2000, and 13.5 million copies around the world in its first month in the stores.

BEST-SELLING ALBUM BY A TEENAGE SOLO ARTIST

Released in 1999 *Baby One More Time* by Britney Spears (USA) sold 13 million copies in the USA alone in less than two years.

BEST-SELLING US ALBUM BY A FEMALE SOLO ARTIST

Canadian country singer Shania Twain's album *Come On Over* has sold a total of 19 million copies in the USA and 30 million worldwide since its release on 4 November 1997.

BEST-SELLING ALBUM ON UK CHART

The album to have sold the most copies in the UK is *Sgt Pepper's Lonely Hearts Club Band* by The Beatles, with a reported 4.5 million sales since its release in June 1967. Music critics often vote the album as one of the best ever recorded.

BEST-SELLING GROUP OF ALL TIME

The Beatles have amassed the greatest sales for any group. All-time worldwide sales have been estimated by EMI at more than one billion discs and tapes to date. Up to 2001 the band were certified for album sales of 163.5 million in the USA alone.

BEST-SELLING SINGLE

The biggest selling single of the rock era is Elton John's (UK) 'Candle In The Wind 1997'/'Something About The Way You Look Tonight'. It was released in September 1997 and sold 33 million copies worldwide in just three months. The song, originally written about US actress Marilyn Monroe, was re-recorded in tribute to the late Diana, Princess of Wales after her death in 1997.

HIGHEST ANNUAL TOUR EARNINGS BY A COUNTRY MUSIC ARTIST

Shania Twain's 1999 US tours grossed $36.6 million (£23.2 million). This amount was more than any other country music performer, and $3.1 million (£2 million) more than she earned on the road in 1998.

BEST-SELLING RAP ARTIST

US rap legend 2Pac (born Tupac Shakur) has certified US album sales of 33.5 million up to the end of 2001, and has had more hits after his death (at the age of 25 in September 1996) than he amassed while he was alive. The hits include two US No.1 albums, *The Don Killuminati* (1997) and *Until The End Of Time* (2001) and a dozen US R&B chart singles.

HIGHEST ANNUAL EARNINGS BY A BAND

Despite breaking up in 1970, The Beatles were still the highest-earning band in 2000. The group earned a total of $150 million (£100.5 million) according to the *Forbes* Celebrity 100 List released in 2001. Surviving members Paul McCartney and Ringo Starr (both UK) are among the richest musicians in the world.

LONGEST MUSIC VIDEO

American pop star Michael Jackson's part-feature film, part-music video *Ghosts* (1996) is 35 minutes long and was based on a concept by horror writer Stephen King (USA).

HIGHEST ANNUAL EARNINGS BY A FEMALE SINGER

Britney Spears earned $38.5 million (£25.5 million) in 2000, according to the *Forbes* Celebrity 100 List of 2001.

LARGEST ATTENDANCE AT A FREE ROCK CONCERT

British singer Rod Stewart's free concert held at Copacabana Beach, Rio de Janeiro, Brazil, on New Year's Eve 1994, reportedly attracted a total audience of 3.5 million.

MOST AWARDS WON BY A MALE CANTONESE POP ARTIST

As of April 2000, Hong Kong's Andy Lau has won 292 awards for a singing career that began in 1988. Since 1992 Lau has appeared in concert 179 times. He has also featured in 101 movies since 1981.

BEST-SELLING TEENAGE ARTIST

Before she turned 20 years old on 2 December 2001, Britney Spears had sold 37 million records around the world – the best ever sales figures for a solo teenage artist.

MOST SUCCESSFUL VIRTUAL BAND

Gorillaz (above) are the world's most successful virtual band, with global sales of 3 million for their eponymous debut album. The animated band was created by Blur frontman Damon Albarn and cartoonist Jamie Hewlett (both UK).

MOST
BRIT AWARDS

Robbie Williams (UK), has won
13 BRIT (British Record Industry
Trust) Awards during his career –
more than any other artist or act. His
most recent win was for Best British
Male Solo Artist, at the ceremony on
20 February 2001. Singer Williams
was in the hugely successful British
band Take That before he launched
his own stellar solo career.

MOST CHARTS
TOPPED WORLDWIDE
BY ONE ALBUM

Since 13 November 2000, the album
1 by The Beatles has topped
the music charts in 35
different countries.

MOST PSEUDONYMS
USED BY A POP STAR

John Lennon (UK), one of the founder
members of The Beatles, recorded
and produced music under 15
different names until his murder
in New York City, USA, in 1980.

MOST WEEKS AT NO.1 IN
THE US SINGLES CHART

Elvis Presley's 18 No.1 records have
occupied the top of the charts for a
combined total of 80 weeks. US
singer Presley holds a total of 14
Guinness World Records.

FASTEST-SELLING POP
ALBUM IN THE USA

The record for the greatest first-week
sales of an album in the USA is held
by US pop group *NSYNC who sold
2.41 million copies of their album
No Strings Attached when released
on 21 March 2000. The album sold
one million copies on the first day,
shipped 7 million copies in the
first two weeks and sold more
than 100,000 copies a week
for a world record 26
successive weeks.

HIGHEST-EARNING SOLO AUSTRALIAN POP PERFORMER

Kylie Minogue (below) sold 200,000 tickets and grossed £3.52 million ($5 million) for a
16-date Australian tour in 2001 – a record for an Australian solo act. The singer played
nine sold-out nights in Sydney, NSW, and another seven in Melbourne, Victoria.

YOUNGEST PERSON AT NO.1 IN THE CLASSICAL CHARTS

In November 1998 Charlotte Church (UK, above) entered the UK classical album charts with her debut album *Voice of an Angel* at the age of 12 years 9 months. The album was certified double platinum in the UK within four weeks. In May 2000 she was named Artist of the Year at the first annual Classical BRIT Awards.

MOST PROLIFIC COMPOSER

Georg Philipp Telemann (Germany, 1681–1767) wrote 12 complete sets of services – one cantata for every Sunday for an entire year – 78 services for special occasions, 40 operas, between 600 and 700 orchestral suites, 44 passions, plus concertos, sonatas and other chamber music.

LARGEST ORCHESTRA

On 15 May 2000 the world's largest orchestra, consisting of 6,452 student and professional musicians, assembled at BC Place Stadium, Vancouver, BC, Canada, to play 'Ten Minutes Of Nine', an arrangement from Beethoven's Ninth Symphony. The orchestra was conducted by Bramwell Tovey (UK), the music director of the Vancouver Symphony Orchestra.

LARGEST CLASSICAL CONCERT ATTENDANCE

An estimated 800,000 spectators attended a free open-air concert by the New York Philharmonic conducted by Zubin Mehta (India), on the Great Lawn of Central Park in New York City, USA, on 5 July 1986 as part of the Statue of Liberty Weekend.

LONGEST INTERNATIONAL SITARIST CAREER

Indian classical sitarist Ravi Shankar celebrated his 60th year in concert as a musician in 1999. Shankar's first sitar performance took place in Allahabad, India, in 1939, and his first international sitar concert was in New York City, USA, in 1956. However, Shankar's first international stage appearances in Europe and the USA took place much earlier, when he toured as a dancer and musical accompanist in his brother Uday Shankar's troupe in 1932, at the age of 12.

HIGHEST AND LOWEST NOTES

The extremes of orchestral instruments (excluding the organ) range between a handbell tuned to g^v (6,272 cycles/sec) and the sub-contrabass clarinet, which can reach C_{11} (16.4 cycles/sec).

The highest note on a standard piano is C^v (4,186 cycles/sec), which is also the limit of a violin's range.

OLDEST PLAYABLE INSTRUMENT

In 1999 archaeologists uncovered a 9,000-year-old Chinese bone flute and managed to play a tune on it. The flute is 22 cm (8.6 in) long, has seven holes and is made from the leg bone of a red crowned crane. It was found at Jiahu, the site of an ancient farming village on the Yellow River flood plain, China.

FASTEST TIME TO CONDUCT ALL 28 VERDI OPERAS

Vincent La Selva (USA), the Artistic Director and Principal Conductor of the New York Grand Opera Company, has conducted – in strict chronological order – the original versions of all 28 operas written by Giuseppe Verdi (Italy) since the first 'Viva, Verdi!' summer season in Central Park, New York City, USA, on 6 July 1994. The final opera was conducted on 1 August 2001.

LONGEST OPERATIC CAREER

Danshi Toyotake (Japan), who died in 1989, sang *Musume Gidayu*, a traditional Japanese narrative, for an astonishing 91 years from her debut at the age of seven. Her professional career spanned 81 years.

LARGEST VIOLIN ENSEMBLE

On 15 June 1925 at Crystal Palace, London, UK, 4,000 local child violinists gathered together to play *Recollections of England – Selection by Mareston*, conducted by Arthur Payne (UK) and accompanied by HM Grenadier Guards Band.

MOST MUSICIANS TO PLAY A DOUBLE BASS

Twenty-two members of the BBC National Orchestra of Wales played a double bass simultaneously in a rendition of Ravel's *Bolero* on 13 November 2000.

LARGEST ORGAN

The largest and loudest musical instrument ever constructed is the Auditorium Organ in Atlantic City, New Jersey, USA. Unfortunately, it is now only partially functional but when it was completed in 1930, it had two consoles (one with seven manuals and another, which was movable, with five), a remarkable 1,477 stop controls and 33,112 pipes. These ranged in length from 4.7 mm (0.2 in) to 19.5 m (64 ft). The organ had the volume of 25 brass bands, and a range of seven octaves.

MOST PERCUSSION INSTRUMENTS PLAYED IN TWO MINUTES

Shovell (Andrew Lovell, UK), formerly of pop group M People, played 66 percussion instruments in two minutes in a successful televised record attempt on 8 July 2001.

LARGEST OPERA HOUSE

The Metropolitan Opera House (above) at the Lincoln Center, New York City, USA, has an audience capacity of 4,065. The stage measures 70 m (230 ft) wide and 45 m (148 ft) deep. It cost $45.7 million (16.3 million) in 1966.

LARGEST CHOIR

Excluding sing-alongs by stadium crowds, the world's largest choir is the 60,000 singers who sang in unison as the finale to a choral contest held among 160,000 participants in Breslau, Germany, on 2 August 1937.

LARGEST DRUM KIT

A drum kit consisting of 308 pieces – 153 drums, 77 cymbals, 33 cowbells, 12 hi-hats, eight tambourines, six wood blocks, three gongs, three bell trees, two maracas, two triangles, two rain sticks, two bells, one ratchet, one set of chimes, one xylophone, one afuche and one doorbell – was built by Dan McCourt (USA) and was unveiled on 6 December 1994 for a show at the Sanctuary Nightclub, Pontiac, Michigan, USA. It took a remarkable 12 hours for a 10-man crew to assemble the kit on the day before the performance.

LONGEST OPERATIC ENCORE

The longest encore listed in the *Concise Oxford Dictionary of Opera*, was of the entire opera *Il Matrimonio Segreto* by Cimarosa (Italy) at its première in 1792. This was at the command of the Austro-Hungarian Emperor Leopold II.

LONGEST PUBLISHED HYMN

'Sing God's Song', a hymn by Carolyn Ann Aish (New Zealand), is 754 verses or 3,016 lines long, with a four-line refrain to each verse.

MOST DURABLE ORGANIST

Florence Gunner (UK) was organist at Far Forest Church, Worcestershire, UK, for 83 years until she was 94. She played every Sunday, and was resident organist for weddings and funerals. She is buried at the church, by the wall close to the organ.

YOUNGEST VIOLINIST TO RECORD BOTH THE BEETHOVEN AND TCHAIKOVSKY CONCERTOS

Vanessa-Mae (UK, below) is the youngest soloist to record the Tchaikovsky and Beethoven violin concertos, both of which she accomplished at the age of 13. The recordings were released on the Trittico label in 1991 with proceeds pledged to charity. Vanessa-Mae made her debut with the London Philharmonia aged 10 in 1989.

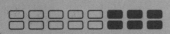

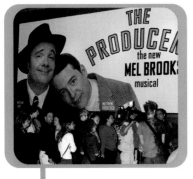

MOST TONY AWARDS FOR A MUSICAL
The Producers (above), written by American comedian Mel Brooks, was nominated for a record 15 Tony Awards on 7 May 2001 winning 12 of them. It beat the previous record of 10 awards won by *Hello Dolly!* in 1964. The Tony Awards, named after US actress Antoinette Perry, are one of theatre's most coveted accolades.

LARGEST CONTRA LINE
An amazing 806 people danced a contra for more than five minutes on 6 September 1998 in Ann Arbour, Michigan, USA, to the dance 'Only in Arbour', played to the tune of 'Reel Beatrice'.

LARGEST TAP DANCE
The most tap dancers in a single routine were the 6,951 who gathered at the City Square in Stuttgart, Germany, on 24 May 1998. Their display lasted 2 min 15 sec.

LARGEST LOCOMOTION DANCE
At the Darlington Railway Centre and Museum, Durham, UK, 374 people were able to 'do the locomotion' dance for 15 minutes on 1 October 2000. The participants danced round *Locomotion No 1*, the world's first passenger steam train, which was built by George Stephenson (UK) in 1825.

LARGEST CHORUS LINE
On 28 September 1997, 593 people from the Roy Castle Foundation (UK), performed for the finale of the *Roy Castle Record-Breaking Extravaganza* at the Royal Liverpool Philharmonic Hall, Liverpool, Merseyside, UK.

LARGEST PURPOSE-BUILT THEATRE
The purpose-built theatre with the greatest capacity is the Perth Entertainment Centre, WA, Australia, with 8,500 seats and a main stage measuring 21.3 x 13.7 m (70 x 45 ft). It was opened on 26 December 1974 and was the first venue for HM Queen Elizabeth II's 1976 Australian tour.

FASTEST FLAMENCO
Sandro Guerrero Toril (Spain) recorded a world's best 507 taps in one minute in Munich, Germany on 6 November 2000.

The record for most taps per second is 16 heel taps by Solero de Jérez (Australia), set in September 1967 in Brisbane, Queensland, Australia.

LONGEST RUNNING ONE-MAN WEST END SHOW
An Evening with Tommy Steele opened at the Prince of Wales Theatre, London, UK, on 11 October 1979 and closed on 29 November 1980 having run for 414 days. Steele, a British singer and actor, then took the show to Australia and Sweden.

OLDEST WORKING MIME ARTIST
Born on 13 January 1914, Arnold Jones (USA) is still working as a mime artist six hours a day, five days a week entertaining crowds in Hollywood, California, USA. He has been a professional mime artist for more than 70 years, starting at 14 as 'The Mechanical Man' at fairs throughout America's Midwest.

MOST EXPENSIVE STAGE PRODUCTION
The stage adaptation of Disney's 1994 film *The Lion King* is the most expensive theatrical production ever. The show opened in November 1997 on Broadway, New York City, USA, and cost around $15 million (then £9.3 million). The British production, which opened in London on 19 October 1999, was not much cheaper, costing more than £6 million ($9.6 million).

LONGEST RUNNING ANNUAL THEATRE REVUE
The longest running annual revue, a theatrical production of comic sketches and songs based around star performers, were *The Ziegfeld Follies*, which went through 25 editions between 1907 and 1957 at numerous venues in the USA.

LARGEST COUNTRY DANCE
A total of 1,914 people gathered in Edinburgh, Lothian, UK, to dance the world's largest 'strip the willow' on 30 December 2000. The display was organized by Unique Events Ltd (UK) as part of the city's 'Night Afore Fiesta' Hogmanay celebrations.

MOST ONE-MAN SHOW PERFORMANCES
The longest run of one-man performances is 849, by Victor Borge (Denmark) in *Comedy in Music* from 2 October 1953 to 21 January 1956 at the Golden Theater, Broadway, New York City, USA.

OLDEST INDOOR THEATRE
The oldest indoor theatre in the world is the Teatro Olimpico in Vicenza, Italy. Designed by Italian architect Andrea di Pietro, it was begun three months before his death in 1580 and completed by his pupil Vicenzo Scamozzi (Italy) in 1583. The venue is preserved today in its original form.

LONGEST DANCE MARATHON
Mike Ritof and Edith Boudreaux (both USA) logged 5,152 hr 48 min to win $2,000 (£411) at the Merry Garden Ballroom, Chicago, Illinois, USA, between 29 August 1930 and 1 April 1931. Such marathon ballroom dances were extremely popular in America during the Great Depression of the early 1930s, when hundreds of people would dance for days for cash prizes.

LARGEST ARTS FESTIVAL
The world's largest arts festival, the Edinburgh Fringe Festival (above) held annually in Edinburgh, Lothian, UK, began in 1947. In its record year of 1998, a total of 9,810 artists gave 16,141 performances of 1,309 different shows.

LONGEST SHAKESPEARE PLAY

Hamlet is the longest of British playwright William Shakespeare's 37 plays. Written in 1604, the play consists of 4,042 lines of 29,551 words. *Hamlet* also contains the longest of any of Shakespeare's 1,277 speaking parts, with Hamlet, the Prince of Denmark, having 1,569 lines of 11,610 words.

LONGEST TIME SPENT IN BED TOGETHER BY A STAGE COUPLE

Jessica Tandy and Hume Cronyn (both USA) have the distinction of having spent more time in bed together than any other stage couple. In October 1951 they opened at the Ethel Barrymore Theater, New York City, USA, in Jan de Hartog's (Netherlands) *The Fourposter* and continued to play the parts for two years.

FASTEST TAP DANCER

James Devine (Ireland) recorded the fastest rate ever measured for tap dancing, producing 38 taps per second in a display in Sydney, NSW, Australia, on 25 May 1998.

MOST STAGE FLIGHTS

Ichikawa Ennosuke (Japan) has flown across the stage more than 5,000 times since April 1968 while performing a Japanese stunt called *chunori*. Accomplished through pulleys and a safety belt, *chunori* has been a popular Japanese stage trick for nearly three centuries.

LONGEST RUNNING WEST END MUSICAL

The longest running musical still playing in the West End is *Les Misérables* (below), which opened at the Palace Theatre, London, UK, on 4 December 1985. The longest running musical in history is *Cats*, which closed in May 2002 after 8,538 UK performances.

LONGEST-RUNNING TV DRAMA

ITV's *Coronation Street* (UK, Jean Alexander as Hilda Ogden shown above), made by Granada, ran twice weekly from 9 December 1960 until 20 October 1989. It is now aired four times a week. As of 6 March 2002, 5,226 episodes have been shown. William Roache (UK) has played Ken Barlow without a break since the outset – a record 42 years.

LONGEST RUNNING TV QUIZ SHOW

University Challenge (UK) has been broadcast for 33 years. The first edition was broadcast on 21 September 1962, but the show stopped in 1987 for a seven-year break. It re-started in 1994 and is still running, currently once a week on BBC2.

LONGEST RUNNING PRIME-TIME ANIMATED SERIES

Matt Groening's (USA) *The Simpsons* has had 282 episodes aired on the Fox (USA) network as of 10 March 2002. *The Simpsons* originally featured as a 30-second spot on *The Tracey Ullman Show* in 1987. After 50 cartoons were aired, Groening was offered his own series, first seen as a Christmas special on 17 December 1989 and then as a regular series from 14 January 1990. It is the longest running prime-time

series still releasing new episodes and it holds the record for the most celebrities featured in a cartoon TV series, with 256 cameos to date.

LARGEST TV PHONE VOTE

During the final of Thames Television and 19 Television's (both UK) *Pop Idol*, broadcast on ITV on 9 February 2002, the communications firm, Telescope (UK), registered 8.7 million votes over a 2-hr 15-min period. During the course of the show British Telecom (UK) received a massive 94 million call attempts to the voting lines as viewers tried to get through.

MOST EXPENSIVE TV DOCUMENTARY PER MINUTE

The BBC's (UK) documentary series *Walking with Dinosaurs*, which showed how dinosaurs lived, reproduced and became extinct, cost over £37,654 ($61,112) per minute to produce. It took more than two years to make the six 27-minute episodes at a total cost of £6.1 million ($9.9 million).

MOST EXPENSIVE TV PROGRAMME

In January 1998 Warner Brothers (USA), makers of the hospital drama *ER*, the USA's No. 1 show with a then weekly audience of 33 million, agreed to a three-year deal with NBC (USA), earning $857.6 million (£536 million) for 22 episodes at $13.1 million (£8.2 million) per one-hour episode. In April 2000, NBC paid $640 million (£400 million) for three more series until 2004, which works out at $9.6 million (£6 million) an episode.

HIGHEST PAID TV DRAMA ACTOR PER EPISODE

In August 1998 actor Anthony Edwards (USA), *ER*'s Dr Mark Greene, saw his salary increase from $125,000 (£77,160) per episode to $400,000 (£246,900) an episode in a four-year, $35-million (£21.6-million) deal.

HIGHEST CURRENT ANNUAL EARNINGS BY A TV ACTRESS

Jennifer Aniston, Lisa Kudrow and Courteney Cox Arquette (all USA) – the female leads in NBC's *Friends* since 1994 – earned $1 million (£703,334) each per episode of the 2002 season. With around 24 episodes per season, each of the actresses will earn $24 million (£16.8 million) for the ninth series. In 1994 they each earned $40,000 (£26,000) per episode.

HIGHEST PAID TV COMEDY ACTOR PER EPISODE

Kelsey Grammer (USA) is to be paid a salary of $1.6 million (£1.1 million) per show for playing psychoanalyst Frasier Crane in the 2002 and 2003 series of *Frasier*.

LONGEST RUNNING POP SHOW

The first edition of the BBC's *Top of the Pops* was aired on 1 January 1964. Artists appearing included Dusty Springfield, The Rolling Stones, The Dave Clark Five and The Hollies. The Beatles and Cliff Richard and The Shadows (all UK) were shown on film.

LONGEST RUNNING TV SHOW

NBC's *Meet the Press*, first transmitted on 6 November 1947, was subsequently shown weekly from 12 September 1948, and has had 2,708 shows aired as of 24 March 2002.

LARGEST ANNUAL RADIO AUDIENCE

Surveys in over 100 countries show that the global estimated audience for the BBC World Service (UK), which is broadcast in 41 languages, was 140 million regular listeners in 1995.

MOST RADIO STATIONS

The USA has over 10,000 authorized radio stations, more than any other country in the world.

MOST EXPENSIVE TV ADVERTISING CAMPAIGN

The $8.1-million (£5.7-million) ads for Pepsi Cola (USA) equate to a spend of $89,700 (£63,000) per second. They were first aired during the American Superbowl, at the Louisiana Superdome, New Orleans, USA, on 3 February 2002. The commercials starred pop singer Britney Spears (USA).

LARGEST TV AUDIENCE FOR A REALITY SHOW

On 24 August 2000, for the final episode of CBS's *Survivor* programme in the USA, around 51 million people, or 41% of America's viewing public, watched Richard Hatch (USA, above left) win the $1-million (£660,000) prize money.

LONGEST RUNNING RADIO PROGRAMME

Rambling with Gambling, aired six days a week on WOR radio in New York City, USA, was first broadcast in March 1925 and was continued by three generations of the Gambling family. The final broadcast by the latest family member, John Gambling (USA), was on 11 September 2000; thus the show ran for more than 75 years.

RADIO DJ MARATHON

DJ Kristian Bartos's (Sweden) broadcast on WOW 105.5 radio, Stockholm, Sweden, lasted for 103 hr 30 min. Beginning at 6:40 am on 8 October 2001 he finally closed his programme at 2:10 pm on 12 October 2001.

The longest radio talk show was one of 33 hours on BBC Three Counties (UK). The show ran from 5:00 am on 16 November until 2:00 pm on 17 November 2001. Presented by Nick Lawrence (UK), the show was in aid of the BBC's Children in Need.

LONGEST RUNNING RADIO DRAMA

BBC Radio 4's *The Archers,* created by Godfrey Baseley (UK), was first broadcast on 1 January 1951. Actor Norman Painting (UK) appeared in the first episode as the character Philip Archer and holds the record for the longest career as a radio actor in the same role.

EARLIEST BROADCAST

The first advertised broadcast was made on 24 December 1906 by Prof Reginald Aubrey Fessenden (Canada) from the mast of the National Electric Signalling Company at Brant Rock, Mass, USA. The transmission included Handel's *Largo*.

HIGHEST EARNINGS FOR A TV CHILD ACTOR

Twins Mary-Kate and Ashley Olsen (USA, below) began their TV careers aged nine months when they starred in *Full House*. By the age of nine they earned a combined total of $79,000 (£56,000) per episode. Now 15, they star in Fox Family Channel's *So Little Time*. Their merchandise empire generates around $1 billion (£696 million) annually and they are said to be the most powerful girls in Hollywood.

EARLIEST ALPHABET
The earliest example of alphabetic writing is that found on clay tablets (similar to the above) showing the 32 cuneiform (wedge-shaped) letters of the Ugaritic alphabet, a now-extinct Semitic language of Syria. The tablets were found in 1929 at Ugarit (now Ras Shamra), Syria and were dated to around 1450 BC.

LARGEST ADVANCE FOR FICTION
It was reported in August 1992 that publishing house Berkeley Putnam (USA) had paid $14 million (then £7.3 million) for the North American rights to the novel *Without Remorse* by Tom Clancy (USA).

MOST OVERDUE LIBRARY BOOK
A German book about the Archbishop of Bremen, published in 1609, was borrowed from Sidney Sussex College, Cambridge, UK, by Colonel Robert Walpole (UK) between 1667 and 1668. Prof Sir John Plumb (UK) found the book 288 years later in the library of the then Marquess of Cholmondeley (UK) at Houghton Hall, Norfolk, UK. No fine was exacted when he returned it.

BEST-SELLING AUTHOR
The world's best-selling fiction writer is the late Dame Agatha Christie (UK), whose 78 crime novels have sold an estimated 2 billion copies in 44 languages. Agatha Christie also wrote 19 plays and, under the pseudonym Mary Westmacott, six romantic novels. Annual royalty earnings from her works are estimated to be worth millions.

BEST-SELLING NON-FICTION BOOK
Although it is impossible to obtain exact figures, there is little doubt that the Bible is the world's best-selling and most widely distributed book. A survey by the Bible Society concluded that around 2.5 billion copies were printed between 1815 and 1975, but more recent estimates put the number at more than 5 billion.

BEST-SELLING CHILDREN'S BOOKS
The 80 titles in the *Goosebumps* series by RL Stine (USA) have sold 220 million copies worldwide since the first book, *Welcome to Dead House*, was published in 1992.

LARGEST DICTIONARY
Deutsches Wörterbuch consists of 34,519 pages and 33 volumes. It was started in 1854 by Jacob and Wilhelm Grimm (both Germany) – best known for their collection of fairy tales – and was completed in 1971.

LARGEST ENGLISH LANGUAGE DICTIONARY
The printed version of the second edition (1989) of the *Oxford English Dictionary* (also available on CD-ROM), contains 21,543 pages in 20 volumes, comprising over 231,000 main entries. In 1993 a series of Additions Volumes, containing entries for additional vocabulary, began to appear: around 4,000 new entries are produced annually.

LARGEST LIBRARY BOOK FINE PAID
On 15 December 1959, Art Ogg (USA) borrowed a copy of *Snow Dog* by Jim Kjelgaard (USA) from the Prairie Creek Library in Dwight, Illinois, USA. In 1999 he discovered the book in his mother's attic and returned it on the 40th anniversary of the due date, 29 December 1999, paying an overdue fine of $292.20 (£180).

HIGHEST ANNUAL EARNINGS BY AN AUTHOR
According to the *Sunday Times* Rich List 2002, *Harry Potter* author JK Rowling's (UK) net worth increased from £65 million ($93 million) in 2001 to £226 million ($325 million) in 2002, largely due to royalties from the hit film *Harry Potter and the Philosopher's Stone* (UK, 2001).

HIGHEST ADVANCE FOR A FIRST NOVEL
In 1999 *Sunday Times* journalist Paul Eddy (UK) was reported to have been paid a record $2.8 million (£1.7 million) by British and American publishers for his first novel, *Flint*, and its unwritten (at that time) sequel.

LARGEST MAGAZINE
A 100-page special edition of the March 2002 Paris Gallery magazine, measuring 67 x 98 cm (26.3 x 38.5 in) and weighing 10 kg (22 lb), was produced for the 2002 Dubai (UAE) Shopping Festival. Around 150 high-quality big copies were printed, identical to the normal-sized version.

MOST PULITZER PRIZE WINS BY A FICTION WRITER
Three American writers have twice won the Pulitzer Prize for fiction: Booth Tarkington (*The Magnificent Ambersons* in 1919 and *Alice Adams* in 1922); William Faulkner (*A Fable* in 1955 and *The Reivers* in 1963) and John Updike (*Rabbit is Rich* in 1982 and *Rabbit at Rest* in 1991).

MOST BOOKER PRIZE WINS BY A WRITER
JM Coetzee (South Africa) and Peter Carey (Australia) have both won the Booker Prize twice. Coetzee won with his novels *Disgrace* (1999) and *Life & Times of Michael K* (1983). Carey first won in 1989 with *Oscar and Lucinda*, and again in 2001 with *True History of the Kelly Gang*.

LARGEST ADVANCE FOR NON-FICTION
Former US President Bill Clinton (USA, above) agreed to sell the worldwide rights to his memoirs to Alfred A Knopf Inc (USA) for an advance of more than $10 million (£7.1 million). The book is scheduled for publication in 2003.

LARGEST CIRCULATION FOR A MAGAZINE

Parade, a syndicated colour magazine, is distributed with 330 newspapers across the USA every Sunday and currently has a circulation of around 35.9 million, the highest in the world for any magazine. It has a readership of 77.6 million and in 2001 had advertising revenues of around $570 million (£400 million).

HIGHEST CURRENT DAILY NEWSPAPER CIRCULATION

Yomiuri Shimbun (founded 1874) published in Tokyo, Japan, had a combined morning and evening circulation of 14,323,781 in January 2002.

HIGHEST EVER DAILY NEWSPAPER CIRCULATION

Komsomolskaya Pravda (founded 1925), the youth paper of the former Soviet Communist Party, reached a peak daily circulation of 21,975,000 copies in May 1990. Its name means 'Young Communist League Truth'.

LARGEST ATTENDANCE FOR A BOOK READING

British author JK Rowling, author of the record-breaking *Harry Potter* series, was one of three authors who read excerpts from their works to an audience of 20,264 at the SkyDome Stadium, Toronto, Ontario, Canada, on 24 October 2000, as part of The Harbourfront Centre's International Festival of Authors. Canadian author Kenneth Oppel read from his novel *Silverwing*, while his compatriot Tim Wynne-Jones presented an excerpt from *The Boy in the Burning House*. Rowling's reading came from the fourth Harry Potter novel, *Harry Potter and the Goblet of Fire*.

MOST VALUABLE TYPEWRITER

Ian Fleming (UK), former spy and creator of fictional British agent James Bond 007, commissioned a gold-plated typewriter in 1952, which was custom made in New York City, USA, and cost the author $174 (then £62). On 5 May 1995 it was sold for £56,250 ($89,229) at Christie's, London, UK. Fleming wrote all but his very first novel (*Casino Royale*) on this typewriter.

MOST SYNDICATED COMIC STRIP

Garfield, created by Jim Davis (USA) and circulated by Universal Press Syndicate (USA), is the world's most syndicated comic strip, appearing in 2,570 journals worldwide.

LONGEST RUNNING COMIC BOOK

The Dandy has been published continuously by DC Thomson & Co of Dundee, UK, since its first edition of 4 December 1937. The weekly comic's best-known character is Desperate Dan, an unshaven cowboy from Cactusville, whose favourite food is cow pie cooked in a dustbin lid.

BEST-SELLING BOOK OF ALL TIME

Excluding non-copyright works such as the Bible and the Qu'ran, the world's all-time best-selling book is *Guinness World Records* (formerly *The Guinness Book of Records*). Since it was first published in October 1955, global sales in 37 languages have exceeded a massive 91,941,000 (to June 2001).

SMALLEST PRINTED BOOK REPRODUCTION

A tiny version of the Bible (left) was made by Massachusetts Institute of Technology (MIT) scientists Pawan Sinha, Pamela R Lipson and Keith R Kluender (all USA) in 2001. Using microlithography, a process similar to that used in the manufacture of computer microchips, they reprinted the full New Testament text of the King James Bible in 24-carat gold on a crystalline silicon tablet measuring just 5 x 5 mm (0.196 x 0.196 in).

AMERICAN FOOTBALL

MOST INTERCEPTIONS IN NFL CAREER

Paul Krause (USA) is the leading interceptor of all time, with 81 steals during his 16-season career playing for the Washington Redskins and the Minnesota Vikings. He retired in 1979.

MOST PASSES IN NFL CAREER

Dan Marino (USA) of the Miami Dolphins completed a total of 4,967 passes between 1983 and his retirement in 2000. His other records include most yards gained through passing in both a career – 61,631 yd – and in a season – 5,084 yd in 1984. In 1998 he was named NFL Man of the Year for his charity work.

MOST TOUCHDOWNS IN NFL SEASON

Marshall Faulk (USA, below) scored 26 touchdowns for the St Louis Rams during the 2000 National Football League (NFL) season. Eighteen were runs from scrimmage and eight were pass receptions. Faulk has also had four 1,000-yard rushing seasons and 14 100-yard rushing games in his career.

MOST PASSES RECEIVED IN NFL CAREER

The most pass receptions in a NFL career is 1,306 by Jerry Rice (USA) of the San Francisco 49ers and the Oakland Raiders from 1985–2001.

MOST PASSES COMPLETED IN NFL SEASON

Warren Moon (USA) of the Houston Oilers completed 404 passes in the 1991 NFL season. Moon was named NFL Man of the Year in 1989 for his service to the community.

MOST FIELD GOALS IN NFL MATCH

Three US players have each scored seven field goals in one NFL match: Jim Bakken of the St Louis Cardinals against the Pittsburgh Steelers on 24 September 1967, Rich Karlis for the Minnesota Vikings v. the Los Angeles Rams on 5 November 1989 and Chris Boniol for the Dallas Cowboys v. the Green Bay Packers on 18 November 1996.

MOST NFL TITLES

The Green Bay Packers have won a record 12 NFL titles – 1929, 1930, 1931, 1936, 1939, 1944, 1961, 1962, 1965, 1966, 1967, 1996.

MOST GAMES PLAYED IN NFL CAREER

George Blanda (USA) played 340 games in 26 NFL seasons. From 1949 to 1975, he played for the Chicago Bears, the Baltimore Colts, the Houston Oilers and the Oakland Raiders.

HIGHEST NFL SCORE

The highest team score in a regular NFL game is by the Washington Redskins (originally the Boston Braves), who beat the New York Giants 72-41 at Washington, DC, USA, on 27 November 1966. The aggregate score of 113 is also a record.

MOST YARDS RUSHED IN NFL SEASON

Eric Dickerson (USA) gained 2,105 yards rushing for the Los Angeles Rams in the 1984 season. In 1989 he became the first player in NFL history to gain more than 1,000 yards in seven consecutive seasons. He is the fastest in NFL history to gain more than 10,000 yards.

MOST YARDS RUSHED IN NFL CAREER

Walter Payton (USA) gained 16,726 yards rushing over his career with the Chicago Bears from 1975 to 1987. During this period he set eight NFL records, including a single-game rushing mark of 275 yards, and 28 Bears records. As well as the yards rushing record, he holds NFL records for attempts (3,838) and combined net yards from scrimmage (21,803).

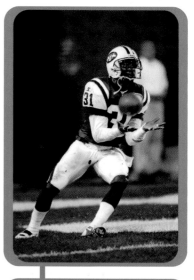

LONGEST RETURN OF A MISSED FIELD GOAL

The longest return of a missed field goal for a touchdown was one of 104 yards by Pro-Bowl-selected Aaron Glenn (USA, above), playing for the New York Jets against the Indianapolis Colts on 15 November 1998.

MOST PASSES RECEIVED IN NFL SEASON
Detroit Lion player Herman Moore (USA, above), received 123 passes in the 1995 season. He is one of only two players in NFL history to have recorded three consecutive seasons with 100-or-more receptions (1995–97); the other is Jerry Rice (USA). On 20 December 1998 Moore became the fastest player to reach the 600-career-reception mark.

MOST TOUCHDOWNS IN NFL CAREER
Jerry Rice (USA) of the San Francisco 49ers and the Oakland Raiders scored a record 190 touchdowns between 1985 and 2001. He holds the Superbowl career record for touchdowns (seven), yards gained receiving (512) and pass receptions.

MOST TOUCHDOWN PASSES IN CAREER
Between 1983 and 1999, Dan Marino (USA) threw 420 touchdown passes.

MOST TOUCHDOWNS IN ROOKIE SEASON
NFL rookie Gale Sayers (USA) scored 22 touchdowns for the Chicago Bears in the 1965 season. A total of 14 were runs, six were pass receptions and two were kick returns.

MOST WINS BY NFL HEAD COACH
The most games won by a coach in the NFL is 347 by Don Shula (USA), who coached the Baltimore Colts from 1963 to 1969 and the Miami Dolphins from 1970 to 1995.

MOST SAFETIES IN ONE GAME
Fred Dryer (USA), playing for the Los Angeles Rams against the Green Bay Packers on 21 October 1973, made two safeties – the most in one game.

MOST POINTS IN CAREER
Gary Anderson (USA, Pittsburgh Steelers, 1982–94; Philadelphia Eagles, 1995–96; San Francisco 49ers, 1997; Minnesota Vikings, 1999–2001) has scored a record 2,080 points in his career. Anderson was born in South Africa and moved to the USA as a child.

HIGHEST SCORE IN A NON-NFL GAME
Georgia Tech from Atlanta, Georgia, USA, scored 222 points, including a record 32 touchdowns, against Cumberland University, Lebanon, Tennessee, USA, on 7 October 1916. Georgia Tech are one of the most successful college football teams.

LONGEST FIELD GOAL
The longest field goal in a NFL game is 63 yards by Tom Dempsey (USA) of the New Orleans Saints v. the Detroit Lions on 8 November 1970 and by Jason Elam (USA) of the Denver Broncos against the Jacksonville Jaguars on 25 October 1998.

The longest claimed field goal is one of 78 yards, barefooted, by Ching Do Kim (USA) at Honolulu Stadium on 23 November 1944.

SHORTEST NFL PLAYER
Jack Shapiro (USA), halfback for the Staten Island Stapletons in 1929, was 1.54 m (5 ft 0.5 in) tall. He played just one game, in which he rushed for seven yards (in two attempts) and returned a punt 12 yards.

MOST SUPERBOWL TITLES
The Superbowl was first held in 1967 between the winners of the NFL and the AFL. Since 1970 it has been contested by the winners of the National and American Conferences of the NFL. The most wins is five by the San Francisco 49ers (1982, 1985, 1989, 1990 and 1995) and the Dallas Cowboys (1972, 1978, 1993, 1994 and 1996).

MOST SUPERBOWL MVP AWARDS
Joe Montana (USA), quarterback with the San Francisco 49ers, was voted Most Valuable Player (MVP) in the Superbowls of 1982, 1985 and 1990.

MOST GAMES OFFICIATED
Raymond Longden (USA) has officiated well over 2,000 games, more than any other referee.

HIGHEST ATTENDANCE AT A GREY CUP FINAL
The largest crowd for a Grey Cup Final is 68,318, who saw the Montreal Alouettes beat the Edmonton Eskimos 41-6 in Montreal, Quebec, Canada, on 27 November 1977.

In the same game, Montreal's Don Sweet (Canada) scored a Grey Cup final record 23 points.

LONGEST COMPLETED PASS IN CANADIAN FOOTBALL
The longest recorded completed pass in the professional Canadian football league is 109 yards and has been achieved by two players – Sam Etcheverry (Canada) for the Montreal Alouettes in a game against Hamilton Tiger-Cats on 22 September 1956 and Jerry Keeling (Canada), while playing for the Calgary Stampeders against the Winnipeg Blue Bombers on 27 September 1966.

MOST YARDS PASSING IN CANADIAN FOOTBALL SEASON
Doug Flutie (Canada) threw a record 6,619 yards in one season for the British Columbia Lions in 1990/1991.

MOST SACKS IN NFL CAREER
Reggie White (USA, above) made 198 sacks during his NFL career, playing for the Philadelphia Eagles from 1985 to 1992, the Green Bay Packers between 1993 and 1998 and the Carolina Panthers in 2000.

MOST RUNS IN CAREER

The most runs scored in a Major League career is 2,248 by Rickey Henderson (USA, above) up to the end of the 2001 season. To date, Henderson has played 23 seasons for seven franchises and he also holds the record for most stolen bases in a career, with 1,380. Henderson, who was born on Christmas Day 1958, played for the Boston Red Sox in 2002.

BASEBALL

LONGEST HOME RUN

The longest measured home run in a Major League game is 193 m (634 ft) by Mickey Mantle (USA), when playing for the New York Yankees against the Detroit Tigers at Briggs Stadium, Detroit, Michigan, USA, on 10 September 1960.

MOST HOME RUNS IN CAREER

Hank Aaron (USA), who played for Milwaukee (later the Atlanta Braves), scored a record 755 home runs between 1954 and 1976. Aaron, from Mobile, Indiana, was one of the first black players to play Major

League baseball. When he scored the home run that set the new record on 8 April 1974 the game had to be suspended for 15 minutes while the crowd celebrated.

MOST HOME RUNS IN ONE GAME

The most home runs scored in a Major League game is four, first achieved by Robert 'Bobby' Lowe (USA) for Boston against Cincinnati on 30 May 1894. The feat has been equalled 11 times since then.

MOST HOME RUNS IN CONSECUTIVE GAMES

Three players have hit home runs in eight consecutive Major League games; Richard Dale Long (USA) for the Pittsburgh Pirates in May 1956; Donald Arthur Mattingly (USA) for the New York Yankees in July 1987 and Ken Griffey Jr (USA) for the Seattle Mariners in July 1993.

MOST HOME RUNS IN ONE WEEK

The most home runs hit in a week is 10, scored in six consecutive games by Frank Howard (USA) for the Washington Senators in May 1968.

MOST HOME RUNS IN ONE MONTH

Sammy Sosa (Dominican Republic) of the Chicago Cubs holds the record for the most home runs in one month, after he smashed 20 in 22 games in June 1998.

MOST CONSECUTIVE HITS

The most consecutive hits in the Major League is 12. The record is shared by two players and first to achieve the feat was Michael Franklin 'Pinky' Higgins (USA) of the Boston Red Sox in June 1938. He was followed by Walter 'Moose' Dropo (USA), playing for the Detroit Tigers in July 1952.

HITS IN MOST CONSECUTIVE GAMES

Joe DiMaggio (USA) connected in 56 successive games for the New York Yankees in 1941; he was 223 times at-bat, with 91 hits, scoring 16 doubles, four triples and 15 homers. DiMaggio is considered to be one of the finest players to have picked up a bat and also found fame through his 1954 marriage to American actress and pin-up Marilyn Monroe.

MOST STRIKEOUTS IN A WORLD SERIES MATCH

The record for most strikeouts in a World Series match is 17, and was set on 2 October 1968 by the St Louis Cardinals pitcher Robert Gibson (USA). Gibson's World Series records include seven successive complete-game victories. He was such a skilled sportsman that he even played for legendary basketball team, the Harlem Globetrotters.

MOST STRIKEOUTS IN CAREER

Nolan Ryan (USA) pitched 5,714 strikeouts during his Major League career with the New York Mets, the California Angels, the Houston Astros and the Texas Rangers from 1966 to 1993. In 1979 Ryan became the first player in Major League history to sign a contract worth $1 million when he joined the Houston Astros.

HIGHEST ATTENDANCE AT WORLD SERIES

The record attendance for the World Series is 420,784 over the six-match series between the Los Angeles Dodgers and the Chicago White Sox from 1 to 8 October 1959, which the Dodgers won 4-2.

The single game best is 92,706 for the fifth game of the series, at the Memorial Coliseum in Los Angeles, California, USA, on 6 October 1959.

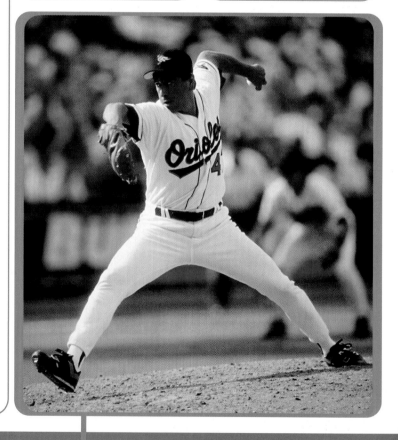

MOST GAMES PITCHED IN CAREER

In a career that saw him play for six different teams, California-born Jesse Orosco (USA, above turning out for the Baltimore Orioles) pitched a record total of 1,093 games from his first season in 1979 until April 2000.

LONGEST GAME

The Chicago White Sox and the Milwaukee Brewers played a game that lasted 8 hr 6 min on 9 May 1984. The White Sox eventually won 7-6 in the 25th innings of the match.

MOST CONSECUTIVE GAMES WON BY A PITCHER

Carl Owen Hubbell (USA) won 24 consecutive games for the New York Giants in 1936 and 1937.

MOST VALUABLE CATCHER

In 1998 Mike Piazza (USA) signed a contract with the New York Mets that made him the world's most valuable catcher. He will earn a total salary of $91 million (£56.2 million) over seven years, has the use of a luxury box for all home games and a hotel suite while on the road.

MOST GAMES PLAYED IN CAREER

Peter Rose (USA) played in a record 3,562 games and had a record 14,053 at-bats in a career that spanned two decades, mostly for the Cincinnati Reds.

MOST CONSECUTIVE GAMES PLAYED

Cal Ripken Jr (USA), who made his debut in 1981, featured in 2,632 consecutive Major League games for the Baltimore Orioles from 30 May 1982 to 19 September 1998.

MOST BASE HITS IN A SEASON

Ohio-born George Harold Sisler (USA) made a record 257 base hits in one Major League season while playing for the St Louis Cardinals in 1920.

MOST HOME RUNS IN A SEASON

The most home runs scored in a season is 73 by Barry Bonds (USA, below) of the San Francisco Giants in 2001. Bonds has also won more Most Valuable Player awards than anyone else in baseball, with four. He won his fourth for his achievements with the Giants in 2001.

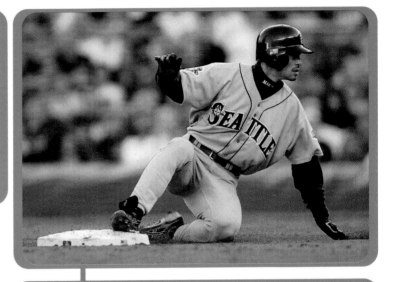

MOST HITS IN A ROOKIE SEASON

The most hits by a rookie in a Major League season is 242 by the prodigious Ichiro Suzuki (Japan, above) playing for the Seattle Mariners in 2001. In doing so, Suzuki broke the 90-year record set by 'Shoeless' Joe Jackson (USA) for the Cleveland Naps (later the Cleveland Indians) in 1911.

OLDEST WORLD SERIES PLAYER

Jack Quinn was 47 years 91 days when he pitched in the World Series for the Philadelphia Athletics on 4 October 1930. Quinn is also the oldest player to hit a home run in the Major League, which he did at 47.

OLDEST PLAYER

Leroy 'Satchel' Paige (USA) was aged 59 years 80 days when he pitched for Kansas City As in his final match on 25 September 1965.

YOUNGEST PLAYER

The youngest Major League player was the Cincinnati Reds pitcher Joseph Nuxhall (USA), who played his first game at 15 years 314 days in June 1944. He did not play again in the National League until 1952.

MOST AT-BATS IN A SEASON

Playing for the Kansas City Royals in 1980, Willie Wilson (USA) made a record 705 at-bats in one season.

PITCHING PERFECT GAME

A perfect nine-innings game, in which the pitcher allows the opposition no hits, no runs and no man to reach first base, was first achieved by John Lee Richmond (USA), playing for Worcester against Cleveland in the National League on 12 June 1880. There have been 13 subsequent perfect games over nine innings, but no pitcher has achieved this feat more than once.

LARGEST REPLICA BAT

The world's largest replica baseball bat is 36.5 m (120 ft) high and weighs 24,380 kg (68,000 lb). The giant bat was made by Hillerich & Bradsby, from Louisville, Kentucky, USA, and can be found outside the Louisville Slugger Museum.

Manute Bol (Sudan), who also played for the Bullets among other teams. Both players are 2.31 m (7 ft 7 in) tall.

The tallest player to be selected for a NBA team was 2.33-m (7-ft-8-in) Yasutak Okayamo (Japan), who was picked by the Golden State Warriors in 1981 but never played in the NBA.

MOST INDIVIDUAL POINTS IN NBA MATCH

Wilt 'The Stilt' Chamberlain (USA) scored a record 100 points when playing for the Philadelphia 76ers against the New York Knicks on 2 March 1962.

MOST FREE THROWS IN AN NBA SEASON

Jerry West (USA, above right) scored 840 free throws for the Los Angeles Lakers during the 1965/66 National Basketball Association (NBA) season. Nicknamed 'Mr Clutch', a reference to his knack of being able to pull his team through tight matches, West's image is immortalized in the current NBA logo.

BASKETBALL

LONGEST GAME

Members of the Suncoast Clippers played out a 24-hour epic basketball game at Maroochydore Eagles Basketball Stadium, Queensland, Australia, on 21–22 November 1998.

TALLEST PLAYER

Suleiman Ali Nashnush (Libya) was reputedly 2.45 m (8 ft 0.25 in) when he played for his country in 1962.

TALLEST NBA PLAYERS

Two men tie for the title of tallest players ever to turn out for a team in the NBA: Gheorghe Muresan (Romania), who currently plays for the Washington Bullets, and

LONGEST GOAL THROWN

Christopher Eddy (USA) scored a field goal from a distance of 27.49 m (90 ft 2.25 in) for Fairview High School against Iroquois High School at Erie, Pennsylvania, USA, on 25 February 1989. The shot came in overtime and the last-ditch long-range effort won the game for Fairview, 51-50.

OLDEST NBA PLAYER

Robert Parish (USA) was aged 43 years 231 days old when he played his last game for the Chicago Bulls on 19 April 1997.

HIGHEST POINTS AVERAGE IN NBA CAREER

Michael Jordan (USA, below) holds the highest point-scoring average for players who have registered over 10,000 NBA points. His average of 31 came from almost 30,000 points in just under 1,000 games for the Chicago Bulls from 1984 to 1998 and the Washington Wizards in 2001/02.

MOST WINS IN NBA SEASON

The greatest number of wins in a NBA season is 72 by the Chicago Bulls in the 1995/96 season.

MOST POINTS IN NBA SEASON

Wilt Chamberlain (USA) scored 4,029 points for the Philadelphia Warriors in the 1961/62 season.

MOST NBA TITLES

The Boston Celtics have won more NBA Championship titles than any other team. They took the title in 1957, 1959 to 1966, 1968, 1969, 1974, 1976, 1981, 1984 and 1986.

HIGHEST TEAM SCORE IN NBA MATCH

On 13 December 1983 the Detroit Pirates beat the Denver Nuggets 186-184 in Denver, Colorado, USA, a record for the highest score ever achieved by a team in a NBA game.

MOST MINUTES PLAYED IN NBA CAREER

Kareem Abdul-Jabbar (USA) was on court for 57,446 minutes in the course of his career. He played for the Milwaukee Bucks from 1969–75 and the Los Angeles Lakers from 1975–89.

MOST CONSECUTIVE FREE THROWS IN NBA SEASON

Between 24 March and 9 November 1993 Mike Williams (USA) racked up 97 consecutive free throws for the Minnesota Timberwolves.

MOST NBA PLAY-OFF APPEARANCES

Kareem Abdul-Jabbar (USA), took part in a record-breaking 237 NBA play-off games in his career.

HIGHEST AVERAGE POINTS IN NBA PLAY-OFFS

The highest points-scoring average in play-off games is 33.4 points by Michael Jordan (USA), who scored 5,987 points in 179 games as a member of the Chicago Bulls.

MOST FOULS IN NBA CAREER

Kareem Abdul-Jabbar (USA) notched up 4,657 fouls over 1,560 games between 1969 and 1989.

MOST WINS IN MEN'S WORLD CHAMPIONSHIP

The men's basketball World Championship was instituted in 1950. The most successful nation in the tournament is Yugoslavia with four titles in 1970, 1978, 1990 and 1998.

MOST MEN'S PARALYMPIC TITLES

The USA have won a record five men's Paralympic basketball titles. Their wins came in 1960, 1964, 1972, 1976 and 1988.

MOST WOMEN'S PARALYMPIC TITLES

The greatest number of women's Paralympic basketball titles won by one country is three by Canada in 1992, 1996 and 2000.

MOST FREE THROWS IN 10 MINUTES

On 6 March 2001 Jeff Liles (USA) scored 285 free throws out of a total of 326 attempts in 10 minutes at Prairie High School, New Raymer, Colorado, USA.

HIGHEST SCORE IN COLLEGE BASKETBALL

The National Collegiate Athletic Association (NCAA) aggregate record for the highest score in a college basketball match is 399. The record total was reached when Troy State beat De Vry Institute, Atlanta, 258-141 at Troy, Alabama, USA, on 12 January 1992. Troy's score represents the highest individual team points total in a match.

YOUNGEST PLAYER TO START AN NBA MATCH

The youngest player to start a NBA game is Kobe Bryant (USA, above right), who was 18 years 158 days when he played for the Los Angeles Lakers against the Dallas Mavericks on 28 January 1997.

MOST BASKETBALLS DRIBBLED BY ONE PERSON

Joseph Odhiambo (USA) dribbled six basketballs simultaneously at his home in Mesa, Arizona, USA, on 15 August 2000.

GREATEST NUMBER OF PEOPLE DRIBBLING BASKETBALLS AT ONCE

On 10 March 2001, 50 basketball fans set the world record for the most people to dribble basketballs at one time in Nashville, Tennessee, USA. Led by ex-Washington Bullets and Chicago Bulls star Charles Davis (USA), each participant dribbled their basketball constantly for a period of five minutes.

MOST BASKETBALLS SPUN SIMULTANEOUSLY

The greatest number of basketballs spun simultaneously is 28 by Michael Kettman (USA) on 25 May 1999 on the set of *Guinness World Records* in London, UK. The balls were Franklin Hardcourt No. 1

regulation basketballs, and Kettman spun them on a specially designed frame for five seconds.

MOST LAY-UPS WHILE JUGGLING THREE BASKETBALLS

Joseph Odhiambo (USA) achieved 38 lay-ups in one minute while juggling three basketballs at Rehoboth Christian High School, Gallup, New Mexico, USA, on 8 June 2001.

MOST THREE-POINT SHOTS BY A TEAM IN ONE MATCH

The greatest number of three-point shots made in one game by a team is 32 by the Garrett Falcons Varsity Boys Basketball team, Garrett Academy of Technology, North Charleston, South Carolina, USA, in their game against Bowman Academy on 2 January 1998.

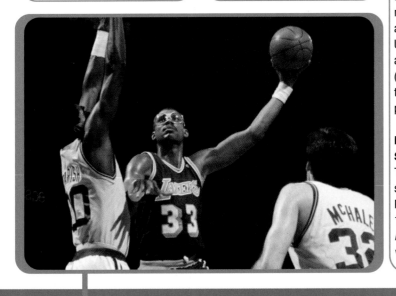

MOST POINTS IN NBA CAREER

The most points scored in a career in the NBA is 38,387 (at an average of 24.6 per game) by Kareem Abdul-Jabbar (USA, above centre) from 1969 to 1989, first as a member of the Milwaukee Bucks and then with the Los Angeles Lakers.

ICE HOCKEY

HIGHEST SCORE
Australia beat New Zealand 58-0 in a World Championship game at Perth, WA, Australia, on 15 March 1987.

LONGEST MATCH
The Labatt's Ice Cats women's team played for 25 hr 2 min 14 sec at Powell River, BC, Canada, on 29 and 30 September 2001.

MOST ASSISTS IN STANLEY CUP GAME
The most assists by a player in a Stanley Cup game is six and is shared by Mikko Leinonen (Finland) for the New York Rangers against the Philadelphia Flyers on 8 April 1982, and by Wayne Gretzky (Canada) for the Edmonton Oilers against the Los Angeles Kings on 9 April 1987.

MOST GOALS IN STANLEY CUP GAME BY INDIVIDUAL
Five players have scored five goals in a Stanley Cup game: Newsy Lalonde for the Montreal Canadiens v. the Ottawa Senators on 1 March 1919; Maurice Richard in the Montreal Canadiens' 5-1 win over the Toronto Maple Leafs on 23 March 1944; Darryl Sittler for the Toronto Maple Leafs v. the Philadelphia Flyers (8-5) on 22 April 1976; Reggie Leach for the Philadelphia Flyers v. the Boston Bruins (6-3) on 6 May 1976, and Mario Lemieux for the Pittsburgh Penguins v. the Philadelphia Flyers (10-7) on 25 April 1989. To date, only Canadian players have achieved this feat.

MOST TEAM GOALS IN NHL SEASON
The Edmonton Oilers scored 446 goals in the 1983/84 National Hockey League (NHL) season. The Oilers also achieved a record 1,182 scoring points in that season.

MOST GOALS BY PLAYER IN NHL MATCH
The greatest number of goals scored by one individual in an NHL game is seven by Joe Malone for the Quebec Bulldogs in their game against the Toronto St Patricks in Quebec City, Canada, on 31 January 1920.

MOST GOALS BY PLAYER IN NHL SEASON
The most goals scored in an NHL season is 92 by Wayne Gretzky (Canada) for the Edmonton Oilers in the 1981/82 season.

MOST GOALS BY ROOKIE IN NHL SEASON
Teemu Selanne (Finland) scored a total of 76 goals in his first season for the Winnipeg Jets in 1992/93.

MOST GOAL ASSISTS IN NHL GAME BY INDIVIDUAL
The record for the greatest number of goal assists by an individual in an NHL game is seven, and is shared by two players. Billy Taylor (Canada) achieved this feat when playing for the Detroit Red Wings against Chicago Blackhawks on 16 March 1947. Wayne Gretzky (Canada) achieved the same record three times with the Edmonton Oilers:

against the Washington Capitals on 15 February 1980, against the Chicago Blackhawks on 11 December 1985 and against the Quebec Nordiques on 14 February 1986.

MOST SHUTOUTS IN NHL CAREER
The most goaltending shutouts in an NHL career is 103 achieved by Terry Sawchuk (USA) for the Detroit Red Wings, the Boston Bruins, the Toronto Maple Leafs, the Los Angeles Kings and the New York Rangers between 1949 and 1970. Sawchuk also made 971 appearances in the NHL, the most by a goaltender.

MOST INDIVIDUAL WINS IN NHL SEASON
The greatest number of individual wins in an NHL season is 47 by Bernie Parent (Canada) for the Philadelphia Flyers in the 1973/74 season.

MOST POINTS IN NHL CAREER
The greatest number of points scored in an NHL career is 2,857 by Wayne Gretzky (Canada), who played for four teams – the Edmonton Oilers, the Los Angeles Kings, the St Louis Blues and the New York Rangers – between

1979 and 1999. Gretzky's points total comprises 894 goals and 1,963 assists achieved in 1,487 games.

Wayne Gretzky also holds the record for the most points scored in an NHL season – 215 for the Edmonton Oilers in the 1985/86 season. Included in the points total are 163 assists, another record.

In his professional hockey career, Gretzky scored a record 1,072 goals. In addition to his 894 NHL regular season goals and 122 Stanley Cup goals, he scored a further 56 times in the World Hockey Association (WHA) in the 1978/79 season.

MOST STANLEY CUPS
The most Stanley Cup wins by a team is 24 by the Montreal Canadiens who won the cup in 1916, 1924, 1930, 1931, 1944, 1946, 1953, 1956 through to 1960, 1965 1966, 1968, 1969, 1971, 1973, 1976 to 1979, 1986 and 1993. Their 32 appearances in the final is also a record.

MOST INDIVIDUAL STANLEY CUP WINS
Henri Richard (Canada) achieved a total of 11 Stanley Cup wins with the Montreal Canadiens between 1956 and 1975, the year in which he retired.

MOST WINS IN NHL SEASON
The most wins in an NHL season is 62 by the Detroit Red Wings in the 1995/96 season.

HIGHEST PERCENTAGE OF WINS PER MATCHES
The highest percentage of wins to games in an NHL season is the 87.5% achieved by the Boston Bruins, who amassed a total of 38 wins from 44 games in 1929/30.

MOST WOMEN'S TEAM OLYMPIC GOLD MEDALS
Women's ice hockey was first contested at the 1998 Nagano Olympics in Japan. The winners were the USA (US goalkeeper Sara DeCosta pictured above) who defeated Canada 3-1 in the final.

MOST HAT TRICKS IN NHL CAREER

The greatest number of hat tricks scored in an NHL career is 50, by Wayne Gretzky (Canada, above). Gretzky, perhaps the finest ice hockey player ever, won numerous trophies including a gold medal at the 1998 Winter Olympic Games.

FASTEST GOAL

The fastest time for a goal to be scored in an NHL match after the opening whistle is five seconds. It is shared by Doug Smail (Canada) for the Winnipeg Jets against the St Louis Blues at Winnipeg, Manitoba, Canada, on 20 December 1981; Bryan John Trottier (Canada) for the New York Islanders v. the Boston Bruins at Boston, Massachusetts, USA, on 22 March 1984, and Alexander Mogilny (Russia) for the Buffalo Sabres against the Toronto Maple Leafs at Toronto, Ontario, Canada, on 21 December 1991.

MOST NHL CAREER WINS BY GOALTENDER

Patrick Roy (Canada), goaltender for the Colorado Avalanche, had logged 516 NHL wins up to the end of April 2002. The record was set on 17 October 2000 in a game against the Washington Capitals.

MOST MATCHES IN A CAREER

Gordon 'Gordie' Howe (Canada) played in 2,421 games as a professional. He achieved his record over 26 seasons between 1946 to 1979.

MOST POINTS BY INDIVIDUAL IN ONE MATCH

The record for the greatest number of points scored by an individual in a professional ice hockey game is 10 and is shared by Jim Harrison (Canada) with three goals and seven assists for Alberta – later renamed the Edmonton Oilers – in a WHA match at Edmonton, Alberta, Canada, on 30 January 1973, and by Darryl Sittler (Canada), who managed six goals and four assists for the Toronto Maple Leafs against the Boston Bruins in an NHL match at Toronto, Ontario, Canada, on 7 February 1976.

MOST MEN'S INDIVIDUAL OLYMPIC GOLD MEDALS

The greatest number of gold medals won by any player is three, achieved by Soviet players Vitaliy Semyenovich Davydov, Anatoliy Vasilyevich Firsov, Viktor Grigoryevich Kuzkin and Aleksandr Pavlovich Ragulin in 1964, 1968 and 1972; Vladislav Aleksandrovich Tretyak in 1972, 1976 and 1984, and Andrey Khomutov in 1984, 1988 and 1992.

MOST MEN'S TEAM OLYMPIC GOLD MEDALS

Ice hockey was first contested at the Olympic Games in 1920. The most wins is eight by the USSR, in 1956, 1964, 1968, 1972, 1976, 1984, 1988 and 1992. In 1992 the team competed as the CIS, or Commonwealth of Independent States, although all the players were from Russia.

LONGEST MEN'S OLYMPIC CAREER

The longest Olympic career is that of Richard Torriani (Switzerland) between 1928 and 1948. He competed in 1928, 1936 and 1948, winning bronze medals in 1928 and 1948.

MOST MEN'S WORLD CHAMPIONSHIP TITLES

The World Championship was first held for amateurs in 1920 in tandem with the Olympic Games, which were also regarded as the World Championship until 1968.

Since 1976 the World Championship has been open to professionals. The USSR took 22 world titles from 1954 to 1990 (and won as Russia in 1993), including the Olympic titles of 1956, 1964 and 1968.

MOST WOMEN'S WORLD CHAMPIONSHIP TITLES

The women's World Championship has been held since 1990, and has been won each time by Canada, in 1990, 1992, 1994, 1997, 1999, 2000 and 2001. In winning seven straight titles, Canada have not lost one game.

MOST PENALTY MINUTES

Dave 'Tiger' Williams (Canada) amassed 3,966 penalty minutes in 17 seasons from 1971 to 1988. He played for the Toronto Maple Leafs, the Vancouver Canucks, the Detroit Red Wings, the Los Angeles Kings and the Hartford Whalers.

MOST POINTS BY INDIVIDUAL IN STANLEY CUP MATCH

The most points scored by a Stanley Cup player is eight, shared by Patrik Sundström (Sweden), with three goals and five assists in the New Jersey Devils' 10-4 win over the Washington Capitals on 22 April 1988, and Mario Lemieux (Canada, below), with five goals and three assists for the Pittsburgh Penguins against the Philadelphia Flyers on 25 April 1989.

FOOTBALL

MOST EXPENSIVE FOOTBALL PLAYER

The highest reported transfer is the £47 million ($68 million) that took France's Zinedine Zidane (below) from Juventus (Italy) to Real Madrid (Spain) in July 2001. Manchester United (UK) paid Lazio (Italy) a UK record £24.7 million ($34.6 million) for midfielder Juan Sebastian Veron (Argentina) in the same month.

MOST WORLD CUPS

The World Cup was initiated by the Fédération Internationale de Football Association (FIFA) and held for the first time in July 1930. It is contested every four years and Brazil have won the most tournaments, lifting the trophy four times – in 1958, 1962, 1970 and 1994.

A women's competition has been held every four years since 1991. The USA won in 1991 and 1999 and Norway were the winners in 1995.

YOUNGEST AND OLDEST PLAYER IN WORLD CUP

Norman Whiteside (UK) played for Northern Ireland against Yugoslavia on 17 June 1982 when he was 17 years 41 days.

Roger Milla (Cameroon) played and scored for Cameroon against Russia on 28 June 1994, at a given age of 42 years 39 days, although some records suggest he was even older.

MOST WORLD CUP APPEARANCES

Antonio Carbajal (Mexico) appeared in five World Cup finals tournaments, keeping goal for Mexico in every competition between 1950 and 1966. He played 11 games in all.

This was equalled by Lothar Matthäus (Germany) who played in 1982, 1986, 1990, 1994 and 1998 taking part in a record 25 games.

YOUNGEST WORLD CUP SCORER

Edson Arantes do Nascimento (Brazil), better known as Pelé, was 17 years 239 days when he scored for Brazil against Wales on 19 June 1958 in Gothenburg, Sweden.

FASTEST WORLD CUP GOAL

The quickest goal scored in a World Cup finals match came 15 seconds after kick off from Vaclav Masek of Czechoslovakia (now Czech Republic) against Mexico in Veña del Mar, Chile, on 7 June 1962.

In qualification matches, Davide Gualtieri of San Marino scored after just seven seconds against England in Bologna, Italy, on 17 November 1993.

HIGHEST INTERNATIONAL SCORE

The highest score in an international match is Australia's 31-0 defeat of American Samoa in a World Cup qualifier at Coffs Harbour, NSW, Australia, on 11 April 2001. Striker Archie Thompson's 13 goals for Australia in the game is also an international scoring record.

MOST EUROPEAN CHAMPIONSHIPS

The European Championship, which was first held in 1960 and takes place every four years, has been won a record three times by Germany – in 1972, 1980 and 1996 (on the first two occasions as West Germany).

A women's tournament was inaugurated in 1984 and has been won four times by Germany – in 1989, 1991, 1995 and 1997.

MOST MEN'S OLYMPIC TITLES

Great Britain have won a record three Olympic titles – in 1900 (an unofficial competition), 1908 and 1912. Hungary have also won the competition three times – in 1952, 1964 and 1968.

MOST COPA AMERICAS

The Copa América, the South American national championship, has been won 15 times by Argentina between 1910 and 1993.

MOST CONCACAF CHAMPIONSHIPS

Costa Rica have won the CONCACAF (Confederation Of North, Central And Caribbean Association Football) Championship (now Gold Cup) on 10 occasions between 1941 and 1989.

MOST ASIAN CUPS

Iran in 1968, 1972 and 1976 and Saudi Arabia in 1984, 1988 and 1997 have both won three Asian Cups.

MOST INTERNATIONAL CAPS

The most international appearances is 160 by Hossam Hassan (Egypt) from 1985 to March 2002.

The women's record for international appearances is 225 by Kristine Lilly (USA) between 1987 and 2000.

MOST GOALS SCORED BY A GOALKEEPER

Paraguayan goalkeeper José Luis Chilavert (above) scored a hat trick of penalties for Vélez Sarsfield in their 6-1 defeat of Ferro Carril Oeste in the Argentine league.

Chilavert scored a record 54 league and international goals between July 1992 and October 2000, largely from penalties and free kicks. He is the only keeper to have scored in a World Cup qualifying game (against Argentina in 1997).

MOST APPEARANCES

Goalkeeper Peter Shilton (UK) made a 1,389 appearances, including a record 1,005 League appearances – 286 for Leicester City (1966–74); 110 for Stoke City (1974–77); 202 for Nottingham Forest (1977–82); 188 for Southampton (1982–87), 175 for Derby County (1987–92); 34 for Plymouth Argyle (1992–94); one for Bolton Wanderers (1995) and nine for Leyton Orient (1996–97); 125 internationals; 13 under-23 internationals; 86 FA Cup; 102 League Cup; one League play-off; four Football League XI and 53 other European and club competitions.

MOST CONSECUTIVE PREMIERSHIP MATCHES SCORED IN

Ruud Van Nistelrooy (Netherlands) scored in eight consecutive English Premiership matches for Manchester United (UK) during the 2001/2002 season. In doing so, he bettered the efforts of Mark Stein (UK), Thierry Henry (France) and Alan Shearer (UK), who had all managed seven.

MOST GOALS IN ONE SEASON

William 'Dixie' Dean (UK) scored 60 goals in 39 matches for Everton in 1927/28. With three more in cup ties and 19 in representative matches, Dean's total was 82.

The Scottish League record is 66 in 38 games by James Smith (UK) of Ayr United, also in 1927/28.

YOUNGEST HAT TRICK SCORER IN BRITISH FOOTBALL

The youngest scorer of three goals in a single game in British football is Trevor Francis (UK), who was aged 16 years 307 days when he scored four goals in the old Second Division for Birmingham City against Bolton Wanderers on 20 February 1971.

The youngest hat trick scorer in England's top division is Alan Shearer (UK), who was 17 years 240 days when he scored three goals for Southampton against Arsenal on 9 April 1988.

Since the formation of the English Premiership in 1992, the youngest hat trick scorer is the Liverpool and England striker Michael Owen (UK), who was 18 years 62 days when he netted three times while playing for Liverpool against Sheffield Wednesday on 14 February 1998.

Ian Dickson (UK) was 18 years 215 days when he scored the youngest hat trick in the Scottish League. Remarkably, it came on Dickson's debut for Montrose against Third Lanark on 22 October 1966.

MOST CONSECUTIVE HAT TRICKS

Masashi Nakayama (Japan) scored hat tricks in four successive matches when playing for Jubilo Iwata in the J-League. His scoring spree began with five goals against Cerezo Osaka on 15 April 1998 and ended with a hat trick against Consadole Sapporo on 29 April 1998. In total, he scored 16 goals in the four games.

HIGHEST WOMEN'S SCORE

The highest score in a women's match is Willenhall Town Ladies 57-0 victory over Burton Brewers Ladies at Willenhall, West Midlands, UK, on 4 March 2001.

MOST SEASON TICKETS SOLD

Every year Spanish club Barcelona sell around 98,000 season tickets (the total capacity) for their home ground, the Nou Camp, making it the football stadium with the greatest number of season-ticket holders.

HIGHEST ATTENDANCE

The greatest recorded crowd at any match was 199,854 at the Brazil v. Uruguay World Cup match in the Maracanã Municipal Stadium, Rio de Janeiro, Brazil, on 16 July 1950.

The official British record is 149,547 at the Scotland-England international at Hampden Park, Glasgow, Strathclyde, UK, on 17 April 1937.

The Scottish Cup final at Hampden in 1937 attracted a non-international official record 146,433, but the UK's largest estimated attendance was at the FA Cup final between West Ham United and Bolton Wanderers at Wembley Stadium in London, UK, on 28 April 1923, where there were serious congestion problems. Thousands gatecrashed and although official admissions were 126,047, it is estimated that as many as 160,000 to 200,000 people were at the game.

MOST PITCHES

The National Sports Center in Blaines, Minnesota, USA, has 57 pitches – 55 of which can be used at any one time – making it the largest such soccer complex in the world.

MOST FEDERATIONS IN WORLD CUP QUALIFIERS

A record 198 federations registered to play the FIFA qualifiers for the 2002 World Cup, which was played in South Korea and Japan. Supporting the fun were the tournament's trio of mascots, Nic, Ato and Kaz (above, from left).

MOST PENALTIES MISSED IN A SOCCER INTERNATIONAL

Martín Palermo (above) has the unfortunate record of missing three penalties in one international, while playing for Argentina against Colombia in the 1999 Copa América held in Paraguay. Palermo first hit the bar, put the second into the crowd and the third was saved. Unsurprisingly Argentina lost, 3-0.

MOST EUROPEAN CUPS

Spanish club Real Madrid have won a record nine European Cups. The tournament, now known as the Champions League and considered to be the most prestigious in European football, was first held in 1956. Real Madrid won the first five between 1956 and 1960 and also won the cup in 1966, 1998, 2000 and 2002.

MOST EUROPEAN CUP-WINNERS CUPS

Until it was disbanded in 1999, the European Cup-Winners Cup was contested annually by the winners of Europe's national cups. The trophy was won a record four times by Spain's Barcelona in 1979, 1982, 1989 and 1997.

MOST SUCCESSIVE NATIONAL LEAGUE TITLES

The record number of successive national league championships is 11 by the Al-Ansar Sporting Club of Lebanon between 1988 and 1999.

MOST FA CUP MEDALS

Three players have won five FA Cup winners' medals – James Henry Forrest (UK) with Blackburn Rovers in 1884, 1885, 1886, 1890 and 1891; the Hon Sir Arthur Fitzgerald Kinnaird (UK) with the Wanderers in 1873, 1877 and 1878 and Old Etonians in 1879 and 1882; and Charles Harold Wollaston (UK) with the Wanderers in 1872, 1873, 1876, 1877 and 1878.

The most Scottish FA Cup winners' medals won is eight by Charles Campbell (UK) for Queen's Park in 1874, 1875, 1876, 1880, 1881, 1882, 1884 and 1886.

LONGEST BRITISH UNBEATEN RUN

Nottingham Forest went undefeated for 42 consecutive English First Division matches from 20 November 1977 to 9 December 1978.

In Scotland, Celtic went undefeated for 62 successive matches from 13 November 1915 to 21 April 1917.

HIGHEST SCORE IN A NATIONAL CUP FINAL

In 1935 Lausanne-Sports beat Nordstern Basel 10-0 in the Swiss Cup Final and two years later suffered defeat by the same margin at the hands of Grasshopper of Zurich.

BIGGEST TOURNAMENT

The second Bangkok League Seven-a-side Competition, which was held from 9 January to 25 April 1999, was contested by 5,098 teams (35,686 players), a world record for a football competition.

LONGEST GOALKEEPING CLEAN SHEET

The longest time that a keeper has succeeded in preventing a goal from being scored past him in first-class competition is 1,275 minutes (just over 14 matches) by Abel Resino (Spain) for Atlético Madrid in 1991.

The record in international matches is 1,142 minutes (nearly 13 matches) by Dino Zoff (Italy) from September 1972 to June 1974.

The British record is 1,196 minutes by Chris Woods (UK), playing for Glasgow Rangers from 26 November 1986 to 31 January 1987.

MOST VALUABLE MEDAL

A record £124,750 ($177,280) was paid for the 1966 World Cup winner's medal owned by England goalkeeper Gordon Banks (UK) at Christie's, London, UK, on 23 March 2001.

MOST LUCRATIVE SHIRT SPONSORSHIP

In 2000 American sportswear giant Nike agreed to pay Manchester United, who play in the English Premiership, a record £302.9 million ($431.9 million) to become the club's official shirt supplier.

MOST EXPENSIVE GOALKEEPER

In July 2001 Gianluigi Buffon (Italy) moved from Serie A club Parma to Juventus for a reported transfer fee of £32.6 million ($46.8 million).

HEAVIEST GOALKEEPER

England international Willie 'Fatty' Foulke (UK) stood 1.90 m (6 ft 3 in) and weighed an average 141 kg (22 st 3 lb). His final games in the early 1900s were for Bradford City, by which time he had ballooned to 165 kg (26 st). Foulke once halted a game by snapping the crossbar.

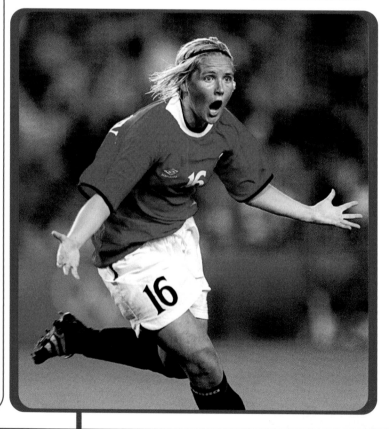

MOST WOMEN'S SOCCER OLYMPIC TITLES

Women's football was introduced to the Olympic Games in 1996. The winners in 1996 were the USA, while in Sydney in 2000 Norway (goalscorer Ragnhild Gulbrandsen pictured above) beat the USA 3-2 in the final to claim the title.

MOST PREMIERSHIP GOALS

The most goals scored in the English Premiership is 204 by Alan Shearer (UK, below). Shearer began his goal-scoring career with Southampton, before moving to Blackburn Rovers and next to Newcastle United in July 1996, for a then British record transfer fee of £15.6 million ($22.4 million). Shearer, an England captain, was also top scorer in the 1996 European Championship.

GREATEST DISTANCE TRAVELLED BY TEAMS

The greatest distance travelled between two clubs in the top division of a national league is 4,766 km (2,979 miles). The journey is between the home grounds of LA Galaxy and New England, based on the west and east coasts of the United States respectively, in the US Major League.

EARLIEST COMPETITION

The oldest trophy is the Youdan Cup, won in 1867 by Hallam FC in Sheffield, South Yorkshire, UK. The trophy was sponsored by local enthusiast Thomas Youdan (UK), and was contested on only one occasion.

MOST INDISCIPLINED MATCH

In the local cup match between Tongham Youth Club, Surrey, UK and Hawley, Hampshire, UK, on 3 November 1969 the referee booked all 22 players, including one who went to hospital, and one of the linesmen. The match, which was won by Tongham 2-0, was described by a participating player as a "good hard game".

All 11 players and two substitutes of Glencraig United from Faifley, near Clydebank, UK, were booked in the dressing room before a 2-2 draw with Goldenhill Boys' Club on 2 February 1975. The official, who had refereed Glencraig before, took offence to a crude chant that greeted his arrival and decided to take appropriate action.

MOST AFRICAN CUP OF NATIONS TITLES

Three countries have won the title on four occasions – Ghana in 1963, 1965, 1978 and 1982; Egypt in 1957, 1959, 1986 and 1998 and Cameroon (Salomon Olembe pictured above, centre) in 1984, 1988, 2000 and 2002.

LONGEST PENALTY SHOOT-OUT

In a West Riding Amateur League Cup tie between Littletown FC and Storthes Hall at Heckmondwike, W Yorkshire, UK, on 29 December 2001 a total of 34 penalties were taken when the match ended 1-1 after extra time. All 34 penalties were scored – 17 apiece – until the match was abandoned due to the failing light.

LONGEST TIME SPINNING A FOOTBALL ON ONE FINGER

Raphael Harris (Israel) spun a regulation-size football continuously on one finger for 4 min 21 sec on 27 October 2000 in Jerusalem, Israel.

FURTHEST DISTANCE TRAVELLED WHILE CONTROLLING A BALL

Jan Skorkovsky (Czech Republic) juggled a football for 42.195 km (26.219 miles) while completing the Prague Marathon in a time of 7 hr 18 min 55 sec on 8 July 1990.

OLDEST PLAYER

The oldest English League player was Neil McBain (UK), who played for New Brighton at 51 years 120 days in a Third Division North match against Hartlepool on 15 March 1947. McBain played as goalkeeper because of injuries to other players.

LONGEST WOMEN'S CONTROL OF A FOOTBALL

Cláudia Martini (Brazil) juggled a ball for 7 hr 5 min 25 sec using her feet, legs and head at Caxias do Sul, Brazil, on 12 July 1996.

LONGEST CONTROL OF A FOOTBALL WITH HEAD

Goderdzi Makharadze (Georgia) kept a football aloft with his head for 8 hr 12 min 25 sec in a record display of control at the Boris Paichadze National Stadium, Tbilisi, Georgia, on 26 May 1996.

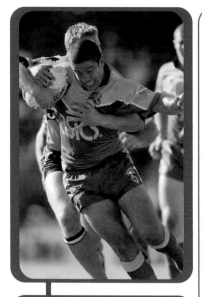

HIGHEST RUGBY LEAGUE ATTENDANCE
Stadium Australia in Sydney, NSW, Australia, was built for the 2000 Olympic Games and holds the record for highest attendances in both rugby codes. On 7 March 1999 a crowd of 104,583 gathered at Stadium Australia for a rugby league double-header. In the first game, the Newcastle Knights beat the Manly Sea Eagles 41-18. This was followed by a match between the Parramatta Eels (above) and the St George Illawarra Dragons, which the Eels won 20-10.

RUGBY LEAGUE

MOST CLUB APPEARANCES
Wales-born Jim Sullivan (UK) made 774 appearances in his career for Wigan between 1921 and 1946. In total, Sullivan took part in 928 first-class matches.

MOST GOALS IN CAREER
Jim Sullivan (UK) kicked 2,867 goals in his club and representative career for Wigan from 1921 to his retirement in 1946.

MOST TRIES IN CAREER
Brian Bevan (Australia), a wing-threequarter, scored 796 tries in 18 seasons, during the period 1945 to 1964. Bevan spent 16 seasons with Warrington, who named a stand at their home ground after him, and a further two years with Blackpool Borough. He scored a total of 740 points for Warrington – 17 points for Blackpool Borough and 39 points in representative matches. Surprisingly, he never played at international level.

HIGHEST SCORE
Ngati Pikiao of Rotorua beat Tokoroa United 148-0 in a Bay of Plenty under-17s league match in New Zealand on 10 July 1994.

HIGHEST SCORE IN AN INTERNATIONAL MATCH
The highest score in an international match is Australia's 110-4 defeat of Russia during the Rugby League World Cup at Hull, East Yorkshire, UK, on 4 November 2000.

MOST CONSECUTIVE HAT TRICKS
Richard Lopag (UK) of Deighton New Saracens scored hat tricks in 12 successive matches during 2000/01. His 26 hat tricks in the season is also a record.

MOST GOALS IN A SEASON
David Watkins (UK) scored a record total of 221 goals in 47 matches when playing for Salford in the 1972/73 season.

MOST CONSECUTIVE DEFEATS
Runcorn Highfield lost 55 successive matches from 29 January 1989 to 27 January 1991. The run finally ended with a 12-12 draw against Carlisle on 3 February 1991.

YOUNGEST INTERNATIONAL PLAYER
The youngest rugby league player to have represented Great Britain is Paul Newlove (b. 10 August 1971), who played in the first Test against New Zealand on 21 October 1989 at Old Trafford, Manchester, UK, aged 18 years 72 days. Newlove, a centre, has played for Featherstone Rovers, Bradford Northern and St Helens.

GREATEST NUMBER OF WORLD CUP WINS
The Rugby League World Cup was first held in 1954. Australia have taken the trophy more times than any other country to date, with eight wins in 1957, 1968, 1970, 1977, 1988, 1992, 1995 and 2000, as well as a win in the International Championship of 1975.

MOST TRIES ON A BRITISH LIONS DEBUT
Former rugby league star Jason Robinson (UK, below) scored five tries on his debut for the British Lions – a team of the best players from the British Isles – in an 83-6 win over a Queensland President's XV in Townsville, Queensland, Australia, on 12 June 2001.

MOST RUGBY UNION INTERNATIONAL TRIES IN A CAREER
Australia's David Campese (above) scored 64 tries in 101 matches for his country between 1982 and 1996, commencing with a try on his international debut against New Zealand. Campese is also Australia's most capped player.

RUGBY UNION

MOST CLUB APPEARANCES
Roy Evans (UK) played 1,193 games, all as prop. His overall total includes 1,007 appearances for Osterley from 12 September 1950 to 29 April 1989.

The record for the greatest number of appearances with one team is held by Allan Robertshaw (UK), who played 1,075 times for York.

MOST TRIES IN A SEASON
John Huins (UK) scored a record 85 tries during the 1953/54 season – 73 were for St Lukes College, Exeter, UK, and another 12 came for Neath and in trial games.

FASTEST TRY IN A CLUB MATCH
Andrew Brown (UK) scored a try only eight seconds after the kick off while playing for Widden Old Boys against Old Ashtonians at Gloucester, UK, on 22 November 1990.

FASTEST TRY IN AN INTERNATIONAL MATCH
Herbert Leo 'Bart' Price (UK) scored 10 seconds after the kick off for England versus Wales at Twickenham, London, UK, on 20 January 1923.

LONGEST KICK
The record for the longest place kick is reputed to be 91 m (300 ft), at Richmond Athletic Ground, London, UK, by Douglas Francis Theodore Morkel (South Africa). The kick was an unsuccessful penalty attempt for South Africa against Surrey on 19 December 1906.

In a match between Bridlington School 1st XV and an Army XV at Bridlington, Yorks, UK, on 29 January 1944, Bridlington's Ernie Cooper (UK) landed a penalty from 74 m (243 ft).

The record distance for a place kick scored in an international match was set at 64.22 m (210 ft) by Paul Thorburn (UK) for Wales against Scotland on 1 February 1986.

HIGHEST ATTENDANCE
New Zealand's 39-35 victory over Australia at Stadium Australia, Sydney, NSW, Australia, on 15 July 2000 was watched by a world record rugby union crowd of 109,874.

MOST INTERNATIONAL APPEARANCES
Philippe Sella (France) played 111 internationals for France from 1982 to 1995, scoring 30 tries – including one in every game of the 1986 Five Nations Championship – and appearing in three World Cups.

MOST PENALTIES KICKED IN AN INTERNATIONAL
The greatest number of penalties successfully kicked during an international fixture is nine. The record is held by two players: Keiji Hirose (Japan), who kicked nine penalties against Tonga (44-17) in Tokyo, Japan, on 9 May 1999, and Andrew Mehrtens (New Zealand), who slotted his nine penalties against Australia (34-15) in Auckland, New Zealand, on 24 July 1999.

MOST POINTS BY A PLAYER IN AN INTERNATIONAL
In a World Cup qualifying match between Hong Kong and Singapore at Kuala Lumpur, Malaysia, on 27 October 1994 Hong Kong's Ashley Billington scored a record 50 points, made up of 10 tries.

MOST FIVE NATIONS GRAND SLAMS
The most Grand Slams (winning all four matches in the Five Nations Championship) is 11 by England in 1913, 1914, 1921, 1923, 1924, 1928, 1957, 1980, 1991, 1992 and 1995. Since 2000 the tournament has been extended to the Six Nations with the inclusion of Italy. France won the first Grand Slam in this format in 2002.

MOST POINTS BY AN INDIVIDUAL IN AN INTERNATIONAL TOURNAMENT
In 2000 Jonny Wilkinson (UK) scored 78 points – 18 penalty goals and 12 conversions – for England in their five Six Nations championship games.

HIGHEST SCORE IN A WORLD CUP MATCH
New Zealand beat Japan 145-17 at Bloemfontein, South Africa, on 4 June 1995. During the same World Cup tie, the All Blacks, as New Zealand are widely known, scored a record 21 tries and New Zealand's Simon Culhane scored 45 points, the greatest number recorded by an individual in the finals.

MOST WORLD CUP TITLES
Australia have won the Webb Ellis Trophy in 1991 and 1999, more than any other country. The trophy, named after the supposed inventor of the sport, was inaugurated in 1987.

MOST CONSECUTIVE INTERNATIONAL RUGBY UNION APPEARANCES
New Zealand's Sean Fitzpatrick made 63 successive international appearances from 1986 to 1995.

The UK record for most consecutive international appearances is jointly held by Willie-John McBride (Ireland), who played 52 successive matches for Ireland between 1964 and 1975, and Gareth Edwards (UK), who didn't miss a match during his career for Wales between 1967 and 1978. McBride also played a record 17 times for the British Lions.

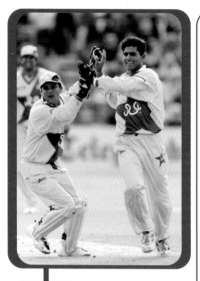

MOST DISMISSALS BY A WICKETKEEPER IN ONE-DAY INTERNATIONALS

The most dismissals is 257 (191 catches, 66 stumpings) by Moin Khan (Pakistan, above left, with team-mate Abdul Razzaq) over 190 matches from 1990 to 2001. The 1999 World Cup was a career highlight for Moin, when he made the most dismissals (15) and combined that with a batting average of 34.

CRICKET

LONGEST TEST MATCH

The lengthiest recorded cricket match was the 'timeless' Test between England and South Africa at Durban, South Africa, which lasted from 3 to 14 March 1939. It was abandoned after 10 days (eighth day rained off) because England's ship home was due to leave. The total playing time was 43 hr 16 min and a record Test match aggregate of 1,981 runs was scored.

MOST TEST 'DUCKS'

The player who has the dubious honour of recording the most 'ducks' in Test cricket is West Indies bowler

Courtney Walsh (Jamaica) with 43 scores of zero in 185 innings from November 1984 to April 2001.

MOST FIRST-CLASS CENTURIES

In 1,315 innings Sir Jack Hobbs (UK) scored 197 centuries while playing for Surrey and England between 1905 and 1934.

HIGHEST MAIDEN TEST SCORE

The highest maiden Test score is 365 not out by Sir Garfield Sobers (Barbados) for the West Indies v. Pakistan at Kingston, Jamaica, on 27, 28 February and 1 March 1958.

HIGHEST FIRST-CLASS BATTING AVERAGE

Sir Donald Bradman (Australia) holds the record for the highest batting average at 95.14, while playing for New South Wales, South Australia and Australia between 1927 and 1949. In total, he notched 28,067 runs in 338 innings, including 43 not outs.

MOST RUNS BY AN INDIVIDUAL IN A TEST

Graham Gooch (UK) scored 456 runs for England against India at Lord's, London, UK, in July 1990, the most ever scored by one player in a Test match. Gooch scored 333 in the first innings and 123 in the second.

MOST TEST RUNS

Between 1978 and 1994, Australia's Allan Border scored 11,174 runs in 156 Tests at an average of 50.56.

MOST TEST RUNS IN ONE DAY

The most runs scored in a single day during a Test match is 588 at Old Trafford, Manchester, UK, on 27 July 1936. England added 398 and India were 190 without loss at the close of their second innings.

HIGHEST TEST SCORE

Sri Lanka scored a Test match record total of 952 for six against India at Colombo, Sri Lanka, on 4–6 August 1997, during which Sanath Jayasuriya (340) and Roshan Mahanama (225) scored a second-wicket Test match record partnership of 576.

MOST CONSECUTIVE TEST VICTORIES

In March 2001 Australia recorded their 16th successive Test victory by beating India by 10 wickets at Mumbai, India.

HIGHEST INDIVIDUAL TEST INNINGS

Brian Lara (Trinidad) scored 375 for West Indies v. England at the Recreation Ground, St John's, Antigua, from 16 to 18 April 1994.

LOWEST TEST INNNINGS

New Zealand recorded a Test low of 26 against England at Auckland, New Zealand, on 28 March 1955.

HIGHEST INDIVIDUAL INNINGS

West Indies batsman Brian Lara (Trinidad) scored 501 not out in 7 hr 54 min for Warwickshire against Durham at Edgbaston, Warwks, UK, in June 1994. His innings included the most runs scored in one day (390 on 6 June) and the most runs scored from strokes worth four or more – 308 with 62 fours and 10 sixes.

MOST RUNS IN ONE DAY

Australia scored 721 in 5 hr 48 min against Essex at Southend-on-Sea, Essex, UK, on 15 May 1948.

BEST CRICKET ALL-ROUNDER

India's Kapil Dev (above) is recognized as being the world's best 'all-rounder'. He scored 5,248 runs (average 31.05), took 434 wickets (average 29.64) and held 64 catches in 131 matches between 1978 and 1994.

MOST RUNS OFF ONE OVER
Sir Garfield Sobers (Barbados, above) hit six sixes off Malcolm Nash (UK) at Swansea, W Glam, UK, on 31 August 1968. Ravishankar Shastri (India) hit the same off Tilak Raj Sharma (India) at Bombay, India, on 10 January 1985.

MOST TEST EXTRAS CONCEDED
The West Indies conceded a record 71 extras during Pakistan's first innings at Georgetown, Guyana, on 3 and 4 April 1988. These were made up of 21 byes, eight leg-byes, four wides and 38 no-balls.

DOUBLE CENTURIES IN BOTH INNINGS
Arthur Fagg (UK) is the only player to score double hundreds in both innings. He made 244 and 202 not out for Kent against Essex at Colchester, Essex, UK, on 13–15 July 1938.

MOST DOUBLE CENTURIES
Sir Donald Bradman (Australia) scored a career record 37 double hundreds between 1927 and 1949.

MOST RUNS OFF A BALL
Garry Chapman (Australia) scored 17 (all run, with no overthrows) off a single delivery while playing for Banyule against Macleod at Windsor Reserve, Victoria, Australia, on

13 October 1990. Chapman had pulled the ball to mid-wicket, where it disappeared into 25 cm (10 in) of high grass.

MOST TEST CATCHES
Mark Taylor (Australia) held 157 catches in 104 Test matches for Australia between 1989 and 1999.

TEN WICKETS IN AN INNINGS
The only bowler to clean bowl all 10 wickets in an innings is John Wisden (UK) for North *v.* South at Lord's, London, UK, in 1850.

Only one bowler has taken all 10 wickets in an innings on three occasions – Alfred 'Tich' Freeman (UK) who played for Kent between 1929 and 1931.

MOST CONSECUTIVE WICKETS
No bowler in first-class cricket has yet managed to take five wickets with five consecutive balls. The

closest was Charles Warrington Leonard Parker (UK) in his own benefit match for Gloucestershire against Yorkshire at Bristol, Avon, UK, on 10 August 1922, when he struck the stumps with five successive balls but the second was called as a no-ball.

The only man to have taken four wickets with consecutive balls more than once is Robert James Crisp (South Africa) for Western Province against Griqualand West at Johannesburg, South Africa, on 24 December 1931 and against Natal at Durban, South Africa, on 3 March 1934.

Patrick Ian Pocock (UK) took five wickets in six balls, six in nine balls and seven in 11 balls for Surrey against Sussex at Eastbourne, Sussex, UK, on 15 August 1972.

At Lord's, London, UK, on 22 May 1907, Albert Edwin Trott (Australia) of Middlesex took four Somerset wickets with four consecutive balls and then achieved a hat trick of three in three balls in the same innings.

MOST DISMISSALS BY A FEMALE WICKETKEEPER
Lisa Nye (UK) claimed a Test record eight dismissals in an innings for England against New Zealand at New Plymouth, New Zealand, in February 1992.

MOST WOMEN'S INTERNATIONAL APPEARANCES
From 1979 to 2000, Deborah Hockley (New Zealand) made 126 international appearances (19 Tests, 107 one-day internationals).

Hockley is the youngest person to have played Test cricket, aged 16 years 80 days.

LARGEST CRICKET BAT
At the National Stadium, New Delhi, India, on 16 April 1999, a 430-kg (947-lb) cricket bat measuring 15.24 m (50 ft) long and 1.82 m (6 ft) across at its widest point was unveiled by LG Electronics India Pvt Ltd.

FASTEST TEST DOUBLE CENTURY
When playing against England at Jade Stadium, Christchurch, New Zealand, on 17 March 2002, Nathan Astle (New Zealand, below), scored 200 in 153 balls and went on to score 222 off 168. England won the game by 98 runs, making Astle's effort the highest individual innings in a lost game.

HIGHEST BEACH VOLLEYBALL CAREER EARNINGS
Karch Kiraly (USA, above) won a record $2,841,065 (£1,995,770) in official Association of Volleyball Professionals (AVP) Tour earnings up to the end of the 1999 season. His 141 AVP Tour titles in his career is also a record.

VOLLEYBALL

MOST MEN'S TEAM OLYMPIC TITLES
The USSR have won three men's Olympic titles – in 1964, 1968 and 1980. The men's team failed to win a medal only once, in 1992, when they entered as the Commonwealth of Independent States (CIS).

MOST WOMEN'S TEAM OLYMPIC TITLES
The USSR have won four women's team titles in Olympic volleyball – in 1968, 1972, 1980 and 1988.

MOST MEN'S OLYMPIC MEDALS
Three players have three Olympic medals – Yuriy Poyarkov (USSR) won gold medals in 1964 and 1968 and a bronze in 1972; Katsutoshi Nekoda (Japan) won gold in 1972, silver in 1968 and bronze in 1964 and Steve Timmons (USA) won gold in 1984 and 1988 and bronze in 1992.

LARGEST AMOUNT OF PRIZE MONEY WORLD CHAMPIONSHIP
In 1998, $2.2 million (£1.6 million) was awarded in prize money, which at the time was a record in the world championships of any team sport. A total of $1 million (£710,000) for individuals and $1.2 million (£850,000) for teams was at stake.

MOST MEN'S WORLD CHAMPIONSHIP TITLES
The first men's World Championship was held in Prague, Czechoslovakia (now Czech Republic), in 1949 and was won by the USSR, who have taken five more titles since – in 1952, 1960, 1962, 1978 and 1982.

MOST WOMEN'S WORLD CHAMPIONSHIP TITLES
The USSR have dominated the women's World Championship, winning the title on five occasions – in 1952 (the year the women's tournament was introduced), 1956, 1960, 1970 and 1990.

NETBALL

MOST WORLD CHAMPIONSHIP TITLES
Australia have won the Netball World Championship (instituted in 1963) eight times – in 1963, 1971, 1975, 1979, 1983, 1991, 1995 and 1999.

LONGEST MATCH
Members of Sasol Netball Club, Evander, South Africa, played a game of netball for 50 hours from 30 March to 1 April 2001.

HIGHEST SCORE IN WORLD CHAMPIONSHIP MATCH
On 9 July 1991 the Cook Islands defeated Vanuatu 120-38 during the Netball World Championship at Sydney, NSW, Australia.

ROLLER HOCKEY

MOST WORLD CHAMPIONSHIP TITLES
England won the first roller hockey World Championship and took all the titles from 1936 to 1939. Since then, Portugal have won the most titles, with 14 between 1947 and 1993. Portugal remain the world leader in this sport today, having joined the Fédération Internationale de Patinage à Roulettes (FIPR) in 1946.

KORFBALL

LARGEST TOURNAMENT
Invented by Nico Broekhuysen, a Dutch teacher, korfball was first played in the Netherlands in 1901. Similar to netball and basketball (*korf* is Dutch for 'basket'), the sport can be played by mixed-sex teams.

On 12 June 1999, 1,796 competitors played in the Kom Keukens/Ten Donck international youth korfball tournament in Ridderkerk, The Netherlands.

HIGHEST TEAM SCORE IN WORLD CHAMPIONSHIP FINAL
The highest team score in the final of the World Championship is The Netherlands' 23-11 defeat of Belgium in 1999, in Adelaide, SA, Australia. The margin of victory, 12, is also the greatest ever attained in the final.

MOST POINTS AT NETBALL WORLD CHAMPIONSHIPS
The most points scored by one player at the Netball World Championship is 543 by Irene van Dyk (South Africa, above) in 1995. Van Dyk is pictured in a New Zealand shirt, who she played for after leaving South Africa in 2000.

LACROSSE

HIGHEST MEN'S INTERNATIONAL SCORE
The highest score ever achieved in a World Cup match is Scotland's 34-3 win over Germany in Manchester, UK, on 25 July 1994.

In the World Cup Premier Division, the record score is the USA's 33-2 win over Japan, also in Manchester, UK, on 21 July 1994.

HIGHEST WOMEN'S INTERNATIONAL SCORE
Great Britain and Ireland defeated Long Island 40-0 during their 1967 tour of the USA.

MOST MEN'S WORLD CHAMPIONSHIP TITLES
The USA have won seven of the eight World Lacrosse Championships – in 1967, 1974, 1982, 1986, 1990, 1994 and 1998. After what was the first drawn international match, Canada won the world title in 1978, beating the USA 17-16 in extra time.

MOST WOMEN'S WORLD CHAMPIONSHIP TITLES
The first Lacrosse World Cup was held in 1982, replacing the World Championship, which had been held three times since 1969. Including both competitions, the USA have won six times, in 1974, 1982, 1989, 1993, 1997 and 2001.

MOST WOMEN'S INTERNATIONAL APPEARANCES
Vivien Jones (UK) played in a record 97 international matches – 85 games for Wales, nine for the Celts and three for Great Britain – from 1977 to 2001. Her club career was with Putney and St Mary's College.

HOCKEY

FASTEST INTERNATIONAL GOAL
John French (UK) scored seven seconds after the bully-off for England against West Germany at Nottingham, UK, on 25 April 1971.

MOST INTERNATIONAL GOALS
Paul Litjens (Netherlands) scored 267 goals in 177 international games.

HIGHEST SCORE IN MEN'S INTERNATIONAL
The record international score is India's 24-1 defeat of USA in Los Angeles, California, USA, in 1932.

HIGHEST SCORE IN WOMEN'S INTERNATIONAL
The highest score in a women's international match occurred when England beat France 23-0 in Merton, London, UK, on 3 February 1923.

MOST MEN'S WORLD CUP TITLES
Pakistan have won the Fédération Internationale de Hockey (FIH) World Cup four times, in 1971, 1978, 1982 and 1994. The men's cup was inaugurated in 1971.

MOST WOMEN'S WORLD CUP TITLES
The Netherlands have won the FIH World Cup five times, in 1974, 1978, 1983, 1986 and 1990. The women's cup was first held in 1974.

MOST MEN'S INTERNATIONAL HOCKEY APPEARANCES
By January 2001 Jacques Brinkman (above) had represented The Netherlands 337 times since his international debut in 1985.

LARGEST ATTENDANCE
A record number of 65,165 spectators watched England play the United States in an international fixture held at Wembley Stadium, London, UK, on 11 March 1978.

MOST WOMEN'S OLYMPIC TITLES
A women's hockey tournament was added to the Moscow Olympics in 1980. Australia have won Olympic hockey titles in 1988 and 1996.

MOST HOCKEY OLYMPICS UMPIRED
Graham Dennis Nash (UK) umpired in five successive Olympic Games from 1976 to 1992 and officiated 144 international hockey games.

GAELIC FOOTBALL

MOST ALL-IRELAND CHAMPIONSHIP TITLES

The greatest number of All-Ireland Championships won by one team is 31 by Kerry between 1903 and 1997. The greatest number of successive wins is four by Wexford (1915–18).

HIGHEST ATTENDANCE

The Down v. Offaly final at Croke Park, Dublin, Ireland, in 1961 was watched by a record crowd of 90,556.

HURLING

MOST ALL-IRELAND CHAMPIONSHIP TITLES

The most All-Ireland Championships won by one team is 28 by Cork between 1890 and 1999.

HIGHEST ATTENDANCE

In 1954, 84,865 spectators attended the All-Ireland Final between Cork and Wexford at Croke Park, Dublin, Ireland.

LOWEST ALL-IRELAND FINAL SCORE

The lowest score in an All-Ireland Final was in the first championship at Birr, Ireland, in 1887, when Tipperary (1 goal, 1 point) beat Galway (0).

HANDBALL

HIGHEST INTERNATIONAL SCORE

The highest international score was USSR's 86-2 defeat of Afghanistan in the Friendly Army Tournament at Miskolc, Hungary, in August 1981.

MOST MEN'S WORLD CHAMPIONSHIP TITLES

For the dominant indoor version of the game, the most men's titles is four by Romania in 1961, 1964, 1970 and 1974, and Sweden in 1954, 1958, 1990 and 1999. However, West Germany won the outdoor title five times between 1938 and 1966, and have won the indoor title twice, in 1938 and 1978.

MOST WOMEN'S WORLD CHAMPIONSHIP TITLES

Three women's titles have been won by Romania in 1956, 1960 (both outdoor) and 1962 (indoor); West Germany in 1971, 1975 and 1978 (all outdoor) and the USSR in 1982, 1986 and 1990 (all outdoor).

CROQUET

MOST HOOPS SCORED IN 24 HOURS

The most hoops scored in 24 hours is 819 in the 24-hour challenge match between Orange City and Bathurst City Croquet Clubs at Orange, NSW, Australia, on 26 and 27 January 2001. Orange won by 413 hoops to 406.

JAI-ALAI

FASTEST SPORT

The fastest speed a projectile moves in any ball game is around 302 km/h (188 mph) in jai-alai, a sport that originates from the Basque areas of Spain and France. The jai-alai ball is three-quarters the size of a baseball and harder than a golf ball. The speed at which it is hurled compares to the electronically measured 273 km/h (170 mph) of a golf drive.

SHINTY

MOST CHALLENGE CUPS

Newtonmore, Highland, UK, has won the Camanachd Association Challenge Cup (instituted in 1896) a record 28 times between 1907 and 1986. Shinty, a game similar to Ireland's hurling, is a sport that is played almost exclusively in Scotland.

FOOTBAG

MOST PARTICIPANTS

A record 946 people formed one circle of footbag or hacky sack – a small, soft ball or beanbag that is juggled in the air by foot – at the Cornerstone Festival, Bushnell, Illinois, USA, on 6 July 2001.

BEST MEN'S CONTROL

The record for keeping a footbag airborne is 63,326 consecutive kicks in 8 hr 50 min 42 sec by Ted Martin (USA). Martin set this record at Lions Park, Mount Prospect, Illinois, USA, on 14 June 1997.

BEST WOMEN'S CONTROL

The women's record for keeping a footbag in the air is 24,713 kicks in 4 hr 9 min 27 sec, achieved by Constance Constable (USA). She set the record in a display at the California Athletic Club, Monterey, California, USA, on 18 April 1998.

TENPIN BOWLING

MOST WOMEN'S PROFESSIONAL BOWLING TITLES

As at 31 December 1999 Shinobu Saito (Japan) holds a record 67 professional bowling titles.

MOST TITLES

Earl Roderick Anthony (USA) won a career record 41 PBA titles and was the first player to earn $1 million (£600,000) in tenpin bowling.

MOST WORLD CUP TITLES

Paeng Nepomuceno (Philippines) has won the annual World Cup four times – in 1976, 1980, 1992 and 1996. He won his first world title at 19 years old, also a record.

HIGHEST SCORE OVER 24 HOURS

A team of six tenpin bowlers scored 251,630 at Eastways Lanes, Erie, Pennsylvania, USA on 25–26 July 1997. During this attempt a member of the team, Cory Bithell (USA), set an individual record of 59,702.

LONGEST BOWLING SESSION

The longest tenpin bowling session is 37 hr 8 min by Steve Taylor (UK) at the Sutton Superbowl, London, UK, on 17–19 September 2001.

HIGHEST HURLING ALL-IRELAND FINAL SCORE

In 1989 Tipperary beat Antrim 41 (4 goals, 29 points) to 18 (3 goals, 9 points) to win the final (above). The aggregate record was when Cork 39 (6 goals, 21 points) defeated Wexford 25 (5 goals, 10 points) in the 1970 final.

LONGEST BOWLS MARATHON
Six members of Durie Hill Bowling Club, Wanganui, New Zealand (above), played outdoor bowls for a record 40 hr 8 min from 13 to 14 April 2001. The attempt was hampered by torrential rain, but a pump kept the surface playable.

BOWLS

MOST OUTDOOR TEAM WORLD CHAMPIONSHIP TITLES
Instituted in 1966, the Leonard Trophy has been won four times by Scotland in 1972, 1984, 1992 and 1996.

MOST CONSECUTIVE CHAMPIONSHIPS
The Herrington Workmen's Flat Green Bowling Club of the Sunderland and District Bowling Association, Co Durham, UK, won the Swan Cup 25 times in a row from 1967 to 1991.

MOST OUTDOOR INDIVIDUAL WORLD CHAMPIONSHIP TITLES
David Bryant (UK) won a record three singles titles in 1966, 1980 and 1988. With the triples in 1980, and the Leonard Trophy in 1980 and 1988, he won a total of six World Championship gold medals. Bryant also won the English indoor singles a record nine times between 1964 and 1983, and claimed five gold medals in the Commonwealth Games between 1962 and 1978.

HIGHEST OUTDOOR SCORE
The highest score in a fours match of 21 ends – played by teams of four – is Sorrento Bowling Club's 67-5 win over Sportsmans at Duncraig, WA, Australia, on 14 March 1998.

HIGHEST OUTDOOR INTERNATIONAL SCORE
During the World Championships at Melbourne, Victoria, Australia, on 16 January 1980, Swaziland beat Japan by a record 63-1. The World Championships were first held in 1966 in Sydney, NSW, Australia.

HIGHEST INDOOR SCORE
The highest total in fours is 64-0 by Durbanville against George Lee Park during the 1997 South African Women's Bowling Association National Championships in Cape Town, South Africa, on 10 March 1997.

OLDEST LAWN GREEN PLAYER
Ron Buchan (New Zealand, b. 1907), began playing lawn green bowls in 1926. He was national singles champion in 1964 and 1965, and fours champion in 1957.

AFL

MOST CAREER GOALS
The most goals scored in an Australian Football League (AFL) career is 1,357 by Tony Lockett (Australia) from 1983 to 1999.

HIGHEST TEAM SCORE
The highest Australian Football League (AFL) score by one team is 239 (37-17) by Geelong against Brisbane on 3 May 1992. Australian Rules Football dates back to 1858. The earliest games featured 40 players on each side and goalposts that were 1.6 km (1 mile) apart.

MOST MATCHES
Michael Tuck (Australia) played 426 AFL matches between 1972 and 1991. He was only the second league player to reach the 400-game milestone before retiring in 1991.

MOST AFL TITLES
Australia has three major football leagues – the Australian Football League, the South Australian National Football League and the Western Australian Football League. The AFL is the biggest and has been won by the Carlton Blues (Justin Murphy pictured below) a record 16 times between 1906 and 1995.

MEN'S 3,000-M STEEPLECHASE

Brahim Boulami (Morocco, below) holds the record for the men's 3,000-m steeplechase. When he ran 7:55.28 in Brussels, Belgium, on 24 August 2001 Boulami became the first non-Kenyan athlete to hold the world record for 23 years.

MOST OLYMPIC GOLD MEDALS

The most Olympic gold medals won by any sportsman is 10 by Ray Ewry (USA). Ewry's medal came in the standing high jump and standing long jump in 1900, 1904, 1906 and 1908, and the standing triple jump in 1900 and 1904. (The Athens 1906 Intercalated Games were officially staged by the International Olympic Committee [IOC], but the medals won are not recognized by the IOC.)

Fanny Blankers-Koen (Netherlands) is the only woman to have won four gold medals at one Games – in the 100 m, 200 m, 4 x 100-m relay and 80-m hurdles – in the 1948 Olympic Games, in London, UK.

Blankers-Koen's total of four gold medals has since been equalled by Elizabeth 'Betty' Cuthbert (Australia) over two Olympics (1956 and 1964) and Evelyn Ashford (USA) in three Olympics (1984, 1988 and 1992).

MOST GOLD MEDALS AT ONE OLYMPIC GAMES

Paavo Nurmi (Finland) won a record five gold medals in the Paris Games of 1924 in the 1,500 m, 5,000 m, 10,000-m cross-country, 3000-m team and cross-country team event. Nurmi, nicknamed the 'The Flying Finn', won 12 medals in total (nine gold and three silver) in the Games of 1920, 1924 and 1928, which is also a record for overall Olympic medals won by an athlete.

The most golds won in individual events at one Games is four by Alvin Kraenzlein (USA) in 1900. He won the 60 m, the 110-m hurdles, the 200-m hurdles and the long jump.

MOST WOMEN'S TRACK AND FIELD OLYMPIC MEDALS

The most athletic medals won by a woman is eight by Merlene Ottey (Jamaica), with three silver and five bronze in the Games of 1980, 1984, 1992, 1996 and 2000. Seven of these medals were won in individual events, which is also a record.

Shirley Barbara de la Hunty (née Strickland) (Australia) won seven medals – three gold, one silver and three bronze in the Games of 1948, 1952 and 1956. However, the photo-finish from the 200 m race in 1948 indicates that she finished third, not fourth, thus unofficially increasing her medal haul to eight.

Irena Szewinska (née Kirszenstein) (Poland) won three gold, two silver and two bronze medals in 1964, 1968, 1972 and 1976, and she is the only woman to win an athletic medal in four successive Olympic Games.

WOMEN'S INDOOR 3,000 M

Ethiopia's Berhane Adere (above, centre right) ran an indoor 3,000 m in a record 8:29.15 in Stuttgart, Germany, on 3 February 2002.

MOST WORLD INDOOR CHAMPIONSHIPS GOLD MEDALS
First held in 1985, the World Indoor Championships are now staged biennially
and the most individual gold medals won is the five taken by Cuba's Iván
Pedroso (above) in the long jumps of 1993, 1995, 1997, 1999 and 2001.

MOST WOMEN'S WORLD INDOOR CHAMPIONSHIPS GOLD MEDALS
The most individual gold medals
won by a woman at the World Indoor
Championships is four, a record shared
by Stefka Kostadinova (Bulgaria) in the
high jump of 1985, 1987, 1989 and
1993; Gabriela Szabo (Romania) in the
3,000 m of 1995, 1997, 1999 and the
1,500 m in 1999, and Maria Mutola
(Mozambique) in the 800-m races of
1993, 1995, 1997 and 2001.

YOUNGEST TRACK AND FIELD OLYMPIC GOLD MEDALLIST
The youngest Olympic athletic gold
medallist was Barbara Pearl Jones
(USA), who was 15 years 123 days
when she was one of the runners in
the US 4 x 100-m relay team in
Helsinki, Finland, on 27 July 1952.

1 mile 3:43.13
Hicham El Guerrouj (Morocco)
Rome, Italy
7 July 1999
2,000 m 4:44.79
Hicham El Guerrouj (Morocco)
Berlin, Germany
7 September 1999
3,000 m 7:20.67
Daniel Komen (Kenya)
Rieti, Italy
1 September 1996
5,000 m 12:39.36
Haile Gebrselassie (Ethiopia)
Helsinki, Finland
13 June 1998
10,000 m 26:22.75
Haile Gebrselassie (Ethiopia)
Hengelo, The Netherlands
1 June 1998
20,000 m 56:55.6
Arturo Barrios (Mexico, now USA)
Le Fléche, France
30 March 1991
25,000 m 1:13.55.8
Toshihiko Seko (Japan)
Christchurch, New Zealand
22 March 1981
30,000 m 1:29:18.8
Toshihiko Seko (Japan)
Christchurch, New Zealand
22 March 1981
1 hour distance 21,101 m
Arturo Barrios (Mexico, now USA)
La Fléche, France
30 March 1991
110-m hurdles 12.91
Colin Jackson (UK)
Stuttgart, Germany
20 August 1993
400-m hurdles 46.78
Kevin Young (USA)
Barcelona, Spain
6 August 1992
3,000-m steeplechase 7:55.28
Brahim Boulami (Morocco)
Brussels, Belgium
24 August 2001

MEN'S OUTDOOR WORLD RECORDS
100 m 9.79
Maurice Greene (USA)
Athens, Greece
16 June 1999
200 m 19.32
Michael Johnson (USA)
Atlanta, Georgia, USA
1 August 1996
400 m 43.18
Michael Johnson (USA)
Seville, Spain
26 August 1999
800 m 1:41.11
Wilson Kipketer (Denmark)
Cologne, Germany
24 August 1997
1,000 m 2:11.96
Noah Ngeny (Kenya)
Rieti, Italy
5 September 1999
1,500 m 3:26.00
Hicham El Guerrouj (Morocco)
Rome, Italy
14 July 1998
4 x 100-m relay 37.40 (shared)
USA (Michael Marsh, Leroy Burrell,
Dennis Mitchell, Carl Lewis)
Barcelona, Spain
8 August 1992
USA (John Drummond Jr, Andre Cason,
Dennis Mitchell, Leroy Burrell)
Stuttgart, Germany
21 August 1993
4 x 200-m relay 1:18.68
Santa Monica Track Club (Michael Marsh,
Leroy Burrell, Floyd Heard, Carl Lewis, all USA)
Walnut, California, USA
17 April 1994

4 x 400-m relay 2:54.20
USA (Jerome Young, Antonio Pettigrew,
Tyree Washington, Michael Johnson)
New York City, USA
23 July 1998
4 x 800-m relay 7:03.89
Great Britain (Peter Elliott, Garry Cook,
Steve Cram, Sebastian Coe)
Crystal Palace, London, UK
30 August 1982
4 x 1,500-m relay 14:38.8
West Germany (Thomas Wessinghage, Harald
Hudak, Michael Lederer, Karl Fleschen)
Cologne, Germany
17 August 1977
High jump 2.45 m (8 ft 0.25 in)
Javier Sotomayor (Cuba)
Salamanca, Spain
27 July 1993
Pole vault 6.14 m (20 ft 1.75 in)
Sergei Bubka (Ukraine)
Sestriere, Italy
31 July 1994
Long jump 8.95 m (29 ft 4.5 in)
Mike Powell (USA)
Tokyo, Japan
30 August 1991
Triple jump 18.29 m (60 ft 0.25 in)
Jonathan Edwards (UK)
Gothenburg, Sweden
7 August 1995
Shot 23.12 m (75 ft 10.25 in)
Randy Barnes (USA)
Los Angeles, California, USA
20 May 1990
Discus 74.08 m (243 ft)
Jürgen Schult (East Germany)
Neubrandenburg, Germany
6 June 1986
Hammer 86.74 m (284 ft 7 in)
Yuriy Sedykh (USSR)
Stuttgart, Germany
30 August 1986
Javelin 98.48 m (323 ft 1 in)
Jan Zelezny (Czech Republic)
Jena, Germany
25 May 1996
Decathlon 9,026 points
Roman Sebrle (Czech Republic)
Götzis, Austria
26–27 May 2001
Day 1: 100 m: 10.64; LJ: 8.11 m (26 ft 7.25 in);
Shot: 15.33 m (50 ft 3.5 in); HJ: 2.12 m
(6 ft 11.25 in); 400 m: 47.79
Day 2: 110-m h: 13.92; Discus: 47.92 m (157 ft
2.5 in); Pole vault: 4.80m (15 ft 9 in); Javelin:
70.61 m (230 ft 2 in); 1,500 m: 4:21.98

WOMEN'S POLE VAULT
Stacy Dragila (USA, below) holds the record for the women's pole vault after she cleared 4.81 m (15 ft 9 in) at a meet in Palo Alto, California, USA, on 9 June 2001. California-born Dragila started her pole-vaulting career in 1993. Her nickname, 'The Goat Roper', derives from the rodeo goat-tying competitions she took part in when she was growing up.

MOST WORLD RECORDS IN ONE DAY
Jesse Owens (USA) set six world records in 45 minutes at Ann Arbor, Michigan, USA, on 25 May 1935 with a 9.4-sec 100-yd race at 3:15 pm; an 8.13-m (26-ft 8.25-in) long jump at 3:25 pm; a 20.3-sec 220-yd race (which also included a record for the 200 m) at 3:45 pm; and a 22.6-sec 220-yd low hurdles (which included the 200-m hurdles record) at 4 pm. Owens's four gold medals at the 1936 'Hitler Olympics' in Berlin, Germany, are a legendary moment in sport, as the success of the Afro-American athlete visibly annoyed Germany's Nazi leader Adolf Hitler, who believed in white supremacy and had hoped the Games would be dominated by white or Aryan athletes.

OLDEST TRACK AND FIELD RECORD HOLDER
Gerhard Weidner (West Germany) set a 20-mile walk record on 25 May 1974 when he was aged 41 years 71 days. This makes him the oldest person to set an official world record in an event open to all ages and recognized by an international governing sporting body.

The women's record is held by Marina Styepanova (USSR), who was aged 36 years 139 days when she completed the 400-m hurdles in a time of 52.94 sec at Tashkent, Uzbekistan, on 17 September 1986.

YOUNGEST TRACK AND FIELD RECORD HOLDER
The youngest man to set an official world record is Thomas Ray (UK), who was 17 years 198 days, when he pole-vaulted a height of 3.42 m (11 ft 2.75 in) on 19 September 1879.

Wang Yan (China) set a women's 5,000-m walk record at the age of 14 years 334 days with a time of 21 min 33.8 sec at Jian, China, on 9 March 1986, making her the youngest woman to hold a record in an individual event.

MOST SUCCESSIVE WINS IN ONE WORLD CHAMPIONSHIPS EVENT
The International Association of Athletics Federations (IAAF) World Championships have been held biennially since 1983 and come second only to the Olympic Games.

From the inaugural games until 1997, Ukrainian pole-vaulter Sergei Bubka was dominant in his event, winning it seven times in a row.

The greatest dominance on the track is shared by Michael Johnson (USA) in the 400 m and Haile Gebrselassie (Ethiopia) at 10,000 m. Both won their events at four consecutive championships from 1993–99.

Astrid Kumbernuss (Germany) holds the women's record, with three wins in a row in the shot from 1995–99.

MOST WORLD CHAMPIONSHIPS GOLD MEDALS
Michael Johnson (USA) has won nine World Championships gold medals in his career: in the 200 m of 1991 and 1995, the 400 m in 1993, 1995, 1997 and 1999 and in the 4 x 400-m relay in 1993, 1995 and 1999.

The women's record is five medals, held by Gail Devers (USA). Her wins were in the 100 m of 1993, the 100-m hurdles in 1993, 1995, 1999 and the 4 x 100-m relay in 1997.

MEN'S 5,000 M, 10,000 M AND INDOOR 5,000 M
Distance runner Haile Gebrselassie (Ethiopia, above) is the first man to hold world records in both 5,000 m and 10,000 m since 1978 and set his indoor world record for 5,000 m within one week of running his first indoor race.

WOMEN'S INDOOR 1,000 M

Mozambique's Maria Mutola (above) holds the indoor 1,000-m record of 2:30.94 in Stockholm, Sweden, set on 25 February 1999. Between 1992 and 1995 Mutola won every one of the 42 races she entered.

MOST WORLD CHAMPIONSHIPS MEDALS

Merlene Ottey (Jamaica) has won a staggering 14 medals in the IAAF World Championships, which is more than any other athlete has achieved. The sprinter claimed three gold, four silver and seven bronze medals between 1983 and 1997.

The most medals won by a man is 10 by the formidable Carl Lewis (USA). He won eight golds – 100 m, long jump and 4 x 100-m relay in 1983; 100 m, long jump and 4 x 100-m relay in 1987; 100 m and 4 x 100-m relay in 1991 – a silver in the 1981 long jump and a bronze in the 200 m in 1993. Lewis also won nine Olympic gold medals in his career, including four at the 1984 Games in Los Angeles, USA, thus emulating his hero, the American athlete Jesse Owens.

MOST MEDALS IN WORLD INDOOR CHAMPIONSHIPS

The most medals won at the World Indoor Championships in individual events is six by Merlene Ottey (Jamaica). The sprinter claimed three gold medals (60 m in 1995; 200 m in 1989 and 1991), two silver medals (60 m in 1991 and 200 m in 1987) and one bronze medal (60 m in 1989).

The men's record is five medals by Ivan Pedroso (Cuba) in the long jump, who took gold medals in 1993, 1995, 1997, 1999 and 2001, and Javier Sotomayor (Cuba) in the high jump, who took the gold medal in 1989, 1993, 1995 and 1999 and had to settle for a bronze medal in 1991.

LONGEST TRACK AND FIELD WINNING SEQUENCES

Iolanda Balas (Romania) won a record 150 successive competitions at the high jump from 1956 to 1967.

The record for a track event is held by Ed Moses (USA), who won 122 400-m hurdles races in a row from 16 August 1977 to 4 June 1987. His domination of the event was so complete that at one time he held the 13 fastest times ever recorded.

WOMEN'S OUTDOOR WORLD RECORDS

100 m 10.49
Florence Griffith-Joyner (USA)
Indianapolis, Indiana, USA
16 July 1998
200 m 21.34
Florence Griffith-Joyner (USA)
Seoul, South Korea
29 September 1988
400 m 47.60
Marita Koch (East Germany)
Canberra, ACT, Australia
6 October 1985
800 m 1:53.28
Jarmila Kratochvílová (Czechoslovakia)
Munich, Germany
26 July 1983

1,000 m 2:28.98
Svetlana Masterkova (Russia)
Brussels, Belgium
23 August 1996
1,500 m 3:50.46
Qu Yunxia (China)
Beijing, China
11 September 1993
1 mile 4:12.56
Svetlana Masterkova (Russia)
Zurich, Switzerland
14 August 1996
2,000 m 5:25.36
Sonia O'Sullivan (Ireland)
Edinburgh, Lothian, UK
8 July 1994
3,000 m 8:06.11
Wang Junxia (China)
Beijing, China
13 September 1993
5,000 m 14:28.09
Jiang Bo (China)
Beijing, China
23 October 1997
10,000 m 29:31.78
Wang Junxia (China)
Beijing, China
8 September 1993
20,000 m 1:05:26.6
Tegla Loroupe (Kenya)
Borgholzhausen, Germany
3 September 2000
25,000 m 1:29:29.2
Karolina Szabó (Hungary)
Budapest, Hungary
23 April 1988
30,000 m 1:47:05.6
Karolina Szabó (Hungary)
Budapest, Hungary
23 April 1988
One hour distance 18,340 m
Tegla Loroupe (Kenya)
Borgholzhausen, Germany
7 August 1998
100-m hurdles 12.21
Yordanka Donkova (Bulgaria)
Stara Zagora, Bulgaria
20 August 1988
400-m hurdles 52.61
Kim Batten (USA)
Gothenburg, Sweden
11 August 1995
3,000-m steeplechase 9:25.31
Justyna Bak (Poland)
Nice, France
9 July 2001
4 x 100-m relay 41.37
East Germany (Silke Gladisch, Sabine Rieger, Ingrid Auerswald and Marlies Gohr)
Canberra, ACT, Australia
6 October 1985

4 x 200-m relay 1:27.46
United States 'Blue' (LaTasha Jenkins, Chryste Gaines, Nanceen Perry and Torri Edwards)
Philadelphia, Pennsylvania, USA
29 April 2000
4 x 400-m relay 3:15.17
USSR (Tatyana Ledovskaya, Olga Nazarova, Maria Pinigina and Olga Bryzgina)
Seoul, South Korea
1 October 1988
4 x 800-m relay 7:50.17
USSR (Nadezhda Olizarenko, Lyubov Gurina, Lyudmila Borisova and Irina Podyalovskaya)
Moscow, Russia
5 August 1984
High jump 2.09 m (6 ft 10.25 in)
Stefka Kostadinova (Bulgaria)
Rome, Italy
30 August 1987
Pole vault 4.81 m (15 ft 9 in)
Stacy Dragila (USA)
Palo Alto, California, USA
9 June 2001
Long jump 7.52 m (24 ft 8.25 in)
Galina Chistyakova (USSR)
St Petersburg, Russia
11 June 1988
Triple jump 15.50 m (50 ft 10.25 in)
Inessa Kravets (Ukraine)
Gothenburg, Sweden
10 August 1995
Shot 22.63 m (74 ft 3 in)
Natalya Lisovskaya (USSR)
Moscow, Russia
7 June 1987
Discus 76.80 m (252 ft)
Gabriele Reinsch (East Germany)
Neubrandenburg, Germany
9 July 1988
Javelin 71.54 m (234 ft 8 in)
Osleidys Menédez (Cuba)
Réthymno, Crete, Greece
1 July 2001
Hammer 76.07 m (249 ft 6 in)
Mihaela Melinte (Romania)
Rüdlingen, Germany
29 August 1999
Heptathlon 7,291 points
Jacqueline Joyner-Kersee (USA)
Seoul, South Korea
23–24 September 1988
Day 1: 100-m hurdles: 12.69; high jump: 1.86 m (6 ft 1.25 in); shot: 15.80 m (51 ft 10 in); 200 m 22.56
Day 2: Long jump: 7.27 m (23 ft 10.25 in); javelin: 45.66 m (149 ft 10 in); 800 m: 2:08.51

FASTEST TIME TO COMPLETE MARATHON FOR WOMEN ONLY

Paula Radcliffe (UK, above) finished the women's race in the London Marathon on 14 April 2002 in London, UK, in 2 hr 18 min 56 sec. This is the record completion time for a marathon in which only women are allowed to take part.

FASTEST MARATHON

The marathon is traditionally run over a distance of 42.195 km (26 miles 385 yd). Its title and length are derived from the ancient Greek legend of a messenger who ran more than 25 miles from Marathon, Greece, to Athens, Greece, to bring news of the Greek army's victory over the Persians in 490 BC.

The men's record is 2 hr 5 min 38 sec by Khalid Khannouchi (Morocco) set in the London Marathon, in London, UK, on 14 April 2002.

The fastest time a woman has run a marathon is 2 hr 18 min 47 sec by Catherine Ndereba (Kenya). This was on 7 October 2001 in Chicago, Illinois, USA, in a race in which both male and female athletes were competing.

A record 11 men finished a marathon in under 2 hr 10 min in Boston on 18 April 1994.

A record nine women ran under 2 hr 30 min in the first women's Olympic marathon in Los Angeles, California, USA, on 5 August 1984.

OLDEST MARATHON

The Boston Marathon, the world's longest running major marathon, was first held on 19 August 1897 in Boston, Massachusetts, USA. It was originally run over a distance of 39 km (24 miles 1,232 yds) and was first won by John J McDermott (USA) in a time of 2 hr 55 min 10 sec. John Kelley (USA) completed the Boston race 61 times between 1928 and 1992, winning in 1935 and 1945.

MOST MARATHON COMPETITORS

The record number of confirmed finishers in a marathon is 38,706 at the centennial Boston Marathon, Massachusetts, USA, in 1996.

FASTEST AGGREGATE TIME FOR MARATHONS ON EACH CONTINENT

The fastest aggregate time in which a marathon on each of the seven continents has been completed is 34 hr 23 min 8 sec by Tim Rogers (UK). The achievement took Rogers from 13 February to 23 May 1999, which is also the shortest length of time in which it has been completed. Rogers began with the Antarctica Marathon on King Jorge Island and went on to complete a marathon in the United States (North and Central America), South Africa (Africa), France (Europe), Brazil (South America) and Hong Kong (Asia), before finishing with a marathon at Huntly, New Zealand (Oceania), to complete the record-breaking set of seven in just 99 days.

The fastest aggregate time by a woman for the same record is 37 hr 20 sec by Kimi Puntillo (USA). She completed the feat between 3 November 1996 and 4 October 1998 and her seven marathons in 700 days is also a record. Puntillo began with the New York Marathon (North and Central America) and then ran further marathons in Antarctica (Antarctica), London, UK (Europe), Mount Everest, Tibet (Asia), Mount Kilimanjaro, Tanzania, (Africa) and Sydney, NSW, Australia (Oceania), before finishing in Argentina (South America).

HIGHEST ALTITUDE MARATHON

The biennial Everest Marathon was first run on 27 November 1987. It begins at Gorak Shep at 5,212 m (17,100 ft) and ends at Namche Bazar at 3,444 m (11,300 ft). The men's record for this high-altitude marathon is held by Hari Roka (Nepal) in a time of 3 hr 56 min 10 sec, while for women, Anne Stentiford (UK) has completed the run in 5 hr 16 min 3 sec.

FASTEST THREE MARATHONS IN THREE DAYS

The fastest combined time for three marathons in three days is that of 8 hr 22 min 31 sec by Raymond Hubbard (UK). He ran the marathons in Belfast, UK, London, UK, and Boston, Massachusetts, USA, on 16, 17 and 18 April 1988.

MEN'S MILE, 1,500 M, 2,000 M, INDOOR MILE AND INDOOR 1,500 M

Hicham El Guerrouj (Morocco, below) is one of modern athletics' greatest middle-distance runners, as can be seen by the five world records he held in May 2002. In 1996 El Guerrouj became the first man to beat Noureddine Morceli (Algeria) since 1992.

MEN'S 1,000 M
Noah Ngeny (Kenya, above) set the record for the men's 1,000 m when he ran 2:11.96 on 5 September 1999 in Rieti, Italy. Ngeny's success beat British runner Sebastian Coe's record that had lasted since 1981.

OLDEST MARATHON FINISHERS
The oldest man to complete a marathon was Dimitrion Yordanidas (Greece) in Athens, Greece, on 10 October 1976 at the age of 98. His finishing time was 7 hr 33 min.

Jenny Wood-Allen (UK) holds the women's record after she completed the 1999 London Marathon, London, UK, aged 87 in 7 hr 14 min 46 sec. It was her 13th London Marathon.

MOST MARATHONS ON SUCCESSIVE WEEKENDS
Richard Worley (USA) ran either a marathon or an ultramarathon – a race longer than a regular marathon, normally 50 km (31 miles) – on 159 successive weekends. First was the Disney World Marathon in Orlando, Florida, USA, on 5 February 1997 and last was the Houston Methodist Marathon in Houston, Texas, USA. In the course of the record Worley ran a marathon in all 50 US states every year for three successive years.

MOST INDIVIDUAL WINS IN HALF-MARATHON WORLD CHAMPIONSHIP
The most individual wins at the (International Association of Athletics Federation) IAAF Half-Marathon World Championship is three in successive years by Tegla Loroupe (Kenya) in 1997, 1998 and 1999.

The most individual wins in the men's event is two by Paul Tergat (Kenya) in 1999 and 2000.

FASTEST HALF MARATHON
The world best time on a properly measured course is 59 min 5 sec by Paul Tergat (Kenya) at Lisbon, Portugal, set on 26 March 2000. However the official world best as recognized by the IAAF is one of 59 min 17 sec, also by Tergat in Milan, Italy, on 4 April 1998.

The women's official half-marathon record is 66 min 43 sec by Masako Chiba (Japan) recorded in Tokyo, Japan, on 19 January 1997.

MEN'S INDOOR WORLD RECORDS
50 m 5.56 (shared)
Donovan Bailey (Canada)
Reno, Nevada, USA
9 February 1996
and
Maurice Greene (USA)
Los Angeles, California, USA
13 February 1999
60 m 6.39
Maurice Greene (USA)
Madrid, Spain
3 February 1998
and
Atlanta, Georgia, USA
3 March 2001
200 m 19.92
Frank Fredericks (Namibia)
Liévin, France
18 February 1996
400 m 44.63
Michael Johnson (USA)
Atlanta, Georgia, USA
4 March 1995
800 m 1:42.67
Wilson Kipketer (Denmark)
Paris, France
9 March 1997
1,000 m 2:14.36
Wilson Kipketer (Denmark)
Birmingham, W Mids, UK
20 February 2000
1,500 m 3:31.18
Hicham El Guerrouj (Morocco)
Stuttgart, Germany
2 February 1997
1 mile 3:48.45
Hicham El Guerrouj (Morocco)
Ghent, Belgium
12 February 1997
3,000 m 7:24.90
Daniel Komen (Kenya)
Budapest, Hungary
6 February 1998
5,000 m 12:50.38
Haile Gebrselassie (Ethiopia)
Birmingham, W Mids, UK
14 February 1999

LARGEST HALF MARATHON
The world's largest half marathon is the BUPA Great North Run, which takes place between Newcastle-upon-Tyne and South Shields, Tyne and Wear, UK. The event that took place on 22 October 2000 had a record 36,822 finishers.

5,000-m walk 18:07.08
Mikhail Shchennikov (Russia)
Moscow, Russia
14 February 1995
50-m hurdles 6.25
Mark McCoy (Canada)
Kobe, Japan
5 March 1986
60-m hurdles 7.30
Colin Jackson (UK)
Sindelfingen, Germany
6 March 1994
4 x 200-m relay 1:22.11
Great Britain
(Linford Christie, Darren Braithwaite, Ade Mafe and John Regis)
Glasgow, Clydeside, UK
3 March 1991
4 x 400-m relay 3:02.83
USA
(Andre Morris, Dameon Johnson, Deon Minor and Milton Campbell)
Maebashi, Japan
7 March 1999
High jump 2.43 m (7 ft 11 in)
Javier Sotomayor (Cuba)
Budapest, Hungary
4 March 1989
Pole vault 6.15 m (20 ft 2 in)
Sergei Bubka (Ukraine)
Donetsk, Ukraine
21 February 1993
Long jump 8.79 m (28 ft 10 in)
Carl Lewis (USA)
New York City, USA
27 January 1984
Triple jump
17.83 m (58 ft 6 in)
Aliecer Urrutia (Cuba)
Sindelfingen, Germany
1 March 1997
Shot 22.66 m (74 ft 4 in)
Randy Barnes (USA)
Los Angeles, California, USA
20 January 1989
Heptathlon 6,476 points
Dan O'Brien (USA)
Toronto, Ontario, Canada
13–14 March 1993
Events: 60 m: 6.67; LJ: 7.84 m (25 ft 8.5 in); shot: 16.02 m (52 ft 6.5 in); HJ: 2.13 m (6ft 11.75 in); 60 m-hurdles: 7.85; pole vault: 5.20 m (17 ft 0.75 in); 1,000 m: 2:57.96

MEN'S JAVELIN
Jan Zelezny (Czech Republic) holds the record for men's javelin with a 98.48-m (323-ft 1-in) throw in Jena, Germany, on 25 May 1996. Zelezny dominates his sport – his best 100 efforts average more than 90 m (295 ft) and he has won three Olympic titles in a row. In 1996 he had trials as a pitcher for the Atlanta Braves baseball team.

MOST MEN'S TEAM CROSS-COUNTRY WORLD CHAMPIONSHIP TITLES
The greatest number of team victories in the cross-country World Championship (first held in 1973) is 16 by Kenya, from 1986 to 2001.

MOST WOMEN'S TEAM CROSS-COUNTRY WORLD CHAMPIONSHIP TITLES
The USSR won a record eight women's team victories in the World Championship – 1976, 1977, 1980, 1981, 1982, 1988, 1989 and 1990.

MOST WOMEN'S INDIVIDUAL CROSS-COUNTRY WORLD CHAMPIONSHIP TITLES
The women's race has been won five times by Grete Waitz (Norway) in every year from 1978 to 1981 and in 1983.

MOST TEAM SHORT-RACE CROSS-COUNTRY WORLD CHAMPIONSHIP TITLES
Kenya have won the team short-race championship four times from 1998 to 2001.

In the women's team event, no country has won the title on more than one occasion.

MOST MEN'S INDIVIDUAL CROSS-COUNTRY WORLD CHAMPIONSHIP TITLES
The greatest number of men's individual victories is five by both John Ngugi (Kenya) from 1986 to 1989 and in 1992, and Paul Tergat (Kenya) from 1995 to 1999.

FASTEST MEN'S 100 X 1,000-M RELAY
The rarely run 100 x 1,000-m relay has been completed in a record time of 5 hr 13 min 21.9 sec by a men's team from the Centro Universitario Sportivo, Bari, Italy, on 14 March 1999.

FASTEST 100 X 1-MILE RELAY
The record time in which 100 people have run 100 miles is 7 hr 35 min 55.4 sec. This was achieved by the men's Canadian Milers Athletic Club at York University, Toronto, Ontario, Canada, on 20 December 1998.

The women's record is also held by the Canadian Milers Athletic Club of Toronto, Ontario, Canada. Their run was on 27 December 1999 and they completed the distance in a time of 9 hr 23 min 39 sec.

LONGEST RACE
The longest race ever staged was the 1929 trans-continental race from New York City, on the east coast of the United States, to the west coast city of Los Angeles, California, USA – a distance of 5,850 km (3,635 miles). The race was won by Johnny Salo (Finland), who completed the run over 79 days from 31 March to 17 June in 525 hr 57 min 20 sec, finishing just 2 min 47 sec ahead of the second-placed runner, Britain's Pietro Gavuzzi (UK).

MOST PARTICIPANTS IN AN ATHLETIC CHAMPIONSHIPS
A record 11,475 athletes – 9,328 men and 2,147 women – took part in the 1993 World Veterans' Athletic Championships in Miyazaki, Japan.

NON-COMPETITIVE RECORDS

FASTEST 200 M BACKWARDS
Timothy Badyna (USA) ran the 200 m backwards in a world record time of 32.78 sec on 17 January 2001 at Santa Clarita, California, USA.

LARGEST ATTENDANCE FOR A SINGLE-DAY EVENT
An estimated 2.5 million people line the streets of New York City, USA, every year to cheer on participants in the New York Marathon.

'END-TO-END' WALKING
The fastest time in which anybody has completed the 1,426.4 km (886.3 miles) between Land's End, Cornwall, and John O'Groats, Highland – respectively, the most southern and northern points of the UK – is 12 days 3 hr 45 min by Malcolm Barnish (UK) in 1986.

MOST INDIVIDUAL SHORT-RACE CROSS-COUNTRY WORLD CHAMPIONSHIP TITLES
The championship was instituted in 1998 and the most individual wins in the men's short race is two by John Kibowen (Kenya, above) in 1998 and 2000.

MEN'S DECATHLON

The men's decathlon record, a competition that consists of 10 different disciplines, is held by Roman Sebrle (Czech Republic, below in the long jump). He scored 9,026 points in Götzis, Austria, on 26 and 27 May 2001.

GREATEST DISTANCE RUN IN 1,000 CONSECUTIVE HOURS

Arulananthan Joachim (Sri Lanka) ran 3.495 km (2.172 miles) every hour for 1,000 consecutive hours in Columbo, Sri Lanka, from 19 August to 29 September 1996. Joachim decided to become a record-breaker when he received a copy of *Guinness World Records* in 1991 and thought that it would be a good way to spread charitable ideas and earn money for his war-torn home country. His aim is to become the most prolific record holder in history and to raise $1 billion for charity.

LONGEST DISTANCE COVERED ON FOOT

Gary Parsons (Australia) completed a run of 19,030.3 km (11,824.8 miles) in 274 days 8 min, starting and finishing in Brisbane, Queensland, Australia, from 25 April 1999 to 25 January 2000. As well as completing a circuit of Australia he also ran round the island of Tasmania and broke three further records along the way – fastest 10,000 km in 135 days 9 hr 50 min; 15,000 km in 205 days 23 hr 18 min, and 10,000 miles in a record time of 221 days 1 hr 7 min.

WOMEN'S INDOOR WORLD RECORDS

50 m 5.96
Irina Privalova (Russia)
Madrid, Spain
9 February 1995
60 m 6.92
Irina Privalova (Russia)
Madrid, Spain
11 February 1993 and 9 February 1995
200 m 21.87
Merlene Ottey (Jamaica)
Liévin, France
13 February 1993
400 m 49.59
Jarmila Kratochvílovà (Czechoslovakia)
Milan, Italy
7 March 1982
800 m 1:55.82
Jolanda Ceplak (Slovenia)
Vienna, Austria
3 March 2002
1,000 m 2:30.94
Maria Mutola (Mozambique)
Stockholm, Sweden
25 February 1999
1,500 m 4:00.27
Doina Melinte (Romania)
East Rutherford, New Jersey, USA
9 February 1990
1 mile 4:17.14
Doina Melinte (Romania)
East Rutherford, New Jersey, USA
9 February 1990
3,000 m 8:29.15
Berhane Adere (Ethiopia)
Stuttgart, Garmany
3 February 2002
5,000 m 14:47.35
Gabriela Szabo (Romania)
Dortmund, Germany
13 February 1999
3,000-m walk 11:40.33
Claudia Iovan (Romania)
Bucharest, Romania
30 January 1999
4 x 200-m relay 1:32.55
SC Eintracht Hamm (Helga Arendt, Silke-Beate Knoll, Mechthild Kluth and Gisela Kinzel, all West Germany)
Dortmund, Germany
19 February 1988
and
LG Olympia Dortmund (Esther Moller, Gabi Rockmeier, Birgit Rockmeier and Andrea Phillip, all Germany)
Karlsruhe, Germany
21 February 1999
4 x 400-m relay 3:24.25
Russia (Tatyana Chebykina, Svetlana Goncharenko, Olga Kotlyarova and Natalya Nazarova)
Maebashi, Japan
7 March 1999
50-m hurdles 6.58
Cornelia Oschkenat (East Germany)
Berlin, Germany
20 February 1988
60-m hurdles 7.69
Lyudmila Narozhilenko (Russia)
Chelyabinsk, Russia
4 February 1993
High jump 2.07 m (6 ft 9.5 in)
Heike Henkel (Germany)
Karlsruhe, Germany
9 February 1992

MEN'S 800 M, INDOOR 800 M, INDOOR 1,000 M

Kenya-born Danish national Wilson Kipketer (above) became the first man to set an indoor 800-m record in a heat rather than a final in the 1997 World Indoor Championships.

Pole vault 4.75 m (15 ft 7 in)
Svetlana Feofanova (Russia)
Vienna, Austria
3 March 2002
Long jump 7.37 m (24 ft 2 in)
Heike Drechsler (East Germany)
Vienna, Austria
13 February 1988
Triple jump 15.16 m (49 ft 8 in)
Ashia Hansen (UK)
Valencia, Spain
28 February 1998
Shot 22.50 m (73 ft 10 in)
Helena Fibingerová (Czechoslovakia)
Jablonec, Czhechoslovakia
19 February 1977
Pentathlon 4,991 points
Irina Belova (Russia)
Berlin, Germany
14–15 February 1992
Events: 60 m-hurdles: 8.22; HJ: 1.93 m (6 ft 4in). shot: 13.25 m (43 ft 5.6 in); LJ 6.67 m (21 ft 9.6 in); 800 m: 2:10.26.

WINTER OLYMPICS

MOST INDIVIDUAL OLYMPIC GOLD MEDALS

Bjørn Dæhlie (Norway) won eight Olympic gold medals in Nordic skiing between 1992 and 1998.

The women's record is six by Lidya Skoblikova (USSR) in speed skating from 1960 to 1964, and Lyubov Yegerova (Russia) in Nordic skiing from 1992–94.

MOST MEN'S ALPINE SKIING OLYMPIC GOLD MEDALS

Four skiers have won three gold medals in the Winter Olympics – Anton 'Toni' Sailer

MOST MEN'S ALPINE SKIING OLYMPIC MEDALS

Kjetil André Aamodt (Norway, below) has won the most men's Alpine Olympic medals. In addition to his record three gold medals, he has won two silver (downhill, combined 1994) and two bronze (giant slalom 1992, super-giant slalom 1994).

(Austria) in the downhill, slalom and giant slalom races of 1956; Jean-Claude Killy (France) in the downhill, slalom and giant slalom in 1968; Alberto Tomba (Italy) in the slalom and giant slalom in 1988 and in 1992's giant slalom, and Kjetil André Aamodt (Norway) in the super-giant slalom in 1992 and 2002 as well as the combined event in 2002.

MOST WOMEN'S ALPINE SKIING OLYMPIC MEDALS

The most medals won at the Winter Games is five – by Switzerland's Vreni Schneider, who in addition to golds in the 1988 giant slalom and the 1988 and 1994 slaloms, won silver in the combined and bronze in the giant slalom in 1994. Katja Seizinger (Germany) also has five – bronze in the 1992 and 1998 super-giant slaloms and golds in the downhills of 1994 and 1998 and the combined in 1998.

MOST INDIVIDUAL OLYMPIC MEDALS

Norway's Bjørn Dæhlie won 12 medals in Nordic skiing between 1992 and 1998. The women's best is 10 by Raisa Smetanina (USSR/Russia) in Nordic skiing from 1976 to 1992.

MOST NATIONAL TOTAL OLYMPIC GOLD MEDALS

Norway has won 94 gold medals in the Winter Olympics between 1924 and 2002. Norway also has the most medals won overall, with 263 medals in 78 years.

MOST NATIONAL OLYMPIC GOLD MEDALS AT ONE GAMES

The USSR won 13 gold medals in 1976 at the Innsbruck Winter Olympic Games, in Austria.

MOST NATIONAL OLYMPIC MEDALS IN ONE GAMES

The most medals won by a single country at a Winter Olympic Games is 35 by Germany at the Winter Games that were held at Salt Lake City, Utah, USA, in 2002.

OLDEST WINTER OLYMPIC COMPETITOR

The oldest competitor in the history of the Winter Olympic Games is British participant James Coates, who came seventh in the skeleton event at St Moritz, Switzerland, in 1948, aged 53 years 328 days.

Anne Abernathy (US Virgin Islands) was 48 years 307 days when she took part in the luge event at the 2002 Salt Lake City Games in Utah, USA, making her the oldest female competitor in Winter Olympic history.

MOST WOMEN'S ALPINE SKIING GOLD MEDALS

The most Olympic gold medals won by a woman is three, a feat achieved by four competitors: Vreni Schneider (Switzerland), Katja Seizinger (Germany), Deborah Campagnoni (Italy) and Janica Kostelic (Croatia, above).

MOST FREESTYLE SKIING OLYMPIC MEDALS

Since freestyle skiing was introduced to the Games in 1992, no skier has won more than one gold in the discipline. However, six skiers have won two medals (either gold, silver or bronze): Edgar Grospiron (France), Janne Lahtela (Finland, above), Elizaveta Koshevnikov (Russia), Stine Lise Hattestad (Norway), Kari Traa (Norway) and Tae Satoya (Japan).

YOUNGEST WINTER OLYMPIC COMPETITOR

Britain's Magdalena Cecilia Colledge was aged just 11 years 74 days when she took part in the figure skating competition at the Winter Games of 1932, held at Lake Placid, New York, USA.

The youngest male competitor is Jan Hoffman (East Germany), who was aged 12 years 113 days when he competed in the figure skating competition at the Calgary Winter Olympics, Alberta, Canada, in 1988.

MOST COUNTRIES TO WIN OLYMPIC MEDALS

Medals were won by a record 25 different countries at the most recent Winter Games, held at Salt Lake City, Utah, USA, in 2002.

MOST OLYMPIC COMPETITORS

The 2002 Winter Olympic Games at Salt Lake City, Utah, USA, involved competitors from a record number of 77 different countries.

PARALYMPIC GAMES

MOST PARALYMPIC MEDALS

Since the first Winter Paralympics, held in 1976 at Örnsköldsvik, Sweden, the most medals have been won by Austria, with a total of 301.

MOST INDIVIDUAL PARALYMPIC GOLD MEDALS

Between 1988 and 2002, Norway's Ragnhild Myklebust won 17 gold medals in the Winter Paralympics. The record for men is 12, held by Frank Hoefle (Germany), also between 1988 and 2002.

MOST INDIVIDUAL PARALYMPIC MEDALS

The most medals won by an individual at the Winter Paralympic Games is 19 by Frank Hoefle (Germany), who took 12 gold, four silver and three bronze in biathlon and Nordic skiing between 1988 and 2002. The women's record is 18 by Ragnhild Myklebust (Norway), who won 17 gold and one bronze in the biathlon and Nordic skiing disciplines between 1988 and 2002.

MOST NATIONAL PARALYMPIC GOLD MEDALS

Norway has won the most overall gold medals, with a total of 118.

MOST PARALYMPIC MEDAL-WINNING NATIONS

The most nations to win a medal at the Paralympics is 22 in the 2002 Games at Salt Lake City, Utah, USA.

MOST ALPINE SKIING PARALYMPIC GOLD MEDALS

Reinhild Moeller (Germany) and Sarah Will (USA) share the record for most gold Alpine skiing medals, with 12 apiece. The men's record is 11 by Rolf Heinzmann (Switzerland).

MOST BIATHLON PARALYMPIC MEDALS

The most medals won in biathlon is four by Frank Hoefle (Germany) from 1992–2002. The women's record is three, held by Ragnhild Myklebust (Norway) in events between 1994 and 2002, and Marjorie Van de Bunt (Netherlands) from 1994 to 2002.

MOST BIATHLON PARALYMPIC GOLD MEDALS

The most gold medals won is three by Frank Hoefle (Germany) between 1992 and 1998. The women's record is two by Ragnhild Myklebust (Norway), Marjorie Van de Bunt (Netherlands) and Verena Bentele (Germany).

MOST NORDIC SKIING PARALYMPIC GOLD MEDALS

The most gold medals won in Nordic skiing is 15 by Ragnhild Myklebust (Norway) from 1988 to 2002. The men's record is nine, shared by Terje Loevaas (Norway) between 1984 and 1994 and Frank Hoefle (Germany) between 1988 and 2002.

MOST NORDIC SKIING PARALYMPIC MEDALS

The most medals won in Nordic skiing is 15 by Ragnhild Myklebust (Norway), all gold, between 1988 and 2002, and Frank Hoefle (Germany), who won nine gold, four silver and two bronze between 1988 and 2002.

SKIING

GREATEST DISTANCE SKIED EVERY DAY FOR ONE YEAR

In 1994 Arnie Wilson and Lucy Dicker (both UK) skied every day in a round-the-world expedition. They covered 5,919 km (3,678 miles) at 237 resorts in 13 countries on five continents. Dicker tragically died in an avalanche in the French Alps soon after completing the expedition.

MOST ALPINE SKIING PARALYMPIC MEDALS

Switzerland's Hans Burn (above) holds the record for most Alpine skiing medals at the Winter Paralympics. He won 14 medals between 1988 and 2002 – six gold, five silver and three bronze.

MOST MEN'S OLYMPIC BIATHLON TITLES

Ole Einar Bjorndalen (Norway, above) has won a record four individual titles in his Olympic career – the 10 km in 1998 and the 10 km, 20 km and pursuit in 2002. He also won a relay gold medal in the 4 x 7.5 km in 2002.

SKIING

MOST MEN'S BIATHLON WORLD CHAMPIONSHIPS TITLES

Frank Ullrich (West Germany) won a record six individual world titles, four at 10 km from 1978 to 1981 (including the 1980 Olympics) and two at 20 km in 1982 and 1983.

Biathlete Alexander Tikhonov was in 10 successful Soviet relay teams between 1968 and 1980 and also won four individual titles.

MOST WOMEN'S BIATHLON OLYMPIC GOLD MEDALS

A women's competition was first held in 1992 and five people have two titles – Anfissa Restzova (Russia),

Myriam Bédard (Canada), Uschi Disl (Germany), Katrin Apel (Germany) and Andrea Henkel (Germany).

MOST WOMEN'S BIATHLON WORLD CHAMPIONSHIPS TITLES

The first World Championships were held in 1984 and the most titles won by an individual is four, by Petra Schaaf (Germany). She won the 5 km in 1988 and the 15 km in 1989, 1991 and 1993. Kaya Parve (USSR) has won six titles, but four of these were in relay events and only two were individual.

MOST MEN'S ALPINE SKIING WORLD CHAMPIONSHIPS TITLES

The World Alpine Championships were first held in 1931. Anton 'Toni' Sailer (Austria) has won seven titles: all four – giant slalom, slalom, downhill and the non-Olympic Alpine combination – in 1956, and also the downhill, giant slalom and combined in 1958.

The women's record is held by Christl Cranz (Germany). She won seven individual events and five combined from 1934–39.

MOST WOMEN'S NORDIC SKIING TITLES

The first World Nordic Skiing Championships were at the 1924 Winter Olympics in Chamonix, France. The most titles won by a woman is 17 by Yelena Välbe (USSR and Russia) from 1989–98, made up of 10 individual and seven relay. She has 14 World Championships gold medals and 41 World Cup victories.

MOST WOMEN'S NORDIC SKIING OLYMPIC MEDALS

Raisa Smetanina (USSR, CIS in 1992) has won 10 Olympic medals – four gold, five silver and one bronze – from 1980–92.

MOST WOMEN'S NORDIC SKIING OLYMPIC GOLD MEDALS

Lyubov Yegorova (Russia) has won six Olympic gold medals: three in 1992 (for CIS) and three in 1994.

MOST NORDIC SKI-JUMPING WORLD CHAMPIONSHIP TITLES

Norway's Birger Ruud won five Nordic ski-jump titles between 1931 and 1935. He is the only person to win Olympic events in each of the Alpine and Nordic disciplines.

MOST MEN'S WORLD CUP WINS

Introduced for Alpine events in 1967, the most individual event World Cup wins is 86 (46 giant slalom and 40 slalom from a total of 287 races) by Ingemar Stenmark (Sweden) in 1974–89. This included a men's record 13 wins in one season in 1978/79, 10 of which were part of a record 14 successive giant slalom victories between 18 March 1978 and 21 January 1980.

MOST WOMEN'S WORLD CUP WINS

Annemarie Moser (Austria) won a women's record 62 individual events from 1970 to 1979. She had a record 11 consecutive downhill wins from December 1972 to January 1974.

MOST WORLDLOPPET MASTERS TITLES

The most times an individual has qualified as a Worldloppet Gold Master is nine by Jan Jasiewicz (Switzerland) up to the end of the 2001 season. To qualify as a Gold Master a skier must complete 10 cross-country skiing marathons in the Worldloppet series, all in different countries and over at least two continents.

MOST NORDIC COMBINED OLYMPIC GOLD MEDALS

The most Nordic combined gold Olympic medals won is three by Sampaa Lajunen (Finland, above) in the individual, sprint and relay of 2002, and Ulrich Wehling (East Germany) in the individual events of 1972, 1976 and 1980.

MOST 'VERTICAL FEET' SKIED BY MEN

On 29 April 1998 Edi Podivinsky, Luke Sauder, Chris Kent (all Canada) and Dominique Perret (Switzerland) skied 107,777 m (353,600 ft) in a time of 14 hr 30 min on a slope at Blue River, British Columbia, Canada.

MOST 'VERTICAL FEET' SKIED BY WOMEN

Jennifer Hughes (USA) skied a total of 93,124 m (305,525 ft) for almost 15 hours at Atlin, British Columbia, Canada, on 20 April 1998. Hughes was accompanied by snowboarder Tammy McMinn (Canada). They were lifted from the bottom of the run to the top by helicopter.

LONGEST MEN'S COMPETITIVE SKI-JUMP

Andreas Goldberger (Austria) leapt a staggering 225 m (738 ft) in a ski-jump competition held at Planica, Slovenia, on 18 March 2000.

LONGEST WOMEN'S SKI-JUMP

The women's ski-jumping record is 112 m (367 ft), held by Eva Ganster (Austria) at Bischofshofen, Austria, on 7 January 1994.

LONGEST SKI-JUMP ON A DRY-SKI SLOPE

On 30 June 1981 Hubert Schwarz (West Germany) jumped 92 m (302 ft) at Berchtesgarten, Germany.

MOST SNOWBOARDING OLYMPIC MEDALS

Karine Ruby (France) has won two Olympic Games snowboarding medals – gold in the 1998 parallel giant slalom and silver in the same event in 2002. Ross Powers (USA, above) also has two medals – the half-pipe gold in 2002 and the bronze in 1998.

MOST FREESTYLE WORLD CHAMPIONSHIPS TITLES

Since the first World Championships in Tignes, France, in 1986, Edgar Grospiron (France) has won three titles – in the moguls in 1989 and 1991, and the aerials in 1995. He also won an Olympic title in 1992.

The most world titles won by a woman is also three, held by Candice Gilg (France). She won the moguls in 1993, 1995 and 1997.

MOST MEN'S FREESTYLE WORLD CUP TITLES

The Freestyle World Cup, instituted in 1980, has been won five times by France's Eric Laboureix, in 1986, 1987, 1988, 1990 and 1991.

MOST WOMEN'S FREESTYLE WORLD CUP TITLES

Connie Kissling (Switzerland) won a record 10 Freestyle World Cup titles between 1983 and 1992.

MOST SOMERSAULTS AND TWISTS IN A FREESTYLE AERIAL JUMP

Matt Chojnacki (USA) managed a remarkable quadruple-twisting quadruple back flip during a freestyle jump at the Winter Park Resort in Colorado, USA, on 4 April 2001.

LONGEST DOWNHILL RACE

'The Inferno' in Switzerland is 15.8 km (9.8 miles) from the top of the Schilthorn to Lauterbrunnen.

FASTEST SKIER

The highest recorded speed for a skier is 248.105 km/h (154.165 mph) by Austrian Harry Egger at Les Arcs, France, on 2 May 1999.

The fastest female skier is Karine Dubouchet (France), who reached 234.528 km/h (145.728 mph) at Les Arcs, France, on 2 May 1999.

SNOWBOARDING

MOST WORLD CUP TITLES

Karine Ruby (France) won 16 World Cup titles from 1995 to 2002 in four disciplines. Mathieu Bozzetto (France) has won the most men's titles – six.

MOST WORLD TITLES

The most titles won (including Olympic titles) is three by Karine Ruby (France). She took the giant slalom in 1996, the snowboard cross in 1997 and the 1998 Olympic title.

FASTEST SNOWBOARDER

Darren Powell (Australia) recorded a highest ever snowboarding speed of 201.907 km/h (125.459 mph) at Les Arcs, France, on 2 May 1999.

MOST WOMEN'S BIATHLON OLYMPIC MEDALS

Uschi Disl (Germany, above) has won eight Olympic biathlon medals: two gold, four silver and two bronze.

MOST MEN'S OLYMPIC MEDALS

In addition to his record five gold medals, Clas Thunberg (Finland) won a silver and one tied bronze, giving him seven Olympic medals in total. This record is shared with Norwegian Ivar Ballangrud, who won four gold, two silver and a bronze between 1928 and 1936.

MOST WOMEN'S SHORT-TRACK OLYMPIC MEDALS

The most Olympic medals won by a woman in short-track speed skating is five by Chun Lee-kyung (South Korea) with four gold and one bronze, and Yang Yang (China), who has four silver and one bronze medal.

MOST SHORT-TRACK SPEED-SKATING OLYMPIC MEDALS

The greatest number of Olympic medals won by a man in short-track speed skating is five by Marc Gagnon (Canada, below). He won three gold and two bronze medals between 1994 and 2002.

FASTEST MEN'S 1,500 M

Derek Parra (USA) skated 1,500 m in a record 1:43.59 at the 2002 Winter Olympics in Salt Lake City, Utah, USA, on 19 February 2002.

FASTEST MEN'S 3,000 M

Gianni Romme (Netherlands) skated 3,000 m in 3:42.75 at Calgary, Alberta, Canada, on 11 August 2000.

FASTEST WOMEN'S 3,000 M

Claudia Pechstein (Germany) skated 3,000 m in 3:57.70 at Salt Lake City, Utah, USA, on 10 February 2002.

FASTEST MEN'S 5,000 M

Jochem Utydehaage (Netherlands) skated 5,000 m in a record time of 6:14.66 at Salt Lake City, Utah, USA, on 9 February 2002.

FASTEST WOMEN'S 5,000 M

Claudia Pechstein (Germany) skated 5,000 m in 6:46.91 at Salt Lake City, Utah, USA, on 23 February 2002.

FASTEST MEN'S 10,000 M

Jochem Uytdehaage (Netherlands) skated 10,000 m in 12:58.92 at Salt Lake City, Utah, USA, on 22 February 2002.

FASTEST MEN'S SHORT-TRACK 500 M

Jeffrey Scholten (Canada) skated a short-track 500 m in a record time of 41.514 at Calgary, Alberta, Canada, on 13 October 2001. Short-track differs from long-track in that it is a race between two opposing skaters rather than against the clock.

FASTEST WOMEN'S SHORT-TRACK 500 M

Evgenia Radanova (Bulgaria) skated a short-track 500 m in a world record time of 43.671 at Calgary, Alberta, Canada, on 19 October 2001.

FASTEST MEN'S SPEED SKATING 1,000 M

Gerard van Velde (Netherlands, above) skated 1,000 m in a time of 1:07.16 at Salt Lake City, Utah, USA, on 16 February 2002.

SPEED SKATING

MOST MEN'S OLYMPIC GOLD MEDALS

Two skaters have secured five golds in this sport – Clas Thunberg (Finland) in 1924 and 1928 (one of which was a tied gold) and Eric Arthur Heiden (USA), who uniquely won all his golds at just one Olympic Games at Lake Placid, New York, USA, in 1980.

MOST WOMEN'S OLYMPIC GOLD MEDALS

Lidya Pavlovna Skoblikova (USSR) won six Olympic speed skating gold medals: two in 1960 and a further four in 1964.

MOST WOMEN'S OLYMPIC MEDALS

Karin Kania (East Germany) won three golds, four silvers and a bronze from 1980–88.

FASTEST MEN'S 500 M

Hiroyasu Shimizu (Japan) skated 500 m in 34.32 at Salt Lake City, Utah, USA, on 10 March 2001. This record was set at the traditional long-track distance, in which skaters race in pairs against the clock counter-clockwise on a standard oval course that measures 400 m (1,312 ft).

FASTEST WOMEN'S 500 M

Catriona LeMay Doan (Canada) skated 500 m in 37.22 at Calgary, Alberta, Canada, on 9 December 2001.

FASTEST WOMEN'S 1,000 M

Christine Witty (USA) skated 1,000 m in 1:13.83 at Salt Lake City, Utah, USA, on 17 February 2002.

FASTEST MEN'S SHORT-TRACK 1,000 M
Steve Robillard (Canada) skated a short-track 1,000 m in a record time of 1:25.985 at Calgary, Alberta, Canada, on 14 October 2001.

FASTEST WOMEN'S SHORT-TRACK 1,000 M
Yang Yang (China) skated a short-track 1,000 m in a record time of 1:31.871 in Calgary, Alberta, Canada, on 20 October 2001.

FASTEST MEN'S SHORT-TRACK 1,500 M
Steve Robillard (Canada) skated a short-track 1,500 m in 2:15.383 at Calgary, Alberta, Canada, on 12 October 2001.

FASTEST WOMEN'S SHORT-TRACK 1,500 M
Choi Eun-kyung (South Korea) skated a short-track 1,500 m in a record time of 2:21.069 at Salt Lake City, Utah, USA, on 13 February 2002.

FASTEST MEN'S SHORT-TRACK 3,000 M
Kim Dong-sung (South Korea) skated a short-track 3,000 m in 4:46.727 at Szekesfehervar, Hungary, on 8 November 1998.

FASTEST WOMEN'S SHORT-TRACK 3,000 M
Choi Eun-kyung (South Korea) skated a short-track 3,000 m in 5:01.976 at Calgary, Alberta, Canada, on 22 October 2000.

FASTEST WOMEN'S SHORT-TRACK 3,000-M RELAY
A South Korea team consisting of Park Hye-won, Joo Min-jin, Choi Min-kyung and Choi Eun-kyung skated a short-track 3,000-m relay in 4:12.793 at Salt Lake City, Utah, USA, on 20 February 2002.

FASTEST MEN'S SHORT-TRACK 5,000-M RELAY
A Canada team of Eric Bédard, Marc Gagnon, Jean-Francois Monette and Mathieu Turcotte skated a short-track 5,000-m relay in 6:43.730 at Calgary, Alberta, Canada, on 14 October 2001.

FIGURE SKATING

MOST GRAND SLAMS
The greatest number of figure skating grand slams – victory in the European, World and Olympic titles in the same year – ever achieved by a man is the two claimed by Karl Schäfer (Austria) in 1932 and 1936.

YOUNGEST FIGURE SKATING WORLD CHAMPION
The youngest winner of a world title is Tara Lipinski (USA, above), who was aged just 14 years 286 days when she won the individual figure skating World Championship on 22 March 1997 in Lausanne, Switzerland.

Two women have achieved the same feat – Sonja Henie (Norway) in 1932 and 1936, and Katarina Witt (West Germany) in 1984 and 1988. Witt won two Olympic gold medals before retiring in 1988.

MOST MEN'S OLYMPIC GOLD MEDALS
Sweden's Gillis Grafström won three figure skating golds in successive Olympic Games from 1920 to 1928. He also won the World Championship three times – the last in 1929 – and a fourth Olympic medal, a silver, in 1932, after which he retired. The Grafström spin is named after him.

MOST WOMEN'S OLYMPIC GOLD MEDALS
Sonja Henie (Norway) won three Olympic figure skating gold medals at the Games of 1928, 1932 and 1936. Henie, the 'Pavlova of ice', was trained by Gillis Grafström (Sweden), who won three figure skating Olympic gold medals himself before his retirement in 1932.

MOST MEN'S WORLD CHAMPIONSHIP TITLES
Ulrich Salchow (Sweden) won a record 10 figure skating world titles from 1901 to 1905 and 1907 to 1911. His contribution to the sport is forever commemorated by the Salchow jump, which is named after him.

MOST WOMEN'S WORLD CHAMPIONSHIP TITLES
The most individual figure skating World Championship titles won by a woman is 10 by Sonja Henie (Norway) between 1927 and 1936.

MOST ICE-SKATING CONTINUOUS SPINS
The most continuous spins made on one foot is 60 by Neil Wilson (UK) at the Spectrum Centre, Guildford, Surrey, UK, on 1 July 1997.

FASTEST WOMEN'S 1,500 M
Anni Friesinger (Germany, above) skated 1,500 m in 1:54.02 at Salt Lake City, Utah, USA, on 20 February 2002. In so doing, she broke her own record of 1:54.38 over the same distance, which she had set 11 months earlier.

MOST WOMEN'S BOBSLEIGH WORLD CHAMPIONSHIP MEDALS

The most medals won by an individual is two: Susi-Lisa Erdmann (Germany) won bronze in 2001 and 2002 (with Nicole Herschmann, both above), Jean Racine and Jennifer Davidson (USA) took silver in 2000 and 2001 and Swiss pair Francoise Burdet and Katharine Sutter won gold in 2001 and bronze in 2000.

BOBSLEIGH

MOST WOMEN'S WORLD CHAMPIONSHIP AND OLYMPIC TITLES

A women's World Championship was introduced in 2000 and debuted at the 2002 Winter Olympic Games. The winners have so far been Germany, Switzerland and the USA, with no country winning more than once.

MOST WORLD CHAMPIONSHIP TITLES

The most individual world titles won is 11 by Eugenio Monti (Italy) from 1957–68. The most successful bobsleigher of all time, he won eight two-man and three four-man titles.

MOST OLYMPIC GOLD MEDALS

East Germany's Meinhard Nehmer and Bernhard Germeshausen both won three gold medals – in the 1976 two-man event and the 1976 and 1980 four-man races.

MOST OLYMPIC MEDALS

Between 1980 and 1992 Bogdan Musiol (East Germany and Germany after 1990) won seven bobsleigh medals – one gold, five silver and one bronze – the most ever won by any bobsleigher at the Olympics. Musiol took part in four Games and never came home without a medal.

MOST FOUR-MAN WORLD CHAMPIONSHIP AND OLYMPIC TITLES

The world four-man bobsleigh title, instituted in 1924, has been won 20 times by Switzerland, including a record five Olympic victories (1924, 1936, 1956, 1972 and 1988).

YOUNGEST OLYMPIC BOBSLEIGH CHAMPION

William Guy Fiske (USA) was 16 years 260 days old when he won the gold medal with the five-man bobsleigh team during the 1928 Winter Olympics held at St Moritz, Switzerland.

OLDEST OLYMPIC BOBSLEIGH CHAMPION

Jay O'Brien (USA) was 47 years 357 days old when he won the gold medal with the four-man bobsleigh team during the 1932 Winter Olympics held at Lake Placid, New York, USA.

SKELETON

MOST WORLD TITLES

Skeleton features riders on sleds, negotiating a winding course on their stomachs. Alex Coomber (UK) has won a record four world titles – the World Cups of 2000, 2001, 2002 and the 2000 World Championships.

FASTEST CRESTA RUN COMPLETION TIME

The Cresta Run in St Moritz, Switzerland, dates from 1884. It is a 1,212-m-long (3,977-ft) ice run with a drop of 157 m (514 ft) and a gradient of between 1:2.8 to 1:8.7. Carved from ice, the run uses natural contours to form its curves. The racers lie head-first on skeleton toboggans, hurtling down the track only inches above the ground, and steer with their shoulders. The fastest time is 50.09 seconds (an average of 87.11 km/h or 54.13 mph) by James Sunley (UK) on 13 February 1999.

OLDEST CRESTA RUN RIDER

Prince Constantin von Liechtenstein (b. 23 December 1911), successfully completed the Cresta Run on 15 February 2000 at the incredible age of 88 years 54 days.

MOST CRESTA RUN WINS

The greatest number of wins in the Cresta Run Curzon Cup competition (instituted 1910) is eight by the 1948 Olympic champion Nino Bibbia (Italy) between 1950 and 1969; and by Franco Gansser (Switzerland) in 1981, 1983–86, 1988–89 and 1991.

LUGE

MOST WOMEN'S OLYMPIC GOLD MEDALS

Luge is similar to skeleton, but the riders lie on their backs and negotiate the curves using their legs to steer. The most women's Olympic gold luge medals won is two, by Steffi Walter (East Germany) with victories in the women's single-seater luge event in 1984 and 1988.

MOST MEN'S WORLD CHAMPIONSHIP AND OLYMPIC TITLES

The most luge World Championship titles won is six by Georg Hackl in the single-seater bob in 1989 and 1990 (for East Germany) and 1992, 1994, 1997 and 1998 (for Germany). Stefan Krausse and Jan Behrendt (East Germany/Germany) won six titles in the two-seater bob, one lying on top of the other, from 1989–98.

MOST WOMEN'S WORLD CHAMPIONSHIP TITLES

Margit Schumann (East Germany) won the World Championship four times between 1973 and 1977. She won the Olympic bronze in 1972, the World Championships in 1973–75 and 1977, and the 1976 Olympic title.

MOST TWO-MAN BOBSLEIGH WORLD CHAMPIONSHIP AND OLYMPIC TITLES

Switzerland (above) have won the two-man bobsleigh World Championships 17 times and have a record four Olympic golds (1948, 1980, 1992 and 1994).

SALT LAKE 2002

MOST CURLING OLYMPIC GOLD MEDALS
The ancient Scottish sport of curling was introduced to the Winter Olympic Games as a medal sport in 1998 and no country has picked up more than one gold medal. In 1998 the first winners were Switzerland (men) and Canada (women). In 2002, Norway (men, above) and Great Britain (women) were triumphant.

FASTEST SPEED
Tony Benshoof (USA) reached a speed of 139.39 km/h (86.6 mph) on the 2002 Olympic luge track at Park City, Utah, USA, on 16 October 2001. The speed was reached during training for the 2001 Luge World Cup Series. Benshoof was a member of the USA 2001/02 Luge Team and participated at the 2002 Olympics in Salt Lake City. The run was timed by a 'speed trap' consisting of timing lights spaced 5 m (16 ft 5 in) apart.

CURLING

FASTEST GAME
Eight curlers from the Burlington Golf and Country Club, Ontario, Canada, curled an eight-end game in a time of 47 min 24 sec, with penalties of 5 min 30 sec on 4 April 1986, using rules agreed with the Ontario Curling Association. Originally introduced to Canada by Scottish immigrants, curling is a competitive sport between two teams of four players each. The intention is to propel a 20-kg (44-lb) object called a stone down a sheet of ice toward a target ring of concentric circles.

MOST MEN'S WORLD CHAMPIONSHIPS
Canada has won the men's World Championship on 27 occasions between 1959 and 2002. The tournament was first held in 1959.

MOST WOMEN'S WORLD CHAMPIONSHIPS
The Canadian women's team have won a record 12 World Championships between 1980 and 2001. The first women's curling club was founded in 1895, but the World Championships were not held until 1979.

LONGEST THROW
The longest throw of a curling stone was an impressive 175.66 m (576 ft 4 in) by Eddie Kulbacki (Canada) at Park Lake, Neepawa, Manitoba, Canada, on 29 January 1989. The attempt took place on a specially prepared sheet of curling ice that was itself a record 365.76 m (1,200 ft) in length.

ICE SLEDGE HOCKEY

MOST PARALYMPIC ASSISTS
Ice sledge hockey is contested at the Winter Paralympic Games. Athletes move on sledges with two blades that allow the puck to pass beneath and have picks to propel themselves and move the puck across the ice. Each team has five players and a goaltender. The most assists in the sport at the Paralympic Games is 15 by Helge Bjoernstad (Norway). His total of 10 in 2002 is a record for a single Games.

MOST PARALYMPIC GOALS
Jens Kask (Sweden) has scored 16 goals in three Paralympic ice sledge hockey tournaments between 1994 and 2002. The most goals scored in a single Games is 11 by Sylvester Flis (USA) in 2002.

MOST PARALYMPIC POINTS
Since the introduction of the sport to the Winter Paralympic Games in 1994, the most points scored by an individual player is 26 by Helge Bjoernstad (Norway).

The most ice sledge hockey points scored at a single Paralympic Winter Games by an individual player is 18 (11 goals, 7 assists) by Sylvester Flis (USA) in 2002.

MOST ICE SLEDGE HOCKEY PARALYMPIC MEDALS
Since its introduction in 1994, no country has won the Paralympic ice sledge hockey title more than once. The winners have been Sweden (1994), Norway (1998) and the USA (2002, left). Norway were second in both 1994 and 2002, and Sweden won the bronze in 1998 and 2002.

FORMULA 1

MOST F1 TITLES
Juan Manuel Fangio (Argentina) first became F1 World Champion in 1951 and then went on to win the title every year from 1954 to 1957 – a record five in total. Fangio retired in 1958, having won 24 Grand Prix races (two shared) from 51 starts.

MOST GRAND PRIX WINS
Michael Schumacher (Germany) has accumulated a record 53 wins from the 162 races he has taken part in up to the end of the 2001 F1 season.

MOST GRAND PRIX RACES
Ricardo Patrese (Italy) has started the most Grand Prix races – 256 between 1977 and 1993.

MOST TITLES BY A MANUFACTURER
Ferrari, the Italian manufacturer of the famous red racing car (below), holds the record for Formula 1 constructors' championships, with 11 titles between 1961 and 2001. Ferrari's total of 145 wins in Grand Prix races up to the end of the 2001 season is also the best achieved by any manufacturer.

MOST GRAND PRIX RACES WITHOUT WINNING
Andrea de Cesaris (Italy) took part in 208 races over 14 years for 10 different racing teams without managing to record a single victory.

CLOSEST RACE
The smallest winning margin for a Grand Prix was when Peter Gethin (UK) beat Ronnie Peterson (Sweden) by 0.01 sec in the Italian Grand Prix at Monza, Italy, on 5 September 1971. Since 1982 timing for all races has been to thousandths of a second, and on 13 April 1986 Ayrton Senna (Brazil) beat Nigel Mansell (UK) by just 0.014 sec in the Spanish Grand Prix at Jerez, Spain.

MOST POLE POSITIONS
The most pole positions a driver has registered in their career is 65 by Ayrton Senna (Brazil), coming from a total of 161 races (41 wins) when driving for the Toleman, Lotus, McLaren and Williams teams. Senna's career was tragically cut short when he was killed in an accident on 1 May 1994 while in qualifying for the San Marino Grand Prix in Imola, Italy.

MOST CONSECUTIVE POLE POSITIONS
French driver Alain Prost recorded seven consecutive F1 pole positions in the 1993 season when driving for the Williams-Renault team. Prost finished the year as World Champion.

MOST POLE POSITIONS IN ONE SEASON
Driving for the Williams-Renault team in 1992, Nigel Mansell (UK) started a record 14 races in pole position on the grid. That year, Mansell won the World Championship. He went on to compete in American IndyCars the following year and won the 1993 IndyCar Series at the first attempt.

MOST POINTS BY A MANUFACTURER IN A SEASON
In the 1988 F1 season, the McLaren team scored a massive 199 points. The team's drivers that year were Ayrton Senna (Brazil) and Alain Prost (France), who between them won 15 out of the 16 races, also a record for a constructor. Senna took eight wins and three second places and Prost seven wins and seven second places.

MOST GRAND PRIX WINS IN A SEASON
The most Grand Prix victories in a year is nine, a record shared by both Nigel Mansell (UK) in 1992, and by Michael Schumacher (Germany), three times in 1995, 2000 and 2001.

MOST CONSECUTIVE WINS OF A GRAND PRIX
Ayrton Senna (Brazil) dominated the Monaco Grand Prix in Monte Carlo, Monaco, winning the race five times in a row from 1989 to 1993.

GREATEST NUMBER OF FASTEST LAPS IN SEASON

Mika Hakkinen (Finland, above) recorded the greatest number of fastest laps in one F1 season with nine in 2000, while competing for the McLaren-Mercedes team. Despite this success, Hakkinen ended the year in second place with 89 points, behind German driver Michael Schumacher, who amassed 108 points for his team, Ferrari.

YOUNGEST AND OLDEST GRAND PRIX WINNERS

The youngest Grand Prix winner was Bruce McLaren (New Zealand), who won the US Grand Prix at Sebring, Florida, USA, on 12 December 1959 when he was 22 years 104 days.

Troy Ruttman (USA) was 22 years 80 days when he took first place in the Indianapolis 500, Indiana, USA, on 30 May 1952, which was part of the World Championship at the time.

The oldest winner of a Grand Prix race (before 1950, when the F1 World Championship was instigated) was the legendary Italian racing driver Tazio Giorgio Nuvolari, who won the Albi Grand Prix held at Albi, France, on 14 July 1946 when he was aged 53 years 240 days.

YOUNGEST CHAMPION

The youngest F1 World Champion is Brazilian driver Emerson Fittipaldi, who was first crowned World Champion on 10 September 1972 aged 25 years 273 days.

YOUNGEST AND OLDEST GRAND PRIX DRIVERS

The youngest driver to qualify for a Grand Prix was Michael Thackwell (New Zealand), who drove in the Canadian Grand Prix in Montreal, Quebec, Canada, on 28 September 1980 at 19 years 182 days.

Louis Alexandre Chiron (Monaco) was a record age of 55 years 291 days when he finished sixth in the Monaco Grand Prix in Monte Carlo, Monaco, on 22 May 1955.

INDYCAR

MOST CHAMPIONSHIP TITLES

IndyCar racing has existed for more than 30 years and has undergone a number of different guises in this time. Formerly known as the AAA (American Automobile Association, 1956–78), USAC (US Auto Club, 1956–78), CART (Championship Auto Racing Teams, 1979–91), IndyCar

(1992–97), and currently the Fed-Ex Series Championship, the most titles claimed by one driver is seven by AJ Foyt Jr (USA); 1960, 1961, 1963, 1964, 1967, 1975 and 1979.

MOST RACE WINS IN CAREER

AJ Foyt Jr (USA) won a record 67 IndyCar races in his career, which spanned from 1958 to 1993. Among those wins is the Indy 500, held in Indianapolis, Indiana, USA, which Foyt won five times. He also won the Le Mans 24-Hour Endurance race and the Daytona 24-Hour race.

MOST POLE POSITIONS

Italy-born US-based Mario Andretti was in pole position for a record 67 IndyCar races from 1965–94.

FASTEST INDY 500 QUALIFICATION

The fastest qualification, taken as an average speed over four laps, for the Indy 500, Indianapolis, Indiana, USA, was achieved by Arie Luyendyk (Netherlands) driving a Reynard-Ford-Cosworth on 12 May 1996. His average speed of 381.392 km/h (236.986 mph) includes a single-lap world record speed of 382.216 km/h (237.498 mph).

LE MANS

MOST LE MANS 24-HOUR ENDURANCE RACE WINS

The most wins by an individual at the Le Mans 24-Hour Endurance race, held in Le Mans, France, is six by Jacky Ickx (Belgium) in 1969, 1975, 1976, 1977, 1981 and 1982.

MOST LE MANS 24-HOUR ENDURANCE TEAM WINS

Porsche, founded in Stuttgart, Germany, has won the most Le Mans 24-Hour races in history. Its cars have won the race 15 times – in 1970, 1971, 1976, 1977, 1981–1987, 1993, 1996, 1997 and 1998.

NASCAR

MOST CHAMPIONSHIP TITLES

Since the competition was first held in 1949, drivers Richard Petty and Dale Earnhardt (both USA) have won seven titles each in the NASCAR (National Association for Stock Car Auto Racing) championship. Petty's seven successes came in 1964, 1967, 1971, 1972, 1974, 1975 and 1979, while Earnhardt was victorious in 1980, 1986, 1987, 1990, 1991, 1993 and 1994.

HIGHEST CAREER EARNINGS

The highest earnings in a NASCAR career is $41,445,551 (£29,011,885) by Dale Earnhardt (USA) between 1975 and 2001.

MOST RACE VICTORIES

Richard Petty (USA) won a record 200 NASCAR races in his racing career from 1958 to 1992.

FASTEST TIME TO COMPLETE INDY 500 RACE

Arie Luyendyk (Netherlands, above) completed the world-famous Indy 500, which was first held in 1911 in Indianapolis, Indiana, USA, in a record time of 2 hr 41 min 18.404 sec driving a Lola-Chevrolet on 27 May 1990.

ISLE OF MAN TT SERIES

OLDEST MOTORCYCLE RACE
The oldest annually contested motorcycle race in the world is the Auto-Cycle Union Tourist Trophy (TT) or Isle of Man TT series. It was first held on the 25.44-km (15.81-mile) Peel (St John's) course on the Isle of Man, UK, on 28 May 1907 and is now run on the island's Mountain circuit.

LONGEST CIRCUIT
The 60.72-km (37.73-mile) Mountain circuit on the Isle of Man, UK, on which the principal TT races have taken place since 1911 (with minor changes in 1920), has 264 curves and corners and is the longest-used circuit for any motorcycle race.

MOST RACES WON IN A CAREER
The most Isle of Man TT race wins in a career is 26 by Joey Dunlop (Ireland, above) from 1977–2000. Dunlop has a remarkable record in TT racing; including his first in 1977, he won a record 19 titles – including the Formula 1 title five times in a row between 1982 and 1986. Dunlop was tragically killed while racing in Estonia in 2000.

MOST SUCCESSIVE WINS IN TWO EVENTS
The first rider to win three consecutive TT titles in two different disciplines was James A Redman (Rhodesia, now Zimbabwe). He won both the 250-cc and 350-cc races in 1963, 1964 and 1965.

MOST EVENTS WON IN A YEAR
The most different classes won in one year is four (Formula 1, Junior, Senior and Production) by Phillip McCallen (Ireland) in 1996.

FASTEST RACE
David Jefferies (UK) registered an average speed of 196.24 km/h (121.94 mph) to set a race speed record time of 1 hr 51 min 22.8 sec to win the 2000 Senior TT on a Yamaha R1 on 9 June 2000.

In the same race, Jeffries also set a record TT lap speed of 207.27 km/h (125.68 mph).

WORLD MOTORCYCLE CHAMPIONSHIPS

MOST TITLES
The World Motorcycle Championships began in 1949 under the Fédération Internationale de Motocyclisme (FIM). The most titles won in a career is 15 by Giacomo Agostini (Italy). Agostini won seven successive 350-cc titles from 1968 to 1974, and eight 500-cc titles, consecutively from 1966 to 1972 and in 1975. Agostini retired from competitive racing in 1976.

MOST 250-CC TITLES
The most 250-cc World Motorcycle Championship titles won by a rider is four by Phil Read (UK) in 1964, 1965, 1968 and 1971. Read also won the 125-cc title in 1968 and a further two 500-cc titles.

YOUNGEST WORLD MOTORCYCLE CHAMPION
Loris Capirossi (Italy, below) is the youngest rider to win a World Championship title. He was aged 17 years 165 days when he clinched the 125-cc title on a Honda on 16 September 1990.

MOST 125-CC TITLES
Angel Roldán Nieto (Spain) won seven 125-cc titles in 1971, 1972, 1979, 1981, 1982, 1983 and 1984.

Nieto also holds the record for most 50-cc World Championship titles, having taken six from 1969 to 1977.

MOST RACES WON IN A CAREER
The most career race wins in the World Motorcycle Championships is 122 – 68 at 500-cc class and 54 at 350-cc class – by Giacomo Agostini (Italy) between 1965 and 1977.

MOST RACES WON IN A SEASON
The most races won in a World Motorcycle Championships season is 19, shared by Giacomo Agostini (Italy) in the 1970 season and Mike Hailwood (UK) in 1966.

MOST SINGLE CLASS WINS IN A CAREER

The most wins in a single racing class in a career is 79, set by Rolf Biland (Switzerland). Biland was racing in the sidecar class.

MOST SINGLE CLASS WINS IN A SEASON

The most wins in a single class in one season was achieved by Australian Michael Doohan, who had 12 wins in the 500-cc class during the 1997 season. Doohan's victory on 4 October 1998 at his home Australian Grand Prix in Brisbane, Queensland, Australia, provided him with his fifth successive 500-cc World Motorcycle Championship title.

MOST TITLES WON BY A MANUFACTURER

Honda, the Japanese company founded by Soichiro Honda in 1948, has won the most World Motorcycle Championships, taking 48 titles in all classes between 1961 and 1999.

OLDEST WORLD CHAMPION

The oldest competitor to win a world title in any class is West Germany's Hermann-Peter Muller, who won the 250-cc title in 1955 at the age of 46.

WORLD SUPERBIKE CHAMPIONSHIP

MOST TITLES

The World Superbike Championship was first held in 1988 and the most titles won by a rider is four, by Carl Fogarty (UK) in 1994, 1995, 1998 and 1999. He claimed all the titles while riding for Ducati.

Fogarty started his career in TT and won the Isle of Man Formula 1 title in 1990. He also holds the record for most superbike race wins with 59 between 1992 and 1999.

MOST POLE POSITIONS

The most pole positions achieved in the World Superbike Championship is the 25 recorded by Troy Corser (Australia) up to March 2001.

MOST RACES WON BY A MANUFACTURER

Ducati (Italy) has won the most World Superbike Championship races, with a total of 161 victories between 1989 to 1999.

SUPERCROSS

MOST SUPERCROSS TITLE WINS

US motorcyclist Jeremy McGrath won the American Motorcycle Association (AMA) 250-cc Supercross Championship title on a record seven occasions between 1993 and 2000.

MOST 250-CC RACES WON IN A CAREER

Jeremy McGrath (USA) had 72 wins in the 250-cc Supercross race class between 1989 and 2001.

MOTOCROSS

WORLD CHAMPIONSHIPS – WINS IN ALL CATEGORIES

Eric Geboers (Belgium) is the only person to have won all three categories of the World Motocross Championships. He won 125-cc in 1982 and 1983, 250-cc in 1987 and 500-cc in 1988 and 1990.

MOST RACES WON IN A CAREER

In a career spanning two decades, Joël Robert (Belgium) won the 250-cc World Motocross Championship title on six occasions – in 1964 and every title between 1968 and 1972.

From 25 April 1964 to 18 June 1972 Robert won a record 50 Grand Prix races in the 250-cc class.

MOST TITLES WON BY A MANUFACTURER

Italian company Ducati (above) has dominated the World Superbike Championship, taking a record eight titles in all. The manufacturer won every title between 1991 and 1996, and also all those from 1998 to 2000.

YOUNGEST WORLD CHAMPION

Dave Strijbos (Netherlands) is the youngest motocross world champion. He won the 125-cc title when he was aged 18 years 296 days on 31 August 1986.

MOST TRANS-AMA CHAMPIONSHIP TITLES

The most Trans-AMA Motocross Championship titles won by an individual rider is four by Roger DeCoster (Belgium) between 1974 and 1977, riding a Suzuki.

SIDECAR

MOST EUROPEAN CHAMPIONSHIP TITLES

The most European Sidecar-Cross Championships won by an individual driver is five by Robert Grogg (Switzerland) in 1972, 1974, 1976, 1977 and 1978. Grogg rode a Wasp Norton motorcycle and rode with three different sidecar passengers over the course of his victories.

COUNTRY WITH MOST SIDECAR-CROSS CHAMPIONSHIP TITLES

Drivers and passengers from Switzerland have won more European and World Sidecar-Cross Championships than any other country, claiming a total of 19 titles between 1971 and 2001. The last European victory by a Swiss team was in 1996, when Andreas Führer's Kawasaki, accompanied by Adrian Kaser in the sidecar, took the title.

MOST ROADRACING NATIONAL TITLES

Milcho Mladenov (Bulgaria) is the holder of 16 consecutive Bulgarian national titles in the motorcycle sidecar 500-cc class. His titles came over 18 years between 1981 and 1999. Mladenov has also won the Balkan Championship on three different occasions.

SPEEDWAY

MOST INDIVIDUAL WORLD CHAMPIONSHIP TITLES
The most individual World Speedway Championship wins is six by Ivan Mauger (New Zealand) in 1968, 1969, 1970, 1972, 1977 and 1979.

MOST WORLD CHAMPIONSHIP TITLES
Hans Hollen Nielsen (Denmark) has been the most successful rider in all World Championship competitions with a total of 21 world titles spread over three different disciplines – pairs, team and indvidual.

MOST WORLD CHAMPIONSHIP FINALS APPEARANCES
Between 1954 and 1972, New Zealand's Barry Briggs made a record 18 appearances in World Speedway Championship finals.

MOST POINTS BY A TEAM IN WORLD CUP
The most points scored by a team in a Speedway World Cup is 68 by Australia to wln the inaugural Ove Fundin trophy in Wroclaw, Poland, held from 1–7 July 2001.

MOST WORLD CUP RACE WINS
At the Speedway World Cup in Wroclaw, Poland, in July 2001, Jason Crump (Australia) recorded 10 wins out of 10 races to help his country win the Ove Fundin trophy.

MOST WORLD PAIRS CHAMPIONSHIP TITLES
The World Pairs Championship (instituted unofficially in 1968, officially in 1970 and renamed the World Team Championship in 1994) has been won a record nine times by Denmark – in 1979, every year between 1985 and 1991, and 1995.

MOST WORLD TEAM CUP WINS
The World Team Cup, instituted in 1960, was won a record nine times by England/Great Britain (Great Britain in 1968, 1971, 1972 and 1973; England in 1974, 1975, 1977, 1980 and 1989), and by Denmark in 1978, 1981, 1983 to 1988 and 1991.

TRIAL BIKES

MOST INDOOR AND OUTDOOR WORLD TRIALS CHAMPIONSHIP TITLES
Dougie Lampkin (UK) has won a record 10 Indoor and Outdoor World Trials Championships, claiming both titles every year between 1997 and 2001. Lampkin entered and won his first trials bike competition when he was only nine years old, and was awarded the MBE (Member of the British Empire) in 2002.

MOST WORLD TRIALS CHAMPIONSHIP TITLES
Jordi Tarrés (Spain) has won a world record seven Outdoor World Trials Championship titles in 1987, 1989, 1990, 1991, 1993, 1994 and 1995.

DRAG RACING

FASTEST FUNNY CAR 440-YD STANDING START
Gary Densham (USA) reached a speed of 526.04 km/h (326.87 mph) from a standing start in a Ford Mustang funny car, or dragster, at Pomona, California, USA, in February 2002.

LOWEST FUNNY CAR ELAPSED TIME
The lowest elapsed time to cover 402 m (440 yd) in a drag car is 4.731 sec by John Force (USA), driving a Ford Mustang, at Reading, Pennsylvania, USA, in October 2001. Force is the most successful funny car driver ever, and holds several records including the most NHRA (National Hot Rod Association) Funny Car Championships, the most successive championship wins and the most career drag car victories. In 1996 Force became the first drag racer to win the national motorsports Driver of the Year award. The NHRA Championships are held as a series of one-on-one elimination races until there are just two drivers left to compete in the final. Up to his hot streak, Force lost nine finals in a row before his first victory, which came in 1987 in Montreal, Canada.

FASTEST SPEED BY PRO-STOCK RACER
For a petrol-driven piston-engined car (Pro-Stock), the highest terminal velocity achieved is 328.86 km/h (204.35 mph) by Mark Osborne (USA) in a Dodge Neon in Reading, Pennsylvania, USA, in October 2001.

LOWEST ELAPSED TIME BY PRO-STOCK RACER
The lowest elapsed time to cover 402 m (440 yd) in a Pro-Stock car is 6.750 sec by Jeg Couglin (USA), driving a Chevrolet Cavalier at Reading, Penn, USA, in October 2001.

FASTEST SPEED BY TOP FUEL RACER
Kenny Bernstein (USA) reached a terminal velocity of 534.59 km/h (332.18 mph) in a Top Fuel drag racer at the end of a 402-m (440-yd) run in October 2001. Bernstein was driving a Hadman dragster powered by a TFX 500 engine.

LOWEST ELAPSED TIME BY TOP FUEL RACER
The lowest elapsed time to cover 402 m (440 yd) in a Top Fuel dragster is 4.477 sec by Kenny Bernstein (USA) in a Hadman dragster with a TTX 500 engine at Chicago, Illinois, USA, in June 2001.

MOST FORMULA 1 INSHORE POWERBOATING WORLD CHAMPIONSHIP TITLES
Guido Cappellini (Italy, above) has won a record six Formula 1 Powerboating World Championship titles from 1993 to 1996 and in 1999 and 2001.

RALLYING

LONGEST RALLY

The longest rally is the Singapore Airlines London-Sydney Rally, which originally covered a distance – the route is subject to alteration – of 16,000 km (10,000 miles) between Covent Garden, London, UK, and Sydney Opera House, Sydney, NSW, Australia. It was first held in 1968 and is next due to take place in July 2004. The longest recognized version of the rally is the 1977 race won by Andrew Cowan, Colin Malkin and Michael Broad (all UK), which covered 31,107 km (19,329 miles) The race is not cheap to enter – it requires a fee of £26,000 ($38,000).

YOUNGEST WORLD RALLY CHAMPION

Britain's Colin McRae was aged just 27 years 89 days when he won his first World Championship title

in 1995. McRae, who has been awarded an MBE and was born in Scotland, comes from racing stock – his father won the British Rally Championship five times. Following in his father's tyre treads, McRae took up rallying in 1986 and entered the World Championship in 1987.

MOST WORLD RALLY CHAMPIONSHIP TITLES BY A MANUFACTURER

Italian car manufacturer Lancia won 11 World Rally Championship titles between 1972 and 1992.

MOST MONTE CARLO RALLY WINS

The most Monte Carlo rally wins is four by; Sandro Munari (Italy) in 1972, 1975, 1976 and 1977 in a Lancia; Walter Röhrl (West Germany) in 1980, 1982, 1983 and 1984, in four different cars; and Finland's Tommi Mäkinen, who won four races in succession from 1999–2002.

MOST RALLY OF BRITAIN WINS

The RAC Rally of Britain was first held in 1932 and the race has been recognized by the Fédération Internationale de l'Automobile (FIA) since 1957. Hannu Mikkola (Finland) has a record four wins, driving a Ford Escort in 1978 and 1979 and an Audi Quattro in 1981 and 1982.

Mikkola's co-driver in all of his victories, Arne Hertz (Sweden), was also the co-driver when Stig Blomqvist (Sweden) won in 1971.

MOST WORLD RALLY CHAMPIONSHIP RACE WINS

Tommi Mäkinen (Finland, below) won 24 Championship races from 1994–2002. Mäkinen set the record when he won the Monte Carlo Rally in Monaco for a record fourth successive time in 2002. Mäkinen also has a record four successive world titles from 1996–99.

MOST WORLD RALLY CHAMPIONSHIP RACE WINS IN SEASON

France's Didier Auriol (above), a former ambulance driver, won a record six races during the 1992 World Rally Championship season. Auriol won his first World Rally Championship race in the Rally of Corsica in 1988 and claimed his first World Championship title while driving for Toyota in 1994.

GREATEST MARGIN OF VICTORY IN A MAJOR TOURNAMENT

Tiger Woods (USA) won the US Open in 2000 by a massive 15 shots, the greatest distance a winner of a Major tournament – the Open Championship, US Open, US Masters and US PGA Championship – has ever finished ahead of the rest of the field. Woods scored 65, 69, 71 and 67 for a 12-under-par total of 272.

MOST OPEN TITLES

Born on the UK-administered Channel Island of Jersey, Harry Vardon won six Open Championships, held in the UK, between 1896 and 1914.

LOWEST WOMEN'S ROUND

Annika Sorenstam (Sweden, below) went round the Moon Valley Country Club in Phoenix, Arizona, USA, in 59 strokes, the lowest 18-hole score by a woman. She was playing in the 2001 Standard Register PING tournament on 16 March 2001.

MOST US OPEN TITLES

Willie Anderson (UK), Bobby Jones Jr, Ben Hogan and Jack Nicklaus (all USA) have each won the US Open four times. Anderson in 1901 and 1903–05; Jones in 1923, 1926, 1929 and 1930; Hogan in 1948, 1950, 1951 and 1953 and Nicklaus in 1962, 1967, 1972 and 1980.

MOST US WOMEN'S OPEN TITLES

Betsy Rawls and Mickey Wright (both USA) both won a record four US Women's Open titles – Rawls' successes came in 1951, 1953, 1957 and 1960 and Wright's were in 1958, 1959, 1961 and 1964.

MOST US AMATEUR TITLES

Bobby Jones Jr (USA) won five US Amateur titles in 1924, 1925, 1927, 1928 and 1930. Jones, who never turned professional, also won the US Open on four occasions, the Open Championship three times and the British Amateur Championship once before he retired at 28.

MOST BRITISH AMATEUR CHAMPIONSHIP TITLES

John Ball (UK) won eight British Amateur Championship titles, the last at the age of 60, from 1888–1912.

MOST US WOMEN'S AMATEUR TITLES

Glenna Vare (USA) won six US Women's Amateur Championship titles between 1922 and 1935. She remained an amateur until her death.

MOST WORLD CUP TEAM TITLES

The World Cup of Golf, which was instituted as the Canada Cup in 1953, has been won most often by the USA with a record 22 victories between 1955 and 1999.

LOWEST INDIVIDUAL WORLD CUP SCORE

From 18 to 21 November 1999 Tiger Woods (USA) completed the four rounds of the World Cup in a record total of 263 strokes at Kuala Lumpur, Malaysia.

MOST WORLD CUP INDIVIDUAL TITLES

The only men to have been on six winning World Cup teams have been Arnold Palmer (USA) in 1960, 1962, 1963, 1964, 1966 and 1967 and Jack Nicklaus (USA) in 1963, 1964, 1966, 1967, 1971 and 1973.

Nicklaus has also taken the individual title a record three times in 1963, 1964 and 1971.

LOWEST WORLD CUP TEAM SCORE

The lowest aggregate score for the World Cup's 144 holes is 536 by the US team of Fred Couples and Davis Love III at Dorado, Puerto Rico, from 10–13 November 1994.

HIGHEST US LPGA SEASON'S EARNINGS

Sweden's Annika Sorenstam earned $2,105,868 (£1,477,269) on the US LPGA circuit in 1999, a record for a single season's takings.

HIGHEST US LPGA CAREER EARNINGS

The record career earnings for a woman on the US LPGA Tour is by Annika Sorenstam (Sweden). She had banked a total of $6,957,044 (£4,874,371) up to April 2001.

HIGHEST US PGA CAREER EARNINGS

The career winnings record on the US PGA circuit is held by Tiger Woods (USA). He had earned a total of $23,767,307 (£16,652,285) from August 1996 to April 2001.

OLDEST RYDER CUP PLAYER

The oldest player to compete in the Ryder Cup is Ray Floyd (USA, above), who was 51 years 20 days in 1993. The biennial tournament between the USA and Europe (British Isles or Great Britain prior to 1979) was first held in 1927.

HIGHEST US PGA SEASON'S EARNINGS

The season's record for the US PGA Tour is $9,188,321 (£6,155,504) by Tiger Woods (USA) in 2000.

HIGHEST MEN'S EUROPEAN TOUR SEASON EARNINGS

Lee Westwood (UK) won £1,858,602 ($2,775,822) in European Order of Merit tournaments in 2000.

LONGEST PUTT

Jack Nicklaus (USA), in the 1964 Tournament of Champions, and Nick Price (South Africa), in 1992's US PGA Championship, have both holed 33.5-m (110-ft) putts in professional golf tournaments.

Bob Cook (USA) sank a putt of 42.74 m (140 ft 2.75 in) on the 18th hole at St Andrews, Fife, UK, in the International Fourball Pro-Am Tournament on 1 October 1976.

On 5 August 2000 Alan Schofield and Robin Kershaw (both UK) both successfully sank a putt measuring 50.79 m (166 ft 8 in) at Fishwick Hall Golf Club, Preston, Lancashire, UK.

MOST RYDER CUP TITLES

The first Ryder Cup match was held in 1927 at the Worcester Country Club, Worcester, Massachusetts, USA. Up to the 1999 event, the USA had won 24 tournaments and Europe seven, with two drawn.

MOST INDIVIDUAL RYDER CUP WINS

Nick Faldo (UK) holds the record for match wins, having won 23 of the 46 Ryder Cup games in which he has played. Faldo also has the overall points record, taking 25 and halving another four. The US record is held by Arnold Palmer (USA), with 22 wins from 32 played. Billy Casper (USA) has the US record points total of 23.5 from 37 matches.

MOST SUCCESSFUL RYDER CUP CAPTAIN

The most successful Ryder Cup captain in the tournament's history is America's Walter Hagen, who skippered four winning US teams in 1927, 1931, 1935 and 1937.

YOUNGEST RYDER CUP PLAYER

Sergio Garcia (Spain) was aged 19 years 8 months 15 days when he played for Europe in 1999.

MOST SOLHEIM CUP TITLES

The Solheim Cup, the women's equivalent of the Ryder Cup, is contested biennially between the 12 top professional players of both Europe and the USA. It was first held in 1990 and the American team have since won on four occasions – 1990, 1994, 1996 and 1998. The European team were successful in 1992 and 2000.

MOST INDIVIDUAL SOLHEIM CUP WINS

The most wins by a player in the history of the Solheim Cup is 13 by Laura Davies (UK) from 23 matches between 1990 and 2000, and also by Dottie Pepper (USA), who played 20 matches over the same period. Both have scored a record 14 points.

MOST CURTIS CUP TITLES

The biennial women's Curtis Cup match between amateur players from the USA against their contemporaries from Great Britain

and Ireland was first held in 1932. The USA have won 22 up to 2000, with Britain and Ireland taking six. Three matches have been tied.

MOST CURTIS CUP INDIVIDUAL WINS

Carole Semple-Thompson (USA) played a record 11 ties and won a record 16 matches from 1974–2000.

Mary McKenna (UK) played her ninth match in 1986, a record for Great Britain and Ireland, and for the first time finished on the winning side.

WOMEN'S LOWEST US LPGA TOURNAMENT SCORE

The lowest four-round total in a US LPGA Championship event is 261. It is shared by Se Ri Pak (South Korea) with scores of 71, 61, 63 and 66 at the Jamie Farr Kroger Classic, Sylvania, Ohio, USA, on 9–12 July 1998 and also by Annika Sorenstam (Sweden) with scores of 65, 59, 65 and 68 in the 2001 Standard Register PING tournament at Moon Valley Country Club in Phoenix, Arizona, USA, on 15–18 March 2001.

OLDEST COMPETITOR IN A MAJOR EVENT

Ed Alofs (Netherlands) took part in the 1997 Compaq World Putting Championship in Orlando, Florida, USA, at 95 years 289 days.

MOST NATIONALITIES AT A TOURNAMENT

A record 72 different nations were represented at the 2000 Junior Open Championship at Crail Golf Club, Fife, UK, in July 2000. The event was organized by the Royal and Ancient Golf Club of St Andrews, Fife, UK.

MOST RYDER CUP MATCHES PLAYED

Nick Faldo (UK, above) played 11 Ryder Cup tournaments between 1977 and 1997. The US record is a shared eight – Billy Casper from 1961 to 1975, Ray Floyd between 1969 and 1993 and Lanny Wadkins from 1977 to 1993.

LOWEST NINE-HOLE ROUND

Nine holes were completed in 25 strokes (4, 3, 3, 2, 3, 3, 1, 4, 2) by AJ 'Bill' Burke in a round of 57 (32 and 25) on the Normandie course at St Louis, Missouri, USA, on 20 May 1970.

The tournament record is 27 strokes and has occurred on eight occasions. The first recorded nine-hole 27 was by Mike Souchak (USA), on the closing nine holes of his opening round in the 1955 Texas Open.

Most recently, Billy Mayfair (USA) scored 27 on the final nine holes of the fourth round of the 2001 Buick Open at Warwick Hills, Grand Blanc, Michigan, USA, on 12 August 2001.

FASTEST ROUND BY AN INDIVIDUAL

The fastest round played by one player, with the ball coming to rest before each new stroke, is one of 27 min 9 sec by James Carvill (Ireland) at Warrenpoint Golf Course, Co Down, Ireland, on 18 June 1987.

FASTEST ROUND BY A TEAM

On 9 September 1996 the Fore Worcester's Children team of golfers completed a round of 18 holes in 9 min 28 sec at the Tatnuck Country Club, Worcester, Massachussets, USA. Collectively, the team went round for an impressive score of 70.

LONGEST CONTROL OF GOLF BALL

Rick Adams (UK) used a sand wedge to keep a ball aloft for 1 hour 17 min on 21 March 2002 in London, UK.

On 17 November 2001 in Brisbane, Queensland, Australia, Henry Epstein (Australia) took alternate touches with two sand wedges to keep a golf ball aloft for 33 min 33 sec.

MOST HOLES IN 12 HOURS

Using a cart to get around the course, Brennan Robertson (USA) played 476 holes in 12 hours at Foxfire Golf Club, Sarasota, Florida, USA, on 19 August 2000.

MOST HOLES IN SEVEN DAYS

Colin Young (UK) used a golf cart to play 1,706 holes in seven days at the Hill Valley Golf Club in Whitchurch, Shropshire, UK, from 26 July to 2 August 1999.

MOST HOLES IN A YEAR

The most holes of golf played in one year is 10,550 by Leo Fritz (USA) of Youngstown, Ohio, USA, in 1998.

MOST HOLES PLAYED BY A FOURSOME IN 24 HOURS

A team of Harold Hagens, Piet van Schaijk, Daniel Kameier and John Neophytou (all Sweden) achieved a score of 5,861 in 24 hours, playing a record 290 holes as a foursome at the Ronnbacken Golf Club, Skelleftea, Sweden, on 10–11 July 2000. Each round took an average of 1 hr 24 min.

LONGEST THROW OF A GOLF BALL

Stefan Uhr (Sweden) threw a golf ball 120.24 m (394 ft 5 in) at Prästholmen, Mora, Sweden, on 20 August 1992.

LONGEST SINGLE 'HOLE' COMPLETED IN 12 HOURS

The longest 'hole' completed in under 12 hours measured 70 km (44 miles) from South Ice Cave, Lake County, Oregon, USA, to the ninth green of the Meadows Course at Sunriver, Oregon, USA. It was played on 25 September 2000 by John Bladholm, Gene Molenkamp, Sean Guard and Mike O'Connell (all USA) in 1,187 strokes. They lost 147 balls in the process.

MOST GOLFERS ON ONE COURSE IN 24 HOURS

A record 605 golfers completed a round in one day at the Rhodes Ranch Country Club, Las Vegas, Nevada, USA, on 21 June 1998.

NORTHERNMOST COURSE

The island of Uummannaq, located to the west of Greenland at a longitude of 70ºN, is the location of the annual World Ice Golf Championship. The course varies considerably in layout from year to year, in accordance with variations in ice floes and snow distribution. Frostbite is a constant hazard for competitors.

FIRST TRANS-AMERICAN ROUND

Floyd Satterlee Rood (USA) used the whole of North America as a course when he played a coast-to-coast round from the Pacific to the Atlantic between 14 September 1963 and 3 October 1964. This 5,468-km (3,397.7-mile) journey took 114,737 strokes and cost Rood 3,511 balls.

GREATEST DISTANCE TRAVELLED BETWEEN TWO ROUNDS ON SAME DAY

Nobby Orens (USA) played two 18-hole rounds – at Stockley Park, Uxbridge, London, UK, and at Braemar Country Club, Tarzana, California, USA – on 20 July 1999. This involved travelling a distance of 9,582 km (5,954 miles).

Orens is a keen golfer – during 1999 he played 134 rounds on 36 courses in 27 cities, five states, six countries and two continents.

HIGHEST SHOT

Vladímir Mysík (Czech Republic) played a shot from the peak of Gasherbrum I – a height of 8,068 m (26,470 ft) – in the Karakoram Range, Kashmir, on 9 July 1997.

HIGHEST EUROPEAN TOUR CAREER EARNINGS

Between 1986 and 2001, Britain's Colin Montgomerie (above) took part in the European Order of Merit, earning a record £8,424,498 ($12,008,908). In his European tour career, Montgomerie had won 25 titles as of April 2002.

HIGHEST WOMEN'S EUROPEAN TOUR SEASON EARNINGS

The record for a season's earnings on the women's European Tour is £204,522 ($330,818) by Laura Davies (UK, above crouching) on the 1999 tour. In 1994 Davies became the first European golfer to be ranked women's world No.1.

LIGHTEST CLUB

The lightest full-size club is the driver JBeam Win.1 manufactured by Japan Golf Equipment Co Ltd of Tokyo, Japan. It weighs just 220 g (7.75 oz) in total. The titanium head weighs 160 g (5.64 oz), the carbon fibre shaft is 35 g (1.23 oz) and the grip is 25 g (0.88 oz). The club is specially embossed with the *Guinness World Records* logo.

LONGEST USABLE CLUB

The longest club that can be used by an individual to hit a golf ball is a driver owned by Brad Denton (USA), which is 3.36 m (11 ft) long. The definition of 'usable' is that the club must be able to be used from a regular stance, have a normal-sized head and be capable of hitting the ball at least 91 m (100 yd).

LARGEST BUNKER

The world's biggest bunker, or sand trap, is Hell's Half Acre on the 535-m (585-yd) seventh hole of the Pine Valley course, Clementon, New Jersey, USA. The course, which covers 253 ha (623 acres), was designed in 1912 by George Crump (USA) and is regarded by most experts as the world's greatest and most challenging golf course.

LONGEST HOLE

The longest hole in the world is the par-seven seventh hole of the Satsuki Golf Club, in Sano, Japan, which measures 881 m (964 yd).

MOST HOLES-IN-ONE BY HUSBAND AND WIFE AT SAME HOLE

Elmer James and his wife Marilyn (both USA) scored consecutive holes-in-one on the 16th at Halifax Plantation Golf Club, Ormond, Florida, USA, on 19 April 1998.

MOST BALLS HIT IN ONE HOUR

The most balls driven by a single golfer in a time of one hour, over a distance of 91 m (100 yd) and into a designated target area, is 2,146 by Sean Murphy (Canada) at Swifts Practice Range, Carlisle, Cumbria, UK, on 30 June 1995.

MOST PARTICIPANTS IN A LESSON

The most people to take part in a single golf lesson is the 389 pupils who were taught by Scotland-born professional golfer Colin Montgomerie in a lesson that took place at the Army Golf Club in Aldershot, Hampshire, UK, on 16 February 1999.

LONGEST CARRY

Karl Woodward (UK) hit a ball a record 373 m (408 yd) at Golf del Sur, Tenerife, Spain, on 30 June 1999.

A golf ball has been hit further than this – Jack Hamm (USA) recorded a drive of 418.79 m (458 yd) at Highlands Ranch, Colorado, USA, on 20 July 1993. This shot, though, came at an altitude of more than 1,000 m (3,280 ft), where the thinner atmosphere would have helped the ball carry a greater distance then if it were hit closer to sea level.

LARGEST GOLF BALL COLLECTION

Ted Hoz (USA) has collected a total of 70,718 golf balls since 1986. Each bears a logo from 7,014 courses, 51 countries and 1,689 tournaments and they are on display at his home in Baton Rouge, Louisana, USA. If the balls were set side-by-side they would cover a distance of almost 3.2 km (2 miles) and their total weight is estimated at 4.6 tonnes.

MOST VALUABLE BALL

On 1 July 1995 Jaime Ortiz Patiño (Spain) paid £19,995 ($31,855) for a Victorian golf ball that was made of leather and stuffed with feathers.

MOST US PGA DRIVING DISTANCE TITLES

John Daly (USA, above) won 10 US PGA Driving Distance titles from 1991 to 2001. Drives at two holes are measured in each round, and the average provides the Driving Distance figure. The holes must face in opposite directions to counteract the effects of wind.

RACKET SPORTS

SPORT

TENNIS

HIGHEST ATTENDANCE

A record total of 30,472 people were at the Astrodome, Houston, Texas, USA, for the 'Battle of the Sexes' exhibition match on 20 September 1973 when Billie-Jean King beat Robert Riggs (both USA).

The competitive match record is the 25,578 who saw Australia's Davis Cup Challenge Round contest against USA in Sydney, NSW, Australia, on 27 December 1954.

BEST WIMBLEDON WILDCARD PERFORMANCE

Goran Ivanisevic (Croatia, below) was ranked 125th in the world when he was invited by the All England Club to take part in the Wimbledon Championships in 2001. Despite his lowly status, Ivanisevic reached his fourth final, beating Pat Rafter (Australia) 6-3, 3-6, 6-3, 2-6, 9-7 to claim the title.

MEN'S GRAND SLAM

The first man to have won all four of the world's major championship singles titles – Wimbledon and the US, Australian and French Opens – was Fred Perry (UK) when he won the French title in 1935.

The first man to hold all four championships simultaneously was Don Budge (USA) in 1936. Having won Wimbledon and the US Open in 1937, he won six successive grand slam tournaments.

The first man to achieve the grand slam twice was Rod Laver (Australia) as an amateur in 1962 and again in 1969 when the titles were open to professionals.

WOMEN'S GRAND SLAM

Four women have achieved the grand slam and the first three won six successive grand slam tournaments: Maureen Connolly (USA) in 1953; Margaret Court (Australia) in 1970, and Martina Navrátilová (USA) in 1983–84. The fourth was Steffi Graf (Germany) in 1988, when she also won the women's singles Olympic gold medal.

Pam Shriver (USA) and Navrátilová won a record eight successive women's grand slam doubles titles and 109 successive matches in all competitions between April 1983 and July 1985.

MOST GRAND SLAM SINGLES TITLES

The most successful player in terms of grand slam singles titles is Margaret Court (Australia), who won 24 titles between 1960 and 1973. She won the Australian Open 11 times, five US Open titles, five French Open titles and three Wimbledon titles.

MOST MEN'S WIMBLEDON SINGLES TITLES

The first Lawn Tennis Championships were held at Wimbledon, London, UK, in 1877. The men's title has been won seven times by Pete Sampras (USA) – every year from 1993 to 1995 and from 1997 to 2000.

MOST MEN'S WIMBLEDON TITLES

The most Wimbledon titles won by a man is 13 by Laurie Doherty (UK). He won five singles titles from 1902 to 1906 and eight men's doubles titles between 1897 and 1906.

MOST WOMEN'S WIMBLEDON TITLES

Billie-Jean King (USA) won 20 titles between 1961 and 1979 – six singles, 10 women's doubles and four mixed doubles titles.

YOUNGEST MEN'S WIMBLEDON CHAMPION

Boris Becker (West Germany) won the men's singles title in 1985 aged 17 years 227 days.

YOUNGEST WOMEN'S WIMBLEDON CHAMPION

Martina Hingis (Switzerland) was 15 years 282 days when she won the women's doubles in 1996.

LONGEST WIMBLEDON CAREER

Jean Borotra (France) took part in the men's singles competition 35 times between 1922 and 1964. He then went on to compete in the men's veteran doubles and mixed doubles events from 1965 to 1977. Borotra retired when he was 78 after 55 years of competition.

YOUNGEST WOMEN'S WORLD NO.1

Martina Hingis (Switzerland, above) was 16 years 182 days when she became women's world No.1 on 31 March 1997. Hingis had turned professional less than three years previously, on 14 October 1994.

MOST MEN'S US OPEN SINGLES TITLES

The US Open was first held in 1881 and three players have won seven US Open men's titles to date – Richard Sears (USA), from 1881–87; William Larned (USA), in 1901, 1902 and 1907–11; and Bill Tilden (USA), from 1920–25 and 1929.

MOST WOMEN'S US OPEN SINGLES TITLES

Molla Mallory (Norway) won eight US Open women's singles titles in 1915–18, 1920–22 and 1926. She also won two women's doubles titles and three mixed doubles titles.

YOUNGEST MEN'S US OPEN SINGLES CHAMPION

'Pistol' Pete Sampras was aged 19 years 28 days when he won the US Open singles championship on 9 September 1990.

YOUNGEST WOMEN'S US OPEN SINGLES CHAMPION

The youngest woman to win the US Open singles title is Tracy Austin (USA), who was 16 years 271 days on 9 September 1979.

OLDEST US OPEN SINGLES CHAMPION

William Larned (USA) was aged 38 years 242 days when he won the men's singles title in 1911.

OLDEST US OPEN CHAMPION

Margaret Du Pont (USA) won the mixed doubles title when she was aged 42 years 166 days in 1960.

YOUNGEST US OPEN CHAMPION

Vincent Richards (USA) was aged 15 years 139 days when he won the US Open men's doubles title in 1918.

MOST MEN'S AUSTRALIAN OPEN SINGLES TITLES

The Australian Open Championships were first held in 1905 in Melbourne, Victoria, Australia. Roy Emerson (Australia) won a record six titles in 1961 and 1963–67. In total, Emerson won 12 grand slam singles titles and 16 grand slam doubles titles.

MOST MEN'S AUSTRALIAN OPEN TITLES

Adrian Quist (Australia) won 13 titles at the Australian Open – the men's singles title three times in 1936, 1940 and 1948, and 10 consecutive doubles titles from 1936 to 1950.

MOST WOMEN'S AUSTRALIAN OPEN TITLES

The most Australian Open tennis titles is 21 by Margaret Court (Australia), who won the women's singles title 11 times (1960–66, 1969–71 and 1973), the women's doubles eight times (1961–63, 1965, 1969–71 and 1973) and the mixed doubles twice (1963 and 1964).

YOUNGEST MEN'S AUSTRALIAN OPEN SINGLES CHAMPION

Rodney Heath (Australia) was aged just 17 years old when he won the first men's singles title in 1905.

YOUNGEST WOMEN'S AUSTRALIAN OPEN SINGLES CHAMPION

Martina Hingis (Switzerland) won the women's singles title at the age of 16 years 117 days in 1997. Hingis also went on to take the women's titles in the following two years.

MOST WOMEN'S FRENCH OPEN SINGLES TITLES

The most French Open singles tennis titles won by a woman is seven by Chris Evert (USA) in 1974, 1975, 1979, 1980, 1983, 1985 and 1986.

LONGEST TENNIS MATCH

The longest match in a grand slam tournament is one that lasted an exhausting 5 hr 31 min between Alex Corretja (Spain) and Hernán Gumy (Argentina) in the third round of the French Open on 31 May 1998. Corretja won 6-1, 5-7, 6-7, 7-5, 9-7.

MOST DAVIS CUP TITLES

The most wins in the Davis Cup, the men's international tennis team championship, is 31 by the United States between the first tournament in 1900 and 1995.

The most individual appearances in winning Davis Cup teams is eight by Roy Emerson (Australia) from 1959 to 1962 and 1964 to 1967.

Bill Tilden (USA) played in a record 28 matches in the final, winning a record 21 – 17 out of 22 singles and four out of six doubles. He was in seven winning sides (1920–26) and then four losing sides (1927–30).

OLDEST DAVIS CUP PLAYER

The oldest player to feature in the Davis Cup is Yaka-Garonfin Koptigan (Togo), aged 59 years and 147 days on 27 May 2001 against Mauritius.

YOUNGEST DAVIS CUP PLAYER

Kenny Banzer (Liechtenstein) played for Liechtenstein against Algeria at 14 years 5 days on 16 February 2000.

FASTEST WOMEN'S SERVE

The fastest service recorded by a woman in competitive play is one of a scorching 205 km/h (127.4 mph) by Venus Williams (USA, above), during the European Indoor Championships in Zurich, Switzerland, on 16 October 1998.

TENNIS

FASTEST MEN'S SERVE
The fastest service by a man (measured with modern equipment) is 239.8 km/h (149 mph) by Greg Rusedski (UK) during the ATP Champions' Cup at Indian Wells, California, USA, on 14 March 1998. Rusedski was born in Canada of a British mother and was granted British citizenship in May 1995.

LONGEST RALLY
The longest contrived rally is one that lasted 17,062 strokes between Ray Miller and Rob Peterson (both USA) at Alameda, California, USA. The attempt took 9 hr 6 min and was set during the United States Tennis Association's 'Tennis Festival' on 4 July 2001.

MOST VALUABLE RACKET
A racket used by the legendary Fred Perry (UK) at Wimbledon was sold at Christie's auction house, London, UK, in June 1997 for a record £23,000 ($37,724). Perry was also world singles table tennis champion in 1929.

MOST BALLS VOLLEYED IN A THREE-HOUR LESSON
The most balls volleyed during a single three-hour lesson is 6,177 by John Forster (USA). He was teaching a group of 456 students at the Cornwall Elementary School, Cornwall, Pennsylvania, USA, on 14 May 2001.

MOST CONSECUTIVE SERVES
The most consecutive serves landed successfully without recording a double fault is 8,017 by Rob Peterson (USA) at Port Aransas, Texas, USA, on 5 December 1998. Peterson was hitting tennis balls for a gruelling 10 hr 7 min during his record-breaking performance.

REAL TENNIS

OLDEST COURT
Real tennis, or court tennis, is the world's oldest racket sport, with a recognizable ancestry that dates back to the 11th century. The most noticeable difference to lawn tennis, which was defined by its own regulations in around 1875, is that the court in real tennis is walled. The oldest active court in the UK is at Falkland Palace in Fife, UK, built by King James V of Scotland in 1539.

MOST MEN'S WORLD CHAMPIONSHIP TITLES
The first recorded real tennis world champion was Clerg (France) in around 1740. Jacques Edmond Barre (France) held the title for a record 33 years from 1829 to 1862. Pierre Etchebaster (France) holds the record for the greatest number of successful defences of the title, with eight between 1928 and 1952.

MOST WOMEN'S WORLD CHAMPIONSHIP TITLES
The women's World Championship (instituted 1985) has been won five times by Penny Lumley (UK) in 1989, 1991, 1995, 1997 and 1999.

RACQUETBALL

MOST MEN'S WORLD CHAMPIONSHIP TITLES
The Racquetball World Championship was held for the first time in 1981 and the tournament has taken place biennially since 1984. Since its institution, the USA have won nine team titles – 1981, 1984, 1986 (jointly won with Canada), 1988, 1990, 1992, 1994, 1996 and 1998.

MOST WOMEN'S WORLD CHAMPIONSHIP TITLES
The most titles won by an individual is three by Michelle Gould (USA) in 1992, 1994 and 1996.

TABLE TENNIS

LONGEST MATCH
Danny Price and Randy Nunes (both USA) played for 132 hr 31 min at Cherry Hill, New Jersey, USA, on 20–26 August 1978.

LONGEST DOUBLES MATCH
The longest doubles marathon is one of 101 hr 1 min 11 sec by brothers Lance, Phil and Mark Warren and Bill Weir (all USA) at Sacramento, California, USA, on 9–13 April 1979.

MOST OLYMPIC GOLD MEDALS
Deng Yaping (China) has won four Olympic gold medals – the women's singles in 1992 and 1996, and the women's doubles (both with Qiao Hang) in 1992 and 1996.

MOST OLYMPIC MEDALS
As well as Deng Yaping (China), who took four medals – all gold – in the Games of 1992 and 1996, Yoo Nam-kyu (South Korea) has also won four Olympic medals – one gold and three bronze from 1988–96.

MOST MEN'S OLYMPIC GOLD MEDALS
The most men's Olympic titles is two by Liu Guoliang (China) in the singles and doubles competitions in 1996.

LONGEST RALLY
John Duffy and Kevin Schick (New Zealand) achieved a 5 hr 2 min 18.5 sec rally at Whangarei, New Zealand, on 5 November 1977.

The longest rally in competition was in a 1936 Swaythling Cup match in Prague, Czechoslovakia (now Czech Republic), between Alex Ehrlich (Poland) and Paneth Farcas (Romania). It lasted 2 hr 12 min.

FASTEST 5,000 COUNTER-HITTING
With a paddle in each hand, S Ramesh Babu (India) completed 5,000 consecutive volleys over the net in 41 min 27 sec at Jawaharal Nehru Stadium, Swargate, India, on 14 April 1995.

SQUASH

SHORTEST MATCH
Philip Kenyon (UK) beat Salah Nadi (Egypt) 9-0, 9-0, 9-0 in 6 min 37 sec in the British Open at Lamb's Squash Club, London, UK, on 9 April 1992.

YOUNGEST TENNIS MEN'S WORLD NO.1
When Marat Safin (Russia, above) won the President's Cup tournament in Tashkent, Uzbekistan, on 17 September 2000 he became the world men's No.1 at the age of just 20 years 234 days.

MOST WORLD OPEN TITLES

Jansher Khan (Pakistan) has won a record eight World Open titles in 1987, 1989 and 1990 and from 1992 to 1996. The Khan family has dominated squash, winning 29 British Opens since 1950 and 14 World Opens since 1975.

MOST CLUB CHAMPIONSHIPS

The most club championships won by an individual at the same club is 19 by Pauline Brown (UK) at the Leamington Spa Lawn Tennis and Squash Club, Leamington Spa, Warwickshire, UK, from 1978–93 and 1995–97. Her 16 consecutive titles is also a record.

FASTEST SQUASH BALL

At Wimbledon Squash and Badminton Club in January 1988, Roy Buckland (UK) hit a ball with an overhead service at a measured speed of 232.7 km/h (144.6 mph) against the front wall. This is equivalent to an initial speed at the racket of a remarkable 242.6 km/h (150.8 mph).

BADMINTON

MOST WOMEN'S TEAM WORLD CHAMPIONSHIP TITLES

The most wins at the women's World Championships for the Uber Cup (instituted in 1956) is eight by China in 1984, 1986, 1988, 1990, 1992, 1998, 2000 and 2002. The only other nations to have won the biennial competition are the USA, Japan and Indonesia, who have shared the remaining 11 trophies.

MOST THOMAS CUPS

The most wins at the World Team Championships – or Thomas Cup – is 13 by Indonesia between 1958 and 2002. Hendrawan (below) was a key member of the team of 2002.

LONGEST MATCH

In the men's singles final at the World Championship at Glasgow, Strathclyde, UK, on 1 June 1997, Peter Rasmussen (Denmark) beat Sun Jun (China) 16-17, 18-13, 15-10 in a match that lasted 124 minutes.

SHORTEST MATCH

Ra Kyung-min (South Korea) needed just six minutes to beat Julia Mann (UK) 11-2, 11-1 during the 1996 Uber Cup in Hong Kong on 19 May 1996, a record for a competitive badminton match.

MOST OLYMPIC MEDALS

Badminton was first contested at the 1992 Olympic Games in Barcelona, Spain, and since its inauguration no individual has won more than one gold medal. The most medals of any colour won to date is the three taken by Gil Young Ah (South Korea). She has claimed the full complement – a gold medal in the mixed doubles in 1996, a silver medal in the women's doubles in 1996 and a bronze medal in the women's doubles in 1992.

FASTEST SHUTTLECOCK

On 5 November 1996 at Warwickshire Racquets and Health Club, Coventry, Warwicks, UK, Simon Archer (UK, above) smashed a badminton shuttlecock at a world record measured speed of 260 km/h (162 mph).

MOST WORLD CHAMPIONSHIP SINGLES TITLES

Four Chinese players have won two individual world titles – in the men's singles the record goes to Yang Yang, who was successful in 1987 and 1989. Three players have made this achievement in women's singles – Li Lingwei in 1983 and 1989; Han Aiping in 1985 and 1987, and Ye Zhaoying in 1995 and 1997.

MOST WORLD CHAMPIONSHIP TITLES

A record five titles have been won by Park Joo-bong (South Korea) in the men's doubles in 1985 and 1991 and mixed doubles in 1985, 1989 and 1991.

MOST CONSECUTIVE SWIMMING OLYMPIC GOLD MEDALS

Two swimmers have won the same event on three occasions. Dawn Fraser (Australia) took the 100-m freestyle in 1956, 1960 and 1964, while Krisztina Egerszegi (Hungary) triumphed in the 200-m backstroke in 1988, 1992 and 1996.

MOST INDIVIDUAL SWIMMING OLYMPIC GOLD MEDALS

Krisztina Egerszegi (Hungary) won five Olympic gold medals with the 100-m backstroke in 1992, the 200-m backstroke in 1988, 1992 and 1996 and the 400-m medley in 1992.

The most Olympic gold swimming medals won by a man is four. The feat has been achieved by five swimmers to date: Charles Daniels (USA) in the 100-m freestyle in 1906 and 1908, 220-yd freestyle in 1904 and the 440-yd freestyle in 1904; Roland Matthes (East Germany) in the 100-m and 200-m backstroke in 1968 and 1972; Mark Spitz (USA) in the 100-m and 200-m freestyle in 1972 and the 100-m and 200-m butterfly in 1972; Tamás Daryni (Hungary) with the 200-m and 400-m medley in 1988 and 1992 and Alexander Popov (Russia) in the 50-m and 100-m freestyle of 1992 and 1996.

WOMEN'S 200-M BUTTERFLY

Susan O'Neill (Australia, left) won the women's 200-m butterfly race at Sydney, NSW, Australia, in a time of 2:05.81 on 17 May 2000. Known affectionately as 'Madame Butterfly', O'Neill has won medals at every swim meet she has entered since the 1990 Commonwealth Games.

MOST WOMEN'S SWIMMING GOLD MEDALS AT ONE OLYMPIC GAMES

Kristin Otto (East Germany) won six gold medals in the Games of 1988 – in the 50-m freestyle, the 100-m freestyle, the 100-m backstroke, the 100-m butterfly, the 4 x 100-m freestyle and the 4 x 100-m medley.

MOST MEN'S SWIMMING OLYMPIC MEDALS

Mark Spitz (USA) won nine gold medals: the 100-m and 200-m freestyle (1972); the 100-m and 200-m butterfly (1972); the 4 x 100-m freestyle (1968 and 1972); the 4 x 200-m freestyle (1968 and 1972) and the 4 x 100-m medley (1972). All but one set new world records. He also won a silver (100-m butterfly) and a bronze (100-m freestyle) in 1968, giving him 11 Olympic medals in total.

Spitz's seven medals at one Games, in 1972, was equalled by Matt Biondi (USA) who took five gold, one silver and one bronze in 1988. Biondi has also won a record 11 medals in total, winning a gold in 1984, and two golds and a silver in 1992.

MOST WOMEN'S SWIMMING OLYMPIC MEDALS

Dawn Fraser (Australia) won eight medals – four gold and four silver – between 1956 and 1964; Kornelia Ender (East Germany) took four gold and four silver medals in the years 1972 and 1976; and Shirley Babashoff (USA) won two gold and six silver medals in 1972 and 1976.

MOST WOMEN'S SWIMMING WORLD RECORDS

Ragnhild Hveger (Denmark) set 42 world records from 1936 to 1942. For currently recognized events (only metric distances in 50-m pools) the record is 23 by Kornelia Ender (East Germany), between 1973 and 1976.

The men's record is 32 by Arne Borg (Sweden) from 1921 to 1929. For currently recognized events the record is 26 and is held by Mark Spitz (USA) from 1967 to 1972.

MOST SWIMMING WORLD CHAMPIONSHIPS MEDALS

The greatest number of medals ever won at the World Championships is 13 by Michael Gross (West Germany). This comprises five gold, five silver and three bronze medals, which Gross won between 1982 and 1990.

Kornelia Ender (East Germany) holds the women's record of 10 medals, with eight gold and two silver in 1973 and 1975.

The most gold medals won by a man is eight by Ian Thorpe (Australia) in 1998 and 2001. The most medals won at a single championship is seven by Matt Biondi (USA) in 1986 – three gold, one silver and three bronze.

MEN'S 50-M BACKSTROKE

Lenny Krayzelburg (USA, above) set a new record of 24.99 for the men's 50-m backstroke in Sydney, NSW, Australia on 28 August 1999.

MEN'S LONG-COURSE WORLD RECORDS

Men's 50-m backstroke
24.99
Lenny Krayzelburg (USA)
Sydney, NSW, Australia
28 August 1999

Men's 100-m backstroke
53.60
Lenny Krayzelburg (USA)
Sydney, NSW, Australia
24 August 1999

Men's 200-m backstroke
1:55.15
Aaron Peirsol (USA)
Minneapolis, Minnesota, USA
20 March 2002

Men's 50-m breaststroke
27.39
Ed Moses (USA)
Austin, Texas, USA
31 March 2001

Men's 100-m breaststroke
59.94
Roman Sloudnov (Russia)
Fukuoka, Japan
23 July 2001

Men's 200-m breaststroke
2:10.16
Mike Barrowman (USA)
Barcelona, Spain
29 July 1992

Men's 50-m butterfly
23.44
Geoff Huegill (Australia)
Fukuoka, Japan
27 July 2001

Men's 100-m butterfly
51.81
Michael Klim (Australia)
Canberra, ACT, Australia
12 December 1999

Men's 200-m butterfly
1:54.58
Michael Phelps (USA)
Fukuoka, Japan
24 July 2001

Men's 50-m freestyle
21.64
Alexander Popov (Russia)
Moscow, Russia
16 June 2000

Men's 100-m freestyle
47.84
Pieter van den Hoogenband (Netherlands)
Sydney, NSW, Australia
19 September 2000

Men's 200-m freestyle
1:44.06
Ian Thorpe (Australia)
Fukuoka, Japan
25 July 2001

Men's 400-m freestyle
3:40.17
Ian Thorpe (Australia)
Fukuoka, Japan
22 July 2001

Men's 800-m freestyle
7:39.16
Ian Thorpe (Australia)
Fukuoka, Japan
24 July 2001

Men's 1,500-m freestyle
14:34.56
Grant Hackett (Australia)
Fukuoka, Japan
29 July 2001

Men's 4 x 100-m freestyle relay
3:13.67
Australia (Michael Klim, Chris Fydler,
Ashley Callus, Ian Thorpe)
Sydney, NSW, Australia
16 September 2000

Men's 4 x 200-m freestyle relay
7:04.66
Australia (Grant Hackett, Michael Klim,
William Kirby, Ian Thorpe)
Fukuoka, Japan
27 July 2001

Men's 200-m medley
1:58.16
Jani Sievinen (Finland)
Rome, Italy
11 September 1994

Men's 400-m medley
4:11.76
Tom Dolan (USA)
Sydney, NSW, Australia
17 September 2000

Men's 4 x 100-m medley relay
3:33.73
USA (Lenny Krayzelburg, Ed Moses,
Ian Crocker, Gary Hall Jr)
Sydney, NSW, Australia
23 September 2000

WOMEN'S LONG-COURSE WORLD RECORDS

Women's 50-m backstroke
28.25
Sandra Voelker (Germany)
Berlin, Germany
17 June 2000

Women's 100-m backstroke
1:00.16
He Cihong (China)
Rome, Italy
10 September 1994

Women's 200-m backstroke
2:06.62
Krisztina Egerszegi (Hungary)
Athens, Greece
25 August 1991

Women's 50-m breaststroke
30.83
Penny Heyns (South Africa)
Sydney, NSW, Australia
28 August 1999

Women's 100-m breaststroke
1:06.52
Penny Heyns (South Africa)
Sydney, NSW, Australia
23 August 1999

Women's 200-m breaststroke
2:22.99
Hui Qi (China)
Hangzhou, China
13 April 2001

Women's 50-m butterfly
25.64
Inge de Bruijn (Netherlands)
Sheffield, S Yorks, UK
26 May 2000

Women's 100-m butterfly
56.61
Inge de Bruijn (Netherlands)
Sydney, NSW, Australia
17 September 2000

Women's 200-m butterfly
2:05.81
Susan O'Neill (Australia)
Sydney, NSW, Australia
17 May 2000

Women's 50-m freestyle
24.13
Inge de Bruijn (Netherlands)
Sydney, NSW, Australia
22 September 2000

Women's 100-m freestyle
53.77
Inge de Bruijn (Netherlands),
Sydney, NSW, Australia
20 September 2000

Women's 200-m freestyle
1:56.78
Franziska van Almsick (Germany)
Rome, Italy
6 September 1994

Women's 400-m freestyle
4:03.85
Janet Evans (USA)
Seoul, South Korea
22 September 1988

Women's 800-m freestyle
8:16.22
Janet Evans (USA)
Tokyo, Japan
20 August 1989

Women's 1,500-m freestyle
15:52.10
Janet Evans (USA)
Orlando, Florida, USA
26 March 1988

Women's 4 x 100-m freestyle relay
3:36.61
USA (Jenny Thompson, Courtney Shealy,
Dara Torres, Amy van Dyken)
Sydney, NSW, Australia
16 September 2000

Women's 4 x 200-m freestyle relay
7:55.47
East Germany (Manuela Stellmach,
Astrid Strauss, Anke Möhring, Heike Friedrich)
Strasbourg, France
18 August 1987

Women's 200-m medley
2:09.72
Wu Yanyan (China)
Shanghai, China
17 October 1997

Women's 400-m medley
4:33.59
Yana Klochkova (Ukraine)
Sydney, NSW, Australia
16 September 2000

Women's 4 x 100-m medley relay
3:58.30
USA (Megan Quann, Jenny Thompson,
BJ Bedford, Dara Torres)
Sydney, NSW, Australia
23 September 2000

MEN'S 4 X 200-M SHORT-COURSE FREESTYLE RELAY

An Australian team comprising William Kirby, Ian Thorpe, Michael Klim and Grant Hackett (above) completed the men's 4 x 200-m short-course freestyle relay in a record time of 6:56.41 in Perth, WA, Australia on 7 August 2001.

GREATEST DISTANCE SWUM

Between 25 June and 23 August 2000 Martin Strel (Slovenia) swam the length of the river Danube followed by three other stages to complete a record total distance of 3,004 km (1,866.6 miles).

FURTHEST DISTANCE SWUM IN 24 HOURS IN 25-M POOL

Anders Forvass (Sweden) swam 101.9 km (63.3 miles) in the 25-m Linköping public swimming pool, Sweden, on 28–29 October 1989.

MEN'S FURTHEST DISTANCE SWUM IN 24 HOURS IN 50-M POOL

Grant Robinson (Australia) swam a world record distance of 101.1 km (62.82 miles) in a 24-hour period in a 50-m pool at the Mingara Leisure Centre, Tumbi Umbi, NSW, Australia, on 28–29 June 1997.

WOMEN'S FURTHEST DISTANCE SWUM IN 24 HOURS IN 50-M POOL

Kelly Driffield (Australia) swam a world record total distance of 95.657 km (59.44 miles) in a period of 24 hours in a 50-m pool at the Mingara Leisure Centre, Tumbi Umbi, NSW, Australia on 28–29 June 1997.

FASTEST 50 M SWUM UNDERWATER

Maarten Sterck (Netherlands) swam 50 m (164 ft) underwater in 38.98 sec on 11 March 2001 at Valkenswaard, The Netherlands.

HIGHEST SHALLOW DIVE

Danny Higginbottom (USA) dived from 8.86 m (29 ft 1 in) into 30 cm (12 in) of water at the Therme Erding Spa, Munich, Germany, on 1 April 2000.

MOST CONTINUOUS ROTATIONS UNDERWATER WITH ONE BREATH

Marta Fernández Pèrez (Spain) completed 28 rotations in one breath in a tank in Madrid, Spain, on 18 October 2001.

MOST DIVING WORLD CHAMPIONSHIP TITLES

Greg Louganis (USA) won five world titles – highboard in 1978, and both highboard and springboard in 1982 and 1986 – as well as four Olympic gold medals in 1984 and 1988.

Philip George Boggs (USA) won three gold medals in one event, the springboard, in 1973, 1975 and 1978.

MOST PARTICIPANTS IN ONE-HOUR SWIMATHON

The most people to take part in an hour-long swimathon charity event is 2,533. The event was organized by BT Swimathon 2000 and occurred at more than 500 British pools from 6 to 7 pm on 18 March 2000.

MEN'S SHORT-COURSE WORLD RECORDS

Men's 50-m backstroke
23.42
Neil Walker (USA)
Athens, Greece
16 March 2000

Men's 100-m backstroke
50.75
Neil Walker (USA)
Athens, Greece
19 March 2000

Men's 200-m backstroke
1:51.17
Aaron Peirsol (USA)
Moscow, Russia
7 April 2002

Men's 50-m breaststroke
26.20
Oleg Lisogor (Ukraine)
Berlin, Germany
26 January 2002

Men's 100-m breaststroke
57.47
Ed Moses (USA)
Stockholm, Sweden
23 January 2002

Men's 200-m breaststroke
2:03.17
Ed Moses (USA)
Berlin, Germany
26 January 2002

Men's 50-m butterfly
22.74
Geoff Huegill (Australia)
Berlin, Germany
26 January 2002

Men's 100-m butterfly
50.10
Thomas Rupprath (Germany)
Berlin, Germany
27 January 2002

Men's 200-m butterfly
1:51.21
Thomas Rupprath (Germany)
Rostock, Germany
1 December 2001

Men's 50-m freestyle
21.13
Mark Foster (UK)
Paris, France
28 January 2001

Men's 100-m freestyle
46.74
Alexander Popov (Russia)
Gelsenkirchen, Germany
19 March 1994

Men's 200-m freestyle
1:41.10
Ian Thorpe (Australia)
Berlin, Germany
6 February 2000

Men's 400-m freestyle
3:35.01
Grant Hackett (Australia)
Hong Kong
2 April 1999

Men's 800-m freestyle
7:25.28
Grant Hackett (Australia)
Perth, WA, Australia
3 August 2001

Men's 1,500-m freestyle
14:10.10
Grant Hackett (Australia)
Perth, WA, Australia
7 August 2001

Men's 4 x 50-m freestyle relay
1:26.78
USA (Bryan Jones, Matt Ulricksson, Robert Bogart and Leffie Crawford)
Minneapolis, Minnesota, USA
23 March 2000

Men's 4 x 100-m freestyle relay
3:09.57
Sweden (Johan Nystrom, Lars Frolander, Mattias Ohlin and Stefan Nystrand)
Athens, Greece
16 March 2000

Men's 4 x 200-m freestyle relay
6:56.41
Australia (William Kirby, Ian Thorpe, Michael Klim and Grant Hackett)
Perth, WA, Australia
7 August 2001

Men's 100-m medley
52.63
Peter Mankoc (Slovenia)
Antwerp, Belgium
15 December 2001

Men's 200-m medley
1:54.65
Jani Sievinen (Finland)
Kuopio, Finland
21 April 1994
Atilla Czene (Hungary)
Minneapolis, Minnesota, USA,
23 March 2000

Men's 400-m medley
4:04.24
Matthew Dunn (Australia)
Perth, WA, Australia
24 September 1998

Men's 4 x 50-m medley relay
1:35.51 (achieved in same race)
Germany (Thomas Rupprath, Mark Warnecke, Alexander Luderitz and Stephan Kunzelmann)
Sweden (Daniel Carlsson, Patrik Isaksson, Jonas Akesson and Lars Frolander)
Sheffield, S Yorks, England
13 December 1998

Men's 4 x 100-m medley relay
3:29.00
USA (Aaron Peirsol, David Denniston, Peter Marshall, Jason Lezak)
Moscow, Russia
7 April 2002

WOMEN'S SHORT-COURSE WORLD RECORDS

Women's 50-m backstroke
26.83
Hui Li (China)
Shanghai, China
2 December 2001

Women's 100-m backstroke
57.08
Natalie Coughlin (USA)
New York City, USA
28 November 2001

Women's 200-m backstroke
2:03.62
Natalie Coughlin (USA)
New York City, USA
27 November 2001

Women's 50-m breaststroke
29.96
Emma Igelström (Sweden)
Moscow, Russia
4 April 2002

Women's 100-m breaststroke
1:05.38
Emma Igelström (Sweden)
Moscow, Russia
6 April 2002

Women's 200-m breaststroke
2:19.25
Hiu Qi (China)
Paris, France
28 January 2001

Women's 50-m butterfly
25.36
Anna-Karin Kammerling (Sweden)
Stockholm, Sweden
25 January 2001

Women's 100-m butterfly
56.55
Martina Moravcova (Slovakia)
Berlin, Germany
26 January 2002

Women's 200-m butterfly
2:04.16
Susan O'Neill (Australia)
Sydney, Australia
18 January 2000

Women's 50-m freestyle
23.59
Therese Alshammar (Sweden)
Athens, Greece
18 March 2000

Women's 100-m freestyle
52.17
Therese Alshammar (Sweden)
Athens, Greece
17 March 2000

Women's 200-m freestyle
1:54.04
Lindsay Benko (USA)
Moscow, Russia
7 April 2002

Women's 400-m freestyle
4:00.03
Claudia Poll (Costa Rica)
Gothenburg, Sweden,
19 April 1997

Women's 800-m freestyle
8:14.35
Sachiko Yamada (Japan)
Tokyo, Japan
2 April 2002

Women's 4 x 50-m freestyle relay
1:38.21
Sweden (Annika Lofstedt, Therese Alshammar, Johanna Sjöberg and Anna-Karin Kammerling)
Valencia, Spain, 15 December 2000

Women's 4 x 100-m freestyle relay
3:34.55
China (Le Jingyi, Na Chao, Shan Ying and Nian Yin)
Gothenburg, Sweden
19 April 1997

Women's 4 x 200-m freestyle relay
7:46.30
China (Xu Yanvei, Zhu Yingven, Tang Jingzhi and Yang Yu)
Moscow, Russia, 3 April 2002

Women's 100-m medley
59.30
Jenny Thompson (USA)
Hong Kong
2 April 1999

Women's 200-m medley
2:07.79
Allison Wagner (USA)
Palma de Mallorca, Spain
5 December 1993

Women's 400-m medley
4:27.83
Yana Klochkova (Ukraine)
Paris, France
19 January 2002

Women's 4 x 50-m medley relay
1:48.31
Sweden (Therese Alshammar, Emma Igelström, Anna-Karin Kammerling and Johanna Sjöberg)
Valencia, Spain
16 December 2000

Women's 4 x 100-m medley relay
3:55.78
Sweden (Therese Alshammar, Emma Igelström, Anna-Karin Kammerling and Johanna Sjöberg)
Moscow, Russia
5 April 2002

WOMEN'S 50-M SHORT-COURSE BREASTSTROKE

Emma Igelström (Sweden, left) holds the world record for the fastest women's 50-m short-course breaststroke with a time of 29.96 sec in Moscow, Russia, achieved on 4 April 2002. In Moscow two days later (6 April 2002) Igelström also swam a world record time of 1:05.38 in the women's 100-m short-course breaststroke competition.

FASTEST WOMEN'S
SINGLE SCULLS – 2,000 M
The women's single sculls record over 2,000 m is 7 min 11.68 sec by Ekaterina Karsten (Belarus, above) at St Catharines, Ontario, Canada, on 28 August 1999. Her average speed during the race was 16.68 km/h (10.36 mph).

ROWING

MOST MEN'S
OLYMPIC GOLD MEDALS
Steven Redgrave (UK) holds the record for winning the most gold medals in rowing at the Olympic Games, with a total of five. His victories have come in the coxed fours of 1984 and 2000 and the coxless pairs of 1988, 1992 and 1996. For winning five golds in five successive Olympics in such a physically demanding sport, many experts consider Redgrave the greatest Olympian of the modern era.

MOST WOMEN'S
OLYMPIC GOLD MEDALS
Canadian pair Kathleen Heddle and Marnie McBean have both won three Olympic gold medals for rowing – in

the coxless pairs and the eights in the 1992 Games in Barcelona, Spain, and in the double sculls in 1996 in Atlanta, Georgia, USA.

MOST UNIVERSITY
BOAT RACE WINS
The first University Boat Race, which Oxford won, was from Hambledon Lock to Henley Bridge, London, UK, on 10 June 1829. Outrigged eights were first used in 1846 and the course now goes along the Thames from Putney to Mortlake, London, UK. In the 148 races to 2002, Cambridge have won 77 times, Oxford 70 times and there was one dead heat, on 24 March 1877.

UNIVERSITY BOAT RACE –
MARGINS OF VICTORY
The closest finishes to the boat race were in 1952 and 1980. Oxford won both by a canvas – 1.8 m (6 ft).

Apart from when one boat has sunk, the greatest winning margin was by Cambridge with 20 lengths in 1900.

OLDEST UNIVERSITY
BOAT RACE PARTICIPANT
The oldest rower is Cambridge's Donald MacDonald, who was 31 years 3 months when he took part in the 1987 race. However, Cambridge cox Andrew Probert was 38 years 3 months in 1992.

YOUNGEST UNIVERSITY
BOAT RACE PARTICIPANT
Robert Ross was 18 years 200 days when he rowed for Cambridge in the 1977 University Boat Race.

LONGEST SEA
ROWING RACE
The longest rowing race held on the open sea is the biennial Celtic Challenge, which takes participants across the Irish Sea. The course taken by the rowers measures a

record 78 nautical miles (144.5 km) from Arklow, Co Wicklow, Ireland, to Aberystwyth, Ceredigion, UK.

FASTEST MEN'S
EIGHT – 2,000 M
The record for 2,000 m on non-tidal water is 5:22.80, at an average speed of 22.30 km/h (13.85 mph), by The Netherlands at the World Championships at St Catharines, Ontario, Canada, on 28 August 1999.

FASTEST WOMEN'S
EIGHT – 2,000 M
The women's record for 2,000 m on non-tidal water is 5:57.02 by Romania at Lucerne, Switzerland, on 9 July 1999. Their average speed was 20.16 km/h (12.53 mph).

FASTEST ROWING
FROM LONDON TO PARIS
A team of 21 Jersey Rowing Club members rowed from Westminster Bridge, London, UK, to the Eiffel Tower, Paris, France, in a time of 90 hr 33 min 33 sec. The journey took from 25 to 28 September 2000 and is the fastest time such a trip has ever been completed.

CANOEING

MOST OLYMPIC
GOLD MEDALS
Birgit Fischer (East Germany to 1990, then Germany) won seven Olympic gold medals between 1980 and 2000. She also won three silvers for a record total of 10 medals.

In addition to her seven Olympic titles, Fischer has won 29 world titles for a record total of 36 titles overall.

The men's record is held by Gert Fredriksson (Sweden), who won a record six Olympic gold medals between 1948 and 1960. He also won a silver and a bronze to make a record eight medals in total.

Fredriksson also won seven World Championship titles, giving him a combined total of 13 Olympic and World titles between 1948 and 1960. He shares this record with Rüdiger Helm (East Germany), whose successes came between 1976 and 1983, and Ivan Patzaichin (Romania), who won his titles from 1968 to 1984.

FASTEST UNIVERSITY BOAT RACE
The race record time for the 6.779 km (4 miles 374 yd) University Boat Race on the River Thames, London, UK, is 16 min 19 sec by Cambridge (above) on 28 March 1998. Their average speed was 24.93 km/h (15.49 mph).

LARGEST CANOE RAFT

A total of 776 canoes and kayaks were held together to form a giant raft on Hinckley Lake in Hinckley, Ohio, USA, on 19 May 2001 at an event organized by Cleveland Metroparks. The rules for this record state that the craft must be held by participants and not tied together.

MOST ESKIMO ROLLS BY HAND

Colin Hill (UK) achieved 1,000 eskimo rolls by hand in a record 31 min 55.62 sec at Consett, Durham, UK, on 12 March 1987.

He also managed 100 rolls in 2 min 39.2 sec at Crystal Palace, London, UK, on 22 February 1987.

MOST ESKIMO ROLLS BY A MAN

Ray Hudspith (UK) achieved 1,000 eskimo rolls with a paddle in a record 34 min 43 sec at Elswick Pool, Newcastle, Tyne and Wear, UK, on 20 March 1987.

FASTEST MEN'S SINGLE SCULLS – 2,000 M

The single sculls world record for completing a distance of 2,000 m on non-tidal water is a time of 6 min 36.38 sec – at an average speed of 18.16 km/h (11.28 mph) – by Robert Wadell (New Zealand, right) at St Catharines, Ontario, Canada, on 28 August 1999.

Hudspith also completed 100 rolls in a record time of 3 min 7.25 sec at Killingworth Leisure Centre, Tyne and Wear, UK, on 3 March 1991.

MOST ESKIMO ROLLS BY A WOMAN

Helen Barnes (UK) completed 100 eskimo rolls in 3 min 42.16 sec on 2 August 2000.

GREATEST DISTANCE IN CANOE IN 24 HOURS

Ian Adamson paddled 327.1 km (203.3 miles) along the Colorado River from Gore Canyon, Kremmling, Colorado, USA, to Potash, near Moab, Utah, USA, on 7–8 June 1997.

FASTEST TIME TO COMPLETE 200 M

At the 1998 World Championships at Szeged, Hungary, the Hungarian four-man team claimed the 200-m title in a time of 31.155 sec, which represents an average racing speed of 23.11 km/h (14.36 mph).

FASTEST TIME TO COMPLETE 1,000 M

The 1996 German four-man kayak Olympic champions covered a distance of 1,000 m in 2 min 51.52 sec to win gold on 3 August 1996 at Atlanta, Georgia, USA. This is an average speed of 20.98 km/h (13.04 mph).

LONGEST FREE-FALL WATERFALL DESCENT

The longest free-fall descent over a waterfall is 19.7 m (64 ft 8 in) achieved by Shaun Baker (UK) over the Aldeyjarfoss on the Skjalfandafljot, a glacial river in Iceland, on 25 September 1996.

LONGEST RACE

The Canadian Government Centennial Voyageur Canoe Pageant and Race from Rocky Mountain House, Alberta, Canada, to the Expo 67 site at Montreal, Quebec, Canada, covered 5,283 km (3,283 miles). Ten canoes represented each one of the Canadian provinces and territories. The winner of the race, which took from 24 May to 4 September 1967, was the *Radisson*, the canoe from the province of Manitoba.

FASTEST 75-FT VERTICAL DESCENT

The fastest time to descend a vertical height of 22.86 m (75 ft) on a river in a canoe is 19.9 sec by Shaun Baker (UK) in Snowdonia, Gwynedd, UK, on 26 August 2000.

PUNTING

LONGEST JOURNEY

The longest known journey that has been completed by punting – pushing a boat using a pole – is a trip of 1,160 km (721 miles) between Oxford, UK, to Leeds, W Yorks, UK, and back to Oxford by John Pearse (UK) – who was accompanied by four crew members – from 19 June to 10 August 1965.

OLDEST
ROUND THE WORLD RACE

The oldest regular sailing race around the world is the quadrennial Whitbread Round the World Race (instituted in August 1973, now called the Volvo Round the World Race), originally organized by the Royal Naval Sailing Association. It starts in the UK and the route taken and the number of legs varies from race to race. The distance covered by the 1997–98 race was 31,600 nautical miles (59,239 km) from Southampton, Hants, UK, and back. The winning boat, *EF Language*, was skippered by Paul Cayard (USA), the first American to win the race.

SAILBOARDING

LONGEST SAILBOARD

The longest sailboard measures 50.2 m (165 ft) and was made in Fredrikstad, Norway. It first sailed on 28 June 1986.

LONGEST SAILBOARD SNAKE

The world's longest sailboard snake was made up of 70 windsurfers in tandem at the Sailboard Show '89 event at Narrabeen Lakes, Manly, NSW, Australia, on 21 October 1989.

YACHTING

MOST PARTICIPANTS IN AN OCEAN RACE

The largest trans-oceanic race was the 1989 Atlantic Rally for Cruisers (ARC), when 204 boats of the 209 starters from 24 nations completed the race from Las Palmas, Canary Islands, Spain, to Barbados, West Indies.

MOST INDIVIDUAL AMERICA'S CUP RACES

Dennis Conner (USA) has raced in six America's Cups as a member of the afterguard, more than anybody else. He made his debut in 1974, was a winning skipper/helmsman in 1980, 1987 and 1989, and a losing skipper in 1983 and 1995.

Charlie Barr (USA) who defended in 1899, 1901 and 1903 and Harold S Vanderbilt (USA) in 1930, 1934 and 1937, each steered the successful winner three times in succession.

NARROWEST AMERICA'S CUP FINISHING MARGIN

The closest finish to an America's Cup race was on 4 October 1901, when *Shamrock II* (UK) crossed the finish line 2 seconds ahead of the American boat *Columbia*.

FASTEST SOLO CIRCUMNAVIGATION

Yachtsman Michel Desjoyeaux (France) circumnavigated the globe in 93 days 3 hr 57 min 32 sec during the 2000 Vendée Globe single-handed yacht race in his yacht *PRB*, starting and finishing at Les Sables d'Olonne, France. He covered 38,600 km (24,000 miles) between 5 November 2000 and 10 February 2001.

MOST YACHTING OLYMPIC GOLD MEDALS

The first sportsman ever to win individual gold medals in four successive Olympic Games was Paul Elvstrøm (Denmark) in the Firefly yachting class in 1948 and the Finn class in 1952, 1956 and 1960. He also won eight other world titles.

GREATEST DISTANCE KITE SURFING

Kite surfing (above) involves using surfboards pulled by kites. On 21 December 2001 Neil Hutchinson, Kent Marincovik and Fabrice Collard (all USA) travelled a record distance of 88 nautical miles (163 km or 101.3 miles) between Key West, Florida, USA, and Varadero, Cuba.

MOST AMERICA'S CUP WINS

There have been 30 challenges for the America's Cup since 1851 at Cowes, Isle of Wight, UK, with the USA winning every time except in 1983 (to Australia), in 1995 and in 2000 (both times to New Zealand - shown above).

WINDSURFING AT THE HIGHEST LATITUDE

Gerard-Jan Goekoop (Netherlands) windsurfed alongside the pack-ice of the Arctic Ocean at 80º 40.3' N, 13º 43' E, north of the Spitsbergen archipelago on 14 July 1985. Goekoop was ship's doctor on board the *MS Plancius*, and went surfing when the boat got stuck in the ice.

MOST WINDSURFING WORLD CHAMPIONSHIPS

World Championships were first held in 1973 and the sport was added to the Olympics in 1984 when the winner was Stephan van den Berg (Netherlands) who also won five world titles between 1979 and 1983.

SURFING

LONGEST RIDE ON A RIVER BORE

The Official British Surfing Association holds the record for the longest ride on a river bore, set on the Severn Bore, UK. The record on a surfboard is 9.1 km (5.7 miles), from Windmill Hill to Maisemore Weir, by David Lawson (UK) on 29 August 1996.

LONGEST RIDE ON SEA WAVES

About four to six times each year rideable surfing waves break in Matanchen Bay near San Blas, Nayarit, Mexico, which make rides of around 1,700 m (5,700 ft) possible.

MOST WOMEN'S SURFING WORLD CHAMPIONSHIPS

The women's professional surfing World Championship was instituted in 1979 and has been won on four occasions by three women: Frieda Zamba (USA) from 1984 to 1986 and in 1988; Wendy Botha (Australia, formerly South Africa) in 1987, 1989, 1991 and 1992, and Lisa Andersen (USA) from 1994 to 1997.

WATER-SKIING

LONGEST WATER-SKI JUMP

The official International Water Ski Federation record for the longest ski-jump is 70.9 m (232 ft 7 in). This was achieved by Jimmy Siemers (USA) at the Tri-Lakes Late Bloomer event at Zachary, Louisiana, USA, on 22 October 2000.

The same record for the longest water-ski jump achieved by a woman is 55.1 m (180 ft 9 in) by Elena Milakova (Russia) at Lincoln, UK, on 27 July 2001.

LONGEST WATER-SKI FLY DISTANCE

The official International Water Ski Federation record for ski-flying is a distance of 91.1 m (298 ft 10 in), by Jaret Llewellyn (Canada) at the Big Air Challenge event at Orlando, Florida, USA, on 14 May 2000. Ski-flying is a similar discipline to regular ski-jumping, but participants have a longer rope, travel behind faster boats and leap off extended ramps to achieve greater distances.

The women's record is 66.6 m (218 ft 6 in), a distance achieved by both Toni Neville and Emma Sheer (both Australia) at the America's Cup event at West Palm Beach, Florida, USA, on 23 and 24 September 2000 respectively.

MOST WATER-SKIERS TOWED BEHIND A BOAT

A record 100 water-skiers were towed on double skis over a distance of a nautical mile (1.852 km) by the cruiser *Reef Cat* at Cairns, Queensland, Australia, on 18 October 1986. This feat, which was organized by the Cairns and District Powerboating and Ski Club, was then replicated by 100 skiers on single skis.

HIGHEST RIDEABLE SURFING WAVES

Waimea Bay, Hawaii, USA (above), reputedly provides the most consistently high waves, often reaching a rideable limit of 9–11 m (30–35 ft). The highest wave ever ridden was a tsunami of 'perhaps 50 feet', which struck on 3 April 1868.

MOST MEN'S PRO SURFING WORLD CHAMPIONSHIPS

The World Professional series began in 1975. Since then, the men's title has been won six times by Kelly Slater (USA, right) in 1992 and 1994–1998. Slater began competing aged eight and won his first competition the same year.

LARGEST PLAYING FIELD

The largest standard playing field for any ball game is the 5 ha (12.4 acres) for polo (below). This area is accounted for by a maximum length of 274 m (300 yd) and a width, without side boards, of 182 m (200 yd). With boards the width is 146 m (160 yd).

HIGHEST POLO SCORE

The highest aggregate number of goals scored in an international match is 30, during Argentina's 21-9 defeat of the USA at Meadowbrook, Long Island, New York, USA, in September 1936.

MOST POLO WORLD CHAMPIONSHIPS

Five Polo World Championships have been contested and three have been won by Argentina, in 1987, 1992 and 1998. The World Championships are held every three years under the auspices of the Federation of International Polo (FIP).

MOST CHUKKAS IN ONE DAY

The most chukkas – a period of continuous play, generally lasting 7½ minutes – played on one ground in a day is 43. This total was achieved by the Pony Club on the No. 3 Ground at Kirtlington Park, Oxon, UK, on 31 July 1991.

HIGHEST JUMP

The official Fédération Equestre Internationale (FEI) high-jump record is 2.47 m (8 ft 1.25 in) by *Huaso*, ridden by Capt Alberto Larraguibel Morales (Chile) at Viña del Mar, Santiago, Chile, on 5 February 1949.

The indoor high-jump record is 2.4 m (7 ft 10.5 in) by *Optibeurs Leonardo*, ridden by Franke Sloothaak (Germany) at Chaudefontaine, Switzerland, on 9 June 1991.

LOWEST OLYMPIC SHOW-JUMPING SCORE

The lowest Olympic show-jumping score obtained by a winner is that of no faults and the record is shared by Frantisek Ventura (Czechoslovakia, now Czech Republic) on *Eliot* in 1928, Alwin Schockemöhle (West Germany) on *Warwick Rex* in 1976 and Ludger Beerbaum (Germany) on *Classic Touch* in 1992.

MOST SHOW-JUMPING OLYMPIC GOLD MEDALS

The most Olympic show-jumping gold medals won by a rider is five by Hans Günter Winkler (West Germany) – four team medals in 1956, 1960, 1964 and 1972 and the individual Grand Prix in 1956. Winkler also won team silver in 1976 and team bronze in 1968, giving him a record seven medals overall.

MOST INDIVIDUAL DRESSAGE OLYMPIC GOLD MEDALS

Henri St Cyr (Sweden) won a record two individual Olympic gold medals in 1952 and 1956. Nicole Uphoff (Germany) has also won a record two gold medals, with successes in 1988 and 1992.

MOST CAREER WINS BY A JOCKEY

Laffit Pincay Jr (USA, above) has ridden 9,311 winners from 16 May 1964 to date. He broke the previous record, by Bill Shoemaker (USA), with a win on 12 October 1999, taking his then total to 8,834. Pincay won the Eclipse Award five times, in 1971, 1973–74, 1979 and 1985, the Belmont Stakes three times and the Kentucky Derby once, in 1984.

MOST TEAM SHOW-JUMPING OLYMPIC GOLD MEDALS

The most team wins in the Prix des Nations at the Olympic Games is seven by Germany in 1936, 1956, 1960, 1964 and 1996, and as West Germany in 1972 and 1988.

MOST TEAM DRESSAGE OLYMPIC GOLD MEDALS

Germany have won a record 10 team gold medals, in 1928, 1936, 1964, 1968, 1976, 1984, 1988, 1992, 1996 and 2000. The country competed as West Germany from 1968 to 1990.

MOST SHOW-JUMPING WORLD CHAMPIONSHIPS

Two men have won the Show-Jumping World Championships

twice: Hans Günter Winkler (Germany) in 1954 and 1955 and Raimondo d'Inzeo (Italy) in 1956 and 1960.

MOST SHOW-JUMPING WORLD CUPS

The greatest number of Show-Jumping World Cup wins is three by Hugo Simon (Austria) in 1979, 1996 and 1997, and Rodrigo Pessoa (Brazil) in 1998, 1999 and 2000.

MOST THREE-DAY-EVENT OLYMPIC GOLD MEDALS

Charles Ferdinand Pahud de Mortanges (Netherlands) won four three-day-event Olympic gold medals (team event in 1924 and 1928, and individual in 1928 and 1932, when he also won a team silver medal).

BEST RACEHORSE WIN-LOSS RECORD

The best career win-loss record for a racehorse is 100% wins by *Kincsem*, a Hungarian mare foaled in 1874, who was unbeaten in all of her 54 races throughout Europe, including the Goodwood Cup of 1878.

HIGHEST PRICED HORSE

The largest amount of money paid for a yearling is $13.1 million

(£9 million) for *Seattle Dancer* on 23 July 1985 at Keeneland, Kentucky, USA, by Robert Sangster and Partners. Part ownership of potential stallions often vastly inflates their value before they go to stud, when in fact the horse would not command that price if it were available on the open market.

FASTEST RACE

The highest speed recorded in a horse race is 69.62 km/h (43.26 mph) over a distance of 402 m (0.25 mile) by *Big Racket* at Mexico City, Mexico, on 5 February 1945 and also by *Onion Roll* at Thistledown, Cleveland, Ohio, USA, on 27 September 1993.

The record speed over 2,413 m (1.5 miles) is 60.86 km/h (37.82 mph) and was achieved by *Hawkster* at Santa Anita Park, Arcadia, California, USA, on 14 October 1989.

OLDEST RACE WINNER

The oldest horses to win on the Flat have been the 18-year-olds *Revenge* at Shrewsbury, Shropshire, UK, on 23 September 1790, *Marksman* at Ashford, Kent, UK, on 4 September 1826 and *Jorrocks* at Bathurst, NSW, Australia, on 28 February 1851. At

the same age *Wild Aster* won three hurdle races in six days in March 1919 and *Sonny Somers* won two steeplechases in February 1980.

MOST CAREER WINS BY A RACEHORSE

Chorisbar (foaled in 1935 in Puerto Rico) won 197 out of 324 races between 1937 and 1947.

MOST CONSECUTIVE WINS BY A HORSE

The longest winning sequence for a racehorse is 56 races by *Camarero* (foaled 1951 in Puerto Rico) from 19 April 1953 to 17 August 1955.

MOST RACES WON IN A YEAR BY A JOCKEY

The most races won in a year by a jockey is 598 from 2,312 rides by Kent Desormeaux (USA) in 1989.

MOST WINNERS IN ONE DAY

Chris Antley (USA) rode nine winners on 31 October 1987, consisting of four in the afternoon at Aqueduct, New York, USA, and five in the evening at the Meadowlands, New Jersey, USA.

The most winners ridden on one card is eight by six riders, most recently (and from fewest rides) by Patrick Day (USA) from nine rides at Arlington International, Illinois, USA, on 13 September 1989.

The longest winning streak is 12 by Sir Gordon Richards (UK) in 1933 (one race at Nottingham, UK, on 3 October, six out of six at Chepstow, Gwent, UK, on 4 October and the first five races next day at Chepstow); and by Pieter Stroebel (Zimbabwe) at Bulawayo, Southern Rhodesia (now Zimbabwe).

RICHEST DAY'S RACING

The Dubai World Cup meeting on 23 March 2002 at Nad Al Sheba, Dubai, UAE (above), had $15.25 million (£10.4 million) in prize money on offer. The seven races included the world's richest race, the Dubai World Cup.

GREATEST PARAGLIDING ALTITUDE GAIN
The paragliding height gain record is 4,526 m (14,849 ft) by Robbie Whittal (UK, above) at Brandvlei, South Africa, on 6 January 1993.

The women's record is 4,325 m (14,189 ft) by Kat Thurston (UK) over Kuruman, South Africa, on 1 January 1996.

GLIDING

HIGHEST ALTITUDE
The absolute altitude record in a glider is 14,938 m (49,009 ft) by Robert Harris (USA) over California City, USA, on 17 February 1986.

For women, the single-seater world record is 12,637 m (41,460 ft) by Sabrina Jackintell (USA) over Black Forest Gliderport, Colorado Springs, USA, on 14 February 1979.

GREATEST ALTITUDE GAIN
The greatest height gain in a glider is 12,894 m (42,303 ft) by Paul Bikle (USA) over Lancaster, California, USA, on 25 February 1961.

GREATEST DISTANCE
The greatest free distance flown in a glider is 1,460.8 km (907.7 miles) by Hans Werner Grosse (Germany) from Lübeck, Germany, to Biarritz, France, on 25 April 1972.

Karla Karel (UK) flew 949.7 km (590.1 miles) in New South Wales, Australia, to achieve the women's record on 20 January 1980.

FASTEST GLIDER SPEED
The official FAI world record speed for a glider is 247.49 km/h (153.96 mph) by James and Thomas Payne (both USA) over California City, USA, on 3 March 1999.

Pamela Kurstjens-Hawkins (UK) set a women's record of 153.83 km/h (95.58 mph) over Tocumwal, NSW, Australia, on 3 January 2000.

MOST WORLD CHAMPIONSHIP TITLES
The most World Individual Gliding Championships won is four, by Ingo Renner (Australia) in 1976 (Standard class), 1983, 1985 and 1987 (Open).

PARAGLIDING

GREATEST DISTANCE
The men's paragliding distance record is 335 km (208.16 miles) by Godfrey Wenness (Australia) from Mt Borah to Ennera Station, Queensland, Australia, on 16 November 1998.

GREATEST DISTANCE FLOWN IN A TANDEM PARAGLIDER
Richard Westgate and Jim Coutts (both UK) piloted a tandem paraglider 220.4 km (136.95 miles) from Quixada, Brazil, on 30 November 2000.

HANG-GLIDING

MOST WORLD CHAMPIONSHIP TITLES
The world championships were first held in 1976, and the most individual wins is three by Tomas Schanek (Czech Republic) in 1991, 1993 and 1995.

The women's world championship was first held in 1987 and the most individual wins is two – Judy Leden (UK) in 1987 and 1991 and Kari Castle (USA) in 1996 and 2000.

The World Team Championships have been won most often by Great Britain (1981, 1985, 1989 and 1991).

GREATEST DISTANCE
The Fédération Aéronautique Internationale (FIA) record for the greatest distance covered in a single flight by a hang-glider is 559.7 km (347.78 miles) by Davis Straub (USA) on 10 August 2000.

The FAI straight-line distance record by a woman in a hang-glider is 370.87 km (230.44 miles) by Tove Heaney (Australia) from Garnpung Lake, NSW, to Bealiba, Victoria, Australia, on 2 December 1998.

PARACHUTING

LARGEST MASS PARACHUTE JUMP
A total of 588 military and civilian parachutists from five nations parachuted from seven aircraft flying at 3,660 m (12,000 ft) over the Santa Cruz Air Base, Rio de Janeiro, Brazil, on 18 April 2000.

MOST PARACHUTE JUMPS IN 24 HOURS
Michael Zang (USA) completed 500 parachute jumps in 24 hours at an airfield near Decatur, Texas, USA, from 18–19 May 2001. He completed a 640-m (2,100-ft) jump every 2 min 53 sec on average, raising money for the Special Olympics.

FASTEST PARAGLIDING SPEED
Patrick Berod (France) attained 28.26 km/h (17.56 mph) over Albertville, France, on 27 June 1995. Fiona Macaskill (UK, above) holds the women's record with 19.86 km/h (12.34 mph) at Plaine Joux, France, on 21 April 2000.

GREATEST ALTITUDE GAIN IN A HANG-GLIDER

The greatest height gain in a hang-glider by a male pilot is 4,343 m (14,250 ft) by Larry Tudor (USA), over Owens Valley, California, USA, on 4 August 1985.

Judy Leden (UK, right) holds the women's record, with a gain of 3,970 m (13,025 ft) over Kuruman, South Africa, on 1 December 1992.

FREE-FALL

LARGEST FREE-FALL FORMATION

The World Team '99 completed a free-fall formation of 282 skydivers on 16 December 1999 above Ubon Ratchathani, Thailand, holding a link for 7.11 seconds. The skydivers fell from 7,010 m (23,000 ft).

LARGEST FREE-FALL EVENT

The 10-day World Free-fall Convention 2000, held in Quincy, Illinois, USA, from 4–13 August 2000, attracted 5,732 registered skydivers from 55 countries, who between them made in excess of 63,000 jumps. The busiest day was 11 August, when 8,104 jumps were made, requiring flight operations on average every 1.08 minutes.

BALLOONING

MOST TO JUMP FROM A BALLOON

Twenty skydivers from the Paraclub Flevo (Netherlands) jumped from a Cameron A-415 PH-AGT balloon over Harfsen, The Netherlands, on 22 April 2000. Two skydivers travelled on top of the balloon and jumped from 1,219 m (4,000 ft). Then the balloon climbed to 1,828 m (6,000 ft) and dropped 12 more skydivers. The six remaining left in two groups of three.

AEROBATICS

MOST WORLD CHAMPIONSHIP WINS

Petr Jirmus (Czechoslovakia, now Czech Republic) is the only man to become world aerobatics champion twice, in 1984 and in 1986. The competition, which is known as the Aresti Cup and has been held biennially since 1960, consists of a known and unknown compulsory and a free programme.

Svetlana Kapanina (Russia) has won the overall women's competition, first held in 1986, a record three times – in 1996, 1998 and 2001.

LONGEST INVERTED FLIGHT

The longest inverted flight lasted 4 hr 38 min 10 sec, and was performed by Joann Osterud (Canada) flying from Vancouver to Vanderhoof, Canada, on 24 July 1991. Osterud also holds the record for the most outside loops – with 208 achieved in a Supernova Hyperbipe over North Bend, Oregon, USA, on 13 July 1989.

MOST INSIDE LOOPS

On 9 August 1986 David Childs (USA) performed 2,368 inside loops in a Bellanca Decathlon over North Pole, Alaska, USA.

MOST INVERTED FLAT SPINS

The most inverted flat spins performed in one attempt is 78 at 4,500 m (15,000 ft) by Wayne Handley (USA) in super-light stunt plane G202, on 2 April 1999. After forcing his plane into an inverted flat spin, he attempted several upside-down rotations per thousand feet. At around 609.6 m (2,000 ft) Handley pulled out of this position and resumed flying as normal.

MEN'S 90-M ARCHERY

Oh Kyo-moon (South Korea, below left) scored 332 points out of a possible 360 at Wonju, South Korea, in November 2000. Kyo-moon also set a record of 1,379 out of a possible 1,440 in Wonju, South Korea, in November 2000. He is shown here with Kim Chung-Tae (below centre) and Jang Yong-Ho (below right) with the gold medals they received for winning the team archery competition at the Sydney Olympic Games in 2000.

ARCHERY

OLDEST ORGANIZATION

The oldest archery body in the world is the Ancient Society of Kilwinning Archers, Ayrshire, UK. The Society's first recorded Papingo shoot (in which archers aim at a wooden model of a bird positioned on a pole at the top of a tall tower) was in 1483.

MOST POINTS SCORED FROM HORSEBACK

The greatest number of points scored from horseback in 12 hours is 4,238.18 recorded by Kassai Lajos (Hungary) at Kaposmero, Hungary, on 6 June 1998.

HIGHEST MEN'S INDOOR 18-M SCORE

Michele Frangilli (Italy) scored 597 points from a possible 600 at the indoor 18-m distance in January 2001 in Nîmes, France.

HIGHEST MEN'S INDOOR 25-M SCORE

Michele Frangilli (Italy) scored 598 points out of a possible 600 at the indoor 25-m distance in November 2001 in Gallarate, Italy.

HIGHEST WOMEN'S INDOOR 18-M SCORE

Lina Herasymenko (Ukraine) scored 591 points from a possible 600 at the indoor 18-m distance in March 1997 in Istanbul, Turkey.

HIGHEST WOMEN'S INDOOR 25-M SCORE

Petra Ericsson (Sweden) scored 592 points out of a possible 600 at the indoor 25-m distance in March 1991 in Oulu, Finland.

HIGHEST SCORE IN 24 HOURS

The highest score in 24 hours over 18 FITA (Fédération Internationale de Tir à l'Arc) rounds is 26,064 by Michael Howson and Stephen Howard (both UK) at Oakbank Sports College, Keighley, W Yorkshire, UK, on 11–12 November 2000.

The highest score in 24 hours by two archers is 76,158 in 70 Portsmouth Rounds (60 arrows per round shot at 60-cm FITA targets from 18.29 m, or 20 yd) by Simon Tarplee and David Hathaway (both UK) at Evesham, Worcs, UK, on 1 April 1991. During the attempt Tarplee set an individual record of 38,500.

HIGHEST WOMEN'S 50-M SCORE

In November 1996 Kim Moon-sun (South Korea) scored 345 points from a possible 360 at 50 m in a single FITA round in Ch'ungju, South Korea.

HIGHEST WOMEN'S 70-M SCORE

Lee Hee-Jeong (South Korea) scored 348 points from a possible 360 at 70 m in one FITA round in Ch'ungju, South Korea, in October 2001.

POOL

FASTEST TIME TO CLEAR TWO TABLES

Nicolaos Nikolaidis (Canada) cleared two tables in 1 min 33 sec on 14 August 2001 at Bar and Billiard Unison in Québec, Canada. He broke the record on his way to potting the most balls in 24 hours – 16,723.

FASTEST CLEARANCE

The record time for potting 15 balls is 26.5 sec by Dave Pearson (UK) at Pepper's Bar And Grill, Windsor, Ontario, Canada, on 4 April 1997.

The women's record is 37.07 sec by Susan Thompson (UK) at the Phoenix Pool & Snooker Club, Wallasey, Merseyside, UK, on 1 December 1996.

Pearson also holds the record for most tables cleared (15 balls) in 10 minutes, with 10 in Las Vegas, Nevada, USA, on 25 May 1998.

The break involved a free ball, creating an 'extra' red, with all 15 reds still on the table, and therefore making a maximum break of 155 possible.

The only '16 red' clearance in a professional tournament was by Steve James (UK), who made 135 against Alex Higgins (UK) on 14 April 1990 in the World Professional Championships at Sheffield, S Yorks, UK.

DARTS

MOST BULL'S-EYES IN 10 HOURS
Perry Prine (USA) hit 1,432 bull's-eyes in 10 hours at the Lake Erie Classic Dart Tournament in Mentor, Ohio, USA, on 27 March 1998.

WOMEN'S OUTDOORS MARATHON
Anne Herlihy (New Zealand) played darts outside for a record 64 hours at The Bridge Tavern, Waitara, New Zealand, from 26–28 March 1999.

HIGHEST WOMEN'S SCORE IN 24 HOURS
The highest score achieved by a team of eight women is 830,737 by a side from The Cornwall Inn, Killurin, Wexford, Ireland, on 1–2 August 1997.

FASTEST DARTS 'ROUND THE CLOCK'
Dennis Gower (UK) worked his way round a dartboard clockwise, hitting doubles in a time of 9.2 sec at The Millers Arms, Hastings, E Sussex, UK, on 12 October 1975.

Jim Pike (UK) achieved a similar feat, with the distinction that he struck the doubles in numerical order, in 14.5 sec at The Craven Club, Newmarket, Suffolk, UK, in March 1944.

FASTEST TIME TO FINISH THREE GAMES OF 301
The shortest time taken to complete three games of 301, finishing on doubles, is 1 min 37 sec by Mervyn King (UK) on 29 August 1997. The successful record attempt was recorded on BBC TV's *Record Breakers* and took place at the BBC TV Centre, London, UK.

PÉTANQUE

LONGEST MARATHON
The longest pétanque, or boules, marathon is one of 24 hours recorded by members of the Half Crown Pétanque Club at The Crown Inn, Stockton, Warwickshire, UK, on 26–27 June 1999.

MOST WORLD CHAMPIONSHIP TITLES
Two players have won five World Championships as members of a pétanque team. Didier Choupay (France) took a team gold medal in 1985, 1988–89, 1994 and 1998. Philippe Quintas (France) won in 1991, 1993, 1995–96 and 1998.

MOST WORLD CHAMPIONSHIP TEAM TITLES
France have won the Pétanque World Championship team title 18 times, most recently in 2001.

CLAY SHOOTING

FASTEST TIME TO BREAK 500 CLAY TARGETS
Scott Hutchinson (USA) shot and broke 500 sporting clay targets in a record time of 30 min 31 sec at the Silver Harbor Lodge, Lake Placid, Florida, USA, on 18 September 1999.

MOST CLAY TARGETS BROKEN IN ONE MINUTE
Esa Kölegård (Sweden) shot and broke a record total of 29 clay targets in one minute at Bräcke, Sweden, on 26 September 2001. The event was filmed by *Guinness Rekord TV*, Sweden.

TRAPSHOOTING

MOST CONSECUTIVE TARGETS HIT
The greatest number of trapshooting targets consecutively hit by one person is 675, achieved by Cathy Wehinger (USA) at a shooting range at Ackley, Iowa, USA, in July 1998.

HIGHEST SCORE FOR ARCHERY WOMEN'S INDOOR 36 FINAL
The highest score achieved for a 36 Final is 358 (out of 360) by Natalya Valeeva (Italy, above) at Caorle, Italy, in March 2002.

SNOOKER

FASTEST MAXIMUM BREAK
The fastest 147, or maximum break, recorded in a professional snooker tournament came in 5 min 20 sec. It was achieved by Ronnie O'Sullivan (UK) during the World Championship at the Crucible Theatre, Sheffield, S Yorks, UK, on 21 April 1997.

O'Sullivan (UK) is also the youngest player to achieve a competitive maximum break of 147. He achieved the feat aged 15 years 98 days during the English Amateur Championship (Southern Area) at Aldershot, Hants, UK, on 13 March 1991.

HIGHEST BREAK
Wally West (UK) recorded a break of 151 in a match at the Hounslow Lucania, London, UK, in October 1976.

MOST DARTS WORLD CHAMPIONSHIP TITLES
Phil Taylor (UK, above) has won 10 darts world championship titles, more than any other individual. Taylor took the WDO (World Darts Organization) title in 1990 and 1992, and the PDC (Professional Darts Council) title from 1995 to 2002.

MOST REGAINED WORLD HEAVYWEIGHT TITLES

Three boxers have twice regained the heavyweight title: Muhammad Ali (USA), Evander Holyfield (USA) and Lennox Lewis (UK, below). In 1988 Lewis won an Olympic gold for Canada, where he moved at the age of 12, and first took the World Boxing Council (WBC) title in 1993. He regained it in 1997 and 2001.

BOXING

LONGEST REIGNING WORLD HEAVYWEIGHT CHAMPION

Joe Louis (USA) was world champion for 11 years 252 days, from 22 June 1937 when he beat Jim Braddock (USA) in Chicago, Illinois, USA, until 1 March 1949. Louis made a record 25 successful defences of his title.

YOUNGEST WORLD HEAVYWEIGHT CHAMPION

Mike Tyson (USA) was aged a record 20 years 144 days when he beat Trevor Berbick (USA) to win the WBC heavyweight title in Las Vegas, Nevada, USA, on 22 November 1986. He added the World Boxing Association (WBA) title when he beat James 'Bonecrusher' Smith (USA) at 20 years 249 days on 7 March 1987. He became undisputed champion on 2 August 1987 when he beat Tony Tucker (USA) for the International Boxing Federation (IBF) title.

LIGHTEST WORLD HEAVYWEIGHT CHAMPION

Bob Fitzsimmons (UK) weighed just 75 kg (165 lb) when he won the heavyweight title by defeating James Corbett (USA) in Carson City, Nevada, USA, on 17 March 1897.

HEAVIEST WORLD HEAVYWEIGHT CHAMPION

Primo Carnera (Italy), the 'Ambling Alp', weighed 118 kg (260 lb) when he won the world heavyweight title from Jack Sharkey (USA) in New York City, USA, on 29 June 1933. His peak weight was 122 kg (269 lb) and his reach was a record 217 cm (85 in) from fingertip to fingertip.

LONGEST FIGHTS

Fighting under Queensberry Rules, lightweights Joe Gans (USA) and Oscar Matthew (Denmark) fought for 42 rounds – a record for a title fight – in Goldfield, Nevada, USA, on 3 September 1906. In the end, Gans won on a foul.

The longest recorded duration of a fight with gloves was between Andy Bowen (USA) and Jack Burke (USA) in New Orleans, Louisiana, USA, on 6–7 April 1893. It lasted 110 rounds, 7 hr 19 min (9:15 pm to 4:34 am) and was declared a no contest (later changed to a draw).

The most rounds ever recorded was 276 in 4 hr 30 min when Jack Jones beat Patsy Tunney (both UK) in Cheshire, UK, in 1825. Before the Queensberry Rules were introduced in 1867, fights were not timed and rounds were limitless – a round would only end when one of the boxers was knocked down.

MOST KNOCKDOWNS IN ONE FIGHT

Vic Toweel (South Africa) knocked down Danny O'Sullivan (UK) 14 times in 10 rounds during their world bantamweight fight in Johannesburg, South Africa, on 2 December 1950.

OLDEST WORLD CHAMPION

Archie Moore (USA) was believed to be aged between 45 and 48 when his world light heavyweight title was removed on 10 February 1962 due to his inactivity. Moore, the only boxer to fight both Rocky Marciano and Muhammad Ali (both USA), had first taken the title in 1952.

SHORTEST REIGNING WORLD CHAMPION

Tony Canzoneri (USA) was world light welterweight champion for 33 days from 21 May to 23 June 1933 – the shortest time for a boxer to have won and lost a world title in the ring.

YOUNGEST WORLD CHAMPION

US-born Puerto Rican Wilfred Benitez was 17 years 176 days when he won the WBA light welterweight title in San Juan, Puerto Rico, on 6 March 1976.

Stadium, Mexico City, Mexico, on 20 February 1993, headed by the successful WBC super-lightweight defence by Julio César Chávez (Mexico) over Greg Haugen (USA).

The non-paying record is 135,132 to see Tony Zale v. Billy Pryor (both USA) at Juneau Park, Milwaukee, Wisconsin, USA, on 16 August 1941.

SMALLEST ATTENDANCE AT A WORLD HEAVYWEIGHT TITLE FIGHT

A meagre 2,434 turned up to see Cassius Clay (USA), who had just converted to Islam and become Muhammad Ali, beat Sonny Liston (USA) at Lewiston, Maine, USA, on 25 May 1965. A small venue was chosen because Ali had received death threats before the fight.

LONGEST UNBEATEN RUN

As of March 2002 Ricardo López (Mexico) remained unbeaten throughout his professional career, with 50 wins and 1 draw from 51 fights over 17 years.

MOST CONSECUTIVE KNOCK-OUTS

The record for consecutive knock-outs is 44 by Lamar Clark (USA) from 1958 to 1960. Clark once knocked out six opponents in one night (five in the first round) at Bingham, Utah, USA, on 1 December 1958.

MOST KNOCK-OUTS IN A CAREER

Archie Moore (USA) recorded 145 knock-outs (129 in professional fights) in his career.

MOST COMPETITIVE FULL CONTACT ROUNDS

The most competitive full contact rounds fought in boxing and other martial arts is 5,962 by Paddy Doyle (UK) from 1993 to February 1999.

MOST REGAINED WORLD TITLES

US middleweight 'Sugar' Ray Robinson (above) beat Carmen Basilio (USA) in the Chicago Stadium, Illinois, USA, on 25 March 1958 to regain the title for the fourth time, a record for a boxer at any weight.

MOST WORLD TITLES SIMULTANEOUSLY HELD AT DIFFERENT WEIGHTS

Henry 'Homicide Hank' Armstrong (USA) held world titles at a record three different weights at the same time. He was the world champion at featherweight, lightweight and welterweight between August and December 1938.

It is claimed that Barney Ross (USA) held the world lightweight, junior welterweight and welterweight titles simultaneously from 28 May to 17 September 1934, but there is some dispute as to exactly when he relinquished his lightweight title.

HIGHEST ATTENDANCE AT A BOXING MATCH

The greatest paid attendance at any boxing match is 132,274 to watch four world title fights at the Aztec

JUDO

MOST WORLD CHAMPIONSHIPS

The most successful man in World Championships history is Yasuhiro Yamashita (Japan), who won five world and Olympic titles from 1977–85 – the world over-95 kg title in 1979, 1981 and 1983, the world Open title in 1981 and the Olympic Open category in 1984. By the time he retired he had recorded 203 successive wins and no defeats.

The women's record is held by Ingrid Berghmans (Belgium), who won six world titles between 1980 and 1989.

KARATE

MOST INDIVIDUAL WORLD KATA CHAMPIONSHIPS

Kata is a form of karate that consists of sequences of specific moves. The most individual world titles ever won is four by Yuki Mimura (Japan). She was victorious in 1988, 1990, 1992 and 1996.

The most men's titles is three by Tsuguo Sakumoto (Japan) in 1984, 1986 and 1988 and Michael Milan (France) in 1994, 1996 and 2000.

MOST INDIVIDUAL WORLD KUMITE CHAMPIONSHIPS

Kumite is a freestyle form of karate. The most successful world champion is Guus van Mourik (Netherlands), who won four titles at over-60 kg in 1982, 1984, 1986 and 1988.

The men's record is three by José Manuel Egea (Spain) at Open (Sanbon) in 1988 and under-80 kg in 1990 and 1992, and Wayne Otto (UK) at Open (Sanbon) in 1990 and under-75 kg in 1992 and 1996.

MOST TEAM WORLD KUMITE CHAMPIONSHIPS

Great Britain has won a record six world titles (instituted 1970) at the men's kumite team event – in 1975, 1982, 1984, 1986, 1988 and 1990.

A women's team competition was introduced to the tournament in 1992 and has been won twice by Great Britain in 1992 and 1996.

MOST JUDO TITLES

David Douillet (France, top right) won six world and Olympic titles – three of each – up to 2000.

WEIGHTLIFTING

MOST OLYMPIC GOLD MEDALS

Naim Suleymanoglü (Turkey) won three weightlifting gold medals at the Olympic Games of 1988, 1992 and 1996. Pyrros Dimas (Greece) accomplished the same feat in 1992, 1996 and 2000.

MOST OLYMPIC MEDALS

Norbert Schemansky (USA) has won the greatest number of Olympic weightlifting medals, picking up four between 1948 and 1964.

MOST WOMEN'S WORLD CHAMPIONSHIP TITLES

The most gold medals won at the women's World Championships is 13 by Li Hongyun (China) in the 60/64-kg class from 1992–96.

MOST WOMEN'S POWERLIFTING WORLD CHAMPIONSHIP TITLES

The winner of the most women's world titles is Natalya Rumyantseva (Russia), who won seven at 82.5 kg between 1993 and 1999.

OLDEST WORLD RECORD BREAKER

The oldest weightlifting record holder is Norbert Schemansky (USA), who was aged 37 years 333 days when he snatched a record weight of 164.2 kg in the then unlimited heavyweight class at Detroit, Michigan, USA, on 28 April 1962.

YOUNGEST WORLD RECORD BREAKER

Naim Suleymanoglü (Turkey) was aged just 16 years 62 days old when he set the world records for clean and jerk 160 kg and combined total 285 kg at Allentown, New Jersey, USA, on 26 March 1983.

SUMO

GREATEST TOURNAMENT DOMINANCE

Yokozuna Mitsugu Akimoto (Japan), whose sumo name was Chiyonofuji, won one of the six annual tournaments – the Kyushu Basho – for eight years in a row, 1981–88. He also holds the record for the most career wins, with 1,045, and Makunouchi (top division) wins, with 807.

MOST CONSECUTIVE TOP DIVISION BOUTS

Jesse Kuhaulua (Hawaii), known as Takamiyama, was the first non-Japanese to win an official top-division tournament in July 1972. In September 1981 he set a record of 1,231 consecutive top-division bouts.

MOST BOUTS WON

Ozeki Tameemon Torokichi (Japan), or Raiden, won 254 bouts and lost only 10 for the highest winning percentage of 96.2 between 1789 and 1810.

MOST CONSECUTIVE WINS

Sadaji Akiyoshi (Japan), alias Futabayama, holds the all-time record for consecutive sumo wins, with 69 victories from 1937–39.

MOST EMPEROR'S CUPS

Yokozuna Koki Naya (Japan), alias Taiho or 'Great Bird', won the prestigious Emperor's Cup 32 times up to his retirement in 1971.

WRESTLING

MOST INDIVIDUAL DISCIPLINE OLYMPIC MEDALS

The record is four individual discipline medals by; Eino Leino (Finland) at freestyle from 1920–32; Imre Polyák (Hungary) at Greco-Roman from 1952–64; and Bruce Baumgartner (USA) at freestyle from 1984–96.

MOST OLYMPIC GOLD MEDALS

The record is three golds by: Carl Westergren (Sweden) in 1920, 1924 and 1932; Ivar Johansson (Sweden) in 1932 (two) and 1936; Aleksandr Vasilyevich Medved (USSR) in 1964, 1968 and 1972 and Aleksandr Karelin (Russia) in 1988, 1992 and 1996.

MOST WORLD CHAMPIONSHIP TITLES

Aleksandr Karelin (Russia) won a record 12 world titles in the Greco-Roman under-130-kg class between 1988 and 1999.

WEIGHTLIFTING WORLD RECORDS

From 1 January 1998 the International Weightlifting Federation (IWF) introduced modified bodyweight categories, thereby making the existing world records redundant. This is the new listing with the world standards for the new bodyweight categories. Results achieved at IWF-approved competitions exceeding the world standards by 0.5 kg for snatch or clean and jerk, or by 2.5 kg for the total, will be recognized as world records.

Men's 56-kg clean and jerk
168 kg
Halil Mutlu (Turkey)
Trencín, Slovakia
24 April 2001

Men's 56-kg snatch
138.5 kg
Halil Mutlu (Turkey)
Antalya, Turkey
4 November 2001

Men's 56-kg total
305.0 kg
Halil Mutlu (Turkey)
Sydney, NSW, Australia
16 September 2000

Men's 62-kg clean and jerk
181 kg
Genady Oleshchuk (Belarus)
Antalya, Turkey
5 November 2001

Men's 62-kg snatch
152.5 kg
Shi Zhiyong (China)
Osaka, Japan
3 May 2000

Men's 62-kg total
No record yet set.

Men's 69-kg clean and jerk
196.5 kg
Galabin Boevski (Bulgaria)
Sydney, NSW, Australia
20 September 2000

Men's 69-kg snatch
165 kg
Georgi Markov (Bulgaria)
Sydney, NSW, Australia
20 September 2000

Men's 69-kg total
357.5 kg
Galabin Boevski (Bulgaria)
Athens, Greece
24 November 1999

OLDEST WRESTLING COMPETITION

The world's oldest continuously sanctioned sporting competition is the Kirkpinar Wrestling Festival (above), which has been held since 1460. The event is currently staged on the Sarayici Peninsula, near Edirne, Turkey.

WOMEN'S 48-KG SNATCH AND 48-KG TOTAL
On 6 June 2000 Liu Xiuhua (China, above) broke the existing world record for the 48-kg snatch by lifting 87.5 kg in Montreal, Quebec, Canada. Liu also holds the record for the 48-kg total – she lifted 197.5 kg on 6 September 1999, also in an event in Montreal.

Men's 77-kg clean and jerk
210 kg
Oleg Perepetchenov (Russia)
Trencín, Slovakia
27 April 2001

Men's 77-kg snatch
172.5 kg
Plamen Zhelyazkov (Bulgaria)
Doha, Qatar
27 March 2002

Men's 77-kg total
377.5 kg
Plamen Zhelyazkov (Bulgaria)
Doha, Qatar
27 March 2002

Men's 85-kg clean and jerk
218 kg
Zhang Yong (China)
Tel Aviv, Israel
25 April 1998

Men's 85-kg snatch
181 kg
Georgi Asanidze (Georgia)
Sofia, Bulgaria
29 April 2000

Men's 85-kg total
No record yet set.

Men's 94-kg clean and jerk
232.5 kg
Szymon Kolecki (Poland)
Sofia, Bulgaria
29 April 2000

Men's 94-kg snatch
188 kg
Akakios Kakiashvilis (Greece)
Athens, Greece
27 November 1999

Men's 94-kg total
No record yet set.

Men's 105-kg clean and jerk
No record yet set.

Men's 105-kg snatch
198 kg
Vladimir Smorchkov (Russia)
Antalya, Turkey
10 November 2001

Men's 105-kg total
No record yet set.

Men's over-105-kg clean and jerk
No record yet set.

Men's over-105-kg snatch
212.5 kg
Hossein Rezazadeh (Iran)
Sydney, NSW, Australia
26 September 2000

Men's over-105-kg total
472.5 kg
Hossein Rezazadeh (Iran)
Sydney, NSW, Australia
26 September 2000

Women's 48-kg clean and jerk
113.5 kg
Donka Mincheva (Bulgaria)
Athens, Greece
21 November 1999

Women's 48-kg snatch
87.5 kg
Liu Xiuhua (China)
Montreal, Canada
6 June 2000

Women's 48-kg total
197.5 kg
Liu Xiuhua (China)
Montreal, Canada
6 September 1999

Women's 53-kg clean and jerk
125 kg
Yang Xia (China)
Sydney, NSW, Australia
18 September 2000

Women's 53-kg snatch
100 kg
Yang Xia (China)
Sydney, NSW, Australia
18 September 2000

Women's 53-kg total
225 kg
Yang Xia (China)
Sydney, Australia
18 September 2000

Women's 58-kg clean and jerk
131.5 kg
Ri Song Hui (North Korea)
Osaka, Japan
3 May 2000

Women's 58-kg snatch
105 kg
Chen Yanqing (China)
Athens, Greece
22 November 1999

Women's 58-kg total
235 kg
Chen Yanqing (China)
Athens, Greece
22 November 1999

Women's 63-kg clean and jerk
133 kg
Nataliya Skakun (Ukraine)
Thessaloniki, Greece
3 July 2001

Women's 63-kg snatch
112.5 kg
Chen Xiaomin (China)
Sydney, NSW, Australia
19 September 2000

Women's 63-kg total
242.5 kg
Chen Xiaomin (China)
Sydney, NSW, Australia
19 September 2000

Women's 69-kg clean and jerk
143.5 kg
Valentina Popova (Russia)
Brisbane, Queensland, Australia
1 September 2001

Women's 69-kg snatch
115 kg
Valentina Popova (Russia)
Antalya, Turkey
8 November 2001

Women's 69-kg total
257.5 kg
Valentina Popova (Russia)
Antalya, Turkey
8 November 2001

Women's 75-kg clean and jerk
142.5 kg
Sun Tianni (China)
Osaka, Japan
6 May 2000

Women's 75-kg snatch
116 kg
Tang Weifang (China)
Wuhan, China
4 September 1999

Women's 75-kg total
257.5 kg
Sun Tianni (China)
Osaka, Japan
6 May 2000

Women's over-75-kg clean and jerk
165 kg
Ding Meiyuan (China)
Sydney, NSW, Australia
22 September 2000

Women's over-75-kg snatch
135 kg
Ding Meiyuan (China)
Sydney, NSW, Australia
22 September 2000

Women's over-75-kg total
300 kg
Ding Meiyuan (China)
Sydney, NSW, Australia
22 September 2000

MEN'S 1-HOUR UNPACED STANDING START

Chris Boardman (UK, below) cycled a record 49.441 km (30.7 miles) in one hour from an unpaced standing start in Manchester, UK, on 27 October 2000. Boardman became the first British cyclist to win an Olympic gold for 72 years when he won the 4,000 m pursuit in Barcelona, Spain, in 1992.

MOST TOUR DE FRANCE WINS

The Tour de France, the most difficult and prestigious cycling race in the world, was first staged in 1903, organized by the French cyclist and journalist Henri Desgrange. Eddie Merckx (Belgium) shares the record of five overall victories in the Tour with Jacques Anquetil (France), Bernard Hinault (France) and Miguel Indurain (Spain).

MOST CONSECUTIVE TOUR DE FRANCE WINS

Miguel Indurain (Spain) won a record five successive Tour de France titles between 1991 and 1995.

MOST TOUR DE FRANCE STAGE WINS

The rider with the most stage wins in the history of the Tour de France is Eddie Merckx (Belgium) with 34.

LARGEST SPORTING EVENT ATTENDANCE

The largest attendance for a sporting event is the estimated 10 million that gather every year over a period of three weeks for the Tour de France.

CLOSEST FINISH TO TOUR DE FRANCE

In 1989 Greg LeMond (USA) beat Laurent Fignon (France) by a mere eight seconds after racing for 23 days for 3,267 km (2,030 miles). LeMond recorded a race finishing time of 87 hr 38 min 35 sec to win the second of his three Tour titles.

FASTEST AVERAGE TOUR DE FRANCE STAGE SPEED

The fastest average speed recorded over a stage of the Tour de France is 50.355 km/h (31.29 mph) by Mario Cipollini (Italy) in the 194-km (120-mile) fourth stage from Laval to Blois on 7 July 1999.

LONGEST TOUR DE FRANCE SOLO ESCAPE

The longest solo escape in the Tour de France was 253 km (157.2 miles) by Albert Bourlon (France) to win the 14th stage – Carcassonne to Luchon – in 1947.

OLDEST TOUR DE FRANCE WINNER

Firmin Lambot (Belgium) won the second of his two Tour de France titles in 1922 when he was aged 36 years 4 months.

YOUNGEST TOUR DE FRANCE WINNER

In 1903 Henri Cornet (France) won the Tour de France at the age of 19 years 350 days. Cornet actually finished the race in fifth position, but was awarded the victory after the first four cyclists were disqualified.

GREATEST DISTANCE CYCLED IN 24 HOURS

The furthest anybody has cycled over a 24-hour period behind a pace setter is a distance of 1,958.196 km (1,216.8 miles) by Michael Secrest (USA) in a successful record attempt at Phoenix International Raceway, Arizona, USA, on 26–27 April 1990.

Solo and unpaced, Secrest was able to cover a distance of 857.36 km (532.74 miles) – another world record – at the Olympic Velodrome, California State University, Carson, USA, on 23–24 October 1997.

MOST MEN'S MOUNTAIN BIKE DOWNHILL WORLD CUP WINS

Nicolas Vouilloz (France) won a record seven successive mountain bike downhill World Cup titles between 1992 to 1998.

MOST WOMEN'S MOUNTAIN BIKE DOWNHILL WORLD CUP WINS

Anne-Caroline Chausson (France) won 13 mountain bike downhill World Cups from 1993 to 1998. Chausson began her career in BMX-racing and in 1993 finished French, European and World BMX champion.

MOST MEN'S MOUNTAIN BIKE CROSS-COUNTRY WORLD CUP WINS

The most cross-country World Cup wins on a mountain bike by a man is 15 by Thomas Frischknecht (Switzerland) from 1991 to 1998.

MOST MOUNTAIN BIKE CROSS-COUNTRY WORLD CHAMPIONSHIP TITLES

The most cross-country World Championship titles won by a man is three by Henrik Djernis (Denmark, above) from 1992 to 1994.

MOST WOMEN'S MOUNTAIN BIKE CROSS-COUNTRY WORLD CUPS

The most women's mountain bike cross-country World Cup wins is 28 by Juli Furtado (USA) from 1991–96.

LONGEST EXERCISE BIKE MARATHON

Bruce Wallis and Arthur Soares (both South Africa) spent 60 hours on a static spinning machine at the Gateway Theatre of Shopping, Umhlanga, Durban, South Africa, from 1 to 4 November 2001.

LARGEST RACE

The most participants at a cycling event is the 48,615 who took part in Udine Pedala 2000, organized by Rolo Banca 1473 at Udine, Italy, on 11 June 2000. The cyclists completed a circuit that measured 29.3 km (18.2 miles) around the surrounding area of Udine.

The most finishers of a tour of more than 1,000 km (621.4 miles) are the 2,037 (from 2,157 starters) who completed the Australian Bicentennial Caltex Bike Ride from Melbourne, Victoria, to Sydney, NSW, from 26 November to 10 December 1988.

FASTEST COMPLETION OF THREE PEAKS

Dave Jones (UK) completed a journey from Caernarvon, Gwynedd, UK, to Fort William, Highland, UK, via the three tallest mountains in Wales, England and Scotland – Snowdon, Scafell Pike and Ben Nevis respectively. Jones cycled between the peaks and ran to the summits in 40 hr 57 min in July 1999.

FASTEST CYCLIST ON SNOW

Christian Taillefer (France) reached a speed of 212.139 km/h (132 mph) on snow when cycling down a glacier at the Speed Ski Slope in Vars, France, in March 1998.

FURTHEST DISTANCE CYCLED UNDERWATER ON AN EXERCISE BIKE

Without the use of any kind of breathing apparatus, Benjamin Franz (Germany) was able to record a distance of 636 m (2,086.61 ft) on a submerged Kettler 'Racer' exercise bike in a single breath in Munich, Germany, on 25 July 2001.

FASTEST TEAM TRANS-AMERICA CROSSING

Going from Irvine, California, USA, to Savannah, Georgia, USA, Ricardo Arap and Alexandre Ribeiro (both Brazil) cycled across America in 7 days 9 hr 56 min in July 1998.

FASTEST MEN'S 200 M UNPACED FLYING START

Curtis Harnett (Canada) cycled 200 m in 9.865 unpaced, from a flying start at Bogotá, Colombia, on 28 September 1995.

FASTEST WOMEN'S 200 M UNPACED FLYING START

Olga Slyusareva (Russia) cycled 200 m in 10.831 unpaced, from a flying start at Moscow, Russia, on 25 April 1993.

FASTEST MEN'S 500 M UNPACED FLYING START

Alexandre Kiritchenko (USSR, now Russia) cycled 500 m in 26.649 unpaced, from a flying start at Moscow, USSR, on 29 October 1988.

FASTEST WOMEN'S 500 M UNPACED FLYING START

Erika Salumäe (USSR, now Russia) cycled a distance of 500 m in a record time of 29.655 from an unpaced flying start in a race at Moscow, USSR, on 6 August 1987.

FASTEST WOMEN'S 500 M UNPACED STANDING START

Felicia Ballanger (France) cycled a distance of 500 m in a record time of 34.017 at Bogotá, Colombia, on 29 September 1995.

FASTEST MEN'S 1 KM UNPACED STANDING START

Arnaud Tournant (France) cycled a distance of 1 km in a record time of 1:00.148 unpaced, from a standing start at Mexico City, Mexico, on 16 June 2000.

FASTEST WOMEN'S 3 KM UNPACED STANDING START

Marion Clignet (France) cycled a distance of 3 km in 3:30.974 unpaced, from a standing start at Manchester, UK, on 31 August 1996.

FASTEST MEN'S 4 KM UNPACED STANDING START

Chris Boardman (UK) holds the men's 4 km unpaced standing start record of 4:11.114, which was set at Manchester, UK, on 29 August 1996.

FASTEST MEN'S 4 KM TEAM PURSUIT

A team representing Germany (Robert Bartko, Guido Fulst, Jens Lehmann and Daniel Becke) covered a distance of 4 km in a record time of 3:59.710 from an unpaced standing start in Sydney, NSW, Australia, on 19 September 2000.

WOMEN'S 1-HOUR UNPACED STANDING START

Jeannie Longo-Ciprelli (France, above) cycled 48.159 km (30 miles) in one hour in Mexico City, Mexico, on 26 October 1996. Longo-Ciprelli has won the Tour Cycliste Feminin three times and has been French road champion 18 times.

HEAVIEST WORLD CHAMPIONS IN ANY SPORT

The World Elephant Polo Association (WEPA) has hosted a tournament every year since 1982 on a grass airfield in Megauly, Nepal. The sport is played by riders on elephants (below), four to a team. Indian elephants reach up to 5,000 kg (11,000 lb) in weight. It is against competition rules for participants to lie down in front of the goal.

MOST KINNAIRD CUPS

Eton fives is played by teams of two, hitting a ball against a court modelled on the chapel wall where the game was first played. The Eton fives amateur championship, or Kinnaird Cup, has been won 10 times by Brian Matthews (UK) and John Reynolds (UK) from 1981–90. Reynolds won an additional 11th title with Manuel de Souza-Girao in 1991.

MOST RUGBY FIVES NATIONAL DOUBLES

Rugby school's National Doubles Five Championship has been won 10 times by David Hebden (UK) and Ian Fuller (UK) between 1980 and 1990. Wayne Enstone (UK) won the title 13 times with three different partners between 1975 and 1997.

Enstone also won the Rugby National Singles Championships, or Jester's Cup – 22 times from 1973–95.

MOST HORSESHOE PITCHING WORLD TITLES

The horseshoe pitching World Championships were originally only held at irregular intervals, but have been held every year since 1946. Ted Allen (USA) has won a record total of 10 World Championships from 1933–40, 1946, 1953, 1955, 1956, 1957 and 1959.

The most women's titles is 10 by Vicki Chappelle Winston (USA). She won her first in 1956 and pitched successfully for the last time in 1981.

FASTEST TIME ROUND MANHATTAN ISLAND BY PADDLEBOARD

Seven members of the Southern California Paddleboard Club circumnavigated Manhattan island, New York, USA, by paddleboard in 6 hr 8 min on 11 June 1999.

FASTEST 500 M ROLLER-SKATING

Alessio Gaggioli (Italy) recorded a speed of 44.631 km/h (27.732 mph) when covering a distance of 500 m in 40.330 sec on a road in Padua, Italy, on 7 September 1996.

GREATEST DISTANCE ROLLER-SKIING 24-HOUR RELAY

A quartet of roller-skiers – Simon Tinning, A Adamson, Mark Walker and A Simpson (all UK) – travelled 488.736 km (303.686 miles) in a 24-hour period at RAF Alconbury, Cambs, UK, on 23–24 May 1998.

MOST TOE WRESTLING WORLD CHAMPIONSHIPS

Alan Nash (UK) has won the men's toe wrestling World Championship four times – in 1994, 1996, 1997 and 2000. Karen Davies (UK) has won three women's titles from 1999 to 2001. The competition is held annually on the first Saturday in June at Ye Olde Royal Oak, Wetton, Staffs, UK. Players push their opponent's foot to the other side of a ring called a 'toerack' using only their toes.

OLDEST SLED-DOG TRAIL

The oldest established sled-dog trail still in use is the Alaskan 1,688-km (1,049-mile) Iditarod Trail (above) from Anchorage to Nome, Alaska, USA, which has existed since 1910 and has been used as the route of an annual race since 1967.

LONGEST SLED-DOG RACING TRAIL

The longest sled-dog race takes place on the 2,000-km (1,243-mile) Berengia Trail across east Russia from Esso to Markovo, which started off as a 250-km (155-mile) route in April 1990. Now established annually, the fastest time in which anybody has completed the journey is 10 days 18 hr 17 min 56 sec by Pavel Lazarev (Russia) in 1991.

FASTEST SANDBOARDER

On 12 April 1999 Erik Johnson (USA) reached a record speed of 82 km/h (51 mph) at the Sand Master Jam at Dumont Dunes, California, USA. The women's record of 71.94 km/h (44.7 mph) is held by Nancy Sutton (USA) and was set at Sand Mountain, Nevada, USA, on 19 September 1998.

LONGEST SANDBOARDING BACK FLIP

Josh Tenge (USA) performed a back flip that measured a world record distance of 13.6 m (44 ft 10 in) at Xwest Huck Fest, Sand Mountain, Nevada, USA, on 20 May 2000.

HIGHEST SPEED ON A LAND YACHT

The highest speed officially recorded for a land yacht – wheeled vehicles with large sails – is 187.8 km/h (116.7 mph) by Iron Duck, piloted by Bob Schumacher (USA) at Ivanpah Dry Lake, Prim, Nevada, USA, on 20 March 1999.

MOST EXPENSIVE PIGEON

The highest sum paid for a pigeon is £110,800 ($160,000) by Louella Pigeon World of Markfield, Leics, UK, to Martin Biemans (Netherlands) on 23 July 1992 for Invincible Spirit, a four-year-old cock that won the 1992 Barcelona International race.

GREATEST COMPETITIVE DISTANCE FLOWN BY A PIGEON

Between 1990 and 1997, Brazilian Beauty, a blue-check hen, owned by Robert Koch (South Africa), flew a record 41,050 km (25,507 miles).

MOST CONSECUTIVE PEA SHOOTING TITLES

The most consecutive pea shooting World Championship titles is three by David Hollis (UK) in 1999, 2000 and 2001. Hollis is also the youngest champion, aged just 15 when he won in 1999. The championships have been held every year since 1969 in Witcham, Cambs, UK. The skill is to aim at a target the size of a dartboard and smeared with putty, gaining five points for the inner ring, three for the middle and one for the outer circle from a distance of 3.2 m (10 ft 6 in). The only rules are that the pea shooter should be no longer than 30.48 cm (12 in), although in an effort to get back to basics, laser sights were banned from use for the 2002 competition.

MOST TIDDLYWINKS WORLD CHAMPIONSHIPS

Larry Kahn (USA) claimed the tiddlywinks World Championship singles title on 16 occasions from 1983 to 1997 and the pairs title 10 times between 1978 and 1998.

Geoff Myers and Andy Purvis (both UK) won a record total of seven consecutive World Championship pairs titles together from 1991–95.

FURTHEST WINK SHOT IN TIDDLYWINKS

Ben Soares (UK) holds the record for the furthest wink shot in tiddlywinks, scoring from 9.52 m (31 ft 3 in) in Cambridge, UK, on 14 January 1995. A wink is the small counter that is flipped into the pot by a larger disc.

FASTEST POTTING OF 24 TIDDLYWINKS

The record for potting 24 winks from a distance of 45 cm (18 in) into the pot is a time of 21.8 sec by Stephen Williams (UK) in May 1966.

FASTEST POTTING OF 10,000 TIDDLYWINKS

Allen Astles (UK) potted 10,000 winks in 3 hr 51 min at Aberystwyth, Dyfed, UK, in February 1966.

HIGHEST ALLEY SKITTLES SCORE

Skittles, or nine pins, is a traditional pub game that predates bowling as we know it. Players take turns to throw wooden balls ('the cheese') down a lane to knock over nine wooden skittles. The highest score is 94,151 in a period of 24 hours by a team from The Carpenter's Arms, Dorset, UK, on 10 March 1995.

HIGHEST TABLETOP SKITTLES SCORE

Tabletop skittles is a miniature version of alley skittles. A popular pub game, nine skittles stand on a table and are knocked over by a ball swung from a pole. The highest score recorded over a 24-hour period is 116,047 skittles by 12 players at The Castle Mona, Newcastle, Tyne and Wear, UK.

MOST ROLLER-SKATING TITLES

Andrea González (Argentina, above third from right) won 14 gold medals at the South American ODESUR games (a multi-discipline South American event), which were held in Cuenca, Ecuador, in October 1998.

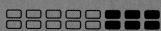

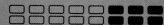

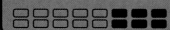

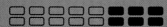

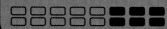

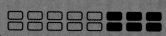

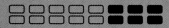
Special thanks go to the following people for their work during the production of this year's edition:

Kat Aalam
Louise Bate
Scott Christie
Ann Collins
Jo Crawford
Neil Hayes
Paul Hearn
Iforce
Joyce Lee
Vicki Miles
Shazia Mirza
Paul Reardon
Amanda Sprague
Caroline Toms
Kate White
Sophie Whiting

The team also wish to thank the following individuals and organizations:

Ernest Adams
Leslie Aiello
American Society of Plastic Surgeons
Amnesty International
Ron Baalke
Healey Baker
Bank of England
Peter Barham
BBC
Guenter Bechly
David Billington, Casella CEL Inc
Biowarfare & Bioterrorism: A Brief History, on www.hospitals-doctors.com
Board of Film Classification
Richard Bourgerie
Bowers and Merena Galleries
James Bradley
Sean Breazeal
Bristol University
British Antarctic Survey
British Geological Survey
British House Rabbit Association
British Telecom
British Tourist Authority
Mike Brown
Lucy Bunker
Caribbean Journal of Science
Clive Carpenter
Mark Carwardine
Ian Castello-Cortes
CERN
Hubert Chanson
Christie's
CIA Factbook
Cinefex
Pamela Clarke, The Royal Archives

Columbia University
Cornell University
Croham Valley Support
Mike Coughlan
Pamela Dalton
Peter D'Amato
Diamond High Council
Martin Dodge
eBay
Economic History Services
Economist Intelligence Unit
Ecoworld
Encyclopaedia Britannica
Louis Epstein
Everestnews.com
FBI
Federation of American Scientists
Forbes
Foreign and Commonwealth Office
Mike Foster, Jane's Defence Weekly
Fremantle media
Geological Society of London
Andy Gillard, Scootering magazine
Simon Gold
Michelle Gonsalves
Google
Stan Greenberg
Richard Gue
Bruce Guettich
Guinness – Die Show Der Rekorde, ARD
Guinness el Show de los Records, Antena 3
Guinness Rekord TV, TV3
Guinness World Records, ITV
Guinness World Record, Nelonen, Channel 4
Guinness World Records, NTV
Guinness World Records: Primetime, Fox Television
David Hancock, Screen Digest
Michael Hanlon
Mary Hanson
Claire Hegarty
Hello! magazine
Home and Garden Television website
David Horne
Yvonne Hussey
IMDB
Immigration and Naturalization Service (USA)
Imperial Cancer Research Fund
International Association of Fire Fighters
International Astronomical Union
International Carnivorous Plant Society
International Centre for Prison Studies
International Confederation for Plastic, Reconstructive and Aesthetic Surgery
International Monetary Fund
International Tanker Owners Pollution Federation

International Union for the Conservation of Nature
Kathryn Jenkin
Steve Jones
Ove Karlsson
Nichol Keith
Michael Feldman
Keo Films
Lancaster University
Rolf Landua
Roger Launius
Anthony Liu
Hugh Gene Loebner
Robert Loss
Joe Lynham
Dave McAleer
Jessica Marantz
Giles Marion
Brian Marsden
Koen Martens
Massachusetts Institute of Technology
Peter Matthews
Metro newspaper
Andy Milroy
Eugene Mirman
Edgar Mitchell
Moody's
Rick Moss
Munich Re
NASA
National Bank of Hungary
National Federation of Master Window & General Cleaners
National Geographic
National Museum of Science and Industry
National Science Foundation
Natural History Museum
Nature Magazine and Dr Chris Gunter
NBC
New York City Police Department
Barry Norman, WKVL Amusement Research Library
Numismatic Guarantee Corporation
OANDA
Official Website of the British Monarchy
Organization for Economic Co-operation and Development
Hilary Pearce
People.com
Edwin Perry
David Power-Fardy
PPL Therapeutics
Prison Activist Resource Center
Private Islands online
Rainforest Foundation UK
Rapaport
Simon Rasalingham
Recording Industry Association of America
John Reed, WSSRC

Martin Rees
Rees Entertainment
Dave Roberts
Royal Armouries
Royal Astronomical Society
Royal Horticultural Society
Rutherford Appleton Laboratory
salon.com
Search Engine Watch
Captain Scott Shields and Bear
Bill Slaymaker
Malcolm Smith
Sotheby's
Southampton Oceonography Centre
Standard & Poor's
Jo Steel
Danny Sullivan
Symantec Corporation
TeleGeography
Telescope
Televisual
Texas Department of Criminal Justice
TF1
The Economist
The Met Office
The New York Times
The Nobel Foundation
The Pentagon
The Sun
The World Bank
The World Economic Forum
Ryan Tunstall
Martin Uman
Understanding and Solutions
UN factbook
United Nations
United States Mint
University of Southampton
US Drug Enforcement Agency
US Geological Survey
USA Today
Variety
Anthony Vestal
Ewan Vinnicombe
Joanne Violette
Juhani Virola
Alice Walker
David Wark
Kevin Warwick
Louise Whetter
David Wynn Williams
Martyn Williams
Tom Wood
World Meteorological Organization
World Roads Federation
World Tourism Organization
Yale University
Richard Yarwood
Robert Young
Paul Zajac, Wards Communications